THE MAMMOTH BOOK OF

SEX, DRUGS
&
ROCK 'N' ROLL

THE MAMMOTH BOOK OF

SEX, DRUGS
&
ROCK 'N' ROLL

Edited by Jim Driver

ROBINSON
London

Constable Publishers
3 The Lanchesters
162 Fulham Palace Road
London W6 9ER
www.constablerobinson.com

First published in the UK by Robinson,
an imprint of Constable & Robinson Ltd 2001

A copy of the British Library Cataloguing in
Publication Data is available from the British Library.

ISBN 1–84119–145–0

Printed and bound in the EU

Contents

"Can't Help Falling in Love"
DOOMED ROCK 'N' ROLL MARRIAGES

Dead End Street
1. "Scary Monsters (And Super Creeps)"
SUDDEN DEATH

2."Don't Leave Me This Way"
DEATH BY THEIR OWN HAND

3."Zoom"
PLANES, TRAINS AND AUTOMOBILES

4. "(You're The) Devil In Disguise"
DEATH BY DRINK AND DRUGS

5. "Don't Go Near The Water"
DEATH BY DROWNING

6. "Jailhouse Rock"
BRUSHES WITH THE LAW
AND ANTISOCIAL BEHAVIOUR

Introduction

Drugs and sex go hand in hand when you're a rock 'n' roll musician. Whereas if I were a violinist, it might be a little different.   *Slash, Guns N' Roses*

No one seems to know where the expression "Sex and Drugs and Rock 'n' Roll" came from. Ian Dury and the Blockheads used it as the title of their first single in 1977, but before that the canvas is blank. We've scoured the Internet, tackled eminent lexicographers and consulted national libraries. Some sources suggest that the phrase has been around since the early- or mid- 1960s, but no one can come up with instances, and that's about as far as we get. If anyone used the term before Ian Dury, then they sure as hell didn't make much of a song and dance about it.

> You could say that I got into music for the sex. I never harboured a burning desire to sing my heart out or be a star. So when I was fifteen it was a big surprise to be suddenly asked to join a rock band. The invitation was extended by the lead singer in a desperate move to seduce me. Until his request I considered him a complete arsehole . . . Then I heard him sing. I can still remember turning my head in shock and horror, thinking, "He has the most beautiful voice." I quickly fell in lust, and as he was very keen on me, I joined his band – and shortly thereafter his bed.   *Shirley Manson, Garbage*

Only the prudish would deny that sex, drugs and rock 'n' roll make a winning team. In the right hands the combination is explosive. In the wrong hands, it's a killer. Inevitably a good proportion of this book is concerned with what happens when things do go wrong. The deaths, the addictions, the injuries, the ego-trips and the degradations of rock 'n' roll are the flip-side of a phenomenon that's altered the course of modern history. If Woodstock is the ying, then Altamont is the yang. What starts out as a dream can quickly become a nightmare, especially with chemicals altering perceptions; but for every Janis or Jimi or Sid there are a million who crave the lifestyle, and it's easy to see why.

> I could be unbelievably horrible and stupid. On tours, I'd get on a plane, then get off it, maybe six or eight times. I'd walk out of a hotel suite because I didn't like the colour of the bedspread. I remember looking out of my room at the Inn on the Park one day and saying, "It's too windy. Can someone please do something about it?" *Elton John*

Despite – or maybe because of – the sex and the drugs side of its nature, rock 'n' roll has become one of the biggest businesses in the world. Becoming a rock star overtook train driver and nurse as every boy and girl's career fantasy around the time Elvis first waggled his hips on American TV. As a way out of the poverty trap, it sure beats training long hours to become a world-beating sportsman (always assuming you've got the talent to knock out Mike Tyson or outmanoeuvre David Beckham in the first place) and the random luck needed to win the lottery. The most enticing aspect of rock 'n' roll from the career point of view is that you don't need to be supremely talented to be supremely successful. Just look at the current charts for confirmation of that. Although only a few succeed to the very summit, the rewards can be high. *Very* high. Members of the Rolling Stones, former Beatles and rock superstars like Elton John and David Bowie are among the richest people on the planet, with offshore bank accounts stuffed full of what was once our money. And even a pervy old has-been like Gary Glitter can hang on to a personal fortune of £11 million without too much trouble.

> If you don't have sex and you don't do drugs, your rock 'n' roll better be awfully good.   *Abbie Hoffman*

Defining rock 'n' roll is an easy way to make enemies. I once collared an American professor of music who insisted that rock 'n' roll is "black music played by white people". It was impossible, he said, for black people to play rock 'n' roll, because then it wouldn't be rock 'n' roll, it'd be R&B or blues. This man is clearly crazy and I'm sure Little Richard and Jimi Hendrix would be able to put him right, given half a chance. In the *Mammoth Book of Sex, Drugs and Rock 'n' Roll* we've taken rock 'n' roll in its widest context, incorporating "rock 'n' roll lifestyle" from the earliest days and encompassing players as diverse as Robert Johnson, Hank Williams, Phil Ochs, Tupac Shakur, Peter Tosh and Madonna. We include reggae, soul, R&B, hip-hop, country, blues, jazz, and even folk music. How on earth can you exclude a man like Hank Williams, who lived his life through a haze of drink and drugs, when someone like Rolling Stone Bill Wyman, a self-confessed Tory with a hamburger restaurant, can't be avoided?

> Let's face it, if I weren't as talented as I am ambitious, I'd be a gross monstrosity.   *Madonna*

This book is not intended as a history of rock 'n' roll, nor is it a definitive guide to the subject. We've scoured libraries and personal collections in search of the best rock 'n' roll writing, and here it is. Not everyone we approached gave us permission to use their material, but over 90 per cent of what we wanted is here. I'd like to thank all those who helped (you know who you are) and offer two fingers to those who didn't (you know who you are, too).

> I am not a saint. I am a noise.   *Joan Baez.*

I've blacked out, had seizures, had my stomach pumped. They took me to hospital in New Orleans once and I came round to find this guy on his hands and knees by the side of my bed going, "Pssst, are you Ozzy Osbourne? Are you dying?" I said, "I don't know." He said, "Before you go, can you give me your autograph?" And shoves this piece of paper into my hand. No respect, these fuckers.

Ozzy Osbourne

If you didn't know anything about Sex and Drugs and Rock 'n' Roll when you picked up the book, you sure as hell will when you put it down.

Jim Driver
London, January 2001

Crazy Blues

Giles Oakley

"There's fourteen million Negroes in our great country and they will buy records if recorded by one of their own, because we are the only folks that can sing and interpret hot jazz songs just off the griddle correctly."

Perry Bradford, a hustling composer, band leader, pianist and singer, with a city-slick line in slang, pestered and badgered executives from the white phonograph recording industry, determined to get a black singer on disc with one of his songs. The man he finally persuaded was Fred Hagar of Okeh Records, a man who had apparently received threatening letters from Northern and Southern pressure groups warning him that to record coloured girls would lead to a boycott of Okeh phonograph machines and records.

"May God bless Mr Hagar, for despite the many threats, it took a man with plenty of nerve and guts to buck those powerful groups and make the historical decision which echoed aroun' the world. He prised open that old 'prejudiced door' for the first colored girl, Mamie Smith, so she could squeeze into the large horn – and shout with her strong contralto voice:

> That thing called love – money cannot buy,
> That thing called love – will make you weep and cry.
> Sometimes you're sad – romantic and glad,
> The most wonderful thrill – you ever had . . .

As Perry recalled in his autobiography *Born with the Blues*, it was a happy moment, "for I'd schemed and used up all of my bag of tricks to get that date; had greased my neck with goose grease every morning, so it would become easy to bow and scrape to some recording managers. But none of them would listen to my tale o' woe, even though I displayed my teeth to them with a perpetual-lasting watermelon grin . . ."

February 14, 1920, was the date of this historic recording session, when Mamie Smith cut *That Thing Called Love* and *You Can't Keep A Good Man Down*. This was the first occasion that a blues singer was recorded. Her first session was made with white musicians, and the songs chosen were much like any ordinary popular song of the day.

That Thing Called Love was commercially a success, the boycott of Okeh products never happened, and in a few months Mamie Smith was called back to make a further record, this time with black musicians. On August 10, 1920, the first blues proper was recorded by Mamie Smith and her Jazz Hounds, which included fine jazz musicians like Johnny Dunn on cornet and almost certainly Willie "The Lion Smith" on piano. This too was another Perry Bradford composition, the famous *"Crazy Blues"*.

I can't sleep at night,   Now, I got the crazy blues,
I can't eat a bite,   Since my baby went away.
'Cause the man I love,   I ain't got no time to lose,
He didn't treat me right.   I must find him today.

Crazy Blues was an astonishing hit, selling 75,000 copies in the first month, at a dollar a time. The fact that the singer was black gave the record a symbolic significance. The sales excitement it generated proved the existence of a large and unexploited market, and the production and sale of blues records started to accelerate rapidly.

The record was a major breakthrough, a turning point in blues history. It was the moment the music ceased to be transmitted exclusively through local folk culture, with all the transience of "live" performances. From the time of Mamie Smith's first recordings it became possible for anyone in any part of the country to hear the same blues and hear it repeated in exactly the same way and as many times as the listener wanted, until the grooves of the disc were worn smooth. The many kinds of blues that had emerged would now gradually become fixed into various, more regular patterns, and the new forms themselves would in turn continue to interact with each other to produce still more variety.

To begin with, blues recordings were dominated by women singers who had come up through cabaret and vaudeville, and for many of them singing blues meant little more than adopting the material that was becoming fashionable. An early advert for a Mamie Smith record referred to her as a "singer of 'Blues' – the music of so new a flavor". In fact she had the clear voice and lightness of a popular singer, with little of the tension and slurred moaning of a country blues singer. Many of the early singers were characterised by this clear enunciation and diction, the style of performers used to projecting popular material with light jazzy dance bands. One of the earliest was the light-skinned Lucille Hegamin, who had a rich voice and a neat, rather jaunty, style of singing. One of her biggest hits was *Arkansas Blues* which was recorded by one company and eventually issued on eleven different labels.

> Ain't got no time to lose,
> I'm tired and lonely, I'm tired of roaming.
> I long to see my mammy in my home in . . .
> I got the Arkansas blues!

Composed by Anton Lada and Spencer Williams, *Arkansas Blues* had a catchy tune, and the jazzy accompaniment of the Blue Flame Syncopaters gave it a good bounce. Like many of the early women singers, with their popular song orientation and lightness of touch, Lucille Hegamin and Mamie Smith seem to reflect a feeling of joy and hope in keeping with the expectations of the black migrants newly arrived in the cities. Lucille Hegamin herself was described in an early record catalogue as "the South's favorite – cyclonic exponent of dark-town melodies". Indeed she had come from the South – she was born in Macon in 1897 – and by 1914 was in Chicago. Billed as Georgia Peach, she sang "nearly all the popular ballads and ragtime tunes of the day", at cabarets and night spots. She told Derrick Stewart-Baxter:

"I was a cabaret artist in those days, and never had to play theatres, and I sang everything from blues to popular songs, in a jazz style. I think I can say without bragging that I made the *St. Louis Blues* popular in Chicago; this was one of my feature numbers."

Here was the ideal background for the breezy hopefulness of people coming to the big city with confident tunes about missing mammy at home in Arkansas. Despite the poverty and over-crowding of the swelling ghetto, Chicago could spell hope and stimulation.

Lil Hardin, the jazz pianist who, according to singer Alberta Hunter, "played a mighty blues", arrived in Chicago with her family from Memphis in 1918.

"I made it my business to go out for a daily stroll and look this 'heaven' over. Chicago meant just that to me – its beautiful brick and stone buildings, excitement, people moving swiftly, and things happening."

Alberta Hunter was herself an immigrant to Chicago. In 1908 she ran away from home at the age of eleven and got a job as a cook, sending her mother two out of her six dollars a week plus board. As she got a bit older, she started hearing stories about girls making as much as ten dollars a week in night clubs. She went looking for such a job and got one in Dago Frank's "where the sportin' girls hung out". Alberta made a career for herself in night clubs and cabarets and was another of the first to sing blues on record.

The clubs and cabarets where singers like Lucille Hegamin and Alberta Hunter started singing were part of the explosion of black entertainment that happened in Chicago in the War years and after; they were part of the glamour and excitement which helped draw people like a magnet. By the 1920s Chicago was in the mainstream of the jazz age, with some of the greatest names playing and recording there – names like King Oliver, Louis Armstrong, Johnny Dodds, Jelly Roll Morton. The Chicago of the 20's has now become part of America's mythology, with

Prohibition, the rise of gangsters like Al Capone, speakeasies, gangland killings, bootlegging, the air of lawlessness, fast cars and tommyguns, a jazz band in every club, everything bright lights and speed. Deplored but avidly explored, it has been written about and portrayed in dozens of Hollywood movies. For some Chicago was to become the essence of America, the melting pot of nationalities and races, a city of opportunities for people of energy, or nerves, a city for the big gesture and extravagance and the big personality like the notoriously and outrageously corrupt Republican Mayor Big Bill Thompson, working hand in glove with the liquor racketeers and the rest.

What is less often remembered of the city is the appalling squalor and poverty of many people's lives, the sheer marginality and instability of their existence. A survey was prepared for the Chicago Council of Social Agencies, *The Hobo: The Sociology of the Homeless Man* by Nels Anderson, based on conditions in 1921 and 1922. It revealed that the number of homeless men in Chicago ranged from 30,000 in good times to 75,000 in hard times, of which probably a third were permanent residents, living in lodging-houses and hotels. In any given year between 300,000 and 500,000 seasonal workers and migrants passed in and out of the city, some seeking and finding work, others becoming down-and-outs.

Chicago had something of the quality of a frontier town, rapidly expanding as an industrial community, a centre of transport, of commerce and of employment, drawing in people by the thousands and spewing them out again in an endless flow. Some settled to regular work, others found a thousand hand-to-mouth ways of hustling a living.

This was the background against which blues and jazz reached a high point of popularity. Many women singers fronted bluesy jazz bands, from the thin-voiced and sophisticated cabaret performer Alberta Hunter with Lovie Austin on piano, to the tough and throaty Bertha "Chippie" Hill with King Oliver's band at places like the Palladium Dance Hall.

Nevertheless the recording world took some little time to catch up with the singers closer to the folk roots. There was still a

tendency to go for the more sophisticated and vaudeville styles
and mainly those readily available near the main recording
centres. With their stagey background, their material often
had carefully contrived lyrics and a well-ordered, dramatically
presented scene, like Sister Harris' *Don't Mess With Me* (1923)

> Miss Lestrange Sarah Brown was the most classical gal
>   in town
> She met honorable Rupert Paul dancing at that Wang
>   Wang Ball.
> He took her home that night, she gave him a kiss,
> But when he went too far she up and told him this:
>
> "Don't mess with me, don't mess with me,
> You work fast that's very true,
> You're in the right church but in the wrong pew,
> Don't mess with me, you better run along an' let me be,
> I've got a razor that's got a nasty blade,
> Just pass on circus, I've seen your parade,
> 'Cause I done picked the ground where your body's
>   gonna be found.
> Don't mess with me . . ."

"Dance, have a stage up there and dance", says Sam Chatmon,
remembering the tent shows of his youth, "and clowns, all like
that – man, they'd have a big time in some places! They called
them the Nigger Minstrels, and the Ringling Brothers, they had a
big show. They had plenty elephants and lions, all like that. The
show was just a street carnival – the one I'm talking about.
They'd show sometime one night or two nights and then they'd
take down and move to the next town."

While in the cities like Chicago cabarets and dance halls gave
work to blues singers, a bigger breeding ground for blues entertainment was to be found in the longer-established world of
travelling black show business.

Following the Nigger Minstrel traditions, numerous shows
travelled the South and Mid-West, playing for the small towns

and plantations. Many of them employed blues singers, both men and women, as part of their bonanza entertainment, bringing colour, extravagance and all kinds of fun – comics, jugglers, dance-routines, wrestlers, ragtime, cakewalk, trapeze artists and wire-walkers. Some blues singers found work with the "second" companies of the big circuses, sometimes following the main show and sometimes touring separately providing entertainment for all-black audiences. But it was mainly the minstrel shows that spread the blues, in many different companies endlessly on the move, from Florida to Texas, Oklahoma to Mississippi, with names such as Tolliver's Circus and Musical Extravaganza, the King and Bush Wide-Mouth Minstrels, the Georgia Smart Set and its rival the Smarter Set, and Pete Werley's Cotton Blossoms Show. Pre-eminent in the field and best remembered of them all were Silas Green's from New Orleans, which started in 1910, and their chief rivals the famous Rabbit Foot Minstrels, organised by F.S. Wolcott from Port Gibson, Mississippi.

The minstrel and carnival shows would perform in huge tents carried in trailers or sometimes their own railroad cars which could be detached from trains and slipped into sidings. As the roustabouts and canvasmen rigged up the tent, a brass band would go parading round the locality "ballyhooing" to drum up an audience, with performers perhaps waving and mugging from atop the back of an elephant. They would play for all kinds of people at levee camps or plantations, or set up outside small towns. Changing facilities might be in a tent or in the rail car, where they also sometimes slept. Ethel Waters recalls sleeping in a stable because "the colored people in Lexington (Kentucky) wouldn't let carnival show girls into their homes, so we couldn't get a room . . . Baby Jim, the show's fat man, had to sleep in the stable, too, but for a different reason. He weighed between four and five hundred pounds. Like all carnival fat men, he was supposed to be the fattest in the world. In all Lexington there was no house with a door big enough for Baby Jim to get through, and no bed strong enough to hold his weight."

At this time Ethel Waters was appearing as one of "The Hill Sisters, Featuring Sweet Mama Stringbean, Singing *St. Louis*

Blues". She was one of the first women to record blues, but hers was the pure-toned, sweet-voiced variety; she later became a very fine jazz singer before entering a career as a movie actress. She came from a rancid and decrepit slum in Chester, Pennsylvania, and was born in 1901 after her mother had been raped at the age of twelve. Her childhood was lonely and isolated in a crowded world surrounded by the sights of groping and fumbling sex in back alleys (she would keep watch while her friends experimented).

"In crowded slum homes one's sex education begins very early indeed. Mine began when I was about three and sleeping in the same room, often in the same bed, with my aunts and my transient 'uncles'. I wasn't fully aware of what was going on but resented it. By the time I was seven I was repelled by every aspect of sex."

She was always a leader in street gangs, stealing and hell-raising, and well acquainted with the local whores. She had much affection for these women and respected them for the way they supported whole families and sometimes even their accidental children through college. Her neighbourhood was not exclusively black; there were plenty of whites, "Hunkies and Jews, and some Chinese". The whores, black and white, worked together, lived together and slept together.

"There was no racial prejudice at all in that big melting pot running over with vice and crime, violence, poverty and corruption. I never was made to feel like an outcast on Clifton Street. All of us, white, blacks, and yellows, were outcasts together and having a fine time among ourselves."

Ethel felt isolated from her aunts and her mother because while "they discussed people and things that happened with considerable intelligence and insight", they appeared to care little for her. It was in the world of showbiz that she found solace, especially in the camaraderie of being on the road with a tent show.

"I liked being in the carnival. The roustabouts and concessionaires were the kind of people I'd grown up with, rough, tough, full of larceny towards strangers, but sentimental, and loyal to their friends and co-workers. The carnival work was colorful and a new experience. But I didn't like it when it rained. It was bad underfoot in the tents because no planks were put down."

Tent show stages were usually made of boards on a folding frame, set up at one end, sometimes lit by candles, but more usually with gasoline mantle lanterns which later gave way to somewhat unreliable electric lamps powered by portable generators. Occasionally the shows would be done "in the round" with four groups of dancers facing each quarter of the audience. Virtually all the famous and great women blues singers of the 20's passed through the rough apprenticeship of the tent show routine. Barnstorming from settlement to township and from State to State gave them the chance to learn their trade as entertainers. The discipline and control of the early blues records reflects the formality of tested professional performance. The blues was taken into a new relationship with its black folk cultural origins; the blues singer – at least the women singers of the 20's – was no longer an ordinary member of black society singing the songs of the working people or playing for the local dances. They were set up on stage, watched and listened to from afar, using every trick and stage device to "present" their songs. The audience was in a more clearly detached position, and if not exactly passive (crowds would wildly cheer, groan, shout and stomp), they were no longer participants on a near-level basis. In fact blues had come close to creating a star system not unlike the world of white showbiz.

Not that blues was the only element in black minstrelsy and carnivals. The chorus girls, the comedy acts, the entertainers of every kind were there too, with jazz musicians bluesy and not so bluesy.

"Every Friday night they had a Midnight Ramble", says Laura Dukes about the Palace Theatre on Beale Street, Memphis. "They had it so they had one night for the white and one night for the colored people. That's when the girls, I don't know, look like they half-stripped you know."

If black showbiz was parallel to white, it was nowhere more apparent than in the world of theatre. At first blacks could perform in segregated white theatres, like on the Western Vau-

deville and the B.F. Keith-Orpheum circuits. These chains of
theatres would book in Negro acts which blacks could watch from
the segregated peanut galleries. But soon the growing tide of
black talent, and the size of the black audiences piling into the
growing cities in the South and North demanded more facilities:
there was clearly money to be made. In 1907 a man from
Memphis started a small circuit of theatres in the South, the
success of which led to the establishment in 1909 of the famous,
and infamous, Theatre Owners' Booking Agency variously
known as TOBA, Toby Time, or Tough On Black Asses. These
white-run theatres provided pretty squalid working conditions;
often there was no backstage and on the smaller stages, no wings.
In some, artists would dress underneath the stage behind thin
partitions, come out through the orchestra pit and climb precariously up a ladder, hoping to get on stage before the lights
came up. The Monogram Theatre in Chicago was so cramped
there wasn't room to stand upright when changing costume and,
being right next to a railway line, every time a train passed
performers had to stop singing or telling their jokes till the noise
died down.

The TOBA theatre hired either independent acts or complete
companies, with bands, chorus girls, comics, and every kind of
vaudeville routine, the show running for perhaps a week before
moving on to another city. None of the theatres paid travelling
expenses so artists would seek to avoid schedules with long
distances involved. It could be a gruelling and humiliating life
for the lesser performers, often harassed by white theatre bosses
like the notorious Charles P. Bailey of the 81 Theatre on Decatur
Street, Atlanta. Bailey was a vindictive and arrogant "czar" in his
own theatre, and his authority ran outside it: he would issue
passes for the black artists to break Atlanta's curfew regulations
(like most Southern cities at that time, Atlanta banned blacks
from the streets after a certain hour).

Soon most cities with a black population of any size had a
Negro theatre – the Pastime and the Beale Avenue Palace in
Memphis, the Lyric in New Orleans, the Lyceum in Cincinnati,
the Dream in Columbus, Georgia, the Koppin in Detroit, the

Bijou in Nashville, the Booker T. Washington in St Louis and others in Florida, Arkansas, Missouri and Alabama. Not every theatre was a TOBA outfit; there were independents in New York, Washington and elsewhere. But all featured the women blues singers alongside their jugglers, snake-charmers, high-kicking "High Brown Chorus Girls", "Sepia Lovelies" and quick-fire comedy routines.

Black audiences were sometimes cruelly demanding. If they didn't think much of a performance they would maintain an impervious independence running up and down the aisles, yelling greetings to friends and even breaking out into fights. But for the best-loved blues singers the emotional rewards could be enormous, appearing in glamorous revues, heading their own companies, singing and moaning the deepest and most emotional of blues. Spellbound audiences would greet the end of a song with whoops and shouts, exultantly screaming for more, applauding wildly and stamping their feet. At such moments the blues stars became virtually racial heroines, symbols of success and glamour, dressed in resplendent outfits, decked in sequins and dazzling jewellery, disappearing for a quick-change to reappear in yet another sumptuous gown. In a society which denied black people the dignity of human equality, denied them the means to even strive for it, the trappings of riches and success were symbols of great potency. That the successes of the great blues singers like Bessie Smith, Ida Cox, Ma Rainey and many others were based on their own intimate knowledge and experience of the blues culture of the poor and dispossessed made the symbolism even more profound.

Bands, Booze & Broads

Sheila Tracy

During the Big Band era, which came to its peak just after the Second World War, the pressures on touring musicians were intense. There was a party every night and even in the days before rock 'n' roll, drink and drugs were readily available. Sometimes it was the only way to keep up. Former Woody Herman sidemen Eddie Bert and Sonny Igoe tell it like it was.

Sonny Igoe Drums   1950–3

I joined Woody Herman after I left Benny Goodman. The bass player with Woody at that time was Red Mitchell, a marvellous bass player, and Shelly Manne was the drummer. They had a small band, and had just come back from Havana and were playing in Philadelphia, but Shelly Manne was going to leave. Red Mitchell suggested me to Woody Herman, so they called me and asked if I'd like to join them, and I said I'd love to.

I joined them in Philadelphia but I didn't play a note there because Shelly hadn't left. We got on a train for three days and went to Duluth, Minnesota. So I'd had my first job with Woody and he had yet to hear me play!

I was with the guys in the band for three days on the train so I got to know everybody, but I was apprehensive because these guys were all so good. Ralph Burns was the piano player, Milt Jackson was the vibes player, Conte Candoli was the trumpet player, and Bill Harris the trombone player, and, of course, there was Woody. I was the rookie!

We went to the job, no rehearsal, he didn't want to rehearse or anything like that. Everybody gets featured and halfway through the night Woody says, "We're going to feature you now, Sonny," so I say, "What am I going to do, with no rehearsal?" So he said, "Just follow me," and he goes into something we later recorded called "Golden Wedding", and so I just follow him. It was a kind of a "Sing, Sing, Sing" type of thing. Everybody had an answer to "Sing, Sing, Sing", Tommy Dorsey had a thing called "Not So Quiet Please" that Buddy Rich played, and Woody had this that all the drummers played. So we did that and luckily we all started and ended together! From then on we did it every night.

That first night it just went beautifully; everybody said, "Hey, that's great," so I was in. I was lucky. Sometimes you get lucky.

After we had the small band for about two months, Woody decided to go back to a big band, and we played in Bop City in New York, and he had a lot of fellas from his previous big bands who augmented our group. We played there for a month, and Sarah Vaughan was on the bill with us. This was 1950 and she was a kid just starting out and sounding marvellous. We did some one-nighters after Bop City and then came back and played the Capitol Theatre.

Woody was a terrific guy to work for. Sometimes I think he was a little too relaxed but he never gave you a hard time and he always respected the musicians for being talented people and let them go their own way, so to speak. I think that was one of the secrets of his success: he was a good organiser but he didn't interfere with how the guys played. That's why he had so many marvellous bands over the years. If you listen to some of those old records, they're just unbelievable.

Bobby Lamb Trombone 1956–8

In November 1955 I heard that Woody was going to reform his big band, so Wally Heider rang Woody who had a small group in Las Vegas. He explained to Wally that Keith Moon, who used to be on the band, was thinking of coming back on the road, in which case all the positions were filled. The other downer was there was a whole heap of guys already there auditioning for the big gig.

We eventually went up to the Sands Hotel where Woody was staying and, just as I went in the door, the elevator opened and out walked Woody. I said who I was and he said, "Well, the good news is Keith Moon has decided not to come back on the band, so there is a place. The bad news is, if you look over there by the bar, all the guys standing there are trombone players who've been auditioning for the past three nights and they're just sizing each other up. So, if you'll come back at midnight and sit in with the band, we'll see how you make out."

I was shattered by all this, but one of the guys at the bar came over to me, I can't remember his name, but I really owe this guy. He said, "You're from Europe, you're a trombone player auditioning for the gig tonight?" and I said, "Yes, I am." So he said, "Well, I auditioned last night so let's have a cup of coffee and I'll tell you about it."

So he told me in detail every single item they were going to play, what key everything was in, what to look out for because there was no pre-look at anything. You went on, there was an audience there, and you played. This guy told me everything so I went back to the hotel with four hours to spare, got in the shower and practised until I was blue in the face!

By the time it came for me to go on stage and play with the band, I practically didn't have to open the book, I knew every bloody thing! Anyway, to cut a long story short, I got the job.

The band was reformed in New York on Christmas Eve as our first gig was a three-hour television show in Philadelphia for New Year's Eve and he wanted the band to be in shape for that. I was a stranger on the band and I had one piece with a solo, Johnny Mandel's *Four Others*. I had the bridge in this, and the show was being televised coast to coast, and, of course, with a week to prepare, I've got to tell you this, I got to know that eight bars upside down, inside out, backwards, forwards, every conceivable way. By the time it came to the actual show, I stood up and played as loud and outrageous as I possibly could and that endeared me to the guys in the band as they could see how hard I was trying. That was the beginning of the Woody Herman years, as I say.

Woody was very, very kind and considerate. He had a lovely philosophy. When a new guy joined the band, he understood perfectly that the mental and nervous traumas that person was going through would inhibit his playing to a large degree so he would leave the guy alone.

In the trombone section we had Wayne Andre who went on to become a big star, and soon after I joined my greatest hero of all time came back on the band, Bill Harris, who for me was the greatest trombone player that ever lived! The magnetism, power and feeling that he used to get into the trombone . . .!

It's a shame that most of the guys around today can't ever, ever hear or see someone play like that – he was tremendous, incredible. I remember when he came back on the band we were in New York and doing a Sunday afternoon concert at Childs Restaurant, next door to the Paramount Theatre. I'm sitting there with Wayne and we're sort of tootling and warming up and through the door came this guy of about 6 feet 2 inches, and very erect. He didn't look the least bit like a musician, more like a bank-manager, but certainly not a jazz musician. Very dignified.

He came up and Woody introduced him and, of course, he was one of the reasons I had taken up the trombone in the first place, so I'm speechless. We got on the stand and Woody, who had a great sense of humour and was very mischievous, decided to call *Not Really the Blues*, another Johnny Mandel piece that featured the trombone section.

I noticed that Bill didn't bother opening the book. Now, he hadn't been in the band for a long time. Anyway, Woody kicked this thing off and the trombones stood up and that was the first time I heard Bill Harris playing in the flesh, and I practically dropped my trombone with fright. I stopped playing and looked across and Wayne wasn't playing either. We were just looking at this giant and wondering at this sound coming out. I looked at Woody who was falling about and he looked at me and said, "That's the way it used to be kid, that's what a trombone sounds like!"

We didn't travel by coach as Woody had some sort of contract with Ford and they gave us four new cars every year, so four guys

were assigned to each car and it made it very good. If you weren't
into booze then you didn't travel in the boozing car, and if you
were straight you travelled in the straight car, or whatever. You
travelled with your own mates and you didn't have to travel in
convoy, you moved when you wanted to as long as you got to the
gig on time. That was the only criterion.

The band did a tour with Louis Armstrong, and we would go
on for the first half of the concert and then Louis Armstrong and
the All Stars would come along and do the second half. At the end
the two bands would get together and we'd all jam.

Edmund Hall, who was playing clarinet in Louis' band, was a
very distinguished gentleman, and I must point out that the
Louis Armstrong All Stars were getting paid a lot more money
than the Woody Herman Roaring Herd. We were at the other end
of the financial scale.

All the distances in America are quite enormous. You can't
really begin to appreciate the size of America unless you're
travelling by road, and we had devised a system whereby we
could save some money on hotel bills. For example, we would
finish Monday night in Philadelphia and the next night we would
be in Virginia or even Ohio. So, instead of going into a hotel that
night, we would drive on and arrive in the next town, say, at
midday. We would check into the hotel, sleep before the gig, do
the gig and sleep that night. You're sleeping twice but paying for
one room and then you move on. It's a crazy way of doing things.

No sleep Monday night, sleep Tuesday and Tuesday night,
leave on Wednesday, do the gig Wednesday night, no sleep
Wednesday night, move on, and so, in 14 days, you would book
into a hotel maybe seven times. Edmund Hall, as I said, was a very
distinguished gentleman and he could see how we were working
this. He said, "Now, look, there's no need for you to do this because
I'm staying in a first-class hotel and I'm not a great sleeper, so why
don't you guys overlap? When you come in for the day, have my
room and sleep in the day. Then when I move on I'll be booked into
the next hotel so you will at least get a sleeping space." It was a very
good idea; but you can imagine the scenario – one black gentleman
books into a very elegant room and four white scruffs leave!

I've got to say this about the American bandleaders that I worked with: I found them all very, very warm human beings, every one of them – Charlie, Stan, Woody. They were all very different in their own ways. Woody's instincts were very sharp, Kenton was the intellectual one, of course, and Charlie Barnet, for me, was the fun one.

Woody was a very instinctive sort of person. I remember we were doing a Carnegie Hall concert and it was the first time the band had been back there since the very famous one in 1945. He was rather keen to emulate the success of the 1945 concert so he picked out the programme very carefully. But the marvellous thing about Woody was he would beat off the very first number and during that first number, his antenna would really be up, in tune with the audience. Then he would calmly turn around, forget the programme and pick the numbers he knew were going to make contact with the audience.

I haven't seen anybody else with this kind of talent. He knew exactly what the audience was going to be like straight away. Not putting down anyone in Europe, but they pick a programme and that's it, like it or not, that is it.

Woody had this instinct with people as well. He only had to look at you and he knew you very well. His way of rehearsing was quite extraordinary, I've never seen anything like it. He must have terrified some of the greatest arrangers in the country but it was an education for them. They would bring in their score and Woody would have a cup of coffee while they rehearsed the band. He would not interfere at all.

Rehearsing in America is a very slow process. They take their time about it. When he was ready the arranger would say to Woody, "Have a listen to this." Woody would listen then he would say something like, "Fine, we'll take the bridge and use that as the intro, take the intro and stick it here, take the first chorus and put it at the back," and he would reshape the entire thing in the space of five minutes, and it worked every time. The funniest thing was the expression on the arranger's face because he would flip having put so much time into it. But then a few nights later, when they were sitting out front listening to the piece, they would come roaring backstage saying, "Man, it works. It really works; that's my arrangement," ignoring the fact that Woody had completely rearranged the arrangement!

It was difficult to do anything that would annoy Woody because he was a nice guy, he was an extremely fair guy but he was a strong guy. He never felt the need to create the famous Goodman "ray", the so-called killer expression. He never, like some bandleaders, created the great freeze-out when they just didn't talk to you for a long time until you finally got the message you were no longer welcome. No, no, he was a different sort of a guy altogether. Very direct, didn't bug you but he let you know he expected the best from you. If you were messing around or just being stupid, he would tell you, like a father figure. He would tell you firm, he would tell you strong but he was never unfair. I never saw him being unfair to anybody.

There were guys fired from the band, but it was like being fired by consensus. I'll give you an idea of what would happen. A saxophone player joined us and straight away we all knew he was not right for the band. I don't mean musically, but he had certain hang-ups, and at that time the law pertaining to these particular hang-ups was extremely severe. If the police had stopped us and begun to search for whatever it was, and say this one guy was caught in a bad situation, we would all have been guilty by being party to this and I would have been deported. It was a very sensitive time for drugs.

This guy had joined the band and it was obvious he was in a bad way. Without anything being said to Woody, all the guys just went and had a chat with this fella and said we didn't think he was right for the band and we, the band, thought it would be a good idea if he just left. So he said, "Now wait a minute, I work for Woody Herman," and we said "Look, here's the situation: we, the band, don't want you on the band, we think you should go."

The following night when Woody turned up to front the band he noticed this guy wasn't there and never said a word but he knew exactly what was going on. And that created a pride and determination and a force within the band that few bands can have where each person is committed to each other. So, you're playing for each other, you're playing with each other, and a spirit develops in that kind of situation which is unique.

I think that's how Woody's bands became known as the Roaring Herds because they were united and had this closeness about them so that when they did arrive in town and started to play, it was awesome. The power and excitement that was generated by the band was tremendous. It was so exciting to arrive at the Blue Note in Chicago or say Birdland or Basin Street East in New York, and every musician in town has turned up to hear the band. So, even before you blow a note, the atmosphere is sky high. Then, when the band starts to play, it takes off, and then a great soloist like Bill Harris stands up to play.

I can remember playing in Hollywood when every trombone player for a hundred miles around was there that night because Bill Harris was in the band. Bill Harris only had to flush the water out of his key and there was a buzz of excitement from all these people, "He's going to play, he's going to play!" He only had to take a breath and they were in ecstasy, I've never seen anything like it. Elvis Presley couldn't come anywhere near this guy!

The first album I made with Woody was for Norman Granz. I remember turning up at the studio and the trombones were Bill Harris, Willie Dennis and myself, and I make no bones about it, of the three players I was by far the weakest soloist. I was very much aware of the situation. Nevertheless, on the first piece, *Stairway to the Blues*, I had the solo.

As it was such an important occasion, I expected Woody to say, "Look, we're recording this, Bobby, so let Bill play that solo," which wouldn't have bothered me at all. But he didn't, so now here I am and nobody has asked me to give away my solo. Just then Dizzy Gillespie walked in, so in the box there's Miles Davis, Norman Granz producing, Dizzy and J.J.Johnson. I can't tell you all the people who came by to say hello.

Here I am standing up, the first guy to play this solo on the first tune. I wasn't too knocked out with the solo at all. It was adequate, but no great shakes, as the situation got on top of me. So when that Verve album came out I rushed out to buy it with mixed feelings. Even though it wasn't one of the best things

I'd ever done, I thought, boy, oh, boy, having my name on the album's going to be great, but having people hear what I sound like is not going to be too good. So it was a strange feeling.

I rushed into the shop, picked up the album, looked down to see the write-up, and Willie Dennis got the credit for the solo! Now, Willie has the most distinctive style of jazz playing ever. He was the first of the doodle tonguers, so for any idiot at all to compare the two was just ridiculous. But here's the punch-line. That night in the band-room in New York, the door burst open and in roared Willie Dennis, screaming, "You're not going to believe this, but you know that load of rubbish you played on the album, they say it's me!"

I was with Woody two and a half years, and by that time I was married with two children, and I wasn't seeing anything of them at all. My wife was bringing them up and I didn't get to spend much time with them.

To give you an idea what being on the road was like and what's involved, I once met Johnny Hodges in Oregon and during the course of the conversation he told me that they had left New York 18 months ago. Now, figure that out. They'd been working their way up and down, up and down, going across America. They hadn't been home in 18 months and it was going to take them nearly a year to work back to New York.

We had a house in Philadelphia and I could leave there and go on the road and might not get back for six months. So, enough was enough. I had a taste and played with some of the greatest people ever, I couldn't be greedy anymore, so we came back to New York, and then we decided we'd come back to London, it was as simple as that.

It's Only Rock 'n' Roll

Wayne "Dang" Dooley

If anyone ever tells you that the term "rock 'n' roll" was coined by American DJ Alan Freed, tell them to take a hike. "Go spin, buddy" – as George Martin might say. The Boswell Sisters recorded a song called *Rock And Roll* in 1934 and rocking and rolling had been Afro-American slang for fucking since long before Freed first set foot on God's good pasture.

The roots of rock 'n' roll run deep. Some hillbilly didn't just wake up one morning and start yelping *Hound Dog* (in fact, Willie Mae "Big Mama" Thornton's original R&B version of the song from 1953 is about as far removed from rock 'n' roll as chopped liver). The birth of rock 'n' roll was a long, messy, and sometimes painful delivery that has no definite conception. It is as American as apple pie and "pleading the First", but with Blues as its surrogate father. Most of the early rock 'n' roll music was performed by black musicians and was termed R&B (rhythm and blues) the more acceptable name for what had been called "race". Back in those days in the States, African-Americans and Caucasians didn't mix too freely, and two distinct markets for music existed: for the black population and for the white.

Louis Jordan, the most popular R&B artist of the forties laid the foundations of rock 'n' roll with his feet-hoppin' "jump blues", and other bastard forbearers of rock 'n' roll weren't slow to sow their own seed. In 1947 Roy Brown recorded a blues called *Good Rockin' Tonight*, which was rockabilly in all but name, and when covered a year later by Wynonie Harris, became so damn rock 'n' roll, it practically spits in your face. Bill Moore's *We're Going To Rock, We're Going To Roll* (1948) and Jimmy Preston's *Rock The Joint* a year later were just two among dozens of records that carried on in pretty much the same vein. Now everybody was "rocking" and if the word "rock" didn't appear in the title of your R&B record in some form or another, you were colder than last week's toast.

At about the same time, a few white boys were unwittingly knocking on rock 'n' roll's door. Hardrock Gunter – now all but forgotten, but once a feature on most white-serviced jukeboxes throughout southern and Mid-West America – was coming up with rockin' boogie cuts like Birmingham Bounce; and on 1950s *Gonna Dance All Night* he actually snarls: "We're gonna rock 'n' roll!" Country artists like Hank Snow, Tennessee Ernie Ford and Hank Williams were travelling a road that ran almost parallel to that of their black counterparts, but without the driving rhythms that pushed R&B straight into the path of rock 'n' roll.

Sam Phillips insists that *Rocket 88* by Jackie Brenston and His Delta Cats, recorded at his Sun Studio in Memphis in 1951 is the first straight rock 'n' roll hit. Although Brenston sang, played sax and is credited as composer, "His Delta Cats" were actually Ike Turner and His Kings of Rhythm, who claimed they should at least have had co-writing credits. Until Phillips placed the master with Chess records of Chicago, Ike thought the song was going to be released under his own name, and he was reportedly seething with rage when he discovered otherwise. *Rocket 88* reached number one in the R&B chart on May 12th, 1951 and was covered a year later by Bill Haley.

Haley, a former yodelling cowboy from Michigan by way of Pennsylvania, led a band called The Saddlemen. Their sound was a cross between Western Swing and Polka, with a prominent beat strapped across it. Despite having an ear on the R&B charts for possible cover songs, they were darlings of the hillbilly set and favourites on country music radio. After the limited success of their cover of *Rocket 88*, a version of Jimmy Preston's *Rock the Joint* sold 75,000 copies and made up Bill's mind. The Saddlemen dropped their snow-white Stetsons and unfeasibly-fringed jackets to become Bill Haley and the Comets. In 1953 Haley wrote *Crazy Man Crazy*, which was to become the first rock 'n' roll record to make the *Billboard* pop top 20. But the song that really gave white kids their first real blast of rock 'n' roll was the Comets' version of a minor R&B hit, *Rock Around the Clock*. It was featured heavily throughout *The Blackboard Jungle*, a film about teenage rebellion starring Glenn Ford and Sidney Poitier (it's said that the song's publisher doubled as the film's musical director), and rocketed to number one in the *Billboard* charts. By some strange quirk of fate, it also made number three in the R&B charts.

This is where Alan Freed comes in. His influence in bringing black music to white audiences began in 1951. A DJ at WKST in Cleveland, he was asked to play black artists' cuts by a record retailer who'd noticed white kids buying R&B and thought he'd sniffed out a new way to make extra bucks. Freed reduced his diet of Perry Como and Dean Martin ballads and changed the name of his show from "Record Rendezvous" to "The Moon Dog Rock 'n' Roll Party", preferring to adopt the Afro-American euphemism for fucking (which white people didn't know anything about, anyway) because it wasn't as overtly black as "R&B". In 1952 Freed almost went to jail for selling 20,000 tickets for a live "Moondog Rock 'n' Roll Party" at a 10,000 seater venue. That the bands were all black (Charles Brown, Tiny Grimes Jump Jive, The Orioles, the Dominoes with Clyde McPhatter, The Moonglows and Jimmy Forest), and the audience half white, says plenty. Soon DJs all over America were playing R&B and calling it rock 'n' roll, and Freed found himself swept off to New York to became a celebrity in his own right. Only accusations of payola would eventually bring him down, and by then (1959), rock 'n' roll was as much part of American culture as hamburgers and handguns.

Although Bill Haley found fame and respect as a rock 'n' roll originator, the chubby-faced geek wasn't really superstar material. Women weren't throwing their soiled underwear at *him*. The world was looking for its first rock 'n' roll star, and the young man waiting in the wings was Elvis Presley.

Sam Phillips had long said that if he could just find a white boy who could sing like a black man, he'd make a million dollars. That dream came true when a pretty-boy nineteen-year-old truck driver came to the studio in 1953, under the pretext of making a record for his mama. Never one to miss an opportunity, Phillips called him back to the studio, organised a couple of Country session-musicians – guitarist Scotty Moore and bassist Bill Black – to see what kind of music the four of them could knock out together. It soon became clear that Elvis favoured soppy ballads, which was a disappointment to Sam Phillips, because the last thing he was looking for was another Perry Como.

Just when he was becoming resigned to cutting his losses and calling it a day, Phillips called a break. Totally unprompted, Elvis started to kick around Arthur Crudup's *That's All Right, Mama*. That was when Phillips knew for sure he had something. He organised a hasty recording and managed to further coax an up-tempo version of *Blue Moon of Kentucky*. When the record was played on the radio a few days later – helped along by mention of Elvis's *white*-only school, thus establishing his race – orders totalling 7,120 copies arrived at the studio.

The combination of timing, talent and musical roots that included gospel, blues and country, made Elvis Presley the star he was. The young Elvis was further helped by the influence of a slightly older Memphis singer, Johnny Burnette, with whom Elvis worked at Crown Electric. Elvis had auditioned for Burnette's trio, but was turned down. Ironically, when Burnette auditioned for Sun Records, they turned *him* down. Isn't Kismet wonderful?

Elvis's first big rock 'n' roll hit came in 1956, once Phillips had sold his contract to the major RCA record company for $35,000. Elvis's share was $5,000 which he characteristically spent on a pink Cadillac. In the three years between his first demo and Heartbreak Hotel becoming a number one pop hit, much had changed. Doo-wop had arrived, heralded by The Penguins' Earth Angel and the all white-Canadian cover version of *Sh-Boom* by the Crew-Cuts (wrongly credited by some academics as the first rock 'n' roll record), both coming out in 1954; the Platters were the first R&B band to have a pop number one with *The Great Pretender* a year later; Little Richard and Chuck Berry were both writing and recording rock 'n' roll (Maybelline was an

R&B chart topper in 1955; *Tutti Frutti* reached number 17 in the *Billboard* chart a few months later), and both singers would later claim to have invented rock 'n' roll. Meanwhile, Ray Charles was developing his own style, which would later be acknowledged as the source of soul music.

Pretty soon rock 'n' roll was here to stay (as the song confidently asserts) and among the best and better-known exponents of the new music were Buddy Holly, Jerry Lee Lewis, Carl Perkins, Eddie Cochran, Gene Vincent and and Fats Domino. By 1959 rock 'n' roll had moved from being dangerous and subversive to as much a part of the cultural mainstream as Marlon Brando, Marilyn Monroe and Abbott & Costello. That the black man's music should have been largely taken over and sanitised was a double-edged sword for the Afro-American community. On the one hand it was obviously more healthy for white and black kids to attend the same concerts and listen to the same music, and it was a far better situation that the black writers to get their work recognised. The downside was that white commerciality made the music acceptable to parents and teachers and in doing so tore the guts out of it.

Music bought the races together to a certain extent, but racism was rife in rock 'n' roll. Guitarist Steve Cropper vividly remembers white kids being segregated at R&B concerts and having to watch from the balcony in Missouri, and it seemed to be an unwritten rule that black performers couldn't have mainstream hits with their own songs, it was a "must" that they be covered and "straightened out" by white acts first. Chuck Berry was outspoken against the racial harassment he was subjected to, and in 1959 he was charged under the out-dated Mann Act with taking a fourteen-year-old hat-check girl across state lines to a club he'd opened in Missouri. His first trial was blatantly racist, the second found him guilty and sentenced him to two years in Federal prison.

In Britain meanwhile, rock 'n' rollers like Billy Fury, Cliff Richard and Adam Faith covered songs by their American counterparts and practised looking rebellious in bathroom mirrors. It wasn't until mavericks like Joe Meek came along and transformed the music into something other than a straight copy of what the Americans were up to, that we saw any major artistic advance. The "Mersey Boom" and the "British Invasion" showed that given a bit of time to percolate ideas, the Brits could rock 'n' roll with the best of them.

Across the Channel, the French discovered rock 'n' roll through Johnny Halliday, a leather-clad bastardisation of Cliff Richard, Liberace and Englebert Humperdinck. Outsiders have often wondered how it is that continental Europeans have never really grasped what rock 'n' roll is all about. It is one of the unsolved mysteries of our age.

What is Skiffle?

Brian Bird

1958: Skiffle was the "in-thing" in Britain. Contemporary author Brian Bird is our guide . . .

Skiffle is a simple form of rhythmic music which has extended rapidly in this country in the last few years. It is Jazz music all right, for it has all the factors of rhythm, melodic improvisation, and the indispensable "beat" necessary to true Jazz. Skiffle is just a simplification of Jazz. For, in playing it, the essential "rhythm section" of a Jazz band is retained, and the "front line" which provides the melody (i.e. trumpet, trombone, and clarinet) is replaced by the human voice of a singer or singers. The obvious advantage of this is that with this simpler line-up many more people can play Jazz in this way, for the expensive instruments – the trumpet, trombone, and clarinet – have been eliminated. This is one reason for the great success of Skiffle, for it is the "poor man's Jazz", available to everyone who has that basic qualification of a genuine, sincere "feel" for the Jazz idiom.

Now, although Skiffle has developed very largely in England in recent years, it came into being originally in America as a part of the growth of Jazz. We must trace its history so that we may see the background and tradition of this musical expression which is so unusually popular.

Towards the end of the last century Ragtime and Jazz were beginning to be played in New Orleans by the early Jazzmen in their bands, using the brass and rhythm instruments, which had become accepted – viz trumpet, trombone, clarinet, guitar, banjo, double bass, drums, and piano. There were, however, many who longed to play but were unable to do so owing to their poverty.

The purchasing of an instrument was far beyond their limited means. These men had the true spirit of Jazz within them, one of the chief characteristics of which is improvisation. They were determined to play Jazz, so they improvised with whatever material they had available, and made their own instruments.

Thus we have the beginning of what were then called the "Spasm bands" – bands which played Jazz on simple home-made instruments. They were sometimes called "Hokum bands", from the American-Indian word "hokum", meaning bogus or imitation. They used anything they could lay their hands on that was cheap or free, to imitate the effects of the more costly instruments. Thus kazoos, combs-and-paper, harmonicas, washboards, bottles, and jugs were all forced into service. And any old boxes or spare pieces of wood were eagerly transformed into fiddles, guitars, banjos, and string-basses by the clever hands of the music-starved Negroes. And with these primitive and extempore tools they played Jazz – and good Jazz, at that. One of the earliest "Spasm bands" appeared in New Orleans in 1896 in Doc Malney's Minstrel Show, and was led by a musician known as "State Bread", who played a zither, supported by instrumentalists with delightfully peculiar names – "Cajun", with a harmonica; "Slew-Foot Pete", playing a guitar built from a cigarbox; "Whisky", a string bass made out of a half-barrel; and "Warm Gravy", a banjo constructed from a cheese-box. They were immensely popular among the teen-agers of that period.

These "Spasm bands" played anywhere they could find an audience – at minstrel shows, in clubs and saloons, on river-boats, and on the streets: the veritable descendants of the wandering minstrels of many a European city of the past. They appealed very much to children, whose homes were the streets, and who found this simple, direct Jazz easy to understand and undoubtedly stimulating. And children are, above all, imitative as well as masters of improvisation. So soon we had the children, with their own home-made instruments, forming their "Spasm bands" and marching as a second line behind the brass bands which subsequently became a feature of the New Orleans streets at that time.

Later on these bands became well established, and in 1924 we have The Mound City Blue Blowers, led by Red McKenzie. He developed "blue-blowing" (i.e. comb-and-paper played in a trumpet-imitation style) to a fine art, using ordinary newspaper with his comb. Other well-known bands of this type were. The Memphis Jug Band and The Dixieland Jug Blowers.

One cannot ignore, and should not despise, these "Spasm bands", for their achievement was perhaps even greater than that of the Jazz bands proper. For, with inferior equipment, they produced Jazz almost as good as, and in some cases as good as, the latter. And it must be remembered that in the course of their musical careers such masters as Louis Armstrong, Johnny Dodds, "King" Oliver, and even the great Jelly Roll Morton played in "Spasm bands" or Skiffle Groups.

In the old days of Mississippi folk-music a free-and-easy party with dancing was known as a Skiffle. And what then became called Skiffle bands were well known in American rural life during the first part of the century – with their informal singing and playing of the old Blues, work-songs, ballads, and Gospel hymns. They also incorporated into their repertoire many of the old English-Scots-Irish-Welsh songs that had been brought over by emigrants, and created accompaniments to these on guitar and banjo. To these was added the influence of the American Negro with his strong sense of rhythm and his deep feeling for life. This produced an unaffected, vital type of Jazz which had a very definite and direct appeal to the country-folk, a special way of playing and singing it which we now know as Skiffle.

It was, however, in the towns, and in Chicago in particular, that the word Skiffle became applied to this sort of music. What were known as rent parties were held there in the 'Twenties, with the obvious purpose of raising money to pay the rent. When the rent was due and there was no money to meet it, families would organize parties at which the Blues, folk-songs, and popular tunes of the day were played and sung. They used whatever instruments they happened to have with them or were able to make, and they played and sang the songs they liked. Nothing was ruled out. Nobody objected to this or that tune as not being correct Skiffle, because everything they played was Skiffle. It was all done in a simple, natural, and unaffected manner. The friends who came would bring contributions in the way of food and drink, and at the end of the evening a collection would be taken to obtain the money required for the rent.

One is reminded of a similar procedure at many a small Jazz club in this country, held in the local pub, where no charge for admission is made, and where, towards the end of the session, an enthusiast goes round casually with an empty pint mug into which contributions in coin may be thrown to help to defray any incidental expenses, part of which is usually the rent of the room. Truly a rent party of our own day! History does have a habit of repeating itself, even in Jazz circles!

There are obviously no records of these early Skiffle parties in America, as their music was purely for local and utilitarian purposes. They had no idea that they were creating something that would sweep across the world and eventually find its echoes in every town and village of England. Their thoughts were centred solely on the rent they had to raise. They would not have imagined, anyhow, that this informal, somewhat ragged music they were beating out on their home-made instruments would have been worth recording. It was just fun to them – fun with a purpose.

But at long last, about the year 1948, some record of this type of music was begun in America. A Harlem newspaper editor named Dan Burley made some piano recordings of numbers he used to hear as a youngster at parties in Chicago, which were called Boogies or Skiffles. He was accompanied by two guitarists, Brownie and Globe Trotter McGhee, and a bassist, Pops Foster, and decided to call the group Dan Burley's Skiffle Boys.

A year later, in England, a Skiffle Group was formed within the Crane River Jazz Band, and in 1952 the well-known Ken Colyer's Jazzmen, one of the foremost traditional Jazz bands in the country, formed a Skiffle Group within its ranks, and another group was used in 1954, when a smaller outfit was required to play the sort of music that Burley had played in America, which was still called by the name he had used – Skiffle. This Skiffle Group of Ken Colyer's has created many charming and intimate ballads, Blues, and work-songs, which have been recorded.

About the same time Chris Barber's Jazz Band, another of our leading "traditional" bands, formed a Skiffle Group, led by Lonnie Donegan, who has since formed and led his own group, and become one of the outstanding Skiffle players of our day. This Chris Barber Group has made some delightful records in which the informal singing and playing are blended in an ideal manner.

Such groups as these were small and relied on very few instruments. Ken Colyer used two guitars (or mandolin), washboard, and bass, in addition to his own singing, while in the group of Chris Barber there were simply two guitars and a string bass, with Lonnie Donegan providing the vocal part. The very simplicity of these first two Skiffle Groups made a great appeal. Young people began to realize suddenly that, with a guitar and a banjo, a home-made string bass, and with a two-and-eleven-penny washboard from the local ironmongers they could make Jazz. Provided, of course, that one of them had a voice!

So, following the example of these two well-known groups, formed in England only a few years ago, the youth of this country became Skiffle-minded, and Skiffle Groups were formed everywhere, in towns and villages, almost as fast as banjos and guitars could be manufactured.

Of all music, Skiffle is the most informal and relaxed. From time immemorial people all over the world have sung simple songs to a simple accompaniment – songs about the things that concerned them in life. They expressed their philosophy in music and song, and this became part of their folk-lore, that rich heritage of the past which enshrines all the feelings and aspiration of ordinary men and women.

Writing about Cecil Sharp, who founded the English Folk Dance and Song Society in England and the Country Dance Society in America, Ralph Vaughan Williams says:

When . . . Cecil Sharp collected and published his new discoveries in English folk-songs (discoveries made on both sides of the Atlantic), he had in mind the ordinary man, the 'divine average' of Whitman. And it is the ordinary man for whose musical salvation the folk-song will be responsible. For here is an ideal music . . . neither popular nor classical, highbrow nor lowbrow, but an art in which all can take part . . . a music which has for generations voiced the spiritual longings of our race.

Real Skiffle is in line with all this, the folk-music of England and America, the ballads, hill-billies, and so on, of both countries, which became welded in the New World into a trans-Atlantic form. The original British folk-songs were regional, and these regional songs were fused together in America and emerged as an American product, with an American twang. (Just as the hordes of emigrants, from practically every country in Europe, poured into the United States during the past hundred years or so, and together have produced the composite American, an almost new race of man.) To this Americanized British music came the influence of the Negro, who added the driving African "beat" which has made Jazz so popular everywhere. The Negroes transformed many British songs and tunes and re-fashioned them in a truly admirable way. By this means, with the spread of Jazz, the music of the whole world is being Africanized today. This thought may bring consternation to some people who view these modern trends with horror and apprehension, and who have mistaken ideas about the Negro and his culture. In passing, the author is reminded of the charming lady of his acquaintance who implored her young daughter not to mention Jazz at the Vicarage tea-party, and the unimaginative father of a young friend of his who told him, in no uncertain terms, to keep off Jazz and politics that evening, when guests were expected! It is a pity that such people do not realize that the Africans have the richest and most joy-filled folk-music of any people on earth. This fact, at any rate, is understood by Skifflers, who play and sing, more and more, this American-amalgamated, British-derived, Africanized music.

It would seem that Skiffle has come along and filled a vacuum in the musical life of Britain. Contrary to popular belief, the

British people are naturally emotional, expansive, and musical. The shy Britisher, unable to express his feelings, is but a character in fiction. We are not a race of shopkeepers, hard-headed business folk with not a soul above making money. We are, racially, like the Americans, an amalgam of many peoples, and wherever you get a mixture of races you get an enrichment of culture. Two or three hundred years ago, and beyond that, back into the Middle Ages, singing and dancing were national pastimes. The music-maker, the troubador, was an important person, and dancing round the Maypole was indulged in by all and sundry at every conceivable opportunity. They danced and sang on all the great occasions of life – births, deaths, and weddings, and at religious festivals, just as the Negroes did in New Orleans. There was a colour, vitality, and rhythm about life in those days which was expressed freely in musical terms.

It was the coming of the Industrial Revolution to Britain which damped all this down, and cast a paralyzing fog not only over the skies of our towns and cities, but also over the cultural expressions of our inhabitants. People no longer sang and made music, as they did in by-gone days. Life had become rapidly urbanized, and singing about gathering nuts in May or coming through the rye seemed rather pointless to the dwellers in the vast, sprawling cities that were speedily distorting the face of our fair countryside. The old music seemed to die in them, and was replaced by a new music from outside – the music of the machines, and the roar of traffic.

Before the advent of Skiffle, just half a dozen years ago, there were not many people in London, or in any of our big cities, who made their own music. Music-making was entirely in the hands of a small group of professionals. The mass of the people just sat back and listened. Such few singers as existed were content to serve out Cockney and provincial music-hall songs, which had little appeal to the younger generation. There was an apathy about individual musical expression which had lasted right through the two centuries of our Industrial Revolution. A pernicious blight had settled on the jolly, care-free Englishman of the past – the blight of a huge commercial system which he had created to serve him, and which now seemed to have become his master. The future, as far as music was concerned, seemed dreary and hopeless.

Then a strange thing happened, as it often does when least expected. Out of the music known as Jazz, which itself came into being under conditions which were gloomy and unpropitious, there developed a simpler, free-and-easy version of itself, a happy, rhythmic combination of music and song which swept through our land and revived in the hearts and souls of our young people the musical heritage of the past – a form of expression which they took eagerly to themselves and which became known by the peculiar, yet fascinating title of Skiffle.

So today our young people are singing again, and making their own music, with confidence and evident enjoyment. Music which during the gloomy decades of the past century had come to be looked upon as an occupation for hack performers only, or as a "cissy" extra to be learned at school by a few abnormal individuals, has now become again a national pastime, with the advent of Skiffle. It is surprising how this suspicion of a great creative art has cropped up from time to time in the course of man's cultural development. Jelly Roll Morton records that when he took on his first job as a Jazz piano-player he was almost ashamed of it, and afraid lest he be considered effeminate. His family thought that all musicians were tramps, trying to dodge honest work, and his grandmother, on learning of his new occupation, announced that a musician was nothing but a bum and a scallywag, and turned him out of the house!

But in our time, happily, things have changed. It is now not thought unworthy that a young man should strum a guitar and sing about the attractions of a girl friend, any more than in the days of medieval Italy a Romeo should serenade his Juliet on a balcony. We are rapidly shedding many of our former inhibitions and prejudices about music, and whereas in the past a young man sang only in his bath, he now does it openly on every occasion when he foregathers with his friends – in pubs and clubs, coffee-bars and dance-halls, and over the radio and television network. The Englishman has become a gayer, livelier person thereby, and has been helped in this metamorphosis by a musical form strange and new to some, perhaps, yet as old and fundamental as mankind itself, which, for want of a better word, has been named Skiffle.

How To Form A Skiffle Group

A Skiffle Group is a small group of people, of either sex, who have come together to sing and play Skiffle music. It is perhaps wrong to talk about "forming" a Skiffle Group, as these usually develop spontaneously and naturally. People of like interest automatically gravitate one to another, and the consequent group decides to make some corporate effort. So a group of instrumentalists gets together and decides to Skiffle.

How large should this group be? There is no hard-and-fast rule about this, but it should not exceed seven in number. A Skiffle Group is, essentially, a *small* group; anything from three to seven can make a good combination.

What instruments are required? Any of the following can be played: guitar, banjo, mandolin, string-bass, drums, and washboard. It is possible to add instruments such as the clarinet, harmonica, and even a fiddle, but it is advisable not to make the group top heavy, but to stick to the usual line-up as suggested above. But there is no rigid canon. Any combination of the above can make good Skiffle.

The essential instrument is the guitar, and if at least two guitars are included, which can play good, strong, correct chords, this will give a sound basis for the singing. Naturally, as good a guitar as can be afforded should be acquired. If a second-hand one is all that the exchequer will run to, then make the best of it. Unless it is very dilapidated, do not try to paint it up, as the original varnishes play an important part in the tune and note quality, and any heavy painting may spoil the instrument. Also do not attempt to convert your guitar into an amplified model, as the insertion of screws, etc, can damage the tone. An electric guitar is not essential for a simple Skiffle Group, but if it is considered that one is needed to amplify solos and it can be afforded, then get a good one at a reputable guitar shop. But start off, like the early

Skiffle and Spasm players, with whatever instrument can be obtained under existing conditions, and produce, as they did, good Jazz from it. And remember to keep the instrument in tune. Frequent tuning is necessary, as the playing of even one number can put the guitar slightly out of tune. Many good guitarists fail to play first-class music simply because they have not bothered to make sure that they are perfectly in tune. And it pays also to indulge in the luxury of a new set of strings frequently. Through use their tone gradually dulls, and a deadness ensues. It is surprising the difference a new set can make to the playing. The same advice applies to the banjo and mandolin.

The string-or double-bass is an important instrument, as it is the musical foundation of the group. But it is probably much too expensive for most groups to consider buying. An old, second-hand one, even if it is cracked, is probably better than a home-made article. One can always stop up the cracks with matchsticks or cover with sellotape to overcome the buzzing. A better sound will naturally be obtained from this than from a box, packing-case, or tea-chest bass.

Nevertheless, a box-bass can be very effective, and this is probably what most groups will start with. One can be improvised very quickly and cheaply. Take an ordinary packing-case or tea-chest, and make a hole in the bottom, large enough to pass a string through. Then turn it upside down. Tie a knot in a length of good string or other suitable material, and pass it through the hole, with the knot on the inside. Now cut a notch in one end of a broom-handle, and, making sure that the string is somewhat shorter than the handle, tie it to the notched end of the handle. Rest the free end of the broomstick on the corner of the tea-chest, and you are ready to start slapping. The note is produced by plucking the taut string in the usual way, and you get your different notes by varying the tension on the string by pulling the handle backwards. High tension gives high notes and low tension low notes. Instead of a tea-chest, an apple barrel, dustbin, tin bath, or oil-drum can be used in exactly the same fashion. And a nylon or gut string can be used, and even steel wire.

Anyone with a keen ear and a sense of rhythm can quickly

become proficient on the box-bass, and it is amazing what good, clear notes can be obtained from this crude, home-made instrument. Some practice will be necessary to get the correct slapping technique, but this will soon come to an enthusiast. It is worth mentioning that this slapping or plucking technique for the string or double-bass was discovered, quite by accident, by Bill Johnson, organizer of the Original Creole Ragtime Band in California in 1911, and one of the earliest string-bass players. He was playing at Shreveport, Louisiana, one day when his bow broke, so he just carried on slapping and plucking unconcernedly, thereby demonstrating that a true Jazzman must indeed be a master of improvisation!

The washboard is a rhythm instrument very popular with Skiffle players, and, incidentally, the cheapest of all to buy, being obtained for a few shillings at any good household store. A metal washboard, backed with wood, is the suitable type, and this should be played by laying it on the knees and stroking the ribbing lightly with metal-thimbled fingers. Heavy-gauge thimbles are the best for the protection of the fingers, and there should be a thimble for each finger of both hands, though some players prefer to use only two or three on each hand. The stroking should be relaxed, and washboard players should remember that it has a very cutting tone, and the sound of the board should be kept in correct relationship to that of the guitars. It should never be played too loudly, as it is only *one* member of the rhythm section, and the beat should come from *all* of them – guitar, bass, and washboard (and drums, if included), as a group. Many a promising Skiffle Group has been ruined by an enthusiastic washboard player bashing away clamorously with great aplomb and a broad smile, quite oblivious of the fact that he is ruining the performance. Washboard players should resist firmly the temptation to steal the show and play to the gallery. A good Jazzman always remembers that he is one of a team and is engaged on a combined operation.

There is no need to have any elaborations of, or additions to, the simple washboard, as such would be unnecessary and distracting from its true purpose, which is simply to supply clear, crisp rhythm. It is true that the great Jazz washboardist, "Washboard Sam", incorporated many refinements into his instrument, including bells, cymbals, and so on. But to do this is merely to take over some of the prerogatives of the drum-set, if this is used. And even if drums are not used, it is always best to err on the side of simplicity and lightness, and to avoid any multiplicity of sound.

Some groups do use a drum-set or a snare drum alone. But here again the question of expense arises. A good drum-kit costs a lot of money, but if a keen Jazz drummer with his own kit is on hand, one who is not an exhibitionist player, then he can be a valuable acquisition. But a snare drum is quite sufficient, or even wood blocks or polished hardboard can be used as a substitute, if played with drumsticks. Good rhythm has even been produced by a hearth-brush and a small empty suitcase as an alternative to a drum. But if you have a good rhythm player on the washboard, and the other rhythm instruments such as bass, banjo, and guitar are all working well in with this, full drum effects would seem hardly necessary, and would produce a top-heavy condition. So much depends on the combination available, and the decision can be taken only when it is seen what each player can achieve. The choice would, inevitably, lie between the washboard or drums, and in the interests of the group's performance, the best player should win!

And last but certainly not least in importance we come to the singer. A Skiffle Group is at its best when accompanied by a vocalist, or vocalists in chorus. The human voice is a melodic instrument, and the singer has to maintain the melody, and even improvise on it. It is essential that would-be Skiffle singers should possess a good musical voice. It is not sufficient to think that one can get away with a spot of casual crooning with an American twang and a fancied resemblance to some leading radio or TV star. This is not Skiffle singing. Skiffle is folk-music, and a vocalist should have a fair knowledge of Blues style singing, as many of the old Negro Spirituals, work-songs, ballads, and Blues are some of the best material for a Skiffle Group to use. He should sing with both intelligence and emotion, really understanding the song he is singing, and identifying himself with its context and message. He should feel within himself that he is not just a paid hack singer churning out popular music, but engaged in a creative art – the age-old art of the music-maker – and is in line with all the great troubadors of the past. And it should be remembered that in any Skiffle Group the voice is the principal instrument and must be heard clearly and to advantage at all times. All other instruments are subsidiary to the voice, and any that are found to be uncomplementary should not be used.

So, having assembled a group of the above-named instrumentalists, plus, naturally, a lot of enthusiasm, one has to decide, at first, which ones shall be included, or whether all of them can be retained. The usual line-up is one, two, or three guitars, a washboard or drums, and a string-bass or box-bass. But one is not tied to this. A banjo can replace a guitar, obviously, but a choice will have to be made in some cases, particularly as to whether drums or washboard are retained. Most groups would probably retain the washboard, in the interests of economy, facility of transport, and general lightness of the group.

It is a good thing to keep the group small, as the more instruments played, the more difficult it is to achieve cohesion. Theoretically, there are no laws or traditions regarding the instrumentation of a Skiffle Group, and some large groups are attempted, but it is important not to over-staff it, and to try to keep the sound light. A heavy, ponderous, unwieldy sound will not be attractive to the ear, and will limit the group to the playing of slow numbers only.

Inevitably, when a too-large crowd of enthusiasts turns up one or two may have to be dropped. This need not cause any undue heart-burning or bad feeling, if the true Jazz spirit is present. In the interests of the group balance, members are usually prepared to stand down. The author remembers a tall, bearded banjoist turning up at one session he was connected with, and, realizing that there were banjos galore, just sitting week after week with his instrument in its case by his side, and enjoying the music of the others! It is, however, possible to practise alternative combinations, using spare musicians, so that reserves are available in case of emergency.

We have outlined the customary set-up for the average Skiffle
Group, but it might be well to add that Skiffle music can also be
played on the very primitive instruments of the early "Spasm"
bands – viz kazoos, combs-and-paper, harmonicas, cigar-box
fiddles, jugs, bottles, and the like, and some groups today are
introducing such into their line-up. What one might call the
"purists" of the Skiffle Movement are going back to the earliest
sources, and re-discovering this first known type of Skiffle-
playing. Thus, we find Russell Quaye's City Ramblers – an
inventive group of Skifflers – reviving this kind of "Spasm"
music, and using a kazoo and a trumpet mouthpiece attached to a
small paraffin funnel, as well as a jug. The Bill Bailey Skiffle
Group also uses a kazoo and a comb-and-paper imitating a
trumpet.

Whatever line-up is finally decided on, the main thing to
remember is to keep the presentation as simple as possible. Skiffle
is essentially a free-and-easy, happy, living music. If one con-
centrates over-much on achieving technical perfection, one may
lose its appealing simplicity and that pleasing folk-tune atmosphere which is its very essence.

And, as Skiffle is based on rhythm, so a varying rhythm,
expressing the words, music, and feeling of the players, should
be developed. Every melody should be presented with its own
distinct rhythmic appeal. For, as in all Jazz, rhythm is the vital
connexion between the players and their audience. It stirs their
feelings, sets their feet tapping, gives an added allurement to
simple melodies, and creates that mystic "swing" which it is the
ambition of all true Jazzmen to achieve when playing.

A Skiffle Group should present a number in a sincere and
unaffected manner. There should be no striving for theatrical
effect, and it is not necessary to wear startling costumes or adopt
dramatic poses when playing. Skifflers are players and singers,
not chorus-boys. The group, however, should not look untidy,
but have the appearance of coherence about it. It is a help to have
them uniformly dressed, and ordinary casual clothes are perhaps
the best. The instruments should be well kept, and it is permis-
sible to paint the box-bass and the washboard. The group should

be placed in positions which are most natural and happy for each member, but need not remain fixed in such positions, which can be varied with the songs and music sung. Natural, relaxed movements should be made when changing position, and these come from a realization on the part of the players that they are not taking part in a stage show, but creating from their hearts, minds, and souls real music, and giving it freely for the benefit of others. This should give Skifflers a true sense of enjoyment, and when this is achieved, self-consciousness disappears. Many of the early Negro Jazzmen have admitted simply, "I've played plenty of Jazz in my time; I never made much money out of it, but I've had an awful lot of fun!" It is in this spirit that Skiffle should be played and sung.

And, lastly, the question arises as to where a Skiffle Group is to play. The answer is: anywhere, at any time. Skiffle is party music, and wherever there are people gathered together seeking relaxation, then they can be entertained by Skifflers. It may be in a coffee-bar, a pub, a club, at a concert, at a picnic, at a holiday camp, in a cave, in a stage show, on the radio, on TV, and even in a church. This last venue may not be so strange or shocking as at first may appear, as will be explained in a later chapter. But, in passing, it is sufficient to say that many a clergyman might consider the possibility of inviting a good Skiffle Group to sing a programme of some of the fine old Negro Spirituals in his church. He would be assured of a good congregation, and of a message that might be more easily understood than some of the sermons he has spent so much time on and preached so painstakingly and conscientiously.

And, by way of contrast, a holiday camp is an ideal background for the performance of a Skiffle Group, and at most of these camps Skiffle contests are arranged. There is the story told of young Barry Barron, from Portsmouth, who took his guitar with him on holiday to Butlin's Skegness Camp. A Skiffle contest was announced. He quickly formed a pick-up group, and scoured the camp for instruments. They finished up with a tea-chest, a dustbin lid, a tin waste-paper basket, and an oxtail soup tin filled with stones. With this motley collection of implements they entered the contest, and walked off with the first prize! These boys were true inheritors of the Jazz tradition. They had the right spirit – the spirit of creative improvisation found in the pioneer Jazzmen of old, and their example must be a stimulation to many a budding Skiffler.

But it is helpful for a Skiffle Group to be attached to some sort of organization, an environment where the Jazz spirit exists, and where there is a congenial atmosphere in which to play, somewhere where they can meet regularly, where they can re-create, before going out and entertaining all and sundry. It must be a friendly place where Jazz matters are of paramount importance and discussed freely. It is possible for a Skiffle Group to have its own organized club of supporters where the necessary background would be available, and some groups may find this adequate. But, as Skiffle is part of the great Jazz Movement, Skifflers should always remember the source from which it derives its inspiration, and it is in a Jazz Club that they will find their true spiritual home. Here, where Jazz music is played, either by a band or on records, the Skiffle Group can take its rightful place. This is where many a group has started, playing and singing with the band, and, at times, filling in intervals with its own efforts. There are Jazz Clubs established all over the country, and it is in such surroundings that Skiffle Groups inevitably find a happy and suitable climate in which to grow and develop.

Gene Vincent – The Genesis of the Dark Side

Mick Farren

He looked for all the world like a man in the grip of some dark, wrenching religious experience. The contorted figure in the black leather suit stood with one leg forward, knee bent, and the other, held rigid in a steel brace and thrust awkwardly out behind him. The stance was unnatural, you could maybe call it unholy. His body seemed twisted, almost tortured. At peaks in the act, his whole frame would appear to vibrate as he clutched the microphone stand with his gloved hands, desperately, as though it was all that prevented him from being born away by the rage and passion of the moment. His corpse pale face was framed, Dracula style, by the upturned collar of his leather jacket, and a sweat soaked bunch of grapes had collapsed on his forehead. He had this trick of raising his eyes to an imaginary point, high in the auditorium, higher even than the cheap seats in the upper balcony, as though he was staring into some unknown place, invisible to the rest of us.

That I can remember it so vividly after more than thirty years has to be the clearest indication of the intensity of Gene Vincent on stage. Maybe, in later life, towards the end, he was little more than an overweight, disorientated drunk, but that still doesn't detract from the virgin impact. Gene Vincent at the Brighton Essoldo in 1960 first convinced me of the awesome power of a live rock 'n' roll show when the envelope was truly being pushed.

Around the same time, Jack Good was producing the pioneer TV rock show, *Boy Meets Girl*, for Granada Television in Manchester. Good must have experienced some of the same

impact when he decided to change Gene's image for his spot on
the show. Lose the rockabilly cat clothes – the Elvis-looking, high
rise pants and sport shirts. It was Good who first put Vincent in
the black leather suit that was to become his trademark, con-
ceptualising the look as "the rock 'n' roll Richard III". Jack
Good, who later went to the US and produced *Shindig*, may have
been pompous, and loudly over educated, but his instincts and
perceptions were usually in the right place. He had clearly sensed
Gene's air of the sinister and the dangerous.

It was certainly the black and white segment of Gene Vincent
on *Boy Meets Girl*, doing the song Baby Blue; backed by Joe
Brown and The Bruvvers, that caused me to move heaven and
earth to get tickets for the show in Brighton. Up in Newcastle, a
kid called Steve Aynsley, who'd later become President of the
Gene Vincent Fan Club in Great Britain, experienced a similar
epiphany. "Gene picked up the mikestand and walked towards
the camera until his face filled the screen. I'd never seen anything
like it in my life. And I realised that nobody could ever make such
an impression on me again. He wore black leather and the light
faded as he moved around. He looked like a demon." Back in
those days, us kids who were too young to drive got around on
Southern Region commuter trains that mercifully came without
corridors. On that train back home, my hands were all over my
date's body and hers were all over mine. No alternative and
damned if we wanted one.

We had just been part of a dark invocation of post-fifties
teenage lust backed by the loudest electric guitars we had ever
heard in our young lives. We had passed childhood's end but
would kick and scream bloody murder before we'd allow ourselves to be forced into what was currently being promoted as
maturity. Almost two decades later, when, in the song Sweet
Gene Vincent, Ian Dury wrote the line "there's one in every
town", I knew exactly what he was talking about – the kid who
watched Gene Vincent and then went out and shot the works for
rock 'n' roll.

Gene Vincent seemed to wear menace like the aura of some
Stephen King creation. Jim Morrison would later talk about rock

'n' roll as a demonic shamanism. Gene simply and inarticulately conjured it. Tommy Facenda, one of Gene's original back-up singers, tells stories of what came to pass when the mojo went to overdrive. "Globe Arizona was another wild gig and it soon erupted into a full scale riot. A fight broke out when Gene was dragged from the stage by the local sheriff in the middle of doing Lotta Lovin. They had to shoot teargas into the joint. Navahos and Apaches were going at it." Grady Owen, rhythm guitar with The Blue Caps, tells much the same story in Britt Hagarty's Vincent biography *The Day The World Turned Blue*: "The sheriff had arrested Gene for wrecking a motel room, being drunk around minors and doing a lewd show. They dragged him off stage bodily and took him to jail. The whole thing erupted so the sheriff came back and shot tear-gas bombs in the place and cleared it." Bet you thought that kind of thing started with Keith Moon.

According to legend, Elvis Presley, Bill Black and Scotty Moore first heard Gene Vincent singing Be-Bop-A-Lula on the car radio while travelling between gigs. Bill Black, never one to forego aggro, immediately accused Elvis of moonlighting with another band, on another label, under an assumed name. Elvis, of course, denied it. He had his work more than cut out being Elvis Presley without starting a second clandestine career under the unlikely name of Gene Vincent.

Black, however, whose neck was apparently as stiff as it was red, wouldn't let it go. He continued the argument even when Elvis pointed out the obvious vocal dissimilarities, that Vincent's range was considerably higher than his and that, where he, Elvis, was influenced by the likes of Dean Martin and The Inkspots, this Vincent character, although singing rock, was straight out of the Hank Williams' school of degenerate, cousin-marrying, country.

If Capitol A&R man Ken Nelson had heard this conversation in the Presley Cadillac, he would have been overjoyed. Nelson had been responsible for spearheading a 1956 corporate talent search for a performer whom Capitol could promote as their answer to Elvis, and Gene Vincent had been the result. With his debut single, Be-Bop-A-Lula selling 200,000 copies in the first month of release, Capitol were already fairly convinced that Nelson had delivered. The fact that Gene and his sidemen reminded Nelson of a "motorcycle gang" at their first meeting didn't seem to strike any warning notes with the Capitol suits. It was only down the line that they would realise Gene very definitely wasn't Elvis. Where Elvis would prove to be polite and hopelessly malleable, Gene turned out to be wilful, difficult, often drunk and possibly a little insane. Where Elvis attempted to be all things to all people, Gene embraced the evil heart of rock 'n' roll, staying in its arms until it ultimately killed him.

Back in those days, A&R men knew next to nothing about the inner workings of rock 'n' roll metaphysics, the dubious ways of rock 'n' rollers, or of the generation gap that they were unwittingly fostering. Initially, the debut single by Gene Vincent and The Blue Caps was to have been the gasping, grinding Woman Love, with Be-Bop-A-Lula on the B-side.

Advance promo on Woman Love, however, ran into a massive wall of resistance from radio stations all across the USA, plus an outright ban in Great Britain by the BBC. Elvis was bad enough, but Woman Love, with its overt sexual rage and frustration, and Gene's near orgasmic breathing on the slap echo vocal track, was ten times worse. No way was Woman Love fifties radio friendly, reinforcing as it did the popular prejudice that rock 'n' roll would trigger "promiscuity, delinquency and the mixing of the races." At this point, Capitol merely flipped the emphasis. Be-Bop-A-Lula became the A-side and history continued.

It didn't seem to occur to the guardians of morality that the two or more million kids who ultimately bought the record would hear Woman Love anyway and cherish it as their private dirty secret.

Gene Vincent was born Vincent Eugene Craddock, in the shipyard town of Norfolk, Virginia, supposedly on February 11th, 1935, just thirty-four days after Gladys Presley's surviving twin first saw daylight (although, as with many things in Gene's confused life, some dispute exists regarding his exact birthdate.)

His childhood appears unremarkable except that he "liked music and girls". His sister Evelyn is quoted delivering a standard cliche of Norman Rockwell rock 'n' roll origins. "A black man lived down the street and he'd come to the store, an old country store, and we had chairs out there and he sang while Gene played." At age seventeen, like many Norfolk boys without skills or future, Gene Craddock enlisted in the Navy, just in time to miss the Korean War, and, after basic training, was assigned to the tanker USS *Chuckawan* as a deck hand. After three years in the service, he re-upped for a further six, and that might have been that, except that he blew a sizable chunk of his reenlistment bonus on a 500cc Triumph Tiger similar to the one ridden by Marlon Brando in *The Wild One*. One weekend in July 1955, in the Norfolk suburb of Franklin, a woman in a Chevy ran a red light and smashed into Gene on his Triumph and his left leg was crushed. He was no more use to the Navy, and it looked as though he might spend the greater part of his life in and out of VA hospitals.

Gene Vincent's bad leg looms large in both legend and reality. It provided him with his unique stage stance, a massive biker credibility, and limitless sympathy. It also tipped him into the drug and alcohol problems that would dog him through his entire career.

"Gene was his own worst enemy. He popped a lot of pills . . . He'd break his cast in every town. Then, in the next town, we'd have to hunt up a doctor and get a new cast." Red Gwynn, his chauffeur during the first surge of fame, tells the story that would be repeated endlessly down the years. The leg caused Gene chronic pain and quickly led to a painkiller habit; the painkillers made him slow so he took speed to get back in gear; the speed made him edgy and thus he drank to mellow out. In the morning, he'd wake with a hangover and his leg still hurt. The cycle was repeated on a daily basis, a process that gradually eroded his heath, talent and stability.

Just to complicate matters, Gene also had a raving hillbilly passion for knives and guns and an increasing tendency, as the deterioration deepened, to pull weapons on wives, girlfriends, managers and promoters when he felt robbed, disrespected or betrayed. It all added to the general mosaic that Gene Vincent was mad, bad, armed and dangerous. Perhaps this was something else that he'd learned in the school of Hank Williams. Certainly in the arena of booze and pills, Gene was following in the master's footsteps. Gene had his leg as the ultimate excuse. Hank had a congenitally deformed spine.

Again, according to legend, it was Gene's leg that provided him with the accidental window to rock stardom. During the six months he spent in Portsmouth Naval Hospital, he's supposed to have fooled around with a guitar and come up with the tune Be-Bop-A-Lula, inspired by the newspaper strip cartoon "Little Lulu". In the face of legend, however, Dickie Harrell, who, at fifteen, was the first drummer with The Blue Caps, tells a different, if somewhat less lovable story. "Actually the song was written by a guy from Portsmouth named Donald Graves." Vincent and his first manager Bill "Sheriff Tex" Davis, a chubby individual with a taste for cowboy outfits who appeared to have fancied himself as a potential rival to Colonel Tom Parker, brought the tune outright for 25 bucks. "It happened a lot in those days. Guys would take the sure money."

If Gene Vincent was simply judged by his legacy of recording, it might be hard to figure what all the fuss and nostalgia are about. This is not to say that he didn't come up with seminal gems, but, for every masterpiece like Race With Devil, Baby Blue, Who Slapped John? or Git It, his Capitol albums contained a whole bunch of bizarre and often ponderous ballads and antique pop songs like The Wayward Wind, Over The Rainbow, This Old Gang Of Mine and Now Is The Hour. When confronted by a recording session and a choice of material, Gene proved all but clueless, and also demonstrated a taste for throbbing saccharine that caused critic John Morthland to refer to him as "a closet schlockmeister". When Gene did it right, however, the finished product could be little short of awe inspiring, and the master-works frequently broke what, at the time, was wholly new ground in rock 'n' roll. In addition, Gene had a unique ability to pick a guitar player. Both Cliff Gallup, who played the celebrated solo on Be-Bop-A-Lula, and Johnny Meeks, who took the lead on the later Capitol albums, have both been cited by everyone from Jeff Beck to John Lennon as primal influences.

The Gene Vincent sound began as fairly sparse, atmospheric rockabilly, but quickly bulked up to a more elaborate and much denser rock 'n' roll, without making the usual concessions to the kind of multi-layered pop so freely embraced by Elvis and Buddy Holly. The song Baby Blue, recorded in 1958 for the low budget teen exploitation movie *Hot Rod Gang* (released in Britain under the title *Fury Unleashed)*, is the perfect example of Vincent's more constructed approach to rock. In what was essentially a deluxe and loaded second look at Heartbreak Hotel, Vincent went for pounding percussion, that broke with the traditional rockabilly snare and high-hat. The mood was locked by threatening piano triplets and a heavy overlay of back-up vocals chanting "baby-baby-baby-baby", until an almost hypnotic pulse was achieved. In a 1970 *Rolling Stone* retrospective on Vincent, Simon Firth sums up Gene's approach to rock 'n' roll when he was at his best. "The interplay of voices and instruments are perfect, the total effect being built up by the between conflict all the elements . . . these tracks quite transcended the normal rock 'n' roll singles of 1957–8." In a world that is all too often blinded by an obsession with guitars and guitar heroes, the crucial part played by backup vocals in the music of Gene Vincent has been largely overlooked.

From about 1958 onwards, the arrangements became more lavish, and back-up vocals took an increasingly important role. On some tracks like Peace Of Mind and the classic Git It, Vincent actually started to stray cross culturally close to the New York goomba doo-wop, the turf of which Dion and the Belmonts were masters.

Gene not only went heavy on backing vocals in the studio, but also took a singing duo, Tommy Facenda and Paul Peek, dubbed the Clapperboys, on the road with him.

Unlike Elvis's Jordanaires, the Clapperboys were fully integrated in the general hoodlum image of The Blue Caps. Instead

of a square gospel quartet, standing uncomfortably apart from the
star's gyrations, the Clapperboys flanked Gene like something
out of a demented version of *West Side Story*.

On the Git It sessions, Vincent was also greatly aided by the
input of Eddie Cochran. Cochran had dropped by these March
1958 sessions at Capitol studios in Los Angeles to sing a third,
bottom line harmony along with Peek, Facenda and Vincent.
Although this first and only formal collaboration between Vincent and Cochran doesn't look like too much in the fine print of a
discography, it represented a budding relationship that would go
sufficiently deep to qualify, both in fact and legend, as one of the
great rock 'n' roll might-have-beens.

Both Gene Vincent and Eddie Cochran filmed song sequences for
the Jayne Mansfield movie *The Girl Can't Help It*. They may
have first on met the set, but according to Dickie Harrell, the
friendship was really cemented at The Rock 'n' Roll Jubilee Of
Stars, a kind of week long, proto rock festival in Philadelphia at
which both men had been given star billing. "Eddie was just
down-to-earth and really good people. He and Gene had a lot in
common. They were a bit like each other and seemed to understand each other. So they started to pal around together." This
palling around continued through a package tour of Australia
headlined by Vincent, Cochran and Little Richard. While Vincent and Richard seemed to have engaged in regular bouts of
butting egos, Gene and Cochran remained friends and drinking
buddies, often joining each other on stage to close their respective
sets. With the advantage of hindsight, it's easy to identify the
growing ties between Vincent and Cochran as having the potential of those symbiotic musical relationships of the Lennon/
McCartney, Jagger/Richards, Jones/Strummer variety that
would later prove the backbone and creative wellspring of truly
great rock 'n' roll bands.

Unfortunately, in 1958, and even in 1960, the world had yet to
recognise this kind of male bonding for what it was, and the
record business had no structure to accommodate it.

In the fifties, the marketing moguls liked their teen idols, in every sense, single and separate. The only double acts they recognised were obvious duos like the Everly Brothers or Les Paul and Mary Ford. Bands invariably meant instrumental ensembles like The Ventures and groups were vocal units like The Four Seasons or The Coasters. In a few short years, rock bands who collectively shared not only the spotlight and the fan worship but also the creative focus, would become the commercial bedrock of the entire pop industry. Unfortunately, the times didn't change quickly enough to give Vincent and Cochran a context in which they could work together as visible equals.

Although the fantasy that Gene and Eddie might have formed the world's first truly kick-ass rock 'n' roll band can be nothing more than pure speculation, they certainly seemed to have what was required. Their personalities were exactly complementary. Vincent was the consummate showman, the wildman who was always prepared to go the extra mile. Cochran was an innovator, a low budget recording wizard who could work wonders with the primitive studio equipment of the time. Although surviving film clips show Eddie Cochran as not altogether comfortable with the hip-swiveling, post-Elvis role into which he'd been cast, he certainly had the writing talent and the technical flair to counteract Vincent's erratic approach to making records.

The truth, as we all know, is that it was never to be. Short of the Git It sessions and some BBC radio tapes, Gene Vincent and Eddie Cochran would never formally work together.

Cochran's death in the car crash outside Bristol, while touring England double-billed with Gene brought all possible plans for the future to a brutal finality.

Gene never seemed to quite recover from the death of Eddie Cochran. When I talked to him in 1969, after he'd played the Country Club in Belsize Park, backed by Brit rock revivalists The Wild Angels, he was drunkenly obsessive on the subject. By that time, he'd totally convinced himself that Eddie's death was the product of a sinister conspiracy by his then manager, the notorious Don Arden. I recall a very drunk Vincent repeating over and over that "Eddie was alive when we got him into the ambulance."

He appeared to have latched on to the belief that somehow, on the way to hospital, Arden had somehow contrived to murder Cochran, intending to cash in his posthumous fame and royalties. Although, the story was patently the paranoid invention of a very fucked up mind – there's even evidence that Gene was out cold when they put Cochran in the ambulance – it does demonstrate just how deep the emotional injury must have been. Vincent clearly believed that something very important had been taken from him, and that things were never the same afterwards. A photograph exists of Gene at Heathrow, walking to the plane home a few days after Cochran's death, one arm in a sling and an overcoat thrown over his shoulders. He looks like a totally broken man, and if one has to look for a starting point for the decline and fall of Gene Vincent, that fatal accident seems to be it.

This is not to say that Gene took an immediate plunge or that other factors didn't come into play. Back in the USA, the payola scandals and the resulting congressional investigations had gone down and almost all of the first generation of rockers seemed to be tainted to a greater or lesser degree by this rock 'n' roll witch hunt. Alan Freed had gone to jail for accepting bribes, Chuck Berry was doing time for pimping. Jerry Lee Lewis was sinking in his personal morass of marriage scandals. Elvis was safely out of it in the Army, and Little Richard had decided that maybe he was better off preaching. The cross that Gene had to bear was a ruthless IRS tax audit which stripped him of his home and most of his possessions. He found himself all but penniless and even had to burn The Blue Caps on their salary cheques. To compound his troubles, Dick Clark, the host of the squeaky clean *American Bandstand* who, since the fall of Alan Freed, had become the arbiter of what was acceptable in US pop, virtually blacklisted Gene after accusing him of being too drunk to make it to his show. The only possible future appeared to be in Europe.

At first, things seemed to go pretty much okay. Gene picked up the ultra-professional Sounds Incorporated as a back-up band, and excelled on a European concert circuit that was being simultaneously criss-crossed by Bo Diddley, a recovering Jerry Lee Lewis, Brenda Lee, Fats Domino as well as home product like Billy Fury, Marty Wilde, Cliff and the Shads, and dubious Frenchmen like Johnny Halliday. Gene's contract with Capitol was anglicised and he cut tracks with Cliff Richard's producer Norrie Paramor at Abbey Road, occasionally using Georgie Fame on keyboards. For a time, his singles, like I'm Coming Home and Wild Cat could still find their way into the charts. Bit by bit, things began to slide, however.

Gene wasn't hurt as badly as some by The Beatles upheaval. It helped a great deal that Lennon and McCartney acknowledged him as a major influence right down to their leather suits, but even Gene's superior grease eventually began to turn to anachronism, and, when it did, he hardly had anyone to blame but himself. While Johnny Kidd, his chief rival in the leather and sideburns business could cut contemporary sounding hits like Shaking All Over and I'll Never Get Over You, and even Vince Taylor, the Parisian pretender could come up with Brand New Cadillac, Gene floundered in the studio turning out either grotesqueries like Lavender Blue or admissions of defeat like Be-Bop-A-Lula '62 and '69.

And with the slide came the drink and drugs, and with the drink and drugs came the slide.

(Shall I stop here or take another couple of rounds on the hell-bound carousel?) Pretty soon Gene was brandishing guns in hotel lobbies, getting stopped at borders without working papers, and hanging with some of the worst low lives in the rock business who I basically can't name here because some of them are now exceedingly rich and powerful. His leg continued to deteriorate and every so often a doctor wanted to cut it off. Gene resisted any such suggestion but, when osteomyelitis set in, amputation seemed only a matter of time. Gene continued to tour, but the quality of the bands he hired took a noticeable dive. From Sounds Incorporated, he descended to a Liverpool group called The Shouts, another British band dubiously called The Puppets and a couple of laughable French outfits, Le Rock 'n' Roll Gang and Les Chats Sauvage. On the recording front, he was dropped by Capitol and drifted from label to label, cutting tracks that best remain buried, although they do show up now and again on those cut price tapes racked in drugstores and gas stations.

By the end of 1965, Gene's health and career had both hit bottom. He returned to California and, for all effective purposes, retired for close to eighteen months, watching in horror as a second revolution changed the face of rock, and "a bunch of long haired hippies" took over.

Gene didn't have the financial base to stay retired for too long. Any number of ex-managers, ex-wives and weird business associates ate up his royalty cheques, and the need to return to work loomed large. And why not? At the age of just thirty-one, Gene should, in theory, have had a long life in front of him. 1967 saw him back on the road, back in Europe, but, unfortunately back into the same self destructive lifestyle cycle. The unpleasant truth was that Gene now only had a scant five years to live. Indeed, that might effectively been the end of the story if it hadn't been for an intervention by the unlikely combination of John Peel in London and Jim Morrison in Los Angeles.

One of the things I used to share with John Peel when I saw him regularly was a unreasonable love for Gene Vincent. Even during the full bloom of the Perfumed Garden, we talked about Wild Cat and Who Slapped John when the hippies weren't listening. Once, when I was on a stoned rant about the evils of private property, Peel suggested that I should put my money where my dialectic was and give him my complete set of Vincent Capitol albums. Collapse of loudmouth anarchist. In 1969, Peel, along with Clive Selwood, the then boss of Elektra UK, formed the Dandelion label. When some pretty sub-standard Vincent tapes came by him, they triggered the idea that Dandelion should put Gene in the studio to cut a album. Whether Peel instinctively sensed that Gene was already three parts into the twilight zone and it might be a last chance to get him on vinyl is open to debate, but, any way you sliced it, the sessions were strange, with Johnny Meeks on guitar and Skip Battin on bass and, of all people, Kim Fowley producing.

Around the same time, Gene had struck up a bar buddy relationship with Jim Morrison at a shot and beer joint called the Shamrock at the Silver Lakeend of Santa Monica Boulevard. The Dandelion sessions rapidly became frequented by assorted Doors and hangers on, who watched while the musicians did the best they could, and Fowley and Gene smashed egos. Skip Battin recalls: "Gene was a perfectionist and Fowley like to move pretty quickly. Gene tried very hard, but he was pretty sick at the time. His leg was bothering him and he was in constant pain." Johnny Meeks is less charitable. "They [Vincent and Fowley] slaughtered that damned album." Slaughtered or not, I'm Back And I'm Proud wasn't without its moments, most particularly a fine reading of J.P Richardson's White Lightning with a sound not unlike that of The Band.

Even though it wasn't Gene's last record, it stands as more of a final testament than the two Kama Sutra albums that followed. Rather than being slaughtered, these went meekly to their doom.

Jim Morrison was also instrumental in a different kind of final moment for Gene. It was essentially Morrison that smoothed the way to Gene's appearance at the Toronto rock 'n' roll Revival Festival that would be mythologised by the one time only appearance of John Lennon and the Plastic Ono Band. The original plan was that Gene should have been backed by the Doors, but, because of scheduling problems, he came on instead with Alice Cooper's band whose pre-metal guitar rock was actually better suited to his style. At the end of an emotional Be-Bop-A-Lula, Lennon came on stage and embraced a weeping Gene. In the movie of his life, this should have been the final triumphant moment, the redemption at the end of the third act. Unfortunately life is never quite as idealised as the movies, and Gene went on to do one more, totally disorganised tour of Europe on which he was all but incapable of performing, before he returned to Los Angeles to die.

Among Gene Vincent's last words was the promise, "If I get through this, I'm going to be a better man." Reform and survival, though, were not on the cards. Returning to LA, he had found that his wife Jackie had left him, cleaning out his bank accounts, and taking the kids and most of their possession. He had promptly gone on a intensive three day drunk that had finally destroyed the already ulcerated lining of his stomach. Soon after stumbling into his mother's house in the LA suburb of Saugus, Gene apparently fell to his knees and began vomiting blood. He looked up at his mother and told her, " Mama, you can phone the ambulance now." Within an hour, he was dead.

Even in death, things didn't go smoothly for Gene. The reappearance of his wife Jackie turned the funeral into an hysterical circus. His sister Donna had recently fallen under the thrall of con artist and guru Tony Alamo, a one time garment district hustler from New York's 7th Avenue who, in the name of God, tended to divest the faithful of their savings and then set them to work in slave labour sweatshops manufacturing rhinestone cowboy clothes for the likes of Glen Campbell and Dolly Parton. Cult vultures descended on Gene's few remaining possessions, carrying off guitars, memorabilia and stage outfits. Johnny Meeks sums up the irony of it all. "It was crazy. I thought, 'Man, typical Gene, He can't even die right. There's always gotta be some kinda problem'."

Gene Vincent was a drunk, a pillhead and, at times, a dangerous and creatively erratic asshole, but that may have been the true power of the man. If rock was literature, he'd probably have been Jean Genet. He was the true pioneer of rock 'n' roll self destruction in the grand manner. He made it clear, from first to last, that rock was about the darkside and the underbelly, and he conducted his career as though the music he played was some kind of mortal combat with destiny. His leather clothes have been copied so many times down the generations that they have become one of rock's visual cliches. His attitude has been borrowed in some part by most of rock's wannabe philosopher desperadoes and pretend warrior poets. His mikestand clutching stance has been aped by everyone from Patti Smith to Stiv Bators to all those grunge geezers in lumberjack shirts, although they probably don't even know it.

The history of this unholy conflict between Gene and his fate is reasonably well preserved.

EMI have a boxed CD set on catalogue that cover all of Gene's Capitol and Columbia Recordings from 1956 to 1964, and if all the out takes and false starts are really too much of a good thing, there's also the twenty track CD *The Best of Gene Vincent And the Blue Caps* in the Capitol Rock 'n' Roll Masters series which is probably all anyone would need in the way of a Vincent selective menu without verging on the obsessive. Britt Hagarty's biography *The Day The World Turned Blue,* while no great piece of literature, will tell you just about everything you ever needed to know about the man and his work. Beyond that, all one has is hearsay and the memories of old timers. All else is speculation and legend.

Perhaps, though, in the final distillation, the legend is Vincent's real legacy. Without becoming unduly metaphysical, Gene Vincent has to be one of those totemic spirits, in the company of Robert Johnson, Johnny Ace, Morrison, Moon, and Sid Vicious, who watch over rock 'n' roll in all its diverse forms, doing their best to ensure that an excess of mental health and sobriety don't reduce the music to the predictable, that the sweat, tears and suicidal stupidity continue, and that the bop they died for never sinks to mundane bloodlessness.

1961: The Legendary Joe Meek

John Repsch

No one has ever lived a life like Joe Meek. Surrounded by intrigue and controversy, he was Britain's first truly independent pop producer and set the ball rolling for the hundreds who envelop the scene today.

He was the man who against all the odds produced hit after hit in his flat in London's busy Holloway Road. In the pre-Beatles era when the British music industry was being run by the likes of EMI and Decca, and Britain was lying stranded in a sea of tepid cover versions of American teen idols, he decided to go it alone and battle it out with the giants.

From an Aladdin's Cave of dusty wires and ropey old spinning tape machines he developed a unique sound which made his records instantly recognizable. It gave them an exciting, spiritual feel which is still to this day so attractive that his discs are collectors' items and sell for very high prices. He even has a fan club!

Working from two bedrooms, his fine-fingered electronics wizardry was a wonder to behold, and the incredible sounds he created could make your hair stand on end. Like an eccentric scientist he worked all hours bending every rule in the book, turning music inside out and reconstructing it. He was the master of cramming everything onto one single track and for years was so advanced that no one in Britain could touch him.

Some of the equipment was new, some homemade. Much of it had been completely reassembled from old EMI and Saga cast-offs and secondhand stuff from junk shops and army surplus stores. His main tape recorders were a Lyrec twin-track stereo recorder and an EMI TR51 mono recorder.

As for the famous Meek method of recording, compared with modern multi-track techniques it sounds as out of date as whalebone corsets, and even then was generally despised for being slow, complicated and losing clarity. But unless everything was recorded at once, as was traditionally done in the large studios, there was no other way.

His technique was almost exactly the same as the one he had started back at home in 1950 using two tape recorders: overdubbing. By layering one sound on top of another – sometimes up to half a dozen times – it meant in effect that when you listened to a Meek record you were hearing not one but several recordings! He much preferred this way because it allowed him to concentrate on one section of the recording at a time, getting the performance he liked best and giving him the chance to change his mind as he went along. Now though, life was much easier with the aid of the Lyrec twin-track. The finished recording would end up on its two tracks – songs having the backing on one track and the voice on the other – and this gave him much more leeway than ever before.

First of all he would deal with the backing. The rhythm section would go into the studio and play while the singer sang along as a guide, unrecorded behind an old screen. While this performance was going on, he would be recording it onto the one track of the TR51. He might record 20 "takes" before deciding which one he wanted and moving on to the first overdub. This time he might want to add an extra drum sound; so he would simply choose the rhythm "take" he liked best and relay it out into the studio for the drummer to play along to. Thus the two sounds combined would be channelled onto one track of the Lyrec. When he again had a "take" that satisfied him he would perhaps overdub a guitar and do exactly the same again, playing the last recording out and collecting both sounds together on the track of the TR51.

Depending on the sound he was after, he would gradually add more and more instruments, spinning spools back and forth until his backing track was done. And while all that was going on he had other machines running. Apart from feeding sounds through echo units he had to watch out for loss of quality; each time he transferred from one track to the other, a little of the original sound was lost. So he had to use limiters and compressors which gave him a louder signal. They could also gave him the sound of pumping. This he would often use to add to the overall excitement, besides which it played an integral part in his unique Joe Meek sound.

When all the backing was happily on one track of the Lyrec, he would have the vocalist sing along to it. The only difference this time was that he liked to keep the singing separate, so would give the singer headphones and play the backing through them instead. Then eventually, probably after more messing around on his own adding sound effects and so on, he had two finished tracks on his Lyrec.

Off he would go with them to one of the outside cutting studios where facilities were better than his own. Surprisingly in the months to come his choice of studio would usually be IBC. Engineers there were still the best and now there was less reason for him and the Studio Manager, Allen Stagg, to be at each other's throats. There he would supervise having his two tracks mixed down to one – the "master tape". Ten shillings in the engineer's pocket assured him of an extra good cut and helped make it the "loudest in the juke box"; and preserving his thick, solid bass drum beat meant that some should get through to the kids who were listening on little portable radios. He would also have two or three demo acetates made with varying levels of bass, treble, etc, and the one he judged best he would hawk round the record companies. If he found a taker he would give that record company his "master tape" and help cut the "master disc", so it kept most of its original quality. This practice was not to be "on" at the prudish EMI and only grudgingly permitted at Pye and Decca. After all that it was clean out of his hands when it went off to the factory for the pressing process.

February 2 1967. Evening. 304 Holloway Road. Meek's final hours, described by his office assistant, Patrick Pink: "He looked clearly sort of sick. He wasn't talking – writing things down. In the evening we watched some TV and had something to eat. That would be about 7 o'clock. I think I cooked it. He was writing on bits of paper; he was afraid the place was bugged and that he was being listened in to. He suddenly asked me after dinner, 'Let's go up, let's make your record. You're more or less up to standards now.' I'd only recorded demos before but this particular one was promised to come out in March, my own. I have a feeling he had it planned. That was *the* night. After all those years I'd been with him and I'd stayed sometimes the night – and that particular night: 'Come on, let's see if we can get a record out of you now'.

"About 9 o'clock we went up into the studio. He had some tracks already made up: the backing tracks. I just did a couple of old ones he had stored away and I'd learnt the words from the acetates – very quick attempts: about an hour. Then I did another one which I'd learnt. It was a backing that was laid down for Heinz; he had already voiced it and the voice had been taken off of it. Heinz had sung it years ago: 'There goes my baby – look at the way she walks.' Joe wrote it. Went on the radio once – Heinz did it 'live'. Nothing had been put out on record, and Joe said I could have it and get it released.

"Then all of a sudden he went really weird and told me to start miming to my own recording – said, 'Just stand there and mime – they're watching us through the walls. They're watching and listening.' I've no idea who these people were. Possibly EMI, because days previously he'd pointed out to me people in cars sitting down the road, possibly with listening devices, had his place bugged, and they were watching him every time he came in and out and following him everywhere. He got worse then and it started to play on his mind. It might well have been true and he wasn't nuts completely. I genuinely believe, even though he was going off his rocker, that there were people bugging his place. I genuinely believe it now; or whether it was the police watching his place, I've no idea. Maybe the police had it bugged; might have been the Drug Squad.

"I was recording the same song over and over and over and over again. I don't think he knew what he was doing at all. He was putting on a show basically for the benefit of earholes, people listening in. On the bits of paper he was writing: 'Sing it again', 'More coffee'. I had to keep going down to make coffee. The session would have been about three hours. I went to bed at midnight absolutely shagged out.

"I was in bed when he came up to get the gun. It was a single-barrel shotgun. He kept it under the bed for protection. He said, 'I'm taking this downstairs'. I never gave it a thought.

"At 8 o'clock in the morning he was still working, running tapes and things. I got up. 9 o'clock I made toast for breakfast and called him down from the studio: 'Breakfast'. He came down, drank the coffee. I don't think he ate the toast – pretty sure he didn't eat at all. He wouldn't talk at all. He wrote little notes, passed them over and burnt them after he'd wrote them. After he'd drunk his coffee he went out in the kitchen and had a burn-up. First of all he was burning a lot of documents, letters and things in the kitchen; it was in a small tin dustbin. He had a bonfire in that. Angry about something – no idea what; he was very angry. The previous day he had just been dazed. Now he'd changed. I think he had his senses – I'm bloody sure he had. He was absolutely paranoid but tense and angry. He wrote two or three messages: 'They're not getting this'. 'They're not getting these'. He went mad and he wrote: 'They aren't going to f—— get this', and he started to burn that painting on the wall: the one with the little black boys dancing naked round a fire. He put the painting on top of a fire – the two-bar fire – which scorched it all up. I thought it was strange but I didn't think it was coming to what happened. I thought at the time he was going out of his head and I was going to call Dr Crispe and he stopped me. He was down for about half an hour. Then he disappeared upstairs to the studio for a little while. I thought, 'Crikey, I'll be safer to stay down here.' So I stayed downstairs. And he came back down to the living room. I think it was about quarter to ten. Give me a little note saying: 'I'm going now. Goodbye.' And I didn't know what it meant. I laughed. I thought, 'where?' The note got burnt and upstairs he went. I thought, 'Well everything's OK then.' Cause he was upstairs playing tapes – my stuff from the night before. That went on for ten to fifteen minutes.

"Then Michael arrives. Michael and Dennis – they'd just left school and they were looking for work, and Joe'd give them a job stacking tapes for a few days for a few quid. There was no set hours with them or whatever; they came and they were told to piss off – they went; that was the arrangement. One came, just Michael. I went up the stairs to tell Joe. Michael stayed at the door. I think he sensed there was something wrong straight away. Whether he'd been there the day before when I'd not been around, I don't know. Whether he knew there was something going on, I don't know, but he knew there was something wrong straight away. He said, 'Is it all right?' I went up to the landing and said, 'Michael's here.' I didn't actually see Joe at that point; he was in the control room. He called out: 'Tell him to f— off – get rid of him', but I'd already started coming downstairs having told him that Michael was here. Then he came to the top of the landing and looked down on me, and said, 'Get Mrs Shenton [his landlady] up here.' I in turn said to Michael, 'Joe don't want you today. Do us a favour, tell Mrs Shenton to come up for me'.

"She came up and she came to me. I was in the room before the office, the waiting room, more or less at the bottom of the stairs. She said, 'What's up?' I said, 'I don't know. Joe wants you.' I took her two or three steps up. She said, 'Oh, hold this for me a minute. I don't like to smoke up there.' I took her cigarette off her, she went on her way upstairs and I went in the office. I think she said, 'Hallo Joe, how are you?' and all the usual rubbish 'cause she did ask me what sort of mood he's in. I said, 'He's in a bad mood again.' I thought everything's going to be OK now; she'll calm him down. Within about half a minute there was a lot of shouting. It was after I put the cigarette out. I was walking back in the living room when I heard him say, 'Have you got the book?' God knows what it was: probably the rent book or rates book or lease or something. He shouted it very sternly. They weren't both shouting, just him. I think she said, 'I haven't got it with me; I'll bring it in tomorrow,' and asked him if he'd like to come down for a cup of tea and a chat. The shouting went on for a couple of minutes, I think. It was all him; he was getting frantic. I was trying to eavesdrop on the conversation, being the nosy kind of person that I am, walking to and fro, but I didn't hear very much.

"I was in the office when I heard a big bang. I didn't know what it was. It was such a f—— big bang, I was stunned. I rushed out and she was falling downstairs and I sort of grabbed her as she came to the bottom, and felt her. I was sitting on the stairs with her flapped over me. I wondered what it was for a minute. Then I saw the blood pouring out of these little holes in her back. And she died in my arms – I'm bloody positive she went still. I had quite a bit of blood over me. Her back was just smoking. He must have been close range, he must have been right at her back. I held her in my arms; clearly there was nothing I could do. She was dead as far as I was concerned and I sort of pushed her over and I shouted out, 'She's dead'. Joe was leaning over the landing banister and I thought I was next. He just had a stony-faced cold look.

"A few moments later I rushed halfway upstairs and looked across the landing and caught sight of Joe outside the control room and I think he was reloading, and before I could get at him he'd pulled the trigger on himself, and there was Joe's body with his head like a burnt candle. Blood everywhere, including over me as well; I was treading in blood . . ."

1963: The Beatles On Tour

Michael Braun

Psychologists have been trying to discover why the Beatles send teenage girls into hysterics. One of them came up with this explanation:

"This is one way of flinging off childhood restrictions and letting themselves go.

"The fact that tens of thousands of others are shrieking along with her at the same time makes a girl feel she is living life to the full with people of her own age.

"This emotional outlook is very necessary at her age. It is also innocent and harmless. It is a safety valve.

"They are also subconsciously preparing for motherhood. Their frenzied screams are a rehearsal for that moment. Even the jelly-babies are symbolic."

News of the World

The Beatles have been on a tour of one-night stands for almost six weeks. They arrive in a new town at about four in the afternoon and are rushed under cover to the dressing-room of the theatre, where they remain until the show. After the curtain goes down they rush out of the stage door and are driven to their hotel. Since most English hotels outside the large cities stop serving dinner at nine o'clock, the Beatles' evening meal has more than once consisted of cornflakes eaten in their hotel bedroom. The next day they are up around noon and the routine begins again.

The Beatles were in Lincoln. After the press conference Ringo developed a severe ear-ache. A woman doctor was summoned, and it took her twenty minutes to talk her way through the suspicious guards. In the midst of her examination Aspinall came in and asked her just what she thought she was doing there, then hastily apologized.

It was finally decided to bring Ringo to the hospital before the show. Dressed in an oversized coat, a hat pulled over his eyes, and glasses, he looked like Brecht being smuggled out of Germany. As he left the theatre a photographer took his picture.

At the hospital the doctor starts to examine him. The assistant area manager for ABC theatres is sitting on a bench outside the consultation room. "He has to be on stage in fifteen minutes," he says. "Everybody's in a merry flap. You have to take charge. I like a drink and parties as much as the next fellow but there's a time for everything."

The nurse comes out. "It's a Beatles' occupational disease," she explains, "all that hair getting in their ears."

Coming out, Ringo offers cigarettes to everyone. The doctor declines. "He's a throat man," explains the nurse. At the door the chief porter asks for an autograph and is warned not to say anything to the press.

At the cab a man walks over and announces: "*Daily Express*. Are you ill or did you come to see a friend?"

ABC man: "He's come to see a friend."

Express: "What's wrong with him?"

Ringo: "Don't know. He's still under observation."

Returning to the theatre, he is greeted by shouts of "Ringo", "Ringo", and "Operation Ringo's Ear" is over.

In their dressing-room the Beatles are shaking their heads like dogs after a swim, preparatory to going on stage. On Ringo's dressing-table is a fresh tube of Yardley's Shampoo for Men, to which someone has appended " – and Ringo".

In the front of the house they are clearing the last stragglers from the first show.

"Search the toilets," says the manager.

An assistant goes into the Men's Room.

"No, you sod, I mean the Ladies!"

*   *   *

In the manager's office beneath citations for "Good Management and Public Relations" two assistant managers are talking.

"I'd make a pot if I was doing the booking," says one.

"They wanted them to leave by helicopter in Nottingham but I said where would you land? On top of those old theatres?"

"The police are competing against one another to see who can get them out the quickest."

After the show they were rushed, still wearing make-up, to police headquarters, to change clothes. As they were about to leave the police chief came over to their car, which was surrounded by about twenty policemen.

"I hope you don't mind," he says, "but my daughters will kill me if I don't get your autograph."

They sign their autographs and as the car pulls away Paul rolls down the window, sticks his head out, and says, "Ta, thank you, thank you very much."

"Dirty sods," says John.

They were to spend the night at a hotel on the outskirts of Doncaster. As they drove, the car kept lurching over to the right-hand side of the road.

"Uh, hey, driver," says John, "we're not on the Continent. This is England, where we drive on the left."

For the next twenty minutes the car kept weaving on the road. John and Paul began to mumble prayers, and at one point Ringo began reciting the Lord's Prayer. Paul, sitting in the front, wrote "Help!" in the frost on the window. Gradually the car came to a halt. The driver had forgotten to fill the tanks with petrol.

Aspinall climbed out and after a few minutes managed to hail a lorry. The four Beatles clambered into the cab with the surprised driver.

"As soon as we get to the hotel I'm ringing up Brian about this driver," says George.

It was then 1.30 in the morning. By 10 a.m. the Beatles had a new driver.

*   *   *

A mixture of sounds is coming through the window of the dressing-room at Sunderland – the wind, as it slices off the Tyneside, and the screaming of hundreds of girls in the alley below.

In the room the Beatles are talking with a priest. Paul is asking him, "Why are there so many big churches in countries where people are starving?" The priest doesn't answer.

Ringo pours himself a Scotch and Pepsi-Cola and offers one to everybody in the room. The priest takes one and George jokingly asks if he is allowed to drink. John quips about Aleister Crowley and black masses.

Paul starts to discuss the financial aspects of Catholicism. The priest says he is paid only a small salary. Paul replies that the Beatles are paid only "the going show-business rates" and that if the priest wishes they can entertain at his church for nothing.

To convince them that money is really unimportant to him the priest tucks a ten-shilling note in Paul's pocket.

Aspinall sticks his head in the room and announces it is almost time to go on stage. The Beatles rush around getting dressed.

"I wish I had time to convince you fellows about the benefits of religion," says the priest. "We'd have a real bang-up fight. Naturally, I wouldn't say the same things to you boys as I say to my parishioners."

"Why?" say Paul and John simultaneously, as they run out of the room.

The priest doesn't answer.

The Beatles managed their escape from the Sunderland Theatre by rushing through the darkened auditorium to the fire-house next door and sliding down a fire-pole. Then, while engine number one clanged out as a decoy they rode off in a police car.

At the hotel they gathered in John and George's bedroom for a call from Australia. They were being recorded by a disc jockey in Melbourne. As they talked to him several girls standing beneath their window began throwing stones at the glass. Paul walked over and told them to stop because they were talking to Australia.

The stones stopped. When the call was finished they turned the lights out and spent a few minutes looking at the girls through a slit in the curtains before going to bed. The next morning as the Beatles left Sunderland several girls were still gathered in front of the hotel, huddling against the winds blowing from the North Sea.

The De Montfort Hall in Leicester is set deep in a large park. Around the perimeter is a high iron fence with many gates. Tonight they are all with one exception locked. The audience all file through this one gate.

The hall inside resembles a large meeting-room rather than a theatre. There is no proscenium arch on the stage. The performance takes place on a large platform in front of flats masking the pipes of a giant organ. Before the performance begins, a girl in the front row, with "Beatles" written in gold on her red jacket, has to be forcibly held down by her friend in the next seat.

Backstage, Paul is playing the piano with a sweater over his head. Ringo and George are putting on make-up, and John is ostentatiously removing the glasses he constantly wears offstage. "Mustn't spoil the image," he says. They come on to the platform, and the screaming begins.

Paul announces the numbers and the girls sit with their hands clenching their faces as if they have just seen a vision. John makes threatening gestures to the audience with his fist. It brings more screams. "In sweet fragrant meadows" sings Paul, nodding his head angelically. "With a love like that," sing Paul and George, and a blonde woman starts to rush the stage. The policewomen in the aisles move in and lead her away. "Twist and shout," bawls John. "C'mon, work it all out." The sound is deafening. Hordes of jelly-babies are thrown on stage. Several autograph books, a doll, a shoe, and an umbrella wind up there also.

As they finish, a girl in a red sweater is reaching for the stage, shouting "John, John". "The Queen" starts. She is comforted by her friend. As the anthem ends she walks out limply.

The house lights start to dim. On the littered stage is a plush doll with a note addressed to "John Lennon – the most fabulous Beatle of them all":

Leicester
Dear John,
Although all the Beatles are "fab" in every way and form, you are the "fabbiest" of them all. I love you, John, so much that I bought you this cuddly toy, which is what I think of you as.

Perhaps you would give it to your baby. Please, John. Will you write to me and say that you received it. Please. It would make just one girl so happy, if you wrote, it wouldn't take you long, although I would wait for ever. Because, as I've already said, you are "fab".
  All my love,
    Susan XXXX

Backstage, the Leicester Chief of Police, moustache bristling, swagger-stick at the ready, is waiting for the departure he had been planning for weeks. As he mobilizes his forces, the rest of the entertainers board the coach they use on tour. As it pulls out of the driveway the crowds who have been waiting for the Beatles scream at the other performers who scream back. Any glory they have achieved has been reflected from their four colleagues, who are even now being shown out of town by the police.

> *Our correspondent does not get from Mr Epstein the impression of a brilliant manipulator, but of a shrewd young man who has caught the lightning.*

Observer

> *Young television actress Jane Asher is the luckiest girl in the world. Because she is being constantly seen in the company of Beatle Paul McCartney. Jane met Paul while writing about popular music but says, "He is just one of many nice boys I know."*

Daily Express.

The north-west corner of the huge lobby of Grosvenor House in London was filled with clusters of people fidgeting. As an apple-cheeked young man carrying an Aquascutum package approached, several of them rose and surrounded him. A room clerk came over and handed him a sheaf of papers. "Mr Epstein," he said, "the telephone just hasn't stopped ringing all day."

Later, in his suite, Brian Epstein relaxes and pours himself a drink. He has just spoken with the last of the people who have waited in the lobby. She is a woman who has flown over from New York to try to get him to endorse a jewelled live beetle. "They're rather fun," he said, looking at one she has left, 'but it does seem rather strange, having to make money from insects."

He explains that he first heard the Beatles while running his family's record business in Liverpool. Before that he was a student at the Royal Academy of Dramatic Art, but he says that when he heard them "I knew they would be bigger than Elvis. I knew they would be the biggest theatrical attraction in the world."

Epstein excuses himself to change his clothes and then suggests dinner. "I've heard the Coq d'Or is amusing. Why don't we go there?" At the table he studies the wine list carefully and when he has finally decided on a dry white wine he leans back and recalls that his task with the Beatles at first was to let them retain their vitality, "but make them dress more tidily". He says he flogged their demonstration records for a year before anyone would listen. During the meal he talks about the other groups he is managing. He seems to be slightly hesitant about moving his office from Liverpool to London, "but I guess it's inevitable".

Over coffee he thinks for a while. "Most managers are L.s.d. [money] men," he says finally. "I guess I have to be one too but I'm not really one at heart. I'd much rather be out on the road with the boys, looking after them. My one dream is seeing the four boys in their dressing-room. No journalists, no fans, no theatre people – just the boys."

Outside the Associated TeleVision studios at Elstree there was a crowd of girls carrying signs reading "We want the Beatles". Inside Studio C, the objects of their affections were rehearsing for an appearance on *The Morecambe and Wise Show*. They were appearing in a sketch, wearing striped blazers and straw hats.

While they were singing "Moonlight Bay", Eric Morecambe put
on a Cardin jacket and a Beatle wig and accompanied them by
shouting "Yeah, Yeah, Yeah". Morecambe asked them how it
feels to be famous. "Not like in your day," said John. "My father
told me about you." They continued rehearsing the sketch. "If
you don't get a laugh on short hairy heads," said Wise, "try
saying . . ." He is interrupted by a tall blonde in a leopard coat
who asks them to pose for some photographs.

They line up.

"Head up," says Dezo Hoffmann. "Paul, up the head."

"Get a camera in there," says a man from ATV. "That's
important."

"George, could you look more interested?"

After a few minutes of posing in several groupings Wise says,
"Do you want us to fly?" and the photo session is over.

Sitting on the side observing were Epstein and a balding man
with a county accent and a three-piece suit. He is Brian Sommerville, the Beatles' new personal-publicity man.

A few seats away the producer of the programme is telling a
colleague, "The show won't be aired for a couple of months.
Let's hope they're still popular then." His secretary asks Paul for
his autograph. "It's not for me, but my niece will kill me if I don't
get it."

After the show was taped, the chief writer accompanied by his
two children visited Paul in his dressing-room. The Beatles were
appearing in cabaret for the first time in a charity benefit at
Grosvenor House, and Paul asked him for a line to introduce their
act. "We thought of something about being at the hotel and
trying to get room service and then suddenly we were at this great
big ball, but that sounded kind of soft."

"You must get a laugh," said the writer. "If you start to
announce and John starts to announce, so you're saying it
together; then you stop and look at each other; then you both
start again at the same time; then you look at each other and *then*
Ringo from way up there announces the number – *Must* get a
laugh!"

Noticing Paul's look the writer told him to think about the opening and thanked him for the autographs for his children.

That night in a suite in Grosvenor House they were still trying to think of an opening line. Someone suggested one based on the news in the evening papers. "No," said John, "nothing topical, I just couldn't say it."

Epstein recalled that at the Command performance he had asked John how he would get that kind of audience to join in. "I'll just ask them to rattle their fucking jewellery," John had said, and with obvious deletions the statement had remained, and become the Beatles' most widely quoted line.

The Grand Ballroom of Grosvenor House was crowded with the elite of British show business. Girls in Diors sat at the edge of the dance floor. Whatever opening line the Beatles *did* use was drowned in the screams that greeted their appearance. During their first number the wires on their electric guitars got crossed and a drunk in a dinner jacket started heckling. "Shuddupp," said Paul, and the audience applauded. After their second encore they were rushed by a mob of people in gowns and dinner jackets. In an effort to get people to dance Cyril Stapleton led his orchestra into *Twist and Shout*.

In the corridor Sommerville was frantic. "I must get hold of a doctor," he says. "John is very sick but the press mustn't know." When he gets to the suite he asks how John is. "He's fine," says Paul. "We just said he was sick so we could get away from the mob."

Sommerville looks at him querulously and asks, "Did you see Dora Bryan?"

"Yeah," says George, "she put her hand on my shoulder and kept screaming 'Twist and shout, twist and shout'."

Sommerville tells them that the chairman of the ball, the Countess of Westmorland, wants to see them.

"Tell her to piss off," says John who is sitting on a sofa, looking glum. "If anybody tells us we were good tonight I'll spit in their faces; we were awful."

While John reflects on the performance, Paul goes into the hallway of the suite to talk with Lady Westmorland. Suddenly he comes running back to the sitting-room.

"Hey, c'mon and look," he says. "She's not an old hag at all . . . she's kinda cute."

1966: Voices from the Underground

Jonathan Green

UFO: "Suddenly there was somewhere to go in London on a Friday night"

SUE MILES: Hoppy started UFO to finance the underground newspaper, *IT*, because it couldn't make enough money out of advertising.

JOHN HOPKINS: There was a church hall off Westbourne Park Road – All Saints Hall. We started putting on weekly events, on Thursday nights, around October 1966. I started doing it as a desperate measure, not to make a profit, but just to pay the debts of the Free School, which must have been a few tens of pounds. Pete Jenner was around, a guy called Jack Braceland came along, and there was a light-show, some Americans from California. We'd never seen a light-show before. They started doing this light-show in the hall and it all got very popular. Joe Boyd was around. He was into music and he saw what we were doing and said, "This is popular; if I find a place in the West End, what do you think about moving it all over there and seeing if we can make a go of it?"

JOE BOYD: Hoppy and I had this conversation about doing something on a regular basis and we formed a partnership to do a club and we had to find a place. Hoppy found the Blarney Club in Tottenham Court Road. We went down and met Mr Gannon. He was very amiable and he agreed to rent it to us for £15 every Friday night. He had the soft-drink concession. We didn't have a

lease, it was an arrangement between us and him. Hoppy and I
didn't sign anything, we just divided up the money every week.
And some weeks I might take £50 or £75. We were debating
between calling it "Night Tripper" and "UFO". Like many
things that happened with me and Hoppy, we each had ideas and
rather than argue about them, we synthesised them. So we made
up these handbills saying "UFO – Night Tripper" and handed
them out in Portobello Road.

JOHN HOPKINS: So he found this place called the Blarney
Club and he came back and said, "Look, I've found this place,
how about it?" So we said, "OK, we've got enough resources to
put on two gigs: one on 23 December, and one on 30 December.
Each side of Christmas: if we can't do it then, it ain't going to
work." Mike McInnerney had been doing some graphics for the
London Free School and he helped with posters, so did Mike
English and Nigel Waymouth, and it worked. Joe looked after the
musicians, I looked after some of the other stuff and it was
amazing. It went off like a forest fire. People got paid, and I
don't think a lot of money got ripped off there. It cost ten
shillings, maybe a pound to get in.

MILES: UFO was started almost immediately after *IT* began.
We had enormous cash-flow problems of course, so we tried a
number of different ways of making money. We had the Un-
common Market, which was a sort of jumble sale held in the
Roundhouse, with various performances at the same time. To get
some proper money turning over we started a night club. I had
very little to do with it. Joe chose the music, Hoppy was in charge
of everything else. It was held in an Irish dance hall on Tottenham Court Road called the Blarney Club. It had a wonderful
polished dance floor.

JOE BOYD: We had these two dates at the Blarney Club, either
side of Christmas '66. UFO – Night Tripper: Pink Floyd,
whoever else, a lot of different people. They played the first
four, they were the resident band, but we also had a lot of other

things like theatre groups, avant-garde jazz, Kurosawa movies at four o'clock in the morning. It was great. It was packed from the first night. I wasn't surprised, but I was pleased. I thought there was an audience there. You could tell, you didn't have to be a genius to look around the streets and see there were a lot of people dressing in funny ways.

MILES: Because our 24-hour city programme hadn't quite worked out yet, we ran it from ten at night until eight in the morning, so that people could catch the morning tubes. By about five in the morning it got a bit funky, an awful lot of people curled up on the floor snoozing, meanwhile psychedelic music was blasting out. The Floyd and the Soft Machine were the main house bands, but we also had Procol Harum's second and third ever gigs, when they already had a Number One hit. The Crazy World of Arthur Brown. Enormous amounts of psychedelic drugs being consumed. Micky Farren had by then joined *IT* and he was on the door of UFO. He and Joy [Farren]. They used to stand on the door and trip out. Micky was in black leather, his James Dean/Elvis Presley phase.

MICK FARREN: Suddenly there was somewhere to go on a Friday night – this old Irish showband ballroom with a revolving mirror ball and stuff. I imagine if we were transported back there it would probably look like little more than an adventurous high-school dance, but at the time it was quite mind-blowing.

RUSSELL HUNTER: Micky was on the door with Joy. Before I knew him I used to go there. There was a guy called Manfred, who was very famous for dealing acid there. This terrible fat German. Jim Haynes was there, Miles . . . most people were there, only you didn't know their names. David Medalla and the Exploding Galaxy, who lived at 99 Ball's Pond Road where the door was kicked in so often that they didn't bother to put it back. They were a free-form art group, but mostly they were a lot of speedfreaks dancing.

STEVE SPARKS: Then I discovered UFO. I sort of wandered down the stairs and there was Micky and Joy and I blagged my way in, I looked round and I thought, "This'll do, this looks interesting."

UFO was magic, I really liked UFO. Having come from running all sorts of clubs, dances and folk scenes in the East End, UFO was so wonderfully naïve. It was so innocent. You really didn't need heavy bouncers. This was a great shock to me, because you used to need bouncers in the folk clubs that I ran, cos they'd come in – seventeen pints and ready to kill. The gentleness and the naïveté of the whole thing . . .

JOE BOYD: We originally decided to do UFO as an experiment, two weeks, and two weeks only. It went very well, everybody enjoyed it, everybody said, "You've got to do it again." We needed a rest, we didn't have anything booked for the next two weeks, and we decided to do two-week bursts. We'd book everything in a two-week lump and we'd do one poster for two weeks. So we had a bit of money and we decided that now we wanted to make it even more successful and we wanted to have some fun with the promotion and not just hand out leaflets in Portobello Road. That's where we came to the posters. I said I have this friend named Nigel who would do a great poster and Hoppy said I have this friend called Michael who would do a great poster. So, following our usual policy, we said, "Let's put them together." They'd never met each other and we basically locked them in a room and said, "Come out with a poster." And they came up with the best thing they ever did. The gold candy-stripe UFO poster, for the second lot of two weeks, in January 1967.

MARK BOYLE: Mike English did the two great posters of the era, for UFO. I remember walking down the street and seeing one of them for the first time and thinking, "God! what a poster," not knowing what it was, then starting to think, "What's it actually advertising?" and working it out and realising, "That's us!"

CRAIG SAMS: My connection to the underground came through Michael English who I had known in Ealing and who now did the posters for UFO. UFO was every other weekend, so on a lot of the alternate weekends Michael, his girlfriend Angela, and Pete Townshend and Karen his girlfriend and me would get together at Karen's place in Eccleston Square and trip the night away. We had our own little UFO. That gave us something to do on the alternate Fridays. Once we were all walking down the street just past the Victoria Coach Station, it was really freezing cold but Townshend had stripped down to his shirt – "Cold is just a state of mind, man" – and we were all barrelling along, just full of our own incredible strength, and some car pulls up. The classic scene: a head comes out and somebody says, "Hi, Pete Townshend. I think your last album was fucking great!" and then the guy drunkenly heaves all down the side of the car. Suddenly you realised the huge distance between where we were going, into spiritual realms, and fifteen pints of lager, which was where a lot of the mods had gone. But we'd all come from the same roots – soul, dancing and mild pharmaceuticals.

JOE BOYD: It was during that period that I was informed that not only was I going to get rowed out as the producer of the Pink Floyd, but they were going to put their prices up. So we then brought in the Soft Machine. That actually began a kind of quest for a constant turnover of new groups being brought into the orbit of UFO. We had Arthur Brown, the Bonzo Dog Doo-Dah Band, Procol Harum, Tomorrow.

PETER BROWN: My hero, the best dancer I've ever seen: Arthur Brown. A fantastic dancer. And if you see any character in the entertainment business who dedicates their whole being to make every night's performance like an opening night, then you know they'll never last. Well, Arthur was like that. It was obvious that he was going to burn out, because every performance was a total performance, the man literally burnt himself out every night.

JOE BOYD: Arthur Brown was playing in a supper club in Mayfair, doing a novelty act in this weird little bar in Mayfair, which was rather posh, with the fire, the whole bit. He suddenly emerged on this tiny stage wearing this fiery crown, with Vincent Crane on the organ. Victor Schonfield told me about him. I just went down to see him and, "Hey! Great. Let's have him at UFO," and two months later he's swinging from the chandeliers at the Roundhouse and his record is Number One.

ROBERT WYATT: When you arrived at UFO, early on, they were usually playing Monteverdi or something. I was probably more awestruck by the place than most of the punters, who I felt took it for granted.

It wasn't any easier playing UFO than the circuit, but the demands were our own. We were able to develop our own idiosyncrasies. Our management had immediately put us on the road on a circuit where you had to play for dance audiences. We weren't very good at that. So the great thing for us about UFO was that the audiences weren't demanding in the same way. They were sitting about, most of them were asleep as far as I could see. The very things that were our faults on the regular circuit – that of all the bands playing *Midnight Hour* or *Knock on Wood* on any particular evening we would play it worst, if we played it at all – became bonuses at UFO. We couldn't play that stuff, or if we did people didn't realise that was what we were playing.

CHRIS ROWLEY: UFO, down in this cellar, was a disgusting-looking place in the daylight but transformed by the light works and Jack Henry Moore's little team of people putting up screens and shining the blobshows around. Manfred, the German acid dealer, attended and distributed the product on a handsome level. At the third UFO he gave out 400 trips. A lot of Americans: Suzy Creamcheese, who was Hoppy's woman. I saw Suzy Creamcheese and two other girls love-bomb a bunch of rather uptight young mods who got into the club. The third or fourth UFO. These mods were standing there pilled up, chewing, looking around them, semi-freaked-out. And the girls noted that these mods were semi-hostile, almost lashing out at the hippies round them. So these girls descended on them semi-naked, clad in gauzy stuff with flowers and all the rest of it, and caressed them. These guys did not know what had hit them. But they calmed down and later on they were to be seen holding flowers and talking to Manfred.

PETER SHERTSER: We used to go down to UFO and we would cause so much trouble. We figured the best way to pull was the ladies' toilets. There's so many people around: to save milling around stand in the bog and you're going to see them all at some point in the evening. So that's where we used to go – very good. We used to disrupt everything at UFO, throw buckets of water over people, all kinds of silly, childish things, but because they were all so crazy, they never knew any different. This was before we got into acid and we were saying: "What is it with these people?" Bit by bit we learned and we were there every weekend.

DICK POUNTAIN: Just about anyone could turn up and perform if they wanted. I saw [Mick] Farren there for the first time, before the Deviants even. I can't remember what the band was called but they were unspeakably awful. It was garage stuff, punk thrashing years before it was thought of, basically because they couldn't play. A bit Velvet Underground-ish; Farren was wearing black leather from head to foot.

MICK FARREN: We called ourselves the Social Deviants and that didn't do much good until basically we started playing UFO. And Jack Braceland who was one of the people doing lights there made us house resident band at this converted strip club he ran down on Gerrard Street. A psychedelic joint. And we laboured in that mine long and hard and met a lot of strippers who came down after work. Being a resident band in a converted strip club in the middle of Soho was quite an education for a young lad.

CHRIS ROWLEY: Happening 44 was a small psychedelic club that ran for about five or six months on Gerrard Street in Chinatown just round the corner from Ronnie Scott's. It was basically run by a couple of old . . . beatniks isn't the right word, but they had connections with the film world: the Bracelands. They had a nudist colony out in Watford. One night I went out to a party there: grass, champagne, and slightly fleshy women in their late thirties who were very ready to take off all their clothing and drag anybody away into a series of nest bunks at the back.

JOE BOYD: We had Jack Braceland, fifty years old, doing a light-show at UFO. He came from Watford where he ran a nudist colony and had Happening 44 on Gerrard Street, the place I first saw the Fairport Convention. It was this strip club in the daytime, just a little hole in the wall. He did a promotion there one night a week. Hoppy knew him and we gave him a little corner of UFO. He didn't have the main light-show but he had a corner and people could go dance in his lights. Basically he was a nudist. And there were a lot of people like this, it wasn't just a generational thing.

PAUL McCARTNEY: You'd go down UFO and see the early incarnation of the Floyd. They'd be down there, a lot of projections, lots of people sort of wandering about, that was nice. It was all like a trippy adventure playground really. Chaplin films going here, Marx Brothers here, Floyd up there, conjuror over here or something – just a nice circus-cum-adventure playground.

JOHNNY BYRNE: I found it curiously tacky, but in retrospect it contained all the best of the cultural movements because it was still young and naïve enough not to doubt what it was doing, there was no cynicism there, there genuinely was the coming together of the various strands.

JIM HAYNES: There was a lot going on in UFO but the main thing was people meeting and gossiping. The human, social side was almost more important than anything else.

CHRIS ROWLEY: You'd circulate: do UFO for two or three hours, then hang out at 44 for a little while, then back to UFO.

The next night, when Middle Earth was open, you'd do the same thing between UFO and Middle Earth. Eventually 44 closed and Middle Earth became much bigger.

Light-shows: "You had to have things going 'Pow!'"

PHILIP HODGSON: John Massara and I were doing light-shows in our school holidays, that's where it all started. In 1966, after we'd both left school, we started doing lights at UFO in Tottenham Court Road. Then Middle Earth. John was working full-time on the lights but I spent a year in the civil service the first year out of school and doing light-shows at the weekends. There were a lot of people doing that – weekend freaks.

It was all very easy doing lights. You got some glass slides, got some ink, slapped them together and slapped them in front of the projector. Mark Boyle was one of the big originators over here. He'd still be classed as daddy of the UK light-shows. Joe Gannon was also involved. Loads of people did it. If you worked for any of the groups at UFO you'd tend to cross over. One group would finish and you'd just stay on for the next one until your ink ran out or whatever and then you'd push off and someone else would step in.

MARK BOYLE: We had already been doing what came to be known as light-shows in '63. It was a natural development from our work. We realised that our pieces were fixed and permanent presentations of chunks of the world, but we also realised that the world's not a fixed and permanent place. So we started to make a series of performances to show our awareness of that. The first light-show we did was in '63. We did some work with Horovitz's *New Departures*: there were a few gigs there with avant-garde musicians and composers and we would come and contribute a light-show element. We would make our light-show into another instrument. Then we did this piece "Suddenly Last Supper" in '63 in our house and I suppose that was the first light-show that was done publicly in this country.

The problem for us was the spread of bad light-shows. According to *IT*, three weeks after we did our first show at UFO there were 120 groups in London doing it. The question was one of quality, and of having new things all the time. We prided ourselves on having a completely new effect each week. And there was always this row of guys sitting in front of us who'd turn round with a cheerful smile and say, "We'll have that!" We saw it more in terms of explosions. There were bubbles and so on, but to get the real quality you had to have these things going "Pow!!!" right across the screen in three colours, lightning effects, turbulence.

It was certainly the visual medium of the underground and from our prejudiced point of view it was one of the elements that made that particular cultural scene so different from any that had gone before. That there *was* a visual side to it. In none of the other "music revolutions" had there been this visual side.

ROBERT WYATT: Mark Boyle was burning himself to pieces doing these experiments with different coloured acids. You just saw him with these goggles, looking all burnt and stuff, high up on some rigging. He used to play tricks, he used to make bubbles come out of people's flies and things. You couldn't see exactly what he was doing from on stage, but the atmosphere was good.

PETER JENNER: I don't think, with all due respect to Mark, that his lights were art. It was just that he called himself art, I don't think he was any different from Peter Wynne-Wilson or any of the others. He sussed that it was a good idea to call himself art; some of the others should have been a bit more hip and called themselves art – they might have done rather better.

ROBERT WYATT: The Floyd always had their own lights people, but no one else did and Mark used to do the place, not particularly the groups, but the walls, everything. The light-shows meant that what we shared with the Floyd was that as personalities you could hide and the overall group effect could be more important than the individuals. The normal thing would be that there would be a focus on one or two individual performers, even in the R&B bands, the lead guitarists would get that focus. Whereas we and the Floyd would hardly be recognised off stage, nobody knew what they looked like through the light-show. The anonymity of light-shows was nice – the fact that you were almost in the same swirly gloom that the audience were in was relaxing and you could get a nice atmosphere going.

JOHN MARSH: Light-shows in those days were desperately unsophisticated. Pre-laser, even pre-video era. Everything very crudely mechanical, very crudely assembled, but for the time, pretty effective. The Floyd had two effects which no other band had, both built by Peter Wynne-Wilson – one called the Daleks, the other was flashes – and these put them, in light-show terms, streets ahead of everybody else. But this was still manually operated, switch-oriented kind of stuff. We had one marvellous effect: projecting the polarised stress patterns in condoms. That was wonderful. This was a time when jo-bags were still essentially thick, unlubricated rubber. What we did was cut them up into flat sheets of material, placing them between two sheets of polaroid film and stretching the things so that the stress patterns in the rubber, which was semi-transparent, were projected onto the stage: it was a beautiful effect. We were stopped one time for some minor traffic offence: I was sitting on the front seat of the van, a pile of Durex in front of me, a pair of scissors and a record sleeve, cutting up these johnnies. The police were absolutely aghast. "That's just our roadie," says Peter. "He's cutting up johnnies, but he's crazy . . ."

SAM HUTT: I went to UFO quite a lot. Saw the bands, the very loud music, the oil lights and Joe Gannon, who used to run a light-show. I remember near the end with Syd [Barrett], him coming up and somebody had given him a bottle of mandies. Mandies were the big bouncing-around drug, very dodgy indeed, and probably a very good idea that they took them off the market. Syd appeared on stage with this jar of Brylcreem, having crushed the mandies into little pieces, mixing them up with the Brylcreem and putting this mixture of Brylcreem and broken mandy tablets all over his hair, so that when he went out on stage the heat of the lights melted the Brylcreem and it all started to drip down his face with these bits of Mandrax.

JOHN PEEL: Being a timorous chap, I found UFO slightly intimidating. In California we hadn't bothered much with the clothes and stuff. I'd gone along to things like the recording sessions that produced *Surrealistic Pillow* and done a lot of gigs, especially at Pandora's Box which produced the Sunset Strip riots when they closed it down, which was what [Buffalo Springfield's] *Hey, Look, What's That Sound?* was all about, but people weren't that much into hippie clothing. I hadn't got any of the stuff. So I had to buy myself a pair of ghastly, vast trousers and a very, very expensive kaftan made out of a bedspread, and the obligatory bells and beads. I felt incredibly foolish in them, I must admit, and even in UFO I felt rather out of place.

SUE MILES: John Hoyland, the writer not the painter, lived above the opticians in Tottenham Court Road, on the corner of Percy Street. He said that every Saturday morning it used to sound like a herd of goats in an Alpine pasture were going by when all the hippies and their bells were finally decanted from UFO and trolled off up the road.

The Soft Machine:
"The only other bloke in Kent with long hair."

PEARCE MARCHBANK: I never really liked the hippie ethos. I could never, for example, understand why people regarded the Grateful Dead as the next best thing to Jesus Christ. The Velvet Underground were obviously *far better*. They were to do with *black leather:* who wanted all these smelly old caravans hanging around with wigwams and so on? They were clean, New York, hard-edged. The Soft Machine were the same: Mike Ratledge in his long leather coat.

ROBERT WYATT: In Canterbury I got into a local sort of beat group, the Wild Flowers. The name had nothing to do with flower power; we lived in the country and Hugh Hopper had a book called *Wild Flowers* and I think he thought it up. Wild Flowers was the beginning of what became the Soft Machine. Hugh Hopper's brother Brian, who played saxophone, was a friend of Mike Ratledge and when Mike Ratledge came back from university and wanted to play, we were the only people there to play with. So he joined the band, playing piano. But nobody in the band was trying to do the same thing at all, which is why it was quite original and why, after a couple of years, it fell apart. It was a constant process of disintegration really, getting in new people to fill the gaps. Which in the Sixties was rare, because most bands were quite stable. I talked to Nick Mason of the Pink Floyd about that once. I said, "How come you lot have stayed together so long?" and he said, "We haven't finished with each other yet." But it kept changing, we kept on tinkering with it and tinkering with it and throwing each other out of it and leaving it until eventually all the kinks were ironed out of it and in the end it became a standard British jazz-rock band. I don't know what happened in the end. I stopped listening after a while – I stopped listening before I even left.

When we came up to London there were two connections: Daevid Allen had the connection with people like Hoppy. The other connection was Kevin Ayers, who played bass guitar and wrote songs. He was the only other bloke in Kent with long hair.

The name Soft Machine came through Mike Ratledge. He had books like *V* and all that kind of thing. I knew the name was taken from Burroughs but I don't think it intrigued me enough to get a copy. Wild Flowers more or less became the Soft Machine. We trickled up to London and then regrouped, one by one.

Kevin Ayers was important in that he knew the Animals office, where Hilton Valentine and Chas Chandler were already starting to manage, and they signed us up really on the basis of Kevin's songs. They were looking for something commercial. Chas was always looking for Slade, and eventually he found them, meanwhile he had to put up with people like us and Jimi Hendrix. Shortly after we joined Chandler Hendrix came to London and musically that was tremendously important for lots of people. For

me too, if for nothing else than that what he let Mitch Mitchell do
on drums gave me space for what I wanted to do on drums. We
were using a lot of jazz ideas on drum kits that there hadn't been
room for in the constricted time-keeping stuff I'd been doing
before. Of course this was quite the opposite of what Nick Mason
was doing with the Floyd: he was a kind of ticking clock there –
which is just what they needed. For electronic rock his approach
was more suitable – uncluttered. People like me and Mitch were
probably too busy, but at the time it seemed exciting. So Kevin
actually got us a deal and turned us into a group that had a
manager and so on. He liked bossanova and calypso. Ray Davies
and the Kinks, who started using stuff like that quite early on,
were a big influence on him. One record company bloke told us,
"I don't know whether you're our worst-selling rock group or our
best-selling jazz group."

The Macrobiotic Restaurant:
"getting the message across."

CRAIG SAMS: On February 14 1967 I opened the Macrobiotic
Restaurant in a place called the Centre House off Campden Hill
Road. They had radionics and various other new-age activities
going on. The guy who ran it was into health foods so he let us
have the restaurant in the basement. It became an instant success
and people just came flooding in. It was the only alternative
restaurant-type venue anywhere in London. It went on for a
couple of months and one night we had a party at which Graham
Bond played and around 1 o'clock in the morning it got too much
of a party and the next morning the writs started to arrive from
our neighbours. So we got thrown out. They were upset with us
upstairs as well; I remember Christopher Hills, who ran the
Centre House, calling down one day, "Can you *please* not smoke
marijuana – we can smell it on the third floor." After that we put
in a guest book which said, "I am not in possession of any kind of
drugs," and everybody signed it including Yoko Ono and various
other customers. Brown rice and vegetables was 2/6, felafel were
1/3 each. Nothing ever came to over five bob. People wrote out

their own chits for what they'd had, someone would watch the till and take their money. It was very trusting. But one night I did a check on the tickets and found out that we had moved 24 slices of apple crumble and only one had been paid for; so after that we went onto a slightly more structured basis. The restaurant generated about £70 a week in sales, of which ten or twelve was profit. At UFO they had this little tea and sandwiches bar and I would bring down rice rissoles and vine leaves stuffed with brown rice – portable macrobiotic food – and give it to the people in the catering area and they would sell it and I would charge them a price for that. And I'd collar people after they'd bought this macrobiotic food and bore them about macrobiotic food, and when they came into the restaurant we'd sit down and give them a two-minute speech – just getting the message across.

An Afternoon
with Syd Barrett

Jenny Fabian

I often thought about Syd, he was the first, the most magical, the most spaced-out, of them all. I'd originally seen Pink Floyd at All Saints Hall, Notting Hill, I was living round the corner and the vibe was out about their freaky music. I went to see them again, at UFO, and I was on my first acid trip. I couldn't take my eyes off the slender dark-haired one hunched over his guitar, making extraordinary cosmic sounds and singing wonderland songs. Great blobs of colour swirled across the stage, illuminating him like a mystical being. By the time I got close to Syd he was permanently tripped-out, and if he seemed more preoccupied with other-worldly things, it didn't matter, it was the same for me. Acid took us somewhere else, except that Syd never came back. I thought he was being poetic when he spoke about mental exile.

Now I'd moved on, written *Groupie* with Johnny Byrne, and had become "Underground Editor" of *Harpers & Queen*. The Floyd had replaced Syd, who wandered off to be a fractured solo artist. Someone had played me an acetate of *The Madcap Laughs,* and I wanted to interview him for my column. It wasn't hard to find him, the underground scene was a small world. I wasn't sure how he'd react, for it was three years since I'd last seen him and the word was that he'd flipped beyond repair. He answered the phone himself, and I was surprised at how friendly he seemed. He told me to come to his flat in Earls Court the following afternoon.

I was on my own doomed roller coaster ride at the time, rich from advances, infamous from sleazy publicity, and heavily into drugs. My previous interview with Arthur Lee had been in the spirit of the times, because as soon as I'd walked through the door of Love's hotel suite they laid a tab of Sunshine on me and I forgot what I'd come for. Part of me knew I was only pretending to be a writer, I was really just a groupie. That's all I felt like as I stood nervously outside Syd's front door. What if he'd forgotten where he lived and had given me the wrong address?

But he hadn't, and he opened the door. He was barefoot and his dark hair hung wild and matted round his waxy white face. He still wore one of those skinny art-deco scarves round his neck like a counter-culture cravat. "Oh, it's you," he said, with a little smile. I shut the front door and followed him into the kitchen, which was bare and bleak. He was boiling an egg in the kettle. He offered me a grimy glass of water, it's all there was, he told me. After hunting for a spoon and breaking his egg open onto a stale slice of bread, he led the way to his room.

The first thing I noticed were the floorboards, which were painted alternate orange and purple. He'd painted the floorboards himself, though he found them rather disturbing to look at, he said. It was a large room, no furniture, just a sound-system and some battered LPs strewn all over the floor. A guitar and some paintings were over in the corner. We flopped down on a mattress covered in lumpy bedding. Syd ate his egg and I rolled a joint. We must have sat there for several hours, most of the time in silence, and he didn't seem inclined to put any sounds on. I felt no need to get through to him because I knew he was out the other side and miles away. His thoughts were like currents in the air, as though they had exploded uncontrollably from a brain that had been boiled in acid and split like a tomato skin.

Now he mostly lived in the fuzzy-land of mandrax, a soft and floaty place that I knew well. He gradually sank back into a pile of crumpled clothes and lay gazing up at me. I wondered if he remembered who I was. I could feel myself changing into a million different chicks as though he was watching me through a kaleidoscope. When he spoke it was vague and disconnected, sad stuff about broken guitars and too many people. I couldn't be sure if he was talking to me, or just thinking out loud, each sentence died away unfinished, and he found it hard to remember what he had said. His voice was soft and gentle, and he smiled a lot to himself.

The room had an eerie glow due to the light filtering in through thin green curtains. He told me his mother had made them and he kept them closed all day because it made the room feel like a tank. It made Syd look very spectral. He said his brain was like a cream slice, and he could stand outside himself and contemplate it. This contemplation would give rise to another creation and so on. He was completely self-indulgent with his imagination, never trying to control or direct it within any bounds of reason. Reasoning was inconclusive and unnecessary to him, because one reason led endlessly to another. I asked him if any reason ever led to an answer. He looked startled at the sound of my voice. Then he told me that as there is no reason, there is no answer. It seemed there was nowhere left to go, and he knew it.

"It gets boring," he said, "lying here all day and thinking of nothing."

I didn't believe him because to me he would always inhabit the world of his songs, full of gnomes and cats and stars and weird fairy tale things. The skin around his violet eyes was bruised with LSD overload, he was irresistibly tragic, and I leaned over and kissed him. He started to laugh, and tumbled me back into the heap of clothing. I couldn't believe my luck and once again forgot the notebook. Our clothes got all muddled up in the heap already there.

We lay there into the darkness, Syd staring at the ceiling, still feeding off his brain's output, until he finally got up and turned on the bare orange light bulb that hung from the ceiling, Suddenly the room took on a new perspective. He put on a Beach Boys LP and it played over and over again until I couldn't stand it any longer and had to leave.

Are You Experienced?
The Death of Jimi Hendrix

Carmen Geddes

"If I seem free, it's because I'm always running"
                                          Jimi Hendrix

The Monterey International Pop Festival was scheduled for June, 1967. In the back of everybody's mind it was to be the opening event for the "Summer of Love". This was a portentous time. In the same month The Beatles released *Sergeant Pepper's Lonely Hearts Club Band*, and the song *San Francisco (Wear Some Flowers In Your Hair)* by Scott McKenzie was about to help set a mood that would influence a generation.

The Monterey Festival organisers were former Beatles publicist Derek Taylor (who was to bring a reluctant Paul McCartney on board), LA businessman Lou Adler, Mamas and Papas mainman John Phillips and music biz wheeler-dealer Alan Pariser. Their aim was to set-up a non-profit making event showcasing "a diversity of international talent". Among those booked to appear were Indian sitar maestro Ravi Shankar, The Byrds, Simon and Garfunkel, The Grateful Dead, the Mamas and Papas (natch), The Who, Otis Redding, Big Brother and the Holding Company and a young American guitarist all-but unknown in his native land, Jimi Hendrix.

The festival ran for three days and proved a huge success. Otis Redding put in a performance that literally took breaths away. He was the only major representative of American soul music, but the power of his voice coupled with his intensity of performance revitalised a style of music that had been largely disregarded by

white American record buyers. That he should die in a plane
crash a few months later would only serve to heighten the
remembered poignancy of his performance. The Who showed
that they were world class rockers and Big Brother and The
Holding Company, featuring rough diamond vocalist Janis Joplin, knocked everybody sideways.

But it was Jimi Hendrix who stole the show. Introduced by
doomed Rolling Stone Brian Jones, who was there for that
express purpose, Hendrix performed as if he were on stage in
an intimate London venue. Although high on acid, he teased
notes out of his guitar even he must have been surprised at. His
banter between numbers was restrained but spot-on, and the
band played the gig of their lives. At the end of the set, Hendrix
set fire to his guitar and smashed it against his amp. Jimi Hendrix
had arrived.

To consolidate on the success of Monterey, he was booked into
a series of American showcases and, although an over-eager agent
had booked him as tour support to the Monkees, this was aborted
after a few mutually-confusing gigs, by summoning up the ogre
of the right-wing pressure group, The Daughters of the American Revolution.

Back in Europe, Hendrix finished the *Axis: Bold As Love*
album in London, and toured extensively in Britain, Scandinavia,
France and Holland; sometimes playing two shows a night. On
January 4th, 1968, Jimi cracked. The combination of fatigue,
acid, booze and frustration resulted in an explosion of temper-
ament, and after smashing up a Gothenburgh hotel room, he was
arrested for criminal damage.

Despite this warning sign, there could be no let up in the
ruthless schedule. By February the band were back in the USA,
headlining a British package with producer-manager Chas Chandler's former band, The Animals, Soft Machine and the Alan
Price Set. Stakes were high and nerves were being rattled, not
least in the management team. Chandler allowed himself to be
bought out by dubious co-manager Mike Jeffrey, a man with a
shady past and supposed mob connections. Bassist Noel Redding
– who resented being told exactly what notes to play and when –

was only persuaded to stay on board by a mixture of threats and promises. It was obvious to everyone at their shows that the band were not getting on, but it was still genius and by now the Jimi Hendrix Experience were the best paid band on the circuit, commanding fees of $50,000 upwards. When it came to getting in the limousine and driving to his first $100,000 concert in Cleveland, he was worried that the band were being over-paid. "What will the kids think?" he asked a friend. "Will they think I've sold out?" Not ready to be convinced that he was worth fees of $100,000, Hendrix refused to get into the car and ran away down the street. On this occasion he was missing for two days.

By 1969, due to a dispute with a former manager, all Hendrix's American royalties were frozen and plans to build his own Electric Lady Studio in New York were stalled until the record label could come up with extra money. At the end of a set at the appropriately-named Mile High Stadium in Denver, Hendrix announced on stage: "This is the last gig we'll ever be playing together" which came as news to Redding, who knew nothing about leaving the band. Jams with John McLaughlin and Miles Davis were meant to lead to a new double album, but despite a distinguished appearance with his new five piece A Band of Gypsys (sic), at the 1970 Woodstock Festival, Hendrix was becoming tired and frustrated. He was busted for heroin possession in Toronto – a "plant", he insisted – and his manager wasn't allowing him the freedom he needed to try new things. Jeffrey seemed eager that his star should give the punters what they wanted, and if that meant more of the same, then so be it. Also, Hendrix felt that Jeffrey was ripping him off and would often talk about "getting his shit together" and leaving him.

Hendrix was tired, and tired of being a star. As a favour to some of Jeffrey's former "associates", Hendrix opened a club called Salvation, but he was kidnapped by supposed mobsters and held in a remote hideout for two days. The cavalry arrived in the shape of Mike Jeffrey, but in his increasing drug-induced paranoia, Hendrix was convinced that his manager had orchestrated the kidnapping to "teach him a lesson". In his eyes it was possible that the heroin planted in Toronto could have come from the same source. Jimi was later acquitted, but the experience haunted him every time he crossed a frontier, which with Jeffrey at the helm, was often.

By the end of August 1970, the Electric Lady studios were finally completed and Hendrix and A Band of Gypsys flew to New York to work on a double album, provisionally titled, *First Rays of the New Rising Sun*. *Angel* was dedicated to Hendrix's mother, Lucille, and *Dolly Dagger* to a girlfriend, Devon Wilson. But right in the middle of the recordings, Jeffrey arranged for Hendrix to play at the Isle of Wight Festival in England and fit in a quick European tour. Tired and playing at a festival that had slumped from being "Britain's answer to Woodstock" to a bankrupt enterprise fought over by French anarchists, Hell's Angels and security staff who probably wouldn't get paid, Hendrix put in a poor set that was poorly received by those still awake to hear it. A few days later, at another festival in Germany, bassist Billy Cox had his drink spiked with acid and his first trip pushed him to the edge of a nervous breakdown.

Dates were cancelled and Hendrix and the band returned to London for a rest. A telegram was dispatched to Noel Redding, asking him to come and take over on bass for as many of the dates as could be salvaged. There was nothing else to do but wait, rest and lie low. Hendrix kept a suite at the Cumberland Hotel at Marble Arch, but as usual, law suits were flying about, and he dodged process-servers, journalists and officials by staying at a private flat in Notting Hill with Monika Danneman, a Danish skating instructor he'd met whilst on tour in Germany. On September 15th, Hendrix and Danneman bumped into Devon Wilson at Ronnie Scott's club in Soho, and Wilson is said to have kicked Monika out of her chair. Two nights later Devon invited Hendrix to accompany her to Who manager Kit Lambert's party. The facts as to what happened next are as hazy as they come. Danneman insists that Hendrix had asked her to marry him and that they'd spent their last days together planning for babies and wedded bliss. Most of Hendrix's friends dispute this and say Jimi had no plans to marry anyone, least of all a woman he'd seen for just a few days in an entire year.

At some time after 1.30 a.m. Monika called to collect Hendrix from the party. Her version of events is that they stayed up talking until the early hours and that she fell asleep in his arms. At around ten o'clock the next morning, she says she awoke and, knowing that he'd run out of cigarettes, went out to the shop to fetch more. When she returned she saw that he was still fast asleep but noticed that there was "something dripping out of the corner of his mouth." She tried to wake him, but couldn't, rang Eric Burdon at his hotel to try and find out who Hendrix's doctor was, before eventually dialling 999. Waiting for the ambulance to arrive, she tidied up "some incriminating evidence" and noticed that some – maybe nine – of her sleeping pills were missing. According to Danneman's version of events, the ambulance crew didn't seem concerned about Hendrix's plight and joked with her that they'd all be laughing about it by the afternoon.

In an interview with journalist Tony Brown, quoted in Pamela des Barres' book, *Rock Bottom*, the ambulance crew, Reg Jones and John Sua, tell a different story. They say that when they arrived only Hendrix was in the flat. "It was horrific," said Jones. "He was covered in vomit. There was tons of it all over the pillow – black and brown it was . . . I knew he was dead as soon as I walked into the room." Monika says that she went in the ambulance to St Mary Abbots Hospital, a fact hotly denied by the ambulance crew and discounted in a later official enquiry. As he was pronounced "dead on arrival" an admissions card was never made out for Hendrix, but at the hospital Monika insists that the medical staff gave her some hope that Hendrix could still be saved. And once she'd been told that he was dead, Danneman says she was allowed to see the body. The authorities dispute this and say that the remains were identified by Hendrix's roadie, Gerry Stickells.

There appears to be further confusion as to the time Hendrix was discovered to be dangerously ill. Stickells is adamant that Danneman called him between 8.30 and 9 a.m. and said that she couldn't wake Jimi. In his autobiography Eric Burdon says that he received her call "at the crack of dawn". But records show that the ambulance wasn't called until 11.18 a.m. What happened in the intervening hours?

When Monika Danneman published her version of events in the book, *The Inner World of Jimi Hendrix*, in 1995, Kathy Etchingham, another former Hendrix girlfriend, sued for libel. Etchingham had already won costs and a thousand pounds from Danneman for saying that Kathy was "an inveterate liar". Two days after the court found her "in contempt", Monika was found dead in her Mercedes car, asphyxiated by carbon monoxide. Within two years of Hendrix's death, Devon Wilson had fallen (or been pushed) from a window at New York's Chelsea Hotel, and in March 1973, Mike Jeffrey was killed in a plane crash on his way to find out who would be inheriting Jimi Hendrix's British musical royalties.

"I'm the one that's got to die when it's time for me to die, so let me live my life the way I want to."   *Jimi Hendrix*

And In The Beginning . . .

Deke Leonard

I joined the Manband in November 1968. I would have joined them a few months earlier but for love. Whatever you do, don't fall in love. The moment that love is declared and reciprocated the world starts travelling at a different speed. A terrible sense of commitment descends upon the proceedings and you are required to invest tremendous amounts of emotional capital with frightening regularity. Judgement is impaired, priorities are distorted and, worst of all, your taste in music changes; in extreme cases this can lead to listening to Johnny Mathis records. For a songwriter this can be disastrous. If you start listening to crap, sooner or later you will start to write crap. The whole business is a pain in the neck and is to be avoided at all costs.

When they first offered me the job in July, I had turned it down because I had just fallen in love with Frances Morris. Accepting the offer would have meant moving to London, where the band was based; something I couldn't contemplate, consumed, as I was, by the fires of love. I write this, you understand, with a deep sense of shame. However, by November, while the fires still raged, a glimmer of reason glinted in the fog. The Bystanders, as they were then called, were a great band; the most successful in Wales. They had left the Motherland, they had a recording contract and they had bucketfuls of work. The Dream, the band I was in, were doing well but we had failed, with a few notable exceptions, to break out of the Welsh gig-circuit. And we didn't have a recording contract. Without a recording contract, life is not worth living. I just wanted to make one record. Just one. *Recordo ergo sum* – I record, therefore I am. The Bystanders' offer was too good to turn down.

I phoned them up and asked if the job was still going. It was and it was still mine, if I wanted it. I arranged to meet the band in Manchester, where they were playing the northern club circuit. Reluctantly I said goodbye to the Dream, bought my ticket and boarded the train. As it pulled out, I waved Fran and Llanelli out of sight.

Now, Manchester has two main stations and, naturally, I got out at the wrong one but, naturally, the boys came to pick me up at the wrong one too. Already we were establishing a *modus operandi*.

We were staying at an hotel called "The Biz", a large, ramshackle building in the Whalley Range district. It was the perfect showbiz hotel, run by Phil Lynott's mother, a wonderfully kind and generous woman. She had a large rehearsal room in the basement, available at no extra charge to the clientele. We were in one of the band rooms; cavernous, ten-bed dormitories. As I settled in, they brought me abreast with the circumstances. There was little ice-breaking to be done. We were old friends; we'd played the same Welsh gig-circuit for the last five years and shared many a curry. No auditions had been necessary, they knew what they were getting. They were Ray Williams, the bass player, Jeff Jones, the drummer, Clive John on keyboards – hereafter referred to as Clint – and Micky Jones, guitar player. And they all sang like angels.

I was Vic Oakley's replacement. Six months earlier, by mutual consent, Vic, their singer, had left the band. The band had a flat in Streatham but Vic's wife, Maggie, still lived in Wales and he was getting increasingly homesick. Also, there were musical difficulties. The Bystanders, like the Dream, had embraced psychedelia with glee but Vic, a singer in the classical sense – like Ray Charles is a singer – found that there wasn't much room for what he excelled at. It wasn't what he wanted to do. It became apparent that it wasn't going to work. So Vic left.

Ray, acting spokesman, said that they were fed up of doing covers, they were fed up of doing the northern club circuit and they were fed up of chicken in a fucking basket. From now on they were only going to do original material (as it was quaintly called in those days), they had played their last nightclub gig and they were never going to do another single. They were going to make an album. Pye, their record company, had agreed to it. For about a year, Pye had been trying to ditch the Bystanders on the usual company grounds that outlay exceeded income, blah, blah, blah. John Schroeder, their producer, had fought to keep the band on the label but had, in the end, to defer to corporate blindness. He was ordered to sack the band. He went to a Bystanders gig to do the dirty deed but was surprised to hear an embryonic Manband, churning out yards and yards of original material. He held fire, returned to the company and persuaded them to keep the band. Even the blinkered idiots at Pye knew they were in the middle of a music revolution; they didn't know what it was, but they knew they were in it. They had set up an offshoot label called Dawn, and like all the other record labels, they were signing anything in loon-pants. John got them to renew the contract and move the band over to Dawn. It was a five-year contract, one album a year at 0.75 per cent royalty. This is not a misprint. Three-quarters of a fucking per cent.

John Schroeder had a formidable reputation. As the brains behind Sounds Orchestral he had a hit with the sublime *Cast Your Fate To The Wind* and his production credits included many of the major stars of the day, including Helen Shapiro and Cliff Rich . . . Cliff R . . . I'm sorry, I can't bring myself to write the name without running to the nearest toilet and puking my guts up. John had signed the Bystanders to the label and produced a series of singles. Some got close. A cover version of an American hit called, rather inaccurately, *98.6* got heavy airplay but was pipped when the Americans had the temerity to release the original recording. Another, *When Jesamine Goes*, later became a hit for somebody-or-other who stole the Bystanders' arrangement, note for bloody note.

"We're changing the name of the band," said Ray, warming to his task.

I felt a bit miffed. I had been under the impression I was joining the Bystanders. I'd enjoyed telling people I'd joined the

Bystanders. "Ooh," they'd say, impressed to fuck. Well, at least I'd been in the Bystanders for about ten seconds.

"What's the new name?" I asked.

"Man," said Ray.

"Man?" I said. I didn't like it. I liked the name Bystanders. I rather liked the idea of a bunch of chaps who happened to be standing around when something happened. Ray could tell I wasn't too keen on it.

"Well," said Ray, "there's the anthropological aspect. Man means the human species, the people of the planet, the lords of creation."

I still wasn't impressed, although I like a bit of understatement.

"And people say man all the time, man," he said. "Man, everybody'll be walking around saying our name, man."

That, it seemed to me, had some merit but I still wasn't convinced.

"It's only three letters," he said, showing signs of exasperation, "it'll be huge on posters."

Now that I couldn't argue with.

"OK, man," I said, trying, but failing, to sound enthusiastic. A newcomer has very little purchase on events. Shut up Leonard, or they might kick you out.

"So, what's the plan?" I said. "Phase out the Bystanders gigs and phase in the Man?"

"No," said Ray, "we're making a clean break. From now on it's just Man gigs. No more Bystanders gigs."

My leg began to twitch. The Bystanders were earning a grand a week, and that's in 1968 money. This was recklessness on a Balaklavian scale. I heard the clank of sabre, I heard the fatal command shouted down the line and I heard the distant rumble of the Russian guns. This was courage way above and beyond the call of duty. This was professional suicide.

"Fine," I said.

I think it's worth breaking off here to tell you how the Bystanders went about earning a grand a week. Let's take the last week of November 1967 as an example. They were booked for a week's residency at two clubs on the opposite sides of Manchester. The early show in one club, then a mad dash across town to the other one for the late show. There were three day-trips to London for BBC Radio sessions, doing a couple of covers and the latest single. Then on Saturday, thanks to special dispensation from both clubs, back down to London for the British Airlines Annual Ball at the Royal Albert Hall with Acker Bilk and the Cyril Stapleton Orchestra. Engagements undertaken – 16. Miles covered – 1,500. Income generated – a grand and change.

They were a frighteningly well-oiled machine. They had three sets of gear; two on the road and one in London. The band travelled in a top of the range Daimler. The driver had to be good, and he was. Nobody can remember his name but he was an ex-getaway driver for a South London firm. He was going straight-ish and he supplemented his income with stunt work for the now defunct British film industry. Watch a re-run of *The Italian Job* and you'll spot him. But all this was coming to an end.

"After this fortnight, we've got one outstanding Bystanders gig to do and that's it," said Ray.

"So, how many Man gigs are in?" I asked.

"Well, er . . . none, actually," said Ray, "but I expect things will start looking up once we've got the album out."

"Great," I said, nodding automatically.

The Bystanders had a history of madness. This wasn't the first time they'd burned their boats. A couple of years earlier they had abruptly left Wales, where they were playing seven nights a week, and headed for the big city lights. They ended up in Streatham, which is neither here nor there, but the intent was there; the commitment; the single-mindedness. They had starved for a year but gradually things had turned around and now they were doing rather well. But just when they seemed to be within striking distance of the prize, they were throwing it all away again.

There is a simple explanation for this behaviour. These poor, unfortunate souls came from Merthyr Tydfil. Some are born and bred, others driven there by catastrophic accident. Those whom the gods wish to destroy, they first send to Merthyr. The Merthyrites spend most of their tragic lives trying in vain to overcome this serious anthropological obstacle, but providence has set its hand against them, and that's that. Descended from one of the seven lost tribes of Tydfil, they are stubborn, mean-spirited, socially-inept weasels. Dante's *Divine Comedy* would have been a lot funnier if, instead of following Virgil down to Hell, he had gone to see the Bystanders playing Merthyr town hall on a Saturday night.

Llanelli, on the other hand, is the Athens of South Wales. Athletic in build, Byronic in spirit, the citizenry stroll the town's balmy boulevards, discussing the great issues of the day, stopping only to admire some new architectural wonder. Our civic buildings exude a knowing grandeur, an ongoing testament to the wisdom and foresight of our elected elders. We are a tolerant, open-hearted, generous people whose life is dedicated to the pursuit and exaltation of beauty.

"Yeah, though I walk amongst the behemoths, I will remain a butterfly," I remember thinking to myself.

We settled into a punishing routine, more for them than me. We'd rehearse all afternoon in the basement then, about six, they'd go off and do the gigs while I hung around the hotel, writing songs and reading. They'd already written half a dozen songs and they played them for me. They were a revelation. They had gone through a startling metamorphosis. Freed from the strictures of the three-minute pop song, they were flying. I'd never heard anything quite like it. My favourite – which didn't make the album – was one of Ray's songs, a fabulous piece of nonsense called *Sesquipedalarianisticpsychomaticmotor*. I couldn't wait to get stuck in. I was so fucking happy.

We were writing furiously, we were playing like demons, and we had more ideas than you could shake a plectrum at. Separately, we had been listening to the same music; the Beatles – *The White Album* at the time – Hendrix and the sublime *Freak Out* album by the Mothers of Invention; this had been spectacularly on my turntable for a good year. Separately, we had been smoking particularly large quantities of dope. Separately, we had embraced psychedelia with loving arms. And we continued to do so with application and delight.

Although everyone had opened their musical shoulders, Micky

was particularly frightening. He was making some extraordinary noises. I'd never heard anybody, anybody, play that good. I was getting my first blast of Jones Unchained, so to speak, and it made me want to roll over and sing *Sweet Sue*.

There's something I ought to get out of the way. It's about Jones and me. My musical soul requires that I maintain the conceit that, as guitar players, we are equals, even though, if truth were told, I'm not fit to lick his boots. I have played with Jones, now for nigh on 25 years and I still don't know what he's going to do next.

Daily, he blows my mind. And the worst thing is that I know that he knows that I know that he's better than me. I know this. He knows this. Occasionally, he reminds me of the fact. He sometimes cushions the blow by pointing out that we have different strengths, that he isn't much cop at writing lyrics, but this is freezing cold comfort in the long dark watches of night. The upshot is that I will have to content myself with being the second-best guitarist in the world. I'd appreciate it if you didn't mention any of this to Jones should you run into him one day – remember my musical soul.

After a week of rehearsals we were all happy with the way things were going but I was getting a little stir-crazy, so, one night I went with them on the gigs. Co-starring at both clubs was David Whitfield, a brittle tenor who had known better days. The high-water mark of his career had been a hit with *Poppa Picolina*, a ghastly quasi-Italian singalong.

> "All over Italy he played his concertina,
> Poppa Picolina, from sunny Italy."

The Bystanders did a 30-minute spot that included *Mrs Robinson* and *I Am The Walrus*, which scared the shit out of David Whitfield fans. All three of them. To be fair, it was the early show. Only obsessives went to the early show. And the three David Whitfield fans were certainly that.

There were three generations; a grandmother, a mother and a daughter. They were identical. The daughter could see what she would look like when she was old, and the grandmother could see what she had looked like when she was a girl. Rather plain women, they wore identical clothes and they all wore identical tortoise-shell glasses. During Whitfield's sets – they followed him from club to club – I examined their profiles for subtle differences, but there were none. While Whitfield sang, they sat in a trance, clutching their David Whitfield records and their David Whitfield Souvenir Programme, gazing, unflinchingly, at their hero. Ray said they were there every night; somehow, I already knew that.

I watched them getting his autograph at the stage door. They were in sensual overload. They flirted furiously with him, laughing hysterically at everything he said. Three generations of unfettered coquettishness. Whitfield treated them like royalty, gently teasing them out of their nervousness, and by the time they walked off into the night, they were in a state of sublime otherness. If I'd been Whitfield, I'd have taken them back to my hotel and fucked their brains out, but that's just the idealist in me.

By the time we left Manchester, we had an album's worth of material. All good stuff. Or so we thought. How is one to judge these things? We were in uncharted waters. We were travelling fast, but we didn't know where we were going. Seneca once said that if a ship does not know to which port it is sailing, then no wind is favourable. With some presumption, I would like to point out to the noble Seneca that the opposite is also true – that all winds are favourable (I've always found Seneca a little stoical in such matters). Let's say we were satisfied. With certain reservations, obviously. We were happy. Sort of.

We headed back to London. 66 Tierney Road, Streatham – mission control. When the Bystanders left Wales, they had no plans. They just got in the van and drove to London. They found themselves in Streatham. They stopped in a residential street called Tierney Road. Picking a house out at random, number 66, they knocked on the door. A sharp-suited man answered.

"Have you, by any chance, got any rooms to let?" they asked.

"Yes, as it happens, I've got the ground floor flat for rent," he replied, in a Welsh accent.

"How much is it?"

"Ten quid a week. A month in advance."

"We'd like to take it," they said, "but we haven't got the advance."

"You're bloody lucky you're Welsh," he said. "Come on in."

During the first few weeks they trawled the London agencies looking for representation, while funds dwindled. They needed something to tide them over. They asked the landlord if he knew of anything.

"Well," he said, "I've got a business selling knitting machines, and I need someone to stick advertising leaflets through people's letterboxes. You can do it in lieu of rent."

"I walked fucking miles," recalls Micky, fondly.

They signed with the George Cooper Agency and the gigs started coming in. More often than not they wouldn't have enough money to get to the gigs, so the landlord would lend them the petrol money and a couple of quid on top for a bit of food. Not entirely altruistic; if they didn't do the gig, he didn't get the rent.

The landlord, it turned out, had other business interests.

"I run an agency that sends go-go dancers to Tehran. That's in Persia," he said. "Know any good looking girls?"

It's astonishing how many of the girls who hung around Tierney Road ended up in Tehran. Ten minutes of conversation with the landlord and they'd be headed, starry-eyed, for the Persian Embassy, clutching their passports.

The band signed a deal with Pye. The singles picked up radio play. The work poured in. They became regulars on the Jimmy Young Show; these were the days when the BBC was obligated to devote a certain percentage of their time to live music. There was the odd TV show. Leeds Music, a publishing company run by Ronnie Scott – no, not *that* Ronnie Scott – and Marty Wilde – yes, that Marty Wilde – was charged with the task of finding the song that would catapult the Bystanders into the big time. Scott and Wilde were hot. They'd just written *Pictures of Matchstick Men* and *Ice In The Sun* for Status Quo, Mark I. Aside from their own prodigious output they administered the interests of a stable of young songwriters, all straining at the leash. They needed a band to demo the avalanche of new songs. Would the Bystanders

be interested? Yes, they would. Every spare minute was spent at
RG Jones Studios in Morden. A great way to learn the trade.

One by one, wives and girlfriends moved up from Wales, and,
one by one, the band moved out into nearby flats. By the time I
got to Tierney Road, only Clint and Plug were there.

Somewhere along the way Plug moved in. Like me, Plug came
from the Forbidden City. He was a drummer by trade, an ex-
Screaming Lord Sutch's Savage, no less, who in between bands,
had got a job in Carnaby Street. From there, he brought home the
latest records, the latest drugs, and the occasional herring-bone
jacket. More importantly, he kept the landlord and his wife, a
lady of Maltese extraction, in a state of high, sexual t-t-tension.
One day, the landlord happened to mention, in passing, that he
liked nothing better than watching another man fuck his wife.
Plug, a man of delicate sensibilities, offered his services, explaining that discretion was his watchword. He was, he said, the man
for the job. The deal was struck and for a while everybody was
happy, until one day the landlord, short of one go-go dancer, sent
his wife out to Tehran. She never came back, having taken up, it
is alleged, with one of the Shah's bodyguards. The landlord was
inconsolable. Plug, if I remember correctly, was rather relieved.
He felt used, he said, and somewhat cheap. I couldn't understand
what was wrong with feeling used and cheap, but I, I freely
admit, have always had trouble with matters ethical.

When I arrived I moved a spare mattress into the front room,
which doubled as a rehearsal room, and unpacked. The following
day I re-packed and went to Swansea to start the album. We were
going to play two nights at the Langland Bay Hotel in Swansea.
Both nights were to be recorded by the Pye Mobile and used as
the foundations of the new album. We would then take the tapes
to Pye Studios in London for overdubs and mixing. It had been
John Schroeder's idea. His rationale was impeccable. As it was
our first album, he thought we would feel more comfortable
playing the new songs in front of a hometown audience rather
than in a cold, impersonal studio. The live atmosphere might also
give the tracks that little extra oomph, he added convincingly.

We hummed and hawed. Surely, we argued, we'd have more

control in a studio and, surely, not all studios were cold and impersonal. The live atmosphere might even detract from the precision of execution we felt the tracks required. Had he made some dark satanic pact with Pye Records? Was he trying to do it on the cheap?

We knew the real reason he wanted to do it in Swansea. He was fed-up with boring old Pye Studios. He wanted an all-expenses-paid junket to the seaside. Most of all, he wanted to sample the legendary graces and perfections of Celtic womanhood. Many times he had heard us extol, at some length, their reputation for baroque sensuality, and now he was ready to face the Argonautian tribulations inherent in a head-to-head with a lissom, but bolshie, Welsh girl. We listened to his pleadings for a suitable time, then we relented. We even fixed him up with Maureen the Mod. Wasn't this, I hear you ask, throwing him in at the deep end? Indeed, it was. What did you expect us to do? Throw him in the shallow-end?

The gigs were great, the recordings immaculate, and I got to sleep with my wife. A day off, and then back to London and into Pye Studios in Marble Arch. We recorded in three-hour sessions, always late in the evening – John didn't like daylight and neither did we.

It seems ridiculous in this day and age, when a studio is block-booked for months on end and 18-hour days are not unusual, but, at least we learnt to work fast. Worse, there would be a half-hour break in the middle of the session when John and Alan Florence, the engineer, would slope off around the corner to the Cumberland Hotel for champagne and smoked salmon. We used the time to hone and burnish the songs and sort out any problems.

When we started to do the vocal, I received an artistic hammerblow. We were recording *And In The Beginning*, the first track on the album. I had sung it during rehearsals, so naturally, I went down into the studio to do my first vocal, in a proper studio, for a proper record. I'd been waiting for this moment all my life and I gave it everything I had. When I finished, there was silence. I could see everybody in the control room talking among themselves.

"Was it alright?" I asked.

"Hang on a second, Deke," came the reply. The conversation continued. I couldn't stand it any longer.

"Is there a problem?"

"Well," came the reply, "we, er, think that, er, well . . . the consensus here is that, er, Micky should do the vocal."

I felt a chill, way down in my soul. My stomach began to churn. This was it. My life was in ruins. I had to face the truth that, when the moment came, I was found wanting. I was a minor-leaguer who couldn't cut in in the big time.

"OK," I said, lightly, and walked up to the control room with a jaunty gait. They explained their reasons, but I didn't hear them. Clint came over and talked earnestly to me, explaining the situation in his caring, reasonable voice. I hate it when he does that.

"It's OK," I lied. "Really. Whatever's best for the band."

Micky went out and did a brilliant vocal in one take. My misery was profound.

A couple of sessions later my next vocal came up. By now, I'd totally given up on the idea of being a singer. From now on I would concentrate on the guitar.

"Look," I said to the control room in general, "we'll save a lot of time and money if Micky does this vocal too."

No, no, no, they protested, it was just that the last vocal suited Micky's voice better. This, they said, was definitely my vocal. I wasn't convinced but I went down into the studio. The song was called *Love*. I sung the song, trying to sound as little like myself as possible. When I'd finished, I looked up at the control room. Casually I raised an eyebrow.

"That was great," they said. "Come and have a listen."

I went up to the control room and listened to the playback. It was awful. It sounded just like me.

"I think Micky ought to sing it," I said.

No, no, no, they said, this was fine.

"OK," I said. "Micky can always do it again if you change your minds."

They said they wouldn't change their minds, and they didn't. The rest of my vocals went without a hitch, although my confidence was rather illusory for the remainder of the album. If I listen to the album, which, believe me, only happens by chance, my vocals sound stilted and wary. But it's too late to worry about that now.

The album had a loose concept – the word still makes me shudder – that modestly entailed covering all the aspects of existence, from primordial soup to the conquest of space. Along the way, we would cover the nature of time; the structures of societies; the innocence of childhood; the rites, and wrongs, of passage; the pursuit of the dream and the corroding effects of reality; the death of idealism and the rebirth of hope. If it didn't fit, we crowbarred it in.

We had recorded a jam at the Langland Bay. It was good and we wanted to use it, but we didn't know where it fitted in. We decided to eroticise it. Why don't we get a girl to make orgasmic noises over it? John loved the idea. Where could we get a girl at this time of night? John said it would take him about ten minutes. Maureen the Mod, we suggested? Giggling coyly, he disappeared upstairs to the Pye offices and returned with a sassy blonde called Anya, a publicist.

"There's always someone upstairs working late," he said. "Anya always works late."

We were all in a state of high excitement. Anya went down to the studio. We played her the track and she started groaning, rather unconvincingly we thought. Anya, a professional to the core, sensed she wasn't giving her best and brought the proceedings to a halt. She found it hard, she said, to get in the mood. She asked Micky, with whom she had a passing acquaintance, to join her in the studio. John turned the studio lights down and drew a heavy curtain – used for baffling, if you must know – across the studio, giving them some privacy. We played the track again and this time, the squeals were altogether more believable. While Anya, with a little help from Micky, worked herself up to orgasm, the rest of us sat in the control room, masturbating furiously. No, that's not true. Honestly. I don't know why I wrote that.

Only Anya and Jones know what went on behind that curtain. I've asked him, but he won't tell me.

As we approached the end of the album, we decided we needed a little magniloquence. We called for the company boffin and doused the whole album in sound effects. I particularly enjoy the Apollo Space Programme ending, where a voice says "I can see the lights of Rockingham below." I like to think it's Alan Shepard but I've got a feeling it's probably poxy John Glenn.

Somewhere along the way we decided, without a trace of irony, to call the album *Revelation*. The album cover – my idea, I'm afraid – was to have us standing naked in a desert landscape on the front, and dressed in a city street on the back. We did the necessary photo sessions. A studio session, naked, with a dry-ice machine, later to be superimposed on a desert landscape, and a London street session, for which, we decided, we needed some unusual clothes – the Bystanders' love of fancy dress? We went *en masse* to Berman's, the theatrical costumiers. We didn't see much that we liked but Clint got a mountain-man jacket and Ray found a buckskin shirt that Sean Connery had worn in *Shalako*, a dreadful British western, whose only saving grace was Brigitte Bardot who spent much of her time semi-clothed, rubbing herself up against this very shirt. This impressed the hell out of me. Berman's were having one of their occasional stock clear-outs and Ray bought the shirt. I tried it on. I looked stupid. Sean Connery must be about nine feet tall.

The photos went off to Pye but, by the time the idea had been filtered through the art department, the front cover, which was all dry-ice and no desert, looked like an album of rugby songs. This little niggle apart, we were delighted with the album. John had been a great producer, never trying to impose, just getting what we wanted down on tape. His suggestions, and there were many, were just that – suggestions. We listened to what he said, but he allowed us to make all the decisions.

I felt a sense of relief. At last, I had made it onto the musical map. When the history of the performing arts came to be written, I would be there. I might only be a footnote, but I would be there. Finally, I existed.

After we finished the album and before we left for Christmas in Wales, we did the final outstanding Bystanders' gig. It was in a large municipal hall in London – nobody can remember where – and it was the Nurse of The Year Ball, an event held annually. What more could a man want than to entertain 3,000 drunken nurses – they were bound to be drunk – dressed up in their best frocks. I went into taffeta overload. And drunk they were, which was just as well because Jeffrey didn't turn up and I had to play the drums. I am not a drummer. You have to be fit to be a drummer. You have to have stamina to be a drummer. You have to be an idiot to be a drummer.

After the worst hour and a quarter of my life, I was carried back to the dressing room. As I lay there trying to fight the bends, Jeffrey walked in.

"Sorry, I'm late," he said, cheerfully, "I ran out of petrol."

During the ensuing struggle, I collapsed from exhaustion and required immediate medical attention, of which there was no shortage. I would like to take this opportunity to thank Staff Nurse Hitchcock in particular, for services, way above and beyond the call of duty, to the healing arts. She was my Nurse Of The Year. I do like a woman who can evacuate a bowel.

By New Year's Day, we were back in Tierney Road writing the next album. We were monomaniacal. We'd play all day and drop acid at night. Plug had seemingly limitless access to endless supplies of flowery Californian blotter-acid; Carnaby Street's finest. We were listening to Zappa, Beefheart (a lot of Beefheart), Steve Miller, Hendrix and the occasional Quicksilver. A big record for us was an album by an Italian-American band called Touch, who, as far as I know, never made another one.

Clint made us all ear-phones, using the receivers stolen from telephone boxes, with Golden Virginia tins as junction-boxes. We questioned him on the ethics of vandalising something that might be, for some, the difference between life and death. What about the poor, innocent, crippled child, trapped in an orphanage on fire, too weak to call for help, whose only hope of survival is that a passing stranger – a Bystander – would spot the fire, find the nearest phonebox, and call the Fire Brigade? And what does he, or she, find when he, or she, gets there? A note from Clint saying, "Sorry man, but I need some headphones for my stereo?"

"Where are all the people working in the orphanage?" said Clint. "And don't they have fire alarms in those places?"

We asked him, kindly, to address the morality of the matter.

"I only steal from groups of phoneboxes," he said, haughtily. "I always leave one in full working order. I even give it a quick service while I'm there."

Clint – two, Ethics – nil. We put our headphones on, dropped another tab of Sunshine, and got stuck into Capt Beefheart. And when we got fed up with that, we'd wander, gormlessly, down to Brixton High Road, to watch the changing of the traffic lights.

The full gear, including drums and PA, was set up in the front room – there was hardly any room for my mattress – and, given a fair wind, you could hear us in Croydon. But nobody complained. The drive to be original was paramount. Micky was, and still is, positively Jesuitical about the damn thing. Personally, I don't mind a bit of burglary. Our style began to come into focus. Our sound was defined by Micky's addled virtuosity and Clint's swirling organ, underpinned by Jeff's galloping drumming, and Raymond's thoughtful, melodic bass lines. I saw my job as adding a bit of window-dressing. I am a great believer in window-dressing. There is a rather apt Welsh retailing adage, which says – "if you have it, put it in the window". Words to live by Funnily enough, when I first met Fran she was a window-dresser.

Micky came up with a huge riff which became *Spunk Rock*, the first signpost, the first inkling of where we were going. For musical buns, it's in 5/4 time and, if you miss out the downbeat note and come in at it from an oblique angle, it bears a passing similarity to the theme from *Sunday Night At The London Palladium*. Micky also came up with a rolling chord-sequence that immediately conjured up a seascape. Clint added the swell, I made seagull noises, and we had *The Storm*; it seemed to write itself.

But, while the musical side of things was leaping and bounding, businesswise, we were in a fiscal black-hole. Gigs were still occasional events; we were now billed as "Man – formerly The Bystanders". We needed management.

We turned, among others, to David Most, Mickie's brother, who was our publisher at Carlin Music. The Most brothers are extraordinary. When energy was handed out, the Most brothers were at the front of the queue. I am fortunate to have had dealings with both of them and I find their company exhilarating. There is no fat on their conversation, they cut straight to the chase and they're as funny as fuck.

David introduced us to several potential managers including Led Zeppelin's manager, Peter Grant. They all listened politely and then declined.

We went back into the studio to start recording the new album; same set-up: John Schroeder, Alan Florence and Pye Studios. It was tentatively-titled: *Two Ounces Of Plastic (With A Hole In The Middle)*. I had, and still have, no idea whether a record weighs two ounces, but it seemed about right.

With our first album under our belts we were more assured in the studio, wallowing in the recording process. There's nothing quite like total musical freedom and a pocketful of extremely dangerous drugs.

The stars of the Pye stable were Tony Hatch and Jackie Trent. They'd had a few hits but mostly they were famous for soap theme tunes. They had written the *Crossroads* signature-tune, and would later write the ghastly theme from *Neighbours*. A few years later, McCartney did a version of "Crossroads" and the TV show delightedly used it from then on. I think that speaks volumes about young Paul.

Quite often, we followed Tony Hatch into the studio. On one occasion we found a harpsichord still set up. I started picking out a tune on it, Raymond added a bass line, and Plug – Jeffrey was late – played the drums. Schroeder arrived, liked it, and suggested we put it down on tape, which we did. As we finished, Tony Hatch came back. When he saw what was going on, he erupted. His voice boomed over the tannoy.

"If you haven't paid for the hire of an instrument, you should not use it. It's rude. Get off it, now!"

Morally, he was correct, but, artistically, he was being a little petty-minded, I thought. After all, we're all musicians here. Sort of. But, I had to concede, I was guilty as charged. An apology was in order.

"How does 'Fuck off' sound?" I enquired.

A bijou argumentette ensued. I got off the harpsichord – the song was in the can anyway – and he left.

The highlight of the album, for me, came during the mixing of *Spunk Rock*. We were listening to a playback. I had my head down on my forearms, leaning against the end, of the console. A rustling noise made me look up and there, standing at the other end, was Sid James. My first thought was, "Wow, this is good acid", but there was no denying it, it really was the great man. The playback finished, there was a moment of silence, then the great man spoke.

"Well, that's music to move your bowels to." He followed it with a cluster of gravelly laughs. He sounded exactly like Sid James. We pumped him, shamelessly, for Hancock stories and he graciously obliged. During the course of the conversation, the reason for his presence emerged. He was there to interview us. Sid James was going to interview me. Well, I didn't see that one coming. He had a record show on South African radio. It was taped in Britain and sent to the evil republic for transmission. I was so starry-eyed, I ignored the implications of condoning the white boot of oppression that for centuries had been a cancer in the body politic of humanity. I ask not for forgiveness, for there is none. In mitigation, there were extraordinarily extenuating circumstances.

We all sat around a microphone in the studio and he began the interview, introducing us in turn. After he introduced me, he stopped.

"Deke," he said, "that's a funny name, how did you get it?"

I had taken the name from the character Elvis played in *Loving You*. It sounded cool, and I thought I'd never get to be a rock 'n' roll star with a name like Roger. It was hardly rivetting radio.

"It's a very long and not very interesting story," I replied.

"Oh," he said, flatly, looking daggers at me, "well, it's a very long story for a very short name." He continued with the interview but it had gone. I had killed it. Suddenly, he clapped his hands.

"Let's start again," he said, looking pointedly at me, "I think we can do better than that." I was suitably chastened. He began the interview again. Once more he introduced us. After he introduced me, he stopped again.

"Deke," he said, "that's a funny name. How did you get it?" I couldn't believe it and neither could he. He gave a damn-and-blast-it grimace.

"It's short for Deacon," I said. "My mother wanted a preacher."

It wasn't quite the Joke Of The Year, but it made him laugh. I had made Sid James laugh. Further proof that I existed. I can't remember the rest of the interview. As he left we all shook his hand.

"Goodbye, Deacon," he said to me.

"Goodbye, Mr James," I said.

"Call me Sid, son," he said.

It's all been downhill since then.

In April 1969, right in the middle of the album, Fran and I got married. I had two best men. Wes Reynolds, from the Dream, did the church, and Martin Ace, also from the Dream, did the reception. I'd rented a flat in Tierney Road, across the road from number 66, and we spent the honeymoon settling in.

When the album was finished, our thoughts turned to the cover. We tried to make it impossible to look at. We decided on one of those optical things that make your eyes go funny. Individual photographs of us, with our faces painted in garish colours, would appear, strategically, in the design.

At the photo session a make-up artist painted our faces: Clint was blue, Jeffrey was green, Raymond was white, Micky was red – which made him look as if he'd been locked in a sauna for ten years – and I was lilac, which made me look as if I was suffering from some terrible palsy. Clint liked the effect so much, he didn't wash for a week.

We decided to call it *Two Ounces Of Plastic (With A Hole In*

The Middle) by default. Nobody really liked it, but we couldn't
think of anything better. We sent the label copy to Pye and all hell
broke loose. They wouldn't accept "Spunk Rock'". They didn't
mind "Rock" but "Spunk" was an absolute no-no. Neither
would they accept "Shit On The World" – one of Clint's finest
moments; a magnificent assault on the principle of authority.

Clint phoned them up and shouted at them, but to no avail.
They were adamant. No "Spunk Rock".

"Call it what you like," said Clint, exasperated, but offering no
alternative.

"What about 'Shit On The World'?" they asked.

"It is as it must be," said Clint, and slammed the phone down.

When we finally saw the cover, we read the tracklisting with
interest. "Spunk Rock" was now called "Spunk Box" – the prats
had changed the wrong bit – and "Shit On The World" was
called "It Is As It Must Be". Our days with Pye were numbered.

Revelation was released. The music press were universally
indifferent. Most considered Pye's new label, Dawn, to be a
pathetic attempt by an old-fashioned record company to cash in
on a music trend they didn't understand. Which was about right.
Melody Maker was the kindest. It said we were competent and a
great deal of work had gone into our arrangements.

We were luckier in the wider world. The national press picked
up on "Erotica", claiming it to be the sounds of genuine sexual
intercourse, citing, as proof, that some of the album had been
recorded in the Langland Bay Hotel. According to the *Sunday
People*, Pete Murray and Alan Freeman were refusing to play it
on their radio shows and WH Smith were refusing to stock the
album. Things were looking up.

Now, if Pye had rushed out "Erotica" as a single, we could
have ridden this wave of publicity and reached a multi-unit
situation, saleswise, as we say in the business. But Pye slumbered
on. There were people working at Pye who thought the earth was
flat.

It was released as a single in France, where it went to Number 3
in the charts. We went to Paris to do a high profile gig at the
Pavillion d'Armonenaville. They were expecting a sexual extra-

vaganza, and were aghast when they discovered that we hadn't brought "zee Erotica girl" with us. Clint, in a frenzy of irony, simulated sexual intercourse with his Hammond organ, laying across the top and bumping and grinding furiously. The French, being French, missed the irony.

Half way through the mixing of *Two Ounces Of Plastic* I handed in my notice. I'm sorry, I said, but circumstances demanded it. Family troubles. It was agreed that I would do an upcoming Marquee gig, then leave. I really didn't want to go.

David Most called to say that Barry Marshall, from the Arthur Howes Agency, was interested in managing the band and he would be at the Marquee.

I felt awful at the gig. After the set, Barry came into the dressing room and introduced himself. He had loved the music and he wanted to manage the band. I explained my situation and absented myself from the ensuing discussions. With my usual impeccable timing I had left just as the band's fortunes were on the up.

"They Sure Broke the Mould . . ." Cynthia Plaster Caster: Groupie as Craft-Worker

interviewed by Jenny Sylvain

Cynthia Plaster Caster – real name Cynthia Albritton, but don't tell her mother, who still doesn't know what she does – is the leader of a loose group of women centred in Chicago, who make plaster casts of rock star's "members" using dental algenate. She first did it in 1969 and is still at it today. Cynthia Plaster Caster's "business" card describes her as "artist, fan, collector".

So, how did you get into plaster casting?
Cynthia: It was as a result of being a horny virgin in the 1960s. I'd never been laid before and my art teacher gave me the homework assignment of making a plaster cast of something hard. Paul Revere and the Raiders and the Hollies were in town, and me and a girlfriend were looking for ways to meet the stars and maybe get laid.

And did you get your cast?
Cynthia: No, but we sure got laid.

And you kept at it?
Cynthia: At first the plaster casting was an excuse to get to the band. Up until that first weekend I'd never even seen a cock in my life.

Please take us through the plaster casting process.
Cynthia: You start with a plater. A plater is someone who gives a blow-job. It's an English slang term. Nowadays I try and use the subject's own girlfriends and wives, if possible. But often I find myself, at my advanced age, doubling up on roles.

Do subjects ever bring their own platers?
Cynthia: I prefer it when they do. It's often been a spur of the moment thing and we've just had to cope. Believe it or not, the job of mixing this dental plaster is really detailed and intense. You've really got to concentrate.

So what happens once the cock's hard?
Cynthia: You've got to time it just right, because the algenate is this really tricky dental substance that has to be mixed for exactly the right amount of time. Once all the ingredients have been added, the mould starts to set and you've got to get going. Sometimes it doesn't work and then you're looking at a blob rather than an erect penis.

I've heard that you oil the public hairs to stop them sticking to the plaster. Is this true?
Cynthia: Yeah. The pubes get oiled. We had some trouble with Jimi Hendrix, his weren't oiled enough and he got stuck in the mould for fifteen minutes. He was getting off on the fact that the impression of his penis was just the right size for him to fuck, so that's what he did, while we released one hair at a time.

How many castings have you done?
Cynthia: Well, I've tried about 60, but I've only got 44. I document each attempt with a serial number and a description.

What kind of cocks do you go for personally?
Cynthia: Well, I don't like comparing size, y'know, but it's length over width for my personal needs.

So who has the biggest cock in your collection?
Cynthia: Well, it's got to be a tie between Hendrix for width and Clint from Pop Will Eat Itself for length. But you know, you've got to realise that it's a moment thing. On another day the results can be very different.

There was a story going around that Hendrix's mould got broken and that you had to stick it back together. Is that true?
Cynthia: Yeah. I was so anxious to see the cast, I prematurely opened the mould and it was still wet and just about to crumble into lots of little pieces, so I closed it back up and left it for a few days. When I opened it, it was in three sections: the shaft, the head and the balls. I just glued it back together . . .

What was this thing about Frank Zappa financing you in the early days?
Cynthia: Yeah, sort of . . .

And did his manager really steal your casts?
Cynthia: It was more that he wouldn't give them back rather than he stole them. He used to keep them locked up for safe-keeping and he kind of got to think that they belonged to him. I had to go to court and spend two days talking cock on the witness stand to get them back from him.

You won?
Cynthia: Yeah, course. They were mine, not his.

How did Frank Zappa's moulding turn out?
Cynthia: Oh, he never posed for me. Frank was kind of straight and normal.

In The Aftermath of Altamont

John Burks

Rolling Stone, 16 February 1970.

It was perhaps rock and roll's all-time worst day, December 6th, a day when everything went perfectly wrong. Altamont remains Topic A among the musicians who were there.

After all, it's not every day that a rock and roll band's performance, let alone the Rolling Stones, is accompanied by a knifing, stomping murder within a scream of the stage.

"The violence," Keith Richard told the London Evening Standard, "just in front of the stage was incredible. Looking back I don't think it was a good idea to have Hell's Angels there. But we had them at the suggestion of the Grateful Dead.

"The trouble is it's a problem for us either way. If you don't have them to work for you as stewards. they come anyway and cause trouble.

"But to be fair, out of the whole 300 Angels working as stewards, the vast majority did what they were supposed to do, which was to regulate the crowds as much as possible without causing any trouble. But there were about 10 or 20 who were completely out of their minds – trying to drive their motorcycles through the middle of the crowds.

"Really, the difference between the open air show we held here in Hyde Park and the one there is amazing. I think it illustrates the difference between the two countries. In Hyde Park everybody had a good time, and there was no trouble. You can put half a million young English people together and they won't start killing each other. That's the difference."

While Richard was satisfying the British press with his incredibly naive view of Western civilization, Meredith Hunter lay dead.

The Maysles Brothers, the film company which had shot the whole Stones' tour, complete with its violent climax at Altamont, had gotten some remarkable footage of Hunter's killing. No less than three cameras had caught the action, and one of them had the entire sequence from the time Hunter was knifed and down, surrounded by Angels. The face of the knifesman was clear, according to Maysles executive producer Porter Bibb.

Which makes it the hottest film property of 1970. Universal Pictures has already weighed in with the highest bid, (reportedly a higher than $1,000,000.00 guarantee) and will release the movie by early summer.

The principal camera on this sequence was positioned 15 feet over the stage, on the Grateful Dead's truck, perhaps 30–35 feet from the spot where Meredith Hunter was fatally stabbed. Amazingly enough, according to Bibb, the whole sequence is perfectly exposed and perfectly in focus.

He could not let the press see it, he said, because the killer was too easily identifiable – especially by his Angels' colors on his back. If this information were to get out, Bibb and the Maysles fear they would be killed. They won't tell the cameramen's names for the same reason.

But Bibb was willing to give quite a detailed account of what's on the film, as he sees it.

For one thing, the film shows Hunter making at least two charges on the stage during the 45 minutes before his stabbing. Many others did the same that afternoon.

Then the camera picks up Hunter some 18 or 20 rows out in the front-stage audience. (According to *Rolling Stone's* eyewitness in our last issue, the incident began at stage left, with an Angel grabbing Hunter's head, then punching him, then chasing him into the crowd, then knifing him in the back, as Hunter ran. It would be at this point that Hunter would appear back in the crowd, about to pull his gun. Which is what happens. Sheriff's detectives investigating the killing believe – based partly upon photos subpoenaed from *Rolling Stone* – that Hunter *was* at stage left, and *was* chased back to where the Maysles cameras pick him up.)

A pair of white men, one of them an Angel, run by Hunter, the black man. The Angel apparently brushes his arm. It looks as if Hunter is trying to brush something away where the Angel bumped him. He makes a face at the stage (perhaps a grimace), sticks out his tongue, and, as the lights catch his eyes, they look glazed.

With his right hand he reaches within his lime green suit coat – the look on his face is extremely agitated – and pulls a dark object out of his pocket. Simultaneously, he begins lurching forward, but unevenly, so it's difficult to tell what he's doing.

Six or eight Hell's Angels, who are standing at the front of the stage, start toward him, forming what looks like a protective football cup in reverse. A semi-circular cup facing Hunter.

A white girl in a white knit over-blouse grabs Hunter's right arm, and appears to be shouting at him. There is a soundtrack, but none of this can be heard, for the Stones are into "Sympathy for the Devil" at high volume. (The girl is evidently Hunter's girl friend, Patty Bredahoff, who affirms that she was wearing a white knit overblouse. She has been instructed to give no interviews by the sheriff's men, and is following orders. Except to tell *Rolling Stone* that she has no recollection of tugging at Hunter's arm.)

Hunter brushes the girl aside. She grabs his left arm. He keeps on walking dragging her forward.

The Angels begin to close in on him.

"It seems," says Bibb, "to last a thousand years, but it's maybe only five seconds."

For one fleeting moment, Hunter brings his right arm across the girl's white dress, in the camera's line of sight. There seems clearly to be the outline of a gun, though there's no detail on the object itself.

For that moment, the girl is the center of the action, frantically trying to pull Hunter away.

The crowd steps back.

Behind the semi-circle of Angels, between the stage and their backs, another Angel appears. Another of the cameras catches him reaching down to pick something up. It glints.

This Angel is wearing an orange bandanna around his neck – probably a handkerchief knotted at his throat – and full Angels' colors. (Meaning that he is a full brother, not a prospective joiner; it was the *prospects*, as they are called, who were responsible for a good portion of the earlier violence.)

A few frames later it is clear that he is holding a long silvery knife.

Suddenly he leaps through the air, over the backs of the other Angels, like a halfback slicing through the line.

His arm sweeps up to its highest reach, knife in hand, the knife once again clearly visible.

In one sweeping arc, the Angel grabs Hunter's right hand with his (the Angel's) left, spinning Hunter around so that he is facing away from the Angel, away from the stage – and – down comes the long knife, plunging deep into Hunter's right shoulder blade.

The Angel rides Hunter to the ground, knifing him at least once more on the way down, mid-back.

It's a classic street-fighter's move, beautifully executed.

And that is the last we see of Hunter for a long two minutes or so, as the Angels gather tightly around, keeping everyone else at a distance. Before Hunter disappears, blood stains can be seen widening on his suit.

The coroner says there were five stab wounds. The film accounts for only two, once again suggesting the possibility that Hunter may have been stabbed earlier.

Then Angels and others carry Hunter away.

According to Bibb, the killer splits immediately after the other Angels gather around Hunter and is not seen again in another frame. No telling where he went.

In one frame, just before he is jumped, there is an unmistakable orange flash at the end of the pistol, Bibb adds. It lasts only for this one frame. Bibb is not saying this is a gunshot, and he's not saying it's not. It might be, say, a reflection off someone's watch or glasses. "The Angels say there was a shot fired," says Bibb. "I can't tell you. It's impossible, really, to tell *what* it is. None of us heard a shot."

Bibb was eager to make one point: "This film is not going to exploit the killing. We had decided before Altamont to do a film, before we had seen any film of the killing or any of that. It doesn't hinge on the murder. We don't want to exploit the sensationalism of the thing."

The arrangement with the Stones is that they and the Maysles own the film 50–50 and are co-producing it. The Stones will help with the editing. But the Maysles have creative control over the cutting. This should begin before February.

There will be, in addition to the Altamont scenes, footage from the tour in New York, Boston, Florida, and the recording studio sessions in Muscle Shoals.

David Maysles was quoted in *Rolling Stone*'s first Altamont story as telling one of his camera-men not to shoot one especially grotesque scene, to seek out good vibes instead. It's true, he did say that, according to Maysles executive producer Porter Bibb, but that was before the Maysles had truly grasped that ugliness and violence was the true nature of the day.

"We want to make it clear," Bibb said repeatedly, "that this film is going to be about violence – about the relationship between the Stones and their American audience, and about the relationship of both to violence."

It was understood that Allen Klein, the Stones' manager, was going to make some sort of statement concerning Altamont on January 12th. But it never happened, and Klein was said to be en route to England, unavailable for comment, the following day.

Neither did anyone have anything to say about the insurance policy the Stones were said to have taken to pay for any damages during the concert. Plenty of ranchers whose fences were brought down, people whose heads were split, and so on, would like to know about that one.

Though Sam Cutler, who was responsible for paying the Angels $500 worth of beer to police Altamont, claims he's just been taking it easy since Altamont – "my part in it is finished, it's up to others to take care of the left-over details" – Sheriff's investigators have spoken with him twice, it is learned.

Detectives Chisholm and Donovan, who are pursuing the murder case for the Alameda County sheriff's department, say it's very nearly together enough to be presented to the District Attorney and the Grand Jury. They have two eye-witnesses, including Patty Bredahoff, Hunter's girl friend, and are eager to get in touch with the eyewitness quoted in the last issue of *Rolling Stone*, since his testimony would make their case that much stronger.

The eyewitness, who preferred to remain anonymous, fearing that the killer and his friends might get him, should be aware that he is one of several who saw it happen, and would not stand alone, and therefore has, the detectives feel, little to fear. To reach them, the phone number is 483–6520.

"It looks good," says Donovan of the information they've got. Asked whether it was an Angel who killed Meredith Hunter, Donovan said that was "reasonable to assume." Porter Bibb, of the Maysles organization, says the killer is quite recognizable in profile, in full face, and in three-quarter view. Donovan agrees (though Rock Scully, one of the Grateful Dead's managers, has seen the same footage repeatedly and claims identification would be very difficult).

One weird Altamont story has to do with a young Berkeley film-maker who claims to have gotten 8 mm footage of the killing. He got home from the affair Saturday and began telling his friends about his amazing film. His house was knocked over the next night, completely rifled. The thief ripped off only his film, nothing else.

Another far-out (and unconfirmed, because the Angels are not talking with the press) report from someone close to the Angels was that they were in possession of Meredith Hunter's pistol, wanted to turn it over to the Sheriff's investigators – obviously, it would be useful to establish self-defense – but didn't know how to go about doing it. If true, the Angels evidently solved their own problem. It is learned that investigators have had the gun since shortly after New Year's.

Mrs Alta Mae Anderson, Meredith Hunter's mother, still had not been contacted by anyone involved with the free concert by January 5th, when she appeared before the Alameda County Planning Commission to request that the Altamont Raceway, where Hunter was killed, be turned into a public park.

"My son's blood is on the land," she said, "and I would like to see the land serve a useful purpose for the youth of Southern Alameda County. I cannot bring my son back, but by your action you may prevent any more wrongful deaths at Altamont."

In the end, the commission voted to allow the speedway to continue holding races, but barred any future rock and roll events, and limited the number of spectators to 3,000.

One sympathetic mother whose own teen-age son was only a few feet from the killing, Mrs Cayren King, of Oakland, put Mrs. Anderson in touch with Ephraim Margolin, a respected (and tough) San Francisco civil liberties attorney, to represent her interests in the trial that is (reasonably) certain to come.

Meanwhile, many were growing impatient with the length of time it's taken for the District Attorney to move. He hasn't moved yet. Some claim that Alameda County authorities do not want to damage the fragile truce which exists between police and Hell's Angels.

But Rock Scully said it would be a "drag if it has to go through a courtroom scene." He has tried to put Altamont out of his mind, to concentrate on more positive matters. But Scully, the man who worked with Stones road manager Sam Cutler on advance preparations before the Stones' higher managerial echelons arrived in the Bay Area, says everybody he knows "is still upset about the whole thing."

"We were all dupes," he says, rather cryptically. "The thing wasn't ever straight. Everybody got had."

Having met with the Angels a couple of times, Scully says they don't dig having the film shown, because they feel it would be exploitation of the Angels.

(Another source says that the Maysles showed the film to the Angels in San Francisco, privately, and that the Angels' leaders demanded $6000 each for nine different California chapters. A total of $54,000. No confirmation on this from the Maysles. The Angels are said to have demanded the money or else . . .)

In any case, Scully now feels that the whole thing was a disaster, and feels foolish, in a way, about his participation in it.

"The Stones, man," he says, "they wrote the script. They got what they paid for. Let it bleed, man. There's never gonna be another one like it. Anybody should have seen this would have happened – this whole trip, man – if somebody tried to buy another Woodstock. We should have seen it, but we couldn't see that."

On Tour with The Stones

Tony McPhee

In 1970, British blues-based rockers The Groundhogs toured Britain with the Rolling Stones. Groundhogs leader and guitarist Tony (TS) McPhee kept a diary and the following report appeared in rock music paper, Sounds.

The news that we had been invited to be support band on the Stones' tour fell on stony ground with the Groundhogs. We weren't being blase about it – it's just that too often on this kind of tour a second band is treated like a pimple being slowly squeezed out of its half hour set because the house was late getting in, or the main band over-ran in the first house and so on; and to try and get across to an audience in less than half an hour is impossible so we were dubious and apprehensive.

The first night was City Hall, Newcastle, and if anything was going to go wrong, it would be then that all the press would be there, all too eager to slag off in a witty way the unfortunates who stand in the stocks on stage, game for any vindictive reporter with some rotten tomato journalese at his fingertips.

So naturally our amplifiers failed to turn up and we had to use the Stones gear. Trying to get a freaky guitar sound out of a small Fender amp is like trying to get Eric Clapton to support Enoch Powell. So despite a friendly and enthusiastic audience, we couldn't play well.

But the Stones had no problems as everything was handled by their amiable American tour manager Chip Monck, who commanded everything like Montgomery of Alamein (how's that for a metaphor, peace lovers!) and had everything working smoothly for the Stones' first appearance of the tour; and a warm audience gave the tour a good start.

Travelling onto Manchester the next day we were happier with the knowledge that our own gear would be at the Free Trade Hall for the two sets that night.

The Stones performed the same numbers, opening with "Jumping Jack Flash" which gave Mick Jagger the chance to cavort. For the next three numbers the initial rousing welcome applause died down to a more or less polite level, but the excellent "Midnight Rambler" gave the Stones the chance to show how exciting they are musically and visually; and from there they kept the numbers at the same intensity with "Little Queenie", "Brown Sugar" and "Satisfaction".

The farewell stroke of throwing a basket of flower petals over the audience broke all the inhibitions (and probably someone's head) as the raving continued.

 News that Hell's Angels were outside the stage door persuaded us to wait in the hall until everyone had cleared.

At Coventry Theatre on Saturday, Chip was still organising the lights when a rotund little official, backed up by a bored policeman demanded the houselights up and the entrance doors opened. With great aplomb Chip verbally shrank the official to the size of a policeman's boot and then obediently brought up the house-lights with the stage lighting incomplete.

The first house was cool and unresponsive to both us and the Stones, but the second house was good and brought the best out of everyone.

Sunday was a day off, and I came home.

Unfortunately I missed the train for Glasgow on Monday, and arrived at 6.30 p.m. to see a Scottish band doing our set. The band, Merlin, did a good set but unfortunately they were all other people's numbers. But that's the only way to get work out of Scottish agents. Sad.

The Glasgow venue was called Green's Playhouse and it had the reputation of being the biggest theatre in Europe. If this is so, it's probably because they didn't bother about building dressing rooms as we were in rooms underneath the stage, with a constant stream of people going through from one side of the stage to the other.

The audience made up for it as they were noisy and great – and they made the prospect of the 350 miles trip to Bristol the next day a little easier to bear.

More than any other major town, Bristol has a vendetta against hairy people, and the attitude of the people in the street towards you is of hostile derision.

The hairy audience gave us a good reception, however, despite the presence of a dozen or so bouncers who were deployed around the Colston Hall.

As soon as the Stones came on, they lined up against the curved stage, facing the audience with their arms crossed – an impenetrable wall of flesh and bone. Each time anyone rose from their seat they were ushered down by a waggle from the head bouncer's index finger. Power!

One brave soul leapt into the aisle and was carried out bodily, but he retained enough composure to blow a kiss to the Stones as he was hurtled past the stage to the exit.

This set a revolutionary mood and Mick Jagger took it further by whirling his belt just above the bouncer's heads.

The final stroke came when, instead of throwing petals at the rest of the Stones, Mick (Jagger) threw them over the bouncers, and the sight of these stalwarts with petals stuck to their heads blew any fears for them; and the audience stood and raved.

Wednesday was the Big Apple at Brighton, which is above a cinema. We were asked to keep the volume down for our set so it wouldn't disturb the filmgoers below . . . but with two and a half thousand asses acting as sound absorbers in the floor, there was no real problem.

With three days of the show remaining, the single show at Brighton has been the best from the Stones which is great because they used their own sixteen track portable recording gear to get this session on tape.

Despite our apprehension about the tour it's been really enjoyable, the Stones being pleasant and generous people; although some of the myriad of "humpers" around have done their best to put us down without success.

Mr Kardoom

Wilko Johnson

*Before forming seminal 1970s Canvey Island rockers, Dr Feelgood,
guitarist Wilko Johnson travelled the hippy trail to India.*

Mr Kardoom was a massage-man who lived and worked on
Bombay's waterfront, under the Gateway of India. Every evening
I would go to where he sat, surrounded by his few possessions,
take off my shoes and sit down on his little carpet. After a while he
would ask me for two rupees and send a boy for some ganja.

He said that it was beneficial to the health to smoke ganja in the
evening.

"But no *charas*. That makes you go mad."

One evening when I arrived there were two or three other
people there. They were talking excitedly and Mr Kardoom
asked me for four rupees.

"Tonight we smoke *charas*. Bombay black."

While we were waiting some more people joined us. One very
lively guy had a plate of food which he pointed at emphatically –
"this is Indian eat! No eggs, no mutton!"

The boy returned with two small pellets of black hashish. Mr
Kardoom mixed it with ganja and filled a chillum, which he lit
and passed around. When it got to me I took two big hits. By the
time I passed it on, I was extremely stoned. I had just begun to
take stock of my surroundings when the chillum arrived at the
food man. He took a blast which made him cough and a shower of
sparks burst from the chillum. The character beside him slapped
him on the shoulder and rolled over in convulsions of laughter.
Soon we were all helpless, aching with mirth at the splendid
display of sparks we had seen.

Eventually things quietened down and the others drifted off, until there was just me and Mr Kardoom.

Beyond the shoulder of the frayed blue blazer he always wore, I could see the waves lapping to the beach in the darkness. Huge reptiles were marching in infinite solemn processions from the sea up into the streets of Bombay.

I was in a temple staring at the wall where a thousand garish idols were expounding primeval truths with intricate mathematical gestures. They raised their arms and flowed into a massive brightly-coloured mandala.

In the centre sat Mr Kardoom. His eyes met mine.

"You walk in the sky?"

"Yes," I said, and the word echoed and re-echoed in my skull. I stood up and took my leave and began the long walk up to the Victoria Terminus where I slept each night.

Some limousines had pulled up outside the Taj Mahal Hotel and a party of rich people were walking across the red carpet. The men were in immaculate evening dress and the women wore expensive glittering saris.

I suddenly realised how scruffy I was, and that I would soon be walking among them.

It was ludicrous beyond all bearing.

I stepped off the pavement and walked into the middle of the street, threw my head back and laughed out loud.

The Seventies were about to begin.

Janis Joplin

The Rolling Stone *Tribute*

Rolling Stone, 29 October 1972.

HOLLYWOOD – When Janis Joplin failed to show up at Sunset Sound Studios by 6 p.m., Paul Rothschild, her producer, gave in to the strange "flashing" he had been feeling all day and sent John Cooke, a road manager for the Full Tilt Boogie Band, over to the Landmark Motor Hotel to see why she wasn't answering her phone. "I'd never worried about her before," Rothschild said, "although she'd been late lots of times. It was usually that she stopped to buy a pair of pants or some chick thing like that." October 4th was a Sunday however, and there were few places to go, even in Hollywood. Even for Janis.

The Landmark is a big stucco building on Franklin Avenue. It is convenient to the sound studios on Sunset Blvd. and near the offices of the record companies and music publishers. It is painted a garish "sunburst orange" and "bear brown" (according to the man at the desk), and it is the favorite motel for visiting performers. The lobby has large plastic plants and some vaguely psychedelic designs on its walls, but the motel's attraction is its tolerance. The guy behind the desk remembered, laughing, the time a guest called to complain about the noise from a series of rooms where members of the Jefferson Airplane were having a party. "The guy who complained was thrown out," he said. It was Janis' kind of place.

When John Cooke got there it was almost 7 p.m. He noticed Janis' car in the lot, and that the drapes in her first floor room were drawn. She didn't answer her door when he knocked, or even when he banged and yelled. He spoke to the manager, Jack Hagy, who agreed that they should go into the room. Janis was lying wedged between the bed and a nightstand, wearing a short nightgown. Her lips were bloody when they turned her over, and her nose was broken. She had $4.50 clutched in one hand.

Cooke called a doctor, then phoned Janis' attorney, Robert Gordon. Gordon claims he went over the room carefully but found no narcotics or drug paraphernalia. The police were called. When they arrived at around 9 p.m., they too, found no drugs or "works." But they told reporters Janis "had fresh needle marks on her arm, 10 to 14 of them, on her left arm."

By the time the 11 p.m. newscaster had finished his brief report, phone calls were already spreading wild rumors – Janis had been killed by some jealous guy, by a dealer, even by the CIA; Janis had done herself in because of some guy, because she thought she was fading, because she'd always been self-destructive. Each new theory had its "informed" proponents, and each was equally groundless.

The confusion was not helped by Los Angeles County Coroner Thomas Noguchi's preliminary report, issued the following morning. It said she "died of an overdose of drugs," but did not specify *what* drugs – alcohol, sleeping pills or something harder.

Gordon, understandably, tried to counteract many of the bizarre rumors and soften the edge of some of the wilder headlines by saying that he felt the drug inferences were unfounded and that Janis had died in much the way Jimi Hendrix had – from an overdose of sleeping pills followed, in her case, by a fall from the bed.

By Tuesday, however, Noguchi reported that Janis who was 27, had in fact injected heroin into her left arm several hours before she died, and that it was an overdose that killed her. He said an inquest will be held, and that "behavioral scientists" would try to determine if the OD was "intentional".

When questioned about the facial injuries, police said they'd "ruled out the possibility of violence. She could have broken her nose when she collapsed," one detective said. The odd amount of money in her hand remains a mystery, however, and will feed the imaginations of the people who must account in some tangible way for her death. At present, the explanations range from "it was change for a bag" – a bag of heroin goes for about $15 in Los Angeles these days – to grotesques about "change for a call for help"! (but the phone in her room, as in most motel and hotel rooms, did not require change).

Reports on Janis' mood in the last weeks of her life do not help much either. They are perhaps appropriately contradictory. Superstars just fade but culture heroines die hard.

Robert Gordon, the attorney, said Monday that Janis had visited him the previous Thursday (October 1) "on business matters."

"She seemed very happy. She told me she was thinking of getting married. She'd been going with a guy named Seth Morgan for a couple of months. I don't believe he is in music. I think he is from Maine.

"She was also very happy about her album. She'd been in town about a month recording it, and she was enthusiastic about the band and about her own singing. She said she 'felt like a woman.' The band had a tour scheduled for November."

When asked about the "business" Janis had come to see him about, Gordon said: "I might as well tell you. She signed her will." He emphasized however that he didn't think the signing "meant" anything.

"She was happy," Gordon said.

Paul Rothschild, who works for Elektra but who was producing the Columbia session (Janis released the albums on Columbia) "independently," at first reported that she was "thrilled and ecstatic." He said he'd known Janis for a long time, and that she seemed "happier and more turned on than anyone can remember." He said the album was "80 per cent" done. A source at Columbia, however, reported that the recording "had not been going well, that it was "coming slowly," and that after a month of eight to ten-hour days in the studio, 11 tracks had been cut and only four were considered "good enough."

When confronted with this, Rothschild became furious. He pointed out that he'd had to "fight all the Columbia people" all through the sessions, "the staff and the executives." He said the

album was the first by an "outside" producer that Columbia
allowed, and that "the record may not have been going smoothly
for Columbia, but it was for Janis Joplin."

The Columbia source listed the titles of the 11 tracks as: "Me
and Bobby McGhee", "A Woman Left Lonely"; "Ain't Nobody's Business", "Trust In Me; "More, More" "Cry"; "Get It
While You Can", "Half Moon"; "Got My Baby" and "Happy
Birthday, John Lennon."

John Carpenter, music editor of the Los Angeles Free Press
and a former partner of Chet Helms (Chet is credited with having
brought Janis back to San Francisco after she'd returned to Texas
in 1966), at the Family Dog, said he saw Janis last on September
28th at the Troubador on Sunset Strip.

"She talked about her old man, said she 'had a lover now,' and
she seemed cheerful but there was something . . . She had a red
dress on and I asked her what she was doing there. She said 'I got
this new dress and I just wanted to look good.' She was alone. We
had a few drinks and there were a lot of people around us. It was
just audition night, you know, new young bands, nobody big.
Toward the end of the night she kind of announced that she was
leaving. Nobody said anything or offered to take her. Finally I
called her a cab and she went home alone."

The last person to see Janis alive was Hagy, the Landmark's
manager. He told police he spoke to her briefly at 1 a.m.
Sunday morning, and that she "appeared cheerful." Janis
had finished a recording session at about 11 p.m. Saturday
night and went with several members of her band to Barnie's
Beanery. John Cooke said Janis had had "a few drinks" and
then drove her organ player back to the motel, said goodnight,
and went to bed.

Mr and Mrs Seth Joplin of Port Arthur Texas, Janis' parents,
arrived in Los Angeles on Monday but said they had "no
comment for the press." Albert Grossman, her manager, flew
in from New York and also refused comment. However a spokesman at his office said he "felt about her as a daughter."

Myra Friedman, a Grossman press representative and close
friend of Janis, said the image she sometimes cultivated and

sometimes had forced on her, the "Get It While You Can Girl," was not accurate:

"I think Janis knew that wasn't really where she was at. Maybe a part of her believed that, but I think the most honest part didn't. She wasn't a conservative girl – that's ridiculous – but she had a lot of needs that were just like everyone else's. She was accepting of a lot of different kinds of people.

"Recently I met her at the Chelsea Hotel – she always stayed there when she was in New York – and she had been reading a book, I saw it. It was *Look Homeward Angel* by Thomas Wolfe. She told me she read a lot, but 'don't tell anybody'."

Sam Gordon, who ran Janis' publishing firm, recalled going to Aux Puces, a pub at 55th Street near Park Avenue, recently with her for a drink:

"We were rapping about what we wanted from life," he said. "I said I wished I was on the road again instead of in the comfortable suburban life I've been living for a while now.

"She said: 'Oh, I'll take that.' I asked if that was what she really wanted and she said. 'Yeah, that's what I really want'."

But Gordon remembers the first song he ever sent to her. It was a Jesse Winchester tune called. "Quiet About It." It was religious, in a way. Janis said she couldn't use it: "I can't talk to my God quietly."

In April, 1968, shortly after Janis hit New York for the first time, she told writer Nat Hentoff: "I never seemed to be able to control my feelings, to keep them down . . . my mother would try to get me to be like everybody else . . . And I never would. But before getting into this band, it tore my life apart. When you feel that much, you have superhorrible downs. I was always victim to myself. Now though, I've made feeling work for me . . . Maybe I won't last as long as other singers, but I think you can destroy your now by worrying about tomorrow. If I hold back, I'm no good *now* and I'd rather be good sometimes than holding back all the time . . . like a lot of my generation, and younger, we look back at our parents and see how they gave up and compromised and wound up with very little . . . Man, if it hadn't been for the music, I probably would have done myself in."

Kip Cohen, manager of the Fillmore East, remembers her backstage at the annual Thanksgiving Day dinners Bill Graham always throws for friends and stars:

"She would come but we could never get her to sit down with us at the table. She used to hide on the stairway with a friend and sit there and sip champagne.

"I remember once she came backstage to see Santana and I said the audience would love it if she just went on unannounced to introduce the group. And the idea of the 'real' Janis walking on stage and doing something other than performing, singing, scared her to death. She couldn't do it.

"She had a tremendous amount of assurance when she got it all together onstage, but offstage, privately, she seemed to be very frightened, very timid and very naive about a lot of things.

"Once you become a public figure you relinquish your privacy and the toll is there. The audience certainly demands an enormous amount from a performer, much more than they deserve, and Janis would give everything and after you give everything, what do you do when the audience wants more?

"That shows them to be the overfed, spoiled suburban brats that most of them are, and I'm more angry today over Janis' death because of that."

Cohen said the guilt for Janis was collective, however. He said he didn't expect the kids to react "very strongly." "We showed a slide of Jimi Hendrix here after he died and they all cheered. It was supportive, but I expect them both to be forgotten ultimately. Nor do I see them [kids] looking for substitutes, nor anyone else coming along to play their roles."

Bill Graham, speaking from San Francisco, denied the "connections" that were inevitably being made between Hendrix' and Joplin's deaths.

"None. None. As far as timing is concerned, that it's in the stars or something. Absolutely none. Hendrix was an accident – and Janis, nobody knows yet. I'm sure that somebody has thrown the I Ching or somebody is turning over the pages of some book and reading the charts and looking through the stars and saying, 'I knew it, I knew it.'

"I only knock that in that so many people will be looking for reasoning and logic – it doesn't mean *that* man was meant to go, *that* thing was meant to happen, it was not written somewhere . . . We don't really know. If, *if*, hypothetically speaking – if both of them are the result of, let us say argumentatively, heroin, the ironic twist would be that they may have a positive effect in that a lot of young people would get off heroin. But because they weren't, what effect will these two deaths have? I should like to think that some of the people who have become successful will begin to evaluate their use of the success and what they have done with it and whether they control it or does it control them . . . Janis, like anybody else in rock, I don't think ever knew how to handle success . . . I think it created problems for Janis – but it never spoiled her. It has always been questionable – does this kind of success include happiness? People have said to me many times, look at you yelling and screaming all the time, with all your money, are you happy? That's for me to determine . . . Am I trying to do what I think I can serve life best at? Did Janis? Do you?"

Graham also dismissed theories that the deaths of Janis, Jimi and Al Wilson, the breakup of the Beatles, the change in Dylan or the inactivity of the Stones meant the "death" of Sixties rock and roll. He said he saw no parallel with the plane crash deaths of Buddy Holly, the Big Bopper and Ritchie Valens in the late Fifties and the simultaneous disappearance of Elvis into the Army, Chuck Berry into jail and figures like Fats Domino and Little Richard into retirement.

"Janis is not all of rock and roll or music or entertainment or pop and neither was Jimi Hendrix. And it only remains to be seen who is coming along to join who is left, to see what we will have. Nobody can say. Nobody can really say what the creative elements will bring to bear. If Bob Dylan didn't come along in the same era as the Band and the Beatles, would this have happened? So you can't really say are the Sixties dead, what is going to come along to replace it – the people who are stars today are going to remain the stars until new stars bump them, put them aside. There are certain acts that shouldn't even be in showbusiness that are headliners today because nobody is taking their place . . ."

At the Airplane House in San Francisco it was business-as-usual; they knew about Janis, but they weren't talking much about it. It was almost as if putting energy behind it might make it worse. Joey Covington sat in the "office," talking on the telephone about buying a car. The Airplane had played a late gig at Winterland the night before, and were just waking up.

"Did you hear that Janis died?" asked Jackie, the Airplane's office manager.

"Yeah, yeah, that's really a shame," said Joey. "The music world lost a great singer. It's really sort of strange to be riding in your car and think about it – about the Hendrix thing, and Janis. Really sort of strange.

"You know what I flashed on today? I flashed on the Jimi Hendrix thing in *Rolling Stone* about *another* pop star dying. I was thinking it'd be pretty far out if you didn't cop on a dead thing, a death trip in your paper.

"I mean, I read articles today that were really fucking dumb, in the papers: 'Oh, the way she used to let her breasts swing, and she didn't wear a bra. . . .' That shit's so dumb, man. I hope your paper doesn't do that."

Grace, barefoot, padded across the room to the water cooler, filled a vase with water, and disappeared again into her room. I knocked on the door, opened it, and asked her if there was anything she wanted to say about Janis.

"Well," she said, "not really. I think it's kind of . . . well, not corny exactly, but . . . why print all that stuff about someone who's dead? She's gone, it's done. I mean. I'm sorry she's dead, but . . . you know? If I come up with any jewels, I'll send them to you, OK?"

In Austin, Texas, Ken Threadgill, a famous folkie who ran a bar called Threadgill's where Janis first began singing in 1961, said he remembered her as a "wonderful old gal, just good common country people. I thought a hell of a lot of Janis. She always said I helped he get started but I was just here and I liked her and her singing. It's hard to believe she was here in Austin just 85 days ago" (for a birthday party and testimonial for Threadgill).

In New York, Clive Davis, president of Columbia Records said he felt Janis "uniquely personified contemporary rock music in spirit, in talent and in personality. Janis and contemporary music shot out of Monterey together in 1967 and I was fortunate to be there. I will always be personally grateful to her as she more than anyone else at Monterey made me intensely aware and excited about the new and future direction of music."

On the day after Janis died, the offices of Columbia in New York looked pretty much the way they do on any ordinary day, except that a fresh batch of her last album, *I Got Dem Ol Kozmic Blues Again, Mama* had arrived from the Grossman office. Columbia had run out of records.

At the Grossman office everyone looked gloomy. "Janis would run in laughing and disrupted things everytime she was in New York," one employee recalled. Someone else would mention the beginning of an anecdote, or start a story, and then it would fade off. This is probably the toughest, most successful organization in one of the cruelest businesses in the country.

At Sam Goody's (a huge, East Coast record chain in New York), clerks were bringing up Janis and Jimi albums from the basement. They didn't look particularly sad, or happy.

And at the Landmark Motor Hotel, one of Janis' musicians looked at the bright facade and squinted. "It's a hell of a place to die."

On Wednesday, October 7th, Janis Joplin's body was cremated, according to her wishes. A very private service was held for the immediate members of her family – her parents, brother and sister, aunts, uncles and cousins. The location was not disclosed.

According to Robert Gordon, her attorney, the family at first wanted to take her body back to Port Arthur for burial, but later agreed to their daughter's request. "They're not unhappy about that," said John Cooke, Janis' road manager since her days with Big Brother.

Cooke also said Janis' closest friends, including her roommate

Lindall Erb, gathered at the Landmark Motor Inn and did not attend the service. "Lindall's OK now," Cooke said. "We're all here together."

Gordon said Janis' ashes will be scattered at sea off Marin County at some indeterminate date.

Janis Joplin was born on January 19, 1943, the oldest of three children, in Port Arthur, Texas, a medium-small city of 60,000, located approximately 15 miles from the Louisiana border. Her father Seth was once employed by the Texas Canning Company, but now works for Texaco. Her mother, Dorothy, is Registrar at Port Arthur College, a business school. She has a younger sister, Laura, an undergraduate at Lamar Tech in Austin, and a brother, Michael.

Many people in Port Arthur work in the oil refinery business in some capacity, and the city is middle-income and middle-class. It is often smokey and hot. From all reports, Janis hated it.

"In Texas I was a beatnik, a weirdo, and since I wasn't making it the way I am now, my parents thought I was a goner," Janis said in 1968. "Now my mother writes and asks what kind of clothes a 1968 blues singer wears. That's kind of groovy, since we've been on opposite sides since I was 14. Texas is OK if you want to settle down and do your own thing quietly, but it's not for outrageous people, and I was always outrageous. I got treated very badly in Texas. They don't treat beatniks too good in Texas."

Her first interests were painting and poetry. She did some of each, but at 17, got very involved with Leadbelly country blues and then Bessie Smith. She sent away for albums of both performers, and played them over many times, trying to sing along. Then she ran away.

She stayed in Austin, Houston, Venice Beach and San Francisco, singing and working at various jobs. Sometimes she collected unemployment checks. She is first recorded as being in San Francisco in 1962, but Ken Threadgill, an oldtime Texas folk musician, remembers seeing her in Austin in 1961. He claims she'd just been released from a hospital in San Francisco, where she'd been under treatment for drugs. That would place her in California sometime before her 19th birthday.

"I first saw her in late '61,'', Threadgill remembers. "She was just a kid. She came up to Austin to go to school at the University of Texas, and she worked part-time as a keypunch operator to help pay expenses. She was around off and on from '61 to '63."

Threadgill had converted a service station into a bar that featured old-time country music done by young and old performers. Another girl singer, Julie Joyce, who used to work at Threadgill's, saw Janis and a "bluegrass" band, she was working parties and occasional coffee houses with, sitting in the street in Austin. Janis had an autoharp. The other musicians were Powell St. John, a harp player and Larry Wiggins, a banjo picker and guitarist. Julie invited the trio to try out at Threadgill's. In one of her first performances, Janis won two bottles of Lone Star beer. The trio also won a $10 prize in a talent show.

"Actually though, she didn't go over so well around there. She was singing in a high, shrill bluegrass kind of sound. Eventually somebody came around who put her on a coffeehouse circuit and that was that," Threadgill said.

Back in Port Arthur at a party one night, she tried an Odetta imitation and the new sound she was capable of startled even her. She continued to restrain her vocals though, doing Bessie Smith-type songs in bars and folk clubs, right up until the first time she worked out with Big Brother and the Holding Company.

Janis told people she'd been in and out of four colleges over the next years, but she definitely was in San Francisco in 1966. Chet Helms, who was then running a musicians' and rehearsal house in the Haight Ashbury and managing Big Brother, heard and liked her.

Sam Andrew, Peter Albin, James Gurley and later Dave Getz had been hanging around Chet Helms' pad in Haight Ashbury in 1965.

"First time I ever met Peter, he had this weird idea for starting a rock group which would speak to all the children of the nation in their own language." Sam said. "I thought, what's this nut trying to do, what trip is he on?" The band began practicing and took the name Big Brother and the Holding Company. They were Helms' house band at the Avalon.

"Before Janis we were doing a lot of space stuff, kind of what Cecil Taylor and Pharaoh Sanders were doing . . . just hard and very free," Sam remembers. At first it was more experimentation. Peter was doing most of the singing, and when Janis came he taught the songs to Janis.

"We wanted another singer, I think maybe one or two people in the group were thinking of Signe and the Airplane and how that worked out. But most of us were thinking of just any vocalist who came along who was good. And Chet was managing us, and he said, 'I know this great chick.' Janis had come out to San Francisco before and freaked out – she didn't think she was going anywhere – and she went back to Texas. So Chet went back and told her about the scene and she and Travis Rivers came out. So we moved to Lagunitas and got into country living and it was a growing together thing for all of us. The rest of us were still new to each other and Janis was a catalyst, brought people out, made it really easy to talk."

Janis, in 1968: "[Chet] told me Big Brother was looking for a chick singer, so I thought I'd give it a try. I don't know what happened. I just exploded. I'd never sung like that before. I stood still, and I sang simple. But you *can't* sing like that in front of a rock band, all that rhythm and volume going. You *have* to sing loud and move wild with all that in back of you. It happened the first time, but then I got turned on to Otis Redding and I just got into it more than ever. Now, I don't know how to perform any other way. I've tried cooling myself and not screaming, and I've walked off feeling like nothing."

Janis and Big Brother – Sam and Jim on guitars, Peter on bass and Dave on drums – worked the Avalon regularly and other small gigs around the Bay area. They were building a reputation with the city's ballroom goers. Janis had moved back to town, and was living in a second floor apartment near Buena Vista Park in the same block as Peter Albin. Country Joe McDonald of the Fish was going with her for a time. Then Big Brother got an offer to record. The label was Mainstream, a small Chicago outfit, and Sam Andrew still thinks of the incident as a "disaster".

"This cat [Bob Shad] was pushing us – this really far-out mother from New York. They had an audition at the old Spreckels mansion; they wanted to sign us then, and Chet said no. A couple of months later we got rid of Chet, for one reason or another it didn't make it. Then we went to Chicago and signed, because it sounded so attractive . . . we were naive kids. We were in Chicago and it was heavy; the club was burning us and here was this cat saying come on down to the recording studio tomorrow, sign up and let's go to the lawyer and make sure it's cool – and it was *his* lawyer – I think we all wanted to, more or less.

"We asked him for $1,000, and he said no. We said $500? He said no. Well, can we have plane fare home? He said not one penny, and to this day we haven't got one penny from that album. (*Big Brother and the Holding Company*, Mainstream 36099). We got back and it was a good time in San Francisco, small gigs . . ."

And in August, 1967, the Monterey international Pop Festival. The group didn't even have their record released. Mainstream was sitting on it. Janis and Jimi Hendrix got rave reviews and incredible audience reaction, and suddenly, the album was on the streets. It was terrible but, bad as it was, it helped spread the band's name. More important, Clive Davis, president of Columbia Records Division, had been in the audience and liked what he saw and heard. And Albert Grossman, who was in the process of assembling the biggest stable of rock acts in America, was interested.

Monterey was the big break for Big Brother. They had been scheduled to play only on the afternoon show, but the reaction to Janis was so strong that the band was put on the evening show again. The audience was ecstatic once again. It was the beginning of the big time.

Big Brother signed with Albert Grossman in January, 1968. Peter Albin said: "We felt it was important to have someone who was involved in management on a national level working for us. There are a lot more offers and deals being done in L.A. and New

York than in San Francisco. We wanted to get out of San
Francisco and start touring."

Bill Graham, remembering the old Janis with her original
band, said: "I was, as everyone else was, very impressed with
this wild, raucous sound coming from Janis . . . the most endearing old story I can remember about Janis is three years ago
when I told her I had Otis Redding booked and she went crazy.
And Otis was there for three nights at the old Fillmore and all the
local groups wanted to play with him and we had a different
group each night. But the thing about Janis was that each night
she asked me ahead of time, she said 'Bill, please, please can I
come there early before anybody else so I can make sure I see
him,' because she idolized Otis. And every night she would come
to the ballroom at six o'clock and sit herself down on the main
floor, right in the middle, right in front of the stage. She was there
before we even opened the building. When we opened there she
was with all the other kids and she was leaning against the stage
and looking up just like all the other little fans and she was just
amazed at his ability, and then she went backstage and was like a
baseball fan asking Willie Mays for his autograph . . . I remember that more than any other event in all the times we were
privileged to . . . I remember that more than anything.

"I don't think Janis tried to be black. I think Janis sang as a
young person coming out of Texas and having kicked around San
Francisco, and her voice was her voice and that was her interpretation of the songs. She sang blues. And in her own way . . .
you know, when someone is a stylist or the originator of a style
and . . . a particular style of blues, I don't think you can compare
her. And I keep coming back to Hendrix. Hendrix was an
innovator on the guitar, Janis was an innovator in a certain style
. . . very few tried to play like Hendrix – you couldn't. Well, Janis
was that. The mark of great talent, creative talent and original
talent is also in its difficulty to copy that talent. And I think that's
what Janis has.

"I recall a time here at the Fillmore in San Francisco, oh, was it
a year ago the last time she was here? And she had a death of a
cold, and she had some alcoholic beverage with her and some tea

on the stage, she grabbed a hold of me and said, 'Bill, I'm so worried. I hope they like me, I'm in my own home town, you think it'll be all right?' The truth is that Janis is one of those people, she couldn't do any wrong here. But even knowing that she was worried and that's what made her what she was. I don't want to knock somebody else, but I figure it's public knowledge that there are a lot of people in this industry who say 'I don't give a shit, I'll go out there and do my thing or do the best I can – we'll do 10 numbers or whatever, make some revolutionary statements and tell everybody to get up and dance,' but Janis, you know, they talk about troupers being ready to get up on the stage anytime . . .

"The last time she played New York. I called Lindall, who is her roommate here in Larkspur, and I said what is Janis into these days? And she said, 'Well, she likes maroon now – she's buying maroon colors, clothing, whatever – and she's really into guacamole and she's into gin' – this is about a year ago and she's off Comfort. And I called New York. It didn't take much. We painted one of the dressing rooms maroon, put up some nice posters, got a bunch of guacamole and just as an extra touch rented a portable bar and took one of the ushers, who is like one of her real fans, and put him in a tuxedo with a top hat with his long hair and his beard and he schlepped over in a taxi, and she came to rehearsal in the afternoon, and we had just the big tulip in a vase in the dressing room and when she walked in she met Mike, the valet, with the tulip, with the guacamole, with the gin, with the room painted maroon, and it destroyed her – she cried."

By April, 1968, Janis and the band (people had begun to think of it in that way by then) were in New York to record *Cheap Thrills* for Columbia. The band had played the Anderson Theater on 2nd Avenue the previous February, across from what was known then as the Village Theatre – but with the coming of the San Francisco Sound to New York, would change to the *Fillmore East*. Kip Cohen, who worked for Bill Graham then, as now, said: "There was no question that she was a great star then, as much as she was now. Big Brother was a funky and not-so-good band but everyone loved them because it was Janis and pure San Francisco

and the height of the whole thing." (Actually, the Summer of
Love had been the *past* season, Hippie had been declared dead,
and the Haight had begun to decay. *Musically*, however, it may
have been the high point.)

Big Brother had some trouble in the studio. Janis reported that
New York had made everyone aggressive. "San Francisco's different," she told writer Nat Hentoff in the New York Times. "I
don't mean it's perfect, but the rock bands there didn't start because
they wanted to make it. They dug getting stoned and playing for
people dancing. What we have to do is learn to control success."

Cheap Thrills, complete with all the Joplin heavies – "Ball and
Chain," "Piece of My Heart," etc., came out in September of
1968 and sold a million dollars in copies. Janis was the biggest
thing in American rock and roll. Cashbox called her "a mixture of
Leadbelly, a steam engine Calamity Jane, Bessie Smith, an oil
derrick and rot-gut bourbon funneled into the 20th century
somewhere between El Paso and San Francisco." Hentoff said
she "was the first white blues singer (female) since Teddy Grace
who sang the blues out of black influences but had developed her
own sound and phrasing." Bill Graham, asked to talk about her
talent as far as blues/rock singer recently: "I think Janis was a
great performer, one of the few great entertainers in rock . . . as
far as being a white blues singer, she moved . . . what else can a
man say – you can't say she was better than – she moved me."
Janis herself said: "There's no patent on soul. You know how that
whole myth of black soul came up? Because white people don't
allow themselves to feel things. Housewives in Nebraska have
pain and joy; they've got soul if they give in to it. It's hard. And it
isn't all a ball when you do."

By November the rumors of the Holding Company breaking
up couldn't be ignored. Janis played her last gig with the band
December 1st at the Family Dog for Chet Helms. She'd already
begun rehearsing her new band, known variously as The Janis
Revue and Main Squeeze, and there were the usual ugly stories
making the rounds. Two days after Janis died, Peter Albin
recalled what it was like: "It was in New York that she made
the decision to split. There were several gigs where all of us

would feel down. She'd have done her part with an amount of self
assurance, but there was a whole time when the waves started
separating. The kind of performance she would put out would be
a different trip than the band's. I'd say it was a star trip, where
she related to the audience like she was the only one on the stage,
and not relating to us at all."

(Albin had been union representative and spokesman for Big
Brother, and both he and Janis worked on the production of
Cheap Thrills – to the chagrin of producer John Simon.)

Sam Andrew, who went on with Janis to her second band, said
she fought the split for a long time: "People were telling her that
[she was better than the band] very early, but it didn't make any
difference . . . then it got pretty intense for six months. Albert was
coming on heavy to her. One night at Winterland – I don't know,
a couple of guys were sick or something, but afterward she said,
'Man, I go out there and try, and those guys aren't trying.' It was
this one night; it was when I noticed the change. And that was the
year of soul, too – the year that everyone was into horns and shit –
it wasn't hard *feelings*. It was pretty natural. We all saw it coming
for quite awhile."

From the very beginning, the Squeeze had difficulty. The line-
up was Sam Andrew, guitar; Bill King, organ; Marcus Double-
day, trumpet; Tony Clemens, tenor (followed by Snooky Flowers), Brad Campbell, bass; and Ron Markowitz, drums.
Grossman sent Mike Bloomfield to San Francisco on December
18th, 1968, to try to get the band together, Janis was scheduled to
debut in Memphis, Tennessee, three days later at the Memphis
Mid-South Coliseum. The occasion was the annual Memphis
Sound party, presided over by Stax Records president Jim
Stewart. The scheduled acts included the Bar-Kays, Otis Redding's old band, Albert King, the Mad Lads, Judy Clay, Carla
and Rufus Thomas, Eddie Floyd and Janis. These were all hard-
core Memphis soul acts (excluding King), given to flash and show
biz. Janis' band seemed out of place, tuning their instruments and
setting up interminably. Half of the crowd had no idea who she
was, and the others, white teen-agers, had never heard her do
anything but "Ball and Chain" and "Piece of My Heart".

Janis opened with "Raise Your Hand" and followed with the Bee Gees' "To Love Somebody".

There was almost no applause. No encore. Backstage, everyone from her band was in shock. She was told repeatedly that she had sung well, and that the rest had been beyond her control, but she didn't want comfort.

After Memphis, members Marcus Belgrave and Bill King left, and were replaced by Terry Hensley and Richard Kermode. The band did a "sound test" in Rindge, New Hampshire (the most obscure gig the Grossman office could arrange), and then ran a "preview" in Boston before playing the Fillmore East on February 11th and 12th, 1969. It was the biggest event in Eastern rock at that point in the year, and the media was waiting, along with legions of fans.

The first song got only fair response, but things improved when Janis did the Chantells' old hit "Maybe" and "Summertime" from the *Cheap Thrills* album. Janis' hair was flying like a dervish and her long fingers were showing white, clenching a hand mike. "To Love Somebody" was overdone, and so was a new song, "Jazz for the Jack-Offs." The distance between singer and band had never been more apparent. She closed fairly strongly, however, with a then-new Nick Gravenites song. "Work Me Lord."

Later, during an interview Janis kept interrupting the questions with her own interjections. "Hey, I've never sung so great! Don't you think I'm singing better? Well, Jesus, fucking Christ, I'm really better, believe me."

Reporter Paul Nelson observed: "One gets the alarming feeling that Joplin's whole world is precariously balanced on what happens to her musically – that the necessary degree of honest cynicism needed to survive an all-media assault may be buried too far under the immensely likeable but tremendously underconfident naivete."

By the middle of March, 1969, things had not improved much, and word was that Grossman was asking astronomical amounts for a Joplin appearance. In his column of March 24th, in the San Francisco Chronicle, Ralph J. Gleason wrote: "It was almost impossible to believe it but the fact was that in her first appearance here with her own group, after all the national publicity and all the tremendous sales of her album with Big Brother and the Holding Company, her opening night audience at Winterland did not bring her back for an encore.

"Her new band is a drag. They can play OK but they are a pale version of the Memphis-Detroit bands from the rhythm & blues shows and Janis, though in good voice, seems bent on becoming Aretha Franklin. The best things they did were the things which were most like her songs with Big Brother . . .

"The best things that could be done would be for her to scrap this band and go right back to being a member of Big Brother . . . (if they'll have her)."

In the April 19 issue of *Rolling Stone*, Random Notes reported: "The whole Janis Joplin hype has grown to outrageous proportions, whereby impossible goals have been established for her. No singer could deliver an absolute organ with every phrase – not Billie Holiday, not Edith Piaf, not Aretha – and yet somehow Janis is supposed to."

In May, 1969, the British pop newspaper Melody Maker carried an interview with Joplin. The following is an excerpt:

"Janis was to have been on the cover of Newsweek . . . but General Eisenhower's death had elbowed her out. [She was shown the discarded Newsweek cover photo and] in quick succession came a display of pleasure at the way the photo came out and anger at the fact it wouldn't be seen. She grasped it in her hands, stared at it for an instant, stamped her tiny foot bullet-like into the . . . floor and swung a clenched fist skywards. A stream of devastating curses accompanied the action. 'God-dammit, you mother – #&131 You %!' And swinging round to appeal to the gathering. 'Fourteen heart attacks and he had to die in my week. In MY week'."

In August, Janis turned in a great performance at the Atlantic City Pop Festival in New Jersey, and in September her attorney considered bringing suit against a television actress for an ad hype. In November her *Kozmic Blues* album was released to generally favorable reviews. The vocal excesses seemed to have been under control, and the material "Maybe," "Try," "Little Girl Blue," "Kozmic Blues" and "As Good As You've Been to This World" was considered "better."

The Revue played its last gig in Madison Square Garden on December 29th, and the next day, Janis announced she'd "gotten together" with Joe Namath, and dedicated her concert to him. Following the concert Clive Davis threw an elegant party for her at his Central Park West apartment and Bob Dylan, one of her old idols, showed up.

On March 4, 1970, she was fined $200 (in absentia) in a court in Tampa, Florida after having been found guilty of using profane language during a concert the previous year. Janis had reportedly screamed at police who were trying to keep teen-agers from dancing.

On March 20 she announced from a hotel in Rio de Janeiro that "I'm going into the jungle with a big bear of a beatnik named David Niehaus. I finally remembered I don't have to be on stage 12 months a year. I've decided to go and dig some other jungles for a couple of weeks." Janis met Niehaus in Rio, where she'd gone as part of a three-month vacation. When she returned, she got two tattoos, one on her wrist, and one over her heart. "A little something for the boys," she said.

In mid-April Janis appeared with Big Brother and the Holding Company's reformed band (Nick Gravenites had been added to the old members; Sam Andrew was also back with them), at the Fillmore West. She did all of her old numbers, even "Easy Rider" from the Mainstream album and "Cuckoo" from *Cheap Thrills*. "We're really dredgin' up the past for ya, folks," Janis chuckled.

The band was much better technically than they'd ever been, but, as in the old days, it was Janis that the crowd wanted. She reportedly allowed a blind person to touch her.

On June 12 she and her new band, Full-Tilt Boogie, debuted at Freedom Hall in Louisville, Kentucky. There were only 4,000 persons in attendance in the monster indoor stadium, but the show was a knock-out. As soon as Janis began her living introduction to "Try" – "Honey if you've had your eye on a piece of talent and that chick down the road has been getting all the action, then you know what you gotta, do . . . "*Try*, just a little bit harder!" – the crowd began dancing and screaming. "I permit them to dance," she told a burly guard who tried to repress some of the audience.

The Boogie band's members include John Till, lead guitar and Brad Campbell, bass, both of whom were with her in the Revue. The new members are Richard Bell, piano, a former Ronnie Hawkins sideman, and Clark Pierson, a drummer Janis found in a North Beach topless bar.

Everyone who saw them agreed that Janis had finally assembled a band that could back her, who could provide the push she felt she needed.

Her last appearance with them was at Harvard Stadium on August 12th, before 40,000 people. Both Janis and the band then went into recording sessions in Los Angeles. Her album with the new group had been tentatively scheduled for a November or December release date.

Janis Joplin's last public appearance anywhere was in September. She showed up in Port Arthur, Texas for the 10th annual reunion of her graduating class of 1960, Thomas Jefferson High School. She wore flowing blue and pink feathers in her hair, purple and white satin and velvet with gold embroidery, sandals and painted toenails, and rings and bracelets enough for a Babylonian whore.

Janis and entourage swept into the Goodhue Hotel's drab Petroleum Room and commandeered the bar. When she asked for vodka (she'd switched to gin and vodka from Southern Comfort about a year ago), the bartender said he had nothing but bourbon and scotch. "God," she said. "Somebody go out and get a bottle of vodka."

Port Arthur has never seen the like of her.

Last December Janis had finally escaped her adopted city, where she'd lived in the Haight-Ashbury across from Buena Vista Park and Hippie Hill and, later, on Noe Street near the southern tip of downtown San Francisco. She found a hideaway home in Larkspur, across the Golden Gate Bridge, three or four towns into Marin County.

Larkspur is one of those pleasant little places. The freeway
leads comfortably into a small shopping center; the homes are
respectable, middle class. Then, somewhere, you make a left turn
and several roads take you into the woods. Baltimore Avenue is
one of those roads, its width narrowed by huge trees that block its
way now and again. Janis' house was at the end of Baltimore.

It's hidden away more by its appearance than by its location.
It's right there in front of you, behind the rounded off end of the
road. Short, A-framed, shingled, modern, comfortable in a forest
of tall trees that keep everything but the wind away. You can't
even hear the sound of kids at Larkspur School, just up the road
and a few blocks over.

The house is unidentified. A Yuban coffee can is nailed to a
front post. "This is a temporary mail box," it is labeled, and
someone has added, "Temporary Hell." Near the adjacent garage, two dogs are wandering around. A TV cameraman waves his
light meter at the air, then pans his camera from the wooden stairs
near the garage that lead into the woods. He pans across the
house, to the fence Janis had had constructed to keep burglars
away.

This wasn't a very private or a very quiet house for Janis and
the girl friends who stayed there. The place was burglarized
several times, and Janis and her clothesmaker/friend, Lindall
Erb, lost furnishings, jewelry, and other valuables. Several
months ago, Janis had a party there that resulted in complaints
from the neighbors. Cars clogged the road all the way up
Baltimore Avenue, and the music blared out of that shingled
megaphone as far as the cars went.

Now the TV cameraman is back in his car – one of three cars
parked facing the house. A high school girl is seated 100 feet
away, watching. "I came here from Mill Valley to pay my
tribute," she said. "I'm just an acquaintance. I came by once
and gave her a bottle of tequila and it got her off . . ."

Up the road, two neighbors, grandmotherly women, are talking. They're saying something about "overdose" to a couple of
kids on bicycles. One of the women talks with a smirk. "Oh, did
she have parents? . . . There was a lot of noise when the band was

practicing – if you call it a band . . . We never talked to her. She just ran down and ran up again in her car."

"I don't think we'll make the 7 o'clock news," the other, named Betsy, says with a laugh.

Inside the house, it's quite. One man, a member of Janis' second band – the one after Big Brother – steps out to get something from his car. Lindall is in L.A., he says. She left the night before, when she heard the news. The people in the home are friends of Lindall's. And no one wants to talk.

The two old ladies have stopped looking at the TV man, and they're discussing reupholstering an old couch sitting in Betsy's front yard.

Road Rats & Dodgy Boilers

Mark Timlin

.

It's 1971 and The Who are on tour in America. We're all convinced we're delivering a blow for the counter-culture, but the counter-culture's about on its last legs and all we're really doing is paving the way for the corporate rock that's to come. We've all been away from home for weeks and life on the road is taking its toll. That particular day we've travelled from New Orleans in Louisiana, to Austin, Texas. It's not much of a haul for the equipment trucks, unlike some other overnights we've had to do on the itinerary, but even so, a couple of us road crew have stowed away on the plane the band use, and which is known to one and all as Cocaine Central.

The main reason we decided to fly not drive, is that we pulled a couple of groupies after the gig in The Big Easy. A right couple of dodgy boilers, one called Feather, who's all patchouli oil, kohled up eyes, velvet and lace, with ripped stockings and Joan Crawford fuck me shoes with five inch heels. The other, a blonde from the mid-west, is always dressed as a milkmaid with pigtails and a denim dress with a little apron, had found religion and acid all on the same day or maybe vice-versa and now gives all and sundry blow-jobs for Jesus. Her name's MaryLou and later on she followed the band to England, but that's a whole another story. The pair of them fancied hooking up with us, so the next morning we caught a ride to the airport and joined the scrum boarding the Boeing and made camp at the rear of the plane with the two girls, a bottle of Southern Comfort, some cheap speed and bag of grass. Straw hat covering his face, Marlboro burning in one hand, and cowboy-booted feet on the bulkhead is my pal Jimmy. Unlike me, he's a *real* roadie who can re-string a guitar, re-wire an amp, and strip down a Chevy small block engine at he drop of a spanner. A native Texan, thin as a whip, six foot six in his heels and about seven foot in that hat, a few years older than I and a couple of centuries wiser, he's been to Vietnam but doesn't want to talk about it. I roll him joints, and make him laugh with my London accent.

But that day I'm not on joint-rolling duty. The girls are there to do that. In those days that's what they did.

Instead I cut out a few lines on the back of a metal flight attache case and everyone takes a beep. As she's bending awkwardly over the case I stick my hand up Feather's skirt. She doesn't wear knickers. To my English sensibility this is anarchy indeed, for although I'd met many women of loose virtues back home, Feather was the first one I'd ever known to walk around with no underpinnings ever. Jimmy of course is vastly amused at this. In Saigon on R&R if I believed what he'd told me one of the few times I got him out of it and talking about his war experiences, none of the whores he met wore anything under the slit skirted dresses.

"Shit," I told him, "I wished I'd been there with you."

"No you don't," he replied, suddenly sober.

Anyhow, me and Feather started fooling around, and Jimmy took MaryLou to the toilet for some unnamed debauchery, so I slid my fingers up into Feather and she got off, and she promised me a good time later, and sashayed off down the aisle to talk to anyone else that would talk to her, and I imagine by the time she got back I wasn't the only one waiting for a good time that night. But that's a whole other story too.

So the plane touches down at Austin airport and there's a bunch of fans dancing around at the edge of the tarmac being held back by sweating cops, and the temperature's about one-twenty in the shade, but thank God the promoter's laid on a load of Cadillac and Lincoln limos, because by this time the band won't travel in the same car together, and there's animosity between the sound and light guy and they won't ride together either, so the tour manager made sure there were cars to spare to transport the entourage to the hotel.

Jimmy, Feather, MaryLou and me are first off the plane and hijack a Caddy and off we go down the road to town and Feather gives me the blow job on the way, and she opens the tinted side window so's all the truckers we pass get a good view of her doing the biz, but by then we're all so zonked, nobody cares.

That night we're booked into one of those chain hotels that dot America from coast to coast. Walk into your room in Austin and you could be in New York, LA or Milwaukee. Built to the same pattern, the rooms, foyers and bars all identical. The interiors are delivered by truck, slotted into place in a concrete shell like a jigsaw puzzle, and can be taken apart the same way. All you need is a special tool that fits all the nuts and bolts that hold the place together. Jimmy tells me all this as we're checking in the first night we shared a room at the start of the tour. Before his spell in the army, it transpires he'd been a rigger for the company. When he was drafted he did the unforgivable; hung onto the multi-faceted tool and now carries it with him everywhere on his belt. Jimmy looks around this reception area of the Austin, Texas branch of the chain with satisfaction. Keith Moon, as if anyone needs telling, the drummer with the band and the craziest man in rock, had been driving everyone mad with his tricks over the past few weeks and generally making crew life a misery. Jimmy has decided to exact a small revenge. We will not, he informs me, be attending that afternoon's sound check at the local civic forum because "We've got other fish to fry."

We check into our room, smuggling the girls through the fire door at the back of the hotel and up the back stairs, then I go for ice from the machine and we drink Southern Comfort on the rocks out of plastic glasses from the bathroom. Only two, so we have to share. Once we ascertain we're the only members of the troupe still in situ, Jimmy unsnaps the sheath on his belt, pulls out the purloined tool and we head for *chez* Moon. The girls stay behind with orders to roll up enough joints to last us the evening and not finish the speed. Keith's room has the same layout as the rest: two three-quarter sized beds, a built in wardrobe, a sideboard bolted to the wall, a chest of drawers, TV, fridge, table, chair and one bedside cabinet, complete with telephone and

Gideon Bible. Facing us as we enter are the glass doors onto the balcony; to our left, the bathroom.

It takes Jimmy less time to get in with his magic tool than it would using a key.

At the nod from Jimmy, I scoop up Moon's stuff and stash inside the wardrobe with the bedclothes. Meanwhile, Jimmy wrestles the mattresses into the bathroom and starts breaking down the beds. I throw the TV, fridge, table, chair, bedside cabinet, pictures and telephone into the bathroom with the bits of bed Jimmy has dismantled. When the room is empty we pull up the carpet, and stash that in the bathroom too. Then Jimmy starts taking the room itself apart. The sideboard just about fills up the bathroom, so I draw back the curtains and open the doors to the balcony. Boiling Texas air swirls in as Jimmy starts stripping the ceiling, the walls and finally the floor from the fabric of the building.

After a couple of hours we stand bathed in sweat in a bare concrete cube, the floor now about eighteen inches beneath the level of the doors. I carefully close the balcony doors and pull the curtains. We shake hands solemnly, declare ourselves well pleased with our handiwork and go down to the bar. By this time the band are making their way back from the soundcheck. John, Pete and Roger come in with their minders and go to their rooms. Then Keith arrives. Alone. By this time, so bad is his rep, that the management find it hard to get anyone to be Moon's personal roadie. So he's started travelling with the crew, which only leads to more problems as he often gets them so out of it, they find it hard to rig the show, which means Keith often ends up all on his lonesome. So when Jimmy gives him a shout Keith is happy to join us for a drink before we all get ready for the gig.

When it's about that time we split. Up on the fifth floor Keith searches for his key. Jimmy and I hover in the corridor chatting about nothing. Keith definitely smells a rat. He gives us a wink, carefully opens the door, reaches in and switches on the light. Halfway through the doorway he sees what's wrong, and his jaw drops.

Even by his standards this is expert vandalism. He is well

impressed. He swears fulsomely, jumps down into the well of the room and gazes round, declares himself happy with the deal, takes the phone out of the bathroom, plugs it in and summons the manager. Keith meanwhile has phoned round and there's quite a crowd waiting in the corridor when the hotel big cheese steams out of the lift and gives us all a filthy look.

Keith lays on his best phony aristocratic British accent and informs the manager that something is amiss with his accommodation. The manager, a sneer on his face, throws the door open, marches in, and promptly pitches face down onto the hard concrete over a foot below. As he lies there, blood streaming from his nose, Keith looks down at him. "My good man," he booms with patrician hauter much to the appreciation of the crowd. "I think you'd better fetch me another room . . ."

"Hello, I'm Marc Bolan. I'm a Superstar. You'd Better Believe it."

Charles Shaar Murray

Cream, May 1972

TYRANNOSAURUS Rex rose out of the sad and scattered leaves of an older summer. During the hard grey winter they were tended and strengthened by those who love them. They blossomed with the coming of spring, children rejoiced and the earth sang with them. It will be a long and ecstatic summer.

John Peel, 1968,
sleeve note to first Tyrannosaurus Rex *album*

T.Rex are the new Beatles, the teen idols of the seventies, and the biggest pop sensation in years. Now they are verged on international success, following the most exciting succession of chart hits since the days of Bill Haley and Lennon and McCartney.

Blurb to Melody Maker *special* Bolan!

Once again, rock and roll madness has settled over the nation, and someone has reintroduced frenzy and hysteria into a section of the musical environment ruled almost exclusively by the Middle of the Road, Dawn, the balladeers and the Jonathan King Karma Squad. People had realized that it was close on ten years since "Love Me Do" and the psychological need for a new Beatles had become so bad that they were even touting The Bay City Rollers for the part. After all, they went down well in Scotland. A stronger child was required, and despite initial disbelief, what we got was Marc Bolan.

Marc Bolan, superstar. A star is someone who we know about, but a superstar is someone *everybody* knows about – your parents, the milkman, your bank manager, everybody. With a double-page spread in the *Daily Mirror*, Marc Bolan is property as public as no one has really been since those halcyon days of 1964, when we all waited, tense and nervous, on the verge of some great discovery, conscious that Jones and Jagger and Lennon and McCartney were about to lead us to some new places.

To the most important group of people in the country – the adolescents and pre-adolescents – Bolan is more than a superstar, he's a superhero. He's not even a symbol of some force or power or concept; he *is* it, he's the main man. And it makes me laugh, because I can remember 1968 when Tyrannosaurus Rex was a £15 acoustic guitar and a pair of ripped-off bongos, something John Peel kept rambling on about and who couldn't get on TV.

Tyrannosaurus Rex should be stamped out, along with their gaseous aider and abetter, John Peel.
Reader's letter to Melody Maker, *1968*

Bolan's improbable journey from the most esoteric of the esoteric to the very toppermost of the poppermost seems logical when viewed through the lens of hindsight, but if you had said four years ago that Marc Bolan would be the biggest thing in British rock you would have been advised to have a good lie down until you felt better. The only person who would not have laughed himself sick was Marc Bolan.

From acoustic freebies in Hyde Park to Wembley's Empire Pool in four years, flat. A rags-to-riches story in the best Horatio Alger tradition. All that happened was that Bolan added more and more technology, more and more instruments, more and more sounds and production, and when the necessary level of electrical energy had been built up, all hell broke loose. Rock and roll madness, verily.

What's more, hardly anyone saw it coming. 1968 was the year

of the heavy electric summer. "Wheels Of Fire", Joe Cocker, Julie Driscoll, Brian Auger, Arthur Brown, and the blues boom, and the music of Bolan and bongo player Steve Peregrine Took was a welcome clearing in the thick, heavy electric jungle. "'Deborah' sold 750 the first day and it blew my mind," said Bolan. Any gentle freak who believed that Nostradamus and King Arthur were alive and well in a UFO hovering somewhere over Glastonbury Tor, or who read Tolkien and Moorcock over his brown rice and apple juice, just had to own the Tyrannosaurus Rex albums, they were essential. "My People Were Fair And Had Sky In Their Hair, But Now They're Content To Wear Stars On Their Brows" and "Prophets Seers And Sages, The Angels Of The Ages", in terms of heroics and headlines they mattered not at all, but they sold enough to keep Marc and Steve Took warm and functioning. Eventually they started going out for £150 a night on the college circuit (one social sec. told the *MM* "We book anyone John Peel likes") and they got bagged with the Incredible String Band.

"What happened was that when we started, 'Layers Of The Onion' had come out and they were considered to be something very funky, and they were getting a lot of press. No one had ever heard of us, so I immediately said to people, hey man, don't compare us with the Incredible String Band, who were beginning to be big and no one had ever heard of us. So I in fact cultivated a battle between the two and in fact we did become bigger, but it was very deliberate, and I was very aware of the two things. I only did it because we *weren't* similar."

So, as time went on, Bolan got more and more involved with the complexities of electric rock. After the departure of Steve Peregrine Took, Bolan linked up with Micky Finn, percussionist, painter, former leader of a Mod band called The Blue Men and one-time Pill King. The resulting single, "The King Of The Rumbling Spires", and album, *Beard Of Stars*, backed up Bolan's mythological speculations with the tougher support of newly acquired Fenders and Gibsons – and a £12 chord organ from Woolworth's. Finally, the abbreviation from Tyrannosaurus Rex to plain T. Rex so that even Tony Blackburn could pronounce it, the big hit single that made the charts with a bullet and all manner of pandemonium. The cream on the cake was the addition of a bassist and drummer. That's how it's done.

I've never seen so many beautiful fourteen-year-old girls in my life as at the T.Rex Wembley concert. You go through into that big, concrete slaughterhouse and they're all milling around buying Bolan books, Bolan posters, "official Marc Bolan sashes" whatever *they* are, rip-offs of every description, fake programmes, greasy old creeps touting tickets at only twice the regular price, rock and roll madness. And all Marc's children are there – weekend dropout hippieboppers meticulously dressed in Early Roundhouse; a sprinkling of skinheads; bemused mums firmly clutching their primary-school-age tots by the wrists; a few older groovers come to check it all out and maybe get laid, looking incredibly uneasy; some short-haired Members Of The Public, and most self-conscious of all, the kids in the white shirts and dark trousers and bulging duffle bags that indicate they've come *straight from school* – the shame of it all! The biggest and best gig yet and they can't even dress up.

It's a whole new world and I feel like a sixth-former sitting at the second-year dinner table. I'm fascinated by Marc's children – is that skinhead *really* wearing glitter under his eyes? – and I'm wandering about digging the people when suddenly this kid, who's no way over fourteen, is standing next to me looking down at my boots and mumbling "Got any speed?" I send him away with the proverbial flea in his ear, but five minutes later there's three others with the same request. I ask why they think I'm a dealer, and the spokesman points to my briefcase, left over from school days and plastered with promotional stickers. "They all carry cases, man . . ." If I look so suspicious I feel I'd better split before The Man gets interested, because dope dealing is no way for a nice Jewish boy like me to make a living.

Possibly one of the most encouraging aspects of Bolanoia is that T. Rex's audience comes from right across the board – skinheads, straights, freaks alike, and this is what makes him anathema to the cultural elitist division of the rock audience. Heavy rock sociology decrees that if you don't like the audience, you can't like the band, and to sit in the same audience as turns up for a Bolan gig is only fractionally less odious than to *play* to them.

Also, there ain't 'arf a lot of 'em, and if that many people dig a band, there must be something wrong with them, which is why any luckless "underground" band who attempt to raise the standard of radio rock are branded as teenybopper sell-outs by the kind of people who had to wait until 1968, when it became chic to say that Brian Wilson was a genius, before they could admit that they liked The Beach Boys. It should be superfluous to point out that The Beatles, The Stones, The Who, Jimi Hendrix, The Yardbirds, Phil Spector and if you want to get technical, Bessie Smith, Robert Johnson and all the others who recorded before the invention of the long-playing record, began their careers (and changed quite a few heads into the bargain) on singles. But that makes no difference to the kind of oneupman so brilliantly caricatured on the Cheech and Chong album: "No, man, I'm not into . . . AM."

Inside, the stage is dominated by a ten-foot-high cut-out of the Electric Warrior tearing into his Les Paul, and two posters of him waving his white Start. Onstage, Rosko is rapping away at a fantastic rate of watts, fast AM nonsense, unstoppable flow of words. He plays The Drifters'' "Saturday Night At The Movies" and the people sing along. He brings on Quiver, who play a pleasant set, laid-back and funky, Cal Batchelor and Tim Renwick playing some of the sweetest interlocking double lead you ever heard in your life. Bolan will later become indignant at any suggestion that the cut-out is inhibiting or distasteful to Quiver, but it seems a cheap and nasty gesture on someone's part, an unnecessary way to ensure that Bolan's presence hangs over the stage even with him still in the dressing-room.

I'm having difficulty coping with the local geography of the Empire Pool, and by the time I reach my seat, I find a clump of little girls – very young, subteenyboppers – in and around it. When I request them to move, they glance at one another and then unanimously shake their heads. I'm gratified that the younger generation has such an admirable disrespect for the property/

territory ethic, but annoyed that my steely-eyed demeanour and casual authority meet with nothing but a flurry of giggles. Dignity outraged, I stick around until Quiver quit the stage to a polite rustle of friendly applause. They have acquitted themselves well tonight, but they'd be kidding themselves if they think that the audience will remember them when they leave, or even recognize the name the day after. But for now, they've pleased a tough and callous audience, if only momentarily.

Interval time. A bit of prowling around in the grimy corridor and a quick hit of alcohol in the bar. Back in the bullring, Rosko is playing Betty Wright's "Cleanup Woman" and explaining that he was asked to play it by Marc himself. He then announces that the next time you see him he'll be introducing T.Rex. *Yeeek!*

The stage is swarming with roadies and lesser minions. When a roadie scuttles on with an armful of guitars, there's a mass intake of breath from all over the hall. Even for a heretic, the tension is extraordinary. The air is humming with nine thousand people hardly daring to breathe because any second now . . .

Yes! There's Rosko and you can't even hear him because they're all screaming, and I needn't have worried about regaining my seat because the three little girls and half the others surrounding us have all hugged each other, squealed and rushed the stage. Bill Legend behind the drum kit, Steve Currie strolling on casually with his Fender Precision bass and his bright red pants, Micky Finn leaping at his battery of conga drums as if it were a month since he'd seen them and not the two hours since he'd beaten them into submission at the 5.30 house, and then on bops the man of the moment, the little guy who used to sit on the floor going "Oochie-coochie-tie-dye, do the one inch rock." It's only Marc Bolan whom Chris Welch used to call the Bopping Imp and the National Elf, and here's what looks like half the jailbait in London rushing the stage as he picks up a well-worn Les Paul and launches into – what?

Much has been written about Bolan's sexual status with his fans (and T. Rex are one of the very few bands today that really have "fans"). Michael Watts has written that Bolan is a romantic rather than a sexual figure, but some of Bolan's lyrics indicate otherwise. Personally, I rather dig the idea of a very young female audience taking home records with lyrics like "I'm gonna suck you" (from "Jeepster"), "Girl I really dig your breasts" (from "Raw Ramp", the B-side of "Get It On") and "Let's do it like we're friends" (from "Jewel" on the *T. Rex* album), not to mention "She ain't no witch and I love the way she twitch" (from "Hot Love") and all the assorted orgasmic gasps and sighs of "Take me!" that crop up all over "Electric Warrior". It bodes well for the future, despite the fact that a significant proportion of Marc's young Bolanoids wouldn't really know what to do with him if they found him one night tucked up in their beds.

The only parts of Bolan's repertoire which had then reached my ears were the old stuff I used to hear on the radio in 1968 and the big hit singles exposed via Radio One, *Top of the Pops* and the jukebox of my local boozer. His first number is unfamiliar to me, but I'm having difficulty hearing it anyway. The kids are being loud, the PA is shitty, and, besides, I'm not really listening, I'm watching. I've never been to a gig even remotely like this and yet it all seems familiar. Racial memory. Then it hits me, it's the Shea Stadium movie all over again. Seated high up in the stands, with fifty-seven varieties of total hysteria all around me, I feel a strange sense of peace like standing on the top of a Cornish cliff watching the waves roll in . . . "sittin' on the dock of the bay . . .".

So I sit and watch finely formed little rivulets and currents of people coalesce into breakers, to surge up to the cliff top on which Bolan and his buddies are grinding their way through "Cadillac", shatter, retreat and reform, return. Rock and roll madness. And with that sense of utter stillness. I realize that rock has reached its third stage, that with Bolan and T. Rex and all these weird little children, the circle game has begun again. Rock and roll lives, stands, continues. The circle is unbroken.

We can't go back we can only look behind from where we came, going round and round and round in the circle game.

Joni Mitchell

The number ends. Bolan surveys all that he has mastered. "Rock on," he says. He announces "Jeepster" and we're all off again. One guy in the next row is having a bad time. He's tall and skinny and fair-haired, physically totally unsuited to being a Bolan, so he's cut his hair short on top and let it grow into long, thin wisps onto his shoulders, turned into a passable Rod Stewart, the next best thing. He's hopelessly pissed or on downers or just overcome by the occasion, and can't stand up, he's falling about all over the place, and his mates, all of whom look as if they'd be more at home in the Shed, are trying to help him, hold him up, but he just mutters something incomprehensible and turns over and I move my briefcase, my dope dealer's briefcase, in case he falls on it, and Marc's children are storming the stage again.

Between numbers they clap rhythms, and when the band play the crowd have to adjust their beat to Bolan's ("It's terrible, it really is, you just have to shut your ears to it"). When he sends the other three offstage and sits, cross-legged, on the stage to pick his Epiphone jumbo, the mood changes to one of awe and expectancy. The little girls are quiet now as Bolan plays "Cosmic Dancer", one of his better new songs. Though the PA makes his acoustic strumming sound tinny and scratchy and his voice floats out over the congregation:

> *I was dancing when I was twelve . . .*
> *I danced myself right out the womb*
> *Is it strange to dance so soon*
> *I danced myself into the tomb . . .*

A strange, circular, reincarnation song, its protagonist forever dancing himself from womb to tomb to womb. In Empire Pool, I'm impressed. Whenever Bolan does one of his little gasps or sighs, the little girls squeal. He does another song, and then Finn joins him with a pair of bongos for one more. Then it's back to the electricity and Legend and Currie return to get their teeth into "Telegram Sam" and "Hot Love". By now I'm focused enough to start evaluating the playing and they sound rough. Without Bolan's multiple guitars and Tony Visconti's strings, it's all bare and thin, but Marc's children don't mind. As long as they can shriek along with him during the middle part of "Hot Love", what do they care? Later they will begin to evolve standards and perceptions as we did with The Beatles and The Stones or Hendrix and Cream or Berry and Holly or Coltrane and Parker. But right now it's enough to shriek. And why not?

And now it's time for the big finish, folks! as T. Rex unveil the extended version of "Get It On". Again, without Ian McDonald's saxes and Rick Wakeman's piano and Tony Visconti's strings and Bolan's other two guitars, it's not up to expectations and Finn and Currie's backup vocals ain't no way as good as Howard Kaylan and Mark Volman, but Bolan rushes through the song and then freaks out, he drops into a squat, puts a white Stratocaster – *a white Stratocaster*, Marc, you tamper with powerful ghosts doing that – between his legs and belabours it with a tambourine. It sounds horrible and meanwhile Finn is leaping about at stage front throwing little plastic tambourines into the throng, which devours them with a terrible hunger.

When it's over, Bolan and the boys split to an aggrieved howl. The sound of T.Rex's audience is something new and frightful to me. When Rod Stewart struts out to sing it's "'Ello mate – 'ave a drink and give us a song then"; for Chuck Berry it's love and affection and gratitude; for The Dead it's a sense of real joy, and sure it's vociferous, but it's a friendly admiration, a collaboration with Dead and people working together to produce the best possible mutual high. But the Bolan audience have a different cry, *Iwannit-Iwannit-Iwannit* they yell, *Gimme gimme gimme!*

So Rosko comes back out and does his showbiz thing and T. Rex troop back out for their encore. They do "Summertime Blues", which was on the "White Swan" maxi-single. On its release, Mick Farren reviewed it in *I.T.* as follows: "A while back I made a terrible recording of 'Summertime Blues.' Now T. Rex have made a really horrible version. *'Can't help you son cos you're too young to vote.'* Of course he can't help you, you're five years old and mentally retarded."

They don't play it very well. Of course they're shagged out after a hard set, but only Bolan's unmistakable voice distinguishes it from a church hall support band. "The reason I do it is because once you've done . . . um . . . your own thing and you've hit a peak which . . . I hate encores, and it's like a non-encore, it's like a vehicle for the kids to really hang out, it gives them something that they know, that's the only reason I use it . . . I don't like encores, and I don't always do them either, because I consider like we end with 'Get It On' normally, and I consider that a great ender, and I don't know how to top that man. Visually I can't do any more than that. Probably the only way to top it is to come out and play on my own. In fact the impact . . . but that would kill . . . it's like concert two, you've got to do another concert after that, which is twelve encores, which is three hours in. No, it does, because you want to play more, you see, so 'Summertime Blues' I use as a thing for the kids to get off on, they don't have to think too much about it, which is cool. I don't have to think . . . and it allows me . . . each time we always play it differently, and they know it . . . it's just a title of a song, a sequence and a riff that people know automatically. It's just a vehicle . . . we used to do 'Honey Don't' at one point . . . encores are a drag. Hendrix never did an encore in his life."

Finally the house lights go on and the Pool disgorges its prey, some of whom buy, on the way out, the Bolan paraphernalia that they rejected on the way in. The place is full of cute little people looking for other cute little people, and as I don't in the wildest stretches of anybody's imagination classify as a cute little person, I wave one of my magic bits of paper and waft myself past the massed OAPs who act as security and I'm . . . backstage.

In the pressroom I see clustered round the bar and outlying tables a variety of journalists and celebrities. Bernie Taupin striding around in his latest pair of earrings. Bolan's parents, the subjects earlier that week of an excruciatingly banal *Record Mirror* interview by Valerie Mabbs, are there looking faintly bemused but ecstatically proud and happy. Chris Charlesworth from the *MM*, the first man to spot that famous pair of pink panties being flung at the stage, is holding forth at the bar. "Did he eat them then or later?" asks a disgruntled colleague. Valerie Mabbs doesn't seem to want to talk to me, so I engulf some chicken sandwiches, do my best to exhaust the bar's supplies of rum and swap reactions with Steve Peacock from *Sounds* and Tony Tyler from *NME*. Drink drink talk talk.

Enter Bolan sweaty and grinning. He's stockier than I would have imagined, stubbly, harder looking than that almost frightening androgynous beauty he had on the *Beard Of Stars* album cover. With him is B.P. Fallon, known to all as "Beep", Bolan's right-hand man and "information roadie". The Electric Warrior hugs his parents and begins to circulate. I am buttonholed by a quietly demented painter who has some crazed notion of getting the government to sponsor a cartoon film he's working on by getting Bolan to appear in it to preach against drug-taking among the young. "Tell me," he asks, "is Marc and the group on drugs?"

So, in the days that followed I did a lot of thinking about the forces that had been revealed to me. I set about obtaining all the Tyrannosaurus Rex and T. Rex records and I took them home and listened to them all repeatedly, much to the fury of the people I live with. Armed with these, photostats of most of Bolan's recent reviews and cuttings, and the *MM* special (terrible production, embarrassingly bad) and *RM* special (long on information, short on good writing), I moved into the cans to investigate the gradual process of change that led from "Deborah" to "Electric Warrior".

What's apparent right from the start is that Bolan's claim that he has always been a rock and roller is not as absurd as it first sounds. Even on the very first album there are rock and roll songs, or what would be rock and roll songs if played by an electric rock band. "Hot Rod Mama" played electrically would sound like a speeded-up version of Dylan's "From A Buick Six", for instance. "Say something like 'Chateau On Virginia Waters' or one of those tracks, 'Mustang Ford'. If Led Zeppelin did 'Mustang Ford' it would sound just like Led Zeppelin. I mean like Chateau On 'Virginia Waters' done by Elton John would sound like an Elton John song. The only thing was that my

tempos were out with traditional music – you know, rock and roll.
I had no backbeat to what I did, it was all jangly. But I didn't have
– you got to state it for people, man, and I didn't because I'd
never played with a drummer."

Bolan had, in fact, done an abortive stint in John's Children,
which produced the legendary "Desdemona". Tyrannosaurus
Rex was an acoustic band simply because John's Children's
record company, Track, had taken back Bolan's guitars and amps
when he left the band. "With John's Children I had my shit
together so we only ever did four songs on stage. We only did a
tour of Germany with The Who, we did a twenty-minute spot. It
was total smash-up media . . . I used to drag amplifiers across the
stage. All that John's Children were at that period were what I am
now. I'm only doing the same thing I wanted to do then."

Mick Farren once wrote of Bob Dylan that he'd always wanted
to be Elvis Presley, but as there was a vacancy for a Woody
Guthrie he took the gig. Marc Bolan wanted to be Jimi Hendrix,
but found himself cast as a Robin Williamson.

Those first two Tyrannosaurus Rex albums weren't really very
good. Only a few of the songs stand out (like the brilliant
"Strange Orchestras" and "Child Star" which had a good tune),
but due to Bolan's enunciation (or lack of it) and the absence of a
lyric sheet, it's hard to tell what he's going on about, and the
drabness of the production makes it tiresome to listen to just as
sound. In 1969 Bolan told Peter Frame of *Zigzag* that the
production was indeed "very bad. It was the first album Tony
Visconti had ever produced and it was done at Advision on an 8-
track – the first in the country – and they didn't know how to use
it. The stereo was awful. When we were doing it, it sounded good,
but when it was on a record, it sounded very thin and nasty."

The first turning point came with *Unicorn*. Between them
Bolan and Took handled vocals, guitars, harmonium, lip organ,
fonofiddle, bongos, African talking drums, bass guitar, piano,
drum kit, assorted percussion, pixiephone and gong, a far cry
from the simple guitar and bongos they started out with. "I'm
really into Phil Spector. When we did *Unicorn*, the whole of
Unicorn, it was in fact technically a cross between 'Pet Sounds'

all the Phil Spector things. And nobody got it, man, at the time. You listen to the drum sound on 'She Was Born To Be My Unicorn', it's totally a Phil Spector drum sound. It's all Phil Spector, the whole album, and no one knew what I was doing at the time."

Unicorn was the first Tyrannosaurus Rex album that I could comfortably listen to. Bolan and Visconti had learned to use the studios properly; *Romany Soup* had twenty-two tracks on it and took five hours to mix. The album's opening cut, "Chariots Of Silk", is, to this day, one of the best things Bolan has ever done, drum riff straight out of The Ronettes' "I Wonder" contrasting strangely with its strange landscape, full of Mages and Bards and the Huntress: "Chariots of silk she rode/stallions of gold she owned". Depending on how seriously you take such things, Bolan's lyrics were improving. "Catblack" featured Tony Visconti playing what Bolan described as a "Runaround Sue" piano backup, teenage chord progression and all, but with lyrics that were finely constructed as well as evocative:

> *Catblack the wizard's hat*
> *Spun in lore from Dagamoor*
> *The skull of jade*
> *Was pearl inlaid*
> *The silks, skin spun, repelled the sun . . .*

Like the first album, *Unicorn* featured John Peel reading a children's story. It was Steve Took's last album with the band, and Bolan was at his wits' end because promoters assumed that the Tyrannosaurus was extinct and therefore stopped offering him gigs. Eventually he joined up with Finn and the next album, *A Beard Of Stars*, featured Bolan's reintroduction to the electric guitar. He hung out at Eric Clapton's Surrey mansion copping licks. "Because I've spent some time with him lately, the guitar on the new record sounds like Eric to me, because his whole vibe is within me," he told Pete Frame.

Bolan's technical command of his instrument was shaky, and therefore he could not and cannot to this day rely on being

Captain Speedfingers, dazzling the punters with absolutely nothing played at fantastic velocity. Bolan's electric guitar leads are,
like those of nearly every other contemporary player, strongly
Hendrix influenced, but unlike all those who copy the screams
and the feedback and the electronic holocausts, he uses the sweet,
melodic, Little Wing's style. His leads, when he's playing good,
concentrate on tonal and melodic content, simple, clean, elegant
lines which twist and curl and end up in unexpected places.

On the other hand, when he does his practising in public and
gets into long jams, he's quite appalling, because when he's out of
ideas, there's absolutely nothing happening. "Elemental Child",
the last cut on *Beard*, is a fine example of Bolan wanking away at
great length. The song is fine ("Torch girl of the marshes/her kiss
is a whip of the moon") but the guitar solo is interminable and
sounds like any young guitarist in his local music shop going to
town on the Les Paul and Marshall 100 until the assistant comes
back.

The music was, however, getting better and the lyrics becoming less flowery. In "Organ Blues", musically a forerunner of
"Hot Love", he wrote, "We make feasties of the beasties, but the
beasties just live in the wild/You know you're slower now and you
were faster when you were a child."

"For three years I didn't do anything visually. I played sitting
down all the time, never moved, didn't move a muffle! But we had
big albums and things and were what I thought was successful at
the time till all this happened. You spoke of media earlier, and the
credibility of the band was lessened by the fact that people
associated us with Flower Power, and that was a long gone
era, and I wanted people to look at the thing in a new light,
and the only way to do that was to have a label change, and change
the music, and change the name, but not lose any identity either
way.

"I make it sound very controlled, but it wasn't at all, it all
happened in three days, and I got put on Fly Records. I didn't
choose to be there. Legally that happened because the company I
was with signed with those people, who formed Fly Records. The

music grew through three albums to what it is now, and people did all that bullshit about instant overnight electricity, which was ludicrous because it had taken two and a half years. From *Unicorn* upwards, it's very obvious."

> *As God-like I strode the forecourt a small voice hailed from a vehicle which lay mute and lifeless beneath the harsh lights. Drawing my noble sword, Renshaw, I was across the concrete in a trice to find that my tiny friends, T. Rex, were becalmed. Chuckling, I scooped them up in the palm of my hand and laid them gently on top of a soft pile of Green Stamps and bore them so to London town. As we sped straight and true to that fair city they told me of their concert tour and of the new record 'Ride A White Swan' on Fly Records. Doubtless you'll own it before long – if you don't by Christmas, my flock of highly trained hedgehogs will fan out through the land and retribution will be swift and terrible – indeed it will . . .*
> John Peel, Disc, *1970*

> *Ten pounds is a lot of money, man . . . it's a bus fare and strings for your guitar.*
> Marc Bolan, *1969*

"Ride A White Swan" made a number two and won a Silver Disc. The rhythm section of bassist Steve Currie and drummer Bill Legend were added, and the hard-rock T. Rex couldn't go wrong. For more than two years, the singles chart had been tepid and boring except for the odd Jethro Tull single, and T. Rex made consistently excellent singles. "I see no reason why freaks shouldn't be in the charts, but then they turn around and resent you for it," Bolan told Peter Frame in mid-'71, with "Hot Love" at the top for six weeks and "Get It On" awaiting release.

It's easy to tell what sound Bolan is aiming for by the tracks he leaves behind. T. Rex's music is not derivative in the sense that, say, Grand Funk's is, because though you can see where it's coming from, it is a synthesis, and all creative rock music has been a synthesis. In Bolan's head, Tolkien and Berry are collaborating on songs, which are taken to Sam Phillips' Sun Studios in Memphis with Phil Spector at the board, Eddie Cochran playing rhythm guitar, Jimi Hendrix lead, Buddy Holly up front to sing and The Ronettes somewhere at the back and Brian Wilson, David Bowie and Syd Barrett all hanging around offering advice . . .

Does it work? Make up your own mind. It's worked in that someone has revived the single as an art form. Any imbecile can furzle around for seventeen minutes and come up with some good licks, but to lay it all down in 2.15 or 3.38 or whatever is a dying trade.

The album boom was a reaction against constricting, formula singles, but as anyone who has to wade through more than a dozen new albums a week will tell you, right now we're suffering from a surfeit of amazingly tedious long-players, so anyone with a gift for producing listenable music in a concise form is very welcome, and now that singles from The Stones and The Who are few and far between, events rather than regular, punctual occurrences, T. Rex are the best singles band we've got. The art of making singles as opposed to albums is no more odious than that of the short-story writer as opposed to the novelist.

John Fogerty of Creedence Clearwater Revival is another musician who understands this: "A single means you've got to get it across in a very few minutes. You don't have twenty minutes on each side of an LP. All it means is that you've got to think a little harder about what you're doing. We learned from the singles market not to put a bunch of padding on your album. Each song's got to go someplace. Most of this is a built-in uptightness. Singles are what I dug when I was little, therefore I have to change now. I've grown up, I don't like Top 40 . . . which is dumb. Why not change Top 40?"

Marc Bolan has changed Top 40, but it's a shame that not all of his *Electric Warrior* album is up to the standard of the singles. "Cosmic Dancer", a fine song, is spoilt by incongruously heavy-handed drumming from Legend and Visconti's saccharine string writing. "The Motivator" is an inferior version of "Get It On" and "Lean Woman Blues" is unbelievable clumsy, though Bolan raises a smile by counting the band in by yelling, "One – two and BUCKLE MY SHOE!!" "Planet Queen" is an indifferent song rescued only by a fine chorus and the excellent vocal backup by Howard Kaylan and Mark Volman. After all, who could sing a line like "Give me your daughter" better than The Mothers Of Invention?

"Rip Off" is a mess, but entertaining. The structure is like a one-chord "Tutti-Frutti", but every so often Bolan sends a reflective minor chord drifting across the chaos. It ends with Ian McDonald improvising mantrically against a long electronic chord. As the chord changes he plays a beautiful bubbling, looping turnaround and then vanishes into the texture of the sustained chord. It might even turn some people onto Coltrane.

Bolan's new-style lyrics blend cars and chicks into the old sword and sorcery scenes, emphasizing yet again that it's all a matter of technology, that it doesn't matter whether you use a silken chariot or a Cadillac as long as it gets you there on time. Despite its Eddie Cochran guitar riffs, "Ride A White Swan" was, lyrically, mainstream Bolan: "Wear a tall hat just like in the old days ride a white swan with a tattooed gown Take a black cat and put it on your shoulder, and in the morning you'll know all you know." "Hot Love" had lyrics that *sounded* right, whether you consciously listened to them or not: "She's faster than most and she lives on the coast She ain't no witch an' I love the way she twitch. She's my woman of gold and she's not very old" and a guitar solo that merely sent two or three random notes floating across the changes – but it worked.

Like many another performer, Bolan capitalizes on his limitations – he doesn't so much sing as manipulate his vocal mannerisms, and his simple lead guitar style is born of necessity. He only seems to have one rhythm guitar lick, but he knows his rock and roll, and he makes it count. Just at the fade of "Get It On", he murmurs, "And meanwhile, I was *still* thinkin'" . . . the pay-off line of Chuck Berry's "Little Queenie".

"I wanted to record 'Little Queenie', but it wouldn't have worked again, so I wrote my own song to it, and I put that on the end so that someone like you would know and wouldn't say, What a cunt, Bolan, ripping off 'Little Queenie' because in the end, it's only the feel of the song."

Subjectively, Bolan singles sound fine when they slide into your head during the course of the day. On *Top of the Pops* or Radio One or my local pub jukebox, T. Rex's records shine out like diamonds in the mud. But in the more competitive environment of an evening at home playing records, they suffer by comparison with The Who or The Dead, or The Stones or The Byrds, or Steeleye Span, or whoever your own best friends may be. But it's good bopping music, and there'll never be too much of that.

Interviewer: Where's Steve Took these days?
Bolan: Oh, I don't know . . . in the gutter somewhere.

John Peel awarded an MBE for his services to Tyrannosaurus Rex.

> Bob Dawbarn's New Year Predictions,
> Melody Maker, *Christmas 1968*

I went to Newcastle with John Peel to see Beefheart at the weekend, and he said that he'd no social contact with Bolan since they had their first hit. Every time he phones the office someone tells him that Marc's tied up right now, man, can he call back on Saturday, far out.

> Richard Neville

See a tin can at my feet/think I'll kick it down the street,
That's the way to treat a friend . . .

> Randy Newman

At the Republican convention in Miami four years ago, Norman Mailer, working on the principle that you can tell as much from a man's circle as from the man himself, declined to watch Nixon's speech and went to have a look at his elephant. In the rock and roll business you can judge a star not only by his groupies (and vice versa) but by his organization (and vice versa). When the new

Jeff Beck Group went on the road, I tried to get an interview with Beck, but his management spewed out endless miles of red tape, which would be too boring to talk about, and so Beck went off on an American tour uninterviewed. It is still unclear as to whether an interview with Beck will appear in these pages or not, but if it doesn't it is neither Beck's fault nor ours, but that of his boring management.

By contrast, when I went to the T. Rex office the day before Wembley to collect my ticket, everyone was friendly, helpful and cooperative despite being out of their minds "trying to get this boogie together" as B.P. Fallon put it. Beep also gave me an apple and a lift back to the West End. When I called to ask for an interview with Bolan, I was told that he was going to the States, but that I could talk to him for as long as I wanted after the 17th. I said that I had to deliver copy by then. All right, said Beep, come round tomorrow at one and you can have an hour or so. No problem.

So the evening before the interview I went down to the Grove to talk to Steve Peregrine Took. He was watching *Callan* on his colour set in the flat he shares with Russ of The Pink Fairies, and various mutual friends were dotted around the room. We all got blasted, and then we talked about the good old days. Took, formerly the London and Home Counties Mandrax Champion, now works as a solo singer-guitarist, "Ladbroke Grove's answer to James Taylor", and he is working on a single with the former bass player from Curved Air. A tall, skinny, immensely friendly guy, his stubble and leather and shades make him look more like a biker than a former flower-child. He'll probably go down in rock mythology as the Pete Best of the seventies.

"It's really strange," he said. "Little girls come up to me and touch me and squeal and run away. The other day at the Aldermaston gig all these little girls started screaming 'Marc Bolan, Marc Bolan' at me, so I screamed back, 'Steve Took, Steve Took,' till they went away."

He has one or two memories of his one American tour with Tyrannosaurus Rex. "We were staying at the Chelsea in New York and Marc didn't like it. He kept running his finger under shelves and going, 'Oh! *Grubby!*' and so we had to move to this big fuckin' hotel where they kept staring at us all the time. So I said to June, Marc's wife, that I didn't want to be a part of no fuckin' freak show. She said, 'I like to be surrounded by nice things.'" Took puts a world of scorn into the word "nice".

So the following day I went out for the interview. I gave myself too much time in which to find the place, with the result that I had to kill thirty-five minutes in a grimy caff in Gray's Inn Road, drinking abominable coffee and reading about Todd Rundgren and Pete Seeger in *Rolling Stone*. Eventually I stumbled into the office tired, wasted and bleary, all my carefully prepared, tough, hard-hitting questions melting away. Chelita Secunda, ex-wife of Bolan's former manager Tony Secunda, ousted the previous week with a blaze of publicity, smooths my passage, indicates the bored-looking black velvet figure perched on the desk and says, somewhat superfluously, "This is Marc Bolan."

Black velvet suit with diamond shapes embroidered out of sequins. "See if his eyes are pinned," Took had said the previous night, but he wears heavy shades. His head and his hands seem marginally too large for his frame. We shake hands, say hello, and Chelita ushers us into another part of the office.

"What can I do for you?" he asks.

"Tell me things."

"What kind of things?"

"Whatever's on your mind."

"I've got lawsuits on my mind right now. Do you want anything to drink?" I ask for a coffee and he goes out. I deposit my case and coat, get out the cassette machine and turn my attention to the Aria jumbo leaning against a chair. I'm just taking a wrong turning on an Albert King run when Bolan comes back in, sipping a Scotch and Coke. "Rock on," he says and we sit down.

Effectively, I blow the interview. Nothing of consequence really gets discussed, and we just sit and talk about rock and roll for an hour or so. Bolan has this very hard, dry, precise little voice, his pronunciation almost BBC except for the slang. He sits there like a little jewelled snake, very poised, very elegant, and we talk about Chuck Berry and Bo Diddley and Nik Cohn and Jeff

Beck and John Lennon and Phil Spector and Uriah Heep and whether there are wizards in Tooting Bec and Neasden. He's studied his rock and roll for more than fifteen years with maniacal devotion. There's very little that I don't know about rock and roll," he says, on any level. Or pop music, for that matter.

"I'm very erratic," he says, "but that's part of art and I consider myself to be an artist, and I don't feel any compunction to be professional if I don't feel like it or play if I don't want to. It's my right. If I'm committed to do a gig, I'll *be* there and I'll play, if people have paid to see me. Whether or not I can get myself together to play well is totally up to my head. I tend to be able to do it, because that's what I'm here for, and it's karmically very bad for me not to do it. It's also very selfish, not to do numbers, but to allow oneself not to go to bed the night before and be maybe drugged out or whatever, and have to do a concert when you know you're in no condition to. It's a stupid thing to do. Every rock and roller's done it, and it's the sort of thing you only do once. Some people do it all the time, which is sad, but it's the sort of thing one learns not to do. I've seen Sly being carried on, but that's cool as long as . . . he has personal pain, man . . . it's hard, it's very hard. I won't ever judge. I've given up judging people as I've given up criticizing people for no other reason that the more I learn about rock and roll, about the sort of success that I've had to experience and probably always wanted . . . the amount of pain and aggravation and heartbreak that's gone with it has in fact not been worth it. It has musically, because I love the music, I mean this is what I do, but the pain is so fucking great, man, and it's the sort of thing that you can't express, which is how, lyrically, Berry leads into 'Tulane' or one of those things. The man has got a lot of soul, and the one thing that people can't deny me – I don't care if they agree, they can't deny me. I've made my point, you know what I mean? Now whether they can relate to it is . . .I'm not going to say I'm a gas, or that I deserve to be as successful. People have *made* me successful. Without the people, there is no success. And also if my head was different it wouldn't have happened."

Finally Bolan split to go to court. "Write whatever pleases you, man, I don't mind," he said as he closed the door behind me.

I didn't like Marc Bolan. I had enjoyed talking to him immensely, but something in his vibration disagreed with me. He had seemed like a tiny, elegant steamroller, riding over all obstacles, buffeting people with the wind of his passage.

Michael Alfandary, promoter: "We've all heard of the T. Rex ten bob concerts. How many of you have ever been to one? No one, because that's all a bloody hype. I've been on to Chrysalis agency for years saying I will do a concert at Hemel Hempstead and charge ten bob and I will pay T.Rex the fee that justifies ten bob and I will make zero money if T. Rex will do it. The reply from Chrysalis is 'You might not like cash but we do and T. Rex dig it too'."

Bolan: "Maybe that's why we don't have an agency any more."

> *"I only do it for the madness."*
> *"What kind of madness, Marc?"*
> *"Rock and roll madness."*

So the four-man group which is actually a two-man group with two salaried employees which is actually a solo act has sold sixteen million records in fourteen months. In their first fourteen chart months, The Beatles had sold five million. Bolan sells three out of every hundred singles in this country. Rock and roll madness.

But finally, Marc, I have to salute you, because you've made millions of kids who never listened to rock and roll begin listening. They copy your hair and your clothes and those Anello and Davide girls' strap shoes you wear are now advertised in Oxford Street as "Bolan Shoes" with your picture underneath. Whether people like me dig you is irrelevant. You have kept the circle unbroken, you have ensured our survival, you've postponed the day the music died. So go 'head on, Marc, Rock on. But remember all your passengers. These weird kids may not be The Children Of Rarn, but take good care of them, man, because right now at this stage of the game, you hold the keys.

Diary of a Rock 'n' Roll Star

Ian Hunter

On Tuesday 22 November 1972, Ian Hunter "mopped up the cat shit" from his kitchen floor and prepared for a five week tour of the States with his band, Mott The Hoople. He documented this latest trip as a "letter to a fan in the front row of The Rainbow", resulting in one of the finest and funniest insights ever into the world of rock 'n' roll.

For the unitiated: Pete is Overand Watts, Mott The Hoople's bass-player; Mick is Mick Ralphs, guitarist; Phally and Phal are the nicknames of organist, Verden Allen, and Buff/Buffin is drummer, Terry Griffin. Tony is Tony Defries, the band's manager whose more famous charge was David Bowie, and Stan is the band's personal manager.

Wednesday, 6 December 1972

And so today in St Louis the snow lays crisp and even. The sun shines. Pete's gone down to breakfast with Mick so I think I'll nip down as well. We're going out pawn shopping. Stan just rang. He says we have to fly tomorrow even though it's only about 90 miles or so and this is upsetting to Mick. He also says Tony's flying in from New York.

Later . . .

The pawn shops were shut. It's strange to find everything closed in a predominantly black area because of a Jewish holiday, but that's the way it is around here. We went down to Franklin Avenue and Easton, then approached Dr Martin Luther King Drive. This drive may one day reflect the size of the man's heart it is named after. At the moment it could be a tribute to the changin' times or, at face value, could be taken as the street Dylan referred to as Desolation Row.

Barbers, pool halls, underground clubs, cheap auto dealers mad missionaries all have the same fronts. Cheap, hand painted with the nature of their business scrawled do-it-yourself style, the letters dribbling down below their intended endings. An old cleaners, a wall, a tower and a cinema are left looted wrecks. Tiny pieces of grass brave their way through this 16 degree December day surrounded by frost-covered chairs, prams, and other junk, once warm in people's homes.

They are slowly knocking the place apart and a lump comes to my throat as a shivering dog tries to sleep at the side of the road. Another stands in the porch of a vacated house, orphaned by rules laid down by new landlords, and almost too skinny to be alive, waiting for the old days to come back. Old buildings stand here and there, the standard black houses of a bygone day. Brick blocks, maybe three stories high with wooden porches, rails, staircases, chairs and other bits of wood stuck on the front giving the overall impression of a cuckoo clock.

Some are still lived in. Articles of clothing hang here and there but not a soul in sight. It's much too cold, what a bloody sight. At least, as I said, they are pulling it down and sightseers in years to come will probably marvel at the flash hotels and beautiful restaurants and parking lots. But I'll always remember the cold, misery and squalor that is the street called Dr Martin Luther King Drive.

Perhaps the next street over might have been nicer, perhaps upper-class blacks have good lives here and perhaps the Indians are worse off. All I can say is nobody should have to live here. It is 12 noon and a really drunk black man sullenly avoids his chick's outstretched arms. When you hate help, hope's been knocked out of you. It's the end.

Mick makes a few phone calls about 2:30 and we finally find a place open on Olive Street, not too far away, called Sam Lights. An overweight (but dieting) guy shakes us by the hand and announces himself as Larry Bird. Potential star, dreamer of

Las Vegas, he says he destroys the world every night before
supper. Pawn shops here are both creative and destructive. Guns
hang next to guitars, flick knives next to jewellery, suitcases,
drums, T.V.s, clothing – they really get into it. A man told me of a
guy in Albuquerque who walked into a shop with a sub-machine
gun squashed inside a Martin case. Most owners will tell you
stories of young rich college kids or bewildered older people
selling ancient Les Pauls for $10. Alas, we never have that kind of
luck! I make do with about the only decent guitar, and E.B.O.
bass which I buy for $75 complete with battered case.

Larry's a great conversationalist. He rings round friends to see
if they have anything. There's a woman who can't get over the
accents, especially Phally's, and we stay there for about 90
minutes. Phally takes photos before we leave. Hundreds of hats
are in a huge bin. They give us one each and we feel like "dudes".
I give a Negro a cigarette in the doorway. He's frozen stiff and
trying to keep warm, but they won't let him in. Even when I offer
the cigarette though, he smiles gently and asks me if I need
matches. I'm not rich, but I feel fuckin' rotten – really rotten.

My hat says "Barrister of Philadelphia" inside it. I wonder
whose it was. Once again a talkative cabby – who tells us about the
huge Bush Stadium which houses baseball, American football
and soccer, apparently soccer's on the way up here. A sign outside
the Bel Air Hotel just down the street from here says "Welcome
Los Angeles Rams" they'll probably be gigging at the Bush.

The promoter rings up and says half the audience is coming
just to see us, and they have the best groupies in the U.S.A. We're
beginning to realize this is standard business procedure to put
you in a happy frame of mind, but we feel good anyway. I try to
ring Trudy, but she's out picking her Mum up; I'll try again later.

Pete sleeps on the bed as I write. He can sleep 14 hours a day if
he's not working. I haven't seen Buff, and Stan doesn't answer so
he must be at the gig. Phally's gone back to his room with Mick.
As I haven't got a watch I can only guess it's about five o'clock.
There's a Chinese documentary on Channel 2. The sound is off
the telly and Cat Stevens sings about the wind in his hair on the
radio. I think I'll visit the bogs for a marathon. American food

does my staid English gut in, even if it's only salad. I just glanced out the window; it's dusk now. The swimming pool's iced over and there's a light in the church across the street. The other way a bridge spans something I can't see and a huge office block slowly goes to sleep, its windows like hundreds of eyelids shutting as the working day comes to an end. Stan rings; sound check in 20 minutes. There's another band added, Dick Heckstall Smith's new band, but we're still second from the top, so that means we can come back to the hotel to get ready. Pete's £70 thigh-length boots have been mended and Trudy rang to say she's in now so I'll ring her. I still haven't had that shit yet.

It's 7:30 now and the sound check leaves us in the hands of the Almighty. We'd just gotten switched on for it when 4,000 people invaded the front stalls leaving Mick amazed, stranded half way through *Ready for Love*. Needless to say, Stan panicked and a poor second-in-command whose name is Rob takes everything he says with shrugged shoulders.

There's a dispute between Bloodrock and ourselves over second billing. Now this may seem petty, perhaps flash, to the reader, but illusion plays a large part in the game of rock 'n' roll and any guy in a band will tell you this is an important facet. The rows I've been through over billing in my life must be in treble numbers, and the result about 50/50 depending on where we were and how big we were. If you are expendable, if you've got enough bread to carry out your threats and fuck off, that counts too.

I chatted to Mick Fleetwood who was very shy but extremely nice, and a couple of musicians from Heckstall Smith's group including the man himself. They're opening every gig because Dick doesn't want to use Mayall and Hiseman as stepping stones. We wish him luck.

As I said, the promoter's not here yet. Still selling hi-fi's in his stereo shop somewhere, so we don't even know now if we'll go on. The *brrrrr* of the hairdryer signifies Pete's drying his hair before applying that silver stuff which will stink the room out and I'm waiting my turn. Just had a grilled cheese sandwich and orange juice with Stan, Phal and Mick. Buff's had a letter from home saying *Disc*'s called us a one-hit wonder. Silly bastards. Buff's camera lens is missing so he's a bit sad, but he'll come out of it himself. You can't sympathize with him or he gets more angry. Tony's flying in with Melanie from New York, but I haven't seen them yet.

Hangers-on bang on the doors and we have to be rude. If you just say hello you are subjected to endless conversation which leaves you behind your schedule. When you do finally get them away they turn nasty anyway so you might as well do it straight away. Chicks knew our names, but then again they make that their business. I should imagine it happens with every group.

One reporter in L.A. told me he'd seen girls asking me exactly the same questions as they'd asked Bolan a couple of weeks before. Well, at least I'm in good company. The adrenalin starts to build; that excitement we get at every gig no matter how big or small, top of the bill or bottom. It will be a sad day when it's not there anymore.

Thursday, 7 December 1972

Well it's now 5:15 p.m. and I'm sitting yet again on T.W.A. going to New York City in seat 14B. Things have slightly altered so now I'm going to tell you (as much as I can) what really happened yesterday.

We got to the gig last night and it was absolute bedlam. As was expected, Dick Heckstall Smith opened, and then absolutely nothing happened for over an hour. The crowd was really hostile and backstage it was a deadlock. Bloodrock were refusing to go on before or after us. Fleetwood Mac didn't want to end the show but Bloodrock wouldn't either. The arsehole promoters hadn't got a bloody clue, they just stood there hopelessly. Why do these silly sods promote? They'd given Bloodrock a second-on-the-bill contract and we had an identical one. Bloodrock would not budge an inch and neither would we; finally we gave in at the time we'd originally planned to do and went on. The poor kids had waited so long because the promoter was totally ignorant, or extremely snidy and just let the incident occur.

What with no sound check and all the hassles back stage, we

went on pretty miserable. If ever a gig should have been pulled out, it was this one. Tony just wasn't sure of the procedure on down-the-bill acts and let it happen. We went on even though we shouldn't have. The sound, although good out front (as we found out afterwards) was terrible on stage. We slowly dissolved in front of a curious but non-committal crowd. Two spots comprised the entire lighting system, Bloodrock not even allowing one of their lights to be used. And the spots careered crazily around the stage missing most of the points in the music. We bravely carried on, me waggling my arse in a none-too-hopeful attempt to attract a few females. What an act. I felt like a prostitute – it was nothing to do with music. It was a professional con, forced on us by circumstances, and we hated every second of it. *Angeline* fared well and we finished with *One of the Boys*. A good ovation but stamping died too quickly for a reappearance, and we trooped angrily back to the dressing room. The atmosphere was electric. We can't stand bummers, especially those not our fault. We'd sold out on the gig and it left a horrible taste in our mouths. We all knew now it should have been a walk-out. We would have had every right to, but it's too late now. We played.

Tony says it's totally his fault – his first experience of a terribly disorganized gig in the States and he finally decides that things will have to change.

We try to discuss it seriously and Bob C., a light man who's watching us and getting ready to light the five or six other headliners we have to do, gives us the benefit of his considerable experience. Big Bob reckons on him going out early with Ritchie the next day to Springfield to check out the lay of the land. If it's at all dodgey Tony will cancel it altogether. By now Bloodrock have actually gone on and we have a quick look at them before leaving. They are going down about the same as us. I like the singer's red velvet trousers with the squiggly yellow line down them, but that's about all.

I turned, and at the side of the stage the little assistant guy was talking to a couple of at least 50 chicks who were hanging around. As a parting gesture, as I passed him I whispered, "That's what happens when you treat your groups like shit." I walked onto the

ramp, happened to turn and saw him waving his fists egged on by
the girls, who'll agree with anything and anybody. I walked back
and calmly shouted, "The people you work for are a bunch of
utter cunts," into his face.

"What?" came a yell. And five guys, one I knew as a promoter,
ran over. "What the fuck are you talking about?"

"You're fuckin' useless; you shouldn't be allowed to run gigs."

"You fuckin' jackass, get out of here. Go on, get out you
fuckin' jackass, you jumped-up cunt. Your group sucks. Get out
before I put a hole in yuh."

"Bollocks, you load of fuckin' idiots – you fuckin' idiots."

The little one came first, fist pulled back, and I squared onto
him. He held back and the promoter came up near – really near.
He threatened and I just stood there facing them. The blood had
gone from my face and my lips were quivering. Tony pulled them
away as calm as ever and they waved their fists and yelled. All I
could shout was "fuck off".

We walked down to the lower level. There were no bottles
anywhere. My lips were twitching and I was in that cold rage you
get when nothing could hurt you. Tony just took me out and we
got in the car without exchanging a word. I don't know what he
must have thought; I knew what I thought though. I knew I had
been what the guy said I'd been. A jackass. I knew the group had
been bad, but I also knew that the pathetic apology for a
promotion by complete idiots was the reason. The band had
missed the whole episode, Tony and I being the last out of the
Convention Hall and now they all ached to go back. The police
were there now. The streets were silent as we travelled back to the
hotel. How was I going to get rid of the rage? As Pete and I lay on
our beds, we talked of the suspicious disappearance of Wishbone
Ash's equipment from this same town, which put them into debt
again and caused them to break off their tour half way through.
The mirror in the room broke at the top from my badly aimed
ashtray. Pete expertly finished the job off with a tumbler.

Stan rang for another meeting with Tony. This time in his
suite on the 21st floor. And so up we troupe for a rambling
discussion – getting slowly to know Tony better, and he us.

He's decided not to mess about on this kind of gig anymore. Out go three or four suspect gigs straight away, and instead he wants us to speed up the act for the all-important headliners.

Good news from Cleveland where we're doing a three-thousand seater. 1,000 seats have already gone by mail order without the gig even having been advertised. It stands a great chance of selling out. Detroit is also selling well. It's on these gigs we must concentrate. We'll take second or third bill only on proven, upfront, well-organized gigs. Last night had been a lesson in a way, and could prove to be a valuable one.

Mugs. Never again. Go and hit a wall, but don't play at any cost. It'll do more damage in the long run.

The meeting over we go down to Mick's room. It's about 3 a.m. in the morning and the room is packed. Fleetwood Mac turn up to see this guy Ed's guitars. Mick rang him earlier and asked him to come. Various ladies hang around but get pretty much ignored in the quest for Ed's guitar bargains. He's well known in group circles and well respected as a purveyor of musical instruments for English bands. We've met him before in various towns. He buys continually around the pawn shops and then goes to where the bands are and sells them. Mick Fleetwood grizzles a bit about going on late and I don't blame him. I just hope he didn't think it was us who fucked him about. They soon leave and various other people slowly follow. I've had a mandy and try, somewhat the worse for wear, to get Ed's double pick-up, upside-down Firebird down from $300 to $250, but he just won't have it. Mick eventually gets a small Gibson amp for $60 and Peter gets a bargain, a 1941D-18Martin Concert in beautiful condition for only $130. I have no luck at all convincing Ed that $250 is a good price and off he goes into the lift with his friends, covered in amps and guitars.

Pete and I return to our room and survey the damage. It looks like the Armada's been through it. Fuck it. My eyes sag heavily; it's 5 a.m. and we may be going to Springfield later today.

But that was yesterday; now I'll get onto today when we almost missed our flight to New York.

The radio wakes me at ten. There's a cold chill in the room.
The temperature is zero degrees. I pull my coat onto the bed and
huddle back into that nowhere snoozing land. Twelve o'clock
comes and Stan rings to say the Springfield gig is off. Bob C. and
Ritchie think it's as bad, even worse, than last night's mess. Tony
suggests we go to New York instead and do a few interviews
which are outstanding so we set 3:45 in the lobby as the leaving
time for the airport. Room-service coffee takes ages to come and
then, about one o'clock, Pete realizes he has no case for the
Martin. We ring Mick; the pawn shops are open, why don't we go
for a quick shuffle. Trouble is Mick's just ordered breakfast so
it's about 2:30 before we eventually get a cab. Franklin has
nothing, but a lightning dash back to Larry Birds gets Pete a
$5 case. It's great for the price – a black one which looks new. The
time is tight though, and the cabby joins in the spirit of the thing
speeding from one pawn shop to another in case of *that* bargain.
Bingo! A shop called Ace discloses from somewhere in the
backroom of junk, a clean long case. He opens it revealing a
shining Fender Jazz bass in immaculate condition. The guy says
he won't mess around, he'll quote his lowest price and that's that
– $125. Pete's in like a shot. Borrows $70 from Mick and another
25 from me as he is, as usual, broke. With the guitar safely in his
sweating paw we joyfully enter the taxi. A great buy – the feeling
an antique dealer or a stamp collector gets when finding something valuable at a very low price.

A clock on a building lights up 4:06 in bulb letters and we are
almost back at the hotel when Pete discovers he's left behind his
T.W.A. bag containing his various walking-about accoutrements. Sullen moans of "You fuckin' idiot" have no effect on
him and he cheerfully redirects the cab back about 40 blocks to
Ace. Mick and I sit in the back glumly. Stan's going to bollock us
for this. We may miss the plane, and Buff hates it if he's kept
waiting. We get back to Ace. The bag is where he left it and Peter
tries to ring Stan to no avail while I rush to make a last-minute
appeal for a Gibson Melody Maker. The guy's sticking at $100
and I think that's $10 to $20 too much by Detroit prices so I
decide to leave it. Mick says I did the right thing, and we speed

downtown. A couple of cardboard cartons hit the car from a small gang of jeering Negroes. We got away just in time by the look of it. Back once again to the hotel, the limos are waiting, one for us and one for Tony, Mellie, Lee and Stan.

We speed to the airport and I'm still marvelling at how we managed to catch the 5:15 to New York. If it hadn't been for the new search regulations, I think we'd have missed it, and that would have meant another day in St Louis as the other planes are flying out full. I wouldn't have liked that. I'm a bit petulant with Tony about the promoter. I can't forget it – I don't suppose I ever will. But he assures me that neither David or we will do a gig for him again. Nuf said.

And now my ears are beginning to pop signifying our slow descent to La Guardia, New York's domestic airport, and I've forgone chicken and roast spuds to write this lot down.

Ah, the lights of New York City. It seems like returning home after doing a gig in Manchester. How many lights down there? It would take a lifetime to count them. The plane's a metal ball, cruising up the groove at the side of the largest pinball machine in the world! Above the dark blue of the darkest drinking bar.

Elizabeth, Newark and over the river to Manhattan. The Statue of Liberty and we might turn in over the Yankee Stadium. Everybody in the world should see the world. It should be made compulsory. The kids from Bradford, Newcastle, Liverpool, Sunderland and all those northern towns whose only buzz is signing on Wednesdays and Fridays may never get to see the sight I see now and I'm woefully inadequate at translating it to paper. Whoops, a bumpy landing, but a safe one and I've got to go. See you.

Now American hotels are expensive, a single in this place (which is really a double, but only one person is booked) is going to cost you $30, so what we try to do is smuggle Trudy in to save a bit of bread. It's all paid for by the travel agency as are the air flights, but Stan's got to settle up at the end, and obviously the band shouldn't pay for somebody's lady.

Trudy and I have wine and shepherd's pie at the Haymarket with Phally and Elaine, and we return to the hotel via Times

Square. I must compliment Winston fags on their huge sign in the Square. This bloke's smoking away and real smoke comes out of his mouth and forms rings in the crisp night air. The temperature here is about 30 degrees. It's a funny thing about the cold here; it's a dry, clean sort of cold, and providing you're not out for too long, it's not unbearable at all.

Anyway, we go back to the hotel and it's one of "those". Now most hotels are groovy. You're paying a lot of bread for a room so they turn a blind eye if any "guests" happen to drop in, but not this bloody place. You get the feeling a $10 bill will solve the problem but fuck them, they overcharge anyway. The thing is they're being funny about letting the ladies in and this can ruin a good Haymarket meal. Indigestion creeps up on me! Only one way. All great statesmen have used it to great effect throughout evolution. In a word bullshit's required – and plenty of it. We storm the desk.

"What is this, a bleeding kindergarten or something? How old do you think we are, 15?"

"I'm sorry sir, but we have a new general manager here; he won't let guests up after midnight unless they register."

"Fuck your general manager. Ring my manager, Stan Tippins, we're leaving, the lot of us, first thing in the morning. This is disgusting. The lady is my wife and lives on the island with her parents while I'm working here, so what are you implying?"

"Look sir . . ."

"We're not looking anywhere, I'm ringing Stan . . ."

"Nuts." [This time we're at the internal phone.]

"SIR! JUST A MOMENT."

We return to the desk.

"Look sir [he calls me sir, he thinks I'm a twat,] just sign your (ahem) wife in and then it's O.K. No extra charge at all."

"Oh, well all right – that's different. [Cough, feeling like a twat now.]

"But don't forget, sir, no ladies can stay the night, all night."

All fuckin' night – forget it. He's just got to say that so he can say
he said it – but I think it's O.K.

Up to our room, watch a Bob Hope film then try to watch a
Bing Crosby film. Finally move Tru's sleepy head over gently
and nip up to switch the T.V. off. It's just about 3 a.m. and I wish
that episode hadn't happened – it means we've got to watch out.
If it happens again, I think we'll either register properly or move
to another hotel. It makes Tru look like a scrubber, and I'm *not*
having that – NO WAY . . .

Parsons' Folly

Phil Kaufman

Veteran road manager Phil Kaufman was a "smart-ass kid from New York" who got into "road mangling" almost by accident in 1968, when he got the job of making sure Mick Jagger made it to the studio every day. There he met a wild American singer-songwriter called Gram Parsons, who led a band called The Flying Burrito Brothers. After the Stones returned to England, Kaufman "road mangled" for Parsons.

Now read on . . .

After the Burritos, Gram made "GP," and after that he made "Grievous Angel" as Gram Parsons and the Fallen Angels, which was released after his death. He brought Emmylou Harris to L.A. to sing harmonies. My name was included in the credits on both albums, a first for me.

During periods when Gram wasn't recording or in between the Burritos and his own albums, he would hang out with John Phillips of the Mamas and the Papas. Gram had a motorcycle designed by Tony Foutz of the loony club. Tony designed this Sportster model with extended front forks and a coffin tank which, in retrospect, was an ominous sign. One time Gram was racing the bike in Bel Air and the front wheel came off. He was taken to St Joseph's Hospital. I took the peg off the bike and made a trophy out of it and gave him the "Dumb Bike Rider of the Year" award, which he appreciated.

I introduced Bruce Wolfe (the attorney who I got to know while I was in Terminal Island) to Gram. He became Gram's attorney. Gram would do stupid things. One time he left the Chateau Marmont (Chateau Marmont was, and remains, a select hotel and short-term accommodation complex in Hollywood. It catered to transient celebrities who wanted privacy and a low profile retreat. The accommodation units were self-contained cabins or bungalows. Gram Parsons rented a unit with Tony Foutz for approximately 6 months), to go to Schwabs drugstore (which is no longer). It was only about 100 yards away but because he didn't trust his old lady, he took all his drugs with him. He got busted for jaywalking and they found drugs with him. He must be the only guy that got busted for felony jaywalking. Bruce Wolfe was on call, as was Harry Fradkin (a personal bail bondsman: "Don't wait in jail, call Harry for bail"). Gram would call me from jail. I would call Bruce, Bruce would call Harry and we'd get Gram back again. This happened more than a few times.

I spent a lot of my time hiding Gram's dope from him. He couldn't understand how he had done so much the night before when, in fact, I had probably taken half of his drugs or thrown them away – I usually just threw the drugs away. When we were on the Fallen Angels tour, Gram and his charmless wife, Gretchen, were constantly fighting, physically fighting with each other. "*You stole that.*" "*You took that,*" referring to whatever they were taking, reds or Nembutals. (Nembutal is a sedative, or downer). They always had an excuse to take more: they couldn't sleep, or couldn't wake up, or couldn't walk, or couldn't . . .

One of Gram's newest followers (and a very good friend) was a guy called Michael Martin. As our bus was pulling out of my yard to go on the Fallen Angels tour, Michael said to his girlfriend, Dale McElroy, "*Can I go with them?*" He looked at us and said, "*Can I go with you?*" The bus was actually pulling out of the front garden. Dale said yes and gave him about $300. Michael jumped on the bus and went on the tour with us. That's Michael, sperm-of-the-moment Michael. He became Gram's valet *du jour*.

One evening while we were in Boston, the aggravation between Gram and Gretchen got so bad that I sent them off to a club called Olivers. When they got in the tour bus, I went back to their

room and searched for drugs. In typical druggy style, they used to
tape their drugs under the bathroom sink or under the toilet bowl
lid. I would not be denied – I found the drugs and got rid of them.
When Gram and Gretchen came back from the gig, they accused
each other of stealing the stash, when in actual fact, neither had
done it.

The tour took us to Blytheville, Arkansas. We stayed at a
Holiday Inn and my new old lady (Kaphy) and I went right to our
room and got on our bed with our magic fingers. It had been a
long ride. We heard screaming and yelling coming from the room
next to ours. Gram and Gretchen were beating each other up
once again. They couldn't find the stash. The hotel manager
called the police, who came in and maced Gram. That's the first
time I'd ever seen Mace used. They took Gram off to jail and,
being the road manager, I had to go and get him out. At that time,
the necks were extremely red in Arkansas. I had very long hair, so
Kaphy put my hair up in a bun. I put my cowboy hat on in order
to look more butch than the cops, if that's possible. I went to bail
Gram out. I was in the Blytheville police station and could hear
Gram mouthing off. Every time he'd mouth off, I heard the thud
of a nightstick hitting bone. Gram just wouldn't shut up. I yelled,
"*Shut up*," and the cop yelled at me, "*You shut up*." I listen to
cops. I never call a man with a gun an asshole. I think it, but don't
say it. Anyhow, I got Gram bailed out. Of course, his voice was
fucked because they had choked him and he had Mace in his
throat. The next couple of days, his singing wasn't up to par, but
with Gram, who could tell?

The bus driver we hired was a guy named Lance. He was
"liquid-and-romance" Lance. Lance knew every girl at every
little truck stop. The tour bus we were on was pretty raunchy,
with seats in the front (not like the modern ones with beds and
TVs and stereos). The situation was pretty grim, and when we
finally dumped Gram and Gretchen off at New York, they flew
back to California. We drove cross-country from Boston. We had
done a show with a group that to this day is my favorite group. It
consisted of three girls and a couple of guys dressed in Spandex.
They had a Harley on stage and they were called The Shitons.

They would do the "doo-wop" stuff. They were great. We left
Boston with Lance, traveled cross-country and stopped in a little
town which had a hotel, a bar and a couple of whorehouses. Of
course, Lance took us to the whorehouse and treated us to a
round of whorehousing. Whatever they do in whorehouses, we
did. We didn't write the book. We just read the lesson.

As Gram's drug problem got worse, he got more and more
outrageous. One time he was at the Palomino and got wasted with
the head waitress. He got nasty with a cop, was arrested, and it
was back to, "Don't wait in jail, call Harry for bail." But this time
Harry was unavailable. I called Nudie Cohen, the rodeo tailor. I
told Nudie about Gram and he said, *"Ol' Gram is in jail again.
Let's go get him."* So Nudie and I went down in his car. He had a
Cadillac with horns and silver dollars on it, and pistols for door
handles. We went and bailed "ol' Gram" out again. (Gram
Parsons was a keen patron of Nudie Cohen's tailoring establishment. Nudie had fashioned individual stage suits for the Flying
Burrito Brothers, Gram's jacket being festooned with marijuana
leaves and pills. Nudie's western tailor shop still exists on
Lankershim Blvd. The store displays many photos of his celebrity clients. On a large photo of the Flying Burrito Brothers, the
following inscription can be read, "To the best friend a kid could
ever have . . . Gram Parsons.") Gram spent a lot of time in jail.
He was the only guy who had a cell with swinging doors.

Just before Gram decided not to live, he was staying with me in
the back house on Chandler. He had strange habits. He'd have
pharmaceutical people bring him oxygen tanks and he'd breathe
oxygen to help relieve his hangovers. They would also deliver
him some pharmaceutical drugs. I think the tanks were just a ruse
for the delivery. After he died, we found several tanks of oxygen
and oxygen masks that I used later on for scuba diving in case of
decompression sickness.

He'd go out and I'd go in and search for his stash. I'd get the
needles and the drugs, almost all of it. He'd come back later and
think that it was either stolen or that he'd used it. He would say,
*"I was really loaded last night and I must have done it all. I better
get some more."* Occasionally, I'd see the dealers coming in my

house. I'd catch them at the gate and say, *"Oh, yeah, let me have that. Gram said to give it to me."* I'd take it and either cut it in half or not give it to him at all, accusing the dealer of stealing his money. (Everyone knows drug dealers are less than 100 per cent honest.) Gram believed my stories and never suspected that I was rationing his drugs.

One day, we came home and Gretchen's car was parked across the street. Chandler Boulevard is a very wide street with a center divider, so it has a lot of space to park. I guess she didn't recognize my car. Gram and I went around the corner and he said, *"I've got some coke. What should I do?"* We stopped at a street off of Chandler and lifted up the lid of a water meter, one of those meters in the ground for reading your water bill. He hid the coke in there and went back home. In the meantime, Gretchen had gone out, so we went back to get the coke but never found it. We were going up and down the streets lifting meter covers up, trying to find the drugs. I'm sure some meter reader was quite happy to discover the stash.

Gram died of an overdose of morphine and alcohol in a modest room at the Joshua Tree Inn motel. He'd gone there with his girlfriend Margaret Fisher, Dale McElroy and Michael Martin. Dale was giving Gram mouth-to-mouth resuscitation when he checked out. Margaret and her drug connection had gone out to get cheeseburgers, and Michael had returned to L.A. to get a fresh supply of grass. I mean, you figure that out. Earlier, the girls had put ice cubes up Gram's asshole, which woke him up, and then they let him go back to his room where he went back into a lethargic state. Dale tried to breathe life into him but it was too late.

I got a phone call from Dale and immediately left for Joshua Tree with Kaphy. By the time we got there, the police had taken Gram away. Margaret and Dale gave me his drugs (they had cleaned the room out before the cops arrived) so I took the drugs out into the desert and hid them. Even though he was dead, I was still hiding Gram's drugs from him. Kaphy and I stayed in Joshua Tree. Margaret and Dale were still there and were pretty shaken up, so we looked after them. I called the police station to see what was going on. They said they were looking for the two girls. I said, *"I've got them with me, and I'll bring them right over to you."* I got the girls into the car and took them out of the county, back to L.A., where I hid them out. I didn't think they were in any condition to be dealing with a country-bumpkin D.A. out in Joshua Tree. I got them back into town and stashed them.

While in Joshua Tree, I kept making calls. We went to the hospital and tried to get Gram's car because it had been locked. We wanted to go to the car and make sure there were no more naughty things, the things that had killed him. Gram had been drinking booze all day and playing pool with people in a little bar called Blackie's or Charley's or something like that. He'd bought drugs from Scott McKenzie's ex-wife who was living out in the desert. I went looking for her. She knew I was looking for her, but I never found her. I've lost interest in trying to find her now, so she can come out and draw her pension.

The album *Grievous Angel* came out posthumously. Gram had previously chosen a picture for the album cover, a picture of Gram and Emmylou sitting on my motorcycle, my Harley. Gretchen and her father (Larry Burrell, an L.A. newscaster, who was a little bit right-wing of Attila the Hun) found the picture offensive and pressured Warner Bros. to change the album cover. I went up to Joe Smith, the president of Warner Bros. Records, and said, *"That's the picture Gram wanted. That's the picture, damn it. If you change it, you're the chicken-shit man of the year."*

When the album came out, it had a cover photo that is similar to the one on the cover the "Hickory Wind" book, a picture of Gram with his silly little necklace. I bought 50 pounds of *ave guano* ("chicken shit"). I took it down to Warner Bros. in Burbank, poured it in Joe Smith's parking space and stuck the album cover in the middle of it. He got the chicken-shit award. For six months after that, I was never allowed to go into Warner Bros. I was strictly *persona non grata*.

Gretchen accused me of stealing jewelry off Gram's body, and also his clothes. What she had forgotten was that one time the year before when they were both living in Laurel Canyon, both stoned on some downer, the house caught fire from a cigarette. They got up and ran into a closet thinking it was the exit. At that time, most of his stage wardrobe and his good clothing were burned.

Gram had a personal guitar which had been custom made for him and Gretchen made a fuss about that, too. He got it from Fred Wallecei of Westwood Music. After Gram died, the instrument was returned to its maker via Fred. Gram also had a Gibson guitar which I stole and gave to Polly, Gram's daughter, who I considered heir to the guitar. (I don't know if that's stealing or just giving it to the rightful owner.) Polly sold the Gibson to Emmylou Harris who still uses it on stage.

Eddie Tickner summed up Gram, I think. People have often asked him, *"What was Gram really like?"* He says, *"You know, I liked Gram. Gram wasn't a nice person, but I liked Gram."*

The days whittled down to a precious few, and it was coming time for Gram's body to be shipped back to New Orleans. I was sitting around the house playing "shuda". You know, *"I shuda done this, I shuda stayed with him, I shuda taken the body. I shuda done that . . . "* and Kaphy, my old lady said, *"Well, you know, shut your fucking mouth. Do it or shut up."* I said, *"You're right, toots."*

I called Dale McElroy. She was the owner of a hearse, a big old hearse. She liked to go camping in the hearse. When she wanted to go camping, she thought the hearse would be like a Cadillac, the way to go, with sleeping bags in the back. I love her to this day. She's one of my best mates. When I called Dale, I told her I needed her hearse and her boyfriend.

I called up the funeral parlor in the little town before Joshua Tree. They were somewhat suspicious when I kept asking questions like, *"Where are the remains going, what time are they going, how are they going?"* After a while, they stopped giving me information, but I got enough to know that the body was going from LAX on a certain flight at a certain time. I called Michael and said, *"We're going to do it. We're going to take his body as per the deal. A deal is a deal. He's our pal. We're not going to let him go back to New Orleans."* Gram didn't want to go back to his stepfather, Bob Parsons, who was a bad guy. Gram used to refer to Bob Parsons as an *"alligator-shoe and pinkie-ring from New Orleans."* All slick guys in New Orleans wear alligator shoes and pinkie rings.

We had told Gram we wouldn't let him have one of those long, family-and-friends funerals. Gram and I had gotten very drunk at Clarence White's funeral and made a pact whereby the survivor would take the other guy's body out to Joshua Tree, have a few drinks and burn it. (Clarence White was killed by a car driven by a drunken lady while loading his equipment in July 1973, only 2 months before Gram Parsons met his tragic end.) The burning was the bottom line. I thought to myself, *"We're going to steal the body. We are going to go out to the airplane and haul Gram off it. If we have to race across the tarmac and dump the corpse and burn it on the runway, whatever, we have to fulfill the promise."*

I called Continental Mortuary Air Service at LAX and asked if the remains going to New Orleans had arrived. The guy checked and said, *"Yes, they are here."* I was just about to hang up when I said, *"Oh, and what's the name of the departed?"* He said, *"Mrs Goldberg."* Just imagine if I had stolen Mrs Goldberg's body, taken it out to the desert, opened the casket and seen this old Jewish prune. I would have thought, *"Oh, my God, Gram, you look fucking awful, mate. No wonder you're dead."* So I asked, *"Is there a Parsons?"* He said, *"No, that hasn't arrived yet. That will be arriving at 8 o'clock in the evening."* Michael and I got a case of Mickey's and a bottle of Jack Daniel's which we were nipping on. We were wearing our Levi's, cowboy boots, "Sin City" jackets and cowboy hats, which was the wardrobe we had worn on the tour.

We drove to the airport and pulled up at the loading bay at Continental. I said, *"Look, Michael, I'm going to go in there and try and get the body, whatever happens. I may have to hit the guy or whatever to get the body."* As I was getting out of the car, a flatbed truck pulled up with a casket on the back. I walked up to the guy and said, *"Hey, is that the Parsons remains?"* The guy said yeah. I said, *"The family has changed their plans."* This was thinking (and drinking) off the top of my head, so I was at a great disadvantage, but I convinced them. I said, *"The family has changed their mind. They want to fly the body privately by private plane out of Van Nuys."* He looked at me and Michael and our unusual attire. I said, *"Look, man, it's late in the night. We've got a couple of girls lined up, and then we got this call. We want to do this quickly,"* and he said, *"Oh, yeah. I understand. I'll just go inside and get the paperwork."* So the guy went in to get the paperwork.

I was questioning whether we should steal the body right there, and as Michael and I were going towards his truck, the guy came out of the Continental office and said, *"Okay, guys. It's a deal."* He took us around the corner to a hangar where they stored dead bodies. At every international airport, there's a hangar where they store bodies. If passengers are watching a plane load up with their luggage and see a coffin go on, it's a little disquieting. So they actually put the coffin(s) in a container, which is then loaded onto the airplane. That way people don't get upset. We went to this old hangar where they keep stiffs. I was in the office signing the paper-work when a cop car pulled up and blocked the doorway. I thought, *"Uh-oh, now I'm in trouble. I got to get out of here."* I was looking for windows to get out. I said, *"Look, Gram, I've taken it as far as I can."*

The cop just sat there and didn't do anything so I thought, *"Maybe we can pull this off after all."* I told the guy that I had signed the transfer papers (I signed "Jeremy Nobody") and handed over the requisite copies. I walked out waving the papers and yelled to the cop, *"Hey, can you move that car?"* The cop said, *"Oh, yeah. Sorry, man."* Then he helped me shift the casket onto the gurney, then into the back of our hearse. At this point, we were getting a little giddy. I thought, *"Man, we are doing it. We're actually getting the body."* The cop moved his car out of the way.

Michael was driving. You know how big a hangar is? Airplanes fit in it, that's how big. Michael managed to hit the wall of the hangar as we were driving out of it – that's an indication of the condition we were in. We jumped out and the cop looked at us. We said, *"Oh, boy. We're really in fucking trouble new."* The cop said, *"Yeah, I wouldn't want to be in your shoes now,"* and he went away.

We were driving out of the airport. We had Gram. We had our buddy in the back. We were talking to him. We said, *"We got you, buddy."* I took over driving and we pulled out of the airport, pulled into a gas station with Gram in the back. I gave the guy a jerry can and asked for five gallons of high test. (High test was the marketing term for high-octane graded fuel, also called "ethyl." Modern equivalent is "super" or "premium") – this was before leaded gasoline – and the guy looked at the car and said, *"What do you want high test for?"* I said, *"I don't want him to ping."* He didn't get the joke.

I called Kaphy and gave her the code, *"The icing is on the cake,"* to which she replied, *"The preacher is in the pulpit."* We had watched a lot of old movies, as you can tell. Michael and I drove out to the desert, just drinking, singing and otherwise carrying on. If you can believe a hearse with a radio, we were listening to the radio and we got out as far as Cabazon, which is a little gambling town on the way to Joshua Tree. We stopped in Cabazon to get a burger and a beer. We got out of the car and said, *"Hey, Gram, you wait here,"* and we were laughing. We went into the bar and the guy said, *"What you guys got out there?"* We said, *"Oh, some lucky stiff,"* and everybody had a good joke on that.

We had a burger and a beer, then drove through the night. It was very dark. If you've ever been in the desert at night, it's about *f* 5.6 out – the stars are so bright. We were driving through the desert and passed the Joshua Tree Inn where Gram had died and said a few silly things like, *"(belch), Oh, Gram."* We were quite drunk. We drove into Joshua Tree National Monument and kept driving and driving until finally I said, *"This is as far as I can go. We're drunk. We're going to have to get out of here."* It turned out we were near Cap Rock. Later on, people said that was Gram's favorite place and Gram wanted to be buried at Cap Rock. The only reasons we stopped near Cap Rock were: a) we were too drunk to go any further; and b) it was a large enough place that we could turn around and make our escape. That's the only significance of Cap Rock. It was a coincidence. Everybody thinks that Cap Rock is a sacred melting place of spirits or what have you. That's not true. We were just two piss-heads who had gone as far as we could take the body. We stopped there.

There were rollers on the hearse. A casket is normally rolled outside and then goes onto a gurney before it's lowered down. We just lowered it down till one end hit the ground, thud, and Michael pulled forward and it went boom. We said, *"Sorry, Gram."* Michael was getting really edgy now. We were both new to the body-stealing business. He said, *"Okay, man. Let's go. Light it, light it."* I said, *"Light what?"* He said, *"Light it."* I said, *"We got to say goodbye to Gram."* He said, *"Man, you're not going to open the box, are you?"* I said, *"Yeah, we're going to see our mate."* The casket had brass hinges. I think there must be some unwritten law in the casket business that says it's forbidden to oil hinges on caskets because when we lifted up the lid, it creaked loudly. "Casket hinges must squeak," I think that's the Dracula Law. It's like a wake-up call for Dracula. When the casket creaks and squeaks open, *"Oh, time to get up."* This one definitely passed the test. It squeaked open and there was Gram lying there naked. As a matter of fact, later on the police tried charging us with stealing jewelry and clothing off the body. I told them he was naked. All he had was surgical tape on his chest where they had done the autopsy, where they had taken out his organs. He was lying there, and I made some crude comment about his little dick. I did the old trick where you say to someone, *"Hey, what's that on your chest?"* and they look down then you snap up to their nose. I did that to him because Gram and I used to do that to each other. Michael said frantically, *"Don't touch him, man. Don't touch him."* I said, *"He's dead. He's dead. Don't you understand?"* So Michael said, *"Come on, let's go."* Then way in the distance, we saw some car lights. We thought it must be the police. I took the gas, poured it all over Gram, and lit the fire.

When high-octane gasoline ignites, it grabs a lot of oxygen in the air. It went whoosh and a big ball of flame went up. We watched the body burn. It was bubbling. You could see it was Gram and then as the body burned very quickly, you could see it melting. We looked up and the flame had caused a dust devil going up in the air. His ashes were actually going up into the air, into the desert night. The moon was shining, the stars were shining and Gram's wish was coming true. His ashes were going into the desert. We looked down. He was very dead and very burned. There wasn't much left to recognize.

We jumped in our hearse and beat it back across the desert. We took the alternate route across the back of the mountains, up over through Big Bear to avoid – I don't know what. It was paranoia. We were too drunk to make the trip all the way back to L.A., so we spent the night in the desert in the back of the hearse. The next morning, it wouldn't start. The hearse was stuck in the desert. Michael, who weighed about 100 pounds, was soaking wet and said, *"I'll go get help."* He disappeared in the desert and eventually came back with a tow truck and a guy who got the car started. We were still quite hung over and drunk. We were drinking warm beer. We went back to the station, had the car fixed, bought some cold beer and made it back to L.A.

I burned all the paperwork for Gram's body. I wish I hadn't destroyed it, but I was paranoid, burning the evidence. I had the toe-tag that was on his toe and all the paperwork for the body. I later realized it would have been of historical interest – or ghoulish interest, depending how you view it.

We pulled into L.A. on one of those horrible, horrible, smoggy days. The air was abrasive. Michael and I were going along the freeway. There was a pile-up, a chain reaction accident that we got stuck in. We ran into the back of a car. A Highway Patrolman came over, looked at us, opened the hearse door and beer bottles fell out. He said, *"All right, you guys."* He asked for our licenses, but got distracted and forgot to take the licenses. He handcuffed Michael and I together and said, *"You two stay here."* Now Michael, as I mentioned, was a real skinny guy. He had been a street junkie in Bombay, living on the streets, begging for money to get drugs. He just slipped the handcuffs off. I put the car in reverse, backed up, drove off the off ramp backwards and we split. I still had the handcuffs on me. Michael was free. We got back to my house and cut the handcuffs off. We hid the hearse and went into hiding.

The next day, headlines around the world twisted the story with things like, "ROCK STAR'S BODY IN RITUALISTIC BURNING IN DESERT." It wasn't ritualistic, it was a couple of piss-heads taking care of business for their mate.

When Gram died, Bruce Wolfe was in the process of filing Gram's divorce. Gretchen had hit Gram with a wooden hanger a month prior and he was deaf in one ear because of this. I had the divorce papers. I was supposed to serve her. Because of my delinquency, I didn't serve her in time. I was going to serve her the next day, the day after he died, not because he died but because it was on my schedule for that day. As fate would have it, I didn't deliver the papers and Bruce pulled the divorce. If I hadn't been so lazy, she would have got nothing, which is what she deserved.

Ironically, Polly Parsons is suing Gretchen and everybody else. Gram didn't generate a lot of money, but he had inherited a lot of money. A lot of that money is going to lawyers now which is a bit of poetic justice for Gretchen.

Gram's sister, Avis, worked for the Edgar Cayce Foundation. Edgar Cayce was known as the sleeping prophet. He supposedly had a vision during his childhood that left him with psychic powers and a gift for diagnosing illnesses from his sleep. He read auras. Gram's sister, Avis, was working at the foundation in Virginia Beach. She told the story that the night that I did the body snatching, Gram's face appeared in the window of her bedroom and his face was half-charred and half-normal. Gram put his thumbs up and disappeared. To this day, it gives me goose pimples just thinking about it.

The funny thing was that Gram's name was Ingram Cecil Connor, III, and when his real dad died − he died from drinking − his mother remarried. His mother married this alligator-shoe, pinkie-ring from New Orleans who was interested in the Snively estate. The Snively estate was from Gram's grandfather (on his mother's side), who had taken swampland in Florida and turned it into orange groves and lots of lucrative

real estate. I think Disney World is on the old Snively ranch.
They did very well. But Bob Parsons was just interested in the
money. He married her and adopted Gram. Gram became
Gram Parsons, Ingram Cecil Parsons. Gram and his stepfather
never got on. Bob Parsons was trying to get jurisdiction over the
Snively estate to transfer it to New Orleans where he and his
alligator-pinkie cronies could control it. At one time, they had
Avis locked up in an asylum and he had taken power of attorney
over her because he said she was incompetent. But Avis escaped. When she did, I got a call from the New Orleans Chief
of Police and from the FBI asking if I knew where Avis was. I
talked to Bob Parsons and said, *"Listen, you fucking asshole,
don't you ever give the police my phone number again,"* and just
laid into him. Gram thought that was great.

Years later, I was sitting on my porch in Nashville and a man
came to me. By some mistake, his mail had come to my house and
he was coming to collect it. The man was Gram Parsons' uncle
and he was the one who had hidden Avis from Bob Parsons
during that period. This was off the wall – out of nowhere, this
man came to me. I had his mail. The last I heard, Avis is
remarried, very happy and living in Virginia. Gram had a sister
named Diane, by Bob Parsons, and Diane really resembled
Gram. It was frightening how much they looked alike. They
both looked like their mother.

Bob wanted Gram's body sent back to New Orleans. He was
trying to establish residency after death. In other words, if Gram
was buried in the State of Louisiana, then the jurisdiction for his
inheritance would be transferred out of Florida to New Orleans
where Bob Parsons could control it. Well, fate being what fate is,
Bob Parsons died. Ha, ha.

There is more good news in this story. When Bob Parsons
checked out, everything was in flux. Although Gretchen ended
up with Gram's share, Polly Parsons, who was Gram's illegitimate daughter, also received something even though Gram
denied being her father, to the day he died. (One time, we were
in court, Bruce Wolfe to deny paternity. When he was in court,
Gram turned around and said, *"Fuck it. I'll take the kid,"* and

left. She ended up being his child, but I seriously doubt that she was. He doubted it, too, but he wanted a child and that was the only way he was going to get one.) Avis got her money and Gram's half-sister, Diane, got her money, too. Everybody got their money except me. Gram died owing me, and he still does.

After I put Gram to rest, I worked with the Modern Lovers on a record. The police were looking for the culprit who had stolen the body. They had narrowed it down to me. Everybody in L.A. knew who did it, so it's not surprising the cops eventually caught on.

At that time, my home was being used for the film *Night Moves*. The police came looking for me, and Kaphy phoned and said, *"The cops are here looking for you."* I said, *"Just tell them to wait. I'll come. There's no sense in hiding out anymore."* I got on my Harley and rode to the house. The movie crew was filming. The police talked to me, took me in the back room where Gram had lived, and asked me if I had stolen the body. I said no. They said, *"We know you did it."* I said, *"What's the charge? Gram theft?"* They said, *"We're charging you with stealing the coffin. The body has no intrinsic value."* I muttered, *"Well, if I had known that, I would have taken the meat and left the wrapper."* They said, *"We won't handcuff you until you are in the car."* It was obvious that they were police and that I was under arrest. The film crew was looking around and saw the police handcuff me as I got in the car. Arthur Penn and Gene Hackman asked Kaphy what was going on. She related the story to them. Arthur Penn looked at Gene Hackman, put his arm around Kaphy and said to her, *"I think we're shooting the wrong movie."*

When I got to the police station in Venice (the station isn't there anymore), "Don't wait in jail, call Harry for bail" and Bruce were waiting for me. The police booked me and mugged me, and then Harry bailed me out. I appeared with Michael Martin at West Los Angeles Municipal Court on November 5, 1973. (Gram would have been celebrating his 27th birthday.) We pleaded guilty to misdemeanor theft. The judge fined us $300 each and made us pay $708 to the funeral home for the destroyed casket. Dale settled the fine and the funeral home bill, Bruce didn't charge for defending us and Harry Fradkin didn't charge for the bail money. *"Mangler, this one's on us,"* they said. Case dismissed.

The Pilgrims have Landed on Kerouac's Grave

Nat Hentoff

Rolling Stone, 15 January 1976.

Backstage at the Rolling Thunder Revue, Allen Ginsberg (who has just dedicated his book of *First Blues* to "Minstrel Guruji Bob Dylan") asks the convener of these revels, these winds of the old days, "Are you getting any pleasure out of this, Bob?"

The convener, who can use words as if they were fun-house mirrors when he's pressed, fingers his gray cowboy hat and looks at the poet. The first he had ever heard of Allen Ginsberg and the kind of people he hung out with was in *Time* around 1958 while he was still a kid in Minnesota. ("I'm Allen Ginsberg and I'm crazy." "My name is Peter Orlovsky and I'm crazy as a daisy." "My name is Gregory Corso and I'm not crazy at all." That had broken up the kid in Minnesota.)

Now, here on the road with this hooting, rocking carnival of time present and time past, both perhaps present in time future, is Allen, who has survived serene and curious, in a business suit.

"Pleasure?" Dylan finds the word without taste, without succulence. "Pleasure? I never seek pleasure. There was a time years ago when I sought a lot of pleasure because I'd had a lot of pain. But I found there was a subtle relationship between pleasure and pain. I mean, they were on the same plane. So now I do what I have to do without looking for pleasure from it."

"He is putting you on," said a friend to whom Ginsberg, later in the tour, had described Dylan's exorcism of the pursuit of pleasure.

"No," Ginsberg said firmly. "Bob's attitude is very similar to the Buddhist view of nonattachment. The belief that seeking pleasure, clinging to pleasure, evokes pain. It stunned me when Bob said that. It meant that he's reached a philosophical level very few come close to. And it's a long-range, practical, workable, philosophical level. Bob has grown an awful lot. He's alchemized a lot of the hangups of his past. Like his insecurity, which has now become," Ginsberg laughs, "an acceptance of and an ability to work with continuous change."

On the other hand, a musician in Minstrel Guruji's band tells of an epiphany early in the tour:

"Joan and Bob are doing a duet. I forget the name of it, it's one of his old tunes. She's really moving. I mean dancing. She starts doing the Charleston and the audience is digging it and we're digging it, Dylan though, he's plunking his guitar, moving his eyes around quick, like he does, looking at Joanie, looking at us, looking at the audience. Like, 'What the hell is she doing that's going over so damn big?' It's over, and Joan walks offstage, grinning, sees a friend in the wings, and says to him. 'You won't be hearing *that* number again from this little old duo on this tour.' And laughs because neither the friends nor the others standing there can figure out what she's talking about. But she's right. Bob's never called for that tune since. He couldn't stand the competition. Big as he is, in some ways he's still a kid scrabbling for his turf."

"Not true," says Joan Baez of the kid characterization. "Or, not as true as it used to be." She had once described Dylan as "a huge ego bubble, frantic and lost, so wrapped up in ego, he couldn't have seen more than four feet in front of him." But now, "Bob has learned how to share," Joan told me one night after a three-and-a-half-hour show in Waterbury, Connecticut, at an old rococo movie theater that reminded me of Depression nights as a boy when we would go to just such a place to feel good anyhow and come home with some dishes besides. No dishes this time, but the most mellow feelings I've had from a concert since the Duke Ellington band on an exceptionally good night. The kicks were from the genuine mutual grooving of the music makers; but it was Dylan, as shaper of the thunder, who was responsible for lifting the audience and keeping it gliding.

A bounteous dispenser of thunder was Dylan this time around. At least three and a half hours *every* night, sometimes longer. (The first concert in Toronto, one of the tour's more exalted evenings, ran close to five hours.) And yet always, or nearly always, the pacing, though relaxed, didn't go slack.

The right mix of a backup band, driving strong but sinuously so it never sounded like an assault. If you could keep T-Bone Burnett, Steve Soles, Howie Wyeth, Mick Ronson, Luther Rix and David Mansfield together – I was thinking as a once and former A&R man – you could have one hell of a house insurance band. Especially with Mansfield, 19 and the kind of natural whom conservatory students prone to neurasthenia should never be allowed to hear or see. Mandolin, pedal steel, dobro, violin – Mansfield makes them all sing, for God's sake, as if he were the sorcerer, not the apprentice he looks like.

Up front Rob Stoner, who doesn't get in the way, and the authentically raffish Bob Neuwirth who may, he says, be in the movies soon. Finally a Rhett Butler for our time. Put another way, I think you have to see Neuwirth to remember his singing.

Then the substars. Ronee Blakley, who earnestly needs direction, as her albums and her musical aimlessness on this tour rather painfully indicate. Roger McGuinn, who has become a large, jolly, historic rocker, almost right for a Christmas mime show. And surprisingly, most impressive of all in the second line some nights, Jack Elliott. With his rambling white cowboy hat and folk collector's glasses, Jack is real serious, however idiosyncratic, and on this tour quite moving in his seriousness. Watching and feeling what "Pretty Boy Floyd," let's say, still means to him, I started thinking of Cisco Houston. Not that they sang alike, Cisco being more of an original, but they trained a lot of memories. And Jack is still spreading seeds.

All the way up front, Joan Baez and as she calls him, The Kid. Her voice has lowered and so the bodiless sound of medieval caroling in a cathedral is also gone. But now there is more warmth and flesh and survivor's humor ("Love is a pain in the ass"); and still that surging vibrato which is so strong that when Joan sings a cappella, the vibrato becomes her rolling rhythm section.

In her duets with Dylan, Joan, most of the time, is a secondary strand. She could overpower him because her timbre penetrates deeper and because she is more resourceful with her voice than he is but Joan is content to orchestrate Dylan. And Dylan – less coiled, even dancing from time to time – cannot ever be called relaxed but now is so in charge that even he believes he's in charge. His singing, therefore, is more authoritative than ever before. That is, the anxiety in his delivery has to do with the story he's telling rather than with the way he's telling it.

It feels good to him, this tour. The itch was there last summer. One liquid night, if you believe Bob Neuwirth: "Me and Bob and Ramblin' Jack decided we were going to go out and tour in a station wagon, go out and play Poughkeepsie. That didn't turn out to be possible. So we did this instead. And this ain't no Elton John show, you know. This ain't no fucking one-fourth of the Beatles show or nothing like that. This show, we got it all, man. Between us we got it all. And it just gets better and better and better."

"The feeling is good," Joan handed me her glass of wine, "because everybody has some room onstage. Bob made sure of that. He didn't have to and I argued against it. I thought it would slow things up. But Bob insisted. He said the guys in the band have to work day and night, and so each of them ought to get some attention. Not that, as you saw, Bob has sworn off attention for himself."

He no longer seeks pleasure, he says. But what of the pleasure of attention? Why, that comes, it just comes.

Blood on the Tracks has been released and Allen Ginsberg, listening close, is moved to write the poet about a rhyme in "Idiot Wind": "idiot wind blowing like a circle around my skull from the Grand Coulee dam to the Capitol."

It's an amazing rhyme, Ginsberg writes, an, amazing image, a national image, like in Hart Crane's unfinished epic of America, *The Bridge*.

The other poet is delighted to get the letter. No one else, Dylan writes Ginsberg, had noticed that rhyme, a rhyme which is very dear to Dylan.

Ginsberg's tribute to that rhyme is one of the reasons he is here with Bob and Joan and the rest of the merry motley. It was, says Allen, "one of the little sparks of intelligence that passed between Bob and me and that led him to invite me on the tour."

Joan, in faded jeans and multicolored, boldly striped cotton shirt, is talking with amused affection about Dylan, about the tour, about herself. The Ghost of Johanna still marvels at the sparks that never cease coming from this "savage gift on a wayward bus." Throughout the tour, although Lord knows she knew his numbers well, Joan would slip into the audience to hear Dylan's sets or, if she were weary, she'd sit down backstage to listen.

"Bob has so powerful an effect on so many lives," Joan says. She has been saying this for some 13 years and at the beginning, before his pop beatification, she pushed mightily to press that savage gift on those who had come to pay homage only to her. Dylan was the "mystery guest" unveiled at her concerts, lurching on stage to break the spell of high-born doom across the seas in someone else's history as he rasped about freak shows right outside.

"I'm still deeply affected by his songs," Joan says. And by him? "Well, of course, there's that *presence* of his. I've seen nothing like it except in Muhammad Ali, Marlon Brando and Stevie Wonder. Bob walks into a room and every eye in the place is on him. There are eyes on Bob even when he's hiding. All that has probably not been easy for him." She says this entirely without her usual irony.

"Sometimes," Dylan says to me on the phone in 1966, "I have the feeling that other people want my *soul*. If I say to them, 'I don't *have* a soul,' they say 'I know that. You don't have to tell me that. Not me. How dumb do you think I am? I'm your *friend*.' What can I say except that I'm sorry and feel bad? I guess maybe feeling bad and paranoia are the same thing."

Onstage, all during the Rolling Thunder Revue, Joan had put her arm around Dylan's shoulders, wiped the sweat off his forehead, kissed his cheek, and looked into his eyes, giving rise to a frisson of voyeurism among those in the audience who yearn for *Diamonds & Rust* to have a sequel, several sequels, for where else these days can you find that old-time mysterious rhapsody in the romances of the famous? "It's on again," a woman behind me whispers eagerly as Dylan and Baez intertwine in close harmony onstage. "It's on again."

Later I ask the question and Joan laughs. "This is a *musical* tour for me. Actually, I don't see much of Bob at all. He spends most of his time on that movie he's making. The movie needs a director. The sense I get of it so far is that that movie is a giant mess of a home movie."

Joan, sitting back on the couch, as spontaneously straightforward as Dylan is cabalistically convoluted. And as he figures in who knows how many sexual fantasies of how many genders, so she is erotic, still freshly erotic, but probably stars in somewhat straighter fantasies. But who knows?

And she is funny, especially in self-defense. As on the day she showed up for her first rehearsal for the Rolling Thunder Revue.

"I'd like to hear that song off your new album," Dylan asks the once and former girl on the half-shell. "You know, 'Diamonds & Rust.' "

"You want me to do *that* on the show?" Joanie looks at him in solemn question.

"Yeah." There is a distinct collector's gleam in Dylan's eyes. "Yeah, I do."

"You mean," the ex-madonna grabs Dylan by the chin and looks him in the eye, "that song I wrote about my ex-husband."

Dylan has been aced. "I have to keep him spinning," Joan says of the rout, "in order to keep my balance."

"Those duets," Joan says of what she's sometimes been thinking while also wiping Dylan's brow and looking into his eyes, "are a hazard. It's hard singing with him because he's so devilish. There are times when I don't know what song he's plucking on that guitar until he starts singing. And he can be tricky. On one song, we'd been doing two choruses all along the tour but one night, just as I'm about to belt the second chorus, the song was all

over. Done! Thanks a lot. Bob had worked out the new short
ending with the band and hadn't told me. Oh, he's a lot of fun
onstage."

Curtain! The second-half of the nonpareil. Rolling Thunder
What-Might-Have-Been-and-What-Has-Been-Point-to-One-
End-Which-Is Always Present Revue is about to start!

Under the cowboy hat, the *klezmer,* the Jewish hobo musician
with roots – roots by the centuries – turns to the sad-eyed, lady
from Chavez country. That lady who, he used to say, "proved to'
me that boys still grow." Dylan looks up at Baez and says, "Don't
upstage me."

She smiles her luminous smile and says, "I'm going to use
everything I have to do just that."

> "I'm back from goose hunting in Maryland," said President
> Ford. He was disappointed at only bagging one goose in six
> hours. Shifting to the subject of country music, "Joan Baez
> really grabs me." Ford admitted. Party host Senator Wil-
> liam Brock (R-Tenn.) agreed. "I wish I could get her to
> campaign for me . . . at least in some areas," said the
> senator.
>
> – *Women's Wear Daily*, November 19th, 1975

The campaigner is still very fond of the *klezmer.* "I used to be too
hard on him. I used to be too hard on a lot of people." Baez grins,
sipping wine. "Well, I'm not as stiff as I used to be. I've lightened
up on people. I don't expect Bob to champion my causes anymore. I've learned he's not an activist, which does not mean he
doesn't care about people. If that were so, he wouldn't have
written 'Hurricane.' "

Having shrived Dylan of her moral burden ("Singer or savior it
was his to choose. Which of us know what was his to lose"), what
does she want for him now?

"I'd like to see him keep making music, keep creating. Why, I
would like him to be happy."

It all depends, of course. Or, as Jane Ace once said to Goodman
Ace, "*If* it makes him happy to be happy then let him be happy."

And what does she want for herself?

Joan Baez speaks to the wall. "There must be something I can do with my life that will be worthwhile."

You talk, I say, as if you've been a sybarite or a government official up to now.

"Oh, I've already done a fair amount of things; but in terms of what has to be done, how do you measure what you still ought to be doing? And maybe what I did wasn't done as efficiently as it could have been. Screaming at people may not be the most efficient way. I'm going to stay back a little from now on. I'm learning how to listen to people instead of preaching at them so much. And learning to listen to myself again. I'm 30,000 words into a book, an extension of *Daybreak*. And the songs. I'm going to write more personal songs. If they come. I go through some very long dry periods But it's fun when it happens."

She likes to laugh, always has, though in the past, as she knows, she has sometimes come on like Carry Nation, wielding her ax, with, as they used to say, an ":achingly, pure soprano."

At the start of rehearsals for a television show in 1960, she announces what songs she will not sing, with whom else she will appear in her section of the program (no one); the amount of time she will need; the kinds of sets behind her she will not permit. She is not negotiating. She is stating irreducible demands and looking toward the door.

The producer, Robert Herridge, a prideful maverick and wildly ecumenical intellectual who is too honest to last long at CBS, is morose, frustrated. He turns to me, who has brought him this burning bush, and snaps, "The bitch is only 19 years old and she thinks she's Thomas Mann."

She also thought that singing wasn't enough, wasn't nearly enough, and as the Sixties went on, she went on the stump for tax resistance and draft resistance, went to jail twice for helping block induction centres, marched for civil rights North and South, arguing with Martin Luther King much of the way. (King was proud that black bands were coming out of the "revolution," pointing out to Joan that "the black keys and the white keys on the piano are out of tune. We have to get them in tune and this is one way." And Joan the still burning bush, pointed a long, graceful finger at him and said, "But the whole fucking orchestra is shot, so what good are black bands going to do?") And she worked with Cesar Chavez before all the articles and books made it modish to switch table wines and peer at the crates the iceberg lettuce came in.

No other performer came anywhere close to Joan in terms of being continually on the line in those already blurred years. And as the most deeply knowledgeable popular circuit rider for active nonviolence, it was Joan who became a pariah among certain "revolutionaries" pushing holy violence because she insisted early in that self-indulgent game that Tolstoy had been right: "The difference between establishment violence and revolutionary violence is the difference between dog shit and chicken shit."

As she kept getting braver and as her radical pacifist thinking grew more rigorous, Joan was also growing into a woman who loved falling in love, just as in the old songs and who kept learning how to move on just as in the new songs. Nearly 35, the mother of a six-year-old-son, she's still moving on, in a number of directions.

"There are four of me right?" Joan says "A mother, a woman, a musician and a politician. For a long time, I always put politics first. When Gabe was born, being a mother and being political took on coequal importance. Music, like before, kept being shoved into the background. And the me that is a woman kept coming and going, depending on whether there was something going on in that part of my life.

"Then," she goes on, "I went broke, so broke I couldn't even fly East for a demonstration. I had done a series of political albums which hadn't sold and so I had to put music up front, I had to stop being part of everybody's political campaign and I had to go out there and entertain. That was last summer's concert tour. I was frightened. What would they think, the people who came to hear the political Joan Baez? At first, I was so apprehensive. I'd announce during a concert that I was on vacation. But you know what they thought? They thought I was human. And *I* liked it too. I found myself *dancing* during the concerts and

I love to dance. I'd never been so spontaneous onstage. The audiences were having fun and so was I."

So, in the middle of the journey, the newsreel footage of the Sixties having been locked up somewhere, which of the four Baezes is going to be in the forefront, now?

"It's still getting sorted out," says Joan. "I'm always going to be involved in nonviolence, I still feel very close to Chavez and the farm workers, and I expect I'll be working again with Amnesty International. But on the other hand, I want to be with my kid. This is a very important year for him, a kind of transition year to when he starts moving away from as much need as he has now for his mother. I don't want to mess this year up. And then there's music. I can see myself getting more involved with the fun of the music, with allowing myself to be a musician for the sake of the music itself."

And the woman part of Baez?

She grins. "That comes and goes, depending on what happens. No way of knowing what's going to happen."

One part of Baez, interlaced with all the others, remains stubbornly intact. "I am," she says, "your basic camp counselor. I really am."

All campers are to be treated equally, with justice and fairness for all. Or else.

By the 12th stop on the Rolling Thunder Revue celebration of musical egalitarianism, the camp counselor is furious. She is preparing a pronunciamento and a graphic drawing for the tour's internal newspaper. She is protesting rank injustice in the heart of all this here cultural freedom.

"They make the security people, the bus drivers and the crew," the burning bush speaks, "eat at separate places and at separate hours from the rest of us. *That* is segregation."

Who is "they" – Lou Kemp?

"I don't know who it is. But this is going to stop. The drawing I'm putting in shows a pool of blood, and it's going to say that without these guys who are being segregated one of us principals might be stranded, to say the least, in the wake of the Rolling Thunder Revue."

What if your protest is ignored?

"Then a lot of us," says Joan, "will go eat with the security people, the bus drivers and the crew. There are a lot of possible approaches to this kind of problem."

Is Bob aware of this segregation?

Joan, customarily spontaneous, customarily candid, weighs her answer. "I don't know," she says.

Allen Ginsberg also speaks of protest, but as in a vision. Where once was a time to howl, now is the time to begin the harvest and to give thanks to the harbingers, then and now.

In Springfield, Massachusetts, Arlo Guthrie moves onstage to play and sing with his father's other son, the hard-wishing hard-traveling, earnestly self-adopted Jack Elliott. Backstage, the midwestern *klezmer* (to whom Woody was his "last idol") watches and listens.

"That's a strong lineage, Woody's" says Allen Ginsberg, "and Woody, of course, was part of an older lineage, that old good-time Wobbly idealism. That's all still going strong right in this show. Joan sings 'Joe Hill.' And 'Hurricane' is part of that too, an old classic social protest song."

Sound the news of injustice and the people will awake. How else can we begin?

"And look how we end," says Walt Whitman's friend.

The end, a reasonably jubilant "This Land Is Your Land," everybody onstage, even Ginsberg-the-keeper-of-the-vision making silvery his finger cymbals, as Joan soars and swoops from the mountains to the prairies and Dylan, smiling, stands his ground, and all the rest move to the hearty beat of the American *Upanishad*.

"There was a kind of vision of community in the Sixties," Ginsberg says after the show, "and many people thought that, once they'd had the vision, everything was solved. But as Jack Kerouac once said, 'Walking on water wasn't built in a day.' Another thing going on in the Sixties was just people digging each other, digging each other's texture and character, hanging out. You can't do that fast either. You know, there was a lot of hanging out in the Fifties too, in Kerouac."

Dylan had been braced and shaped, in part, way back then by Kerouac. *Doctor Sax, On the Road, Mexico City Blues.* The day after the Rolling Thunder Revue came to Lowell, Dylan, Ginsberg and Peter Orlovsky visited Kerouac's grave. Ginsberg had brought a copy of *Mexico City Blues* and Dylan read a poem from it. The three then sat on the grave, Dylan picking up Ginsberg's harmonium and making up a tune. When Dylan pulled out his guitar, 'Ginsberg began to improvise a long slow, 12-bar blues about Kerouac sitting up in the clouds looking down on these kindly wanderers putting music to his grave. Dylan is much moved, much involved, a state of introspection closely captured by the camera crew that has also come along.

Before Lowell, before Boston, before Plymouth, the day the Dharma Carnival was to leave New York, Allen Ginsberg meets Muriel Rukeyser on the street. This soft-voiced, slow-speaking, hugely honest poet, who of late has been in South Korea trying to stop the terminal silencing of an antideath poet there, is glad to see Ginsberg. She admires people with visions. She asks where he's going.

"I'm going on the bus," Ginsberg says cheerily "It's a minstrel show!"

"But it's more than a minstrel show, isn't it?" she asks me the next day.

"It is a signal to the country," Ginsberg tells me on the road, "What happened in the San Francisco renaissance in the mid-Fifties was one of those signals that characterize the rise of social rebellion. And that happened in the very midst of McCarthyism. Then, in the mid-Sixties, the peace marches and the rise of rock – the Beatles and things like that – were among the signals for a further rising of consciousness, a wider sense of community. Now the Rolling Thunder Revue will be one of the signal gestures characterizing the working cultural community that will make the Seventies."

I would like to truly believe, I tell the poet, but where, except in wish, is the basis for such joyous tidings in a time of torpor?

"Have you read Dave Dellinger's book, *More Power than We*

Knew?" The poet must resort to prose. "Dellinger shows that many of the demands that the youth generations or the left or the movement made in the Sixties have actually been met. Congress *did* cut off funds for the Vietnam war and who would have thought that possible in the mid-Sixties? Then there were all the protests about the police state, and a police state paranoia to go with them. Now a great deal of that has been confirmed and exposed in public investigations. Not that everything has been all cleaned up but the work of the Sixties *did* bear some fruit. It never was in vain.

"So now, it's time for America to get its shit together," the poet says idiomatically. "It's time to get back to work or keep on working, depending on who you are, because the work that went before *has* been good, even though people got discouraged. It's been as good as you can expect, considering what it takes to walk on water or reverse the machine ago or deal with overpopulation or capitalism. Rolling Thunder, with *its* sense of community, is saying we should all get our act together. And do it properly and well." The poet, bouncing his vision, laughs. "Once you have a view of the right path, then you have to travel that path."

That means Dylan's getting his act together too?

"Having gone through his changes in the Sixties and Seventies, just like everybody else," Ginsberg says, "Bob now has his powers together. On the show, he has all the different kinds of art he has practiced – protest, improvisation, surrealist invention, electric rock & roll, solitary acoustic guitars strumming, duet work with Joan and with other people. All these different practices have now ripened and are usable in one single show, just as there is also room for Mick Ronson and his very English kind of space-music rock, Joan and her sort of refined balladry and Roger McGuinn with his West Coast-style rock. All of these different styles turn out to be usable *now*."

"Do you know what Dylan is talking about doing?" a principal of the tour says to me. "Don't use my name but he might start a *newspaper!* That blows my mind. It'll be like a community newspaper, but for a community all over the country."

I wonder who is going to be the music critic and in particular, who is going to write about Dylan's records. Blind Boy Grunt?

"I am not able to tell you any details," says Allen Ginsberg, "but this tour may not end as all other tours have. There is some desire among us to have a kind of permanent community and Dylan is stepping very, very slowly to find out if that can work. Recordings would be one way and there may be other ways. One must proceed slowly and soberly – unlike the Beatles when they tried to expand their sense of community. Remember John Lennon trying to put together that whole Apple enterprise as a sort of umbrella organization for all kinds of collective work? But he didn't have the right personnel and so it wasn't done soberly and practically enough. This would be. Keep watching. The thing is to keep the Rolling Thunder spirit alive."

Joan Baez's denunciation of class segregation aboard the Rolling Thunder Revue has appeared in the troupe's internal newspaper. Her sketch of some nameless star, lying on the ground with blood pouring out of his head, was not printed and has disappeared. But the accusatory text reads:

"We strongly suggest that the security people, the bus drivers and the crew be treated more like human beings and less like bastard children because without them one of the principals might be left dead in the wake of the Rolling Thunder Revue.

[Signed], Joan Baez and a large supporting cast."

Did it work? I ask.

"Well," says the ceaseless strategist of nonviolent direct action, "things kind of came together a bit after that. A lot of people each in his or her own way, began committing small acts of civil disobedience – like taking the bus driver to their table. So the tone has changed and the segregation has lessened." Some people, I am buoyed to see, are still overcoming.

The tour is old enough for retrospection. "When you got that call from Bob," an old acquaintance visiting Joan backstage says, "I suppose you got on the plane without even knowing what you were going to get paid."

Joan looks at the questioner as if the latter has just asked if the tooth fairy has gotten over its cold. "When I got that call," Joan says, "I had already planned my fall tour. So I told the people dealing with the money that although it seemed like fun, they'd have to make it worth my while to change my plans. Well, after my lawyers got involved and we worked out a contract, a very detailed contract, they made it worth my while. Sure, I'm glad I came. This tour has integrity. And that's because of Bob."

"Tell me," the acquaintance asks, "what are his children like?"

Joan hoots. "I've *never* seen any of them. They're like mythology. It does gather around him, mythology. And he certainly helps it gather. Mythology and confusion. Like some of the songs. I know who 'Sad-Eyed lady of the Lowlands' is no matter who *he* says it is."

"But at least we all know who 'Sara' is," the visitor observes.

"Dylan says," Ginsberg has overheard, "that song is about Sarah in the Bible." And Ginsberg laughs.

Mythology has become palpable. Sara Lowndes Dylan has joined the Rolling Thunder Revue, and with her are several Dylan children and a nanny. Allen Ginsberg is impressed. "Sara is very intelligent, very funny and I would say queenly. She's sort of aristocratic looking, like an old-time New York young Jewish lady who's been 'around a lot in the theater, which she has been. Sara and Joan," Ginsberg chuckles, "have had time to compare notes on Dylan."

"No, I had *never* known her before," Joan says of Sara, "and yes, we have been comparing notes, and that is all I'm going to tell you about that. But I will say that for me, Sara is the most interesting female on this tour. Why? Because she's not a bore. That's the best thing I can say about anybody."

Sara Lowndes Dylan has become part of the Rolling Thunder Revue Acting Company, adding her skills and fantasies to what Allen Ginsberg estimates to be more than 100 hours of film already in the can for the giant kaleidoscope being shot by Lombard Street Films which is being financed – I am told for nonattribution by those close to Zeus – by Dylan himself. At least five or so complete concerts have been preserved and some special numbers, such as "Isis," have been filmed more times than that. And there have been scores of scenes enacted by diversely mixed members of the troupe. Sara Dylan, for instance, has now portrayed a madam in a bordello in which one of the nubile employees is enacted by Joan Baez in a brazen French accent.

Joan, at first rather standoffish about what she had earlier regarded as a huge mess of a home movie has now become more involved. In another scene for instance, she and Dylan are in a bar and the bartender is Arlo Guthrie. "My God, she has a lot of energy," says cinéaste Allen Ginsberg. "And what a marvelous mime."

Also intermittently involved are members of the band, virtuosic David Mansfield among them. As an educational insert in the bordello sequence, Allen Ginsberg is seen in his business suit, taking Mansfield (playing a chaste 14-year-old) to lose his cherry, as Ginsberg puts it in the old-time vernacular. This being, in part, a musical, Mansfield of course has his violin along.

Like many of the scenes in this gargantuan movie – which will purportedly be cut and edited in the spring by Dylan and Howard Alk, who worked with Dylan on *Eat the Document* – the bordello section started as quite something else. Ginsberg had suggested a scene involving a number of women in the troupe, in part because he is much taken with the notion that the dominant theme in the Rolling Thunder Revue is respect for the "mother goddess, eternal woman, earth woman principle." He points to the songs in the show such as "Isis" and "Sara" and notes as well that Sara Dylan has diligently researched this theme in such works as Robert Graves's *The White Goddess*.

The women having assembled, there was much discussion as to the roles they would play – perhaps the graces or the goddesses of the nine muses. Somehow however, as Sara Lowndes Dylan said, "After all that talk about goddesses, we wound up being whores."

"Nonetheless," says Allen, "Sara as the madam did talk about Flaubert."

*   *   *

Dylan is consumed by this film. He conceives a good many of the
situations, advises on the transmutation of others, does some of
the directing, peers into the camera and works, picking up
technique with the film crew.

One day after much shooting, Ginsberg, wondering how Dylan
keeps track of the direction of all this footage, asks him. Dylan
wishes he hadn't.

"I've lost the thread," Dylan, with some bewilderment, admits
to Ginsberg.

A couple of days later, Ginsberg asks Dylan if the thread has
been relocated. The singing filmmaker nods affirmatively.

"So what *is* the thread of the film?" the poet asks.

"Truth and beauty," says his ever precise friend.

Along with the Dylan children and their nanny, Joan Baez's
six-year-old son, Gabriel, is now on hand, together with Joan's
mother and a nursemaid for Gabriel. What would Kerouac have
made of this way of doing the road?

Also suddenly triumphantly materialized – a climactic reaffir-
mation of the eternal woman principle – is Bob Dylan's mother,
Beatty Zimmerman.

"A regular chicken soup Jewish mother," Allen Ginsberg says
approvingly. "With a lot of spirit."

Toronto. A cornucopian concert with Gordon Lightfoot and
Joni Mitchell added to the Astartean cast. And also added in
the fertile finale, "This Land Is Your Land" – Bob Dylan's
mother.

Seated at the back of the stage, Beatty Zimmerman is pulled up
and onto stage center and begins to dance and wave to the
audience, none of whom, she is sure, knows who she is.

It is getting near the start of the second chorus and Joan Baez,
chronically gracious, pulls Mrs Zimmerman toward the lead
mike, the principals' mike. "All of a sudden," Joan says, "Dylan
kicks me in the ass. Gently. It was his way of saying, 'I think I'd
rather sing this chorus than have my mother do it.' So I had to
gracefully Charleston Mrs Zimmerman back a few steps and then
leap to the mike and sing with Bob."

And there, back a few steps, is Mrs Zimmerman, arms flailing, dancing to Woody's song and the music of Woody's children and the music of her own child, of all things. The first time she's ever been on stage with that child.

"Sara, Joan, his children, his mother," Allen Ginsberg meditates, "he's getting all his mysteries unraveled."

Not quite. Not yet. Earlier in the tour, listening to him as he chants what I took – wrongly, it turns out – to be kaddish for "Sara," there is that mysterious, demonic force, in and beyond the words, that will last a long while beyond the tour. That cracking, shaking energy which reminds me of another *klezmer* on the roof, another Tateh in ragtime, Lenny Bruce. But Lenny, who certainly had his act together, never learned how to get his defenses together. Dylan, on the other hand, has developed a vocation for self-protection. If he has a mania, it is for survival. ("I'm still gonna be around when everybody gets their heads straight.") And part of the way of survival is keeping some of his mysteries damn well raveled.

One morning, as the caravan is about to break camp, a rock musician says, "You know what makes him different. He sees the end of things. The rest of us, we're into something, it's as if it's going to last forever. Dylan, he's in just as deep, but he *knows it's not going to last.*"

I am mumbling about a stiff singer who phrases, however authoritatively, like a seal and plays nothing guitar on the side. Why, then, do I once again (unlike the '74 tour) find him powerful? "It doesn't matter whether he's musical at all," I am instructed by Margot Hentoff, a writer on these matters. "He has in his voice that sense of the fragility of all things, that sense of mortality which everybody tries to avoid acknowledging, but is drawn toward when they hear it. He's got it and nobody else has."

It was my wife (quoted in a *New York Times* epitaph I had written of the '74 tour) who had greatly annoyed Dylan, a friend of his told me. "He's not 'The Kid' anymore," she had said in print, "so what can he be now?"

A year later, having come upon the Rolling Thunder Revue, she has an answer: "a grown-up. Maybe a suspicious secretive, irritating grown-up. But no longer a kid. He's lost that. And now, as he grows older, he'll get still more powerful because he'll reach the further knowledge that there is no way out of loss, and so he'll have a new truth to talk about."

Late one night, at the Other End, before the trail boss was quite ready to get the wagon train going, Dylan and Bob Neuwirth and the rest of the gang are elevating their discourse.

"Hey, poet, sing me a poem!" one of them yells to Dylan.

"Okay, poet," says the Minstrel Guruji.

Delighted, Allen Ginsberg is saying, "It's like in a Dostoevsky novel, the way they've taken to calling each other poet. It's no more, 'Okay cowboy'. It's 'Okay poet.' They're using 'poet' as an honorific, practical thing, and that means they've grown old enough to see that poetry is tough, that it's a lasting practice bearing fruit over decades."

"Dylan has become much more conscious of himself as a poet," Ginsberg adds. "I've watched him grow in that direction. Back in 1968, he was talking poetics with me, telling me how he was writing shorter lines, with every line meaning something. He wasn't just making up a line to go with a rhyme anymore; each line had to advance the story, bring the song forward. And from that time came some of the stuff he did with the Band – like 'I Shall Be Released,' some of his strong laconic ballads like 'The Ballad of Frankie Lee and Judas Priest.' There was to be no wasted language, no wasted breath. All the imagery was to be functional rather than ornamental. And he's kept growing from there.

"Like he's been reading Joseph Conrad recently. *Victory* in particular. I found out when we were talking about the narrative quality of some of the newer songs – Hurricane and Joey and Isis. Bob related the way those songs developed to what he'd been learning about narrative and about characterization from Conrad. The way characterization and mood shape narrative. Now he's asking about H.P. Lovecraft. I wonder what that's going to lead to?"

It is near the end. In Toronto Joan Baez is backstage. On stage Dylan is beginning his acoustic set. A member of Gordon Lighfoot's band begins to move some equipment. Baez glares at him and he stops.

"The jerk didn't know any better," she says later, "but I didn't want to miss a note. I didn't want to miss a word. Even after all these shows the genius of The Kid was still holding it all together. I'd heard it all, every night and here I'm sitting again as close to him as I can get. And not only me. You look around and you see every member of the band and the guys in the crew listening too."

"What is it? what is it he has?" I ask.

"It's the power," Joan says. "It's the power."

"Oh, I'm hurtin'." It is the next morning. Bob Neuwirth groans and coughs in a most alarming manner. "This is a rolling writers' show," Neuwirth manages to say. "Nobody on this tour who isn't a writer. *Oh, I'm really hurtin'.* Even the equipment guys, the bus drivers, they're all jotting things down. It's a goddamn rolling writers' convention. *Oh my God, I can't even cough.* It's going to be such a drag when this tour is over."

Joan Baez, mildly sympathetic when she's not laughing, says to the audibly aching Neuwirth, "Do let me describe what happened to you last night. Everybody has his own way of dealing with anxieties," she explains to me, "and his way was to get himself black and blue. He got very, very drunk and ornery and for an hour and a half four very large security guards were wrestling him in the hall because they didn't want him to leave the hotel and go wreck Gordon Lightfoot's house where we were having a party. Well, he got there anyhow and he did wreck the house just a little. But everybody had a grand time, and now Neuwirth feels fine too, except he can't walk very well.

"You see, it's going to be rough for all of us when this is over. And Neuwirth's way of handling that was to have an early blowout. God, it's depressing at the end."

*   *   *

At the beginning, in Plymouth, Massachusetts, Elliott Adnopoz (long since transubstantiated into his vision, Ramblin' Jack Elliott) sees an old friend, the replica of the *Mayflower,* on whose rigging he, an expert sailor, had actually worked years before. Climbing to the top of the mizzenmast, Elliott explodes with a long, joyous, "Ahoy!" and waves to the Minnesota poet in the cowboy hat below as Allen Ginsberg proclaims, "We have, once again, embarked on a voyage to reclaim America."

At least it is steady work, especially for a minstrel.

Rolling Thunder Stones

Allen Ginsberg

Nine poems from the troupe newsletter

I

A crystal ball's on the Piano – Is Dylan leading us to the
Mountain, or are we moving out thru vast calm open space
Empty free of God? Kerouac's grave's in Lowell, Sunday
we'll sing over his bones. We land in America today,
Plymouth Rock, step out and discover kingdom.

Oct. 31, 1975

II

Lay down Lay down yr Mountain Lay down God
Lay down Lay down yr music Love Lay down
Lay down Lay down yr hatred Lay yrself down
Lay down Lay down yr Nation Lay yr foot on the Rock
Lay down your whole Creation Lay yr mind down
Lay down Lay down yr Magic Hey Alchemist Lay it down
    Clear
Lay down yr Practise precisely Lay down yr wisdom dear
Lay down Lay down yr Camera Lay down yr Image right.
Yea Lay down yr Image Lay down Light.

Nov.1, 1975

III

Rolling Thunder Sunrise Ceremony Nov 5, 1975 (Verses improvised with Australian Aborigine Song-sticks at request of Medicine-man Rolling Thunder.)

When Music was needed music sounded
When a Ceremony was needed a Teacher appeared
When Student was needed Telephones rang
When Cars were needed Wheels rolled in
When a Place was needed a Mansion appeared
When a Fire was needed Wood appeared
When an Ocean was needed Waters rippled waves
When Shore was needed Shore Met Ocean
When Sun was needed the Sun rose east
When People were needed People arrived
When a Circle was needed a Circle was formed.

IV

Heroic ecstasy!   Nov. 8, 1975

V

Snow Blues
Nobody saves America by sniffing cocaine
Jiggling yr knees blank-eyed in the rain
When it snows in yr nose you catch cold in yr brain.
                                              Nov. 10, 1975

VI

My own Voice rose to Heaven in elation
When Rolling Thunder passed over this Nation
With Lightning flashing thru the whole Creation
I heard whole Cities chanting Jubilation
This land was made for you and me.
                                              Nov. 12, 1975

VII

Local Noise
Eleven hours night bus rolled thru blizzard New York
Honeymoon with Mist-Maiden Niagara Falls
Holy of Holies for Iroquois We're sleepy
He-No Thunder Enter our Music.

                              (with Anne Waldman)
                                    Nov. 15, 1975

VIII

To the Six Nations at Tuscarora Reservation

We give thanks for this food, deer meat and indian-corn soup.
Which is a product of the labor of your people
And the suffering of other forms of life
And which we promise to transform into friendly song and
    dancing
To all the ten directions of the Earth.

            (Adaptation of trad. Zen thanks-offering for food.
                                    Nov. 18, 1975

IX

Snow falls	in thee
Souls freeze	is a drag
Speed kills	dead bag
heart's ease	Smoke grass
Alcohol	Yaas Yaas
fools wills	Shake ass
O slaves	mind's wealth
Who craves	joint's health
junk raves	Ready?
Downer's	Medi –
angers	tations
eyes blur –	patience

I sing   eyes keen
Rolling   serene
Thunder   as graves
Ho Ho!   saves! saves
Macho   nations
frenzy

Dec. 4, 1975

Tubes Help You Thrive More Sleazily

Stann Findelle

New Musical Express, 20 March 1976.

"IT'S DANGEROUS back here, so watch your step, especially during scene changes," says Mort Moriarity, manager and back stage commentator on the Tubes, the group that squirts its letters from a container of "Joy-Jell" marital lubricant.

It's Saturday night in smelly old San Bernardino, a cowtown about thirty road apples down from Los Angeles, and the group is readying up to play the local Civic Firetrap. Mort sports a flesh wound on his pate from a previous evening when he didn't watch his and was struck by shrapnel flying from the group's arsenal of volatile stage props.

Night after night, the twelve or so maniacs furiously mount and discharge off the stage in a programme that plays like a television screen might if someone twirled the channel selector like a roulette wheel.

This writer sits like a voyeur in the foyer as the girls like your mother always warned you about – Re Styles, Mary Nyland, Cindy Osborne, Helene Gauxe and Leila T. Snake – unabashedly pancake make-up their bare behinds and tune up their G-strings in preparation for the mini-Busby Berkeley burlesque of Tom Jones' "It's Not Unusual".

Other quick change costumes are set in order like a brace of loaded muskets for the show's barrage of vignettes.

The girls are only slightly cognisant of my presence as they pad around with their freshly rouged cheeks, although one mistakes me for a security man, and asks where the toilet is. I inform her

that anywhere in the building will qualify and she laughingly
agrees.

Outside, the crowd is damn near ferocious. There are about
3,000 "San Berdoo" no-necks being stuffed into a place where
the walls sweat at 2,300 maximum. Plenty of 'em are bent out of
shape because they have to stand up the whole set. But this is the
atmosphere the Tubes prefer; indeed, perpetuate. They dig
playing the "toilet" circuit. Every night plays like a royal flush.

THE TUBES do it alone these days with no opener or inter-
mission. Nobody would dare share a bill with them. Led
Zeppelin got burned once, when, in front of a 60,000 stadium
in San Francisco, the Tubes stole it all away by throwing giant
amphetamine tablets at the crowd during "White Punks on
Dope".

Then, in 1974, The Kinks mysteriously cancelled (word was
getting out) leaving the vanilla suited John McLaughlin holding
the bag. The Tubes fiendishly dressed up in the white costumes
of Wooder Bread bakers, with loaves of Wonder Bread supplied
by the company that thought they were doing a collage project.

The Tubes threw bread and the crowd threw back everything
they could get their hands on, including bottles, shoes, lettuce,
and grapefruit. The stage looked like a blitz of fruit salad. And
then they introduced McLaughlin . . .

The names of the principals are too good to be fake: John
Waldo (Fee) Waybill is the leader, Maypole, chameleon man,
whose previous experience was an actor and an equipment mover,
skills which have come in handy. More about him in a second.

Re, which rhymes with Fee, is the lead lady, who retired from
films after a meteoric career in the Alexandro ("El Topo")
Jodorowsky "The Holy Mountain". where she played a crazed
art dealer's best piece.

It is she who Fee bodily whips around the stage in their
infamous "Mondo Bondage" S&M leatherette sequence.

There's a lot of other people running around, although drummer Prairie Prince – who has the credentials of playing sessions
with George Harrison, Nicky Hopkins and Journey – artist and

synthesizer Michael Cotton and guitarists Rick Steen and Bill Spooner seem to be heavies in the group's structure. There's also a fellow known as the Sadistic Leroi, who, among other things. guards the girl's flanks back stage.

The programme includes a grand assortment of warp-rock theatrics, with Fee splitting into many weird characters. There's the snarling "Dr. Strangekiss" with arthritic metallic hand-jive, "Space Baby" where their stacked backdrop of 19 in. TV screens are a scream.

If you sit close enough, you can make out Fee in the myopic parabolic claustrophobia typical of broadcasts from astronautical capsules. Fee radios how the space ships are performing a three way "Menage a trois" docking procedure for Project Ur-Anus.

More medical and musical malpractice develops as Dr. Fee conducts surgery on a double neck guitar which gives bloody birth to a ukelele.

There's no need to fret, because the "It's Not Unusual" soon follows with the ladies impeccably choreographing their generous rear ends (this always devastates the crowd).

Finally, there is the finale the emergence of Quay Lewd (Fee in 18 in. stilt platform shoes) and his legendary avalanching KILL amplifiers.

It's rock and psychodrama, where every fantasy and fetish is paid its due. The Tubes even invent a few new ones for different occasions.

BUT AS WORD gets out, the segments lose potency. A cold cream-covered Fee strips down to a decent looking chap back-stage, comes down off his 18 inches and confides, "After our mammoth European tour, we shall record a new album, and develop a totally new Spring show."

What does he expect the European crowds to be like? "I expect them to be very European. A bunch of foreigners, mostly."

Foreigners indeed. And what region of the world first disgorged this mob of misfits, these overdosers of *Howdy Doody*, *Hopalong Cassidy* and *Heels and Hose* magazine?

"We come from Arizona," he says, slyly.

Arizona, besides being from where the yellow streams of Goldwater stem, is a commonwealth with an interesting similarity to Australia.

The current denizens of both sovereignties descend from fixed populations: the Australians from the criminals who were shipped there when it was a penal colony; Arizonians from the seed of thousands of tuberculosis patients that used to be shipped there when arid weather was the only cure.

It figures that many Australian bands and singers commit wholesale larceny on existing styles and gimmicks of flourishing acts and that an Arizonian band would be called the Tubes and act like they're in some terminal stage of the pox.

In this woefully deserted desert region, the Tubes were spawned from the wedding of two hard barbecue rock acts, known uncleverly as "Arizona" and "Beans".

"Arizona had been known to use the alias 'Los Frijoles et Los Radar Man De Uranus?" offered Waybill, to very little avail. "The group used that name to play in Mexico. They were subsequently deported." Arizona mixed with Beans, whose prior credits, make that demerits, included representing San Francisco in Japan's Expo '70 (!?).

Re strokes into the dressing area, arm in arm with Prairie, for a semi-drowsy discussion about how tough it is to get body make-up off. This writer once had the unfortunate experience of playing an Indian snake-charmer in a soft porno flick known as "House of 1,000 Delights", and believe me, it was no delight to find melon-almond yellow greasepaint number 6 on my towel for six months subsequent.

"Well, one way to live with it is not to wash," leaked Re. "But my procedure is to dive, shower, rub-down, scrub – fine. Start over. Di-sh-rub-scrub-fine. Wanna hear it again? Now I suppose you're gonna ask some sexist questions, right?" she snaps good-naturally, if you can imagine one snapping with good nature. "We do all this complicated dancing steps, and all you see is when we push the *big ass*, right?"

She looks at Prairie, who in turn looks uncomfortable. "As to the G-strings, well Prairie here and I used to do a puppet show.

But I used to pull the strings." Prairie has a "please don't say anymore" look in his eyes.

We pan back to Fee with some economic questions.

You see the Tubes usually lose money every show, even though they sell out.

Also, there's a problem mutually shared by other stage acts like Sha-na-na and Flash Cadillac, that the records, unless they're video discs, cannot transmit the essence of the live imagery.

Fee seems to take the posture of a trouper who does it for the love, rather than the money.

"We don't look to graduating towards large stadiums. The loss of intimacy is not what we desire. Perhaps the TV screens could be larger, but there's a lot going on stage as well. We'd rather do two shows nightly in a place like this than lose the impact in a basketball hall".

This was certainly worthy of honourable mention, a group not working towards the easy buck while putting on a hell blaster of a show.

Fee was less open about the new programme in the works. "Well, it's a secret. We're thinking and absorbing many new elements. Some fat girl almost pulled me off the stage in a recent show. We may add that."

Then, after a moment's reflection at my cxaggcratcd dismay, he adds. "Well, I'll tell you this much. I may grown some tits for the Spring show. We might also sell some used TV's at inter-mission".

Fee did not elaborate whether the TVs would be televisions or transvestites . . .

Well, bless-uh muh soul, what's-uh wrong with me?

Mick Farren

New Musical Express, 22 May 1976.

WHEN AN artist hasn't produced anything of note for something like 14 years, the world begins to judge him on just about anything but his talent. When no original work is forthcoming, a superstar tends to be evaluated by his fans, his tastes, his vices and his private life.

This is exactly what happened to Elvis Presley. During the latter half of the 1950s he virtually turned popular music inside out. Then he was drafted into the U.S. Army. When he returned to civilian life his career came to what almost amounted to a full stop.

With a couple of notable exceptions, nothing he produced from 1962 onwards had any creative power whatsoever. His work turned into a constant re-hash of a tried and trusted formula.

The gap between his work and the mainstream of rock widened to the point where Presley became a strange archaic figure, maybe fascinating as a peculiar phenomenon, but hardly valid as part of the on-going path of modern music.

To put it bluntly, he became the last surviving dinosaur, whose rampages through the Las Vegas hotel lounges were entertaining spectacles, social curiosities, but hardly works of art.

A lesser individual would not have survived. He would have been quietly buried in the rock encyclopedias as another star who went nova and quickly burned out.

Probably the most amazing thing about the two-decade Elvis Presley epic is the way in which he generated sufficient energy during the first six years of his career to carry him through 14 years or more when he did nothing.

Presley still has the wholehearted attention of a large section of the public, although it is mainly concerned with his marriage, his waistline and strange reclusive life. Hardly a week goes by without some Presley story turning up somewhere in the press.

So what did happen during those first six years? What was the nature of the 50s explosion that provided Presley with so much momentum that it carried him, as a full blown superstar, clear into the latter half of the 70s?

Exactly 20 years ago (11 May 1956, to be precise), "Heartbreak Hotel" went into the *NME* singles chart, for the first time, at number 15.

So this seems as good a time as any to take a close look at the early career of Elvis Presley.

After 20 years of media overkill, the facts of Presley's formative days have become almost totally obscured by the legend. Research is made even more complicated by his super-isolated way of life.

He has never given what could be called a serious interview, and never made any real mention of his musical roots.

The legend tells us that the truck driving boy stopped at Sun Records' studio and cut a birthday greeting disc for his mama. He was later called back by Sam Philips and proved a total failure as a crooner. Fooling around in the coffee break, rock and roll was discovered by accident.

The legend presents Elvis as a simple-minded hood who had the manners of James Dean and unbeknown to himself, had, both in voice and body, the power to awake teenage America, who promptly carried him to fame and fortune on a hysterical tide.

Yeah?

It does sound something like a fairy tale, doesn't it? It is also hard to believe that Elvis Presley could have been the complete simpleton that legend sets him up to be, and actually do what he did.

On the other hand, could anyone who was all that smart have

participated in those awful films, recorded the dreadful songs and generally acted the creative fool for so many years?

This, my friends, is the basic paradox of Elvis Presley. Was he simply an unwitting product of time and environment, or was he a great deal shrewder than the legend has ever given him credit for?

CERTAINLY IN Britain the environment didn't seem, on the surface, to be in the least ready for Elvis Presley. The *NME* of 11 May 1956 was full of Dickie Valentine, Lita Rosa and Alma Cogan. The cover among other things, featured Max Bygraves playing the drums. The two main features were a Sinatra story and a special welcome home to Ted Heath (the band leader, not the late Prime Minister: in 1956 the grocer was probably only a gleam in the Young Conservatives' eye).

Number one record that week was "No Other Love" by Ronnie Hilton.

In America, the situation was a good deal more acceptable. "Heartbreak Hotel" had been number one for some weeks. Teenage America was still, in its own way, mourning James Dean, who had been dead for just nine months, and Presley was being hailed as the "Hillbilly Cat" or the "King of Western Bop."

More important, the success of "Heartbreak Hotel" was the culmination of a revolution that had been changing the entire course of country music. Presley may or may not have been a leader in this revolution, but he was certainly its figurehead.

In the Southern States, although the Supreme Court had outlawed segregation in 1954, racism was still at its height. It was the era of Governor Faubus and Federal troops being moved into Little Rock, Arkansas, to quell redneck violence. Country and Western was also firmly in the grip of racial discrimination.

The fact that the country establishment had no truck with black music had stifled just about any progress after the death of Hank Williams in 1953. Drums were banned from the stage of the Grand Old Opry. Many young white musicians were in open revolt against the conservative stranglehold.

All over the South, small groups of pickers in their teens and 20s were going directly against the natural order of things and listening in to black radio stations and buying singles of people like Howling Wolf, Junior Parker and Lowell Fulson.

One of these groups was in Lubbock, Texas, centred around a young man called Buddy Holly. Another was in Norfolk, Virginia, around an ex-sailor who used the stage name of Gene Vincent.

But by far the most important was in Memphis, Tennessee, where Carl Perkins, a guitarist called Scotty Moore, a bass player called Bill Black, a young pianist, Jerry Lee Lewis, and a number of other renegade country boys, had a loose association with Sam Philips, the owner of Sun Records.

Sun split its product between country music and so called 'race' records. Philips had already recorded black acts like Rufus Thomas, Doctor Ross, Willie Nix and Little Milton, as well as a comprehensive country catalogue.

The aim of the ol' boys who hung around Philips's tiny, chicken coop studio was to fuse these two musical forms and produce a new, exciting, energetic hybrid that would provide a tangible sound for the restless Dean generation of teenagers.

Unfortunately, this interest in black music tended to upset the rednecks. They had a handy phrase for people who took too sympathetic an interest in the doings of blacks. The epithet was "Nigger lover".

Whether Elvis Presley shared these ideas of combining R&B and country before he met up with Sam Philips and Scotty Moore is doubtful. His main musical interests seem to have been Billy Eckstine, Dean Martin and The Inkspots. Although his list of favourites was not one hundred per cent white, it was hardly jumped-up R&B.

It could be that Presley's musical taste, as published in the fan magazines, may have been tailored to poor white prejudices. His knowledge of bluesmen like Arthur (Big Boy) Crudup, and the way in which his early stage act leaned heavily on the black school of strutting-stud-blues-shouters-who-shook-their-thing indicated that his interest in black music was more than what was considered healthy for a red blooded Southern Boy.

AT THIS point you have to bear in mind that in the middle 50s, it required quite an effort of will for a white boy to tune in to a black radio station or buy black records. Drug stores, restaurants and truck stops, and the juke boxes that went with them, were strictly segregated.

The fact has to be faced, the young Elvis Presley was probably a little weird. He was the protected and, within their restricted income, the pampered only child of a poor white family. A degree of the protectiveness may have stemmed from the infant death of his twin brother Jesse.

Contemporary publicity made a whole big deal about Presley's taste for pink suits, black shirts, white shoes and the entire hoodlum drag for which he became famous. What nobody ever mentioned was the source of his style.

In fact, Presley seems to have directly copied the 50s pimps who hung about in the black neighbourhoods. They were just about the only other people in town who wore the kind of matching pink outfit that Scotty Moore recalls him wearing at their first rehearsal.

The only people who sold those kinds of threads were the sharp stores down in nigger town.

Thus we have this picture of a poor white boy. His parents are indulgent to the point where they buy him a guitar and later his own car when they figure he needs it. He copies the styles of the black pimps from across town, and has at least a passing interest in black R&B. His mannerisms are straight from Dean and Brando.

This is hard to reconcile with the legend of the artless hick who showed up at Sun Records wanting to sound like Dean Martin.

Even the legend makes it pretty clear that when he went into the Sun studios to make his very first demo tapes, he didn't need all that much persuasion to start rocking out on Arthur Crudup's "That's Alright Mama".

It could be that Presley went into the Sun studios without any ides beyond trying to sound like Dean Martin, but was maneuvered into R&B and "That's Alright Mama" by Moore, Black and Philips who recognised his potential. Certainly Scotty Moore became his first ad hoc manager and was a considerable influence in those early days.

After a period of rehearsals, Sam Philips got an acceptable cut of "That's Alright Mama". Once the single was released, one of Philips's first tasks was to prove to the Southern audience that Elvis was white. This was deftly accomplished in an interview with Dewey Phillips (no relation) on the Memphis radio station WHBQ.

By asking Presley what high school he went to, he subtly got the information across. Everyone in and around Memphis knew when Presley replied "Hume Highschool" it was a segregated white school.

Again, contrary to the legend, "That's Alright Mama" wasn't an immediate smash hit. Although it clocked up healthy sales around the South, the next move for Presley was a gruelling period of one night stands around the South.

This time on the road was an intense, make or break episode in the Presley saga. Crowded into beat-up station wagons, covering hundreds of miles a day, eating garbage food and living in cheap motels, the pace was crushing.

Although Presley has never been directly associated with drugs, there is no doubt that the majority of musicians playing these backroad circuits depend heavily on amphetamines, benzedrine and No-Doze. If the speed didn't get to Presley, certainly the strain of seemingly endless one nighters did.

Scotty Moore recounts:

"He had so much energy in those days we'd have to sit up nights and wear him out so we could go to sleep. There'd be pillow fights, we'd wrestle. Anything we could think of. It, like, wore us out.

"Every day, every night was the same. He chewed his fingernails, drummed his hands against his thighs, tapped his feet and every chance he got he'd start combing his hair."

When this bundle of nerves and energy was pushed out on

stage it proved to be the most exciting thing the South had seen
since the civil war.

HAVING GROWN used to the portly, posturing, sequinned
Las Vegas superstar of the 70s, it's hard to realise just how wild
the young Presley actually was on stage.

He was strikingly good-looking in the fashionable delinquent
manner. He was mean, frenetic, and as greasy as any teenage hood
who swaggered down the main street of the small towns where
Presley and his bands played town halls, movie theatres, high
school gyms and National Guard armouries.

Hardly any record remains of those early stage shows, only a
few photographs and the memories of the people who attended
them. Even this scanty evidence, however, proves beyond a
doubt that the young Elvis was an explosive performer. He
used his body with the same outrageous abandon as Mick
Jagger.

His moving on stage seems to have summed up frustration,
barely repressed sexuality and spasmodic violence in the kids
growing up in Eisenhower's paternal and paranoid America.

His tense, braced leg, gunfighter stance that would suddenly
erupt into angry, fluid motion; the dropping to the stage, sliding
on knees and the constantly bumping, grinding hips said it all to
the teenagers in the audience.

The girls in the front row were jerked from their Bible Belt
upbringing into screaming hysteria. They fought to get at the
larger than life stud in the gaudy suits and longer sideburns than
any hot rod punk.

Bob Neal, Presley's manager before Colonel Tom Parker came
into the picture, talks about these primal audiences:

"You'd see this frenzied reaction, particularly from the young
girls. We hadn't gone out and arranged for anybody to squeal and
scream. Not like Frank Sinatra did in the 40s. These girls
screamed spontaneously."

At first, Presley was at the bottom of the bill in these small-
town package shows, but he quickly moved up to the headliner
who closed the show. This wasn't simply because of his popu-

larity. Other acts on the bill flatly refused to face the audience after Presley had finished with them.

Unwittingly he created a good deal of hostility among the other performers. Some of them looked on the near-riot situations that he whipped up in the crowd as a deliberate sabotage of their own careers.

Hostility didn't only come from the performers. Some of the male punks in the audience reacted with as much intensity as the girls. However, the intensity was of a very negative kind. As his fame spread through the South. so did the number of adolescent rednecks who laid in wait to take a swing at the nigger-loving faggot who was getting the flower of Southern womanhood in an uproar which more than likely distracted the ladies' attention from the punk's own backwoods macho posturing.

In Lubbock, Texas, one teenage gang went so far as to fire-bomb Presley's car after a local scandal sheet had printed a phony story suggesting he had been sleeping with the local police chief's daughter.

Bob Neil again: "It was almost frightening, the reaction that came to Elvis from the teenaged boys. So many of them, through some sort of jealousy, would practically hate him. There were occasions in some towns in Texas when we'd have to be sure to have a police guard because somebody'd always try to take a crack at him. They'd get a gang and try to waylay him or something.

"Of course, Elvis wasn't afraid of them and was quite willing to defend himself – and did on occasions."

In fact, it would appear that Presley was not only willing to defend himself, but actually enjoyed a good punch-up.

There was the celebrated incident when he beat up a gas station attendant who ridiculed him while he was having his car filled up. The pump jockey appeared in court looking more than a little battered, while Presley was virtually unmarked. The verdict still, however went in Presley's favour.

Although photographs are about all that remain of those early stage shows, there is what seems to be fairly accurate recreation of their atmosphere in the second of Presley's films, "*Loving You*".

In a lengthy stage show sequence at the end of the picture

there's at least some live show excitement. During the song "Got A Lot Of Living To Do", he cuts loose in a series of the most amazing routines, knee and arm swinging in perfect sync, going through seemingly impossible hip gyrations and moving across the stage on the points of his cowboy boots. He outstrips even James Brown in superlative showmanship.

Of course, it's only a recreation, the movie has obviously watered down and sanitized what must have happened at a real small town concert. The audience of extras remain obediently in their seats, and you get the impression that even Presley was being to some extent kept in check.

AFTER PRESLEY signed with RCA Victor and started on the path to becoming a fully fledged superstar. the documentation of his live acts, although less than satisfactory, becomes a little bit more complete. Footage of the Steve Allen and Ed Sullivan TV shows that provided him with useful stepping stones to nation-wide fame is still intact, although Presley was made to tone down his presentation considerably before he was let loose on TV.

There also exist a number of newsreel clips. One of these of Elvis performing "Heartbreak Hotel" at an open air concert, is little short of magnificent. He slides across the stage, his arms flailing like a windmill and his knee going through wide swinging rotations in time with the beat. Although the photography is patchy and the sound less than a joke, it gives a tantalising glimpse of the power of the man when he was at his youthful peak.

As his popularity rose to greater and greater heights, the controversy that surrounded Presley puffed itself up at the same speed as his income and record sales. It grew beyond the simple physical danger of a few pimply J.Ds wanting to rough him up.

News commentators, syndicate columnists, Bible thumping preachers, bush league sociologists and pop psychiatrists all discovered that knocking Elvis Presley was a cheap and painless way of racking up points with the mums and dads of middle America.

The stream of incentive more than equalled the vilification that greeted the Stones when they first attracted media attention.

He was attributed with almost singlehandedly inventing juvenile delinquency. He was accused of leading civilisation back to the jungle with voodoo rhythms. Some of the most extreme fundamentalists saw him as an agent of the devil.

A gas station owner in Texas (Elvis seems to have had a particular trouble with gas station people) offered to smash a Presley record with every purchase of five gallons or more.

A Massachusetts District Attorney, Garret Byrne, told an eagar press: "Rock and roll gives young hoodlums a chance to get together. It inflames teenagers and is obscenely suggestive."

The *New York Daily Times* went even further. It demanded a crack down on riotous rock and roll, describing the music as a "Barrage of primitive jungle beat set to lyrics which few adults would care to hear." The answer, it went on, was to ban all teenagers from dancing in public without the written consent of their parents and a midnight curfew for anyone under 21.

A shame to say, but even *NME* got dragged into the act – in the issue of 5 October, 1956. From New York, they schlepped up a psychologist called Dr Ben Walstein who attempted to explain why rock drove kids apeshit. After listening carefully to "Blue Suede Shoes", he opined:

"The first impression I get from this has to do with this business of 'don't step on my 'blue suede shoes' . . . don't hurt me . . . allow me to have a sense of independence. I think also there is some sexual component in this in that one might say that the blue suede shoes represent something that has not been tried by the adolescent. There is certainly an anti-formalism in Presley's work, a mood of rebellion."

Heavy stuff, huh?

Time magazine was surprisingly kind.

"Without preamble, the three-piece band cuts loose. In the spot-light, the lanky singer flails furious rhythms on his guitar. In a pivoting stance his hips swing sensuously from side to side and his entire body takes on a frantic quiver, as if he had swallowed a jack-hammer."

It was the *New York Journal American* that really put the boot in.

"Elvis Presley wiggled and wriggled with such abdominal gyrations that burlesque bombshell Georgina Southern (A big league stripper of the time) really deserves equal time to reply in a gyrating kind. He can't sing a lick, makes up for vocal short-comings with the weirdest and most plainly planned suggestive animation short of aborigine's mating dance."

Just so their parents' paranoid fears wouldn't be totally without foundation, the kids went out and obligingly staged a few real-life atrocities of their own.

In Jacksonville, Florida, they tore the clothes off Presley's back. In Whichita Falls, Texas, they took his Cadillac apart, in Fort Worth the local maidens carved his name into their flesh with pen knives. In San Jose, California, teenagers routed the local police department, injuring 11 cops. There was another riot in sedate Boston, at the Massachusetts Institute of Technology.

Probably strangest of all, in Asbury Park, New Jersey (now who the hell is it comes from Asbury Park, N.J.?) 25 "vibrating teenagers" were hospitalised following a record hop.

Yes, gentle reader, as they said in the NME of 15 June, 1956. it was "Presleymania". (Even then you could read it here first).

IT WOULD be an understatement to say that this kind of two-way hysteria must have had profound effect on Presley's person-ality. It would probably be about as profound as being run down by Apollo Seven.

If his subsequent behaviour is anything to go by, the two things that must have loomed large in his consciousness were that he must erect an impenetrable barrier between himself and his maniac fans, and that those same fans were so maniacal that it was pointless to take vast amounts of trouble creating quality product when they'd scarf up just about any crap he cared to dish out.

In 1956 this second idea may have been pretty vestigial. A few years still had to pass before it become the sad hallmark of most of his work.

The first one, however, was a living reality. Elvis had to be guarded day and night if he was to remain in one piece. It's no exaggeration to say that some of his fans were crazy enough to tear him limb from limb and keep the bits as souvenirs.

Other performers, too, were kept at a distance. Squeaky clean Pat Boone tells the story of how they were double billed on a rock spectacular. He had looked forward to a dressing room heart-to-heart with this rock and roll phenomenon.

When Presley finally arrived at the auditorium, Boone realised that no cozy man to man chats were going to be possible – Presley was constantly surrounded by a large team of sinister looking, and possibly armed, bodyguards.

Already in 1956 he was on the way to that life sentence in maximum security places.

Elvis Presley's isolation from what we've come to call "the street" was total. He was far more cut off than either The Beatles or the Stones or even Dylan ever were.

Presley was a rock and roll prince completely on his own. Back in the 50s there were no elite watering places. No Ad Libs, Speakeasys, Max's or Ashleys where stars could pass the time with other rock aristos. Indeed, there were no other rock aristos. If he wanted to relax it was a matter of renting a cinema or amusement park after the common punters had gone home and filling it with vetted chicks and professional payroll buddies.

IT'S A matter of debate whether the isolation of Elvis was the way the Colonel planned it, or simply a set of cumulative circumstances that he exploited. Colonel Tom Parker, always a strange hybrid of W.C. Fields and Machiavelli, certainly seems to have been responsible for shutting down all his boy's cultural inputs and by the time Elvis went into the Army, they were virtually at zero.

The Memphis Mafia was already in embryonic action, and few people got past Cousin Eugene and the other good ol' boys who copped a weekly wage for keeping Elvis amused.

No artist can survive without some kind of line to the outside world. Without that artists stagnate and wilt into a welter of purposeless repetition.

This was exactly what happened to Elvis Presley. His information from the outside world became totally filtered by Colonel Tom and the Memphis Mafia. His faith in Parker was absolutely implicit. After all, hadn't the Colonel turned him into one of the greatest superstars in history?

Tom Parker, a huckster to the core, took the attitude through-out Presley's career that if the bucks came rolling in for inferior product, then why bust a gut making a contribution to culture? You sometimes get the impression that the Colonel was another one who reached for his gun when he heard the word culture.

This was, after all, the man who, even when Presley was a huge star, still liked to strap on a change apron and get out among the crowds and hawk souvenirs or programmes.

His attitude may have made Presley a multi-millionaire, but it deprived the 20th century of one of its greatest white blues singers.

When Elvis came out of the Army he moved into an impene-trable cocoon. He also seemed to stop thinking. In his private world he gave the impression that his ambitions went no further than a constant stream of expensive toys. As long as the go-karts, girls, guns, Cadillacs and colour TVs kept coming, Elvis looked as though he was happy.

Certainly his work declined. The Presley operation took the attitude that anything would do as long as it had the Presley mark of authenticity on it. It was as though Rembrandt had started knocking out quick scenic views because all it took was the signature to get the bucks.

His method of working became grossly simple. When a new song was being considered, a Presley imitator was hired on to work out the vocal part. This would be played to Presley who, unless he felt exceptionally inspired, would merely copy what he heard. It was a ghastly contrast to the pains he took over "Heart-break Hotel" or "Hound Dog". (He did thirty takes of the latter before he was satisfied he had it right).

The young Phil Spector worked on demos of Leiber and Stoller songs for Presley. He gives a frightening insight into Elvis's post-army recordings.

"Songwriters would come to me and say. 'You make the demo

for us, get a good drum sound get a guitar sound, get a kid that really sounds like him, y'know?' There was a kid named David Hill who used to do a lot of Elvis's demos. Brian Hyland was another and P.J. Proby. A lot . . . I forget their names. People you'd call in say 'sing like Elvis Presley'. and they'd do it. Then you stood a much better chance of getting Elvis to record it, because he always followed the demonstration records.

"If there was a lick or a riff that appealed to him, he wanted it in the record. In fact, many times he would use the demonstration track that was used in New York, and just sing over it. And that was released as the new Elvis Presley single. Far out, right?"

Immediately after Elvis came out of the Army, he went into the studio. Although it only took 12 hours to record, "Elvis Is Back" must qualify as one of his best albums.

His version of Lowell Fulson's classic "Reconsider Baby" proved beyond doubt his awesome power when he got down and actually sang the blues. The track also gave tenor player Boots Randolph a chance to lay down one of the great rock and roll brass solos of all time.

Tragically, "Reconsider Baby" was a fleeting swan-song. After that the stream of musical porridge began. Now and then something would surface, "Put The Blame On Me", "Burning Love", parts of his TV spectacular, snatches of live Vegas shows, as tantalising glimpses of what might have been.

At 40, it's probably too late for Elvis to turn back to his roots and stop the slide down to becoming a portly curio. Let's face it, he's now been rich for longer than he was ever poor. The rich don't take to change gladly.

I fear all we have left of Elvis Presley are the old records and a lot of speculation about what might have been and why.

Speculation can go on all night. The only person who can tell us the truth about Elvis Presley is Elvis Presley, and you know he don't talk.

Spitting into the eye of the Hurricane

Phil McNeill

New Musical Express, 15 January 1977.

STREET CORNER *paper seller: "Read all about it! Sex Pistols split up! Read all about it!" Passer-by: "Is it true?" Paper seller: "No, I just like to cheer people up."*
                    Cartoon in London Evening Standard.

THOSE FOUR Scumsurfers of the Apocalypse, their Satanic Majesties The Sex Pistols, have come to terrorise the Netherlands. Two nights ago they played Rotterdam with The Heartbreakers. Now it's Friday and with The Vibrators over from London to join the bill, they are headlining at Amsterdam's famous Paradiso Club for the second consecutive night.

Since they left London all hell has broken loose.

The straw that broke the camel's back was an incident at Heathrow Airport.

Spitting, allegedly puking, and generally horrifying fellow passengers, the Pistols hit the headlines again and EMI responded by terminating the band's contract.

Their manager, Malcolm McLaren, promptly denied that the termination was mutual as claimed, and, while the band checked into some poky down-town hotel, a couple of EMI bigwigs flew over to Amsterdam—the Hilton, natch—to persuade Malcolm to get mutual.

While the nation scanned the news with bated breath for latest developments, *NME's PHIL McNEILL* touched down at Amsterdam airport and zeroed in on the eye of the hurricane . . .

*   *   *

THE PARADISO is much bigger than I'd imagined it to be – at least twice the size of the Marquee, for instance, with the ambience of a much friendlier Roundhouse, a balcony, two quirky bars, pool and pinball, a high (five foot) stage with lighted stained glass windows behind; and hardly any sign of the public dope scene for which it's famed.

Two black guys morosely attempt to sell cocaine outside as *Guardian* rock writer Robin Denselow and I shuffle in just in time for The Vibrators' opening number.

For most of the audience, "No Fun" is their first taste of live English punk rock, and there could hardly be a better way to start: tongue-in-cheek nihilism, stampeding guitars and grotesque flash.

They're amused, seem to enjoy it, give it quite a good reception. The Vibrators' set is reviewed in full in *On The Town*.

Backstage, The Heartbreakers and Sex Pistols wander in as The Vibrators wander out. After a while there's a completely different population in the concrete box dressing room, and I sidle over and set up the tape machine next to Pistols drummer Paul Cook: You done the one at the 'Undred Club that time, didn't ya?

Phil McNeill: Yeah, a long long time ago.

Glen Matlock: Was you the bloke that was gonna "split down the middle"?

No, the main thing I've written about you recently was in the Stranglers piece, actually . . .

Cook: Luring 'em into saying naughty things. (Hugh Cornwell had called Rotten "a paranoid clown'.)

People were saying at the time what a bad deal it was for the Pistols, running into all this trouble, and it seemed to me if anything it was helping you because you were getting all these front pages. I mean, you're a household name now. But I must admit it seems to have changed somewhat since then.

Matlock: Backfired? In some ways, yeah. It's all part of it, though, isn't it, all the mad hassle. The more madder the better.

I don't know how you stand the pressure of it, though.

Cook: We're used to it already. I just think it's a load of bollocks. I don't know why they all write about it.

Matlock: You don't believe it till you've been the other side of it really.

Cook: Like that thing at the airport. I'm not kidding, straight up, we couldn't believe it when we got over here. Someone phoned up, said this that and the other – we just couldn't believe it. There was a press bloke waiting I suppose, just waiting at the airport for something to 'appen. We just acted our natural selves. It just beats me.

Wasn't there anything at all?

Cook: Nothing. Really. The bloke from EMI was with us all the time. He would have said if there was, but he didn't.

I've heard you're gonna refuse to let them (EMI) break the contract.

Cook: Come on, we're not just gonna let 'em say, "Get off the label, do this, do that."

You wouldn't rather just go somewhere else?

Cook: That's the point, innit? We're just letting Malcolm sort it out.

Matlock: A contract's a contract. If you sign a contract, right, and six months later they say you gotta tear it up . . .

Cook: If they do it with us, what chance have other bands got?

But I would have thought that working with a company that was so against you, you'd rather just get out.

Cook: Yeah, but it's the people at the top who are against us. The people in the record company, like the A & R guys, who work on the shop floor, they're behind the band – and they've got absolutely no say in it. It's yer John Reads – he's the guy that's in charge of *all* of EMI, not just the record company.

Matlock: He doesn't normally interfere.

What happened before the Grundy interview? It seemed at the time like you were just sitting there, right, here's our opportunity, we're gonna get on the box and . . .

Matlock: Swear!

Create havoc.

Matlock: No, we just went there and sat in a room for a bit and had a beer each, and he asked us a few questions – we just answered him. That was it. We never even spoke to the guy before it. He was just, like, sitting there, y'know – he looked a bit kinda pissed.

Cook: I think he incited *(obscured)* but he asked John – John said "Shit" under his breath – and he said "WHAT WAS THAT?" He said, "Nothing, no nothing." He said, "Come on, come on, I wanna hear it", y'know. What does he expect?

There's also at the moment a rather nasty rumour going round that you didn't play on the record.

Cook: We 'eard that too. We got on to them straight away and got a letter of written apology. We 'eard it on the radio, couldn't believe that one either. It seems totally wrong to go . . . *(obscured)*

One of the rumours is that Spedding was on the record.

Cook: Spedding can't play as good as that (*laughs*).

You did some work with Spedding though, didn't you?

Cook: Three tracks. A long time ago though. We really rushed in, but we come out of it alright. He produced on 'em. It was alright.

But the single is categorically you lot?

Cook: Sorry.

The single's definitely you lot?

Cook: Oh yeah, yeah. What a question! (*Laughs*). How can you believe it?

I don't believe. I gotta ask it, haven't I?

Cook: Yeah, okay. We 'eard it on Capital Radio, we just couldn't believe it.

How's the audience here taking to you?

Cook: Oh, alright. They was getting going last night.
They seemed to like The Vibrators.

Cook: All the bands went down really well last night.

What are your favourite bands out of the other bands that are around?

Cook: These boys.

The Heartbreakers? What do you reckon to the Vibrators?

Cook: Ah, you're trying to put me in that trap again what the Stranglers fell for.

They didn't fall for anything. They'd decided to give that interview before I walked in the room.

Cook: How other bands can just go out and say things about . . . I think any band that's about at the moment; trying to do something new, give 'em credit for it whether you like 'em or not. Don't just go out and slag 'em off, whether you like 'em or not. I think it's good that they're just doing it, that it's something new.

Jones *(from across room)*: Who's this?

Cook: He's from the NME.

Jones: What's your name?

Phil McNeill.

Jones (*aggressively*): Oh, are you?

Cook: No, they've been good to us lately.

We've been good to you all along. What's all this about spitting at the audience?

Cook: We don't. You been reading too much *Daily Mirror*.

Well, in the wake of reports of John spitting at the audience some bands have started doing it.

Cook: We read that in the press too, and suddenly we were playing and everyone started coming along and spitting at us. That's what they thought we wanted, y'know. Gobbing at us. In Manchester or somewhere.

What's your reaction to seeing people with safety pins through their jaws?

Cook: I've seen that too, yeah.

It seems like it's a development of John wearing safety pins through his shirt.

Cook: Let 'em do what they wanna do, that's what I say. Who cares?

And what about the great nazi thing that's going around now? You got a lotta kids coming to your gigs these days wearing nazi emblems and safety pins through their faces and god knows what else.

Cook: They take it too seriously, they really do. If they wanna wear a nazi armband, let 'em. I don't think kids are that political, really mean what they do. They like the shape of it. It's a good shape.

What about the Pistols? What's your politics?

Cook: Do what you wanna do. That's what we're doing, and getting turned down for doing it. Do you want to talk to John for a while? *(Rotten is standing nearby, back to us. Cook tugs his arm).* John. John! Here, this is Phil.

Rotten: No way.

Cook: He's from . . .

Rotten: *(Obscured, shrugging Cook off).*

Cook *(Slightly put out):* Alright. He don't wanna do it.

THE HEARTBREAKERS' set flashes by. It's been said here already – the Dolls, a heavied Ramones, not so fast though – the reception's comparatively quiet but the friendly atmosphere combined with the blazing rock on stage . . . it's a helluva gig.

I interview The Vibrators in the Paradiso office. They're euphoric because the guy from Amsterdam's other main club, the Milky Way, who blew out the gigs he'd booked for The Vibrators when the Grundy–Pistols thing erupted, came down last night and has booked them in for two days' time.

A charge shivers the room as "Anarchy In The UK" lams out in the background; Malcolm McLaren arrives and huddles heatedly with The Vibrators' manager. Bread.

A few songs into the Pistols' set we wind down the interview: it will appear here sometime soon. But let's go check the naughty boys . . .

THE JOHNNY Rotten Show is well under way. Long time no see. Not much sign of the vast improvements in playing we've heard about: the sound's much clearer than the early days, but the music is still primitive. Without Rotten they're a good, hefty drummer, an ordinary bassist and a mediocre guitarist.

"Substitute" and others go by. The crowd are up for the first time, standing fascinated but diffident. Rotten goes through his ostrich poses, the chin jutting, the mouth leering, the eyes rolling. They're playing what seems to be "No Future". It boasts the title line from the National Anthem.

There's a long break, with a lot of aural and visual aggro between the punters and the Rotten/Matlock duo, then they resume the song, very loud. It's sloppy, and it reaps silence.

A green-haired lady is sitting under a Christmas tree stuck on the wall behind the drums, and as they go into "(We're so pretty, oh so) Pretty Vacant" it occurs to me, vacantly, that it looks like she's wearing some gigantic hat. The Pistols are playing tighter, but it's still mighty basic. Jones compensates for his limited skill with a fair line in one-note breaks.

Johnny Rotten is a perplexing performer.

He has an extraordinary ability to enrage his audience.

At the most basic level it's his insults and his bad behaviour, but Rotten has something deeper. It goes deeper, too, than his contempt for society in songs like "I'm A Lazy Sod". And surely it goes beyond his looks, his fleabitten hunchbacked reptilian cadaver.

Somehow this guy repels virtually everybody, and somehow his power reaches through the taunts to the sensibilities of thousands, maybe even millions, of people who have only ever heard his name and seen his picture.

Yet he is mesmerising. He can't be ignored. He's not just some hooligan who swore on TV, he drags the most casual observer into, usually, a love-hate relationship: probably the most charismatic rock star to emerge since Bowie.

Suddenly a couple of kids at the front who have been hitting Rotten with woollen scarves start throwing beer. Not glasses, just beer – but for this laid-back mob it's the equivalent. While Rotten stands there Cook erupts from his stool and he and the girl chuck beer back, Matlock kicks his mike stand very nastily off the stage, and the rhythm section storms off. Jones is still riffing, and Rotten sends the girl to get the others back. They eventually return for the only really furious piece of music they play all night.

Meanwhile Malcolm McLaren stands impassive upon the mixing desk riser, his three-piece suited solicitor behind him.

The show really begins about now. It's got nothing at all to do with music, but so what? It's Entertainment.

The band have left the stage – all but Rotten, who sneers. "If you want more you can clap for it." Feeble applause. The disco starts, and feet start shuffling out:

But a chant is generating. Yes . . . yes . . . the Pistols are coming back. "Whatcha Gonna Do 'Bout It", nihilism incarnate.

They end but don't go. "You're boring," drones Rotten. This weird challenge to the audience to respond. I look round at McLaren – and see that he is standing there gesticulating to Rotten, the upswept arms of the "Get Up" movement and the hands clapping overhead . . . and Rotten is mimicking McLaren. This show ends when Malcolm says so.

The crowd raise a half-hearted chant. Rotten's response:

"Right, you fuckers, we're gonna do one more, so move or else forget about it."

It's a very good version of "Anarchy", lots of echo on the voice. End of act.

End of act? No way. McLaren is signalling Rotten again, and, puppet-like, Rotten copies him. Whether the audience wants one or not, there's going to be another encore. There is, and this time Rotten stomps off before Malcolm starts signalling.

The point of all these false encores eludes me, unless the Sex Pistols are actually unliberated enough to get an ego-boost out of such conventional trappings of success.

Their music is lumpen, but the spectacle is marvellous. That last sentence could easily be applied, coincidentally, to shows I've seen in the past year by Queen and the Stones – and like those bands today, the Pistols' main success is in show business.

Malcolm has agreed to speak to Robin Denselow and me at his hotel. How the hell do we find it?

We wander off in pursuit of the beleaguered mad scientist. It's freezing and I haven't eaten all day. We walk for miles. As we near our destination Steve Jones runs past, bums five guilders off me virtually in return for showing us where he's staying much to my bemusement . . . finally we're there.

And behold, McLaren appears. For some reason we can't go in so we conduct the interview standing on a hotel step by a canal at 3.00 in the morning. McLaren looks even more wasted than I feel, talking unstoppably like a man possessed, staring into space. There could be 2,000 of us listening.

"WE'VE HAD WORD that most of the majors won't touch us with bargepoles."

You haven't had offers from people like Polydor, UA?

"No, that's all guff, man – who's spreading those kinda rumours? There's nobody after us. We've had, I suppose you call it votes of confidence from the shop floors of various record companies, but you begin to realise that those sort of people don't have any control over the situation, just as it's happened in EMI.

"We've had people like the guy from EMI Publishing, Terry Slater, he rang me up today and he feels totally pissed off that he's been totally overruled. He's the head of EMI Publishing, he signed us four weeks ago for £10,000 and now he's been told that's all got to be quashed. He's been made to look stupid.

"The same goes for Nick Mobbs, who threatened to resign. He's now been told that would be very unhealthy for him, so they can produce a wonderful statement saying on EMI no one has resigned.

"There are different bands with different points of view. The real situation is that people on the board of directors at EMI do not agree with our point. The people who actually work for EMI, they do. But if they come out and make a statement to that effect they will get the sack, or they'll have to resign.

"Those truths have never come out. What appears in the press is that we have been thrown out by all EMI together, a wonderful consensus of opinion."

If it comes to the crunch and they force you to terminate, will you repay the advance?

"How are we going to repay the advance? We've already spent all the money maintaining ourselves here and on the tour. We're out here promoting their single – it's not just *our* single."

Is it out here?

"Yeah, that's the reason we're here. We weren't doing any other European territory simply because EMI sent a memo asking them not to release it. EMI Holland got the record out before that memo reached them. Now they're withdrawing it."

Are they blocking its sale in England?

"Oh yeah, it's being withdrawn in England."

If you do split with them, what happens to any tapes that are in the can?

"Those questions have been raised. They would prefer that we take the lot and go away with it.

"It's been very easy for them. Someone signs a contract for two years: that is an agreement between two parties. If you can tear that contract up in two months because they dislike the opinion of the band – by 'they' I mean the EMI board of directors – it makes a farce of the whole situation.

"What about all these other bands that are coming along? They sign a contract and some guy at the top, not the A & R guy who's responsible for signing, says 'I don't like what I'm hearing about this band, I don't want them on the company anymore. So they go out the window.'"

Who are the guys who've come over here?

"The managing director of EMI and the head of the Legal Department – Leslie Hill and Laurie Hall. They came over to terminate the contract and we haven't terminated it. They want us to have another meeting; at the moment they haven't met any of my proposals, probably because they have been told they can't meet anything.

"We had a two-hour meeting tonight.

"It's been very nice. We've come away to Holland and someone's decided behind our back to 'mutually terminate' the contract. Legally we're still on EMI Records.

"Now people on the EMI board are saying, 'Why the hell did we sign them in the first place? They're musically inadequate, it was too much money . . .

"But I spoke to Leslie Hill, the managing director of EMI Records, prior to us signing. It was him that was exhilarated by the band and thrilled at the idea of signing the act. He was fully aware of their public image, and he will not deny that.

"EMI had all the tapes to all the Pistols' songs. They heard them, they were excited at the prospect of signing this act and commercially gaining through it. We had had offers from other companies, but I went there because the sympathy with EMI was strong on the shop floor.

"Nick Mobbs, Tony Slater on the publishing side, David Munns on the promotion side, Mark Ryder the label manager, Paul Watts the general manager and Leslie Hill the managing director wanted to sign this act.

"Now they're saying, 'We have 4,000 employees on EMI and if we took a consensus of opinion I don't think you would raise the amount of votes necessary.'

"I made a proposal, I said, 'OK, find us an equivalent contract.' If I walk into Warner Brothers they're going to say, 'Well man, you didn't make it with EMI, the bad publicity, etcetera.'

"What they did on TV was something that was quite genuine. They were goaded into it, and being working class kids and boys being boys they said what they felt was . . . O.K. They don't regret it.

"The KLM situation at the airport was fabricated up to a point. Yeah, the band might have looked a little bit extraordinary, they may have spat at each other. Big deal. And someone may have appeared a little drunk. But they weren't flying the plane, they don't need to be that sober.

"There are these bands now that have some sort of petition, like Mud, Tina Charles, all these other Top Twenty acts, and sent round this petition to all the record companies saying that they do not support this kind of music."

(NME talked to Mud's manager, Barry Dunning, on Monday. He denied Mud had signed any petition, nor would they ever do so.)

"My lawyer asked: We'd like a meeting with John Read or the rest of the money. They'd rather give us the rest of the money than have a meeting. John Read speaks on behalf of all the shareholders, he controls the whole of EMI Ltd., which covers far more than just a record company. He wouldn't meet us. He sent Hill instead; every time you just get to speak to Hill. Hill has his orders and he can't move from that point."

How much money have you had of the £40,000?

"Half. The first year. But that has been spent on supporting a tour.

"We ended up selling the fucking record at the bloody door in Rotterdam and at the Paradiso last night. It's a joke."

What's next, a big legal battle?

"I don't know. I asked Hill if they can reconsider their situation, quite simply – and if they can't, why can't Capitol Records, who we're signed to in America? 'Oh well. Capitol Records decided to go along with Manchester Square.' They don't want any part of it.

"I said, 'What happens if we're on another label and the distribution is through EMI? Are EMI gonna distribute the record?' They can't really answer that. It's very difficult, it really is. I feel pretty bad about it.

"Hill's now saying, 'Can't you go to Virgin Records, I hear that's an interesting company.' Bollocks man, we went to Virgin Records before we went to EMI and they didn't wanna know.

"If we walk into another record company, what are they going to say? 'If you can't play anywhere and we can't hear your records on the radio and EMI decided to drop you . . .' What the hell are they going to do?

"It's not just EMI, it's people behind the scenes, guys that go on the radio and say we didn't play on our record, the guy that's scared to put us on *Top Of The Pops* even though we're in the breakers because the BBC don't want to be seen to be associated with us.

"What's it all about?"

UNTIL LAST week I had no sympathy whatsoever for the punks-as- martyrs line, but if what McLaren says about them not being able to land a contract elsewhere is true (I still don't really believe that one), and EMI Records do succeed in breaking their legal contract simply on account of thirty seconds of televised swearing, then I'll, I'll . . .

Phew, for a moment there I Almost Cut My Hair!

The McLaren interview was recorded on an EMI tape.

Fifty Tabs a Day Turned this Man into a Tree (nearly)

Phil McNeill

New Musical Express, 10 December 1977.

Frank Marino would like you to know that he is *not* the re-incarnation of Jimi Hendrix. Frank Marino has this to say: that he does *not* play heavy metal; that he *never* goes to rock concerts; and that punk rock is *not* his "cup of tea".

He also has this to say: that he is a "Deeply religious" man; that he once took 1,500 tabs of acid in one month and spent a year recovering: and that he is *furious* his record company haven't translated his "World Anthem" into Russian.

I say this: Frank Marino is a great guitar player. He says he is the only person in the world who truly *understands* Jimi Hendrix, and I am inclined to believe him.

Frank is tired. So tired he's shaking. He stepped off a plane from New York at 10:00 am, attended a press reception in his "honour" at lunchtime, has already undergone a bout of interviews, and now, at four o'clock, he's sagging painfully and deliriously in his CBS corporate chair, waxing soft and intense about the guy he must spend his life telling journalists about: James Marshall Hendrix.

You'd be forgiven for thinking Marino really was Jimi's ghost. Not only has he got a sublime control of his guitar; not only does his band. Mahogany Rush, line up like the Experience; not only does his drummer, Jim Ayoub, throw himself around the kit almost as delicately as Mitch Mitchell; not only does Frank sing like Hendrix, dance through innumerable subtle guitar tones and drift casually across the

frets like Hendrix . . . but sometimes he even *talks* like the
guy!

Frank Marino is gifted. Literally. Playing guitar came so easy
to him that he now strings a guitar left-handed at home and puts
himself through the tribulations of learning the damn thing, just
to see what it's like.

Can he bear telling the story yet again? Happily, he can, and he
takes it back to the days when he was just a teenager hanging out
on Montreal street corners. The summer of '69 . . .

"I was just a kid who hung around the park and beat up on
other kids and took drugs. What was happening '69 in America
was only just starting to happen there. Montreal was very back-
ward.

"So when the drugs finally hit me. I had nobody to go to.
Hallucinations? What's that? It really hit me, man. I was doing a
lot of acid, and in the last month before I quit – I quit drugs after
that – God, I did easily 1,500 trips of acid.

"And I got very sick. Physically. Demolished myself. I was 14
going on 15. And to make a long story short, I was in this hospital,
fucked up – and believe me, freaking out isn't the word: it took me
a year to recover.

"So here I am half dead, not knowing where I am – in fact
that's where the name Mahogany Rush came from, because I felt
like I was turning into a tree or a lot, like mahogany, and
whenever I felt like that I used to tell to tell my brother I was
having 'Mahogany rush'.

"So I'm in this hospital, thinking of these tunes I'd been
hearing on record players all summer – they happened to be
Jerry Garcia tunes – and there was a guitar there . . ."

AND out came Frank as an overnight acid guitar virtuoso. "I never
had any illusions that I really was Jerry Garcia or Jimi Hendrix." he
insists. That apparently, is a myth that's been blown up from the
first interview Frank ever did, when, a year or so after he left the
hospital, he recounted his experiences to the *Montreal Star*.

Still, Jimi is there, ever-present in the conversation. As Hendrix weaves in and out of the interview, it transpires that Frank, if

pushed, will accept just one categorisation on his music: Jimi's own stated goal, Sky Church Music. He asserts calmly that he understands Hendrix – musically – better than anyone else alive. In the same way that Hendrix was talking, shortly before drugs got *him*, about augmenting his band with guitarists whom he would direct, so Frank toys with the notion of adding three axes and some keyboards to his own trio.

His ambition is Hendrix's achievement; that peak of performance where, you cease to hear guitars, you just hear *music*.

Marino asks me to imagine listening to some glorious filmtrack and picking out the violins, cellos and piccolos. You just don't think about it.

He hasn't quite caught that yet, but on record at least he reckons he's close.

The idea, he assures me, is "never to lose sight of yourself". Religious talk? Well, Frank is a religious person.

He points to the heart-shaped gold locket around his neck. "You may think I'm crazy," he shrugs, "but in that locket there's a piece of the cross of Jesus Christ. My mother is Arabic, and her mother, and *her* mother, straight from the old Arabic country – my father is a Sicilian – and this has been handed down and down and down . . .

"I am a deeply Christian person. People might be cynical about it – that doesn't matter. I'm not pushing it on anybody. I'm not saying: 'Have you heard the good news?' like those people in the street. Nobody wants that. *I* don't even want that."

NEVERTHELESS, he does admit that religion governs some of his music. Lyrics, in fact, are Marino's prime shortcoming, many of his numbers being trivial love songs.

Those that aren't often resound with the skyblown idealism of Todd Rundren.

The prime example is the title track of Mahogany Rush's latest album, "World Anthem". In an explanatory note on the LP sleeve, Frank informs the listener how he's come to realise that what all people are searching for is "ultimately the same thing – peace and unity. I decided that the most useful part I could play in the achievement of this goal would be to create a world anthem."

Here's a sample of "The World Anthem":

> Now we stand united and
> We pledge eternal brotherhood
> Now we sing as one and bring
> Our hearts to all that's good.

The thing is, Frank doesn't sing it himself. The "World Anthem" track is purely instrumental; *you* sing the words yourself: To aid the process, the song is translated into no less than 11 different languages on the cover!

When I compliment him on this ingenious concept, he suddenly shrugs off his weariness and positively leaps across to me.

"Bravo!" he yells. "Let me shake your hand! You're maybe the fourth person who has realised why I didn't sing the words on the LP. Other people have said, 'Why don't you sing it?' But I said, no . . . they'll understand one day.

"Let them have it," he says grandly – "Them" being the people of the world. "Let them put the words on that *they* want. As soon as I put *my* voice on it it would become a Canadian World Anthem, or an American World Anthem."

So who did the translations?

"CBS. I asked them for the translations . . . I asked them for translations that they didn't give me! I wanted it in every language in the world, including dialects, Swahili and everything.

"Okay, they didn't wanna give me everything except the major languages. So why did they not include Russian? *Why* would they not include Russian? I screamed and yelled at them. I said the whole point, the whole *breaking* point in the world today is the Russians and the West.

"It's not . . . France, or . . . the real war is the Russians, that's the whole point. *And you don't give me Russian?* And I'm giving you a World Anthem! A World Anthem, but not for the Russians! That makes me look like I'm stoopid! And I'm *not* stoopid.

"But it was too late, and they wouldn't get me the translation. What could I do?

"I'm a victim of bureaucracy."

In concert, too, Frank Marino is also a victim – of technical limitations. I make no guarantees whatsoever about his onstage performance; at the time of writing, it remains to be seen.

But this I will say. If you have any love for electric guitar *music*, then a record collection without a Mahogany Rush album is like a World Anthem without a Russian translation.

A Clash of Interests

Miles

Time Out, 15 December 1978.

It's been a long time since anybody regarded The Who as a mod band, the Beatles as exponents of Merseybeat, or Bob Dylan as a folk-rocker. Musical movements enjoy even briefer lifespans than the careers of the musicians that emerge from them, and bands that start life in the turmoil of a new departure either vanish when times change or find a direction of their own. This has already happened to the British punk movement, and a magnificent crop of new groups are now developing in very different ways: The Jam, The Stranglers, XTC, The Buzzcocks, Siouxsie and the Banshees, the Only Ones, Wire.

The Clash are the punk band who've stayed closest to their roots, and by being the most uncompromising, they have retained most of that original hard energy. Now they're poised at that difficult stage between local artistic success (which these days means Europe) and a place in the global rock industry. They have embraced the advanced technology of rock and risked the pressures of the market and yet managed to retain their integrity. With a second album produced by the heavily metallic Oyster Cultist Sandy Pearlman and recorded in London, New York and San Francisco, The Clash no longer can feel at home in the dole queue. But they're still broke. The new album, "Give Em Enough Rope", entered the British charts at number 2, the four punks stared balefully from the covers and centrefolds of the four rock weeklies, and even in New York City *Soho Weekly News* headlined its front cover "The Clash, Britain's Best New Band". Yet as journalists rushed to deem them the Rolling Stones of the eighties, the band themselves closed ranks against a flurry of lawsuits from erstwhile manager Bernie Rhodes.

The day after the press reception for the new album, vocalist Joe Strummer and drummer Topper Headon were to be found selling clothes at a cold open air stall in Dingwalls Market in Camden Town. "We're broke, man, so you just have to do what you can," Strummer shrugged. "Bernie's kicked us out of our rehearsal studio and changed the locks." Not long ago The Clash filled the Rainbow Theatre three nights in a row and then had to take the bus home because they couldn't afford a cab.

Once upon a time punk really was the music of the unemployed school-leaver living at home with his parents in a high-rise council block, numbed by TV, harassed by the police and funded by the dole. The supergroup stars living in tax exile might just as easily have been living on the moon. Johnny Rotten: "We have to fight the entire superband system. Groups like the Stones are revolting. They have nothing to offer the kids any more . . ."

Punk energy was negative energy, pure Nihilism. A response born of poverty instead of sixties affluence cancelled the kids' subscriptions to hippy hopes of a counter-culture and replaced them with . . . nothing. They suggested no alternative, they saw no future at all. Perhaps not surprisingly this turned out to be a more universal message than anyone suspected. In Jubilee Week The Sex Pistols "God Save The Queen" made number 1 on the charts despite having no airplay and being banned by most large chain stores. Public school boys scenting doom in the dialectic pointed out that "No Future" could mean even more to them than to the unemployed.

Lead guitarist Mick Jones recalls the community feeling that existed when punk first started. "In them days it was definitely more of a movement in terms of people working together with one aim. It's only since the record companies came in that all the competition and bitchiness started. Before, it was like all other art movements, you know? Like art movements didn't mind having their photographs taken together and they all worked together like one group and it was the *one group*.

"All the people that used to be around were working for one

aim. Some kind of change really, to do something more interesting and different from what we had at the time. Like, if you
wanted to go out there was nothing for us to do . . ."

Joe Strummer used to go on stage with "Hate & War" sten-
cilled on his boiler suit. Not just because it was the opposite of the
hippies' "Love & Peace" dictum but because it was an honest
statement of what is happening today in Britain with our personal
Vietnam in Northern Ireland and ever growing racialism at
home. "Things will get tough," Strummer says, "I mean a fascist
government. But people won't notice like you won't notice your
hair is longer on Monday than Sunday . . . What I'm aimed
against is all that fascist, racialist patriotism type of
fanaticism . . ."

This he sees as the role of The Clash. "There's so much
corruption: councils, governments, industry, everywhere. It's
got to be flushed out. Just because it's been going on for a long
time doesn't mean that it shouldn't be stopped. It doesn't mean
that it isn't time to change. This is what I'm about, and I'm in
The Clash, so, of course, that's what The Clash is about.

"We ain't no urban guerrilla outfit. Our gunpower is strictly
limited. All we want to achieve is an atmosphere where things can
happen. We want to keep the spirit of the free world. We want to
keep *out* that safe, soapy, slush that comes out of the radio. People
have this picture of us marching down the street with machine
guns. We're not interested in that, because we haven't got any.
All we've got is a few guitars, amps and drums. That's our
weaponry."

The band may not be packing any pieces, but they do have an
armoury of ideas – and they weren't welcome on the airwaves:

> *"All the power is in the hands of people rich enough to buy it*
> *While we walk the streets too chicken to even try it."*
>   ("White Riot", their first single)

The Clash began in May 1976 as a drummerless group,
rehearsing in a small squat near Shepherds Bush Green. In
the grand British rock tradition as laid down by John Lennon,

Keith Richards, Jeff Beck, Jimmy Page, Ray Davies, Pete Townshend, Eric Clapton and David Bowie, they were all art school
dropouts.

When guitarist and lyricist Mick Jones formed the band he was
still at Hammersmith Art School. He comes from Brixton. His
father was a cab driver and Jones lived with his parents until they
divorced when he was 8. His mother emigrated to America and
his father moved out, leaving Jones to live with his grandmother.
When he wrote "London's Burning With Boredom" for The
Clash he was still living at his grandmother's flat on the eighteenth floor of a tower block overlooking The Westway. "I ain't
never lived under five floors. I ain't never lived on the ground."

Jones asked Paul Simonon to join his group. Simonon had been
playing all of six weeks, just strumming at a guitar but now he
"found" a bass and began playing. Simonon was also born in
Brixton. His parents had split up and he lived mostly with his
father. "I had a paper round at six in the morning. Then I'd come
back and cook me dad his breakfast. Then I'd fuck off to school.
Then I'd come back back and cook me dad his dinner and do
another paper round after school and then I'd cook me dad's tea
. . ." He got a council scholarship to the Byam Shaw art school in
Notting Hill. "I used to draw blocks of flats and car dumps." At
the time of meeting Mick Jones the only live rock band he'd seen
was The Sex Pistols.

Vocalist Joe Strummer was in an R&B pub band called The
101ers and had even made a single, "Keys To Your Heart"
(Chiswick Records), when he met Mick and Paul. The guitarist
and bass player, together with Glen Matlock of the Sex Pistols,
were just leaving the Ladbroke Grove social security office when
Joe arrived on his bike. They had seen The 101ers play The
Windsor Castle and recognised in Joe "the right look". "I don't
like your group," said Mick, "but we think you're great."

"As soon as I saw these guys," said Joe, "I knew that that was
what a group in my eyes was supposed to look like." Almost
immediately afterwards The Sex Pistols supported The 101ers at
a gig and convinced Joe of what was happening. He broke up his
group the next day. "Yesterday I thought I was a crud, then I saw

The Sex Pistols and I became a king and decided to move into the future. As soon as I saw them I knew that rhythm and blues was dead, that the future was here somehow. Every other group was riffing through the Black Sabbath catalogue but hearing The Pistols I knew, I just knew!" Joe's art school was Central ("A lousy set-up").

The first thing the band did was refurbish an abandoned warehouse in Camden Town, then, with Terry Chimes (nick-named Tory Crimes) sitting in on drums, they began rehearsals. They played their first gig in Sheffield in June 1976. Since places like the Marquee wouldn't book punk bands they often had to create venues such as cinemas or playing The ICA.

The Clash signed with CBS Records; controlled from New York by the mighty Columbia Records Corp. The deal, for something over £100,000, received a lot of press. But it wasn't, in fact, very good since it included no tour support and it is easy to lose £50,000 or £60,000 on a national tour promoting an album. The band remained on £25 a week, though times were better than in November '76, when they had returned to their cold warehouse after flyposting an ICA gig and desperately devoured what remained of the flour and water paste that they had used to put up the posters.

Then came the tour with The Pistols on their ill-fated "Anarchy" dates and an album for CBS. They cut it in three weekends using their sound man as a producer. He'd never been in a studio before and the production was, not surprisingly, muddy. Despite this, the power of the music comes through and "The Clash" remains one of the best punk albums ever made. It entered the charts at number 12 and sold over 100,000 copies in the UK. But Columbia refused to release it in the States because they thought the sound quality would preclude airplay.

This was the period of punk violence. During one particularly unpleasant gig when the spit, bottles and cans were falling like rain, Terry Chimes watched as a wine bottle smashed into a million pieces on his hi-hat. He quit. Life on the road under such conditions took its toll on the others as well. Mick Jones remembers making the first album . . .

"Two years ago we did the band's first interview. On Janet Street Porter's 'London Weekend Programme' it was, and me, being all young and naive, I blamed bands taking too many drugs for the great mid-70s drought in rock. I recall saying it really well. And a year or so later, I found myself doing just as many drugs as them!

"Y'know, taking drugs as a way of life, to feel good in the morning, to get through the day. And it's still something I'm getting over right now. I was so into speed, I mean, I don't even recall making the first album."

They auditioned 206 drummers and rejected them all: Number 207 was Nicky "Topper" Headon, a friend who'd-played briefly with them in the old days. Headon was born in Bromley. His father is a headmaster at a primary school and his mother is a teacher. "I first played drums when I was 13. I was working at the butchers, cleaning up and I saved the money to buy a kit for £30." After school he worked the Dover Ferries and then on the Channel Tunnel before moving to London.

With their lineup complete, The Clash began to tour Britain, always taking with them a number of other bands that they felt close to philosophically or musically: The Buzzcocks, Subway Sect, The Slits, Richard Hell & The Voidoids from NYC and The Lous, a French female punk band. The art-rock bands of the sixties took rock out of the dance hall and placed it, literally, in the concert hall. The Clash took it back to the dance hall again — partly by necessity since their audiences have been known to pogo as many as 200 seats per concert into oblivion. With replacement costs at £20 a chair, the band began to insist on seatless venues.

Nonetheless their concerts were banned by local watch committees, and the police continually busted the band for drugs and vandalism. They survived bomb threats in Sweden and found one of their most devoted audiences in Belfast, a town many English bands refuse to play. Everywhere they went dozens of fans were allowed backstage and their hotel rooms were always packed out with local punks crashing on the floor because they couldn't get home.

After a month-long tour of Europe the band returned to

discover that their everyday movements had become prime fodder for the music press. Anything that could possibly be interpreted as "selling out" was jumped upon. Since the punk stars had not been imposed on their audiences (in the way The Bay City Rollers were) but had risen from their ranks, to "sell-out" was not a concern that the band would lose artistic integrity and produce overtly commercial records, it was a concern that they would sacrifice community to commerce. And it was true, the band was feeling more and more distanced from its audiences. It was a subtle change: the scene's originally negative, yet communal, charge was unavoidably transformed into individual craft pride as the musicians became more professional. The very technology of rock, its expensive amplification equipment and studios, introduces the businessman into the musicians' lives. Playing becomes the band's work, performed while everyone else is at play. In "The Sociology Of Rock", Simon Frith pin-pointed the problem perfectly:

"Their work is everyone else's leisure, their way of life is everyone else's relaxation, escape and indulgence. They work in places of entertainment. What for them is routine is for their fans a special event. Musicians themselves are symbols of leisure and escape, their glamour supports their use as sex objects, as fantasies and briefly held dreams."

The Clash are now a long way from the squat in Shepherds Bush. They remain on a level of intimacy with many of their fans; perhaps a little too intimate at times. (A few months ago Joe Strummer got hepatitis from a well aimed gob of spit which caught him in the mouth.) But as their fame grows, particularly with the release of their new album in The States, the only way they will be able to express their original ideals will be through their music. That is now their job.

Joe Strummer: "I think people ought to know that we're anti-fascist, we're anti-violence, we're anti-racist and we're pro-creative. We're against ignorance." And their music is real fine as well.

Ants Out of Bondage

Paolo Hewitt

Melody Maker, 12 January 1980.

In which Adam and the Ants reconcile their apparent predilection for S/M with their desire to succeed as musicians without grovelling.

> *"I just think you don't understand at all. I don't think you understand what I'm trying to do, as a direct result of not coming to the gigs. None of the papers come . . . and if they do, they don't stay. You want to know why? Because they're scared."*   Adam Ant, December '79.

About three weeks ago, Do-It records-unleashed one of the most eagerly-awaited albums of the year. And that's no exaggeration. In its first ten days, this album shifted some 20,000 copies and may even, fingers crossed, find itself nestling alongside the rest of the post-Xmas dross that finds itself in January chartsville. What makes that fact so exceptional, however, is that it's odds on that you've probably either never heard of the band, Adam and the Ants, or of their album, "Dirk Wears White Sox".

In short, we're dealing with a change-of-the decade phenomenon that no-one, except those with their ears to the ground, either expected or wanted – especially the music press.

For three years now, journalists have hounded, ridiculed or ignored the Ants, causing mistrust and suspicion on all sides. The criticisms, made early on in their career, were based mainly around the belief that the Ants were fascists, sexists and decadent. It seemed that the only people interested were the fans, the fanzines and me.

Yeah, little old me, who wanted to know why (for instance) surviving punks were emblazoning Adam's name across their jackets, why this up-against-the-wall situation had evolved, and why such a growing underground movement had been both misunderstood and, worse still, blatantly ignored. No-one would tell me, so I went to Do-It records to do it myself.

Come in, shut the door and meet the Ants!

At one end of a white table sits dark-skinned David Barbe, Ant drummer. Sullen and suspicious (what did I tell you?), he will open up only occasionally.

Opposite him, guitarist Matthew Ashman, complete with a nervous twitch, emaciated figure, striking black and red jumper and a penchant for bumming my cigarettes. On his right is Lee, the new bass-player who keeps very, very quiet.

The man on my right, though, is definitely ready to get his point of view over. Adam Ant is a small dark-haired man who could probably talk all night, so loquaciously does he want to make himself understood.

Okay, lads. Let's deal with the critics first. They've called you Nazis.

Matthew: "We're not Nazis. Simple as that. Never have been . . . and we don't associate ourselves with Nazism."

So where did the misunderstanding come from?

Matthew: "A song called 'Deutche Girl'."

Which is about?

Matthew: "It's a story, a love story about two kids who happen to be" he falters. "Well, Adam will tell you about it."

Why can't you?

"Because I don't want to."

Can't or won't I wonder.

Adam: "I saw a film once by Leni Reifenstahl, about the 1932 Olympics or something. Anyway, I saw those wonderful German girls, hundreds of them all in a row. Now I'm a great one for history, and there was a war in 1939 and atrocities were committed. But this was very much along the lines of Mel Brooks' *The Producers,* and I just imagined a love story between a member of the Hitler Youth and one of those girls – because every kid in Germany at that time, whether they liked it or not, just had to do it, they had no choice in the matter."

Sounds innocuous enough to me. "When we played in Germany, real fascists turned up at our gig, real Nazis with shooters, and they said they wanted to kill me for having make-up and they wanted Dave because he's half-caste. Now we had a choice, but we went out and played – and that to me was the most scariest thing ever."

Dave: "Another thing, right, about this fascist thing. I've been in the group since the beginning, and we've always been called fascist because at the beginning of punk there was a lot of National Front talk about, and we were made into a scapegoat. But what good would it do me voting NF? My dad's coloured and my mum's Jewish, and I've got a lot of brothers and sisters. Do you get my point?"

Sure.

"That's why I don't like the music press, because it's very wrong and nasty. And you can put that in your fucking interview."

What about the sexist angle, though? I've read statements of yours in fanzines where you've said that your music – Ant music – is designed for "sex-people". I mean, what the hell are "sex people", Adam?

"People who get off on sexual phenomena. People who like sexual imagery and enjoy being sexual."

Maybe that explains the badges that Adam designs depicting sexual repression, by either male or female, accompanied by such witty captions as "What do you mean you don't like Adam and the Ants?"

"My graphics are totally misrepresented because the sado-masochistic element in my earlier work was just pure imagery, and if you look at the work of painters like Hans Bellmer, Allen Jones and all the pop artists, well, what do you do about it? Ignore it? I just happened to respond to it. I thought, yeah, if it works in a painting medium, it may work within the realms of rock 'n' roll.

Malcolm McLaren and Vivienne Westwood did that, to a certain degree, with their shop called Sex."

But those Allen Jones pictures which depict sexually dominated women are still sexist, McLaren or no McLaren. What do you think of that, Adam?

"I look upon him as a genius, a brilliant painter. I don't care what the fucking Time Out people say about him, that's all crapola."

But don't you think it's sexist?

"No, not really. It's quite the reverse in sado-masochism, because usually the female takes on the dominating role."

Wrong. Whether the woman or the man is in charge doesn't matter. It's still an unequal situation, which makes it sexist.

"No it doesn't. It makes it sexual, because they do it in the privacy of their own closet, or their own bedroom, and it's entirely up to them."

In a way, yeah, but via your songs and badges you're taking it out onto the streets. "Yeah, I am bringing it out onto the streets, because I want people to know it exists. What we're basically dealing with here is taboos, and a lot of my work is a kind of musical therapy for certain taboos that I may have."

Adam suddenly scoops up a brown envelope that's been lying at his feet.

"Look, these are just some of the letters we get, and they're all going to be answered. Here you are, here's a fanzine someone's started."

It transpires it's actually been created in Italy, and carries on its back page – well, what do you know – an Allen Jones painting.

Adam: "I don't think it's harmful. I think that imagery is just as tasteful as *Sounds* having a picture of some girl across the-letters page."

True enough, but it's still on the same level. Two wrongs don't make a right.

"No, not at all. These kids are trying to make fanzines which are about presenting imagery and ideas you can't find anywhere else. That's the whole idea of fanzines, and that's why I do them –

because I know they're not going to edit any of the interview down.

"Take this Berlin one. Now those kids are very aware about what happened in the war, because they're reminded of it every day. So they've got to face the taboo of the Third Reich, or whatever. And do you know how they do it? They ridicule them."

So is that what you're into, exposing social taboos and reducing them?

"No, I'm not ridiculing them. I'm just bringing them to people's attention."

And how do you hope they'll react?

"I hope their reaction is going to be that they remember and not do it again. Like with a sexual taboo, if somebody's faced with the fact that someone is gay or a transvestite, maybe they won't ridicule him that much, because they'll understand that a fetish is not something to be afraid of."

CERTAINLY, if you listen to the Ants' new album, you'll wonder what all the fuss is about. All but three of the songs have words whose exact meaning is unclear, which inevitably leads to the conclusion that they were designed purely and specifically for Adam's fans. Adam disagrees at first, but comes round later.

"I tried all the time to challenge structures. The biggest fault for me, looking at the album three months later, is that it tried to do much, it had too many ideas and got too diverse. It didn't quite cut through to anybody outside of our fans."

Exactly. Then again, though, the traditional relationships that exist between a band and an audience have become somewhat twisted in this case. Because of the aforementioned combination of distaste and reticence among journalists, no music paper has afforded Adam the chance to get his views and ideas over to a larger audience.

"It's taken three years for me to say anything to a major paper like yours, because it's the first interview we've ever done with the Melody Maker," Adam says. "And it's got to be said, because kids send in letters to papers like yours – and they never get printed, because we're not a band to like. That's okay. But the thing is that we exist, we're stronger than we ever were, and we're playing better than we ever were."

All of which, granted is quite true, but are they any good? Well yes and no.

No, because although Adam may fancy himself as a kind of modern Lenny Bruce, whom he describes as "a hero, capital letters H-E-R-O", he lacks that particular gentleman's stunning ability to hold up taboos and ridicule them through an acid wit.

And how important are Adam's concerns to the audience he's reaching? Surely the social protestations of such luminaries – however crass – as the Subs and Upstarts would be of more relevance.

Matthew: "It's not, relevant, they're just competing with the rest. The thing is they haven't got the power to change. We can change whenever we like, because that's the only way to innovate."

I don't know about that – most kids I know who follow you are just purely into imitation and idolisation of Adam. I mean, how do you feel about being a hero, Adam?

"That's very flattering. I'm honoured. I hope that if they think I'm a hero I can live up to it, because a lot of heroes don't."

No, they don't – they just lose their bottle and vision, which is the main reason for my admiration of Adam. Against all the odds, he's shown that you don't have to lick record-company boots to succeed.

"I went up North yesterday," Adam muses, "and after eating in a restaurant I came out, and who should I meet but Paul Weller? Our eyes met, and simultaneously our arms shot out and we shook hands. There was like a great feeling of respect for one another, because I began to doubt the original people from '77, and that guy is still as sincere and serious as he was two years ago. And he admired the fact that we were still doing it, because that LP is what everybody was shouting about in '77. It was made out of choice. We had full control over it, it's exactly the way it should be."

It's also been devised and conceived by people under 25, a fact that pleases both Adam and I, as we both agree that far too much control of the music business is in the hands of people who burned out years ago.

I can see, now, why so many kids put so much faith in him. He won't let them down.

So what does the future hold, Adam?

"I want every young kid to say that in 1980 they saw Adam and the Ants without having to go hundreds of miles to see us."

Life in a Simple Mind

Paul Morley

Paul Morley gets into the head of the Simple Minds' Jim Kerr

New Musical Express, 3 October, 1981.

HERE WE GO AGAIN . . . Daylight. What day is it? Should I get up? Is there anything to do? What am I going to do? Where am I today? Liverpool . . .

It was the Royal Court last night. Not much of a response, why bother with an encore? Why does everyone look so bored until it looks like we're not coming back onto the stage? What's it like outside? Do I need to shave? Rotten colour scheme in this room . . . boring hotel. Maybe I should go back to sleep. Fine dreams. A day off today. Some photos to do. Still, the first week of something that's going on for three months. I can't even think what's happening tomorrow.

What is?

What town?

Have I got any clean clothes left?

It's not that late really . . . Really all this is getting more and more like a respectable job, the petty worries and all that. All the things I wanted to get rid of . . . I can't face going out and playing much more, especially in this country. It's getting so oppressive and divisive. I hate . . . I dunno . . . I just feel there's some kind of betrayal.

This whole procedure, roadies, trucks, big halls, hotels, buses, I can't go through with it much more. But then it's so hard to find the alternative. Yeah, I mean what is the alternative?

This whole tour date planning for months ahead, it's like Dr. Feelgood or the fucking Rush. So then why do I do it? We just use the channels that are already provided yet try and do something new and more emotional . . .

I dunno, it's like those two passions, there's that spirit we get playing that we just don't get recording. Last year was so terrible we just didn't want to play Britain again. Yeah . . . I think if I was going for the big alternative I wouldn't sign to a record company I'd get sponsored by a magazine or a vodka company. I think some sort of radical change is needed. I suppose we're not doing much about that side of it but who is . . .

I never honestly thought we'd end up this far in, so tangled up. You're in Glasgow and you hear the first two Roxy LPs and then you hear "Real Life" and you think, Fuck working. You see a couple of great films, read those kind of books, and more and more you get the feeling that you just have to do it for yourself, find out for yourself, and in a way you're play acting. But you get the chance and you go for it.

Early on you think what the fuck ever gave me the backbone, the absolute cheek, to think that I could ever do anything? That horror I have . . . I dunno . . . I do think that people are getting more anxious these days to be adult earlier . . . that word youth is dodgy, this supposed voice of youth that sounded out for two decades . . . what has the voice of youth got to say for itself? What has the point of that voice been? Where is the value in what I'm involved in? . . . Has it been one word, a sentence, an act of violence? What is supposed to be going on? What are we reaching for?

Maybe it's just one moment that can carry you through, that you hold within yourself for the rest of your life. Maybe pop music is like a drug, maybe it does you bad. Drug . . . that's a complimentary word for it. It's more a tranquiliser for a lot of people, an anaesthetic. I don't know . . . Too many words, too much analysis . . . that's why I loved what Morley wrote about Peter Hammill. As fashionable as fuck. All that straightforward way of approaching things and passing on information that just clogs everything up and we've come to accept all this banality, banal music and banal ways of discussing it, and that phrase just brought it right down to what it is.

When I went on Radio One a few days after I read that on *Rock On*, just the name gives you some idea of what's going down, it was probably Ted Nugent the week before . . . and the guy asked me the usual question about how most bands who've been around as long as us would've quit without the conventional success and usually I'd have given the polite rap but I just goes, Well other bands make crap LPs.

I liked that. I'm fed up with patronising myself. This has to be stressed . . . if anyone is going to make music it may as well be Simple Minds. Who else are we going to look up to in this day? That's a better way to feel.

What did Morley say? The difference between sincerity and authenticity . . . some groups are content with being sincere, we have to be authentic. The punk thing seems long ago. I've learnt that there's much more than what was suggested back then. You have to go for it. For what? Does it shine? Is it a glory? Ave . . . it's a glory

People who are truly in love with the world are as cynical as fuck, they don't accept anything straight . . . because they care. I care. I just want to . . . that line in "Love Song": "*America is a boyfriend*", it's so throwaway, it means nothing and it means everything, it's just great. It stands for the whole fucking glory. I hate people who ignore ambition and possibility. I just love . . . celebration.

Today I'd like to have lots of money . . . just today. There are all those people who've helped us and who I owe things to. Not possessions, but I just feel today that I'd like to buy people loads of things . . . I don't have to, they don't expect it, but I'd love to . . . I want a lot of money today. I'd have had that thought a year ago and been ashamed. Today I just feel uplifted. I don't feel guilty. A few years ago it would have been philistine if you didn't have the ultimate conventional social conscience, but now you're allowed, in some ways, room to come in at problems in different ways.

I can sum up all that rock guilt in one line and I can go deeper than just a moan. I accept it both – pleasure and protest, the beauty in fear. Celebrate, that's what it is, there's so much to go on. You have to take things head on. Think of the amount of people I've met who I wouldn't have if I'd listened to those people who said I was being stupid and pretentious. I've never really been stopped from doing anything I wanted to, there's nothing that's been out of bounds in terms of . . . well, there has really . . . Greatness . . .

Like Paul said, that "Empires And Dance" was a genuine high and with the new LP we haven't moved on much, just consolidated that whole.

Yeah . . . I think this has been the end of some kind of phase for us. There were those big leaps between the first and second and the second and third and with the fourth it wasn't nearly as big a move. We've reached the end of something . . . I don't know what the next starting point will be . . . that Greatness I think we've got that at our fingertips . . .

Last year there was hardly anything up there with "Empires And Dance" . . . in time it'll be looked upon up there with the big ones. It just shines so bright, lines, sounds and feelings that come through . . . at the end of last year we'd come so far from being termed the wet and wimpy mascara boys and we were being given some true respect. Then it changes and people expect so much from us . . .

I don't think our songs go on too long, people are missing the point and associating us with totally the wrong images. Our songs deal with trance and gathering forces and motions, and that's just developed maybe to its limits . . . but think about the repetition in my life . . . think about the shape and agility in the songs that is being overlooked.

These people talk about the abstraction in my lyrics . . . just what is abstraction? It's as elusive as the word pretension, using that word to soak up everything I do, it's just a lazy response. Still . . . reviews used to matter, now you can just throw them away . . . the standard is appalling . . .

Morley said he'd read a review of our Manchester show that made him ashamed to write for the same paper . . . just so condescending and simplistic . . .

There is like . . . well . . . Chris Bohn gave me one of the biggest kicks in my life in terms of that go for it when he came to us all cynical and then went away saying the lyrics to "Empires And Dance" could have been words to "Lodger" if Bowie had been younger. That just like elevated me.

Then a year later . . . don't one year give us this king thing and the next year say we're wasted. Don't call us top of the class in one year and then dunces the next. The gap hasn't been as big but we've not crumped, we've not lost our way. Just what are the expectancies, what do people expect from popular music? Chris Bohn what is your expectancy of Simple Minds . . . what should I be writing about, Chris, that has value and vibrancy and where would they difference be to what I'm writing now?

Don't give us the crown and then snatch it away. We deserve better. Do that to the fools.

We know our position, we're not bull shitting anyone and there's no way we're fat and lazy . . .

We've only been together three, four years and this is the first time we've slowed down after tremendous acceleration . . . like the two LP idea was our own because we had to get all our ideas out of the system ready for the next stage. What the fuck does hype matter? In this bloody world, faced with all the crap and superficiality, does it matter if Virgin or the *NME* hype something that has some soul and depth?

The thought of doing a double LP, you just get visions of Masters of Rock and The Clash, but how could we get all those songs out? Of course we know that two LPs at that price is going to get us in the charts. I'm not denying that; and I'm not ashamed of that . . . there are three or four songs on "Sons And Fascination" that are as good as anything put out this year. Am I ashamed of that? No fucking way.

What's it matter who's hyping you? We control the lust in the music. Everyone's hyped by some force, myth or matter. I could say that the second disc is a gift to the people, a gift to our fans. But am I going to say that? Fuck no. It's just a collection of songs that's over two records. There it is. We'll be lucky to break even

. . . a Top 20 LP for a few weeks doesn't matter much. I'm not ignorant. It represents an end of something for the Minds.

What happens next? We travel a few thousand miles and we'll end up with something different. We always respond to change, we get impatient. We've done four LPs . . . it's weird, probably pathetic. No one could have expected that . . . Paul says we've been fucked up because we've toured so much and produced such strong music and we're broke but it's that something that has come to exist within the Simple Minds that is important. No one gets inside us.

Right now I'm broke but that's just a hangover from past bungling . . . we're doing alright in Britain, we're doing alright in Europe; we're taking off in American discos, we're going to make to Australia . . . we're going to make lots of money and as it is we're having a great time and there will always be excitement and possibility . . . we have made something special for ourselves . . .

I'm the front person in the group and I get all the attention . . . Paul just interviewed me yesterday . . . but Charlie and Mick and Derek, it seems not enough to be just musicians or technicians these days, but for me to have the courage and drive to get on a stage and perform I have to have total trust in the people beside me . . . and they're good. They're no way just a backing group. I'm getting to be just like the pulse behind what they do . . . in interviews I always go on about musical heroes but right now Burchill and McNeill and Forbes are my heroes . . . The next stage will emerge out of the great strength we've established amongst ourselves and we're going for an energy that's twelve times greater than what we originally envisaged.

We're not scared to take on any task and what we've achieved in the past has given us the confidence to just go for the next giant jump into some area that might once have appeared hopelessly out of reach. Simple Minds has meant confidence, yeah, and we will take on absolutely anything. For the heck of it. It's a word I wouldn't have thought of using for a few years – but for the sheer *anarchy* of it. For the fun of it. For the necessity. For the vitality.

Any shame I've had about feeling this way about what I'm doing has turned into celebration. Any nervousness I feel about performing or walking down the street relates to the confidence by keeping the edge, keeping us looking. Bands do make crap records. We don't. There's not many bands who've progressed like us. Because we're fucking good. We've got vision, courage, tons of it . . .

I look at things that are so floppy and milky and I see that we're part of something crappy and unlovable and we just want so much to be better than all that. We want to make something that people can touch, that isn't manufactured. We want to exploit the industry ten times more than it can exploit us. If the *NME* says to us you can't go on the cover because you've missed the boat we can just tell them to stuff it up their arse . . . none of that matters any more.

We have a spirit now and nothing can break it. We have this spirit and it's helped us break away from all the silliness and faddiness and it's not sake for sake and it's giving us more and more confidence.

The past two years have elevated me so much. I don't apologise now. I'm more dynamic. I couldn't speak to a person before unless they asked me something. Now I bawl and scream like a madman and I will not feel contrived or embarrassed or any shame. We've got something iron solid whilst other groups are relying on flukes and bits in time . . .

I've found something that I have to do, a way of growing up, owning up, and I'm going for something. I don't stop for no one. We have taken a long road compared to some groups but we've got this energy that just exists and it's strong and we can see it. We're so fucking good and we're getting better all the time.

Yes, I am going to get up. What shall I wear? What can I find out about this world, anyway?

Eddie, the Maiden and the Rue Morgue (Iron Maiden in Paris)

Colin Irwin

Melody Maker, 4 April 1981.

A small hotel in Montmarte

It's the weirdest plot this side of the "New Avengers". A man in a trilby scrabbling through a desert. A Monroe blonde stalking him with a 12-bore. A bunch of civil servants poring over ordnance survey maps.

A herd of pert American nubiles – doing Europe in a week – gaze bemused at the flickering spectacle in the corner pretending to make some sense of it, while their languid chaperone frantically attempts to locate a disco to pack them off for under 20 dollars a head.

The odd off-peak German tourist perches discreetly in a dark corner scribbling a postcard; a Welshman and a New Zealander argue loudly about the French rugby assassination of England earlier that afternoon; three long-haired geezers in satin jackets cluster sullenly around a pot of limp tea; Abdul the crazy Tunisian waiter rushes around with trays of drinks like a demented clockwork mouse; and a nervous English journalist grapples heroically with an uncommonly generous shot of best cognac.

The entrance is brilliant. A real barge-through-the-saloon-doors-and-everyone-dives-for-cover job. The girls titter and nudge one another, the chaperone clamps chastity belts around the lot of them, the pot of tea freezes, the journalist turns on the tape machine, and the rugby screeeches to a halt midway through a vital drop-kick.

He stands there relishing the effect of his own impact; a tall barrel-chested figure clad in black leathers atop knee-length boots, the minutest suspicion of a sneer on his bottom lip. The guy is unquestionably a *star*.

He greets the pot of tea with a lethargic wave, slumps into a chair, and acknowledges the collective attention.

"I can't take all this," he announces to no-one particular . . . "God, I'm missing my old lady."

His name is Paul Di'anno. He was born in Chingford (the name is a result of Sicilian ancestry) and would like to play for West Ham when he grows up. In the meantime he's lead singer with Iron Maiden, doesn't give a fig about your reaction to *that*, and as a result has become one of the most celebrated characters in the strange, wacky world of heavy metal.

Iron Maiden's first album reached number four in the British charts; the new one, *Killers*, has already made the top ten; they've enjoyed a couple of hit singles; they can sell out major concert halls virtually all over Europe. And Paul Di'anno hurls comical abuse across the hotel foyer with fearless hilarity, splashing his charisma like garlic on a French cab driver's breath, the way only a likeably cocky East End street-wise guy can.

A French record company representative attempts to coach him through a bit of local banter to impress the natives. He writes something down which looks incredibly long and complicated, and Paul glares at it with all-disguised hostility. "Okay," says the guy, "we'll try something else. All you need to say at the end is 'Paris, je vous aime'."

"Sheer vooze emm," he repeats dutifully. It's not good enough. "Aw shit, leave it out . . . I don't *need* all this," he grumbles. "We'll go through it later, okay?" and the subject is closed.

The English journalist is introduced. Paul greets him matily, the two-handed shake of paws. "Are you reviewing this?" he bellows across a few minutes later. "Er . . ." "Another slag-off I s'pose. That's all we get these days."

Iron Maiden are feeling the critical backlash . . . *that's* the sort of status they've achieved now.

The Bataclan, Paris

Imagine being in a sauna wearing a fur overcoat, wedged in by dozens of other bodies jammed from wall to wall. That's the deal tonight. Battle across the unseated hall and it's like the Somme, corpses piled high, a dreadful stench, young kids throwing up in the loo. Even the can-can dancers painted on the walls are passing out.

Deadening your senses is the only realist solution to the horror; Iron Maiden fit the part beautifully. They steam on flaunting an arsenal of silver studs around their waists, stalking in and out flashing lights amid a monster crescendo of noise.

Di'anno, belligerent and intimidating, clearly doesn't take the pretty route on long journeys. He goes for the throat and usually gets it, while bass player Steve Harris and drummer Clive Burr set him up for it with a thundering backdrop that's totally devoid of mercy.

"Thisisasongfromoursecondalbumit'scalled . . . MURDERS IN THE RUE MORGUE, and another brain cell disintegrates. "Thisisasongcalled . . . INNOCENT EXILE," and flashes of smoke billow from cans perched on speakers on either side of the stage. "Thisisasongcalled . . . PHANTOM OF THE OPERA," and another five ounces of sweat flees from the journalist's emaciated body.

The French are more resilient. Huge manes of hair fly back and forth in mind-numbing ecstasy. Screeching cheers greet every utterance from Di'anno. A battery of lit matches threaten the ultimate heavy metal orgasm – let's all be sacrificed in a sea of flaming cardboard guitars.

"Thisisasongcalled . . . PURGATORY," More flashes of smoke, more blitzing barrage. Even Maiden are sagging discernibly by now.

It's time for Di'anno to demonstrate his crash course in Francais. He squares up to the audience like John Conteh on a bender, the audience tense, the road-crew hold their breath ready for his party-piece . . . "I dunno if you can understand me, but you've been fucking great tonight."

Another blast. Two strange creatures stride on either side of the band, their faces identical gruesome masks of fanged teeth, weals, bulging eyes, and boisterous white hair. It's the same face that dominates the stage back-cloth, the same face that appears on the cover of "Killers" (clutching an axe dripping blood, leering over a hapless victim). It's called Eddie, a gut-busting mask that started life as a modest marketing ploy and is now beginning to take over the band. It's already become their most instantly identifiable trademark.

The Eddies retreat. The band depart in a flurry of waves, but quickly return to play their excellent first single 'Running Free' in tow with French heavy metal band Trust. The crowd go crazy – Trust are demi-gods in France ("it's like Led Zeppelin turning up to jam with a band in Britain" said Maiden manager Rod Smallwood).

Afterwards somebody asks the English journalist what he thought about it all. Wiped out and washed up, the journalist says he was . . . er . . . *impressed*. You know, the sheer single-mindedness with which they scatter your ashes, the brutal persistence of their warfare on your nervous system, the full-blooded commitment they apply to their task . . . in the end you can't help but gape in awe, admire, and finally capitulate and throw your head against the paintings of can-can dancers in the time-honoured tradition.

One day the world will be comprised solely of young men in leather jackets and studded belts who fling their heads at passing traffic and greet one another not by shaking hands, but by cracking skulls. Yeah, he couldn't go as far as saying he actually *liked* them, but God was he impressed!

They all wanted to be footballers. The classic escapist route. Proud working class East-Enders, not foreign to the odd scuffle, like a knees-up, and home is the Upton Park terraces.

But if Di'anno is the bustling centre-forward, devouring goalkeepers when the ref's not looking, then Steve Harris is Billy

Bonds, the backbone of it all. On stage his bass holds the band together, and off it he writes virtually all the material, is easily their most reasoned, articulate spokesman, and seemingly the one who maintains some modicum of order in the general mayhem of life on the road.

Under the same analogy, lead guitarist Dave Murray, all flowing blond hair and short sentences followed by bouts of giggles, is Alan Devonshire, skilful, sometimes flash, but on his day a match winner. Burr, the drummer, like Di'anno full of mouth 'n' bravado, is obviously Phil Parkes; and new signing Adrian Smith is Geoff Pike.

Steve Harris pulled them together in 1977, when punk was king and God help bands who played anything else. The only thing God wasn't allowed to help was heavy metal. But UFO, Stray and Zeppelin were their gods, so Iron Maiden suffered the scorn, bore the neglect and held firm even in the protracted absence of gigs.

This was the heavy metal Resistance. But it all comes round again and by the end of 1979 they found themselves not only with more work than they could handle, but also being hailed – along with Saxon and Def Leppard – as the vanguard of a movement cutely dubbed by the media as the new wave of heavy metal.

"What upsets people about heavy metal," says Steve Harris, "is the fact that it won't go away. They've tried but they can't get rid of it. And that really annoys them.

"The media had to put a tag on it, but there was definitely an upsurge of young heavy metal bands around the same time – Saxon for example – I think because people were just fed up with punk, so they formed bands to play the music they themselves wanted to hear."

"Personally," adds Clive Burr, "I can't stand new wave, but I can appreciate what it did."

Di'anno is the first to crawl from the lift. He has as much warm blood in him as the average Egyptian mummy, and he growls and becomes more and more agitated by Abdul the waiter's increasingly spectacular attempts to wish him bon matin and ascertain how he liked his kippers.

"Christ," says Di'anno eventually, "I bet Cat Stevens never stayed at this hotel."

Gradually they filter down. All tangle with Abdul. "I've got a mouth like a vulture's crutch," screams Burr loudly, disturbing *everybody's* hangover.

It takes them two hours to piece together the previous night's trail of wreckage. They hit town with Trust, and various members of both bands were left scattered along the route.

Frank Zappa booms out of the Iron Maiden van stereo and clears the streets of Montmartre in seconds. Spirits lift. Zappa is obligatory daily fodder in the Maiden van – a rigid rule of which they all wholeheartedly approve.

"I don't actually listen to much heavy metal at all," says Di'anno (who once sang with an all-white reggae band). "I tend to listen to T Rex a lot now. Oh, and Trust. I listen to them five or six times a day."

They go sightseeing to the Louvre, to the Eiffel Tower, etc. Most of all they want to see the Rue Morgue (the subject of one of Steve Harris' most blood-curdling lyrics). Some hasty research reveals there's no Rue Morgue in Paris. They console themselves by allowing Eddie to run riot frightening tourists at the Eiffel Tower.

The journalist is intrigued by Iron Maiden. He wondered frankly about the precise attraction of heavy metal. The band are patient with him.

"The thing is the energy," says Steve Harris. "You can express yourself. It's a very aggressive music and that's a big part of it. That's not to say it's violent – there's never trouble at our gigs and we never cause trouble."

The journalist foolishly persists. He asks if they're not self-conscious about conforming to a cliche, with leather jackets, the macho image, the numbing music . . .

"If I wasn't in a band I'm pretty sure I'd be wearing the same sort of gear. I've always worn leather jackets. I've had long hair since I was 15, know what I mean? I've never worn a suit. Even when I was a draughtsman I went to work in jeans and a tee-shirt. We wear what's practical."

But, argues the interrogator, they're young working class geezers obviously with hearts of gold, don't they feel any need for their music to express the social concerns of the day, and the frustrations of their class and creed?

Burr: "We're not political, we're not sexist, we're just musicians of a reasonably good standard who want to entertain."

"Obviously," adds Harris, "we've got our view about things but we don't see the need to preach it to other people. Whatever our opinions, they are opinions, and it's not right to try influence people in that way. I know it may sound as if we're shying away from problems, but music is there for people to enjoy, I don't agree with a lot of what Tom Robinson was doing. Okay, he's into his own thing but really he's trying to ram things down people's throats, but to my mind if he wants to do that he should be an MP."

The journalist laughs. "No *really*, if he feels that strongly about it. He was getting involved with thing like Rock Against Racism and getting politically involved and I don't think it's right to try and sway kids' thinking in that way. Music shouldn't be used as a propaganda tool. It should be there purely as a means of escape or whatever."

The Bataclan, Paris

Iron Maiden's second gig is a hundred times better than the first. Cooler and generally more civilized, and even the journalist finds himself succumbing to the odd, involuntary tap of the foot.

It begins to make some sort of sense. The key is that the music is beyond analysis; it's above criticism; it's wildly detached from any other form of music. It's merely *there*.

So the journalist stops worrying about it. He allows himself to join the backstage congratulations, shakes their hands, and wishes them all the best. He heads for the flesh-spots of Paris, an enormous cloud lifted from his head.

And One More Thing, Danny . . .

Ringo Starr interviewed by Danny Baker

New Musical Express, 12 December 1981.

"MORNING RICHARD, what'll it be, eh?" In the old coaching days, such assumed familiarity would've earned the inn-keeper a gentleman's glove around the chops; but today The Gentleman just summons up a half-pint of foaming lager and casts a beady eye over the staggering selection of under-glass fare.

Our scene is taking shape inside one of those synthetic "country" pubs with, in this case, horrible great photos of modern aircraft replacing the obligatory horse-brasses and hunting horns. The clientele are standard and old. Nobody appears to have to go back to work and all conversations are conducted in a pitch something like a sombre Hindu death mantra coming up from the drains. Outsiders, particularly young(ish) outsiders with obvious accents, are not encouraged to stay till the flowing bowl runs dry. (Anton our photographer proved a problem. But I passed him off as a Welsh illiterate from the hills, a role he plays with remarkable ease, and this erased fears that he was not actually British.)

What was most remarkable about this fusion of farm-house and formica was its choice of gentle muzak. Call me a ragged old traditionalist, but I find it incongruous to have delicate clusters of elderly ladies sipping the Pimms and Tia Maria beneath hidden speakers that waft out Johnny Winter's "Progressive Blues Experiment". Bad Casting, I call it.

"Morning Richard," I call out. Sitting here now, the exact reasons why I wanted to talk to Ringo Starr seem fuzzy. All I can grab hold of is that, well, my sister was the girl who climbed Buckingham Palace Gates the day he got his MBE and she would drag me along to any number of strange locations as a cover note to Mum and Dad that we were only going "a pictures". I was raised on Beatlemania from the age of five and today, like Peter Cushing in *Satan's House,* I have no idea why I keep returning to this place. I think I loathe McCartney, although I like quite a few of his records, and Harrison is well and truly the *real* Worzel Gummidge, though he seems to have his Simpleton's Head on permanently.

However, a few weeks back I was quaintly warmed to see Ringo Starr arriving back in England to stay. Whatever he has done musically since The Beatles has been hopeless. But it was a sincere hopelessness and somehow more desirable than all the pretending and sneaking about his mates were doing. Plus, because of a Truly Great acting performance in *That'll Be The Day* – much of it ad-lib – I knew that he was still pretty much sane and sober.

Some people inherit millions, some people achieve millions and some people have millions thrust upon them. Ringo had millions thrust upon him and has always seemed a little bit dazed and wearied by it all. By returning home, Ringo – at the age he was always made for, anyhow – slots in. Slots into Ascot and his big old house, his animals, casual clothes and long leisured afternoons. He has a big garden too. It's called Berkshire.

Ringo is well aware that his musical output is of about the same interest to Britain as that of England Dan & John Ford Coley. He hasn't released a record for two-and-a-half years and is pushing his new one – new label – hard. During our little meet, he did not wish to speak of anything else, that was clear even to the point of such stunts as leaning over to my cassette and loudly saying the name of the album and, later on, the single. The odd scraps of other interest he delivered dutifully but minimally.

Ladies and Gentlemen, the 1981 Ringo interview.

So you're back Ringo. "Yep, back." As I ask why, he begins to order some food.

"I was homesick. Really. Just that. I never planned on staying away forever and I was away for six years. See I met Barbara and decided . . . oh beef and cheese . . . like where were we going to live . . . yeah with french bread . . . and I wanted to be near my kids. And half a lager."

Why here then?

"You can't . . . it's just England y'know? You get used to somewhere and you get to feel it after six years of only being allowed in for a few days – birthdays, Christmas. Plus I say, my kids are here, they live with their mother in London."

I read that Zac has a group.

"Yeah, he has. I think all of them are going to be drummers even though I'd rather they played guitar or something. His band have played this place. It was a big night for everyone. I've heard them and it's heavy. Heavy and hard, but I'm not allowed to call it heavy metal. They've got a big following in Bracknell."

When was the last time you played?

"Me? Ooh, *The Last Waltz* I think. I sometimes get the urge to get a band together and go on the road . . . but then the feeling goes away again."

What about busking it around the pubs like Led Zeppelin are doing?

"No, no. Drummers don't normally just set up and start playing in pubs, do they? Even though there's this guy on children's TV – Johnny Ball – well, he used to be – still is? – a drummer and we both worked at Butlins together years ago. He had this job of getting everyone in the bar dancing just by performing 'Knees Up Mother Brown' on the drums, like, every night. That's hard to do, I'm telling you. That's why I don't need to perform really."

Do you consider yourself a musician or an actor these days, then?

"Oh, always always a musician, a drummer. That's what I am – drummer. That's all there is to it. Can we get to the bit that says "New Album?""

You must know that people consider you to be just getting by in music because of . . .

"The Beatles. Of course. Lucky Ringo. No talent. It's silly, like the big dream where you're just standing in the right place at the right time. Simple. See we all lived in the same town at the same time. Before I joined I was always working, they didn't pick on me for some unknown reason – like I was walking past and they said 'Oi, let's have him' – we worked out well together was the reason I joined. They asked me and I said yes, because well, I thought they were the best band in Liverpool anyway. And yet there's still all that madness about I've never been on the albums and the rest of it. But, y'know, that band split up 11 years ago."

How bored are you by Beatle questions these days?

"Really bored, but I know it has to be said in any article, dunnit? Nobody ever asks me about Rory Storm or The Eddie Clayton Skiffle, Group – they were good bands too."

Have you ever read a good Beatle book?

"No. I've not read many. The new single is called 'WRACK MY BRAIN'."

Do you feel old?

"Age has nothin' to do with it. Musicians can't get old, you don't turn into an old musician. I can play with anybody – OK, I am one of the *older* musicians, I enjoyed watching all the archive film of Cliff [Richard] the other night. Then there was that young band on there doing nothing but old Cliff stuff with the suits and all. I suppose they'll get on to us next."

Why did you stop making records for that period until now?

"Boredom. I was bored with records. Going in every November – I had no enthusiasm at all and it showed through the records. I still enjoyed playing but my own records bored me."

You had a couple of hits early on, yet seemed to think in terms of LPs all the time.

"No, I still think in terms of hit singles. Sure. I'm always looking for a hit. That's the game – hits. But, especially over here, it's been very difficult, so my main market was America. I dunno, maybe because I wasn't here; or whether what I *was* doing just wasn't acceptable here, even though it still was in America. The later albums weren't accepted anywhere, though."

One reason given for your homecoming was that after John was murdered, you were scared of the US.

"No, that wasn't even in it. All that fear trip is exaggerated. For a while, everyone put on a little extra muscle but the reasons I came home were simply homesickness and family. England's much more relaxed, a little more courteous. Of course, it's true I can walk into any pub without bother too. The press like that fear angle. They thought it was callous of Paul and George when only I showed up after the shooting. But nobody knows how you react at times like that. We were holidaying in the Bahamas, which is close by, so once we heard – I was completely blown away – naturally the holiday was up the spout, so we just went over there to say 'Hi'. We spent eight hours there, felt very very close, and went again. But it can't be said that the others were callous in any way."

How about the music press view that LA is just full of zombies walking around making albums?

"Yeah. That's what I am. A zombie walking around making albums. This one's called 'Stop And Smell The Roses'."

THE HOUR I was with Ringo Starr passed quickly, I thought. The hour on playing back the tape I wouldn't wish on Pink Floyd's engineer. Names like Harry Nilsson and Jim Keltner floated around, as well as a long passage about what motivates these people to make dull records. Ringo seems as oblivious of the inconsequentialities of his old circle of friends as he is about the UK music press, his own past and role as Beatle, and the problems inside this "relaxed" and "gentle" land. In the same way as his local would be a traditional, friendly, post-card country inn, Ringo would love to be back in England amongst the street-wit and bottles of brown ale. Both institutions are just playing at it in Surrey's cotton wool surroundings.

There was one lovely moment that seems almost unbelievable. I was talking about rock musicians and the video craze when I mentioned that Pete Townshend is making his new record on film simultaneously.

"Well, we did that," says Ringo casually. "We did that in *That'll Be The Day.*"

That'll Be The Day?

"No, not *That'll Be The Day* . . . what was the studio one? The one where we ended up playing on the roof?"

Let it Be?

"Yeah, yeah . . . *Let It Be* . . . that's the one."

You probably remember it.

Wine, Women and Song

Steve Sutherland

Melody Maker, 11 December, 1982.

You want to read some heavy metal sycophant eulogising White-snake for sounding like a million Panzer divisions? Well, go buy *Kerrang!*

What I want to know is what the hell David Coverdale thinks he's up to further bankrupting the language of pop by releasing a collection of sleep-walking rock cliches like *Saints And Sinners* in this year of our Thatcher, 1982? So I asked him and here's what he said:

"Talking about music's like singing about football – it doesn't make any sense. I don't make statements for the world to follow. I make statements from what I feel. I'm interested in physical and emotional relationships. I'm not preaching to convert, I'm preaching the gospel of the 'Snake which is, in essence, wine, women and song.

"Rock 'n' roll will last as long as people drink and fuck. To me, that's what it is – a release the same as pubs are a release. Look, I don't want this to sound superficial because I don't *feel* super-ficial about it!"

Fine. Time to put Coverdale's words to the test. *"Wine"* suggests to me a publicly unattainable, irresponsible hedonism, something that *separates* rock from the needs, aspirations and real welfare of its audience – something irrelevant outside showbiz careerism.

"No, I think it's striking a chord, people identify with me. I think I'm part of a male fantasy and a female fantasy because I share those fantasies. I don't have any airs and graces, I'm not removed. I don't have a gold-plated Rolls-Royce – we have a very nice selection of cars because I enjoy choice in life, but I write about *emotional* problems and it doesn't matter how much brass you've got, you still have fuckin' hassles.

"I've worked with a few people who've thought they were divine – that's very dangerous. The audience *can* elevate you to a mental status which is not real, but we are not members of the royal family . . . though the business is full of liggers and bullshitters who feed off you like molasses on a whale. I saw a lot of it when I was with Deep Purple and I hated it. Oh, for six months I basked in it, copying everyone else, being a big-headed, ego-maniacal asshole and I was as guilty as any of them for thinking I was God's gift to whatever.

"Then there was a particular incident – and I won't mention any names – when I was an observer and I turned round and said to my old lady 'Can you believe that guy! What he fuckin' said! The way he behaved?' And she said 'Just look in the mirror'. It was a severe eye-opener I can tell you.

"So I learned a long time ago, though I still don't know why Tommy Bolin (the Purple guitarist who died) had to put such much stuff in his system. Why? I don't know because I don't need it. I love a drink, I *adore* a drink and flirting . . . just like you! But I haven't had the feeling to go over the top. If anybody comes around anywhere near my people with smack, they'll have difficulty walking away because, if they offer it to those people, they'll offer it to kids.

"Say what you like about me and my music, but insult my audience and . . . well, kiss my fist! See, they're not as dumb as the media makes out. I deliver honestly and if they thought I was taking the piss, they'd drop me like hot fuckin' potatoes. I will not work or be associated with anybody who takes the piss or takes advantage of the audience. I *hated* Purple's removed, moody, arrogant asshole image and I *refuse* to make fat, lazy, boring records.

"The new album, *Saints And Sinners*, is, I reckon, about 80 per cent artistically successful songwise, though performance-wise it's a different bag of apples. The next album *will* be the live strength of Whitesnake – the best rock 'n'roll act in the world –

captured in the studio. It has to be! I'll never be a cabaret artist, I refuse to be a parody of myself and if I started going through the motions on stage, if I though I was being dishonest, I'd bottle it straight away.

"I don't look upon it as a hobby, although I don't need to make any more money. It's a responsibility, a fuckin' lunatic passion! With Purple it was like having your bollocks tied up. I've got so much more to offer than sturm and drang . . . though, I've yet to get it right."

COVERDALE touts the enormous sales his records notch up and the up-coming sold-out tour as evidence of artistic activity but, if he actually achieves the "communion" with his audience that he boasts, then his attitude to "*women*" could have frightening repercussions. Incapable of treating people as people, even if he denies chauvinism, he still manifests an immature – if honest – inability to see women as anything other than a reflection of what men think of them.

"Some of my cock rock stuff is throwaway, but I do worry about wanting to chin ugly, female militant journalists who are trying to rob women of their feminity. I got a lot of flak for the cover of *Love Hunter* because it looked like this Snake was gonna beat the shit out of this woman. That wasn't the case!

"If you look at the words it was a celebration. I say women are assholes yes, but they're wonderful people as well. I'm not writing songs for men to trample women into the ground, although I am guilty of thinking women are fuckin' marvellous!

"All I can give you is a male statement. If Janis Ian or Joni Mitchell presented me with the women's argument then maybe . . . I mean, I think Tina Turner is sensational and Millie Jackson's a fuckin' maneater – I'd be scared shitless to walk into *her* dressing room to say 'hello', so don't thrown the fuckin' gauntlet at me!

"I don't just meet a woman and go 'Fuck! I'd love to get into your pants!' I'm married, I'm wearing my wedding ring and my four year-old daughter is the love of my life. What more to you want me to say? . . . though I've seen women behind the Iron Curtain where they're supposed to be equal on a social level, doing the same jobs as men, and it's not a pretty sight. It's very refreshing to come back and if I'm guilty of putting women on a pedestal then I apologise to the women who don't like it and POWER to the women who do!

"See, I honestly believe that women control the whole fuckin' game, the whole structure. If they want you in their pants, they'll fuckin' 'ave you, but they'll let you think you're doing all the manipulating. Women are the cleverest fuckin' species on earth. I'm absolutely serious and maybe my tunes are a defence mechanism against that.

"Most of the songs I write are about the hassle the old lady gives me, or the search for personal identity and I don't believe the audience takes it as seriously as you seem to think. I don't believe people leave my concerts wanting to ravage the nearest . . . uuh . . . I don't know . . . *maybe?*

"I believe the people who come to see me, whether they wear denim jackets with patches all over them or not, are responsible individuals. If the media don't, it's tough shit!"

"Song", in Whitesnake's vocabulary, means safe entertainment, satisfied to express itself through the cliched cartoon extremes of superstuds and mistreated victims couched in the long important imagery of the blues. Coverdale disagrees, claiming, as a "Virgo-Libra", he *is* either a "peacock" or a "little boy lost" depending on his mood and maintains his motives are honest and his method effective.

"I will *not* use the stage as a political platform to preach my beliefs and tell people what to do. I ask questions and I make personal statements. I like to do charity work – which is always very on the quiet – but when the pro-and anti-abortionists both came and asked me to do something . . . well, y'know, sometimes I *am* anti-abortion depending on the individual circumstances.

"I'm not fuckin' God! I can't make any statements. I'm worried about the bomb, I'm scared shitless about that warmonger Reagan who's carried over the image of the B-movie cowboy into politics, I'm glad Haig is out. I'm disappointed that Schmidt is out of West Germany, I don't know anything about the Kohn guy . . .

"I read somewhere 'What would you do if you found out you had four minutes to live?' Oh, I'd grab the nearest woman and fuck her!' You'd be lucky if you could get it semi-hard with all that kinda shit going on!

"I'd embrace my family just repeating 'I love you, I love you, I love you' until the shit hit the fan. I don't know, what would you do? What Can you do? I just hope Russia and America can still keep tickling each other's ass because it's such a fine line between having a verbal argument and a fist fight.

"The Falklands? I fuckin' hate the idea of people getting hurt! I heard a story about this SAS guy who, that night they did that forced 30-mile march, was creeping in and he jumped into a trench to gather information and got an Argentinian soldier and was about to top him and it was a 14-year-old boy! Fuckin' horrid!

"But South American politics or any Latin country's politics are obscene really, it's whoever's the strongest. Politically the Falklands may have given too much power to the stiff upper lip British attitude, but I would never make a statement to put down the guys ordered in to defend this kind of situation.

"You're tickling things out of me that I don't particularly want to make statement on. Listen, in private conversation I would give you my opinions; professionally I wouldn't like them to be abused because of lot of families lost their kids. Y'know, I'm proud of it and I'm disappointed that it had to come to that.

"There's no sweeping statement you can make about any fuckin' thing. You can't say love is wonderful because it can be up and down like a pair of whore's tights. If you adore somebody's company and they can reduce you to a snivelling shit and elevate you to an Adonis, what sweeping statement can you make about anything in the world?

"What can I do? I escape from that bullshit the same as I believe my audience does. I want people to enjoy, to have a good fuckin' time! I'd like everybody in the world to have a good time but I'm on no political ticket and I *don't* believe it's unhealthy – okay?"

Eyeball to Eyeball
with The Residents

John Gill

Time Out, 24 June 1983.

Who are The Residents? Why are they pushing journalists off the tops of ferris wheels? Why are we chasing people wearing giant eyeballs through the streets of Harry Lime's Vienna? And who is the drunk lurking in the dressing room?

It all began with a mysterious late night call from San Francisco, the caller claiming to represent The Residents and apparently giving me the green light to join their European tour, and ended, appropriately enough, 209 feet above Vienna, in Car No 2 of the massive Reisenrad ferris wheel. As the car reached the highest point of its journey, a menacing American guy with a cruel laugh and maybe murder on his mind tried to manoeuvre me towards the sliding door, murmuring something about his pal Harry Lime and how he wished he'd brought his Luger along for the ride . . .

Depending on your awareness of The Residents and their links with the film score of *The Third Man*, you'll decide the above lies somewhere between Bible and bullshit, but what the hell. It was a great ride and the point when the wheel hit its zenith was a moment of truth (of sorts).

History will note The Residents as the most secretive band on the planet. I know of only two people who *may* have met them during their 11-year career, and they're not saying. For their first ever European dates, the San Franciscan mystery band have demanded an elaborate security regime, with backstage access limited to crew and performers, and everyone on the road wearing baggy grey boiler suits, black woolly hats and – the final lunatic flourish – plastic and fur Groucho Marx masks, making it difficult to ascertain the gender, let alone the identity of anyone in their 18-strong entourage. Given such a smokescreen, the best one can do is presume that everyone and no-one in the entourage is A Resident.

From their earliest broadsides – "Meet The Residents" (the "Meet The Beatles" cover with crayfish heads replacing the Mop Tops and containing a vinyl nightmare) and "Third Reich 'n' Roll", a brilliant and frequently offensive medley of deconstructed pop classics – it was apparent that The Residents launched off from the zone Frank Zappa was too chicken to explore. Over the years, a stream of bizarre projects – ballets, operas, concept pieces, anthropological studies, movies, videos, rip-offs and sell-outs – has emanated from their independent Ralph Records label. These have been accompanied by rumours, official statements, lies, threats, a demented form of Big Mac University marketing and a thronging mythology somewhere between Lovecraft and Borges. They have peopled their career with real and imaginary collaborators, friends and foes: Snakefinger, onetime Chilli Willi guitarist Phil Lithman; ethnomusicologist N Senada, who travelled the world discovering exotic musics for them; artist Gary Panter, whose shattered mixture of Lichtenstein and Patrick Caulfield gave their visuals the peculiar 'Rozz Tox Aesthetic'; Frank Johnson, who may or may not be their office computer; Penn Jillette, Residents' spokesman, show narrator and alumnus of the Ringling Bros Circus; and the powers behind the shadowy Cryptic Corporation, whom the band have accused of everything bar being a front for the Illuminati.

During the 1970s, their empire expanded; first with the Cryptic Corporation then, under its shadow, Pale Pachyderm Publishing, El Ralpho Studios, Pore No Graphics and WEIRD, their official fan club. Ralph himself signed the likes of MX-80 Sound, Chrome, Yello, Tuxedo-moon, Fred Frith and Renaldo & The

Loaf. During this period, The Residents sometimes had blazing rows with Cryptic, occasionally fleeing the country and turning up, quite literally, anywhere from Macchu Picchu to London. Their marketing campaigns have ranged from limited editions packaged in bits of wrap-up sculptor Robert Cristo's "Running Fence", through "Third Reich" re-issued as 'Third (Censored) 'n' Roll' to cash in on the controversy, Residential care parcels containing "Real Residents Hair" key rings, Residents aspirin, windshield scrapers and pizza coasters, to threats of murder if people didn't buy their records. Their earliest advertisements appeared alongside those for X-Ray Spex and 1,000-Part Toy Soldier Sets in Superman comics.

The Residents' music will confound the most eclectic listener; perhaps intentionally so. When not doing to chart pop what Picasso did to the rule about pictures having an eye on either side of the nose, they wagon-trained out into Red Indian tribal music, gamelan ceremony, Eskimo folklore, Oriental folk music, big band swing and mainstream jazz (Stan Kenton, I'm sure, has a place in their hearts) and film/TV musical scores from the heights of Weill, Rota, Morricone, Herrmann and, er, Lalo Schifrin down to the lowliest B-movie and TV series. Stradding Charles Ives and The Archies, they have repeatedly garnered the critical superlatives like 'revolutionary' and 'inspired'.

Most recently, they've been engaged on the culture-clash trilogy "Mark of the Mole", two acts of which, "Mark of the Mole" and "Tunes of Two Cities", have so far been released and now form the basis of their tour. Ladies and Gentlemen, as Jillette has it, welcome to The Residents' Mole Show.

More a musical than a rock gig, its book follows the oppressed, cowled, pit-dwelling Moles and their attempts to gain entry into the society of the fat and rich Chubbs, all of them individually-wrapped hymns to cholesterol and round-the-clock TV. Although the story has yet to be resolved, the Moles have left their pit and are on the march. However, the cunning Chubbs may only accept them in order to run the Mols into a slave class . . .

Understandably, the innocent observer's reaction may be to cry

"Allegory!" and leap in with theories of women, blacks, gays or Puerto Ricans pitched against Reagan's America. As Jillette said at their press conference in London last month, as the eyeballs nodded behind him and Residential cameras snapped the assembly hacks, The Residents refuse to explain the story. Even to him.

Not only do The Residents refuse to speak, but it soon becomes obvious that you can't hold a sensible discussion with either them or their representatives. Barred from talking about any substantial aspect of their work, you're restricted to the gloss of their anonymity. Some find this infuriating, which often leads to people spying on Ralph employees, "exposing" them as Residents in picture and print, and worse. Most quickly realise that if it *is* a hype, it's totally benign; in fact, a harmless free entertainment for whoever cares to take notice.

All of which, as they intend, leaves you alone with the music, vinyl or live, and here The Residents explain themselves most eloquently. Thirty-odd towering backdrops, numerous "lifesize" cut-outs of Moles and Chubbs, three dancers, a narrator, a teasingly see-through skrim, one wheelchair and a smoke machine accompany the band on stage. Out of the eyeballs (hilarious at a distance but very intimidating up close), they're all back in boiler suits, hats and masks, the lip-hugging moustaches, bushy eyebrows and large spectacle frames giving them a look of caricatured mania. You don't need opera glasses to see that, here, they're sending up both the seriousness and the intent of their anonymity. Though the music veers from thundery Amerindian clangour to exquisitely romantic melody, they're plainly out there to have fun, as their Moulinex job on the Stones' "Satisfaction" attests. Clad in nothing but masks and zeppelin-sized underwear, they rock 'n' roll around behind the skrim doing the most scandalous things to the original.

I connected with their tour in Hanover, where they played a lively, if problematic, gig in an absolute toilet of a venue. The next morning, they assembled in the drizzle outside their scruffy *pension* (no room bars and 24-hour service on this tour) for what promised to be a nightmarish day-long drive to Vienna. The masks were off, revealing a mixture of the sexes, between their late teens and late thirties, all of them normal, healthy young Americans. With the first of two mini-buses loaded and ready, a group of 11 of us found our mini-bus had broken down. As we piled into taxis to go to the railway station, I breathed a sigh of relief and fingered my flask of duty-free gin less anxiously. Promisingly, among our party were two I sorely suspected of being, well, *Them*, and apart from a 12-hour train journey, the next best venue for what I intended would have been a locked cellar supplied with an Anglepoise and thumb screws.

Maybe Miss Marple would have fared better, but the journey was 100 per cent epiphany-free. Cunning or disingenuous comments about favoured bands, books, movies or painters more often than not met with a relaxed "Who?" or "Naw". Hamfisted attempts at spying found one of them with an early Beefheart tape, another with Randy Newman's "Trouble in Paradise". Someone was reading John Kennedy Toole's wonderful "Confederacy of Dunces", and a dogeared copy of Philip K Dick's "Three Stigmata of Palmer Eldritch" appeared, mysteriously, open on the laps of two different people. And even this skimpy evidence could have been left lying around for my benefit.

At the top of the Vienna's ferris wheel the next day, as people recounted favourite scenes from 'The Third Man', I decided to risk A Real Question.

"So," I asked the car in general, "would The Residents admit to having used 'The Harry Lime Theme' in their music?"

"Well, maybe", A Resident said, "But not intentionally."

Big deal? In its context, *that* was down in the underground car park with Deep Throat.

Backstage before the first of their two shows at Vienna's Sezession Club (hard by a main entrance to Harry Lime's sewers), watching the dancers limber up, or Jillette rehearsing what would be a show-stopping Esperanto gloss on his English narration, or masked and boiler-suited characters rushing back and forth with props and costumes, such a monumental confusion set in that, like a character in some Ray Milland psycho-twist B-movie, in all probability *I* was The Residents and these weirdos with the big pink noses and distressing amounts of facial hair were in fact dedicated doctors and nurses about my cure.

Around five in the morning, decanted into a hotel room. A Resident/Doctor took pity and agreed to explain the rationale behind the funny noses and eyeballs.

Their representatives stress repeatedly that the anonymity is not an issue, merely an attempt to short-circuit the personality cultism intrinsic to pop and concentrate attention on the music. It could be said, of course, that this merely replaces one cult with another. The point, perhaps, is that the eyeballs and general mystery scam are less insidious, indeed less obscene, than the padded crotches, silicon tits, jailbait rapist roles and the premiums on age, gender and looks that others use to shore up questionable talent. I was told that, on a personal level, The Residents prefer to stay anonymous simply so they can drink in bars, eat at take-aways, go to the movies and be themselves without suffering the side-effects of dubious stardom.

Most important of all is that the music must (and does) stand on its own. Mystery bands, from Klaatu to Klark Kent, are nothing new, and most disappear or come out of the closet as soon as the gimmick begins to pall. The Residents have kept it up for 11 years and show no signs of giving up. In that light, anyone who tries to penetrate the mystique is, frankly, unhealthy obsessed, jealous or plain mean.

During our ticklish manhunt, the serious side of their anonymity showed itself only once. The morning after the Vienna shows, they were unable to agree with Austrian TV over the security of a live, one-hour film shot the previous evening. Some heavy negotiations took place in the foyer of their hotel, and ended with A Resident grabbing two cans of film, striding out into the street and exposing them to the strong morning sunlight. The audio tape followed suit, and was chopped into tiny strips on the pavement outside. Again, something many other rip-off wary bands would do, but it shows the jesters aren't afraid of showing some muscle.

Goodbyes are bad news, especially when you're going home and they're scudding off for more fun and games in the capital cities of Europe, so I slipped off to the airport. Standing in line for a solo seat back to London, and with no physical or recorded proof of anything that had happened, the thought suddenly struck me: what if the real Residents hadn't even left San Francisco in the first place?

Elephant Fair

Mark Steel

Comedy is not, nor could it ever be, the new – or any other type of – rock 'n' roll. During the early eighties I would sometimes be on with bands at colleges or festivals, in which case they would invariably go out of their way to fulfil every conceivable rock 'n' roll cliche as if it were part of their contract.

Arriving in the dressing room I'd find them lying across armchairs with legs dangling over the side, a tin of lager in one hand and a fag in the other, skilfully holding on to both while receiving a joint, taking a drag and passing it on.

In the background the drummer would be doing his sound check, banging the bass drum once a second for a minute, stopping to suggest something like, "Two rev higher on middle downstroke, Slimey" and then doing it all again with no appreciable difference whatsoever to the sound.

'Hey," someone would begin, "Do you remember Rotterdam?"

Someone else would walk over to the table, open another tin of lager and burp loudly.

Half a minute after the Rotterdam question was posed, one of them would laugh under their breath, and a half a minute later they'd go: "Yeah, Rotterdam," and recount how wrecked they'd been when they were there, and how they were so out-of-their-head on whiz that they'd nicked a bicycle, rode it into a canal and it had turned out to belong to the Dutch Minister for Trade and Industry.

A roadie with a T-shirt too small to cover his beer gut would strut past carrying a two feet wide spool of gaffa tape, an unfeasibly huge bunch of keys dangling from a loop in his jeans, take an exaggerated draw on a spliff and say, "Wow, I hear there's some wild chicks here in Dudley," and yelp like an injured dog.

Someone would start slinging pieces of dried up pizza at the bass player and the guitarist would break into one of the band's songs, accompanied by the roadie using a pair of snapped pool cues as drumsticks on the window. Then they'd all have a discussion about the filthy habits of a bloke called Oily.

Throughout this they would be so engrossed in their own world that they wouldn't notice that I was in the room, quietly nibbling sandwiches and excluded from their universe. It wouldn't be out of rudeness; they just hadn't noticed.

Nor would they notice that when they started to play, there would be only eighteen people in the audience. So that from the way each song was introduced ("This next one's for a very good friend of ours" or: "All right, Dudley are you ready to go crazy?") and from the way the guitarist would go down on one knee and look as if his solo was causing him extreme dental agony, you would imagine they were playing to fifty thousand in Hamburg. Until the song ended and the sorry squeals of a handful of students echoed around the enormous and largely empty hall.

Saddest of all, I'd be watching, thinking, "Great. This looks like more fun than comedy."

So, only once do I remember experiencing anything approaching the lifestyle of the touring rock and roller. Three of us were booked to do a show on each of the three days of the Elephant Fair in Cornwall. We hired a van which broke down in Wiltshire and arrived late. We did the show as soon as we could but the organiser of the event was a hippy called Argos, who docked our money anyway, with the efficiency of a pre-war docks supervisor.

It was pouring with rain, so within hours the entire site was a sea of mud. Several people's tents blew down, including ours which meant we spent the first night in a sleeping bag in the van. The toilets, which began as holes in the ground behind a flapping length of canvas, degenerated from such luxury into a seething cauldron of toxic bile that would have repulsed a medieval serf. Food was veggie burgers and kidney beans served three times a day, with the only variety being a change in the number of kidney beans.

If you could get into a position whereby sleep was a possibility, someone in the vicinity would play the whole of *Simon and Garfunkel's Greatest Hits* on an acoustic guitar. And if you looked up at any given moment, you would see at least one person trying desperately to learn juggling with skittles, and at least one bloke with a beard dancing naked in the mud. And everywhere there was mud. It was impossible to take the merest stroll without mud covering every inch of your clothing, getting into your hair, your shoes and at least two orifices.

So there was nothing to do but get wrecked. Become one more bumbling idiot so out-of-it that the simplest question could only be answered, "Yeah, huh, I'm so out of it, heuugh, heuugh," with the last "heuugh," going so slowly that it actually stopped before the end.

So far then, so rock 'n' roll. Now for the delivery. It's the second day of the festival and there are about a thousand people at the tent where the comedy is scheduled. Going on first is a comedienne from our troupe who strolls on stage.

"Well," she begins. "I expect you're wondering what I'm doing here. Well I'm doing what a lot of you are probably doing; getting out of a very boring dinner party."

"Surely," we think, "She's not going to do the dinner party routine we've seen her perform at twee London theatres."

"I'm just hopeless at dinner parties," she continued, and proceeded with a piece about the drawbacks of hostess trollies.

The entire audience in this packed tent sat puzzling through an abundance of narcotics for a minute, collectively agreed and confirmed that this woman had, in the midst of the most squalid conditions anywhere in the world without refugee camp status, walked on to the stage to talk about dinner parties and hostess trollies. As if militarily planned, a mass of projectiles made from mud were sent hurtling towards the stage, and the poor woman scuttled backstage and burst into tears.

Comedy the new rock 'n' roll? We're not fit to lick their Rizlas.

All I Want for Christmas is My Two Front Teeth

Barry McIlheney

Melody Maker, 20 December 1985.

POGUES BIGGER THAN JESUS SHOCK!

It was a bit like finding a bottle of Guinness where the holy water used to be.

James, the very lovable accordionist, casually lobbed it into the conversation just as we were all beginning to agree that this growing move to canonize Shane MacGowan was getting a touch out of hand. I might have expected it with Geldof, certainly with Lennon, but Shane MacGowan? The man who writes songs that lead family stores to bring the warning stickers out of the closet? The man who gets up on stage every night with a bottle in his hand and wakes up every day with his stomach in his mouth? You're telling me that HE was born on Christmas Day?!

Yessir, this man was once a shiny new arrival on the front of his local paper and ever since has had two celebrations on the day when just the one is enough to send the rest of us into an extended alcoholic stupor. Still, all part of the image, is it not?

NO MORE HEROES, ROIGHT?

No. I say that all this stuff about our latest anti-hero being all our wildest fantasies made flesh is just a touch too comfortable to really get that close. Indeed, if there is one thing that Shane MacGowan now loathes with a rare intensity, it is surely the recent attempts to install him as some kind of alternative deity, the big-eared Buddha with the sun shining out of his gums. Yes, he takes a drink, yes he wears his Irish heritage with pride and yes he regards what he and The Pogues have achieved in the last 18 months as being just as relevant or worthy of respect as the dirty deeds of any of the other pretty boys currently jockeying for position at the end of 1985.

But ask him about his art and he'll tell you that everyone can do it, ask him about his worldview and he'll tell you about the band, ask him about death and he will tell you tales of religion and disease. And ask him about Christmas and he will tell you everything you ever wanted to know.

DRUNKEN PADDIES, PART 96

"What's that you're drinking?"

Large Bloody Mary, thanks Shane.

"I've given up on spirits now. On a life kick. It was after that last piece you printed, no, it was somebody else, no it was you, anyway, me mother read it and she was upset so I gave it up. (Gurgle.) Nah, I don't really have a drink problem now, I only take Guinness and wine."

It should perhaps be pointed out that this means one bottle of wine and one pint of Guinness per order but still, changed days indeed from the now-legendary lost weekend we spent together in Berlin. That'll shut up all those . . .

'Like, we still drink more than other bands, certainly more than any of the ponces who get into the charts. We're just normal people. We like drinking and at least it's not steroids or coke all the time like other people. Plus, our audiences drink a lot and I feel we owe it to them to stay drunk."

THE JANUARY SALES

It is, of course, no big surprise to discover that The Pogues' specially-written Christmas single will not now be available until . . . January.

"Well, we did try to get it out for Christmas but then we decided to put an orchestra on it and it started to turn into 'Bohemian Rhapsody'. So we dropped that idea and it's now a duet, me and Cait, but we just couldn't get it out in time for Christmas. Which is a shame, 'cos it was written with Christmas in mind.

"I sat down, opened the sherry, got the peanuts out and pretended it was Christmas. It's even called 'A Fairy Tale Of New York', it's quite sloppy, more like 'A Pair Of Brown Eyes' than 'Sally MacLennane,' but there's also a ceilidh bit in the middle which you can definitely dance to. Like a country and Irish ballad, but one you can do a brisk waltz to, especially when you've got about three of those inside you.

"Like this. (Hysteria in the camp as he crawls off the sofa to demonstrate) 'Once Upon A Time In America'! Strauss! This last final waltz at Christmas! But the song itself is quite depressing in the end, just like the rest of them, it's about these old Irish-American Broadway stars who are sitting round at Christmas talking about whether things are going okay . . .

"Anyway, it'll be a four-track EP but that's the main one. There's also a cover version of a song called 'Do You Believe In Magic' which was originally done by the Lovin' Spoonful!"

"Yeah. (Gurgled.) But it doesn't sound very like the Lovin' Spoonful the way we do it. And there's an instrumental called 'Planxty Noel Hill' which is for the guy in Dublin who slagged us off on a radio show when we were over there."

The one that called Cait a pig?

"Somebody called her a pig but I dunno who it was. It was like this really mad situation where a press conference had been arranged to go out live on Irish radio. So there's eight of us sitting on one side of the table and all these journalists on the other side and they're asking the usual sort of questions about drunken paddies and perpetuating stereotypes or whatever.

"And all this is happening live on Irish radio and there isn't even a fucking drink in the place! So we're paranoid and they're paranoid and you can imagine what it sounded like. It was all just a misunderstanding and although I'd never been to a press conference before I know now why so many journalists always get beaten up at them. Keeeeeeeeeesh!"

CHRISTMAS PRESENTS (1)

So what do you want for Christmas, Shane?
 "A new brain, thanks."

CHRISTMAS PAST

You probably think that Christmas Day for the birthday boy in the Irish family MacGowan household is a bit of a wild affair, with the booze in plentiful supply and all the old crooners coming out of the woodwork for the double celebration. You're not wrong.

"Yeah, everybody gets pissed and then the relatives come round and everyone gets really pissed . . . shit, you can't print that! Forget it! Nah, we all go down to the pub down the road and there's a bit of singing and everybody has a good time. There are like great Christmas songs, real party pieces that are always done by one of us. Stuff like 'Blue Moon', lots of music if you can call it that the way we sing them! I'm actually considering doing them on stage when I get fat and bored and go to Las Vegas to be a crooner. That's all I want from life really."

But it must be mighty crack having your birthday and Christmas all on the one day?

"What, like I'm one year older and Christ is one more year dead?"

THE HAMMERSMITH WORLD TOUR 1985

If it hadn't been for Live Aid and all its glorious memories, then 1985 would surely have gone down as the year of The Pogues. Starting off back in January as support to Elvis Costello at the Hammersmith Palais, they went on to do what Shane describes as the Hammersmith tour, selling out the Clarendon, the Palais and the Odeon in quick succession, conquering the rest of Britain and

Europe over the summer and selling more than 70,000 albums in the process. And perhaps more importantly, the last year has seen them develop from a bit of a bad joke on stage to the most outrageously exciting live act currently on offer. Anywhere. Not bad for a bunch of drunks who still can't play their instruments. (© The Irish School Of Advanced Purists).

"Yeah, I suppose it's been a bit of a shock. Still is really. I mean, to a large extent, we're still just a band that gets up there and does a few numbers. And why shouldn't a band like that sell lots of records? It's a bit like Los Lobos, they're just a bar band like us really but we both make far better records than any of these philistines who spend half their lives in a recording studio.

"And I always thought that if anybody started doing what we do then it would either be the most awful disaster you can ever imagine or else it would be pretty successful. So I never really expected too much success but now I've got some I'd like to have a whole lot more . . ." Still, there must be the danger of all this becoming a bit, ah, over-professional, a bit too . . . slick, perhaps? Maybe?

"Keeeeeeeeeeeeeeeshuuuuugh!"

SHANE MacGOWAN'S CHRISTMAS MOVIES

"Once Upon A Time In America", *"The Cotton Club"* *"Scarface"*. "I don't really like deep films. Where's Barry Norman, you're Barry, uh . . ."

SHANE MacGOWAN'S CHRISTMAS BOOKS AND PLAYS

"I HAVE never read a book that is less than twenty years old. Apart from the 'Skinhead' series. I know now that the big writers are people like Jackie Collins and I never want to read that. It sounds old-fashioned but I don't give a shit.

"The only play I know in recent years is Brian Friel's 'Translations'. It's a good, but again it's historical, its the sort of thing you can imagine being written by Ibsen or Eugene O'Neill. But this is all a bit highbrow innit? Let's just say that I don't think the best things in Irish culture are highbrow."

RUM SODOM AND BEGORRAH

Do you listen much to the album now?
"Only when I come home pissed and then it sounds great."

THE GHOST OF CHRISTMAS FUTURE

"The idea was always to expand the original line-up and although we've already done that with Phil Chevron and Terry Woods. I think eventually we'll have a lambeg drummer on one side and a badhran player on the other."
I can do that. I can play the Lambegs till my hands bleed.
"You a Prod? Suppose you must be."
Silence.
"C–t."
Gurgle.
"Nah, I'm only kidding. I don't care about that shit. We never get any of that 'which side of the war are you on' stuff. In Belfast and in Glasgow we get Celtic and Rangers fans together with no problems. I dunno, but we seem to light the torch of peace in people's hearts."
I wait for the inevitable gurgle and feel instead a strange glow at the sound of silence.

CHRISTMAS PRESENTS (2)

So what do you really want for Christmas, Shane?
"My two front teeth . . . bastard! If you print that I'll take out a contract on you. Nah . . . I'm actually scared of getting anything done to my teeth or my ears cos I'd probably look even worse than I do now. I think I'll grow a beard instead."
And join Prefab Sprout.
"Are they really relations of yours?"

SAD TO SAY, I MUST BE ON MY WAY

THEY'RE not as it happens, and they're certainly not one of the bands that excited Shane MacGowan over the last twelve months. In this little Christmas list he will include only the Potato Five and The Tall Boys, labelling the former as even better than early Specials ("Jerry Dammers thinks that and he needs two front teeth as well").

But no, like me, and maybe like some of you, the only thing that has really made the hairs rise in '85 has been The Pogues, their memorable live performances, their stunning album, their wonderful attitude, their great drummer, their impish guitarists and everything else about them. I nearly told Shane all of this, nearly wished him a happy Christmas, a great birthday and a prosperous New Year but then he attacked me with a corkscrew, two of them called me fatso before I went to bed and I suddenly remembered that I had come not to praise The Pogues but rather to bring their first great chapter officially to an end and thus make sure that they don't let the bums get them down.

So happy birthday Big Ears and I now say goodbye to all that.

Hell on Wheels: The Cramps

Simon Garfield

Time Out, 7 May 1986.

Pink fur bra straps, gold lamé trousers, no undies, leopard-skin gloves, black glasses, lots and lots of sequins and pearls, and that's just Colin the driver. It's 6.28 on a coach marked "Cramps" in Gloucester Road coach park on a Sunday morning and there are 47 of us set to embark on a journey that none of us will ever forget. Two of us will return with serious injuries. Three will not return. The customs people will reveal three concealed knives and a Sten gun. If I could live my whole life again, I'd do it all exactly the same except I wouldn't travel to see the Cramps in Belgium.

This is no sunny ramble up Pleasure Drive. This is dangerously fanatical psychobilly weirdness. A musical nightmare worse than *Absolute Beginners,* a critical journey with a coachload of great haircuts and strange, expensive habits. Everyone has paid £45 to be here, and with food and alcohol and T-shirts on top it will amount to maybe £60. And for what? For a return coach and ferry trip to see an immensely rough, religiously basic rockabilly band play a warehouse in Deinze, mid-west Belgium, just south of Ghent. Mead Gould Promotions, the Brighton company responsible for the pilgrimage, have organised a demanding schedule. Gloucester Road to Dover to Calais to Deinze to gig to Calais to Dover to Victoria in 25 hours with No Beds Involved.

There are no free drugs (few drugs going at any price, it seems). The seats will not recline, the Channel crossing in early April will be rough, there's no toilet on the coach, there's feeble

air conditioning, and only four people I can see have any excuses
for being here at all. The coachdriver Colin, bemused at his
strange cargo, a man who would later display an awesome line in
sexist and racist humour; Ann-Marie, the early-twenties courier
who is being paid £50 for the nightmare and who's only on her
second such trip (the first was with seven coachloads of Simple
Minds supporters for three days in Paris: "A bit of a disaster –
we missed the ferry"); and the other freeloaders are myself and
seasoned photographer Derek Ridgers, a 35-year-old dad who
spends the first leg of the journey assuring me that all will be
fine. He tells me he was at the Clash gig at the Rainbow in '77
where his seat was taken apart while he was sitting on it. All
musical adventures after that have been a doddle, he says.
Ridgers is a helpless Cramps fan like myself, but we still feel
rather out of place. We decide not to reveal we are travelling on
the *Time Out* passport for two reasons: one, we want the story
straight, want the psychobilly psyche with no adornments; and
two, you'll understand that *Time Out* is not the sort of magazine
you might own up to reading on a trip like this, let alone writing
for. Not with these people. Hence once our cover is blown on
production of camera and *UK Press Gazette* (fundamental
error), we make out we're both from *Kill Your Pet Kitten*
fanzine, but this does not last long because there's someone
on a seat near us who claims he's from *Kill Your Pet Puppy* and
knows *all* the opposition.

The others on board are just bobbing along for the fun of it.
There are rockabillies, psychobillies, punkabillies, monsterbillies
and someone actually called Billy. There's an average age of 21, a
5:1 male:female ratio, a straw poll that reveals that the huge
majority either have student grants or regular wages to support
such devotions, and a glance up the coach that shows that few
have come alone, a lot have come in pairs, and the rest have come
in small, knuckly gangs. There are no blacks. As a Jew I calculate
that I'm the only minority rep at all in this hurtling lower-
middle-class crew, united only by a craving to hear a singer
called Lux Interior ask, midway through the set, whether Your
Pussy Can Do The Dog. Mad? Certainly, but tugging out of

Kensington at 6.40 am I reckon there sure must be worse ways to spend a Sunday. Three weeks later I still can't think of any.

Several on the coach have never seen the Cramps before; some have never been outside England before. One guy, a person in a grey Cramps cardigan knitted by his mum, has seen the band on all 13 of their recent UK dates. Another diehard, Flash, admits to paying insane money for rare Cramps vinyl – "like £9 for an LP with one track on it I wanted." He does, however, have a copy of The Cramps' debut UK 12-inch EP 'Gravest Hits' in green, and is the only person he knows to have even seen one. He drinks neat vodka at 11 am on the ferry over, and by showtime he'll be well enough tanked to remove his trousers. Despite his fanaticism, he says he's never met The Cramps, shrugging "They're just not the sort of band you meet".

Which is true on many counts. First, as may later become apparent by examining their lyrics, they're perhaps not the sort of band you *want* to meet, certainly not in a room alone. Secondly, they don't make it over here from their home in LA too often – the last tour was two years ago – and though they no doubt love their fans as much as anyone, blah, blah, their hard sexy sheen will always be maintained far better by can't-touch mythology than by walkabouts with the kids.

And thirdly, and speaking as something of a pro, photgrapher Ridgers will say that their London publicist leaves much to be desired. All the way to Dover he's telling me how badly he feels treated by press officer Vermillion Sands who 'really could have handled things better' over his assignment to Wolverhampton. Can't recall all the details here, but as we board the ferry Ridgers boasts he has seen a picture of Vermillion from her punktime singing days. "Not just any old picture – it's her urinating into a sink." Wowee! Bonanza!

The ferry over. It spills with post-*vacances* schoolkids. It is notable only for the considerable number of 24-unit lager crates escorted by some great haircuts from the upper decks to a coach on the lower deck. Our haircuts, our coach, of course, and this

despite a strange alcohol ban on board. The ban is optimistic. No
real evidential problems though, as the same ferry company will
see the same lager, in a slightly different form, returned with
vigour during a slightly rougher crossing on the return leg.
Something a little nice to look forward to.

A lethal brew as it turned out, but the rest of the outward trip
sure went with a roar after the first nine crates. As with all coach
journeys that have ever been, the most fun is to be found at the
back, and as we enter Belgium in the early afternoon, two huge
flat-top brothers Glenn and Steve make it known that they love
this theory as well as anyone. Whereas most backseats are designed for five, our backseat is only designed for Glenn and
Steve, respectively 22 and 20, both cherub-faced, both lavishly
tattooed, together weighing an easy 30 stone, and each tucked
into an XL/Fe (extra large/fucking enormous) Cramps T-shirt.

These are nice people to do business with, not least, it seems,
on the dancefloor. Glenn shows me four purple fist-size arm
bruises acquired the last time he let loose at a Guana Batz gig tree
weeks ago. "We were stomping and yomping – Whooaa! – and we
heard this crack and we saw that someone had broken his nose.
Blood everywhere. I did it, but of course it was an accident.
Stomping gets rough, but that's the fun."

Glenn then slips a Demented Are Go cassette into the coach
machine and begins to loosen up for the gig. He's still seated,
but his arms are soon locked into a cycle of frantic turkey-style
clucking, prop-forward shoving and praise-the-lord overhead
wrist waving. In mid stomp he tells me he's seen a lot of the
world with his arms engineer dad, that he himself travels from
Bracknell to work a 12-hour day as a buyer for a civil engineer
in Grosvenor Square, and that The Cramps represent the
trashiest, most extreme wing of his devotion to all things
rockabilly.

Demented Are Go are another side of it, possessed of a singer
who makes Lee Marvin sound like Sandra Dickinson, and of a
drummer who's sitting three rows ahead of us offering to sell me a
DAG tape for £9. I demand a press copy and he stares at me for a
while before shaking his head in disbelief. Meanwhile a Cramps

tape has found its way into the coach machine, and is bleeding out a set of desperate stanzas we have all learnt to drill for deeper meanings over the years:

I'm a human fly, and I don't know why, I got 96 tears and 96 eyes . . .

This is the band's second US single from October '78 which now changes hands for £35 (ie you pay someone £35 to remove it from your collection).

When the sun goes down and the moon comes up
I turn into a teenage Goo Goo Muck . . .

– the classic fourth UK single.

Do the eye-gauge, do the eye-gauge, do the eye-gauge
Everybody's doin' it . . .

– from the fifth UK single "The Crusher", the flipside of which opens with the immortal:

Life is short, filled with stuff.
Don't know what for, I ain't had enough . . .

And right up to date with the new, increasingly adult release:

There some things baby I just can't swallow.
Mama told me that girls are hollow.
Uh-Uh, What's inside a girl?
Somethin's tellin' me there's a whole nuther world . . .

All lyrics are anchored to the most brutally plagiarised guitar runs you have ever heard, and delivered in great, bug-eyed, warped style that goes some way to disguise the fact that The Cramps still do not play too well.

"I certainly wouldn't pay £45 to see them," says Julie next to me. "If you think about it too much, you realise they're rubbish. Still, *great* rubbish though." Julie has just bought a £900 R-reg Fiesta with her savings from three jobs, and hence is being sponsored on the trip by friend Danny, whose opening line to me is, "You better kill the Hammersmith Odeon, I fuckin' hate it there." In fact this is his only line, but he repeats it with alarming regularity and conviction throughout the trip.

Thirty minutes from the venue there's a meal break in Kortrijk, an elegant, sluggish, very conservative town where Boy George is recent and still rather alarming news. It's important to know this when walking around with Nelson Piperides, a 20 year-old chemical processor from Loughborough who's dressed as a severe fashion casualty-cum-junior drag queen. He has thick long spills of false black hair, quasi Spiderwoman make-up incorporating lots of white powder that battles in vain against a grimly persistent emergence of stubble, knee-length patent plastic boots, a green and black speckled padded jacket and a black plastic shoulder-bag the size of a large envelope with a red scarf streaming out the side. There's a funfair in Kortrijk today, but only one attraction: Nelson. "In Nottingham people spit and abuse me," he says. "Here their mouths drop open and they can't shut them again. Strange people."

We eat chips, hot dogs and nougat, and Nelson's brother Howard buys candy floss as it matches perfectly the consistency of his heavily lacquered overhang of quiff.

Back on the coach, and only minutes from the huge brick and corrugated iron warehouse that will host tonight's show, I try for a change in mood and slap on a tape of Haydn's "Sunrise". It lasts about ten seconds, a pretty good run I think, and is followed by serious threats to my spine, limbs and throat and cries of more Cramps, more Cramps. In the event that the band have cancelled, I can now see myself as a hostage.

No cancellation. The show, number 18 out of a scheduled 58, is something of a stormer, probably the eighteenth such stormer in a row. By the third song I can just make out a mass of Glenn stomping his heart out, and perceive a slow, sensible Belgian retreat from the immediate area. Somewhere in the lull between numbers I can hear someone shouting: "Kill the Hammersmith Odeon! Kill it!".

By the time of the encore I reach the most obvious conclusion of the night: The Cramps are insane. Each day this crazy travelling, each night a Holiday Inn, each afternoon the sound-check, each show the same build-up, the same snarls, same loopy garbage deluxe played as if their lives depended on it (which, of course, it does). There is guitarist "Poison" Ivy Rorschach, who lists her favourite movie quote as "I don't beat clocks, I beat people" and tonight sports a chunky and glittery gold bikini top and sub-Arabian double slit silk skirt: there's drummer Nick Knox, who lists his sixth favourite thing as "my reflection in my mirror" and his tenth fave as "eating things", tonight, as every night, wearing black boots, black trousers, black skirt, black shades, black hair: singer Lux Interior, who claims his seventh favourite film to be *Take Off Your Clothes And Live*, tonight in bare scarred chest and gold lamé trousers which he struggles to peel off on stage (no undies); and then there's Fur, bassist for this tour only, listing her fourth best phrase as "have a nice trip, see ya next Fall", and wearing leather trousers and pink bikini top outlined with white fluff. After ten years the band are still seeking a permanent bassist. One early Cramp, Bryan Gregory, not only had an interesting kick of collecting earth from every graveyard in every town The Cramps ever played, but one day decided to quit, jumped in the van, and drove away for good with all the band's gear. This has always been a tough act to follow.

One minute before the show tonight I ask Ivy why anyone would possibly want to spend at least £45 to see them. "Because we're the kings and queens of rock 'n' roll and we're the only ones currently reigning. It's just got to be worth it."

It's worth it because, irrespective of the band, the pain is half the fun. Beneath all this hyperbole, there's a decidedly warming atmosphere on board – an adhoc supporters' club with a marked lack of football-fan aggression. Julie next to me is seriously considering going on a Banshees expedition in a few weeks. I tell her she's mad, but it's not impossible to see how even such Cramps lunacy drags people back for more. In the last six years, Mead Gould have organised over 300 rock trips and it's clear that many fans on each journey are not Coach To Hell virgins. And rather a Coach To Hell than all-night queue to see Dylan at Earls' Court.

This makes sense at the time, in a twisted sort of way. By France, four hours later, the sense has long vanished. I don't care to remember too much of the travelling back, for obvious reasons.

If there is a Mr Harris of Harris Coaches, I would guess that he's fairly thin, the height of a small child, has little need for sleep, has a great sense of adventure and an ex-directory telephone number. If Harris is a she, you'll find, perhaps, that she's Alltime Sphincter Queen.

It is an immensely long and painful haul. A few snog. Some spew on the ferry. Quiffs frizzle and sob. Any promise of sleep is dashed by Danny's loud requests to kill a well known London concert hall and by the very real threat of Glenn sleepstomping and landing an entire coachload in A & E.

By Victoria I've stolen about two hours sleep, probably a fair average. It's 7am, and many of those with jobs to go to this morning turn from psycho-and rockabillies into psycho-and rockawilliams. Ridgers slinks back to the wife and kids, clearly distressed at the lack of major international incidents. I detour home past the Hammersmith Odeon, but can only bring myself to shout at it viciously.

Danny, I'm sure, will be furious.

Jackie Wilson Said

Geoff Brown

Time Out, 14 January 1987.

As an infant a highlight of my week was to be taken by my grandfather to one of the nearby Sunday morning street markets – Club Row, Brick Lane or Petticoat Lane. Although he never managed to sell me, I did in fact become sold. On music. While he stall-crawled in search of carpentry tools, I was left browsing in a record shop. It's been somewhat perturbing, though still a great pleasure, to discover that one of the first three records I ever bought there has been number one over Christmas.

The perversity of record sales during the festive season is well known, so the fact that the late Jackie Wilson's 29-year old rock 'n' roll novelty hit 'Reet Petite' (it'll be 30 this October) is a hit again ought not to be a surprise. Even less so given the becalmed, mundane state of white pop and evergreen appeal of outstandingly spirited black soul singers such as Wilson. His other hits, such as 'I Get The Sweetest Feeling' and '(Your Love Keeps Lifting Me) Higher & Higher' are often rereleased and regularly chart.

Unlike last year's Sam Cooke revival, Wilson's posthumous hit has not had the benefit of exposure through an enormous advertising campaign for jeans or similar hip youth product. All it's had is radio airplay and an astonishingly offensive video in which a puppet, presumably meant to represent Wilson, displays an array of racial stereotypes which render one speechless with anger and embarrassment. It would surely not have been made were he alive to issue writs.

Wilson's career effectively finished when he collapsed on stage at the Latin Casino in Camden, New Jersey on September 29 1975.

He was 41. The heart attack was followed by deep coma and severe brain damage. He survived in various remedial homes and care centres, never able to communicate other than through eye movement or minimal mumbling, until January 21 1984, when he died at Mount Holly, New Jersey, aged 49. It was a dreadfully drawn-out, inert death for a man whose stage act had been as vigorous as James Brown's and whose presence and vocal expression was on a par with Sam Cooke. Unlike those contemporaries of his, however, Wilson's career resounded to the echo of unfulfilled potential largely because his voice was so re- markably adaptable to a huge variety of styles.

Shortly before his incapacitating heart attack, Wilson had toured Britain on the back of yet another release of "I Get The Sweetest Feeling" and I met and interviewed him. Must've been one of the last to do so, because in the States interest in him was low and on his return he would set out on the Golden Oldies rock'n'roll revival tour which was to be his last. Jackie wasn't much over five foot six inches tall but carried himself well ("self-assured, almost cocky" my notes at the time said) and you could easily see that he was an athlete. He'd in fact been a Golden Gloves amateur boxer in his home- town of Detroit, where he was born on June 9 1934, and trained at the same place as his hero Joe Louis. He attempted to combine fighting with singing – "I'd finish boxing and if I could get the cold towels to get the mouth down I'd sing" – until his mother ordered him to quit the ring. But the footwork, agility and suppleness Jackie learned there became part of his act: the spins, twists, eye-boggling dance steps, painful knee-drops and splits, just like that other ex-boxer James Brown.

Compulsory gospel experience (the Ever Ready Gospel Singers) was followed in '51 by a brief spell at Dizzy Gillespie's Dee Gee label before he was spotted by R&B bandleader Johnny Otis. But his big break came in '53 when he replaced Clyde McPhatter, who was joining the Drifters, in Billy Ward's Dominoes with whom Jackie sang for four years. Although past their peak, Ward's group got all the work it could handle and the leader gave Wilson a thorough grounding in stage-craft. Unfortunately,

Ward was guiding his act away from R&B and rock 'n' roll and towards Las Vegas and though Wilson sang lead on three hits they were of the ilk of "St Therese Of The Roses", upon which I shall not dwell. But the Vegas experience was illuminating. "They were so polite to the extent that they wouldn't tell you that they didn't allow black and white to mix although we were playing the place. They said 'We got you a great big 40-foot luxurious trailer equipped with everything! And it's all yours for the time you're here.' So that's where we got to change."

Wilson quit to go solo in '57. Short of material to record for Brunswick who'd snapped him up, he turned to an old boxing acquaintance.

By 1957 Berry Gordy Jr had tried his hand at and discarded several careers and was currently hawking his songs around Detroit. Wilson took four of Gordy's co-compositions and they were all hits, though strangely the first, the jaunty "Reet Petite", made only 62 in the US but reached number six here. The next three – "To Be Loved", "Lonely Teardrops" and "That's Why (I Love You So)" – plus a final Grady contribution, "I'll Be Satisfied", established Wilson as a soloist comfortable with a breadth of material – from the rather grandiose barnstorming balladeering of "Loved" through the earthier "Teardrops" to the peppy "That's Why".

Coincidentally, because Gordy was less than enamoured with the royalties he received for these hits, he quickly decided to set up his own label and the very earliest Motown hits often bore traces of arrangement, lyric or melody from one of the Wilson hits. (Wilson never recorded for Motown though one of his later hits, "Higher & Higher", featured the label's house band moonlighting for another label and illustrates all too vividly what a different route Jackie's career might have taken had Gordy signed him.)

But the problems which beset Jackie's recording career were manifest in those first hits. The producer, a white bandleader named Dick Jacobs, tended towards the lavish with strings and although neither he nor any other producer could ever entirely subjugate Wilson's magnificent, rangy high tenor, neither did they exactly enhance the expressive gifts of his voice. Still, there were enough genuine R&B or soul performances – on the LP "Jackie Wilson Sings The Blues" or in singles like "Baby Work-out" and "Doggin' Around" – for one to ignore quasi-operatic outbursts on adapted classics such as "Night" (from Saint-Saens) and "Alone At Last" (Tchaikovsky).

When I asked him about this – why, for instance, didn't he quit Brunswick? – he said, 'My mind would say go but my soul would say stay.' So we talked about the then (in '75) scarcity of good material because for his type of singer it is akin to lifeblood. He answered haltingly, attempting to analyse, almost to himself, his style. "I don't think people worry about the singer anymore. It's The Stylist." Which made his position precarious? "It does a little. But you have to create something. What I think I have is a voice," he paused. "Although I always did use a falsetto note and I actually caught myself creating a style back in those days (of 'Reet Petite') by hitting the high note all the time. But trying to create, I have found it hard in the past. I just don't actually think I could create. I can be me, I can probably sing a little bit this way, a little bit that way but basically I am hoping that an arrangement will *give* me a style."

And this held for what he called his "opera stuff"? He said it did. He'd wanted to try it but was nervous. Instead of his usual studio he was taken to one "where Perry Como had recorded. Now do you understand how I felt?" I said I *thought* I did. "It was a huge palace and there were all these longhairs. I just closed my eyes and thought about Mario Lanza."

However variable his recordings may've been, live his shows were exciting, impassioned entertainments and as with singers whose impact on women was similarly explosive, Jackie had problems in this direction, most notably when a fan/girlfriend shot and seriously wounded him in a New York hotel room in '61. But the wounds on his career left by the variable material with which he worked and the over-wrought orchestrations within which he often found himself were more lasting.

A switch from recording in New York to Chicago with a squad of younger producers and writers – Carl Davis, Sonny Sanders, Eugene Record (of the Chi-Lites) and Willie Henderson – in '66 revived his career and the better tracks from that period keep coming back. "Higher & Higher" was a hit both sides of the Atlantic in both '67 and '69, has charted since and is much covered, most recently by the Inspirational Choir (it was originally written for a gospel group, Wilson told me, "and nobody wanted to try it because it had a churchy flavour"). "I Get The Sweetest Feeling" first came out in '68, wasn't a hit until '72 and repeated in '75. Others in his catalogue, particularly '66's "Whispers (Gettin' Louder)", could easily do the same as maybe could 'You Got Me Walking', a '72 recording and arguably the last good pop-soul track he cut.

After Jackie's heart attack there was an upsurge of sympathy and the Detroit Spinners and Barry White, both red hot at the time, were among the first to do benefit concerts to defray his medical expenses. After two years in hospital he was moved to a retirement community for further, but frankly hopeless, therapy until on January three years ago he was taken back into hospital and died 15 days later. In the way of these things, this was the cue for an outbreak of legal crossfire between his wives and "guardians".

Far better to remember the great showman and the extraordinarily gifted singer who could switch from gospel to rock 'n' roll to R&B to soul to doo-wop to frenetic dancers to the schmaltziest ballad to soaring pseudo-operatic treatments with the ease of a master chef cracking an egg. It's what made Van Morrison write the line "Jackie Wilson said it was Reet Petite". I guess it may've been one of the first three records Van bought too.

Phallus or Fallacy

Mat Smith

Melody Maker, 12 March 1988.

It's ironic but true. While we've all been celebrating the re-awakening of pop's diffracted genius we've allowed its fall into the grasp of the censor to slip by. While its head and heart are still free to flutter around the firmament, its nether regions are unceremoniously but firmly tied down lest they pop up and embarrass its increasingly cossetted audience. As a journalist it's becoming increasingly difficult to represent bands as they truly are. By the time you read this much of it will have already been cut for fear of sanctions from the news-stands.

As every other entertainment industry is allowed to probe the boundaries of its possibilities, pop cowers in the corner, ashamed of its body and trying desperately to forget that it once *celebrated* that thing in between its legs. But enough is enough, The Red Hot Chili Peppers have sat long enough, have had enough of the pratting or rather not pratting around and are charging gull tilt and full frontal at the new morality with everything they hold dear swinging in front of them as they run.

The Red Hot Chili Peppers are putting the three most important letters back into FUNK, taking the piss out of the idiots who forgot what it was for in the first place and are being censored left right and centre because of it.

"From our viewpoint it's impossible to ignore the correlation between music and sex because, being so incredibly rhythmic as it is, it's very deeply correlated to sex and the rhythm of sex, and the rhythm of your heart pounding and intercourse motions and just the way it makes you feel when you hear it. We try to make our music give you an erection."

The Chili Peppers' bassist Flea, star of Penelope Spheeris' "Suberbia" and a slightly unnerving muscular dwarf with an apprentice skinhead haircut takes a gargantuan toke backstage at the Paris Rex Club and blows smoke rings into the atmosphere.

"In terms of the sexist interpretation," he continues "that's really shallow. The fact that we have songs like 'Party On Your Pussy' (changed to 'Special Secret Song' after complaints from EMI) is meant as an endearing compliment to the female race who we treat as total equals and who we love very much. There is *no* sexist attitude in this band.

"To me the closest thing you can call it by conventional categorization is hardedged funk, but there again, to me it's too personal, there's not a tangible way to describe it. The thing is the sense of commitment to the groove. I have to give up all my other thoughts and just wail as hard as I humanly can.

"Today funk isn't very funky to me. It's just too clean. Funk should be dirty music; it's not pristine, it's gotta have that dirty grungy feel. It's not a crashing snare drum or a flashy bass drum pattern. When funk started it was a dirty word and kids would hide their funk records cos their parents didn't wanna know about James Brown, cos that was like saying 'F★★★'.

"A guy slaps a bass now and does supposed funk lick number 63 and disco drum beat number seven and everybody calls it funk. Everytime I play a gig they play this song called 'Pump Up The Volume' and they call that funk? That's not funk man, that's a bunch of sequencers jacking off for androids – it's not for people who like to shake their ass and get down."

The Chili Peppers have hit their stride and aren't gonna be sidetracked by an accusation of boring old fartism. Singer Antwon The Swan takes up the argument.

"The whole reason we started playing music is cos we loved making people feel certain ways and our music is very heavily based on emotion and just the feel you get when you listen to it. The best way to describe our music is like a bowel movement because it comes out of us very naturally and it'll always be like that. We do what we do and we do it as good as we can."

The Chili Peppers call themselves an organic anti-beat box band. Others call them dated – an outmoded amalgamation of slap bass and slapstick, hard funk and hard rock. But then, others miss the point. The Chili Peppers are more than mere dancing fools. They're a primal instinct that's been largely tamed into impotence in modern pop. Others tease and tweek but no one actually has a noisy multiple orgasm in the middle of each and every song. Antwon laughs at the notion but understands the sentiment.

"It's largely a philosophy of ours that we're very pro-humans making emotional music for other humans to listen to. It's our belief that computer rap music is interesting to listen to but it's impossible for a computer to translate the emotions that we find it necessary translate. They don't have penises, they don't have hearts, they don't have soul and they can't play with any of those elements and those are very strong elements in our music. It's about what we are, where we come from, our unity as friends and the chemistry of our four brains put together along with the fact that we have an incredible drummer."

Like most Californian-bands, The Chilis exhibit an insular gang-like existence but deeper than that they share an instinctive and almost tribal celebration of their own male sexuality often result-ing in frequent shows of nudity. The resulting accusations of sexism are predictable, lazy and miles off the mark – nevertheless, there's no denying that in the Chili Peppers' world, the cock is king.

"I'll tell you a secret about 'Fight Like A Brave'," Jack laughs. "When I did the drum track for that song these guys stood at the studio window and pulled their scrotums out and pressed them against the studio window. They gave me scrotes while I was playing to give me energy. That was the main inspiration for that song."

Does it happen often?

"No. But if we've been in the studio all day and we've having a hard time getting a take we'll say 'Testicles out!' and we'll get them out and it'll help us."

Antwon says their penchant for nudity goes way back to the early Seventies fad for streaking.

'We used to streak when we were kids. One night Flea and myself were round my house and we got naked and painted ourselves with my mother's lipstick and took some eggs and we were gonna knock on this one guy's door and throw eggs at him when he answered but he wasn't in so we ended up throwing them at some obscure old man walking down the street.

"Another time when Flea and I had signed to EMI they were having this big meeting with all the heads and we wanted to go in but they wouldn't let us so we took off all our clothes and ran in naked and totally freaked them out."

"It all goes back to when we were young," Jack offers by way of explanation. "Did you ever have those dreams where you're walking round your high school in your underwear or naked and every one else is not and you're going eeeek! I suppose everyone has these dreams when they're growing up. We're just turning them into reality. The sock thing was Antwon's idea. We used to play at this strip club in Hollywood and we wanted to upstage the girls so we went back for the encore one night just wearing a sock each. I laughed so much I pissed in mine.'

How do they stay on?

"Ballpower. As long as he elastic's good you're okay."

And if not . . .

"It hasn't happened yet."

Do you ever get hard-ons on stage?

'We probably would but we move around too much." Says Antwon. "It's more a mental hard-on."

The best thing about The Red Hot Chili Peppers is that they never stop to think about the consequences. Like Jack walking through UK immigration with a tit hat wobbling on his head, Flea and Antwon's childhood sport of throwing themselves off Los Angeles apartments five storeys down into neighbours swimming pools – they only stopped when the singer missed, hit the side and advanced screaming into the water with his back cracked in half. All this comes out in the music and the motto seems to be if something's worth doing, it's worth doing in as extreme a manner as possible. According to Flea, the Chilis are the aural equivalent Dali's "Andalusian Dog" making music with nothing in mind but to enjoy themselves.

We put as much into it every night as we can. Not too many bands do that. Some guys are just too old and take too many drugs to get on stage and put everything into it. Anyone who sees us that doesn't think we take our music seriously has gotta be crazy. I mean to me on that stage if I have a bad show the very thing worse is a death or a heartbreak. You live in it and love it and nurture it and when you do a good show it's great."

Not surprisingly when it came to choosing producers for their new LP, "The Uplift Mofo Party Plan" someone else's idea of using Malcolm McLaren was given the boot straight away. As Flea explains, adopting a dreadful McLaren accent:

"He was going, 'Right, 'ere's wot we do. Anthony, you're gonna be the star and you three can just sit at the back playing simple rock 'n' roll. That was his concept and we did not wanna go for it. After that he went on for about two hours speeching about how important it is to get back to the roots of rock 'n' roll 'cos nothing has ever been done differently, which we don't agree with. We think everything should be done differently and we think we're doing it differently. But he gave this really convincing speech about being in touch with the origins of it."

It was a ridiculous but well-presented argument and on the strength of it McLaren lost himself the job. He made me faint man," Flea exclaims. "I f***ing fainted. I got real stoned and he just started talking and talking, we were in his room and my head started bobbing and then I fainted."

The Chili Peppers have had producer problems before, notably with Andy Gill on their debut LP.

"To tell the truth," Flea explains, "it didn't work out as well as we thought it would. We really loved his earlier work and we wanted to go for a sound like that – not as sparse but with the same raw funkness, but when we go together he wasn't into the same thing anymore.

"We had a few clashes of opinion during our time together that were kind of monumental and he tried to introduce a drum machine to our music, which was the opposite of whatever we had in mind. He thought it was necessary to get on the radio."

When it came to recording "Uplift" with Michael Beinhorn things were much better. Beinhorn spent a full month mixing the album and even went on tour with the band thereby becoming aware that one of their most important assets was the pure physical energy.

"I hit my bass as hard as I can," says Flea. "I pound it 'til my fingers bleed and Michael understood that. It's hard to translate that onto vinyl but he did that."

Beinhorn also captured the Chilis' inane but engaging sense of humour – a vital part of their stageshow sorely missing from their two previous albums.

"I think as people individually we're all naturally driven very ferociously just to make people smile and be happy. We tend to base a lot of our day on making jokes and making funny faces to make people smile and we focus that little more intently in the songs we write."

"But that lady still didn't like it when you patted her on the head walking down the street," says Flea.

Have you ever gone too far?

"I've been slapped a few times," says Hillel, "just for being rude. But being slapped is fun."

The Chilis' understandably object to being called white dopes on funk. Leaving aside the inverted racism of the term Flea reckons they're more psychedelic – in the true sense of the word. "When I think of psychedelia it always hits me as something that's more AAAAAAAAAARGH! than Wow man," Antwon agrees.

"We've been a band now for five years and it just so happens that we're white but that's irrelevant. Our music shouldn't be categorised in terms of colour cos it really sets up barriers that are just negative and so all these years we were inspired to play funk 'cos we grew up in America and we heard beautiful funk music so we got into our own special funk groove and people began saying to us what are you doing playing that groove when you're white and we just thought it was pure bullshit.

"People just tend to categorise us by colour with bands who we're nothing like other than the fact that we have the same colour skin. They may as well compare us to other bands who we don't sound like that are black."

In that way, The Chili Peppers are caught astride the same fence that eventually ripped the balls off Funkadelic back in the Seventies. Flea agrees.

"I would make that same comparison myself. For a start we're not the most commercial band in the world. The way radio is segregated our music is too funky for the rock stations and too rocky for the black stations. Funkadelic had that same problem especially in the early days when they were completely hard rock funk."

Meanwhile The Red Hot Chili Peppers hold the promise of the great night out. The guest list for their recent show at the Clarendon was a Who's Who of anything worthwhile that's around at the moment, and in Paris The Duranies who were in town recording their new LP threatened an appearance but in the end never showed. Jack was a trifle flattered but on the whole underwhelmed by the news.

"Well it's a compliment for anyone to like us but uh . . . Duran are the kind of band that people look at and say, 'Oh I'd like to be like that.' They portray themselves in that light as if they're bigger than something that they really are.

"That really bothers me 'cos I think that glamorisation of the music and entertainment business is ridiculous. It's totally bourgeois and stupid. It's crap for people to think that life is like a little motion picture, it isn't. We want our music to get off their butts and do something positive. That's what 'The Uplift Mofo Party Plan' is all about."

Wrestling with the Devil: The Struggle for the Soul of James Brown

Michael Goldberg

Rolling Stone, 6 April 1989.

The Georgia judge who is about to give James Brown a six-year prison sentence is in a jovial mood as he surveys his courtroom, taking in the television cameras, news photographers and reporters. "You know they're giving out reports of his progress on the radio," says Judge Gayle B. Hamrick of the Richmond County State Court.

Brown, already serving another six-year sentence at South Carolina's State Park Correctional Center, is being escorted to Hamrick's court in downtown Augusta. The singer is expected to plead guilty to misdemeanor weapons and traffic charges that stem from a now infamous interstate chase that began when he entered an insurance seminar carrying a shotgun last September. It is the same series of events that led to his incarceration in South Carolina.

The judge is talking to a bailiff. "Every few minutes it's 'Hey, we got a report in on James Brown – they just passed us in a police car'," says Hamrick, smiling.

"Judge, gonna charge admission?" asks the baliff.

"We're gonna set up three rings out there," Hamrick says.

The courtroom begins to fill. Brown's mother, his aunt and one of his sons, as well as Danny Ray, his longtime master of ceremonies, and Leon Austin, a childhood friend, find seats. Brown's wife, Adrienne, who is here to plead no contest to her own misdemeanor traffic charges, the result of a 1987 incident, bustles in. "Nothing but a zoo," she says with a frown. "Don't these people got nothing better to do?"

Adrienne Brown's case has already been heard by the time her husband is finally brought into the court a little before eleven. Judging by his appearance, no one would know that James Brown has spent the last six weeks in prison. Attired in a three-piece suit and a burgundy silk shirt, a gray silk scarf tied around his neck, he flashes a smile as he greets an acquaintance. But standing before the judge, the singer quickly becomes subdued and somber.

As Brown begins speaking in a low, hoarse voice, reporters strain to catch his statement. "My life has always been a model, and I just don't feel good about it now," says Brown, adding that he is "very sorry for what happened . . . If I had it all to do over again, well, I just wouldn't do it." With his hands clasped behind his back, Brown looks up at Hamrick and says quietly, "I hope this is behind us."

Brown's contrition pays off. After he pleads guilty to the charges, the judge gives him what amounts to a slap on the wrist: a six-year sentence that will run concurrently with his South Carolina term. Brown could be free in August 1991.

Albert "Buddy" Dallas, one of Brown's lawyers, tells the judge that his client is sincere, that he "wants to do good." But three weeks later Brown is on the telephone, calling from prison, complaining wearily that the police have harassed him for the last two and a half years, expressing disappointment that having served on President Reagan's anti-drug task force for seven years, no one from his administration has stepped in to help.

"I was very much surprised that I didn't get a call from the White House," Brown told *Rolling Stone* in late February. "I think I should get some help. I knew President Carter on a one-on-one basis. I know a lot of the state senators, governors. When they get the message, they going to help me out." Comments like these aren't surprising. Brown recently described himself to one of his former backup singers, Vicki Anderson Byrd, as "the only man who can do anything I want."

Brown thinks he should be released. "Special treatment I'm not looking for," he says. "But I don't think I should be in here. I am not a man who breaks the law. That [the insurance-seminar incident] was something that happened very fast, and I think the policemen just wouldn't accept their responsibility once they shot the car up. Thank God I'm living. Regardless of who did it, I didn't protest against the police, because I didn't want to cause problems. I figured if we could work it out some other kind of way, if I had to go to jail for sixty, ninety days, and then we work it out, I would accept that. If I had actually fought it like it actually happened, we'd have a lot of problems in the state, and I didn't want to see that. I didn't want to have a racial problem. So I took it all on me."

James Brown has always had a tremendous ego, and not without justification. He is arguably the greatest artist in the history of black music, and his contribution to American popular culture is, simply, immeasurable. His thirty-three years as a hit maker dwarf the accomplishments of current stars like Bruce Springsteen, Prince, Michael Jackson and U2. He invented funk and rap, and his profound influence on music is international is scope. Brown has sat with American presidents and last year even had an audience with the pope. His words once cooled rioting in Washington, D.C., Boston and Augusta, following the assassination of Dr. Martin Luther King Jr.

According to Joel Whitburn's new book *Top R&B Singles: 1942–1988*, Brown is the most popular black musician of all time. His recorded legacy – 114 charted singles – included such classics as "Papa's Got a Brand New Bag," "Out of Sight," "(Get Up I Feel Like Being a) Sex Machine," "I Got You (I Feel Good)," "Night Train," "It's a Man's Man's Man's World" and "Say It Loud – I'm Black and I'm Proud."

Brown's fall comes at a time when his influence on the pop scene is as strong as ever. You can see it in the dance steps and music of superstars like Prince and Michael Jackson, Mick Jagger and George Michael and dozens upon dozens of other entertainers. His own recordings have been sampled to death by Eighties rappers, like Run-D.M.C., the Beastie Boys, Eric B. and Rakim, the Fat Boys, Ice T and Public Enemy, which takes its name from an old Brown record. "Everybody samples James Brown," says rapper Melle Mel of Grandmaster Flash and the Furious Five. "You can't make a rap record without using some James Brown."

Or as Brown himself put it with a laugh during his telephone call from prison, "The music out there is only as good as my last record."

But another James Brown is now surfacing – one whose bearing is not so regal. Since Brown disappeared behind bars, friends, business associates and musicians have come forward with horror stories about their days with the man. They say that for thirty years he has been beating women; that he has gypped collabora-tors out of record royalties. That he threatened musicians with guns; tried to steal their girlfriends; left band members stranded on the road; and got so high on marijuana and PCP that he thought he could "fly like a bird".

"They don't know, sir," counters Brown, who won't talk about his drug use. "My employees tell you, 'Oh, James Brown smokes a little pot.' I won't say nothing about those gentlemen. I'm going to be more man than they were. I'm a clean man".

But what of the PCP that was found in Brown's blood after his arrest? "They can find anything they want to find, don't you know that?" he says. "I'm just the last of the Afro-Americans to have enough intelligence to deal with the business world. And they would like to kick me out, back over into that fast lane. And they're not going to get me to do it."

Despite such denials, Brown's problems are the dark side of tremendous ego and self-determination that helped a neglected child of poverty to fight his way to the top. But like fellow rocker Jerry Lee Lewis, Brown is a man who has been wrestled to the ground by a host of personal demons.

Some years ago in a fit of rage, James Brown scolded one of his employees by saying, "You know I got the Lord in one hand and the devil in the other, and I can control you. You're nothing without me!"

James Brown might just as well have been shouting at himself.

James Brown is a mess. It is May 6th, 1988, and in his plush suite at the Plaza Hotel in New York City, Brown is tripping on PCP, the potent hallucinogen known on the street as angel dust. He is in such bad shape that the hotel doctor must be called to treat him for high blood pressure and hypertension, and his aides are forced to cancel his show at the Lone Star Cafe.

This is almost unheard of: for decades, Brown has been the self-proclaimed "hardest working man in show business."

This also occurs at what should be a time of celebration for James Brown. He in the midst of a major comeback. In 1986 he was inducted into the Rock and Roll Hall of Fame, and with "Living in America," he made his first appearance on the Top Ten pop charts in eighteen years. His latest album, *I'm Real,* is strong on the black charts. But in the hotel room, there is nothing but misery. "Doc, you just don't understand," says Brown, who is upset by his marital troubles. "You just don't understand."

At the Lone Star, word is brought to Brown's band by his wardrobe mistress, Gertrude Sanders. "Martha, James is really sick," a teary-eyed Sanders tells backup vocalist Martha High. "He's just about gone. I'm scared he's going to die."

A group of Brown associates and employees – including the Reverend Al Sharpton (who is making headlines for his role in the Tawana Brawley debacle), drummer Arthur Dixon, music director Sweet Charles Sherrell, saxophonist Maceo Parker, High and Sanders – head back to the hotel. "You could smell the stuff from the elevator," Sherrell recalls later. "It was heart-breaking. Both of them [Brown and his wife] were just out of it. She could hardly open the door."

Inside, a disheveled Brown sits on the edge of the bed, staring into space. For the next few hours, Brown's visitors try to bring him around by getting him to drink milk, massaging his shoulders and offering their support. "That was a good show tonight," Brown eventually says. "Wasn't that a good show?"

"Man," says Maceo Parker, "I think you're talking about *last* night."

"We supposed to work tonight," Brown says.

"He didn't *know* he'd missed the show," Martha High recalls later. "That's not James Brown. That's *out!*"

*   *   *

Last year the self-styled godfather of Soul continued to make news: in the spring he was arrested after beating up his wife, one-time *Solid Gold* hair stylist and makeup artist named Adrienne "Alfie" Rodriguez; since then he has been repeatedly busted on drug and weapons offenses. It hasn't helped matters that his wife – also arrested and charged with possession of PCP – told her story to the *National Enquirer*, describing the beatings she had received at her husband's hands in an April 26th article headlined 'James Brown tried to kill me' and let the tabloid photograph her bruises.

Drugs were also tightening their grip. Brown had been smoking reefer spiked with angel dust for years, but he was in command onstage. So band members were shocked when he hit the stage stoned and out of control at both the New Orleans Jazz and Heritage Festival and at the Valley Forge Music Fair, in Philadephia. In midsong he would stop the band, stare at the audience and, says Sherrell, "talk about something in left field. It was horrible."

The sad denouement came on Saturday, September 24th, 1988, when Brown, high on PCP and carrying a shotgun, entered an insurance seminar taking place in a building adjacent to his Augusta office. According to Geraldine Phillips of Atlanta, who was leading the seminar, Brown wanted to know who had been using his private restroom and began asking her questions. "I thought if I answered one of those questions wrong, he was going to kill me and everybody else," she said later, although it turned out the shotgun didn't work.

The police were called, and a two-state high-speed car chase ensued in which Brown allegedly attempted to run over two policemen who were setting up a roadblock. The police shot out the front tires of Brown's truck, but that didn't stop him. He drove another six miles on the rims, circling back to Augusta before stoping in a ditch. The police said that after they removed him from the truck, he started singing "Georgia" and "was doing his 'Good Foot' dance" as they gave him a sobriety test. Released on bail, Brown was in trouble again within twenty-four hours, when he was arrested for driving under the influence of PCP.

Brown claims the incident happened somewhat differently:

that he was just trying to find out why people were using his bathroom without permission and that he stopped for police but that they kicked in his window and shot at his truck. "A man fires twenty-three rounds of bullets in a truck, two in the gas tank, and then rush me to the hospital and say I am on drugs and I'm going to kill him – they wanted me to plead guilty to that," says Brown. "Worst day of my life."

People close to Brown – his agent, Jack Bart; his attorney Buddy Dallas; his childhood friend Leon Austin – blame Adrienne Brown for the big man's troubles. "She no good for him," says Austin. But artist manager Joyce McCrae, who has known Adrienne Brown since the early Eighties, believes she is as much "a victim of James's problems as James is himself.

"Alfie has been portrayed as the scapegoat, the cause of all of James's problems," says McCrae. "James certainly knew about drugs long before he ever met Alfie. On the few occasions that I sat and listened to her talk, she reminded me of the women I'd seen suffering from battered-wife syndrome on TV talk shows. For her to bear the blame for the downfall and destruction of James is absurd."

"A scapegoat is right," says James Brown. "She is a scapegoat for some people who have taken advantage of her because they don't like the relationship between she and I. They don't like it because we are third-world people. Third-world people are not recognized.

"I'll tell you what got us into this problem," he continues. "Number one, they didn't like the marriage between my wife and I in that small area. Next, they didn't like my wife leaving NBC, coming and staying with me. Some group of people want me to go to New York or Los Angeles. They want James Brown in a big city, think he's more effective with the business world. They need my guidance because eighty-five percent of the business is all James Brown. But I don't want to live in L.A. I like coming back home.

"I been a human all my life, but we don't get human rights. *Should* get them. I don't have to explain myself. You know who explains my problem? Martin Luther King. Kennedy dying for human dignity, human rights, Adam Clayton Powell, James Meredith, Hubert Humphrey. You all want to spend your time trying to make me a drug addict when you should spend your time trying to get me back on the streets so I can help you with the problem."

There is a small painting hanging in James Brown's private office. The painting shows a bull, its back already bloodied, butting its horns into a red matador's cape.

Most stars of Brown's stature are handled by experienced managers based in New York or Los Angeles. Not James Brown. He didn't have a manager, and when he was not on the road, you could often find him in Augusta handling his own business out of a suite of offices in an anonymous-looking executive park near I-20.

On the afternoon following Brown's Augusta court appearance, his wife is sitting at a big desk with an engraved plaque that reads, "James Brown, President". She is on the phone with *USA Today*. "This has been one of the worst days I've had," Adrienne Brown says. "I almost broke down today. I'm ready for the hospital, but I'm trying to keep going."

Brown hangs up. "How much do they want us to take?" she asks. "We're just two people. They had James and I in the same courtroom today! I told God last night I can't take too much more."

Sitting across the desk from Brown is forty-year-old Ray Ferrill, who looks like a low-rent Tom Waits and says he is James Brown's godson. "What we have is a conspiracy to incarcerate," he says and then proceeds – in a rambling monologue – to tie James Brown's problems to Iran, racism and national security.

Adrienne Brown is exhausted. Her eye shadow is smeared, face puffy. But she is hanging in there, staunchly defending her husband and their marriage. She says his troubles have only helped his career. "This man is so hot right now it's scary," she insists. "There are movie contracts right now they want to negotiate in jail."

Brown pops a diet candy in her mouth. "My husband doesn't take drugs," she says flatly. "They say they want to treat James the same as anybody else. Well, he's *not* anybody else. And then, what they want to do is come down even harder to show that they're not treating him like anybody else."

"Scapegoat and an example," says Ferrill.

Addrienne Brown says she has also been victimized. "We love each other," she says. "And that's where it's at. This bull of me feeding my husband drugs. You can't *make* James Brown do anything."

The phone rings, and this time it's Sharpton.

"Hi, Rev," she says. "These asshole attorneys made him plead guilty. He got another five years. Well, it's because they figured he'd get a deal. He got no deal. I'm telling you, Rev, we're telling you, Rev, we're both doomed people if someone doesn't move on something."

In Adrienne Brown's world, as in her husband's, paranoia runs rampant. She recounts an incident last year in which "a nickel bag of grass" was planted in her husband's coat pocket and insinuates that his lawyer may have had a hand in it. "A month ago, before he went to jail, my husband had his coat hanging here in the office," she says. "We were sitting here in the office – Mr. Dallas, myself, my husband, the people who work here, some reporters. Mr. Dallas says, 'That's a beautiful fur coat – may I see it?' Mr. Dallas walked up to the coat, looked at it, touched it. We went home, and my husband emptied the coat pockets. Do you know what he found? A nickel bag of grass. Now that was put there!"

Adrienne Brown sighs. "Do you understand how we can be set up?" she asks. "These things happen with us. And it's hard for people to believe, because it's like a soap opera. But it isn't. It happens to us *everyday*."

Asked later about the coat incident, Buddy Dallas recalls "being in the office and asking about the cougar coat." He says, however, that he has had nothing to do with – let alone planting illegal drugs of any kind.

Adrienne Brown denies she has been beaten by her husband,

and she doesn't want to talk about the photograph of her bruises that appeared in the *National Enquirer*. But pressed on the subject, she makes it sound like a publicity stunt. "We sold newspapers," she says. "James couldn't get in those newspapers, no matter all the good he's done. There are many P.R. schemes that people use."

But at the moment Adrienne Brown is unhappy with the way she and her husband are being portrayed. "Let these animals talk all they want to talk," she says. "As soon as this is over, I'm taking care of them." She pauses a moment. "If this story is wrong, I will hunt you down."

On the Saturday afternoon before the Augusta trial, Bobby Byrd – a former member of James Brown's Famous Flames and at one time the singer's closest friend – is brooding in the upstairs bedroom of his Atlanta home. Just a few weeks earlier, Byrd, who is in his fifties, suffered a mild stroke when he learned he wouldn't be getting the money – some $25,000 in artist's and writer's royalties – that he claims James Brown owes him.

A spokesman for PolyGram Records, Brown's former record label, says there may be royalties owed to Byrd by Brown. The label currently credits all royalties from James Brown records or productions against monies previously advanced to Brown (Brown's attorney says that figure is about $2 million); it is Brown's responsibility to pay artists like Bobby Byrd who were under his production umbrella.

"Bobby need his name in the paper," says Brown, who denies owing Byrd any money. "Whatever Bobby Byrd did, he did. I know nothing about it. Bobby made a mistake years ago – he quit [Brown's band]. That's his problem. He shouldn't have quit."

"Everything was beautiful when we first started," says Byrd, who co-wrote such Brown classics as "Licking Stick – Licking Stick," "(Get Up I Feel Like Being a) Sex Machine" and "Talkin' Loud & Sayin' Nothing." Byrd is thinking of those early years, in the Fifties, when the whole band would pile into a station wagon and head off to gigs.

"We were playing locally up and down the highway, the girls

screaming and that was all that mattered," says Byrd. "Making a few dollars. We all supposed to be together. It was the Famous Flames. Everybody got an equal share of everything. We gonna stick together till the very end." Byrd pauses a second. "We thought."

Byrd sips from a can of soda pop. "But when it got to the money, then this man changed *completely*," he says. "It was like the difference in night and day."

"James's head just went bigger and bigger and bigger," says Johnny Terry, another former member of the Famous Flames, during a separate interview.

For years the people who worked for James Brown wouldn't talk about these things. To this day, many of Brown's employees won't say a word against their boss. They include Danny Ray, who has been Brown's master of ceremonies for a quarter century; wardrobe mistress Gertrude Sanders; the secretaries in Brown's office; and even former members of Brown's band, such as St. Clair Pinckney, who quit last summer after the band was stranded in Rome with no money for nine days. "He's a loving person," insists Sanders, who has been with Brown for decades. "A nice person."

But many others – some no longer on Brown's payroll, some still in his employ – have had it. They are fed up with the world of James Brown, where he is the self-proclaimed king and mere mortals are expected "to bow", as a former band member puts it.

"That goes for the moon and stars and the air outside," says the Reverend Al Sharpton, who once claimed he and Brown were starting a nationwide chain of Groom Me shoeshine parlors, where "unskilled young people" could make a living shining shoes. "That's the way it's always been."

No more, Brown once ruled the recording studio, dictating every note on some of his records, but before he was imprisoned, he was merely showing up to overdub his vocals after hired professionals wrote and produced the tracks. Since the early Seventies, Brown has had major tax problems; he currently owes the government in excess of $9 million. Once considered an astute businessman – whose properties included a booking agency, three radio station, seventeen publishing companies, a record label, a television show, a production company and a Lear jet and who had millions in an Atlanta bank account – Brown no longer even owns the sixty-two-acre Beech Island, South Carolina, ranch where he lives.

James Brown's almost supernatural ability to create astounding records from street talk and raw rhythms went hand in hand with an obsession for stardom bordering on the pathological. Abandoned as a four-year-old to the care of relatives and friends, neglected and unloved (he says it was twenty years before he was reunited with his mother), James Brown grew up on the streets of Augusta – the "ill-repute area," he calls it – where he learned how to wheel, deal, gamble and steal.

"I wanted to be somebody," Brown has said. "To *be* somebody." He was a tough, street-savvy kid who in addition to working odd jobs – shining shoes, delivering groceries, picking cotton, racking pool balls – put more cash in his pockets by playing dice and directing servicemen from nearby Camp Gordon to the local whorehouses.

"He didn't have nothin'", says Henry Stallings, one of Brown's schoolmates. "He always say that's why he work so hard now. He don't ever want to go back that way. Never, ever again !"

By the time Brown entered the seventh grade, in 1949, he was stealing bicycles, hubcaps, car batteries – anything he could turn into cash. But that came to an end that year, when a night of breaking into cars landed him in Alto Reform School, near Toccoa, Georgia, with a sentence of eight to sixteen years.

"They took me off the street," Brown said this January. "They put me in prison. I thought they were putting me away, but they were saving me. In that prison I found myself."

While serving three and half years in reform school, Brown met Bobby Byrd during a baseball game between the inmates and some of the local Toccoa kids. Byrd liked Brown and persuaded his mother to intervene in his friends' behalf. The Byrds sponsored Brown and took him into their home.

Byrd also took Brown into his group, the Gospel Starlighters.

Before long the members of the group had switched to hard R&B, changing their name to the Famous Flames. In January of 1956, they were signed to King Records, in Cincinnati; four months later "Please, Please, Please" was in the R&B Top Ten. By then Brown's ego had already begun to assert itself: at his insistence, the name of the group was soon changed to James Brown and the Famous Flames.

Brown' first taste of fame sent him into hyperdrive. Over the next decade he relentlessly pushed himself, his band and his business advisers. Along the way he created the baddest rock & roll show the world has ever seen.

Writers have been trying to get the James Brown experience down on paper ever since. "He is in an ecstasy of agony," Wrote Doon Arbus in the mid-Sixties. "It is as if he is gripped by demons and poltergeists," wrote Philip Norman of the London *Sunday Times* in the Seventies. "He does a split, erupts into a pirouette, whirls like a dervish, and ends up at the microphone just in time to shriek 'bayba-a-ay' as the band modulates into the introduction to his latest hit," wrote Robert Palmer in the late Seventies, when he was a pop-music critic for *The New York Times*. "*James!* he was then, shooting out of the wings like a pinball off the spring with a 'pleeeeeeese!' that could pop a hairpin at fifty feet," wrote Gerri Hirshey in *Rolling Stone* in 1983.

Any way you put it, Brown was a phenomenon. As Bill Wyman of the Rolling Stones once said – and as one look at the 1965 performance film *The T.A.M.I. Show* confirms – "You could put Jerry Lee Lewis, Little Richard, Chuck Berry and Bo Diddley on one side of the stage and James Brown on the other, and you wouldn't even notice the others were up there!"

From the late Fifties through the mid-Seventies, James Brown toured year-round, crisscrossing the country in buses and Cadillacs and later a series of private jets, coming up with ideas for songs in dressing rooms, cutting hits between gigs. Business was done on a cash basis, and Brown carried suitcases full of cash from town to town – as much as $250,000 – his employees often passing some of it out to the DJs whom his men hired to "copromote" the shows.

The pace was manic, and Brown gave no quarter. He fined his musicians for infractions ranging from a missed note to a wrinkled stage outfit. "He wanted things to always be razor's edge," says saxophonist Pee Wee Ellis, Brown's arranger during the middle to late Sixties. "He kept people intimidated. Stupid stuff. We had dress-code fines, shoes had to have a certain shine. There were rules about carrying our uniforms."

Brown's passion and obsession made him push harder and harder, fueling a remarkable stream of hit records – seventeen in a row during one two-year period – that didn't stop until the late Seventies. At a time – the late Fifties and early Sixties – when record companies typically chose the song, producer and musicians that would work on a recording session, Brown was a revolutionary. "He insisted on making his records his way," says Alan Leeds, one of Brown's former tour managers who now works for Prince. "He said, 'I'm not going to sound like the Stax sound or the Detroit sound, where everybody has the same studio guys. I got my band, we're gonna play my music, and we're going to play it my way.' And when the record company balked at that, he'd just not record at all. And he'd make them suffer until they needed a James Brown record so badly that they'd take whatever he gave them."

Even disillusioned former sidemen like Ellis and Byrd brighten up as they describe working on the hits. Ellis says that his job was to "act as a translator and a mediator between the bizarre and the guitar, taking the unorthodox ideas of James Brown and making them somewhat conventional but not losing the rawness."

Among the songs Ellis co-wrote with Brown was "Cold Sweat," which became a Number Seven pop hit in 1967. "He called me into the dressing room and mumbled something, hummed a feeling," says Ellis. "I got on the bus, and by the time we got to Cincinnati [where the studios of King Records were located], we fell off the bus, rehearsed the song for a few minutes, cut it, then got back on the bus and went back to work."

Brown recorded live in the studio. Standing in the middle of the room surrounded by his band, Brown would try out new dance steps even as he laid down a track. Unable to read or write music, Brown would sing each part to the musicians. "He'd take the rhythm section, verbally hum the parts out," says St. Clair Pinckney. " 'I want you to play this – *dum-da-dum-da-dum-dum*. Gimme this kind of beat. Play that for a few minutes. Okay, hold that right there, don't forget nothin'. Hold that groove right there.' Then he'd call the horns in and do the same thing with them. Next thing you know, it's 'Okay, roll the tape.' Most times it was first time down."

Former band members, including Byrd, Ellis, Johnny Terry and others, complain that Brown didn't always give them full credit for their contributions. They say that Brown would add his name to songs he hadn't written and that instead of paying someone, he might give them a writing credit. Terry claims he wrote "I'll Go Crazy." Both Byrd and Bobby Bennett, another former member of the Famous Flames, say one of Brown's girlfriends, Betty Newsome, actually wrote "It's a Man's Man's Man's World." Although Brown has disputed this, "It's a Man's Man's Man's World" – which for many years was credited solely to Brown – is now also credited to Newsome.

Wherever the songs actually came from, no one denies that Brown made them his own. "It was his energy that gave it the fire," says Bob Patton, who worked for Brown promoting his records and tours. "If you took James away, the band could play the tunes, but they didn't have the spark. He made the engine run. Damn near burn it out sometimes."

Brown could get crazy on the road. In 1968, Bennett was playing cards with Danny Ray in his room at the Ritz in Paris when a furious Brown burst in, a pistol in his hand. "He came in and pointed it at me," says Bennett. "He told me, 'I'm going to kill you. You told my old lady I had another woman on the plane.' He jumped on me. I tried to throw his head out of the fifteenth-story window. If not for Danny Ray, I'd have driven his head through one of the iron bars they had in the window. Danny was shouting, 'Don't kill him!' "

But Brown saved the worst treatment for his women. "He beat Tammi Terrell terrible," says Bennett. "She was bleeding, shedding blood." Terrell, who died in 1970, was Brown's girl-friend before she became famous as Marvin Gaye's singing partner in the mid-Sixties. "Tammi left him because she didn't want her butt whipped," says Bennett, who also claims he saw Brown kick one pregnant girlfriend down a flight of stairs. Both Bobby Byrd and his wife, Vicki Anderson, say that in the Seventies, Brown abused his wife at the time, Deirdre, "something terrible."

"All the women liked his money and his fame," says Anderson. "They liked being Mrs. James Brown. This is nothing new. The minute he buys you the first thing – if you're his woman – next will come those beatings." Anderson says she has seen Brown repeatedly lure women away from their men with promises of stardom. On a plane flight to London in 1976, Brown even tried to steal his best friend's wife. "He told her that if she left me, she'd have an album and it would be Number One," says Byrd.

"Said he'd make me a millionaire," adds Anderson. "I wasn't going to leave my husband for no hit record."

Brown abruptly ended the prison telephone interview with *Rolling Stone* before he could be asked about abusing his girlfriends and wives over the years, and his lawyer Buddy Dallas said he could not comment because the incidents had occurred before he represented Brown.

Sheriff Carrol Heath is sitting in his Aiken, Georgia, office, where a photograph of himself and George Bush is prominently displayed. "About two and a half years ago we started getting the calls," says the sheriff, running a hand across a pale forehead and through thinning white hair. "Either Adrienne, the wife, or her mother. 'James beat up on me.' 'Get someone out there. He's killing her.'"

The sheriff shakes his head. He picks up a phone and asks for a computer printout. The printout shows that Adrienne Lois Brown called the police once in 1984, three times in 1985, once in 1987 and more than half a dozen times in 1988. "On one occasion she said he was going to take her out into the woods and shoot her," Heath says, putting the printout aside. "You know, if a man and woman can't get along, they should part ways."

Captain Jim Whitehurst, a big man who says his nickname

around the sheriff's office is Wyatt Earp, steps into the office. In apparent homage to the psychotic villain of *The Night of the Hunter*, Whitehurst has H-A-T-E tattooed on the knuckles of one hand, L-O-V-E on the other. "It's a damn Yankee," says Whitehurst. "I can tell just by looking at you."

Whitehurst is followed by Bill Hartman, an investigator who has been to Brown's ranch. Hartman is wearing a belt with a buckle in the shape of handcuffs. "I went out there the day after the car got shot up," he says, referring to an incident that occurred over the 1988 Easter weekend. "I met her at the hospital. She was beat up real bad. Black-and-blue marks all over her body. Legs, back, side."

Hartman takes a seat. "What was supposed to have happened, they had got into an argument because he wasn't going to take her on this foreign tour," he says. "He went in the house, and first he got her mink coat, throwed it on the ground and shot holes all in it. Then he went back in and got one of these here leather jackets with sable collar and sable cuffs, thrown it on the ground and shot it up."

"Did they have holes in them?" asks the sheriff.

"Sir, I don't know," replies Hartman. "Because before she went to the hospital, she had took them to a furrier to have them fixed. The next-door neighbor told me that the night of the incident she wouldn't even go to the hospital until she took them coats over to that furrier to have them fixed."

"You ever recall going out there and finding the house in disarray and the furniture broken up?" asks the sheriff.

"Just bullet holes," says Hartman, smiling. "Plenty of bullet holes in the house. He took a .22 rifle and went into this walk-in closet and shot down through everything on her side of the closet. Found bullet holes in the bedroom walls."

Whitehurst leans forward in his chair. "Ever shot a monkey?" he asks, idly fingering a bullet he has picked up off the sheriff's desk. "Ever seen anyone shoot a monkey?"

James Brown is standing in a small room inside the Law Enforcement Center a few hours after he has received his concurrent sentence. He is smiling, flashing that classic grin, his false teeth glistening. His mother, Susie, her body enveloped in a black fur coat, is seated nearby, staring almost reverently at her son. Seated next to her is Brown's aunt Gerry. "I feel so good," says Brown.

'Yeah, yeah, I'm so happy," interjects his mother.

Brown mentions a Psalm he has been reading; he implies that the spirit has moved him. "At the height of my career, I thought that everything was happening great," he says. "And thank God for it, but the height, the very pinnacle of everything I've ever done in the business, is not ten percent of what's happened in the last ninety days. See, it's almost a rebirth."

And what has happened?

Brown assumes a thoughtful pose. "I'll tell you," he says, "it's like an omen. As a kid in that prison, I found myself. An omen in my life. The same place I'm at right now. That was the beginning of my life, in 1950. This is the beginning of my life again. An omen. An omen.

"I can't give you the kind of interview I'd like to give you in front of my mother," says Brown. "But, you know, once you be lucky enough to do some of the things I've done in life, there's a lot of stress. Christ went off – he didn't want to be around the people when he was praying. I ain't no Christ, but I at least got to go off and think." He laughs. "If Christ had to do it, what about me?" he asks. "I'm no prophet – I'm just a good person trying to do the right thing. But I got to have that time off."

But what about all the trouble he has been in? What about the drugs? What about the violence?

"Being a victim of different kinds of things going in your system," says Brown. "I've been a victim of that. And to stand here and run my history down would be hard to do, but I'll always be behind telling kids not to use drugs, I'll always be behind drug abuse. I can't stop the pushers, but I can stop the kids from being buyers."

It's time to leave; Brown wants some time alone with his family. But he just can't help himself, and he voices bitterness and resentment over his predicament. "If they catch some sports figure snorting coke or any kind of drugs, you know what they do?" he asks. "Have him sit on the bench and then let him play next week. I can go to some of our highest official wives, they just send them to a clinic. But I'm sure when God wanted Moses, he didn't think of all the people younder, he thought only of Moses. Maybe if a man is strong enough and people believe in him, maybe they won't take no for an answer . . .'

Brown flashes that grin again. He is shaking hands, about to turn away. "I thank God that I know what I know," he says. "Everybody help you win. But nobody help you when you lose. So when you get back to winning again, they'll love you again."

Brown's mother and aunt chime in: "That's right, that's right."

"Thank God the Lord gave me something this time to know what I have to do," he says.

"I'm glad to hear you say that," says James Brown's elderly mother. "I was praying for you."

Grin Reaper

Nick Coleman

Time Out, 4 July 1990.

You can look Keith Richards in the eye and ask him if he's spent all his adult life divorced from reality. He stops, inclines his head slightly away, as if to deliver an aside to accomplices behind the drapes, and adopts a look of kiddish insolence. 'Well, if rock 'n' roll ain't reality, I don't know what issss-hh-hhhuuhhuuuu-huuhh-h!'

The laugh takes its shape from the exhaust fumes of his words. It is the tubercular love-child of a waste disposal unit and an espresso machine, a choking press of ragged air, catching lime-scale in the funnel of his throat before belching out in a vapour of aitches. Delighted, you keep on wanting to say "do it again", but he usually obliges before long anyway. He laughs a lot.

Richards has made his funky reply to your 'dangerous' question and now it's name for him to forget about the bluesmen behind the arras. His head comes round slowly again until his coppery eyes catch the light from the window. The face folds into a smile.

"In fact, nobody really knows what my lifestyle is including myself-ffff-uuhuhhuuuhhh. I mean, I always wonder why people want to interview me. I must have such a *weird* point of view on everything because since I was 18, 19 this is all I've done: played guitar and lived in hotels and . . . actually, that's not true, either, Either? I got two families and I was a junkie for ten years. I used to shoot my way out of buildings on the Lower East Side of New York. This 'famous rock 'n' roll star' thing don't mean much to me . . . maybe the dope kept me closer to the ground than most people even though my head was up there . . ."

He has a curious habit of raising one or both of his forearms to parenthesise a point allowing his wrists to hang limply and has head to roll slowly from side to side. There's something faintly gibbon-like about the gesture, and something gentle.

"This glamorous rock 'n' roll life and all that money: aaah-shit . . . I mean I'm shivering in a corner with a shooter in my hand, waiting to shoot my way out of a dealer's place, to get a gram . . . I stayed in touch with the streets that way, I suppose; and that was my own personal thing – I mean. I can't speak for Elton John . . ."

Over that ten years, did you ever ask yourself questions?

"Yeah. But I always replied, 'I'll talk to you later-rrr-hh-hhhhuuuhhhhuhuuh'."

Richards is the first to show, bolting from the darkness to choke-start 'Start Me Up'. Isolated against the dark mouth of the Urban Jungle proscenium like a cave-painting, white on black, chalk white as a hill man, he is pre-historical.

He bestrides the vast stage not so much like a colossus as something altogether less heroic; the Cro-Magnon profile, wreathed in smiles or glowering with concentration, suggests baser enthusiasms than those commonly associated with the pomp of rock pageantry. He might be sawing logs. And it's in the visual bathos of his nerveless comfort on stage that you recognise why it is that Keith Richards is the only man ever to look good in a guitar.

"The funny thing about those riffs, those songs is that if I'm playing them, it's because I still get the same kick out of it, y'know?" he says, eyebrows up. "There're riffs like "Tumbling Dice" where you go [and he kisses his hands and blows on them] 'Jesus *Christ* it's a sweet riff. This is the feeling I been looking for *forever, Jesus Christ is this me!?* HEY, THAT'S ME, BABY. AND I SOUND LIKE *THIS*!'" And he rolls back from the edge of his seat, hands in the air, wheezing like a boiler.

It's in this betrayal of enthusiasm that Richards reveals himself. At 46 he is beyond cool. His eyes glint like sequins in the stiffening reef of his complexion (you want desperately to tap it to see how it sounds), and he still tugs at a stray rope of hair behind

his right ear in a gesture that's been with him since the first
cultivation of his ludicrous assassin's mop. The hipster mannerisms are as deeply etched as the trenches on his face, invisible
from the inside and therefore of no importance. Only he knows
how much of a motherfucker he really is.

We're in Madrid, where the Rolling Stones are cocking the
eleventh leg of their massive European 'Urban Jungle' tour, and
Richards is full of beans following a hugely successful first night.
Not without thinking about it for a moment he suggests that the
band is playing better than ever ("even Charlie's smiling – I
dunno if he's got some secret!") and that the only way to find out
what will ultimately become of the Rolling Stones is "to take it as
far as it'll go. It would be a chicken motherfucker who'd toss the
towel in now." It is indeed a terrific show.

These are uncharted waters for rock music. Not only has there
been no other single group to make it more or less intact from
rock's pubescence to its present stage of incipient middle age –
and no, I do not count The Who, who simply burlesqued
themselves on their "farewell" tour last year – but there is also
no other group to have ridden the changes in rock's agenda
without having to make significant alterations to their own.
The Stone remain indefatigably themselves.

Indeed, whether you regard the Stones' perpetual Stonesiness
as a kind of egregious rejection of the beautiful ephemerality that
makes pop pop, or whether you see their continued existence as
an heroic avowal of some deeper worth in popular culture, it is
impossible to escape the feeling that this group is The Archetype,
the first grunt in which all of rock's useful variations in language
were distilled. That is to say, the Rolling Stones were the first
group fully to realise the notion that rock is first and foremost
about *gangs*.

Keith's gang is his pride and joy. He speaks about them pro-
prietorially, wryly, without sentiment but always with a degree of
generosity.

"Shiiit, Charlie was *mortified* to become a pop star in the first
place. It just wasn't *hip*. He hates being famous because he can't

take it with the same serenity that I can muster, nor with the same enthusiasm as Mick . . . yeah, Mick, he needs to know before he goes to sleep what he's gonna be doing when he wakes up, whereas I don't give a shit – whatever's necessary, y'know, that's my attitude." He lights up and shuffles closer to the edge of his seat until he's cantilevered over the coffee table and the open lips of a bourbon bottle like a vulture. He points a finger.

"But what it comes down to, the only fun in all of this, the only reason I do it, the only way I can get a real *spark* out of anything is by playing with other guys. And it's not what *I'm* playing, either, it's what all of us are doing. I mean, if five guys can work together, then why not everybody?. . . and make the world a little bit easier, y'knowh'ahmean? Shit, this is the only place I can get a little taste of that." And he concludes with a little epicurean gesture of finger and thumb.

The geometry of gangs is complicated. If gangs were merely about the adolescent male's struggle for power then gangs would not be interesting or sexy and no one would ever join them. It would be too frightening, and more than anything else, gangs are about feeling *safe*. All the same, Richards reckons that the only thing that frightens him now is, by definition, "unnamable. Mind you, not being able to play scares me. I suppose I'd be scared of doing a Beethoven, going deaf. I dunno . . . I spent so long trying to scare *other* things . . . but then again that was my way of getting rid of fear."

The first thing he remembers as a child, in his parents' flat in Dartford above the greengrocers, "was pointing up into the sky and trying to say 'wassat?' I couldn't really say proper words then but I could understand them, and my mum understood what I was trying to ask. She said, 'it's a Spitfire.' And even now when I'm walking down a hotel corridor and someone's watching a World War II movie on TV in their room and an air-raid siren goes off and catches me unawares, it puts my hair up, zzzzzschoooouupe!" One hand goes up the back of his head like a tarantula. "Shit, there's bits of me that remembers more than my memory does. My *hairs* have memories."

*   *   *

The geometry of music, indivisible in this case from the geometry of gangs, is how Richards would appear to make sense of the world. He remains a fan, enthusing about his reggae and his blues, keen to talk rock 'n' roll, apparently indefatigable in his search for "spark".

"A lot of rock 'n' roll bands are what I call Brabazons – they go down the runway but they never take off. I've been very lucky with the cats I've worked with. Charlie, who's really a jazz drummer, can make that beat take *off*. If you've got a drummer who plays like a concrete boot you just sink.

"But most of it's done on typewriters these days. If rhythm is concerned with the body, which is what I think it's concerned with, you got to use your whole body to express it. You can't do it like that (he taps an invisible keyboard). And what most people are interested in nowadays is not rhythm itself but the *sound* of the thing that's creating the beat. They got all these new toys, things that'll go CRASH and *wooo-wooo-wooo*, and what is actually lacking is *rhythm*." He sighs and twists the lock behind his ear long-sufferingly. "But since rhythm is as important to people as their own heartbeat, it'll establish itself again. I mean, I'm no Back-To-Mono cat – I don't revere Phil Spector 'cause he's only got one ear – but all this shit don't seduce me. It's like a department store at the moment and nobody can get out of the toy department."

So we discuss what it is that makes the internal geometry of "It's Only Rock 'n' Roll" and "Tumbling Dice" so peculiar; and how it is that bunch of cats with guitars and drums can go to work on a beat 'til it flies. And most of what is said is untranscribable. It's all in the wrist action.

It's also in the mysterious thing about Not Knowing What Happens Next. When the Rolling Stones are playing well it's never a written book; you always have the feeling that the next second might never have happened before; and that is a thing you won't find in any department store.

Richards's accent is very strange, a multiple pile-up of well-formed '60s art school hipster vowels, the wrecked consonants of Dartford, the occasional halt of Jamaican intonation (where he offically resides) and the transatlantic drawl which runs everything together into a refined, husky blur. His accent is a map of his past.

I asked him if he felt growing up the rock 'n' roll way was simply about making yourself tougher – he's rather fond of epithets like "that's the price of an education, man" and, on the prevalence of images of death in the painting of the early Flemish renaissance: "I have a healthy respect for Death, and I try to avoid him at all costs; but at the same time, if you don't try and meet him every now and then you won't know what to look out for." He didn't smile at the question.

"Noooo. Inevitably the older you get the tougher you become. Things like learning how not to give a shit when your girlfriend leaves you, is that toughening up? I dunno. I don't think so. And I suppose you do have to watch that you don't get cirrhosis of *everything* . . .

"But having kids is the most important thing. I mean, you can be a hardened old bachelor – that's dead easy, I know a million of 'em – but living with *kids* . . ." He looks at the ceiling, his Marlboro pointing straight up like an aerial . . . "I mean, that's the reason I have 'em: they keep me soft. They're showing you things you don't remember. They kind of string your life together – instead of it being the '60s, then the '70s, then the '80s, they give you a constant thread, because you can see yourself in them and you remember what it was like to be that pure and trusting. Nobody can look upon that, *live* with it and not understand its worth. In many ways I'm a cynical, hardbitten motherfucker – I *have* to be – but I got these two little chicks at home who can beat me up every time."

Which is all very well, but he is still gangleader, and Buttons to Jagger's Twanky in the on-going media pantomime that's played to rapturous tabloid audiences up and down the country since the latter embarked on his dismal solo career and Keith chilled out altogether on the drug stories.

"The break was a ventilation. To me, the fight – ha! the big fight! – it was regrettable but it was the only way to goad Mick. It got like the only way to find out what was happening was to pick up the *Sun* or the *Mirror* or the *New York Times* to find that Mick was sending me a message. Hhhuhhuh! Y'know 'Just got your letter and YOU CAN FUCK OFF!' When you're working together you can carry on your fights behind closed doors – they're controllable because of doing the gig, y'see? – but the luxury of this particular one was that we *weren't* working together. The only problems I ever have with Mick are when we're not working together and when we're not working together, it's no real problem-mmm-hhuhhhuuh!

"We've been stuffed together for years and one of the consequences of the break was making us realise we were stuck together whether we liked it or not. It's not even like with a wife who wants to divorce you or you want to divorce her; Mick and I can't get divorced. Even if we never wanted to see one another again or work together again we'd *still* have to get together to decide what was to be done with the stuff we'd already done. It'd be like negotiating child visiting rights, y'knowh'ahmean?"

And are the things you like about him now the same things you liked about him then?

"Yeah. I like him playing harp, man. And I like to see his bum in front of me when I'm playing guitar, doing his shit. I like about him all the things he probably hates about himself." Which is solid geometry.

Only the Lonely

Dominic Wells

Time Out, 17 April 1991.

OF ALL LONDON'S punk misfits, The Only Ones were the strangest. Peter Perrett, the lead singer, had long hair, porcelain features and effete clothes rescued from second-hand shops; they played raucous guitar solos at a time when that was an incitement to riot: long before Morrissey, the lyrics to their perversely beautiful melodies were all of poison and decay. "Another Girl, Another Planet", a thinly veiled ode to heroin, regularly crops up now in lists of all-time great singles, but failed to make the Top 75 on release. They recorded three albums for CBS, the last of which peaked at No 37, and they split up in 1980 after a US tour straight out of "Spinal Tap".

They needed a police escort to get out of Birmingham, Alabama, after their gig disturbed a neighbouring pool hall and 30 rednecks came out armed with pool cues. Guitarist John Perry's habit had become so bad that no one would share a room with him, and his girlfriend was busted and imprisoned in LA. And as if that wasn't enough, Peter Perrett had to flee charges of attempted murder when, after a 6 foot 4 inch car-park attendant had hassled him, he got into his car and ran him over. Finally having been smuggled back to London, he developed hepatitis from the dirty needles he used on tour and was confined to bed for six months. He didn't get up again for half a decade.

Around 40, Perrett now looks 25. A heroin habit can do that; it is like ingesting embalming fluid. His handshake is firm and he's brimming with vitality and hope for the future. A retrospective live album last year almost brought him out of hiding and now Virgin Video has released a tape of late '70s Only Ones footage mixed in with a contemporary interview but more importantly he's been recording again, and a solo comeback is just waiting for the right deal. "My voice is much better" he says. "Before, I used to like slurring out of tune. I used to like discord: but now I can appreciate pretty things."

He plays me a demo: "Place of Safety", a gutsy kick in the teeth to today's by-numbers pop, the lyrics as always reflecting a private torment. After their second child was born in 1983, Perrett and his wife Zina turned up at the hospital to find the baby had been spirited away by social workers; the couple regained custody only after a lengthy legal battle.

Perrett is a walking Government health warning: heroin screws you up. In 1986, for the love of his children, he checked into the Bethnal Green Hospital and spent a month drying out. "Although it was a bit like prison, the fact that I had my own brain back, I was thinking again, laughing and crying and just *living* again was great. Taking drugs might be exciting and fun for two years, but after that it's the most boring existence that you can imagine."

"I'm in love with extreme mental torture," he sang on "No Pace For The Wicked". "I'm in love with the way you hold your head and cry." What on earth is wrong with the guy? What makes Perrett run?

A child prodigy, he registered off the IQ scale at the age of four. His dad taught him algebra at five and his mathematical skills later resurfaced in poker; he won so much money once from a couple of drug dealers, killing time before they flew to Brazil, that he was able to accompany them on Concorde. In his first year at public school, he was caned every day; he went through several (befriending Steve Harley at Haberdashers) until he eventually passed four A-levels at Norwood technical college. Liberated from school at the fag end of the '60s, he just got wilder.

"Because I'd been to boarding school I started life late. I used to think infatuation was love and that women were there just to amuse me." He married Zina in 1970; their first baby died three days after birth. Perrett started going out with Cathy, a Playboy bunny who'd been in the hospital bed next to his wife's. A string of affairs ended only when one girlfriend, Lynn, moved in with him and Zina, and froze out all her rivals; when Perrett finally dumped her, Lynn made several attention-getting suicide bids – thus the typically charming Only Ones ditty, "Why don't You Kill Yourself? You Ain't No Use To No One Else".

Now, Perrett says, he's grown up: "I was very immature at the time. After I had kids I realised what is was like for someone to be more important to me than me, and I finally fell in love with the mother of my kids, whom I've actually been married to for 21 years now."

It's tempting to believe that great art can come only from great suffering, that wisdom is born of adversity; if so, Perrett's comeback is well starred. He's experimenting with the new technology on studio time bought by an indie benefactor, and has lost the arrogance that made him disassociate himself from The Only Ones' third album, when CBS foisted a new producer on the band. "I'm really excited," he says. "I'm looking forward to finding a good producer and getting a real quality sound. I hear stuff on the TV and there's some fucking great sounds around." But most of all, one suspects, Perrett is simply glad to be still alive.

In Bed with Mick Jagger

Tony Parsons

Marie Claire, December, 1992.

They say that the only woman in the Rolling Stones camp that Bianca could stand to be around was Shirley, the wife of Charlie Watts. Bianca is said to have liked Shirley because she believed that the drummer's wife was the only Stones woman who Mick hadn't fucked. True or false, it illustrates one central point about Mick Jagger's turbulent love life: he has been spoilt for choice. "Jagger is about as sexy as a pissing toad," said Truman Capote. Armies of women have disagreed and have fallen prostrate before Mick's grotesque beauty.

Jagger squired Marianne Faithfull in the sixties, Bianca in the seventies and Jerry Hall in the eighties (she may yet be his choice for the nineties). All three would, in their day, have been a candidate for any "Most Beautiful Woman in the World" award. But there have been others. "Mick sleeps with many women but he rarely has affairs with them", Bianca said.

"They are all trying to use him. They are all nobodies trying to be somebody. I'm up against this every day," said Jerry Hall. "I'm not talking about just groupies. One girl, a famous singer, said to Mick when she first me him, 'Should I put my diaphragm in? Or should we talk first?' Mick said it put him off so much. It's so unromantic."

But romance has never really suited him, at least not in his public persona. Though he was written some tender love songs, on record Jagger has always seemed most at home when tormenting his women. "Under my thumb is the squirming dog who just had her day," he gloated as a young man, and this theme of crotch-scratching belligerence has dominated his work. And he is

Mick Jagger, the lead singer of the ultimate rock and roll band. Next year he will be fifty. It can't be easy.

In 1992 Jagger became a grandfather for the first time and a father for the fifth time. When he fled Jerry Hall after the birth of their third child for the arms of a young nubile or two, it was tempting to see his errant behaviour as a symptom of Mick's menopause. But while the effect of being called "Grandad" and reaching his half-century should not be discounted, the tabloids who condemned his infidelity as the pathetic antics of an ageing swinger ignored one crucial fact – Mick Jagger had always fucked around.

"Which songs are about me?" Jerry once asked him.

"They all are, darling," he replied.

Sure.

"You can't stop having affairs if they come along," he has said. "But there's a difference between that and trying to be with every girl you meet."

So what kind of women does Mick Jagger like? As we see from the years he spent with Marianne, Bianca and Jerry, he likes women in their prime. Or even a bit younger – many of his brief flings have been with girls who you could imagine getting over the affair by throwing themselves into their A levels.

Those who have chronicled life on the road with the Stones – Robert Greenfield in his book *A Journey Through America With The Rolling Stones*, Stanley Booth's *The True Adventures Of The Rolling Stones* – suggest that when he is touring, Mick will sleep with almost anyone. Playboy Bunnies. Backing singers. Lowly groupies. The wives of the rich and famous. Anyone. In this he is no different from any other rock and roller. But being Mick Jagger, he has a bigger choice than anyone else.

Off the road, his tastes are much more refined. He likes to win girls who are desired by other powerful men. "Far and away the most beautiful lady you have ever seen on a catwalk," said Donald Trump of Carla Bruni, the model Jagger was linked to after the rift with Jerry, while Jerry herself sat between Mick and Warren Beatty on their first big date. "They were both being pretty keen," remembered Jerry. But Jagger can fight off the stiffest competition.

He likes posh girls. The upper class has given him some of his most spectacular erections. Carla Bruni was born into the aristocracy, as was Marianne Faithfull, the daughter of a baroness, and Bianca Rose Perez Moreno de Macias, the daughter of Nicaraguan toffs.

Faithfull and Bianca were both his social superiors and Jagger, a terrific snob, has often used his relations with the opposite sex as a chance for social mobility. He is a sucker for true class. In many ways, Jerry Hall – who comes from a huge brood of dirt-poor Texans – was an aberration. But what Jerry has going for her – apart from the fact that she is a cosmic amalgam of legs, hair and teeth – is that she is an easy woman to be around. She wants to please her man. "My mama told me that a woman should be a maid in the living room, a cook in the kitchen and a whore in the bedroom," Jerry once informed me. Jagger likes a strong woman who doesn't attempt to be his equal.

His first love was Chrissie Shrimpton, the kid sister of Jean Shrimpton. She was a seventeen-year-old student when they began courting in the early sixties. Jagger allegedly proposed marriage but quickly changed his mind when fame deposited a legion of women on his doorstep. They spent four years together. "He kept her under his thumb," said Marianne Faithfull, adding that when the affair with Shrimpton was over, "he never saw her any more." If Jagger stays friends with an ex-lover then it is probably for the sake of the children. He is infinitely more dutiful as a father than he is as a husband and has a deep bond with the son and four daughters that he sired with three different women (three with Jerry, one with Bianca and one with Marsha Hunt). But though he loves his kids, it seems that too much domestic bliss makes him claustrophobic. He will never be comfortable smiling from the pages of *Hello!*, God bless him. Probably a contributing factor in the split with Jerry was that it was all getting a little too cosy.

He never played happy families with Marianne Faithfull. True, she had a small child that Jagger doted on, but domesticity was staved off by jealousy, mental confusion and drugs. There are those who see Faithfull as the love of Jagger's life. "I think of all the girlfriends he's had, he loved her the most," said Jerry Hall.

The daughter of Baroness Erisso, Faithfull was educated at St Joseph's Convent in Reading. She was seventeen when she met Andrew Loog Oldham the iconoclastic young manager of the Rolling Stones (he dreamed up the headline, "Would You Let Your Daughter Marry A Rolling Stone?") Oldham admired her pretty face, her sweet, melancholic grace and no doubt her mother's title. One night she spent thirty minutes recording a Jagger/Richard song called "As Tears Go By". It made her a pop star.

Faithfull was the epitome of liberated sixties womanhood, the First Lady of Swinging London. "I lived in a Renoir painting," she said. "Long blonde hair, sunny days, straw hat with ribbons." The reality was not quite so wistful. "My first move was to get a Rolling Stone as a boyfriend," she told *NME* in 1975, ten years after "As Tears Go By." "I slept with three and then decided the lead singer was the best bet."

She had married a Cambridge undergraduate called John Dunbar but by 1965 it was over and Faithfull – and her young son – were living with Jagger. While most of the Beatles were setting up home with their provincial childhood sweethearts, Jagger and Faithfull were the couple of the age. The fallen convent angel and the neanderthal rocker. He gave her notoriety. She gave him class. He also gave her a paltry £25 a week to keep house in Cheyne Walk. She was the first woman to complain of his stinginess, though not the last.

Perhaps Jagger was not so different from a Beatle husband lording it over his little hairdressing *hausfrau*. Faithfull says that Jagger resented her ambitions. "You can't have two stars in the house," she said, although she admits that she in turn was jealous of his achievements, especially his ability to turn her drug problems into great songs. "I was jealous seeing him going out and doing better and better work," she said. "All my traumas and all my unhappiness he changed into brilliant songs and it made me sick to see him, like a really good writer or any really good artist, turning the traumas in his own home into work. All artists are totally selfish."

Their *amour fou* floundered as the sweet dreams of the sixties were turning very sour. In Sydney, where Jagger was to make a film about Ned Kelly, Faithfull – depressed by her fading relationship with Mick and the death of Brian Jones – took 150 Tuinal sleeping pills. Jagger woke up and summoned help quickly enough to save her life. He is good in a crisis (Jerry Hall says that he was incredibly supportive when she was wrongly arrested in Barbados for possessing 20lb of marijuana).

As the sixties drew to a bitter end, one cold Chelsea night Faithfull grabbed her son and some clothes and left Jagger. For months he tried to win her back. But she was sinking deeper into heroin and one day Jagger walked in to find that she had done something unforgivable. She had become fat. And then he no longer wanted her.

Years later someone asked Jagger if he felt responsible for destroying Marianne Faithfull. "Marianne nearly killed me, man!" he replied. "I wasn't going to get out of there alive." Guilt does not come easily to him. On the rocky road to the seventies, Jagger had a brief relationship with Marsha Hunt, a black American who danced naked in the hippy musical *Hair*. Jagger has always had a soft spot for black girls and their union would have been unremarkable if it hat not produced a child, Mick's first. At the time, Hunt refused to name the father of her daughter – although his identity was widely known. "He's no longer involved with us," Hunt said. "At first I thought I cared for him a lot, but I found out afterwards I didn't really know him at all."

In her autobiography, Marsha Hunt says that Jagger told her he didn't love her and never had, only a couple of weeks after their daughter Karis was born. Happily, Hunt, Jagger and their daughter Karis have since established a much warmer relationship. Jagger can be very adult about these situations.

As the new decade dawned, Narcissus discovered his reflection and was immediately smitten. Apart from looking like a female version of Jagger, the woman who would become his wife (his first and, I believe, his only wife) embodies many of the qualities that Mick seeks in a lover. Bianca had class. She was exotic. And she was hard to get. They met at a Stones show in Paris in 1970 as Faithfull unravelled back in London, and Bianca was "an Inca princess dressed like a Dior mannequin", according to Philip Norman, "watching the proceedings with the slightly contemptuous detachment of an Egyptian royal cat."

And Jagger was on the rebound. The wounds inflicted by breaking with Faithfull were too serious to be soothed by blowjobs from an endless succession of groupies. Mick married his glossy Latin beauty in St Tropez on 12 May 1971.

They had a fight on their wedding day – always a bad omen – because Bianca initially refused to sign a wedding contract stipulating whether their property was to be held jointly or separately (the contract was required by French law rather than Jagger's parsimony). Bianca thought that such clinical legalities had no place in romance and wanted the wedding called off. Jagger got angry. "Are you trying to make a fool of me in front of all these people?" An intensely proud man, he does not like to lose face, and Bianca relented.

After a chaotic civil marriage and a quiet religious ceremony where the organist played the theme from *Love Story* (Bianca's choice), the happy couple retired to their wedding party accompanied by assorted Beatles and Stones. The groom, always the exhibitionist, took to the stage to strut his funky stuff and Bianca stormed off, sulking for reasons unknown. Perhaps she did not want to share Mick Jagger with the crowd. She later said her marriage ended on the day of her wedding. Marianne Faithfull heard about the wedding on her way to Paddington to catch a train to see her parents. She went into an Indian restaurant and eventually became so tired and emotional that she passed out with her lovely face in a plate of curry. She spent the night in Paddington Green police Station. Five months later in Paris, Blanca gave birth to a daughter called Jade.

"The music's not as good," sniffed Marianne Faithfull of Jagger's new muse. But for a while the couple were in Biba heaven, defining the new age as surely as Mick and Marianne had in the sixties.

The St Tropez wedding of these two pouting beauties marked

the start of the transition of rock stars from grubby bad boys to
jet-setting Nigel Dempster fodder, hanging out with Andy War-
hol and Halston in VIP room at Studio 54.

But Mr and Mrs Jagger were soon arguing on two continents.
What did they argue about? Everything. Careers, their daughter,
their friends (none of them mutual). Perhaps the only thing they
didn't argue about were Mick's casual fucks. Bianca was always
too sophisticated to play the part of the jealous wife, and in these
pre-HIV years, the exchange of bodily fluids really did not seem
to count for very much. But like some seminal Princess of Wales,
what Bianca objected to was the privileged, oppressive world
inhabited by her husband. And though widely perceived as a
gold-digger who wanted only to further her career as an actress
and model, she seems to have genuinely hated the sordid scenes
that surrounded the band. She despised the sycophantic cour-
tiers, the sexual and chemical gluttony, the endless travelling, all
the things that look quite appealing from a distance and are no
fun being married to.

Though their marriage would drag on for a few more years
(their divorce was finalized in 1980), Jagger and Bianca were
leading separate lives by the time he found something stirring in
his trousers for a young Texan model called Jerry Hall. She was
going out with someone else at the time. But Jagger never lets that
stop him.

Jagger invited the prairie rose and her boyfriend Bryan Ferry
to a Stones show in 1976 (backstage at a Stones concert is always
Mick's favourite singles bar). After the show they went back to
Ferry's house in Holland Park. Jagger is never shy in declaring
his feelings. "I'd go in the kitchen to fix some more tea and Mick
would follow me and Bryan would follow him," wrote Jerry in
her wonderful autobiography, *Tall Tales*. "He was real jealous
that Mick was flirting with me. Finally Bryan got really upset and
said, 'I'm going to bed.' He stomped off and everyone started to
leave. And Mick tried to kiss me but I didn't let him."

She did eventually. After her dinner date sitting between
Jagger and Warren Beatty at that New York restaurant, Jerry
ended up in bed with Jagger (he enjoys stealing women from

under the nose of another sex god). Jerry was guilt-ridden for betraying Ferry and told the rubber-lipped Lothario that it could not happen again. But it did.

After the dirty deed was done, Jagger sent flowers, he called – he can be the perfect gentleman when he wants to be – and though she tried to fight him off, once again Jerry's long, golden body ended up in Mick's bed. And as Jerry fretted about whether she could stick with Ferry or submit to Jagger's lascivious charms. Mick would sit on the floor, get out his guitar and sing her an old blues song by Robert Johnson. "Stop breaking down/Mama, please stop breaking down/The stuff I've got will bust your brains out baby/Girl, you're going to make me lose my mind." He is quite capable of turning the romance up to full volume. Then Jerry's father died. She was devastated. Ferry was touring. Jagger was there for her and genuinely sympathetic. That clinched it – she would leave Ferry for Jagger. But if this lasts a year it's a miracle, thought Jerry.

Seven years later their first child, Elizabeth Scarlett, was born. Her brother James arrived a year later and baby Georgia was born at the start of this year. They are all cherubs wreathed in golden ringlets with bee-stung lips, little Micks made angels. Typically, Jagger has lavished love and attention on his children but has not let their presence interfere too much with his sex life. During his relationship with Jerry, Jagger has had a number of outside interests. The press has linked him with Catherine Guinness in 1979 and Lord Longford's daughter Natasha Fraser in 1980. "Purely platonic," said Jagger. "He's my new boyfriend," Natasha is said to have told friends. "Stay away from my man," said Jerry.

Then there was teenage New Yorker Gwen Rivers in 1982. The same year Mick was seen dancing at a night club with a US deb Cornelia Guest, eighteen, the *Sun* tells us. "They later had breakfast together."

1982 – the year before he turned forty – was the year of living unfaithfully for Jagger; the year when he went astray in a spectacular fashion. "He decided to take advantage of the way girls are," said Jerry. She immediately retaliated with an affair with horse-loving tycoon Robert Sangster. Stung, Jagger pursued her. And he gives very good phone.

He won her back but, ten years on, Jerry Hall is faced with exactly the same problems with this year's models. At the time of going to press, there are rumours of a reconciliation. Anyway, talk of Jagger and Jerry divorcing is almost certainly academic. Last year they went through a Hindu wedding ceremony in Bali but were unable to supply the Indonesian government with all the documentation needed to make the ceremony legally binding – passports, birth certificates, doctor's letters, divorce papers and – most important of all – a letter from a Hindu priest stating that the couple have converted to the Hindu faith. Neither Mick nor Jerry are practising Hindus. Was it just coincidence that Jagger went through a wedding ceremony that did not actually marry them? Or did slippery old Mick know exactly what he was doing?

And what happens to Mick Jagger's women? Jerry Hall once told me that when Jagger went through his phone book from the sixties, half the people in it were dead. His women have fared slightly better. Chrissie Shrimpton is forty-nine now, the mother of four children and living in south London with her husband Mike Von Joel. In 1976 Jagger won a High Court injunction forbidding her from publishing his love-letters in one of our sleazier tabloids. "I shudder to think of being married to Mick," shuddered Chrissie. "He takes a lot of pleasing."

Marianne Faithfull, the girl from a Renoir, exchanged Mick Jagger for heroin. She spent a lot of time in the early seventies roaming Soho trying to feed her habit. Later she kicked her addiction, worked in the theatre, made some critically acclaimed albums and is currently working on her autobiography. She is philosophical about her love affair with Jagger. "We loved each other," she said. "We wanted to keep it and we couldn't in the end. You need time to be together. He was so busy that I really tried to hold myself back. And it nearly destroyed me. The effort of restraining myself and not working was terrible. And I ended up on drugs."

She does not blame Jagger for her descent into hard drugs. "People always assume I was already a junkie when I was with

Mick – but I wasn't. At that stage it was still an experiment."
Faithfull married a punk rocker called Ben E. Ficial (not his real
name,) but is now single. She does not regret the night she walked
out of Cheyne Walk and Mick Jagger's life. "It would have killed
me staying with Mick," she said. "He has always been quite
brutal towards his women. I still love him in a way but everything
happened for the best. If I was Mick's chick I'd be just that."

Marsha Hunt is now a successful novelist and the daughter she
had with Jagger is a university graduate (Mick attended her
graduation ceremony). Blanca Rose Perez Moreno de Macias
flirted with acting but that didn't work out. Now she does good
works on behalf of her country, raising funds and visiting trouble
zones in Nicaragua and other Central American countries. "I
have survived," she said. "I was the Nicaraguan who married a
rock star and now I am someone else. I have no regrets and we are
still friends."

Bianca was bad-mouthed as an upmarket bimbo but she has
turned out to be a woman of real courage, real integrity, real
substance. And she looks great. She lives in New York, but I saw
her at a private club in London last year and – on the verge of
becoming a grandmother – she looked like dynamite.

Jerry Hall's future is assured. She has hired out her lovely face
to promote goods as varied as Bovril and Bentley, and has
launched her own range of luxurious swimwear. She has such
huge supplies of Texan charm that she will always be loved in this
country. What she has to decide is if she wants to give Jagger
another try or if she has been hurt enough.

The talk of the getting-back-together grows louder every day.
By late summer Mick and Jerry were eating dinner together at the
Mansion On Turtle Creek restaurant in Dallas. They were said to
be spending their son's birthday together at La Fourchette, their
chîeau in the in the Loire valley. Sweetest of all, the happy couple
were spotted cuddling backstage at a Dwight Yoakam concert in
London.

My guess is that they will attempt to drag their relationship
around the block one more time but that eventually there will be
more betrayal, more tabloid headlines, more young lovelies

kneeling before the altar of Mick Jagger's celebrity. And so it will go on until Jerry runs out of patience or Jagger runs out of juice.

But how about some sympathy for the old devil? Warren Beatty may get all misty-eyed every time he smells a soiled nappy but Warren has just become a father for the first time. Jagger has been a father for over twenty years. And Warren is an actor. Mick is no actor – as anyone who has seen any of his films will testify. Mick is rock and roll, where the love of a good woman can never truly compete with the love of a good time. Something that has been inside him all his life refuses to let him settle down. It's a blessing when you are a young man. By the time you are forty-nine, it is a kind of curse.

Jerry might believe that Jagger loved Marianne Faithfull more than any of his other girlfriend. Personally I think his great love is Jerry Hall. Jagger has, I believe, loved her as much as he can love a woman. If she can't hold him, no woman can. Which of course is a distinct possibility. He is, after all, Mick Jagger, the lead singer of the Rolling Stones, growing old disgracefully. What else did we expect?

Virgin on the Ridiculous

Sarah Kent

Time Out, 21 October 1992.

Madonna's *Sex* comes condom-wrapped to protect it from casual
encounters. The material girl's face is printed on the rape
resistant Mylar in a blue swoon – head thrown back, eyes closed,
mouth open. Classic Hollywood ecstatic: blonde and beautiful, a
distant object of desire. But Madonna, dubbed by Martin Amis
"the most post modern person on the planet", refuses to be
merely a dreamy screen on to which people can project their
wishes. She has to be in control, shaping any free-floating
fantasies. We are *her* subjects, not vice versa.

Her book was proclaimed "flagrantly pornographic", even
before it was seen. French customs seized it and the Japanese
censored it. Several printers refused to handle it, before a Mid-
West firm agreed – on condition that it remain anonymous.

Press hysteria has also been phenomenal. Papers all over
Europe (except Germany) have fallen over themselves to condemn the book, sight unseen. The *News of the World* blasted
"Dirty" Don Trelford for serialising the pictures: "Now mucky
toffs can *Observer*". The *Mail* devoted a whole page to saying
they were not going to run a story and *Today* ran a spread
headlined, ironically, "Aren't you sick of Madonna?"

Maybe the publishers know what they are doing, slapping on a
strict embargo; but the press always fill a vacuum with hot air,
much of it spiteful. Whether or not you like or approve of *Sex*, it is
a daring, even career-damaging act which merits proper attention.

I suspect it's not the content the people find objectionable – it
is relatively mild, anyway – but the fact that a woman is on top.
Steven Meisel may have held the camera, but it is obvious who

called the shots: "These are fantasies I have dreamed up," affirms Madonna.

The book comes with its own protection, a cover of sheet aluminium, proclaiming that behind the soft veneer comes a hard layer, like sculpture. Such contradictions permeate the pages. *Sex* starts hard-core black and white – photo edges are roughly torn, prints are tacked viciously down and framed by millions of staples (the graphic equivalent of studs and safety pins) – before getting fluffier, funnier and going full colour. The images alternate between sweet and sour; wanton and innocent; naive and sophisticated; passive and aggressive; vulnerable and predatory. The opening shot says it all. Madonna sits on a chair, clad in leather gear and a mask. One finger is in her mouth, the other in her fanny – a sexually mature child, mean-looking but in need of love. "Love is something we make," she declares, "pass it on." Arch stupidity or disarming simplicity? Like Marilyn, Madonna has an uncanny ability to be wise and foolish adult and infantile, hard-bitten and soft centred – all at the same time.

The book is best when at its most relaxed and humorous, least convincing when Modanna strives for crack-alley cred as a tourist in Manhattan's down-town dives: sex clubs such as the Toilet and the Vault and a burlesque theatre called the Gaiety. She play-acts SM in basements and backyards, whipping a well-covered rump, being tied up by lesbian skinheads who threaten her with teeth and blade. "There's something comforting about being tied up, like when you were a baby and your mother strapped you in the car seat." But the atmosphere is wrong, the threat is unreal and the narrative without dynamic. The pictures are like fashion plates – for rubber goods and swimwear – without serious dread. A genuinely disconcerting shot show a man in evening dress riding a pack of naked slaves, but then it gets ludicrous as he and Madonna, in a full-length sequined sheath, luxuriate amid the bulging beefcake.

But there's a beautiful triple portrait, a nest of heads that contrasts Madonna's soft cheek with the cranial stubble and spindly plait of a lesbian skinhead who kisses her neck, while her partner gives her an adoring peck on her tattooed shoulder.

Another glorious image: Madonna's white neck arches back in a long curve as her teeth tug on the nipple ring of a naked savage. Printed in metallic tones, he looks like a sculpture. A companion picture sizzles with similar tensions. The man, constrained by collar and lead, kisses the instep of Madonna's foot, jammed into a ballet pump held vertical by a high wedge heel. It's an extraordinary image of mutual bondage – both dominatrix and slave seem equally trapped.

The timing of *Sex* is impeccable. "The Body" is in vogue: it's Today's Topic. Jeff Koons and La Cicciolina have been publicly consummating their marriage (art with porn) in full-colour, fairy-story photographs of fudge-packing. Andres Serrano has been outraging God-fearing Senators with elegant come shots, and in this country, Della Grace, the self-styled 'Pussy Licking Sodomite', has been celebrating the lesbian body in stunning photographs of rituals and sexual display. As an art collector – with her own curator to advise her what to buy – Madonna must be aware of these moves. But dubbed the "dirtiest coffee table book ever", *Sex* is actually more like a designer fanzine – searching after street rather than sitting-room or art-crowd cred.

Madonna is at her high-spirited best when pondering her solo obsessions. She simulates innocence better than wickedness – a large chunk of her is still a child. And innuendo is sexier than overkill. "I love my pussy," she proclaims, "it is the summation of my life. My pussy is the temple of learning. Sometimes I sit at the edge of the bed and stare into the mirror . . . Sometimes I stick my finger in my pussy and wiggle it around the dark wetness and feel what a cock or a tongue must feel when I'm sitting on it. I pull my finger out and I always taste it and smell it . . . It smells like a baby to me, fresh and full of life."

We're in the realm of girl-talk, teen confessions for the post-feminist generation, who grew up unashamed of their bodies. Twenty-five years ago women crept to consciousness-raising groups clutching hand mirrors with which to examine their genitals, ridding themselves of shame and ignorance and discovering that their private parts were also for their pleasure, not just the possession of men.

Madonna recalls the moment she discovered masturbation:
"that glorious day when finger found flesh and with legs spread
open and back arched, honey poured from my 14-year-old gash
and I wept." She kneels over a mirror, finger exploring her
crotch. The words are assertive, but the picture is modest. She
keeps her knickers on – no split beavers in this book, no crotch
shots. Bare buttocks and breasts, but scarcely a genital in sight –
no penetration, only fabrication. Ciccone's revelations are demure, indeed, when compared with Jeff Koons and La Cicciolina's shaven-haired shagging: but then her tribe are mostly in
their teens.

One of the most disarming photographs is of the 34-year-old in
a turquoise T-shirt – hair straggly, looking all of 14 – gazing at
her body in the bedroom mirror. It rings true – I remember
spending hours admiring my budding breasts. The silliest shot is
of her ejaculating suntan lotion over a supine black beauty on the
beach; one of the most understated but sexiest, a man's hand
sprinkling talcum powder on her bare behind. The naffest verbals
are girly hints on how to seduce your man – playing hard to get,
wearing garter-belts, sucking your finger and saying "one really
disarming thing" every date. I prefer her other approach –
shaving the pubes of a mean-looking motherfucker.

Women who try to explore their sexual identities come up
against a perennial problem: how to display their nudity without
reducing themselves to titillating titbits. Madonna masterminds
this balance – between subject and object – by constantly changing tack and tempo and by revealing more verbally than visually.
Her words are often sexier than Meisel's pictures. "I've often
dreamed of lying on a beach completely naked . . . the water
comes rushing in assaulting me . . . I am open, I am on display to
the sea." A girl arrives and they make languorous but steamy
love: "I pour the purest of myself into her . . . I drink in every
drop of her sweet nectar.' Dusk falls and she feels at one with
nature: 'I look into the fantastic sky, red now but then pink and
violet. They sky is the colour of pussy. I am content.#' The best
that Meisel can do is to show Madonna kneeling in the shallows: a
cute pin-up – calendar kitsch.

One shot I can't forgive – a fake rape in a gym showing everyone grinning as though assault were fun. Madonna's thoughts on violence are vacuous: "if women are in an abusive relationship . . . and they stay in it, they must be digging it"; her views on the porn industry simple-minded: "I don't think pornography degrades women. The women who are doing it want to do it. No one is holding a gun to their head." The mega-millionairess has obviously forgotten what poverty means.

The wackiest picture is of Madonna tiptoeing naked across a lawn clutching a handbag and water bottle, like some daffy housewife escaping for the day. She hitches starkers beside the freeway and munches pizza naked in a parlour. One of the most inspired images, printed a soft violet, shows her suspended naked from a gantry as though she has just been lifted from the sea – the modern equivalent of Botticelli's Venus, blown ashore on a shell: newly born but fully formed. The most telling fantasy in *Sex* finds her in schoolgirl knickers and socks sitting on the lap of a father figure, smoking, as he adoringly fondles her breast – she is said to be driven by the need for her father's love and approval.

Madonna sees herself as a liberator: "avenger of the libido dead, a sister of mercy or lady of head". But I see her as a prisoner, occasionally breaking the bonds of fame by leaping naked into the light of day and photographing the brief moment of release, before beating a hasty retreat to the safety of a dark-windowed limo.

The most memorable picture in the book shows Madonna in vest and boots perched on a radiator, peeping through the blinds – exposing herself to the world and monitoring the reaction. It's an image of loneliness and longing – of a kid who can't go out to play; of someone tough yet vulnerable, exhibitionist yet reclusive, needing the crowd yet cut off from the street. The summation of a life spent struggling for fame, then learning how, on earth, to deal with it.

Virgin Father

Brian Case

Time Out, 24 March 1993.

I remember mistaking an old woman for a trout stream in Vermont, and I had to beg her pardon. "Excuse me," I said. "I thought you were a trout stream." "I'm not," she said."
(Trout Fishing in America *by Richard Brautigan)*

Few in the sell-out audience for the US Premiere of Mike Oldfield's "Tubular Bells 2" at Carnegie Hall had been around when "Tubular Bells" came out in 1973. Young New Yorkers, they knew little of that Camelot era when Bilbo Baggins walked the land and Flower Children blew bubbles or drilled holes in their skulls to relieve barometric pressure. They'd probably never heard of Constable Zippo and his Electric Commode Band either, nor Boeing Duveen and the Beautiful Soup, and they hadn't taken to their beds, inconsolable, when Blodwyn Pig split up, its leader, the number 8 shirt, leaving to join Wombat.

Nevertheless, when Oldfield sprints on stage in white trainers brandishing a strenuous thumbs-up, the house goes off like a rocket. A small, antic figure, he bounces about like a budgie, working his way through a forest of guitars, belting those tubular bells with a mallet, while the synthesizers hoot like wood flutes or replicate the digestive system. It's larkier than the original, with passages for kilted bagpipers and hoe-down, but it's still the old static stuff. The Oldfield fist in the air at the end seem: disproportionately robust. "That music is *inspiration-based!*" thrills a girl in glasses. "He told the *whole story* in music."

Inspiration-based! The early '70s were rich in progressive rock to fold the arms to. Yes released *Tales from Topographic Oceans,* and Pink Floyd *Dark Side of the Moon*, dealing with lunacy and death and that. Roy Harper released *Lifemask* which, since rumours abounded that he'd been given days to live, was seen as his final testament. In fact, he'd feigned insanity to dodge conscription into the RAF and been convincing enough to undergo ECT. A flap lifted on the sleeve to reveal his staring eyes, but he was back next year with *Flashes from the Archives of Oblivion* and then *When an Old Cricketer Leaves the Crease*, both titles tantalisingly valedictory. Oldfield himself followed through with *Hargest Ridge*, which went to No 1 in the UK while *Tubular Bells* was still at No 2, then *Ommadawn*.

Oldfield is still bucked by the response next day. "It crosses a couple of generations, which is gratifying." His voice is soft as thistledown, even when New Age Music comes up. "They put me in the New Age slots in the record shops. It's not New Age, it's not sausage and chips. American journalists ask me how it feels to be The Father of New Age Music. What? What are you talking about? New Age Music is something session musicians do in their spare time."

He is a veteran martyr to labelling, having been beached by punk. "Until now, I've never felt I could do a good live concert. I've always had musicians with a cynical attitude left over from the punk years. If you were a real musician trying to make music, there was something wrong with you. Punk diluted the musical abilities of practically a whole generation. You were machine-gunned to death in the pop press if you could really play. It was *kill!* Amazing! Underneath, punks were probably unloved children who covered it up by aggressive attitudes. To me that's terrible cowardice. To own up and admit that you're a little child who wants to curl up on the floor and cry like a baby takes a lot of courage."

He'd been amused by the concert narrator supplied by a look-alike agency. He'd wanted a Clinton, settled for a Nixon, and got a Reagan who resembled nobody. Vivian Stanshall, mellifluous and wacky, had been the voice on the original album. "He was *supposed* to be the voice on "*Tubular Bells 2*" but when the producer went to collect him for the session he was asleep in the bath with a pot plant and wouldn't wake up, so we got Alan Rickman," laughs Oldfield. His meat-eating guffaw is a shock.

On his music, however, he is a perfectionist. "It's about playing it with as much love as you can." His large hands wring an imaginary guitar neck as he explains. The piece was scored and conducted; the tempos were correct; pep talks with the band had emphasized *feeling*. "We're not doing a rock 'n' roll approximation of the album – we're actually trying to recreate it in the most minute detail possible." He had chosen the slide projection – Picasso's 'Guernica', Dali, Van Gogh's cypresses. "I thought it'd just be great if you could see a masterpiece up there – something that just connected with the music as I felt it."

Despite the influence of Terry Riley's minimalist systems on early '70s music, *Tubular Bells* seemed to come from nowhere. "I don't know where it came from. I know I discovered music very young and I liked classical, Led Zeppelin, folk, flamenco, so when I got the opportunity to make my own album it was natural to put all these different kinds of things into it. A lot of people are tied down to the vocals and drum kit, but to me every instrument is a vocal. With the guitar you can make vowels and consonants by using the plectrum or vibrato, and the same thing with synthesizers."

Tubular Bells was Virgin's first release in 1973, and sold 16 million copies. Globally, hippies flipped. Richard Branson, who had a chain of discount record shops and wanted to launch his own label, gave the 19-year-old longer studio time in which he overdubbed every instrument himself. The result founded the Branson empire. 'Without it, Virgin Alantic most likely wouldn't exist today,' said Branson when he sold Virgin for £510 million. Oldfield, however, still resents his 17 years with label. Mick Brown's biography of Branson, *The Inside Story*, defines the tycoon: "He was not a child of the '60s at all, nor even of the '70s; but someone awaiting the arrival of the '80s." Oldfield, one suspects, is still fishing Brautigan's trout stream. "Why is everyone ashamed of the hippy times? Loons? Boring old hippies?" he asks. "Is it because of the punks?"

How he hated the biography! "I remember putting it on the fire and watching it go up in smoke. It makes me seem like an awkward, difficult musician whose attitude was to thwart him. There was a total lack of understanding between someone like him and someone like me. We came from totally different backgrounds. He's got these amazingly supportive parents who follow him around the world – *'Well done, Rickie!'* – whereas my mother was carted off to mental hospital every couple of months. He couldn't understand the effects that something like that would have on me."

Success saw him overwhelmed with lawyers, accountants and mental problems. He wouldn't give interviews or do concerts. Cities threw him into panic attacks. In fact, just about the only musician then with worse withdrawal problems was Syd Barrett, founder of Pink Floyd, creator of "Arnold Layne", the banned ballad of a knickers thief. Syd may yet be holed up in a cellar in Cambridge, according to *Terrapin,* his Appreciation Society's monthly magazine. "I was totally introverted and scared of the world. I couldn't even go on an aeroplane. Every kind of phobia you can imagine, I had.

"It just used to annoy Richard. He couldn't relate to it because he's always been *the Hero.* I used to think he was a friend of mine, but he's got that chatty and chummy way of being with people that makes them think that. It was all *Jolly japes! St Trinian's!* But as soon as my sales figures dropped below a certain level, my music was taken off the Virgin shelves and the Sex Pistols put up, and I couldn't reach him on the phone. I don't think I'll ever totally forgive him for not letting me out of that contract, and paying me such a low royalty. Respect was lacking."

Virgin contracts were famously watertight and copyright enforced to the letter. Oldfield's original contract was for ten albums of 5 per cent royalties, which soured as new acts – Steve Hillage, Henry Cow, Gong – were signed to Virgin at better rates. He retained a lawyer and in 1977 got terms amended to 8 per cent, but in 1981 was back for more. A deal was struck: more money, but more albums. A 1985 photo of the two together – something of an up-date on Richard the Lionheart and his Blondel – features rows of the Branson teeth, none of the doleful Oldfield's, the tycoon's arm heavily leaning on the artist's shoulder.

But the relationship wasn't quite Elvis and the Colonel, nor was it as slippery as that between Fleetwood Mac and *their* manager who, tired of their personality clashes, tried to assemble a new Fleetwood Mac with none of them in it. And it had curious medieval survivals. Even after litigation, Branson agreed to continue as Oldfield's manager for one barrel of beer a year. Oldfield ran off with Virgin press officer Al Clark's secretary, and had three children by her. "That *was* a possible source of friction between us!" he roars.

These days, Oldfield is nothing like the haunted wimp peeping out from between those tulip leaf lapels. Exegesis, a coercive therapy in which clients noisily re-enact the birth trauma, has been the making of him. The Oldfield disparities come into focus – the whisper and the guffaw, the sudden loudhailer impersonations, the big-fist gestures. Therapy has bolted stuff on. At 40, he seems at peace with himself. "There's a sixth sense and probably a seventh, ninth and tenth. What we see around us is just a tiny skin of the total reality. I don't *know* anything – and I quite like it that way." He recently founded Tonic, a charity to fund those in need of psychotherapy. "I've written to Branson to get some *money* out of *him!*'

Names are for Tombstones, Baby: The Mission

Martin Roach

This first American tour saw The Mission in a frenzy of drugs, drink and women which swept them inexorably onwards and upwards. It was almost as if the more they took the more they would succeed, because for all the discerning comments and furrowed brows, for many there was a perverse fascination in watching the band's chaotic behaviour. The press found reams of great copy in these tour tales and the public were either compelled or disgusted by the events, but certainly very aware of them. The live shows were relatively unaffected by the lifestyle, and with the band producing a majority of blinding gigs the frenzy offstage created a myth around them that avidly held people's attention. Hinkler feels that this hysteria of excess fuelled the fire that took The Mission so quickly to where they were: "There was a definite level where each person knew they could still produce the goods, after which they just became a drunkard and couldn't play a note. I think we knew our levels, and we benefited from being drunkards most of the time, because people seemed to like that about us, we were just a bunch of knock-about drunks having a laugh". It was the drugs however, that dominated The Mission's band culture, and Hinkler believes it was quintessential to their success: "It was the signature of everything we did. It put a stamp on our relationships, how we worked, what we were like. It affected everybody's character and totally ran the show, especially speed. Decisions were made at the drop of a hat on speed, and we'd just go out and do stuff. It was the fire of the band really, the fuel for the ride we were on, and with the drugs we just ploughed through everything. We were just pissheads together, and did all the things that being four pissheads on a big budget entails. When people applaud you for being a pisshead you tend to be a good one".

There was never any premeditated element in all these escapades however – the band behaved as they did because they wanted to, and on many occasions the consequences were detrimental to the group's welfare, not beneficial. It was never calculated – Perrin felt it was almost inescapable once he had joined the ride back in January 1986, and was swept up in all the activity: "It came along and it was exciting so you get on the ride and go with it, you don't look back to see how big it's got. It's such a rollercoaster ride that it's all you can do to keep your feet on the ground at all, because if you don't strive to keep that perspective you're in trouble. Everything had become so big so fast that the drug use was really no more than a natural extension of the rollercoaster ride that we'd been on. Maybe someone could have said 'Okay, let's put the brakes on and take stock, this is dangerous' but there's never been that degree of planning and it just isn't that simple to stand outside of something so incredibly intense."

Such stories make for good press and great and great profile – they do not however, precipitate the healthiest of lifestyles. As The Mission rollercoaster veered faster and faster, it was inevitably going to lose control and with it one of its passengers. On 15th May it happened – the ride came to a shuddering halt, and the passenger who proved to be the victim was Adams. All the crew and band had been equal participants in the chaos that had gone before, but there had been earlier signs that Adams was becoming disillusioned and losing control. After one gig he was all coked up and moaning about a wart he'd had on his ear since childhood. He stood up, went into the bathroom with his pen knife, squeezed the wart between two fingers and sliced it off. He came back covered in blood, announced 'I've got the bastard', sat down and snorted another line of coke. Apart from such physical manifestations of this volatile edge he also expressed dissatification with some of the politics of touring in the USA: "You're just something to put on while they get drunk; you play places where they have a beer advertisement and a band – the beer was half price and there was an English band on. Nobody was seeing us, why were we playing these places? I don't see any point in going back to Nashville for instance. I know three people liked us there, but they weren't from Nashville, they'd travelled. Nobody in Nashville wanted to see us. We turned up with an artic full of stuff and couldn't get any of it in. We were playing places as big as the bar of The Marquee, eight days on the trot – by day eight you just don't want to know." Having said that he had also rather worryingly expressed an attraction to the extremes America offered: "Everything's better over here – the drugs, you can drink all day if you want, you don't have really stroppy hotels with stupid rules. The extremes are quite open to you and they're a lot cheaper as well as being much more extreme." It was this dangerous and explosive cocktail of disillusionment and excess that was to finally snap Adams' body and mind.

The scenario was the 22nd date of the tour in Los Angeles, the night after a show in Orange County to the south. The catalyst was a live radio broadcast for KRock FM, America's premier alternative radio station – what happened over the next twenty-hours nearly ripped the very heart out of The Mission. KRock FM had arranged two performances, one at 2p.m. and one at 8p.m. to feature in a forthcoming Dudley Moore film called *Like Father Like Son*, and had been plugging the event five times a day for weeks. Then at the last minute, with the band on their way to the venue in Los Angeles, the film company pulled out and effectively rendered the whole day pointless. Perrin, who was driving to the gig separately decided it would be best to cancel the show and let the physically and emotionally burned out band take a desperately needed break. KRock FM refused to cancel however, as Perrin explains: "KRock absolutely hit the roof. I was in the Hyatt on Sunset Boulevard, and I was getting major international grief in minutes. KRock were phoning Polygram in New York saying if this gig is pulled, don't just forget about The Mission's career with KRock, it'll be EVERY Polygram act. So

Dick Asher, the President of Polygram USA phoned Phonogram
UK and they called me at the hotel saying the band had got to do
the gig, it had to happen. So I was faced with the prospect of
having to persuade the band to do it – they did not arrive in the
best frame of mind. By now they were completely fried and the
crew were winding me up about how bad the band had got saying
'I wouldn't like to be in your shoes, they've flipped.' When the
band bus pulled up into the car park the crew got up and legged it
and pretended to be busy."

The band climbed off the bus at 6a.m., all of them wrecked,
and when they heard of the events they immediately refused to
play the gig. Hussey explains why they were so reluctant to fulfil
their slot: "None of us wanted to do it, we were all fucked. Craig's
always been the most violent, he was a bad drinker and the drug
use didn't really help – he was already right on the edge. We'd
finished this show in Orange County at about two in the morning,
driven to LA, and checked in the hotel. We could only get a
couple of hours kip at the most before the planned soundcheck at
9 the next morning, so we obviously did a througher, drugs, coke,
liquid breakfast, Jack Daniels, the lot. We were all absolutely off
our tits, but we were supposed to do these two shows in one day."
Following an angry and protracted hour-long discussion, Perrin
convinced three of the band that it was in their best interests to
play the gig, because of the difficult political repercussions of
pulling the show. But Adams would not be persuaded and flatly
refused to do the show. A vote was taken and he was outvoted
three to one.

With the crisis temporarily avoided, Perrin knew that all was
not well however, and was almost resigned to be a helpless bystander in the events to follow. Having been forced to play the
shows against his will, Adams set out to self-destruct. At 9 in the
morning he arrived at soundcheck clutching a half empty bottle
of Jack Daniels and made it perfectly clear that he fully intended
to finish the rest off soon. As Adams continued drinking, the first
show came and went and was a relative success, despite Hinkler
and the bass player dancing on stage in their underpants whilst on
air. Immediately after this show this show the band could be

found shouting at some kids in the car park for more drugs, and shortly afterwards the biggest drug deal of the tour went down in one of the backstage rooms. By now, however, the drugs and drink could not hid the immense tension that had bottled up in The Mission camp – when they returned from the dressing room, Perrin felt a sense of impending disaster: "I just remember trying to keep out of the band's way, hiding in the production office in the bowels of the venue, because it was out of control and I could see what was going to happen from the minute they walked in."

Retiring to the relative sanctity of their hotel, the band and crew tried to get some rest but nobody could sleep. The atmosphere was wrong, no-one knew how to cope with these new and destructive feelings. Perrin settled down on his bed for brief nap, and was drifing into sleep when he was jolted awake by two police sirens screaming down Sunset Boulevard. He knew they were heading for the hotel and he knew something had gone terribly wrong. He jumped to the window and saw Adams standing in the middle of the Strip, no boots on, ranting and raving like a madman. In horror, Perrin watched helpless as the first police car spotted Adams apparently out of control and drove into him, knocking him flat. Perrin flew down the stairs and out on to the road – by the time he arrived there Adams was lying half under the police car, motionless. He was dragged off the tarmac and bundled into the second car. Perrin explains what had happened to precipitate this incident: "Craig couldn't find his room key, so he had ripped off his boots and hurled them at the hotel manager who'd bundled him out of the hotel where the police car had run him down. I'll never forget his face as he sat there handcuffed in the back of this car, it was the most terrible expression I've ever seen on any man. He just looked like a wild animal, his eyes were completely crazed."

It took all of Perrin's considerable diplomatic skills to get Adams bailed out of the police car and to persuade the hotel manager not to press charges. The gig that night was approaching and they could still make it. They had to. But the nightmare had only just begun. Far from calming down, Adams accelerated his drinking, consuming massive quantities up to an hour before the show. They were all sitting in the crew bus – the atmosphere was fraught with tension and conversation was strained. Some petty comment was made and Adams flew into a wild rage, screaming and ranting violently that he wanted his passport, he wanted it now and he wanted out of The Mission. When nobody moved he smashed his right hand into a window, breaking it badly and increasing his fury, and stormed off the bus. Within three hours he was on a plane back to Britain.

The chaos did not stop there – with Adams lost there was no respite, and the nightmare continued. They went back to the hotel where they were immediately escorted off the premises by an angry manager, and called their agent to cancel the evening's show. They later found out that David Bowie had been on the guest list, along with 200 fans from the show the night before since Hussey had offered them all a free ticket because he felt the band had played a bad gig. The political repercussions of all this were dreadful. The immediate emotional repercussions were worse. With the *LA Times* tracking Perrin down to his hotel to get the full story, and KRock FM running "Mission Up-Dates" with the hourly News Bulletin, the band launched into a massive binge as the only way they could see to shut out the catastrophic events. It was not a good policy. The police were tipped off that Hussey was with an under-age girl – he was, but not the under-age girl the police were told about. So after all that had happened that day they were then raided at five o'clock in the morning by the local force. The police charged into the room and caught hold of Hussey, scaring the girl who started crying. Hussey moved to comfort her but the policeman flew at him and pinned his arms behind his back, face pushed hard against the wall. Pulling out a pair of handcuffs he slapped them around the singer's wrists and whispered into his ear "You're going to get at least a year for this". Meanwhile, the father who had tipped the police off had come to the hotel and found his daughter asleep in a car outside – after prolonged discussions Hussey was released but the whole entourage was immediately ejected from this hotel as well. So Perrin found himself at 5 in the morning trying to flag down cabs to take him and the mountain of luggage to a new hotel, but it was too late. Word had spread around town and The Mission were not welcome anywhere.

With the band in shreds, Adams back in Leeds and the whole crew reeling from the catastrophic events of that day, the survival of The Mission was in serious doubt. Shortly afterwards when asked about the lifestyle that had precipitated Adams' breakdown Hussey said: "Many people we knew of didn't survive. That was a big thing that was frightening me, but I didn't really care. I think to a large extent we were on a death trip – we were just going to blow up or burn out . . ."

Rock of Ages

Laura Lee Davies

Time Out, 12 October 1994.

Nick Mason, Pink Floyd's reserved, greying drummer is sitting on the sofa in the lounge of his extremely civilised hotel suite talking about "very aged bands".

That's a bit rich, you might think, coming from someone who keeps time for a band who have been making music since the '60s first started to swing. For a band who, when they wrote "Shine On You Crazy Diamond", must've sent the price of shares in lighter fuel rocketing. For a band who put a prism on the cover of one of their albums and called it *Dark Side Of The Moon*. Sure, it *was* 1973, but they still talk about it and even *play* it . . . for a band who wrote songs about how awful school is 15 years after they first started the group.

Okay, so Pink Floyd aren't S*M*A*S*H or Manic Street Preachers: they were too old to surf the first wave of new wave, let alone the *new* wave of new wave: and they're not likely to be following L7's stripteasing footsteps on "The Word." But give Nick Mason a break, I think he's at least *half* referring to Pink Floyd too. However, he's making no apologies for the fact that they still sound the same after all these crazy years.

"Whether you're the Who, the Rolling Stones or Take That, basically, once you get into it, you inevitably produce what you sound like without any conscious decision. There's never any 'Does this sound like Pink Floyd? Oh my *God* it sounds like Deep Purple, what are we going to do?' The other thing to bear in mind is that records, especially with these very aged bands we have now, is that even when they think they're being radical, everyone's narrowing down their focus, and what was radical in 1967 is now far less broad."

It's been a long time since "radical" has been a word that people might associate with Pink Floyd. Even before they were drawling "all in all you're just *uh*-nother brick in the wall" Pink Floyd had become the epitome of dinosaur rock, along with all the other daddies who couldn't get their act together in punk's savagely brief time-limit. It didn't stop "The Wall" album and tour selling by the schoolbus-load though, and Pink Floyd albums, despite the lack of former principal songwriter Roger Waters' presence these days, can still shift millions worldwide. Sniff if you will at 11 million fans still willing to buy records called *A Momen tary Lapse Of Reason* and *Delicate Sound Of Thunder* and 14 sell-out nights at Earls Court exhibition centre this month. Resist if you dare the fact that Pink Floyd are HIP AGAIN.

And here's the proof: most of the capacity crowd at a disused film lot on the outskirts of Rome are under 25. What's more, the hippiest trance-inducing dance clubs in London would give their clapped-out smoke machines to have a sound system and a lighting rig like this. Yes, indeed, the musical world has finally caught up with Pink Floyd; hush your mouth if you dare suggest that the best bits of their latest album, *The Division Bell* sound like The Orb; remember where you heard those weird ambient noises first.

Having already sent three million Americans into spin since spring, Pink Floyd are finally catching sight of their tour's London finale as they polish off Europe. Plotting a route which ensured that their films, lights and special effects would be seen in a sufficiently darkened evening sky as they travelled the time-zones, Nick Mason, Rick Wright and Dave Gilmour have trotted across the world with three stage sets, lasers borrowed from the American armed forces, 49 trucks full of rig and 200 backstage staff. In Rome alone they have booked, over five days, the equivalent of 400 nights for crew and guests at a five star hotel, and they all seem to be taking it in their stride. I guess after 30 years doing the experimental rock thing, there's not much to faze you.

"I probably do all this for exactly the same reasons as when I started: essentially I wished to show off in a rather discreet way," Mason laughs. "I still get excited when we're planning and doing the shows. Obviously there are elements of what drove one initially which have disappeared. One wanted to be a proper rock star – have the money and all the rest of it. I still have no regrets about the money, but I no longer wish to be a true pop star, I don't want to be a personality. I've seen that and I realise how lucky I am."

Indeed. They may have sold over 140 million albums and produced, in *Dark Side Of The Moon*, the third biggest-selling album of all time, but when Mason, Wright and Gilmour aren't on stage, they look more like band managers than band members. In fact even *on* stage there is not much more to them than an array of jeans and equipment.

"It probably has been easier for us to stay sane," admits keyboard player Rick Wright. "Pink Floyd is such a huge, big thing, the biggest selling tour at the moment. But there isn't any hysteria when the fans meet us because when people think of Pink Floyd they think of the music, *then* the visuals, *then* us perhaps third. If you think about the Stones, you might think of Mick Jagger, then the songs. . . well, sorry Keith! If you're selling yourself, it's easy to let the person on stage become something other than the person on stage. It's easier to get confused. We don't have that. We're normal, straight, middle-class guys. The madness will not come from what we do as Pink Floyd, it'll come from our private lives."

Of course it's not as if Pink Floyd's history has been without its excesses. Dave Gilmour joined the band in '68, when Syd Barrett's unsociable behaviour became a logistical nightmare. Syd's brief reappearance during the making of *Wish You Were Here* is one of the reasons the album remains a favourite with the rest of the band, but by the early '80s, the band was falling apart again. *The Final Cut* was made almost entirely by Roger Waters, with Rick Wright only employed as a session musician. When lyricist Waters split from the band in '85, Gilmour and Mason decided they would carry on. *A Momentary Lapse Of Reason* which was made almost entirely by Dave Gilmour with help from Nick Mason, was produced amid bitter legal wrangles with Waters over a band name which Syd had originally come up with. With Wright returning as a band member, this year's *The Division Bell* is the first Pink Floyd album in many years written, rehearsed and recorded as a band. Someone was overheard referring to the inflatable tour pigs as Roger and Syd.

While all three remaining Floyders admit things aren't the same without Waters, they also agree that continuing *with* him would have been impossible. Traditionally, the more real a band seem – sweating and grinding through their gigs and their videos – the more authentic and enduring they appear. If Pink Floyd had been more famous for their frontmen than their spacey guitar noises and lonely, ambient rock, they wouldn't have made it into their fourth decade. So no, you won't see Dave Gilmour giving it the "Good evening Rome" treatment.

"Oh, I'm not very good at all that – my Italian's pretty bad and I'm not a very good dancer either," beams a distinctly chipper Gilmour backstage. Despite the sharp glint in his eye which betrays a glimmer of the rock life, he looks no more suited to stadium gigging than the other two. "I have no desire to be an iconic character like Rod Stewart, who seems to me just as much a victim of his own image as he is a success because of it. We're not hiding from being personalities, but we're not that good at it and it doesn't seem terribly important to chase after it. I'd rather let the music speak for itself."

"Luckily we're not expected to provide views of our lovely mop-tops while we're stage," adds Mason, referring to the band's decision not to use the giant video screens which are such a regular feature of rock stadium concerts. Instead, props crash and catch fire, film projections and lasers shoot across the stage, expensive thingies inflate, explode and sparkle. This is what really goes on in the mind of every would-be guitarist when they're standing in a shop in Denmark Street, trying out a guitar they can't afford.

"There's an awful lot of garbage talked about our show being over the top, the figures spent on this, that and the other," shrugs

Gilmour. "But we just try to do it as well as it can be done, given our own abilities. I don't really think what we're aiming for is innovation at the cost of emotion and beauty. In our early days we went for innovation," he smiles. "When I listen to old bootleg gig tapes I think, '*Oh God*'. I'm 48 years old, I don't want to be *quite* that innovative any more! I want it to turn me on. If that makes people think we play it safe, then so be it. In the early days, there was an awful lot of dross among the good stuff, in searching out the highs, we certainly went through some lows, and these days I'd rather avoid them."

With a backstage set up the size of a small Berkshire village, a three-tier mixing desk with room for 30 seated guests and a set-list which is so precisely programmed with the lighting arrangement that sets, songs and even solos can be lengthened or shortened at a moment's notice, Pink Floyd are staging the most extravagant, but also the most flexible and "spontaneous" live show on the move. One song into their set, their press officer, who has already seen the show five times, starts to point out places where they have changed the order of the show. When I tell Mason that by half time (in what turns out to be a permutation of the "Dark Side" option) she told us to forget every thing she had told us on the way to the gig, his chest visibly puffs up with pride. "There's a prevalent view that there's no soul, no heart in Pink Floyd because it's about technology and machinery. I disagree, it's about the music being played. If you're doing a stadium show, you know you've lost the plot if you can see people playing frisbee at the back. We do a lot to surround the audience, to draw them back in. People ask why we don't wanna play in a club," he laughs. "We can do that if we want, but very few people are in the position we're in to do *exactly* what we like. I'd rather keep this band doing what it does particularly well than try to be a blues band at the Marquee."

Rick Wright confesses that, even 120-plus dates into the tour, they still can't agree on which song should kick the show off. "Dave wants to do 'Shine On You Crazy Diamond' first. I disagree, so does the rest of the band and the rest of the planet, basically. So we swap around." While rare shots of the band are being taken, another set-list argument breaks out. But there is little in the way of serious, fret-board snapping tempers being mislaid. For the main part, Pink Floyd are, five months into a non-stop tour, a fairly happy camp. In the hotel foyer, only the occasional ashen-faced hang over-sufferer loiters in the shadow while tour crew, company reps, parents and friends gather each morning to roam around Rome, each evening to get the guest bus to the gig, and each night to celebrate the good health of the show until the bar closes at a sober 2 a.m. With wives and sometimes even kids around, there is less display of rock 'n' roll's higher spirits around the band as there is between the courtesy bus drivers and the darevil local traffic police who escort the Floyd entourage everywhere.

"Generally there are no rules like some bands have about no women and children," explains Mason. "though we don't want to be the Grateful Dead going out with a whole tribe, we have a happy medium. But what I would like is to tour for shorter periods. Between the last tour and this one, I've had two more kids and home life is more important to me. It'd be nice to work for two months and then to go off, but once the stuff is built and you've taken on a crew, every day you're not working, there's a crew sitting in a hotel somewhere – 200 of them all having breakfast, ha ha! you can't let that go on for three months while we all stay home watching television."

Although Gilmour, Mason and Wright aren't yet in need of monthly rest and bathchairs, there are, of course, many who would still regard them as the essence of creaky old rockdom. "That's all bullshit," Wright replies bluntly. "To all those people, I'd say go ahead and write music that proves you're right, that we *are* boring old farts. Do something better. Fine, I'd love to hear it."

"I think most of the other old bands should split up because they're too old, but I don't think we should," giggles Gilmour more lightheartedly. "It's not the way the world works. When we're obsolete, we'll be told by the people who buy our records and come to our concerts. I suppose I ought to be surprised by our popularity 30 years on, but I'm not. *My* children listen to the

old albums and get turned on by them. I can understand younger
people discovering *Dark Side Of The Moon* and *Wish You Were
Here* and recognising the value in them compared to a lot of what
I hear coming out today." As for the ambient, dance-orientated
scene in which the likes of Alex Paterson's Orb have often been
cited as working under the influence of Floyd, Gilmour apol-
ogetically admits that he's not much into dance music, although
he like some of the ideas which float around before the "clanking
beats" begin.

Despite opening with "Shine On You Crazy Diamond" (Gilmour clearly has a gift for picking heads or tails), the lighters take
a while to come out tonight. Instead, the Italians put Pink Floyd
to shame, coming in with the words to their favourite songs in
better time than the band. From the stage, the gathered throng
appears as little more than tiny pink specks, but there is something extremely intimate about the evening, perhaps because
everyone is staring at the shimmering effects and drifting off
with a hazy memory of the first time they listened to Pink Floyd
in their own bedrooms.

"I think we mean different things to different people," says
Mason. "Some people take it desperately seriously. Others come
for the fabulous view. Then some do a joint and think 'Wow!'.
Perhaps our success is down to being a sufficient abstraction that
we are all these things to all these people. It's not as specific as
being Metallica and having to wear those very tight trousers.
Now that *would* be difficult . . ."

Hound Dog Taylor

Bruce Iglauer

They ran on equal parts of brotherly love, vicious adolescent rivalry and Canadian Club. For over ten years Hound Dog Taylor and the HouseRockers made joyous music together five or six nights a week, first in the tiny taverns that dot Chicago's South Side ghetto, later in clubs, colleges and concert halls literally around the world.

They were quite a sight on the bandstand. Hound Dog perched on his folding chair, stomping both feet to keep time, grinning his millions-of-teeth grin, pausing between songs only long enough to light up a Pall Mall and tell a totally incomprehensible joke (which he'd interrupt halfway through, cackling with laughter and burying his face in his hand) before tearing into another no holds-barred boogie. Phillips (no one ever called him Brewer) with his broken teeth and crooked smile, dancing in the aisles, his vintage Fender Telecaster strung around his neck like some giant pendant, his shirt tail hanging out, kicking his leg in the air as he squeezed out a high note, occasionally grabbing the mike to sing in a voice as battered as his guitar. Ted Harvey, his hair clipped tight to his head, yelling out encouragement from behind his minimal drum set, chomping out the rhythm on the wad of gum in his mouth, sometimes drifting off to sleep without ever missing a beat, until Phillips would sneak up behind him in mid-song and wake him with a slap across the back of the head.

They were inseparable, and they played together like brothers, sensing each other's twists and turns before they happened, feeding energy and good spirits from one to the other. They fought like brothers, too, as they criss-crossed the country from gig to gig in Hound Dog's old Ford station wagon, arguing constantly about who was the best lover, who had the best woman, who was the best mayor Chicago ever had, who was or wasn't out of tune the night before. The arguments weren't always in fun either. From time to time a knife appeared, and finally even a gun.

They made a lot of noise for three with two guitars and a drum set. Between the incredible distortion from Hound Dog's super-cheap Japanese guitar, the sustain from his brass-lined steel slide (made from the leg of a kitchen chair), the sheet metal tone of Phillips' ancient Fender, their cracked-speaker amplifiers, and Ted's simple, kickass drumming, they could indeed rock the house.

They played amazingly long sets, two or three hours of driving boogies and shuffles mixed with the occasional slow blues. It was music born in the Deep South juke joints, when electric guitars were still something new and bass guitars were unheard, of music for all-night dancing and partying. The purists called them a blues band, but Hound Dog called it rock and roll.

Hound Dog was already playing guitar and piano when he came to Chicago from Mississippi in 1942 at the age of 27. (He used to haul an upright piano to Delta fish fries on a mule drawn wagon). But he was strictly an amateur musician. He moved in with his sister Lucy in the neighbourhood around 39th and Indiana in the heart of the ghetto, a neighourhood he lived in for the rest of his life. He found a day job as a short order cook, and on Sunday morning he played for tips at the Maxwell Street open-air market, competing for attention with unknowns like Muddy Waters and Robert Nighthawk.

It wasn't until 1975, when Hound Dog lost his last job building TV cabinets, that he began trying to make his living as a musician. He played with almost every guitarist and drummer in the city until he chose a construction worker named Phillips in 1959 and a shipping clerk named Ted in 1965 as the official HouseRockers.

By pricing his band lower than any other on the South Side (when I met them in 1970, the whole band was making $45 a night), Hound Dog was able to get gigs at taverns that usually couldn't afford a band. And by pumping out non-stop music and clowning, he drew one of the most loyal crowds in town. Hound Dog and the HouseRockers played some of the seediest clubs in Chicago, clubs that held fifty or a hundred people (who were usually dancing frantically in the aisles), clubs that didn't even have a bandstand, just a space cleared of tables where the band could squeeze in. Their favourite gig was the Sunday afternoon jam at Florence's at 54th Place and Shields, a gig they held for over ten years. On Sundays at Florence's you were likely to run into Big Walter Horton, Magic Slim, Carey Bell, Lefty Dizz, Son Seals, Lee Jackson, Big Moose Walker, Lonnie Brooks, Left Hand Frank, or Johnny Embury, all waiting to sit in with Hound Dog.

When Wes Race and I recorded them, we did our best to create the atmosphere of one of those club gigs in the sterile environment of Sound Studios. We couldn't bring in all their friends and fans, but we did bring in the same battered amps, cranked them up to the same maximum volume, poured the whiskey, and the band cut the same songs they played every Sunday at Florence's. Because they wouldn't rehearse and hated to play the same song twice, we cut albums in two nights, recording twenty songs a night and choosing among the best takes for the albums. We cut "Hound Dog Taylor and the HouseRockers" in 1971 and "Natural Boogie" in 1973, and the songs on "Genuine Houserocking Music" were recorded and mixed at the same sessions.

After the release of their first album, their three lives changed dramatically. They went on the road, first to Midwest clubs, then to New England colleges, then to New York concert halls, and finally even to Australia and New Zealand. They established fanatical followings in college-town clubs like the Kove in Kent, Ohio and Joe's Place in Cambridge (where they often played six nights a week for three weeks straight to packed houses, and unknown acoustic guitarist named George Thorogood opened the shows). They gave three fantastically successful performances at the Ann Arbor Blues Festivals and headlined festivals in Miami, Washington and Buffalo. They played Philharmonic Hall in New York, the Auditorium in Chicago, and literally

hundreds of other gigs around the country. *Rolling Stone* printed
a feature on them. They even appeared on nationwide Canadian
early morning television (where Hound Dog told everyone how
happy he was to be visiting the home of Canadian Club).

When I think back on the four years I managed, booked,
recorded, drove and carried equipment for Hound Dog Taylor
and the HouseRockers, dozens of incidents crowd into my mind:

- Hound Dog shaking the sleeping Ted Harvey after seven or
  eight hundred miles on the road, and commanding him to 'wake
  up and argue!'
- The delight of the band in locating a Kentucky Fried Chicken
  outlet in Melbourne, after they had decided they were going to
  starve to death rather than eat Australian food.
- A late night slide-guitar duel to the death with JB Hutto at
  Alice's Revisited in Chicago, with no clear-cut winner.
- Hound Dog's pride at being introduced by BB King to the
  audience at the posh London House night club.
- Ted falling asleep in a huge shipping carton backstage before a
  crucial concert and being found only seconds before showtime.
- Hound Dog sitting up all night in a Toronto hotel room with
  the lights, TV and radio on, because he was afraid to go to sleep
  and have another one of his dreams about being chased by
  wolves.
- Phillips stepping in to save me from a knife wielding drunk
  outside of Florence's.
- And Hound Dog, dying in his hospital bed, desperately hanging on to life until Phillips finally relented and came to visit him
  and put to rest their most serious (and violent) argument.
  Brothers indeed.

Hound Dog died on December 17, 1975.

Phillips and Ted still live in the same building on the South
Side (though they are usually feuding and don't speak very much
. . . just like a lot of good friends). Ted regularly plays with
Jimmy Rogers and has become sort of the dean of old style blues

drummers in town, since the deaths of Odie Payne and Fred Below and the virtual retirement of SP Leary. Phillips still sits in now and then, and recently toured Sweden as guest of the Hjalmar Kings – a sort of Hound Dog tribute band (pretty good, too). I don't think they visit Hound Dog's widow Freda very much these days, but I stay in touch with her, and (of course) she gets his royalties.

When they do speak, Phillips and Ted talk about Hound Dog and his music, as do thousands of fans. But Hound Dog said it best himself – "When I die, they'll say, he couldn't play shit, but he sure made it sound good!"

KLF: There's No Success like Failure

Stewart Home

It began with a phone call from a publicist who asked if I'd like an all expenses paid helicopter trip across Dartmoor to witness former KLF star Jimmy Cauty demonstrate his sonic gun. Next came a press release which promised that the formidable and highly dangerous Saracen Armoured Personnel Carrier Audio Weapons System would transmit sonic frequencies and run down photographers for my amusement. The press statement was accompanied by sixteen pages of recent cuttings detailing the deadly effect Cauty's "noise tank" had on cattle when he demonstrated the weapon for the amusement of a few friends.

From the start, I suspected something dodgy was going on. Cauty built his career in the music industry on the back of stunts and scams. The first KLF album *1987* received rave reviews, but the record was soon suppressed by lawyers acting for ABBA who objected to the heavy sampling of their hit single 'Dancing Queen'. Drummond and Cauty milked the legal proceedings for press coverage, then released a new version of the LP with all samples removed and detailed instructions on how to recreate the original sound. Later scams included dumping a dead sheep outside the Brit Awards ceremony at which they were named Best British Group. Shortly after this, the KLF announced that they would not be releasing any new material in the foreseeable future and that their entire back catalogue was deleted.

Having relaunched themselves as the K Foundation, Cauty and Drummond turned up at the 1993 Turner Prize to humiliate winner Rachel Whiteread with a forty thousand pound award for being the world's worst artist. This was followed by a controversial trip to Scotland, during the course of which the duo burnt One Million Pounds. In November 1995, they selected the *Workshop For A Non-Linear Architecture Bulletin* to announce a twenty-three year moratorium on K Foundation activities. This privately circulated newsletter is so obscure that news of the moratorium is only just beginning to seep through to the general public.

While Bill Drummond is currently collaborating with former rocker Zodiac Mindwrap on a series of novels, Cauty is pursuing various solo projects, including an album of his sonic experiments for release on Blast First Records. After my initial dealings with this outfit, I was more that a little perplexed when further details of the Dartmoor trip were faxed to me by a PR company working on behalf of the band Black Star Liner. Having made it as far as one of fifty block-booked seats on a Devon bound train, I was presented with a set of ear plugs and a personal safety waiver to sign. Since most of those present were acting as though they were on some Boy's Own Adventure, I moved along to the next carriage where I was able to relax. After working out that I'd switched seats, publicists began dropping by to ply me with drinks and plug Black Star Liner, who were performing after Cauty had demonstrated his noise tank.

By the time we boarded a helicopter at Exeter airport, the majority of journalists present were at least mildly drunk. Then, after a twenty minute chopper ride, disaster struck. The pilot announced that we couldn't land because a mist had swept across the moor. Instead, we returned to Exeter airport where we were told a coach would pick us up and transport us to the acoustic weapons test site. After an hour of waiting, the PR people were going crazy. Meanwhile, an assortment of journalists and photographers were having luggage cart races around an otherwise deserted passenger concourse. The airport had closed down for the night, until one of our party succeeded activating the public address system and went into pirate DJ mode.

A security guard appeared and attempted to restore order when a bored music journalist switched on a luggage conveyer and one of his friends disappeared down it. Finally, a fleet of cabs conveyed us to the Latern Inn at Ashburton. We'd already missed Black Star Liner. The free bar only mildly improved the gloomy atmosphere that hung over the event. To make us feel better, every journalist present was promised an interview with Jimmy Cauty. We had to go through to another room and talk to Jimmy one at a time. First up was Tony from *i-D,* who came back quietly complaining that all he got was some incoherent babble about drugs.

When my turn came, I began by asking about the burning of the million quid. Jimmy flatly refused to talk about the K Foundation. Next, I asked Cauty if he was up on the latest research into frequency weapons, which got a much better response. "I know very little about military research into the uses of low frequency sound as weapons. All this stuff about Advanced Acoustic Armaments is a joke, all I've done is mounted some disco gear onto my two Saracen tanks. Everything the press has written about the sonic guns I'm supposed to have built is just rubbish, the papers want to believe this stuff which is why they are so easy to hoax."

"The event cost fifty thousand pounds to put on," Cauty cackled after I told him about the debacle at Exeter airport, "and I'm really pleased with it. What happened at the airport was as much a part of the entertainment as what I did up on the moor. I'd intended to detain everyone up there, the fog coming down was a real stroke of luck. The performance was sponsored by Black Bin Liner and their record company because they thought they'd gain some radical credibility from the stunt. It might have blown up on the band, but it will still get their name around. After all, they've just played the most expensive pub rock gig ever!"

So there you have it. Jimmy Cauty the side-splitting avant-garde manipulator of the art of hype, who leaves journalists and PR people trapped in a web of their own making. Or, Jimmy Cauty the pop star whose promotional stunts end in fiasco? The choice is yours. In a knowing post-modern sort of way, I think it's bese to accept both versions of Cauty as true.

Charlie and the Music Factory

Peter Paphides

Time Out, 29 October 1997.

Heroin screws you up. But if you're member of a high-flying rock band, nothing really buggers up an album quite like cocaine – ask almost every rock star who's ever set foot in a studio.

> "Does anyone know where Charlie is, because everyone backstage is asking for him . . ."
>
> Mrs Merton, Brit Awards 1997

> "Now the drugs don't work, they just make you worse . . ."
> from "The Drugs Don't Work" by The Verve

Richard Ashcroft may speak from bitter experience, but for the industry execs laughing knowingly at Mrs Merton's on-stage quip last March, the drugs are working just fine thanks. To say that cocaine is back in the music industry would be to imply that it had ever been away. And yet, as recently as five years ago, the Mrs Merton joke would have seemed inappropriate in an environment where such habits were being conducted furtively. In the aftermath of post-Britpop prosperity and Spice mania though, everyone felt they *deserved* to be off their tits. When business is booming, the music industry does like to congratulate itself. And why shouldn't it? After all, coke is a social drug. And in the nocturnal haze of after-show parties, album playbacks and endless schmoozing, coke allows you to be sociable. "That's exactly it," concurs one press officer at one of Britain's best-known music PRs. "It's just a laugh, you know? You share it with your friends, you all get into the same cubicle and people are impatiently kicking the door. And everyone goes, 'Are you all right?' and you just *laugh*. Everything's funny on coke."

"I'd agree in as much as there's a functional use for coke that might serve the needs of the music industry," says Mick Houghton, PR to Julian Cope, Elastica, Spiritualized and Echo And The Bunnymen. However, having seen many careers threatened by the drug – his own included – Houghton's feelings are mixed: "I think its nullifying effects are its very allure. Especially if you're an artist. Most of the time, being in a band is so boring. And it's not like working at a record company, where you have to function in the office the next morning. Being on tour or in the studio is mainly just waiting around, either to go on stage or for the engineer to finish some fine-tuning. When I started working with Echo And The Bunnymen in the 80s, Mac (Bunnymen singer Ian McCulloch) was pretty anti-drugs, but the thing about coke is that it's there all the time. And really, the moment you get a deal and you realise that you can just phone someone to get you a taxi, that's where the slippery slope begins. You've entered a world where actions have no consequences and someone will always clean up the mess. Consequently, it takes a strong will to say no. Especially when someone else will always get the drug for you."

Simon Raymonde, who has just taken a break from The Cocteau Twins to release an excellent solo album, echoes those sentiments: "It's one thing to be anti-drugs, but the moment you're in a band, it counts for nothing. The reason you take it is that you run out of ways of saying no. And also, you think people won't like you if you don't take it."

Does that seem like a cop-out? Imagine being in a band. *Really* imagine it: three months at a time away from your loved ones; ten hours on a coach from Washington to Buffalo, trying to while away the hours; the pressure of knowing you're only as good as your last album. How would *you* get through? We all saw how Oasis imploded on that aborted American tour last year. But in truth, their legendary cocaine intake – often blamed as the cause of earlier Gallagher spats – was probably what kept them going through so many previous US tours. Coke, you see is second only to sleep for making the hours fly. If there are interviews to do, it'll keep the quotes coming. And it will also help maintain post-gig adrenalin levels. Record and management companies don't just keep coke available for themselves. It's even better for appeasing bands. Take, for instance, the tale of the young band whose breakthough hit a couple of years ago launched a world tour. It was midway through that tour that their manager noticed them falling asleep on stage and introduced them to the wonders of coke as pop Pro-Plus.

As with most drugs, though, prolonged use can distort your judgement. Tales that emerged from the end of that Oasis tour display all the hall-marks of over-indulgence: mood swings; aggression; paranoia; the sense that everything is futile. One fan even alleged that after a Philadelphia show, Liam confessed, "I love Noel, but he hates me. Maybe if I was dead he'd be happy." However, when she suggested they talk it over, Liam snapped, "Fuck you. I'm not leaving". Judgement, however, is something you can manage *without* as long as you're on the road. In recording studio though, it's crucial. "Coke isn't a creative drug," concurs Houghton, "Smack and acid, dope even, are all better for creativity." Is that because one function of coke is to make you like yourself more? "Well, yes, because you lose the ability to discern. I've had more conversations with bands talking gibberish because they've been taking coke than because of other things. Mac's solo career suffered through that lack of judgement. During that period, his life was dominated by coke and alcohol – those drugs do seem to go hand in hand – and that destroyed his sense of what worked musically. Coke albums are always easy to spot. They're incredibly obvious and ham-fisted, and if there's an idea there, they just can't let it go. They pile more ideas, often the same idea, on top of it."

The grandiose mediocrity of Oasis' *Be Here Now* and The Stone Roses' *Second Coming* bear out Houghton's remarks. On *Be Here Now* potentially good songs succumb to bombastic arrangements, meandering outros and general complacency. As for The Stone Roses' disastrous comeback, guitarist John Squire was swift to admit that the delays in completing *Second Coming* were born of his attempts to use coke as a creative drug. Is it possible to make a decent coke album? Well, yes. As long, that is, as artifice and paranoia are the very things you want to make your subject. Hence Bowie's *Berlin* period in the late '70s. For the same reason, first impressions also indicate that Suede pulled it off with *Dog Man Star*. When used about the genesis of "We Are The Pigs", Brett Anderson explained. "I was imagining all these masked gangs smashing through my windows. It's partly paranoia due to taking too much coke. If you're taking coke all night and it gets to 12 o'clock next day, you're paranoid as fuck and imagining a load of big-booted policemen with riot shields smashing your door down.' But Brett has made no secret of the fact that other drugs were involved in the making of *Dog Man Star*: 'At the end of the day, if you take too much cocaine, you become a cabbage . . . sitting indoors and having sex all the time because that's the only thing cocaine is good for."

"In a way", says Houghton, "I think coke's worse than heroin. Heroin kills you whereas cocaine destroys you. People usually kick smack before it kills them so their careers might at least remain intact. You can't say that about coke." Given the unanimity that coke is so detrimental to creativity, it seems bizarre that so many bands (more than we could name here) have succumbed to it.

Flick through most discerning record collections, from The Beatles through Coltrane, the Stones, Spiritualized and Lou Reed, you'll see that heroin has contributed much more to the pantheon of great pop. "There's actually more mileage in any other drugs, be it pain killers, alcohol or whatever," avers Radiohead's Thom Yorke. "The only people I've seen doing it are the dullest fucking people on earth. Have you read *Less Than Zero?* I mean how fucking dull can you get?"

So one can safely assume that "OK Computer" relied on less pernicious sources of inspiration?

"Well, I've never taken it if that's what you mean. I don't agree with taking any drug that people are being shot and killed for. I can understand why people might do it – I'm not assuming the moral high ground – but . . . erm, to me, it seems to make people very boring. And it's a really vulgar, ugly, ugly, ugly, *ugly* drug. For me, it twigged permanently after I read a piece in last month's *Elle* about 'the new debauchery', which confirmed everything I've ever suspected about coke. It was the worst piece of journalism I've ever read."

The piece in question, by Harvey Marcus, does at least manage to capture something of the post-Oasis air of chemical triumphalism so prevalent at those Brit Awards. Spuriously splicing together examples of recent trends in cinema, fashion and pop in order to create a thesis, Marcus concludes: "New Debauchery is all about freedom of expression, however constructive or destructive that might be. Vulgarity, excess, luxurious thoughts, high hopes, it's about all those things we've learned to feel guilty about but needn't any more."

All this new debauchery though, only works if you're not actually the artist. Media types and industry execs can snort themselves into their own rectums and still hold down their jobs. Bands, though, need to connect with their public in some meaningful way. If they don't they jeopardise their careers. Whither the new debauchery in the testimony of Cocteau Twins' guitarist Robin Guthrie? "We started doing it in 1988, I think around the time of *Blue Bell Knoll*," he recalls. "By the time I wanted to stop, everything in my life was based around getting drugs. Music was a by-product, something I did because I was too wired to go home. So I'd stay in the studio for five days. It was worse than death. With death you can switch off. I thought parenthood might straighten me out," continues Guthrie, "but I was dealing with a more powerful force. That's where you realise – when you're sitting bollock naked in your living room at 6 a.m. in the middle of winter with all the windows open, and this little girl comes in and says, 'Dad, are you all right?'"

Coke signals
The rich and famous on powdering their noses.

"If someone's doing coke I can taste it in the back of my throat" *Elton John on a craving that continues seven years after he gave up the drug.*

"By the time I was 23 I was addicted, but it didn't seem to matter in our business. No one thought it was unusual to be up all night doing lines of coke" *Alan McGee, Creation boss*

"I did like cocaine . . . but it would dress you up for a party and never take you there" *George Clooney on why he gave up using*

"Yeah, I liked the high of cocaine. But I was never addicted because I knew it could kill me. You could not do high-level work and be doing coke. No way. You just don't have the energy" *Richard Gere*

"For the successful model, drugs serve different purposes. I remember I'd often be up at 6 a.m. shooting until 4 a.m. the next day and then having to be on a plane. I was so exhausted one day when I was due to go from France to Dusseldorf that I said to the agent: 'I can't go.' He said: 'I'll give you something to keep you awake.' It was cocaine. I was 20, quite old by industry standards. Usually, someone will start a girl on drugs much younger. The drugs help her to work because they make her feel powerful and beautiful. And if she has to get an advance from her agent to buy them, they charge interest in the form of a 10 per cent commission on her earnings.

"It is true that until they destroy a girl's looks, some drugs make you look wonderful. Cocaine was a drug of choice when I was a top model because it shrinks the blood supply to the eyes and makes them look bright. Apart from one agent who finally helped me go to rehab no one lifted a finger to get a girl off drugs, even when it was obvious she was killing herself. I saw one girl's nose pour blood and she was rushed off to hospital.

Her nose had collapsed because of all the cocaine *Paula Hamilton, former mode and ex-addict*

"There's a fucking blizzard of cocaine in London at the moment and I hate it. It's stupid. Everyone's become so blase thinking they're so ironic and witty and wandering around with this stupid fucking cokey confidence. Wankers. I did it, but I can't say I was a cocaine addict" *Damon Albarn (March 1996)*

"Coke is God's way of telling you you've got too much money" *Sting*

"You get up in the morning, surrounded by empty bottles, and the mirror's covered in smears of cocaine, and the first thing you do is lick the mirror" *Elton John on his wild years*

"I take cocaine. Big fucking deal. It's a social thing and I've been doing it since before I was even in a band" *Noel Gallagher*

"I took cocaine once in my life at Edinburgh and I told this to the *Face* magazine. The next thing, it's there on page three next to the girl's knockers: 'My drug hell – Steve Coogan tells how he came close to death from cocaine addiction' *Steve Coogan on tabloid distortion of his drug use*

"Some of them were very good drugs. They work for the moment. I hear even some extroverts like them. All my heroes are drug addicts so it was very easy for me. Saying 'I'm an artist' is a great device when you are in total denial. You say let's talk about Baudelaire, Henry Miller, WC Fields, John Barrymore, blah, blah, blah. But all these people ended up rather tragically. Drugs work for a while and then they don't work any more" *Ex-addict Dennis Hopper who at his peak, would get through three grams of coke a day*

"It was a nightmare time because cocaine is a very spiteful bedfellow. And it really takes it out of you. If you want to lose

all the friends and relationships you ever held dear that's the drug
to do it with. Cocaine severs any link you have with another
human. That's the one thing that really came home to me in the
mid-70s – what I was doing to all my relationships. I didn't have
anyone left who could get anywhere near me.

"Maintaining is the problem. You retain a superficial hold on
reality so that you can get through the things that are absolutely
necessary for your survival. But when that starts to break up,
which inevitably it does – around late 1975 everything was
starting to break up – I would work at songs for hours and hours
and days and days and then realise after a few days that I had done
absolutely nothing. I thought I had been working and working
but I had only been rewriting the first four bars or something.

"[They call it punding.] That's right! Punding! Going back to
the start, over and over again like these poor rats that get fucked
up in experiments. I saw something on CNN where they showed
the effects of cocaine on the human brain. The great physical
holes that cocaine puts in the brain. It just looks like Swiss
cheese. And I have been tempted to go and have my brain looked
at to see how many holes I have. Because they are there for life"
David Bowie to Tony Parsons, on his Thin White Duke years

"Better than gold"
*Millionaire car manufacturer John De Lorean, secretly filmed
making a toast to the cocaine he had unwittingly just sold to FBI
agents*

The Death of Michael Hutchence

Mike Gee

Fame is vapour
Popularity is an accident
And the only earthly certainty is oblivion
Mark Twain

When Vincent Crane of Atomic Rooster sang "Death walks behind you" he didn't know how right he was or how close it was. On February 20, 1989, suffering from recurring depression, Crane committed suicide, a largely forgotten lead singer of an early Seventies spook rock trio that had two hits, 'The Devil's Answer' and 'Tomorrow Night', and three reasonable albums and actually lasted into the Eighties on the back of numerous line-up changes with Crane the only constant. But they were lean, uncelebrated years and nothing Vincent did would bring him close to the original Rooster, not even the presence of Pink Floyd's Dave Gilmour on their final *Headline News*. He ended up guesting with Dexy's Midnight Runners in 1985 and writing some songs for Kim Wilde before taking his final bow. Vincent wasn't wrong – death does walk behind you. And just like love, death is all around you. Death accumulates, never goes away. Learning to live with death is a lesson life itself.

Saturday, November 22, 1997, was another warm Sydney day in a series of warm days that seemed to have begun the summer before the calendar gave it the official nod. But it was a day that hadn't felt right since the moment of waking at about 11 am. Some days are like that: they are out of balance, crotchety, edgy,

wrong – they say hello with a twitch and nagging and a gut sense
of wonk. Wendy (girlfriend, writer, bookworm, sometimes
photographer) and I spoke of it over what constitutes breakfast
on our world time clock. The answer to wonk is – more often than
not – go out and spend money, especially money you can't afford
to spend.

Phantom Records in Pitt Street is part of Sydney and, indeed,
Australian music history. In 1980 Phantom Records was born on
the back of its owners' desire to release music they liked: that it
became a major independent force they never considered. Today,
it still seems to work that same simple philosophy. The store is
small, snuffly, full of smatterings of taste and obscurity. Nosing, I
found three or four CDs that would start the hunt perfectly.
Peculiarly, when I went to buy them, the disc for one was in a
locked drawer. This meant finding a key which turned out to be
with the manager (I think) who was upstairs. And took several
minutes to come downstairs.

The drawer was unlocked, the disc located, when the man with
the key suddenly spread his arms, looked at us and said, "You
heard it first at Phantom. Michael Hutchence is dead." A lot of
stuff can pass through the mind in an instant: I just felt dizzy and
hot and tried to look cool. "The stupid bastard comes back to
Australia just to fucking kill himself on some bad . . ." I missed
the last word completely. "It was on the radio just now. They've
taken a body from the Ritz Carlton Hotel and while it hasn't been
officially identified, it's him. He's dead. How fucking stupid." I
picked up the CDs, I can't even remember what they were now,
negotiated the door and steps and attempted to walk straight. You
don't expect to be standing in a record store idly wasting money
and contemplating wasting even more, only to be assaulted with
the news that somebody you have known in a small-but-big way
and were expecting to see in concert a few days later is dead.

There are several very good secondhand stores further down
Pitt Street where collectors trawl the vinyl and CDs, the smell of
the possessed upon them and a certain madness in their eyes.
Wendy discovered me in one of them about 40 minutes later. She
began speaking and I cut her short, "Michael's dead." "What?

Who?" "Michael Hutchence is dead, maybe a drug overdose."
"No, oh no." She nearly burst into tears. Didn't. Picked her way
through M,N,O and P without seeing one cover and said she
needed coffee.

By 4 p.m. we were in a taxi heading home. The radio news
confirmed – almost immediately – that Michael Hutchence was
dead, and there was a hint of suicide. Michael, suicide? It didn't
make much sense at the time. Michael had never seemed suicidal.
Of all the 'rock' people I'd met Michael seemed one of the least
likely to commit suicide. His beliefs, the books he eschewed, the
philosophies he'd turn to, none of them were those of a potential
suicide. In 1994 he'd said, "There's a lot of seriousness that I
think is totally unwarranted . . . people killing themselves –
literally (the reference was to Cobain) over stuff they shouldn't.
That's sad. Pop eats its young, that's for sure."

Exactly two months short of his 38th birthday, Michael let
something devour him. Or perhaps it had been devouring him for
a while, so maybe it was just finishing him off. Yet, in retrospect,
the signs were there that something was wrong, seriously wrong,
in his life. But we are always wiser with time.

Michael flew into Sydey's Mascot airport at 11 p.m. on Tuesday,
November 18, 1997. He was home. He'd been talking about
coming home for a while. He wanted to bring the family to
Australia and settle here: he also realised that Sir Bob wouldn't
agree to that and that a solution needed to be found.

His last few years had been demanding, erratic, exciting,
testing. He had found his soulmate, become a father, seemingly
survived the worst the paparazzi could throw at him and particularly Paula. Professionally, INXS were back and while not
embraced with the kind of fervour of a decade earlier, at least with
a warmth that was satisfying; they had survived a separation that
had no return date pencilled in when they drifted apart in late '94,
the loss of their manager of 15 years, C.M.Murphy, and personal
dramas within the brotherhood including the break up of Kirk's
17-month-old marriage with Deni Hines, the daughter of Australian music legend Marcia Hines. And Michael had been work-

ing on and off on his debut solo album (news of which at the time
in 1995 was seen by some as a sign that maybe INXS would never
pencil in a return date.)

On Friday, June 9, 1995, somebody within the closed shop that
was MMA leaked the news that Murphy was giving his svengali
role away. It was over. One of the longest and most successful
rock'n'roll marriages ended with a cheap leak to Sydney's street
press that enraged the always emotional Murphy who had intended keeping it secret for several months hence.

On paper it was potentially devastating. Murphy was the
ramrod that pushed INXS into unheard-of zones for an Australian rock band. By using his business brilliance, Murphy built
a platform beneath the sextet that meant they didn't have to look
over their shoulders, worry about whether their business was
being conducted efficiently or whether – as has happened so often
to performers in the past – their assets were being drained by
incompetence and sheer greed. Secure, INXS could concentrate
on what they did best: making records and playing live.

If INXS were shocked by C.M.'s resignation they didn't seem
it and the issue of "what-would-happen-next?" drifted out of the
media as Murphy set about restructuring his business interests,
having decided that now was the time for his family to come first.

Like everything else it seemed to point to the end of old ways. If
INXS were to come back it would definitely be afresh. With
Elegantly Wasted they had begun the process of reshaping. A close
friend of Michael said that he was relieved to be back in Sydney and
positive about the future – despite the perpetual stream of INXS as
iconic has-beens stories that seemed to surface regularly, not to
mention an oft-quoted (in the days after his death) comment what
Michael didn't know where INXS fitted in any longer, which
concerned him, as did the possibility of his own obscurity.

His arrival at Sydney airport was marked by a short and playful
banter with the press who seemed surprised that he actually
stopped to talk to them before heading off to the Ritz Carlton
Hotel in Double Bay where he checked in as "Murray River', a
reasonably straight pseudonym as they go, and moved into the
smallboat harbour-facing room 524.

The Ritz is a high-class elegant mix of old-fashioned furnishings and luxury with plenty of shiny, polished wood and metal and a guest list that would keep celebrity spotters happy for weeks on end. In the past I've shared the lift with former Australian Prime Minister Bob Hawke and his wife Blanche, talked acid daze and halcyon ways in the beautifully appointed lounge with Ray Manzarek of The Doors and their biographer Danny Sugerman, spent three hours dissecting the local music and radio industries over a very long lunch with Richard Clapton who couldn't afford to be there but was, sat in the gym with teen-dream dance/pop sensation Peter Andre who's done so well in recent times in England and Europe, spent half-an-hour by the pool with the gorgeous Heather Nova who has the kind of eyes you really want to fall into, and wandered by the suite in which both Axl Rose of Guns'N'Roses and George Bush, then US President, had both slept – separately, of course.

The next day Michael took it easy, made some phone calls and allegedly caught up with a couple of old friends. On the Thursday he had breakfast with his father Kell, rehearsed with INXS at he ABC Studios in Gore Hill, and managed to sleep through the entire evening, missing a fundraiser for former girlfriends Kym Wilson's theatre company. Michael was also believed to have had several prescriptions filled, including one for Prozac, the anti-depressant medication.

On the Friday he was back at the ABC studios where Channel 9 got the exclusive inside story and film of the band rehearsing. It showed a band honed and shiny, intent and intense. Michael even commented at the end of one song how perfect it was, then muttered "perhaps too perfect". He and they seemed happy, looking forward to the 13-date Australian tour. Maybe not. There was one unforgettable shot on that strip of film. It was taken when Michael wasn't aware he was on camera. Slumped on a stool, he looked utterly drained and exhausted . . . and haunted.

Then again it had been a long year on the record and the road and Yates' custody battle with Sir Bob had become a hard-edged war. Sir Bob wasn't giving an inch, then again as a father and wounded ex-spouse it is hard to see why he would. That is human nature. But for Michael it was more. If you read the hundreds of thousands, perhaps millions of words that have been written about Michael before and after his death, and you sift through all the theories and you try to gauge the truth behind all the hot air, hyperbole and standard responses, there emerges a gut-wrenchingly sad snapshot of a man uncertain about his future, perhaps about his band, certainly about himself, who seemed in the end desperately lonely without his woman and child. Michael said many years ago that he had his mid-life crisis at 24; perhaps, and perhaps not. If this wasn't such a time of crisis in his life, it was a time of change and a depth of feeling that defied words and explanation. It was easy to see what Michael needed most when he arrived back in Australia: Paula, Tiger Lily and the girls.

He would explain how much pressure he felt to his father that night when they met for dinner at the Flavour Of India restaurant in Edgecliff, a few kilometres up the road from Double Bay. Later Kell would tell *The Daily Telegraph* (UK, February 3, 1998) " 'He was in great form: joking, mimicking friends, big smiles . . . He'd just been in LA, screen-testing, for a new Tarantino movie. He was elated – he'd won the part.'

"But Kell also knew that his son was taking Prozac and had been depressed. 'I grabbed his hand and said: "Look, Mike, tell me. What's this all about?" Michael said he was distressed about the legal battle raging between Paula and himself, and Bob Geldof.' This centered on Paula's plan to bring two of her three daughters by her former husband – Peaches and Pixie – to Australia for a three month holiday. Not unreasonably, Geldof had objected because of the amount of schooling the girls would miss. That day, Michael and Paula's lawyers had been arguing their case in the High Court in London.

"According to Kell, his son was 'furious' with Geldof who, in his view, 'would not let go of Paula.' After dinner, the two men went back to the Ritz Carlton. 'We said fond farewells outside the hotel. It was the last time I saw him,' says Kell, his voice breaking."

Fifteen days later, *The Daily Telegraph* (Sydney) quoted an interview with Kell that appeared in the British magazine *Hello!*

In the interview Kell said "his son spoke of a 'vendetta' against him the night before he died.

"Mr Hutchence said he thought Michael's death was due to disappointment over his lover being prevented from bringing her children to Australia, to the pressures of the INXS tour and to 'booze, Prozac and other substances'.

"'Michael was absolutely fed up with the situation over Paula's children', he said.

"'He told me "Dad, I feel there's a vendetta against me and it doesn't matter what plans Paula and I make, something always happens to destroy them".'

"Mr Hutchence said there was no indication that Michael had planned to commit suicide when they dined together the night before he was found hanged in his hotel room in Double Bay.

"'But I feel in my heart it was suicide,' he said."

Kell was also quoted earlier in *New Idea* magazine as saying, "I had never seen him so bubbly. Michael was so full of fun that night – mimicking (an old party trick) and carrying on. I remember saying, 'This is vintage Michael.'"

Kell also said that as a result of the screen tests Michael was wanted in LA straight away but had concluded "I can't walk off the tour."

In mid-December Kell appeared on television in an extensively quoted interview during which he took a swing at Sir Bob. Both *The Sun* and *New Musical Express* reported that Kell said, "He [Sir Bob] made their lives miserable. It's like he was on a vendetta – to get them. And that's really the truth of it. He created extraordinary situations and I think contributed very much to what happened . . .

"Those kids, Pixie and Peaches, loved Michael so much. And he wasn't trying to take the children away from their father."

Back at the Indian restaurant, reports of that final dinner are much the same. Superficially, they don't depict a man considering suicide. But as Kell noted in the press he felt that beneath the surface and the frivolity was a tangled mess of emotion. Michael and Kell drank beer and wine and chose four main courses at which Michael picked throughout the night.

At 10.30 p.m., Kell dropped Michael off at the hotel where he went straight to his room and stayed for about half an hour. *The Daily Telegraph* (December 13, 1997), in an extensive feature of Michael's final days by Marcus Casey, reported that it had interviewed "a Southern Highlands woman – named 'Karen' – who had known Hutchence for more than 15 years, and believes she met Hutchence in his room at this time.

"The woman, nervous and distressed that her name entered the final loop of Hutchence's life, did not have a sexual relationship with the singer.

"She would not elaborate on what went on in the room, but displayed intimate knowledge of prescription medicines and said Hutchence was taking many.

"Adamant that no hard drugs were present when she was in the room, the woman said Hutchence told her he'd been on a variety of medicines for a full month.

"One was Keflex, considered the strongest antibiotic available over the counter.

"Karen would not elaborate on the others.

"'His body was saturated with them that's all I know,' she told *The Daily Telegraph* after being interviewed by police investigating the death.

"Michael was so up when I saw him, but looking back, he was like a volcano waiting to explode with the amount of pharmaceuticals in him."

Exactly why "Karen" visited Michael's room has never been disclosed.

About 11 p.m., dressed in black jacket and pants and alone, he left room 524 and entered the elevator which he shared with two sisters, Zinta Reindel and Tamara Brachmanis, and according to Liz Hannan of *The Sun-Herald* (November 23) ended their plans for a late-night dip in the hotel swimming pool. "'I think it's closed girls,' Hutchence told the sisters and their friend, Tanya Turnbull."

Mrs Reindel also said, "'He looked like he was a bit high on something but stars are always on something . . . But he was happy'."

Michael left the lift and entered the hotel's piano bar where, according to several witnesses, he spoke to two women, applauded the woman who was singing, had a drink and seemed a "happy guy".

In fact, happy seems to have been the key word for the evening so far. And it got happier when Kym Wilson arrived with her boyfriend, Andrew Rayment, a solicitor and son of leading Sydney silk Brian Rayment.

What happened next is best told in Kym's own words.

Kym Wilson was to become the victim of one of the worst pieces of rumour-mongering to erupt in the wake of Michael's death: that she'd committed copycat suicide herself, unable to deal with the guilt she felt for what had gone on with Michael that night or, according to who you listened to, she had hanged herself in a police cell after being charged with manslaughter over Michael's death and that her death had been covered up.

I turned up for work at *The Sydney Morning Herald* about 5 p.m. on November 28 to find the rumour the hottest topic of the day. Journalists were seriously investigating it and at least three people asked me if I knew whether it was true. A few phone calls and I knew it wasn't. It appeared to have started as a sick joke in the Goodbar nightclub in Sydney's inner city Darlinghurst, close to the renowned Oxford strip, the social home to many of the city's gay community. From there it spread with alarming rapidity. Several people told me starting such rumours was a game and the rumour surrounding Wilson wasn't the first.

On December 3 a picture of a very much alive Kym Wilson and a story about her theatre company appeared on the front page of *The Daily Telegraph*. But it wasn't enough and Wilson was forced to surface and tell her story in an effort to reclaim her life: she had been forced to move out of her home at Scotland Island, an hour north of Sydney, where the world's media were camped out on her front lawn, and had spent hours convincing friends that she wasn't dead.

Woman's Day (December 15, 1997) carried the exclusive interview (for an alleged fee of $150,000 which Wilson donated to a

Trust fund set up for Heavenly Hiraani Tiger Lily) by Leigh
Reinhold. The British tabloids had shown her no mercy. The
article records for posterity headlines such as "The Woman
Michael Had Sex With That Night" and "The Woman Paula
Didn't Want At The Funeral". Compassion? What compassion?
Fact? What fact?

Kym Wilson, pretty, strong-willed, independent and in some
ways, according to those who know her best, quite shy and old-
fashioned, was probably the last person to see Michael alive.

"'Because Michael was a rock star, people want to believe
scandalous clichés over what happened,' she says. 'But the night I
spent with him, which was followed, five hours after I left by his
death, was a night with a friend, of catching up with a man who
predominantly was very in love with his life at that time and so in
love with his family.

"'He told me over and over again that night that he loved Paula
and Tiger Lily, who was his pride and joy, and he also felt Paula's
three other daughters were part of his family too. It was one of his
greatest moments of pride in his life that all the girls called him
Daddy.'"

Wilson says they had gone up to Michael's room rather than
stay in the bar where they had met him because he wanted to be
close to the phone in case some news of the custody battle Paula
was fighting with Sir Bob came through from London.

"'He was concerned about the custody hearing but I wouldn't
say he was depressed,' she says. 'His attitude was that he believed
he was right that he and Paula should get custody of the children
and if they didn't have luck this time, they would keep fighting
on. I never for one instant think he thought that would be the
end, that he would give up if the case didn't go their way. He
spoke with such excitement of his future – I had really never seen
him with so much to look forward to.

"'Michael talked about how he desperately wanted the girls to
be with him and he thought that was that they wanted too.
Michael wasn't very fond of Bob Geldof, he didn't paint a good
picture of him at all.'

"While waiting for the phone call, the trio ordered strawberry daiquiris and Michael talked about the exciting ways his life was changing and evolving.

"'He was very excited about his solo career. He had a CD demo of one of his songs which he was desperate to play, but there was no CD player,' she says. 'While we were there, he also had a phone call about a film Quentin Tarantino was very interested in him doing.

"'He'd been working up to that for a long time and he was very excited about the fact – he put his arm around me and said, "Kym, I'm an actor now too!"'

"Michael was anxious to know whether Paula, Tiger Lily and the other girls would be able to join him for the 20th anniversary tour of INXS. Kym told him they would wait until the phone call came through.

"'He took a phone call while we were there, saying that they still hadn't got a judge for the case. By this point, it was about 4.30am. My poor darling boy was falling asleep lying at the foot of the bed. Michael just looked at him and looked at me trying to keep up the conversation and said. 'Oh look, you two go home.'"

Further on in the story Wilson talks about the reaction after the story broke and the rumours that began to emerge.

"'People have wanted to imply that there was a sex and drug-crazed orgy happening in Michael's room that night,' she says. 'Nothing could be further from the truth. It was a night of catching up with a close friend trying to find out the result of a court case about his family.

"'Of course we had a drink. But in the six hours we were there, we would have only had between six and eight drinks and we were hardly drunk. There were definitely no drugs in the room when I was there and there wasn't any sex either.

"'The police have been very public about the fact that Prozac was found in Michael's room and I'm very dubious about that drug. I don't understand enough about it to analyse what potential it had in the situation, but from what I've heard, Prozac may well have been one of a number of things that culminated in Michael's death.

"'Paula, and I thank her, has said she places absolutely no

responsibility on me and she knows there was no sexual activity and attributes no blame for the situation to me at all. She understands even in the enormity of her grief, that I was just a friend of Michael's who happened to be with him at the time.

"'I'm sure she knows from the relationship she had with Michael that none of the rumours are true and the police are in no doubt that there was no sexual activity in the room that night. Nor have I been charged with manslaughter, nor am I dead after hanging myself in a cell after I was charged. It's not true.

"'The insinuation that there was sexual activity in the room was more hurtful than anything because I have a very strong relationship, a monogamous relationship, and Paula and Michael loved each other so desperately. How dare the press insinuate something that didn't happen, especially about someone who can't respond.'

"Kym is quick to defend the friend she met when she was 17, at the birthday party of her best friend Mouche Phillips. . .

"'I remember the night we met vividly, he wore a blue feather boa and there were feathers left wherever we went for a whole week. . .

"'Michael and I had a romance, but it was a very long time ago and it was very brief,' she explains. 'It started a wonderful friendship that would last for many years.'

"'. . .I think that it was a beautiful way for us to get to know each other to become friends. Most of the time we spent together was as friends.'"

The oddest fact in Kym's story though comes at the end. Earlier she has said how she and her boyfriend had left their telephone numbers on a page in Michael's diary and told him to ring if he needed someone.

The last two paragraphs of the story read: "Kym says she knows that Michael appreciated their final hours together because of two words written in his diary where she had left her telephone number.

"'He had written "Thank you" in between my boyfriend's and my name which was not only a wonderful little message from him but it also made it a lot easier for me to cope,' she explains. 'When you're the last person to be involved in that kind of tragedy, the questions that you ask yourself are endless. But I know that I tried to give him as much support as I could that night and there was no way that I could have foretold what was going to happen. I think he wrote that thank you for a reason."

Left unanswered is a question: if Michael Hutchence had intended to live, why would he leave a message for Kym Wilson? Obviously, he could thank her in person or by the phone and just as obviously she wouldn't be likely to see those pages in his diary again. So why the message. . .

In the last five hours of his life, Michael was hardly ever off the phone. He is reported to have made about 10 calls out in that time and received several more. One call was from Paula Yates who rang about an hour after Wilson and Rayment left with the news that the custody hearing had been adjourned until December 17 and she couldn't come out immediately with the children.

This was the first of several crucial calls that some, including current INXS manager Martha Troup, believe caused him to snap. Troup had spoken to Michael about 1a.m. when Wilson and Rayment were with him. On December 5, she told internet e-zine *Addicted To Noise* (http://www.addict.com) senior writer Gil Kaufman that a nervous breakdown in the early hours of the morning had caused Michael to take his life.

"He snapped," said Troup. "He felt pressures and it was snap . . .he snapped for that momentary time. I think [it was] pressures about his child Tiger and Bob Geldof and all the escapades that went on in the last year . . . It just reached a climax. It was the culmination of everything, how he [Geldof] treated Paula and how he was making his [Hutchence's] life miserable."

Troup also confirmed that Michael was indeed happy during that last call. "He was in a brilliant mood when I spoke to him," she said. "He was talking about film things, and he'd read a script. Just the second I got on the phone he was 'Martha I love you,' just lovable, lovable, lovable. And he was very excited that day from rehearsal and he felt it was going really well. He was happy. He loved Australia, he loved it."

After Paula's call an angry Michael then phoned Sir Bob

about 5.30 a.m. on November 22 and according to Sir Bob begged him to allow the children to come to Australia. In the room next door Gail Coward stated that she heard a loud male voice swearing at that time. Sir Bob confirmed the nature of Michael's call. He later said, "We didn't have a row – it takes two people to have an argument. He called up late and I just couldn't understand a word he said. I just put down the phone. Michael had been bombarding me with calls for the past few months. It was impossible to talk to him because he was always off his head."

About three hours passed before Michael made his next call: to his former lover, Michelle Bennett, who lives not far away from the hotel. He left a message saying, "I think it's seven o'clock. I need to talk to you." It was 9 a.m. Ms Bennett told the NSW State Coroner, Mr Derek Hand, that Michael sounded "drunk". During the next hour, he rang Martha Troup at 9.38 a.m. – at the New York-based office of Entertainment Consulting Company and at home. He left a message: "Marth, Michael here. I f. . .ing had enough"; a second call followed 12 minutes later. On both occasions Ms Troup was unable to get to the phone. According to *The Daily Telegraph* he also rang INXS members and other friends and associates, although they have subsequently never been identified. He found more answering machines.

Finally, he called Michelle Bennett again at 9.54 a.m. and began crying. Concerned about him she rushed to the hotel, arriving about 10.30 a.m. She got no answer when she called his room from the hotel lobby and no response when she knocked on the door of his room. She wrote a note and left it at reception. Michelle Bennett had arrived too late. Michael Hutchence was probably already dead. . .on the other side of the door.

Michael Kelland Frank Hutchence died between 10 a.m. and 11 a.m. on Saturday, November 22, 1998, when he tied a leather belt around the self-closing device on his hotel door, put the other end around his neck and – naked – hanged himself.

He was found about 11.55 a.m. by a maid.

Love will tear us apart.

"I don't know whether I'm angry or guilty. . . You always think if it's a mate that there was something you could have done.

"I still find it hard to figure it all out because I had a conversation with him not that long ago where we talked about something like this and we both agreed how dumb and selfish it would be, and Hutch was not all that selfish. . .

"He was very light, whereas I don't think I'm the easiest person in the world, so we balanced each other out. But I hadn't seen him for a while, because we were both off doing our thing. I'm finding the whole thing very hard to understand. . ."

Bono of U2 in *Q* magazine talking about Michael's death and how they had once discussed suicide.

The Pilton Pop Festival

C. J. Stone

Rain.

Rain, rain, rain rattling on the roof of the van, falling in waves, washing down the hillside in muddy streams, gathering in pools: relentless, driving rain, hissing and shifting and blustering about. Rain.

And then mud. Streams of mud. Rivers of mud. Oceans of dark, slimy, greasy, sticky mud. Mud up to your ankles when you walked. Mud splashing your trouser legs and up over your coat. Mud on the toilet seats in the awful festival toilets, looking like shit. Mud to stand up in and mud to sit down in. Mud.

That was Pilton that year. Rain. And then mud.

The reason we were on the litter-pickers field is that Des was organizing the stage there. It was high up on the hillside, overlooking the site. I wasn't working on the field. I was there as part of the entertainment crew. But I liked the idea of serving the litter-pickers. The litter-pickers and the working class of the Pilton Festival. They're there to work, picking up litter. Mind you, they don't get paid very much. They have to buy their tickets. And then, when the Festival is over, if they've done all of their shifts to their supervisor's satisfaction, they get their ticket money back. That's all they get, the chance to come to the Pilton Festival and then work for nothing. It seemed like a raw deal to me.

They also get fed. Unfortunately for them, the food franchise has gone out to a couple of sloppy vegans. So that's what they get to eat: vegan slop. Bowls of vegetables in a runny sauce. The same thing every day. Working hard all day, in the pouring rain, for a bowl of vegetables. But the organizers were well organized.

They'd put out a couple of franchises for vegetarian burger stalls. Not that the burgers were free: the litter-pickers had to pay for them. And being hungry (and unable to face any more bowls of unpeeled potatoes in various bland sauces), they were flocking to them. One of the vegetarian burger stalls was run by the organizers themselves (or by their children, rather). And this was the cause of my first wobbly at the Pilton Festival.

It was getting late into the first day, and we hadn't eaten all day. We'd delivered all of that food and all of that equipment for them – including their poxy vacuum cleaner – but no one was offering to feed us. I was hungry. All I'd had to eat in the last two days was a flimsy slice of pizza. Des didn't seem to be worried about it. He was in his "go with the flow" festival phase. "Something will turn up," he grumbled. I was too hungry to wait. Instead I offered to buy Des and Angelina some food. So Des was right. Something did turn up. I did.

I went to the vegetarian burger stall run by the organizers' children and ordered burger and chips three times. The burgers were £1.50 each, £2 with salad. So I ordered three burgers with salad, and stood back to watch. It was appalling. There were a bunch of kids in there, aged between about eight and fourteen, running around amid all that hot fat and cooking equipment, and they had no idea what they were doing. Not one of them could cook. There were flames leaping and fat sizzling, and a bunch of kids squabbling, and people queuing up, waiting, and I was starving and Angelina was starving, and the kids – who knew Angelina – were taunting her. "Nyer, nyer, nyer Angelina," they were saying in that sing-song way that kids use to effect derision. I was steadily losing my temper, not just with the kids: with the adults who'd put them here. And we were just waiting and waiting while this was going on.

But eventually the food came.

"You said salad, didn't you?" the kid asked.

"Yes," I said.

And he put one slice of cucumber and a bit of lettuce into the bun with the burger. One slice of cucumber.

"What's this?" I asked.

"Salad," the kid said.

"Salad? Salad? One slice of cucumber for 50p. You call that salad?"

"I'm sorry," he said, "it's what I was told to do."

I stormed back to the van.

"I'm fed up," I said. "I'm pissed off. One slice of cucumber for 50p. And the chips are inedible. And it took fifteen minutes to get served. And none of them know what they're doing. I'd be surprised if there wasn't fire in there. It's fucking dangerous. I hate festivals, I really do."

Later Susanna was talking to the organizer of the litter-pickers field. He was moaning on about how hard the work was, how spiritually unrewarding.

"So why do you do it?" she asked.

He paused. And then, enunciating his words very carefully, he named a five-figure sum.

The first Pilton Festival took place on 19 September 1970, after the young Michael Eavis had visited the Bath Blues Festival earlier in the summer. He was suitably impressed. He decided he wanted one of his own.

Perhaps the only mystery is how a person like Michael Eavis came to be at the Bath Blues Festival in the first place. He was a churchgoer, a Methodist. He was also a dairy farmer, working the land that had been worked by his family since 1894. I imagine that his background had been severe; or strict, at least. I imagine that he would have been a cautious man – cautious and practical – being from hardy, hardworking yeoman stock. So how come he was at this festival? That's easy. He hopped the fence.

Well no, he didn't really hop the fence. But the fence had come down, and he walked in for free. I only wanted to say that because it became a feature of my stay at Pilton this year, watching the countless hordes hopping over the fences. It was nice to think that – though he didn't actually hop the fence himself– Michael Eavis had actually blagged his way into his first festival.

He was thirty-five years old.

Anyway, he came away from this festival in love with the whole thing. The light and colour of the scene must have impressed him, probably because it did contrast so severely with his own background. He'd never seen hippies before. He'd never seen clothes like that before. Here we have a bunch of people having fun. A bunch of people ideologically opposed to the very work ethic he'd been brought up to worship, dressed in flowing robes, with patchwork clothes and dangly hairdos. Many of them would have been dancing. Some of them, indeed, may have been dancing naked. Dancing naked was the thing to do if you were a hippie. On top of which, he loved the music. Actually he'd always loved the music. He played Radio One to his cows, and had made a record himself many years before: a 78, which he refuses to let anyone hear. But it crossed his mind that here might be a way of making money, to supplement the income from the farm. So he set out to recreate some of the ingredients on his own land. He booked the Kinks to headline the show, in September that year. In the end they backed out, and Marc Bolan and T. Rex played instead.

The show was not a great success. Only 2,500 people turned up. And Jimi Hendrix had just died, so there was a kind of gloom over the event, an atmosphere of mourning. But Eavis provided free milk, and the proceedings must have gone smoothly enough for him to think that it wasn't such an unmitigated disaster. He must have thought that, since he was to host a similar event the following year. And that subsequent event has since become a legend.

According to the official programme of the 1997 festival, it was called the Glastonbury Fayre, and held over the solstice period in June 1971. I said it was a similar event. It was similar in that bands played and hippies attended. But in every other way it was entirely dissimilar. It was one of the earlier free festivals.

This second festival was Andrew Kerr's idea. Kerr had been the personal assistant of Randolph Churchill from 1959 until his death in 1968. After that he became a free spirit, a hippie. I met him. He came to visit me in my van. He's a dapper little chap, not much younger than my Dad, but a Universe away in terms of his attitudes. Very sprightly, very sparkly, very alive.

He isn't "little" really. He's five foot ten. I only said that because he reminds me of my Dad, and my Dad is little. And also because "dapper little chap" as a phrase suits him. Anyway, it sounds better than "a dapper medium-sized chap."

We met up so that he could correct some of the errors that have accumulated around the event over the years. There's been a number of official histories written. Not one of the writers took the trouble to consult with Andrew Kerr.

The first thing he told me was that the spelling was wrong. All the books I consulted spelled it the same way: as "Glastonbury Fayre".

"It was Fair," he said to me: "F-A-I-R. Glastonbury Fair."

He'd gone to the Isle of Wight Festival in 1970, he told me, and had been appalled at the rank commercialism of the event. It was in his Rover driving back that it had occurred to him that he wanted to create a festival of his own. The car was full of people, and he started telling them of his idea. He said, "Well it's definitely not going to be like the other festivals. We've got to have a festival that's not a hype, that is a celebration of life and gives respect to the environment."

He'd come by what he described as "a little money". I expect it was quite a large sum of money by my standards, but a little money by the standards of those circles he moved around in. He'd been reading the New Testament. "Give all that you have and follow me," it said. So he decided to do that. He decided to give his money away in the form of a free festival.

"Something was kind of inside me over this period," he says to me now, "and I will definitely not say that it was to do with drugs."

So, together with Arabella Churchill (Randolph's daughter) and a number of other people, he formed Solstice Capers Ltd., in order to execute his fantasy. That's when the festival was planned to take place: summer solstice the following year.

Well I was interested in this. I was interested in how the ancient celebration of the solstice came to be revived. I mean, it's such a commonplace now. Almost a whole generation have grown up to recognize its significance. It has become something of a tradition. But back then, when Andrew Kerr was planning his event, there was no such tradition. I was hoping for some mystical revelation, of the kind that Ubi Dwyer had had, before the Windsor Free, or Wally Hope before Stonehenge. But actually he'd read it in a book. It was *The View Over Atlantis* by John Michell, a very influential book amongst the hippies at the time. But it was definitely revelations he was looking for.

And his first thought, in fact, had been to hold it at Stonehenge, on a round stage. It was only later, in the wake of Michael Eavis's mini-festival, that he considered Pilton and opted for the pyramid.

Jimi Hendrix was asked to play. "I'll be there," he said. But, of course, he never lived to fulfil that promise. However, the world premiere of *Rainbow Bridge*, Hendrix's film, took place at the festival. So perhaps he was there in other ways.

By now someone had suggested that Kerr approach Michael Evis, and an appointment was made. The day before, however, Kerr climbed Glastonbury Tor, along with the usual carload of people. They spent the night there. Someone offered him an oat cake. That was Bill Harkin, later to design the pyramid stage. He stayed up all night – "the excitement of the occasion prevented me from sleeping" – and in the morning he went over to visit Eavis.

There was no rainbow, note. This is one of the myths that he wanted me to clear up. He did not see a rainbow over Worthy Farm from Glastonbury Tor, as previous histories have stated it. The rainbow came later.

So, arriving in Pilton Village, and parking up, he met Michael Eavis for the first time.

His first impression was that Eavis's face was shining. "Open, genuine, blazing, outgoing": these were the adjectives he used to describe the young Michael Eavis that day.

Kerr told the farmer of his plan, and offered to pay for the use of the land. "We don't have much money, but we'll pay what we can," he said.

And Eavis didn't even think about it. He just said yes.

"It was the most blessed thing in my life," says Kerr now. "The chance to live out a dream, a really crazy dream.

I met Michael Eavis too, a little before I met Andrew Kerr. It was Michael Eavis who gave me Kerr's address. I interviewed him at Worthy Farm, in his office: the same office from which he runs the festival every year. It's tiny, not much bigger than your average toilet, and packed with files, as well as a desk and two chairs, a computer, telephones, notice boards, all crammed in there, like a pile of junk stuffed precariously into a cupboard. It seemed extraordinary to think that, year after year, that huge event has emerged from this tiny space.

What puzzled me was why Eavis had gone along with Kerr's idea. He wasn't exactly going to make his fortune. He was a straight-laced Somerset farmer, and a Christian to boot. He didn't even drink or smoke cigarettes, let alone go along with the excesses of the hippies who came with Andrew Kerr to invade his farmhouse that year.

"That's a good question," Eavis said. "I'm puzzled about this as well. But I had an affinity with the hippies. I mean, I can always talk to hippies, anywhere I go. Maybe it's that I get more of a dialogue with these people than I do with a lot of other people. But it was all very romantic at the time. It was a very romantic thing to be doing, all lovey-dovey, and I was in love."

Des told me a good story. He said he was driving around the back lanes near Pilton one year, just after the festival, when he came across Michael Eavis, carrying a plastic bag, and scouring around the hedgerows.

"What are you up to, Michael?" he asked.

And Michael showed him what was in the bag. It was human excrement. Apparently one of the local farmers had told him that he would object to the festival unless Michael did this: unless he went round the hedgerows himself to collect the shit. He was not allowed to get contractors in to do the work. He had to do it himself. And such was his dedication to the festival that he had actually agreed. Maybe it was the same spirit that had urged him to accept Andrew Kerr's proposal all those years before.

Anyway, whatever the reason, Worthy Farm soon became the stomping ground for the countercultural elite of the time. Kerr sold up his house on the Thames at Chiswick and moved into the farmhouse. And it was while he was entering the farm gates that first time that he saw the rainbow spanning the house.

All sorts of people were coming and going during the nine months leading up to the festival. Hawkwind practised in the barn, as did the Pink Fairies. The cast of *Hair* turned up. Members of the Grateful Dead. Friends of John Lennon. Some thieves and plenty of phoneys. Even a guru or two. Some of them had peculiar aliases, like Zee and Toad. It was the Beautiful People, hair and floral dresses wafting in the breeze, odorous with patchouli oil. Headbands and sandals. Flappy flares. Waistcoats. Scarfs. Frilly shirts. The smell of hemp and garlic. I'm certain they would have indulged in late-night philosophical conversations under the influence of some high-grade stimulants. Eavis was just tending his herd, letting them get on with it. But there they were, in all their full-blown hippie splendour, talking heaven down from the stars, the Lords and Ladies of the revolution.

What the local people thought about this hippie invasion in the months preceding the festival is not on record. The police were fairly sanguine about it, however. Kerr had to speak to them to make arrangements about traffic flow and access and the rest, and a number of officers came to see him at the farmhouse. In order to get to Kerr's room they had to pass through Bill Harkin's room, which was full of people sitting on the floor blowing chillums. So they tiptoed gingerly through that, like it was an obstacle course. As Kerr stood up from his desk to greet them, he glanced out of the window. He was confronted with the sight of a naked female draped against the wheel of a cart which was parked in the middle of the lawn outside. And there, in front of her, "with a lazy-lob on" (it's a naval term), dancing and wobbling his buttocks about, completely naked, performing what looked like some sort of magical sex rite, was the High Priest. Yes, the High Priest: the same High Priest we've met before. Kerr was embarrassed. He didn't know what to do. The policemen just leaned over to get a better view through the window, and spluttered with laughter. After that they had to pick their way back through the chillum obstacle course in Bill Harkin's room again. No one had moved an inch.

Later they said, "We know they're all smoking pot. But we're not interested in you lot. It's the big boys we're after." They were West Country policemen. A different breed in those days.

The actual festival, the following year, was a high-camp hippie to-do. Kerr had planned it"in the medieval tradition, with music, dance, poetry, theater, lights and the opportunity for spontaneous entertainment". When he introduced the bands to the audience, he said:

> Glastonbury is a place far too beautiful for yet another rock festival. If the festival has a specific intention it is to create an increase of awareness in the power of the Universe, a heightening of consciousness and a recognition of our place in the function of this our tired and molested planet. We have spent too long telling the Universe to shut up; we must search for the humility to listen. The Earth is groaning for contact with our ears and eyes. Universal awareness touches gently at our shoulders. We are creators being created and we must prove our worth.

Bill Harkin designed the Pyramid stage, one-tenth the size of the Great Pyramid itself. It was built out of scaffolding covered with expanded metal and plastic sheeting, and placed on a blind spring, near the so-called Michael line that joins Glastonbury to Stonehenge, in a natural amphitheatre. Kerr dowsed the spot himself. It was certainly a spectacular structure. Officially the festival ran from the 20th to the 24th of June, but what with early arrivals, and late departures, actually managed to stretch out for over a week. The acts were Hawkwind, Traffic, Melanie, Fairport Convention and David Bowie. The Grateful Dead were supposed to have turned up, but never did. Between 12,000 and 15,000 people attended.

So far, so good. A fairly typical rock festival at the time. But it was also a celebration of this peculiar new culture. And that's where things seemed to get a little crazy.

I used the expression "high camp" to describe it earlier. That's because I've seen the photographs. There's something theatrical about the whole event. People are decidedly in costume. The usual things: flowery robes and Afghan coats and bangles and beads and dodgy-looking hairdos. But there's an air of play-acting about the scenes that are presented to you, a feeling of "Look at me!" One oft-used photograph shows a bunch of people worshipping the rising solstice sun. Their hands are all raised in the air, and one or two are kneeling. Is it ecstasy? Or just amateur dramatics?

Well why not? By 1971 the media were all-powerful, as they are now. Why not play them at their own game by adopting costumes – or no clothing at all – and posing in order to set your own agenda?

The photographer was a freelance at the time, working for various West Country publications. He's virtually made a living out of recycling festival memorabilia ever since. He just happened to turn up at the festival. His name is Brian Walker. There's another photograph of his which appears regularly, and which he has resold many times. The magazines always pick the same sets of photographs it seems. It's of three men in a naked embrace, with a Gay Liberation Front poster beside them. "Right On!" the poster says. But the picture editors usually crop the picture. In the full version there's a heterosexual couple looking at them. And their eyes are a picture: a mixture of surprise and distaste. You forget that so much of this was actually very new at the time.

One day Kerr was talking to the men from the Milk Marketing Board. They were running a milk stall on site. Suddenly someone called Gyp turned the corner. He was this classically beautiful man, with a profusion of hair, shrouded in a cape, with a top hat and high boots. Kerr considered him a nuisance and was hoping he wouldn't come over to talk. But he did.

"Hi," he said. "Do you like my clothes? But they are wonderful."

At which point he raised the cape above his head to reveal that he was only wearing the boots and a shirt underneath.

"Go away, Gyp," said Kerr.

But it broke the ice with the Milk Marketing Board men. They were cackling with laughter. They couldn't contain themselves.

That night Gyp went into the village and picked someone's prize gladioli. Then he rang on the door.

"Look," he said, when the woman answered it, "I've brought you these beautiful flowers."

So there was some suspicion among the villagers, naturally. Most of them had no idea what to make of it all. One farm manager accused the hippies of trampling crops, damaging hedges and turning a field into an open lavatory. People were kept awake by the noise, and complained to the local vicar. The vicar's wife said, "But what can he do about controlling pop music which continues into the early hours?" Eavis tried to impose a twelve o'clock curfew, but the hippies always managed to stretch things out. On one occasion he could clearly be seen through the back-lit plastic sheeting chasing the stage manager about, trying to get the music turned off. And the police warned the festival-goers not to walk around naked in public places. Chief Inspector Lewis Clark said, "If people were trying to get into a place with no clothes on we would send them back because it could annoy the residents," And then he added, darkly, "There are laws concerning nude persons in a public place."

The *Sun's* account is the best. LOVE IN THE MUD ORGY, says the headline. And then it goes on to describe a twenty-year-old woman making love to a series of men in a mud pool:

> A police spokesman said, "It was an amazing sight. Our men saw this girl making love in the mud with one man, then several others joined in.
> "About a thousand people stood by and watched.
> "We're not interested in that sort of thing – they weren't annoying anyone or causing any offence as far as we know."
> Later, "Magic Michael", a twenty-four-year-old hippie from a Welsh commune, danced naked on stage for an hour to the accompaniment of bongo drums and frenzied squeals.

Which begs the question, really, of why the police didn't arrest "Magic Michael"?

So, here I am, more than a quarter of a century later, enjoying – if that's the word – the legacy of that first free festival. And I've got a hand-painted WORTHY FARM sign from that era in my van, and a map of Glastonbury on my wall. It must mean something.

I'd told Des that I hated festivals. This is true. I can't see the point, really, of leaving the cities to come into the countryside, only to camp out in another, rudimentary, dirty, uncomfortable city like the Pilton Pop Festival.

But I was trapped here, so I had to make the best of it. I'm only telling you this so you know what privations I went through in order to deliver you this little entertainment. An artist must suffer for his work.

And I did suffer. I suffered all that rain and all that mud. I suffered plates of vegan slop. I suffered listening to Des and Dicken's interminable arguments.

"Dylan, concentrate will you. You're not playing it right."

"The name's Dicken, Des, Dicken. Dickendickendickendicken. Dicken!"

"What?"

"DICKEN!"

And then I suffered sleepless nights because of all those people coming over the wall. It was a concrete wall this year, about nine feet high. I didn't mind them coming over the wall, myself, as long as they did it quietly. It was the security guards chasing and screaming abuse at them that got to me. "I can see you there. Fuck off. Fuck off. Get back. D'ya hear me? Fuck off. If you come over, I'll phone through, and someone will pick you up."

The following day I was talking about it to a friend, when someone overheard me.

"Fucking security guards," I was saying, "keeping me awake. I'd rather people got in for nothing than to have to put up with all that ranting."

"Well I think they're doing a good job," this other person said. "It's the blaggers that are ruining it for all rest."

"What do you expect?" I said. "Most people can't afford the ticket prices."

"Then they should stay away."

"But the fact is, they're not going to stay away, are they? They'll come whether you want them to or not. It's inevitable. If they like the bands, but they haven't got the money, then they'll hop the fence. I even think that Eavis caters for them. He expects them to come."

"Then they should work, like me. I'm a litter-picker supervisor. I've done it every year since the festival began."

"For what? For your ticket money back? Most people aren't that stupid. Anyway, maybe they haven't got the money upfront to pay for the ticket in the first place."

"Then they should come before the wall goes up and find some work to do. It only goes up a month before the festival starts."

"So what you're saying is that you expect people to come a month in advance in order to sit around in a field, waiting for a couple of days worth of festival. And that's all right, but hopping the wall isn't. You're off your trolley," I said, "And anyway," I added, triumphantly, "Michael Eavis blagged his way into his first festival. Did you know that?"

I later heard that the main injuries at the festival that year were spinal injuries, some very serious, from landing badly after leaping the wall. One woman I know broke her spine. The other complaint was trench foot.

Well I had some adventures there, and I'm not complaining. Occasionally I'd even venture out from the litter-pickers field. This was usually so I could get some proper feed inside me. I went over to the sacred field, to visit the Druids a couple of times. The first time Ellie was there, but by the second she'd disappeared. Ellie had been in my van on the solstice, the day of the ceremony on the traffic island. "Where's Ellie?" I asked.

"She's not here."

Susanna and Denny told me that the High Priest had banished her from the field. He'd told her "in no uncertain terms" that had she been Queen Guinevere in a previous life she would have been dragged out by her hair and called a whore and a harlot. This was the first time I became aware that all was not Love and Peace in the hippie camp. I happen to like Ellie.

Susanna told me a story. There were look-out posts all along the top of the wall, manned by security guards. They were like metal cages. Suddenly one of the cages began to collapse, and the security guard was falling. People clapped and cheered.

"He broke his leg," said Susanna. "So the last thing he heard before he broke his leg was a lot of people clapping and cheering. I wonder what he made of that?"

But most of the time was spent in my van in the litter-pickers field, avoiding the rain. Lots of people spent lots of time in my van, avoiding the rain. It became the resource centre for all the musicians. They were practising in there. And in the evenings it became the pub. We'd buy beers from the marquee and bring them back to the van to drink. It's always been an ambition of mine, to own a pub. And now here I was, in a pub with wheels.

Des was having trouble setting up the stage in the marquee. A stage was supposed to be arriving, but it never turned up. So I lent him my Afghan carpet – which I carry for just such an occasion – and that became the stage instead. People had to take their boots off to step on the carpet. That was my only proviso. All the musicians played in their socks, which made them feel very homely, very laid back. It's a surprise that they weren't playing country and western all the time, so laid back were they. So, in this muddy marquee, in this muddy field, in this muddy festival, in this muddy county, in this muddy country, in this muddy June, there was one little patch that never got muddy at all: my Afghan carpet.

There was a musician friend of Des's, a big , gangly, hunched man with a lined face, grey hair, and a little Krishna bob at the back of his head. He had a friend, a dour, sullen, sour-faced woman. She was one of those people who can bully you quietly. She doesn't have to say anything. You can sense her disapproval, like waves in an ocean of toxic waste, washing over you. And she could genuinely psyche you out. She genuinely psyched me out.

I was talking about this woman with a friend of mine, many months after.

"What was her name again?" I asked.

"Er. . .J. . .J. . .J. . .something. Joy was it?"

"No. Misery more like."

So we'll call her Misery.

One day I was doing a reading. It was all part of the entertainment. I was going to read a story I'd written years ago, called "Off the Grails", about the first time I'd met the High Priest. Misery saw the title.

"Do you believe that I have the Holy Grail", she said.

"Hmmm", I said, noncommittally, "have you?"

"Yes. Do you believe the Holy Grail could be a stone?"

I hadn't considered this. "No". But I showed her the last line of the story. "In my story it says that the Holy Grail is a cup of tea."

She huffed angrily and stared. I'd said the wrong thing.

"Look", I added, "maybe the Holy Grail is having a sense of humour, don't you think?"

But she just huffed again and ground her teeth. After that she never took her eyes off me.

I got up on stage (well, onto my Afghan carpet) and started reading the story. I've read it a few times, and it usually raises a few laughs. But Misery was staring at me. I could feel the cold points of her eyes needling into me. So much for the Krishna ideal. I got to one of the lines which usually raises a laugh. Nothing. Not a murmur. Not a titter. Not even a smile. It was awful. And Misery just stared and stared. It was like there was only me and her in the room, and those steely eyes, psyching me out. I read out the next joke, and got the same response.

"It doesn't seem to be going down too well," I said.

I said, "Well if no one's going to laugh, I might as well read out a miserable story." Which I did. It didn't raise any laughs cither. But then again, it wasn't meant to.

Later, Des's friend said. "You did well there, to keep going. You know she was psyching you out, don't you?"

"Was she?" I said. "I hadn't noticed."

And then, on the Thursday, I was sitting in my van late at night drinking a beer, and watching all the brake lights winking on and off in a huge snake leading up to one of the gates. It went on for hours. The cars were shuffling forward slowly, and then stopping again, with the brake lights going on and off. And there were all these lights twinkling in the valley, and across the hill-sides. Fires burning.

Traders' lights along the main drag. Torches and headlights moving about. I was impressed. From a distance it all looked so beautiful. Like a constellation of stars in the deep night. And I imagined Michael Eavis sitting there in the farmhouse watching the same scene. Did I ask myself what he went to all this trouble for? I realized then that he would have been thinking, *I did this. This is mine.*

So the days were spent wandering between my van and the marquee, picking up a few beers now and then, and receiving visitors.

One day someone came to call on Des. She was an attractive young woman with hennaed hair and a kind-looking face. There was one rule in the van, too.

"Take your shoes off before you get in," I called.

She got in and embraced Des, and Des introduced me. Then this man got on board. He was the most astounding sight. He didn't have any shoes on, so he couldn't take any shoes off. He was dressed like an Indian sadhu, with a raggedy yellow robe wrapped over his shoulders. A cadaverously thin man, with tiny round glasses, and long, grey, dreadlocked hair: he was the very picture on an Indian saint.

Goodness, I thought, *I've got Mahatma Gandhi on board.*

"This is Swami Barmy", the woman said. It was some such Indian-sounding name, even though he was clearly a Westerner.

And then he grinned.

"Grin", is simply not a big enough word. There's no word in the English language to describe the sheer extent of his grin. He beamed. He broadcast. He projected that grin, like an anti-air-craft spotlight into the night sky. It stretched from ear to ear. It threatened to split his face in two. It showed all his teeth like a row of tombstones. He grinned at Des and he grinned at me. He grinned so widely and so persistently that I was forced to count his teeth. What else could I do? It was all I could see. Grin, grin, grin. It was most disconcerting. And then he sat down cross-legded on the bench seat and, still grinning, began to rub his feet. He was rubbing the mud off. He rubbed the mud into little balls which he collected in his hand. And once he'd rubbed it all off, he threw it out of the door.

He said a few things, always with that grin on his face. I couldn't tell where his accent came from. It was a cross between mid-Atlantic and Indian. I thought he might have been an American. So I asked him where he was from.

"Basildon", he said.

I almost cracked up.

"So you're a hippie then?" I asked, stifling my laughter.

"Last of the pure spirit", he said, grinning some more. "Went to India in '73. Never came back."

I went to find him later. He was part of the Rainbow Gathering, a circle of hippies meeting in various parts of the world to pray and meditate and visualize for world peace. They were going to Greece next, he told me. I thought I might try and follow them, as part of this project. But no matter where I looked I could never find him again. Obviously he'd raised his vibrational level and ascended into a higher dimension. Either that, or he'd given me the wrong directions.

I have to say that I took an instant and total dislike to the man, though I'm sure he didn't deserve it. His grin got on my nerves. He seemed to be wearing his bliss like a badge. His clothes got on my nerves. I was thinking, *Oh, it's enlightenment as a fashion statement, is it*? His Indian accent got on my nerves. *It's Basil from Basildon pretending to be a guru*, I thought.

But I never could explain why, exactly, I disliked him so much. Actually he'd been totally inoffensive. Polite even. He'd taken the trouble not to dirty my floor with his feet. It's true, there were peculiar moments. At one point I'd been trying to talk to him outside, trying to get directions for the Rainbow Gathering circle. And he'd bent himself back as I was talking, almost bending himself double so that his hands touched the floor behind him. It was odd. But he was harmless enough.

It took me months to realize why I disliked him. In fact, I only realized today, as I sat down to write this. he was me as I had wanted to be. He had fulfilled exactly the dreams I'd had. He'd gone to India and stayed. He was the happy hippie I might have been. It wasn't him I disliked, at all, it was me. The hippie me.

Rhyming and Stealing:
The Beastie Boys

Angus Batey

"It wasn't until 'Fight For Your Right To Party' came out that we started like drunken fools. At that point, our image shifted in a different direction, maybe turning off the kids that were strictly into hip-hop. It started out as a goof on that college mentality, but then we ended up personifying it."

Adam Yauch

Touring to support a No. 1 album should've been a breeze. When the Beastie Boys headed out on the road with Run DMC in what is still possibly the biggest rap package tour in the history of the music, it looked like another inspired move by Simmons on behalf of his charges. A triumphal procession across America was one thing, but by the time the two bands reached the UK the situation had changed.

A short series of dates at three to five thousand capacity venues across Britain during May 1987 was announced, and the majority of the shows sold out quickly. A night at Liverpool's Royal Court Theatre, among a batch added later in response to heavy ticket demand, and one of only a couple of dates on the tour's British leg without Run DMC, was the principal exception. At this point in time, the Beasties were not the bigger draw to UK audiences: a combination of tabloid hysteria and music press over-reaction to the violence at rap concerts in the US, and the linkage made between the music and the activities of street gangs, managed to put off many curious outsiders: and to die-hard rap fans (even in

1987 there were significant numbers of them in Britain) Run DMC were significantly more important than the Beasties.

"We wasn't wild, crazy – we wasn't a story you could sell as big," reasons Run, attempting eleven years later to assess why his band weren't as caught up in the media spotlight as his friends and touring partners. "They created the name 'Beastie' – pretty scary. They had some wilder props on the stage and [the press] was makin' up lies about 'em. Our story I guess, while we was great musically, our story wasn't as notorious or as cover-worthy. Musically we were good, but crazy we were not. They could sell more papers saying "the Beastie Boys turned over cars" and what not. And on stage they were a little wilder, drinkin' beer and throwin' it on each other. It was a different vibe they were trying to sell: this sex and violence vibe [came from] the media."

Contrary to the fans' perspectives, the substantial advance press for the UK tour concerned the Beastie Boys almost exclusively. And, in common with most of the British popular press' reporting of youth cultural movements, almost everything written about the band prior to their arrival in Britain was ill-informed and alarmist. At this time the band's stage show was, like their records, part of a plan to calculatedly offend. A go-go dancer and former stripper, Eloise, appeared on stage with the group, in various states of undress, usually in a cage. The three rappers would habitually prowl the stage armed with cans of lukewarm beer that they spent more time spraying on the audience and one another than drinking. The brewing company took exception to the fact that the band performed occasionally in front of a large Budweiser logo, so they stopped using the backdrop. This seemed a little unfair: after all, the band were using an awful lot of their product. The brewers clearly didn't like the public associating Budweiser too closely with a bunch of pissed-up adolescent oiks.

"Everything we did was stupid," Mike D told *Q* magazine's Howard Johnson in 1996. "When we were asked what kind of stage show we wanted the first thing we could think of was a giant dick, so we had one made! It seemed the obvious thing to do at the time. We used the dick down in Alabama and Carolina and completely freaked everyone out. We were immediately banned and they passed a Beastie Boys Ordnance outlawing outrageous and immoral behaviour in a public place. This was where the British tabloids first picked up on us."

Details of the band's performances on the *Raising Hell* tour were exaggerated from their already cartoonish proportions and splashed across acres of British newsprint. By the time the tour hit Europe, tales of the band's "outrageous" shows, liberally sprinkled with sex and alcohol, had become the stuff of Fleet Street legend. The tabloid press love a band like the Beasties were then; to describe their tour as being eagerly awaited by the media would have been a considerable understatement. Yet press reporting of the band didn't merely fan the flames of a volatile situation: it effectively provided the fuel for the fire and lit the match as well.

The British press has long exuded a veneer of youthful exuberance used to maintain an illusion that it is in touch with the feelings of the majority of the right-minded citizens it seeks to sell newspapers to. But in reality, the various daily titles are often mouthpieces for their proprietors, whose vested interests are promoted *ad nauseam* and who habitually side with a little-England mentality that fears and distrusts change, seeks to shore up so-called "traditional" values in life, art and society and runs screaming with indignation and incomprehension from anything that threatens the *status quo*. Normally, this is restricted to political reporting, which is usually heavily slanted to support the party the newspaper's owner favours, but occasionally the reporting of a youth cultural phenomenon is used to reinforce the newspaper's standing in the eyes of what it believes is its readership. The midmarket tabloid papers in Britain predominantly support an old-style conservatism that would find anything like the Beastie Boys anathema: the mock horror espoused in the writing of the likes of *The Daily Express* and *Daily Mail* was therefore unsurprising. Similarly unlikely to raise eyebrows, but certainly more self-contradictory to anyone unfamiliar with the British media, was the wave of outrage that drenched the band from the tabloids. *The Sun* and *The Daily Star* were apoplectic in their indignation that the band should have stage props such as a 25-foot hydraulically-operated penis and skimpily attired go-go dancers in cages on stage, while remaining oblivious to the double standard they were operating by printing pictures of topless women on page three of their rags every day. As analysed by Sarah Thornton in her dissection of the way the tabloid press switched from attacking to utilising rave music for their own ends a couple of years later, the contrariness of these newspapers seems to know no bounds. Thornton's essay, "Moral Panic, the Media and British Rave Culture", notes that "in Britain, the best guarantee of radicality is rejection by one or both of the disparate institutions seen to represent the cultural *status quo*: the tempered, state-sponsored BBC . . . and the sensational, sales-dependent tabloids." One only has to glance at the tabloids during a major international football tournament to comprehend their obliviousness to what they're doing: during the European Championships of 1996, when the England team played both Spain and Germany, several papers were rebuked by press watchdogs for the xeno-phobic tone of their pre-match writing. ('Achtung! Surrender!' was the *Mirror*'s front page headline on the day England played Germany). Yet when these tabloid-fed chickens come home to roost, and violence erupts involving English so-called "fans", it's the same papers that rush to condemn the thugs' behaviour, even though their jingoism has helped to foster the cultural atmosphere in which such attitudes can breed.

It was into this illogical ferment of reactionary bullshit and media frenzy that the Beasties stepped, improperly prepared for what was about to occur. Their main mistake was in believing that the audience they would play to would all be in on the joke they had created – an illusion abruptly shattered by beer cans and baseball bats a few days later. Even the indignation and offence they were deemed to have caused during their tour of the US with Madonna two years earlier was nothing compared to this.

By the time the group's UK appearances began to draw near, tabloid fury was fast approaching its zenith. By this stage the Beasties had established a reputation for goofing around and acting up, being more than a little boorish and sexist, and for not really giving a shit. And the band's media coverage subsequently split neatly into three areas, too. There was the "ban this evil filth" angle, the "they're outrageous but they're from nice middle class families, so they're even more despicable because it's all a sham" story, and the "this isn't music!" indignation. A fine early example of all three was provided in *The Daily Star*.

"The Beasties are, most people agree, the most obnoxious group ever," railed journalist Ivor Key, a man clearly no stranger to the concept of hyperbole. "They play the sort of music that parents love to hate," he notes, and, clearly excited by accidentally getting something right, he succinctly analyses that "Fight For Your Right" is "nothing like their usual material." He then gives full vent to his ignorance and misconceptions about rap music, taking up the sort of establishment *vs* youth culture moral high ground that has been proved to be so spectacularly out of touch every time it's been since the rock and roll era began.

"There are no melodies, no harmonies, no real singing," he observes, "just a relentless, often obscene flood of depraved words which extol the virtues of raw sex, guns and getting high on alcohol and angel dust. They are loud, talentless and disgusting."

Examining the Beastie live show to add colour and a notion of study to his invective ("They seem to spend much of their time showering each other with beer as they flail and chant to the hammerjack rhythm tracks played by a disc jockey who is up there with them"), Key reads like an amateur anthropologist, always looking in, never understanding or getting close to acknowledging that there's anything here worth more than his contempt. The piece ends with the writer's assertion that the band "have built a reputation on outrage rather than talent" – the notion that you can have a talent for outrage being unthinkable – and stresses a final quote from Mike D to reinforce in his reader's mind that there is nothing in common between either the Beastie Boys and musicians, or rap and music in general: "Next tour we might even play instruments."

This was stock-in-trade tabloid newspaper reporting. Key has looked for what he knows will outrage his readers and gives them gratuitous detail which is designed to titillate as much as to highlight deviant behaviour (the piece is accompanied by a photograph of a woman removing her top while on stage with the band, captioned "DEPRAVED"). It was a piece designed to reconfirm prejudices in order to sell papers. In the tabloid sales war, it would appear, the truth is most certainly the first casualty.

Accompanying Key's piece was a smaller story which quoted the suitably "outraged" Conservative Member of Parliament Peter Bruinvels and outlined his desire to see the group and their records banned from entering Britain. "Their kind of trash is obviously very dangerous," rails the easily offended Tory, who adds "our children will be corrupted by this sort of thing." Bruinvels' fellow Tory MP, Geoffrey Dickens, clearly didn't even wish to concede that the Beasties were human. "I want these diabolical creatures banned from these shores," he told *The News Of The World*. Bruinvels and Dickens belonged to the school of British politicians that felt his or her chances of re-election were best enhanced by being able to provide prospective voters with a bulging file of press clippings to emphasise their high public profile. Consequently, they were always willing to offer an emphatic opinion on any issue and would be quoted frequently in the tabloid press, regardless of the issue or their detailed knowledge of it. They became known as "rentaquotes", and, satisfyingly, many of them found their seats in Parliament rather more difficult to hang on to than they clearly had imagined. That the Beastie Boys are still with us long after Dickens and Bruinvels have been consigned to history's dustbin is perhaps a small victory.

Underlining their own suss and subtly showing the tabloid pack they had a bit more going on upstairs than they were being given credit for, Yauch laughed off the railings of the Tories as the band briefly stopped off in London on their way to the Montreux festival. "All we're doing is having a bit of fun," he told *The Sun*'s Craig MacKenzie. "The problem is we're living in conservative times. With Reagan and Thatcher running the countries, people act like it's a big deal."

"There were debates in parliament about . . . whether we

should be able to bring our 'inflatable' penis, which was actually hydraulic," Diamond recalled to *Q*. "I've always had this visual image of very earnest people in wigs discussing the merits of a hydraulic penis."

There is some truth in the axiom that there's no such thing as bad publicity and, for a band in the Beasties' position, stories like those already printed could do very little harm. *Of course* they're offensive and parents don't understand them: that's what rock and roll's supposed to be about. If you're appealing to the rebel spirit in teenagers you're hardly going to find it a handicap if those teenagers' parents are less than whole-hearted in their praise of your band. Consequently, and in common with the majority of pop acts that find themselves for a time at the centre of the tabloid storm, the Beasties and their representatives decided to play along with the papers and grant interviews and photographs to keep the press coverage ticking over. When the band arrived in Montreux, Switzerland, for an appearance at the city's annual pop festival, where they would perform alongside the legendary likes of Smokey Robinson, the tabloids were foaming at the leash.

"My job with the Beasties was to try and cause as much chaos as possible on the road and build the press story as it went along," John Reid, the band's road manager told *Q* in 1996. "We did deals with a lot of the journalists out there [in Montreux] to keep the press thing moving."

The wheels finally came off, though, when *The Daily Mirror* ran their front page headline story on May 14th. Headlined "POPIDOLSSNEERATDYINGKIDS", the piece accused the band of mocking crippled and terminally ill children. The story, by Gill Pringle, would prove difficult to live down, regardless of the fact that it wasn't true.

"Gill Pringle had been hanging in Montreux trying to get a story and she had asked Adam Horovitz for a few words," Mike told *Q*. "He blew her off because he didn't have time and because she'd been snubbed she just made up the entire story."

Pringle reported that the band had told a group of young "mainly terminally ill leukemia sufferers" to "Go away you

fucking cripples." (The ever-prurient paper replaced the letters
following 'f' in the adjective with asterisks.) Pringle further
maintained that the group had laughed and sworn at the children
and that they were "roughly pushed aside as the three-man cult
band rampaged through a plush hotel after a five-hour drinking
spree which left a trail of destruction." Her attempts to ask the
group to explain their actions met with short shrift: "When the
group's Adam Horovitz was asked about the incident he sneered:
'Who cares about a bunch of cripples anyway?'"

"When I read it, I was really pissed off," explained Mike D. "I
felt powerless to convince anyone it wasn't true. We didn't sue
the paper although we did consider it, it would have been too
costly. There was actually a small retraction printed much later
but by then the damage had been done. I had to phone my Mom
and tell her that I wasn't really a cannibalistic, child-eating mass-
murderer."

The band found an unlikely, if temporary, ally in the shape of
The Mirror's deadly rival in the battle for circulation, *The Sun*.
Previously, on the day Pringle's story had occupied their nemesis'
front page, *The Sun* had also been hot on the Beasties' tails,
though their story stopped some way short of potential libel.
Reporting that the band had got drunk, sworn at reporters and
cameramen and that Yauch had had what appeared to be a fight
over a groupie with Run DMC's Jam Master Jay, the paper's
reporters gleefully described the band's insurrectionary activities. Noting that Yauch was "drunk after knocking back brandy
and vodka cocktails called 'Cold Medinas'" ("Cold Medina"
would become a catchphrase for Public Enemy's Flavor Flav,
and 'Funky Cold Medina' was even later a hit single for Tone
Loc, whose producers, the Dust Brothers, worked on the
Beasties' second LP – further examples of Beastie slang becoming
part of hip-hop's colloquial vocabulary), the paper reported the
rapper's comments at a subsequent press conference as though
they constituted a threat to the fabric of British society. "We're
going to carry on drinking our Cold Medinas, taking drugs and
falling on our faces," Yauch is quoted as saying. "If people in
Britain don't like it they know what they can do." He further

endeared himself to every right-thinking anti-reactionary soul across the globe by suggesting that the appropriate course of action to be taken by the Tory MPs who'd been campaigning to have the group's work permits refused would be for them to "Fuck off".

So it must have been with some heaviness of heart that *The Sun* found themselves running a story supporting the band the following day. While Pringle and *The Mirror* stood by their earlier story, repeating their accusation and supporting in with Pringle's apparent eye-witness claims ("I WAS THERE . . . I SAW the tears spring into the eyes of two children who asked for their heroes' autographs and whose dreams were shattered,"), *The Sun* found themselves sticking up for the band they'd spent a month assassinating the character of, in order to undermine the authority of their main competitor. Quoting a mother of one of the children ("The Beasties were very kind to the children and happily signed autographs for them," said Pauline Hallam), and pop star Paul Young, a patron of the Dreams Come True charity that had paid for the children to visit the festival, *The Sun*'s piece set out to rubbish Pringle's claims. "OK, so we get drunk, fight and smash up bars," admitted Yauch, in half a sentence vindicating the previous day's *Sun* smear, "but we know where to draw the line. Who the hell would want to upset a bunch of kids who haven't got long to live?"

In a side-bar to *The Sun* story, which reported that the band had gone on yet another late night rampage in Montreux, this time – tsk, tsk – attempting to turn over two parked cars, the Beasties received what would for some time come to be one of the most perceptive analyses of their attitudes and psyches. That this should come from the celebrated topless model and, at that time, putative pop star Samantha Fox is surprising enough. Fox became famous as a "page three girl", a peculiar institution to the British tabloid press: a busty young woman is pictured topless on page three of the paper each day, thus making a mockery of the editorial direction – which always leans towards conservatism and prurience – with the oft-voiced opinion that "it's just a harmless bit of fun." The difference between "harmless" Sam and her ilk and the "diabolical" Beastie Boys stage show, with its topless women and ludicrous giant phallus, is rather difficult to discern. So, for that matter, is the difference between three blokes behaving lewdly and talking about sex and a woman famous for baring her breasts having as her first hit single a song that went "Touch me, I wanna feel your body". Unless, of course, you're a tabloid newspaper employee, or a page three girl. "They are the sort of boys," opined "sexy Sam", "whose heads used to be stuck down toilets at school." Clearly a kindred spirit.

Sam was still seething when the third British tabloid on the scene, *The Daily Star,* entered the fray. She told their reporter: "They're awful, horrible – just one big turn-off." *The Daily Star* led with the car incident, and two photographs of the band trying to overturn it, and also quoted Larry Blackmon of Cameo, who said "That band is giving pop a bad name." Blackmon, a past associate of the hardly titillation-shy George Clinton, once appeared on *Top Of The Pops* wearing a bright red (and, one presumes, significantly oversized) codpiece, provoking a record number of complaints to the BBC only broken years later by the programme's broadcast of the Prodigy's "Firestarter" video.

The game, though, was almost up. *The Sun*, exhibiting some of the finer traditions of investigative journalism, had tracked down families and friends of the trio and set out to shed some light on their past. "I could play the outraged parent," explained Yauch's father, Noel, from what the paper described as a "£1 million ten bedroom mansion in Brooklyn", "but I really find the Beastie Boys whole put-on terrifically amusing." Horovitz' father, Israel, whom the paper referred to as "one of America's most respected playwrights" in a manner that gave the mistaken impression their readership gave a shit, supported Noel Yauch. "Don't you think it's fun how much excitement the boys have created?" he asked rhetorically. "They are not irresponsible. Everything about them is on the side of the angels." (A fuller version of this quote, attributed to *Newsday*, appeared in *The Detroit Free Press*: "I'm extremely proud and not at all surprised. They're very anti-drug and pro-get-to-work, and that's on the side of the angels. He has a talent, and a seriousness, and he's having a lot of fun.")

Incredibly, the band had still to set foot in the UK. As if on cue, the tabloid campaign to deny the band work permits for their tour of the UK abruptly stalled. A spokesman for the Home Office, the government department dealing with immigration matters, told *The Daily Mirror* that Douglas Hurd, the Home Secretary, had personally looked at the case but concluded that "it would be an inappropriate use of the immigration laws in this case."

The remaining few days until the band's arrival in Britain passed reasonably quietly. Yet one significant story ran in *The Sun* on the day the band landed in the UK. With a typical scaremonger's flair, Garry Bushell tried to stir a racial subtext into what the press had already decided would be the inevitable violence. Bushell had championed the extremely suspect right wing Oi! skinhead post-punk movement when writing for music weekly *Sounds*, and his new job at *The Sun* seemed to afford him many more opportunities to stir up similar tensions. His story, which was never substantiated and never repeated (except by himself), quoted an unnamed source described only as "an insider" who claimed that in "troubled" Brixton, where the Academy would host the first two shows of the Run DMC/ Beasties tour, "black gangs are giving out leaflets with the slogan 'No Whites Allowed'. They think the Beastie Boys are getting rich from black music and they don't want a load of white kids at the show." Residents of the area saw no such leaflets, and, despite rather than because of a massive police presence, the two gigs passed off without incident. That, of course, didn't stop Bushell from pursuing his own agenda. Here's what he wrote about attending the first Brixton gig: "A leering dreadlocked thug held a Stanley knife to my throat and told me: 'If you want trouble tonight, you're gonna get it.' Student trendies recoiled in terror as Rastas and soccer yobs rubbed shoulders with political nutters in Brixton, south London. Tension was running high from the start, after black extremists had circulated race-hate leaflets warning white fans to keep clear. Throughout the show . . . belligerent black kids tried to pick fights with white fans. They pushed and shouted insults."

Walking to the Academy in Brixton for the first of those two
shows on May 23rd was indeed an unnerving experience, but for
very different reasons than those given by Bushell. The venue is
situated (literally) a stone's throw from the area's police station,
and although concerts there are no rarity, the atmosphere on the
night was charged and volatile. Rows of police on horseback
stood guard in front of the police station, and while the intent
may simply have been to channel concert-goers from the nearby
underground station to the venue, to the untrained eye it appeared as though the police were expecting a riot, and were ready
for Beastie Boys fans to attempt to storm the police building.
Simply getting into the venue from the surrounding streets
became something of a nerve-jangling affair: as the band's future
British press officer, Anton Brookes, who attended the Brixton
shows as a fan, recalled when speaking to *Q* some years later,
"The atmosphere was heavy – there were loads of police everywhere and it felt like you were at a football match." That
atmosphere inevitably found its way inside the venue: that there
was no riot is simply testament to the good-nature of the people
attending the shows.

The Beasties, their dancing girls and their hydraulic penis,
then, became something of a sideshow. Run DMC, the headliners
in everyone's minds but the media and the police, were who the
majority had paid to see. And the threat of some sort of trouble
probably dulled the occasion for many. While the inevitable
edginess surrounding an event held under such circumstances
can add a frisson of excitement, to many people the threat of
trouble, and their own safety in the event of it, became the over-
riding concern.

In what was one of only a handful of pieces written about the
band's trip to Britain to see through the surely transparent
facade, *The Independent*'s Dave Hill gave his own account of
going to the Academy show. "The management of The Academy
had sought to cover themselves by a combination of PR and
heavyweight security, which, had its implications not been so
gloomy, could have been cheerily described as a farce. As teams of
bristling bouncers frisked you from head to toe with crackling

phallic symbols, there was a leaflet to read, urging patrons to behave for fear of losing future promotions 'of this nature.'"

"What the Beasties contrive," Hill continued, "is half low *Animal House* humour and half lumpen role playing. So spectacularly impotent is their libidinal posturing that the offensiveness of having caged go-go dancers on stage comes close to symbolising their comprehensive uselessness to any sane female person. So crass is the sensibility they assume as the springboard for their routine that only the naive could construe them as some sort of ideological vanguard. Few rap punters would be so uncool as to actually *follow* a bunch of loons like that . . . A persona has been filched and perfected so completely that the line between acting off and really meaning it has become blurred: which just about defines most adolescent boys."

So far, then, there'd been no real trouble (aside from that bloke threatening Garry Bushell). In Liverpool, though, a combination of a self-righteous attitude among people who'd bought tickets after reading Pringle's story in *The Mirror*, and felt that the band needed to be "taught a lesson", conspired with the group's and their management's underestimation of the seriousness of the situation to produce a real riot for the press to gloat over.

Fundamentally, perhaps, overestimating their audience was the band's only mistake. "I think anyone who's smart enough can see the joke in it," Yauch had said while touring the States. "It's an inside joke between the three of us; with our success, the joke has become public property. It's worked its way into best-selling records, but the joke's still ours, so it's OK. People don't credit kids with the intelligence to listen to music and see that it's a joke. Parents get too uptight. The music is for the kids; if the parents don't like it, that's their problem."

In the same way that the south Bronx had become synonymous with urban decay through repeated images of the multiple malaises affecting it in the mid-70s before the birth of hip-hop culture, so in the mid-80s, Liverpool had become intractably linked with the failing fortunes of industrial Britain. Margaret Thatcher's Conservative government had done their best to break the spirit of working class people in Britain, most obviously through the protracted attempt to crush trade unionism through the bitter years of the miners' strike between 1984 and 1986. During an overlapping period, Liverpool city council was controlled by a Trotskyist organisation, Militant, who provoked a head-on conflict with the government by refusing to stick to what they maintained was an inadequate budget set by the Conservatives with which to run local services. An area already reeling from the loss of almost all its local industry through the ravages of the global economic recession, Liverpool had further to deal with the systematic erosion of local services as the council and the government played out a war of attrition. It was not the sort of place to play if the press had managed to convince elements of somewhat hopeless local young people that your band was a pampered shower of middle-class brats, playing at being from the street, who thought it was a laugh to take the piss out of crippled kids. Given that the date didn't sell out before the worst of the tabloid stories appeared, it seemed inevitable that some sort of problems would arise.

"The Glasgow and Liverpool dates were added after the tabloid stories broke," Diamond explained to *The Detroit Free Press*, "so there were a lot of people who'd come to see the spectacle rather than the band. Liverpool was unbelievable. The bottles started flying 'cos most of the people there just wanted to get drunk and start a fight. We were in a no-win situation. If we didn't go on there'd be a riot for sure and if we went out and asked the crowd to stop throwing shit then we'd really get bombarded. We just decided to give it a shot and see if we could get through."

"Ah, man, Liverpool," Adrock began, recalling that fateful night in a later interview with *NME*'s Ted Kessler. "Three songs in and we realised that *all* the audience are singing, but not one of our songs. So we asked our English friend, The Captain, what was going on and he said, 'It's really bad, they're singing football songs.' Then the bottles and cans started flying in from everywhere."

The band attempted to play through the hail of debris. Finding the going decidedly tough, they took a brief respite but came back on-stage with baseball bats and tried to hit things back towards the crowd. By the end of the third song, they gave up all pretence of making it through the set and retired to their tour bus. "Once we were on the bus we thought, 'Thank God it's over,'" Mike D recalled. '"All English people are assholes."'

Yet it wasn't. On their arrival back in London in the early hours of Sunday 31st, Horovitz was arrested and charged with an alleged assault of a female fan, who claimed to have been hit in the face by a beer can pelted from the stage by the baseball bat-wielding Beastie. "I spent the weekend in the police cells, which was a drag because it was a long weekend," Adrock told Kessler. "I never threw a thing, I was totally innocent." On advice from tour management and the record company, Yauch and Diamond left the country while Horovitz was questioned at Notting Hill police station. "We weren't being disloyal to Adam," Mike D recalled, "but there was nothing we could do for him." "My friends were sharing it with me, in a way," Horovitz said to Kessler. "Do I recognise myself? Think of the time you were the most drunk, hugging the toilet, fucked up and ugly . . . but happy in a way. Do you recognise that? Me too." Adrock appeared in court on June 1st and was released on bail of £10,000. A court appearance, where the charge of grievous bodily harm to 20-year-old Joanna Marie Clark would be heard, was set for Liverpool Crown Court on July 21st.

Tabloid accounts of the evening in Liverpool were predictably lurid. Most of the reports carried claims from people who heard sectors of the crowd chanting "We tamed the Beasties", *The Daily Star* also quoting Liverpool Royal Court Theatre manager Simon Geddes as saying that a proportion of the audience wanted to give the band "a taste of their own medicine." All laid the blame for the melée squarely at the Beasties' door, with Geddes quoted in *The Sun* in a rather less equivocal frame of mind: "They incited members of the crowd to violence and that is unforgivable. We could have sorted out the troublemakers if the band had simply walked back off the stage when the missile throwing started."

As Horovitz travelled to Japan to meet up with Diamond and Yauch and continue the band's worldwide tour, he could have been excused more than a little room for wondering just what he'd gotten himself into. Although the memories of those close to events suggest that much of what happened was easily shrugged off, some wounds took time to heal.

Speaking in 1998, Bill Adler recalled that "it seemed to me that they could wear the scorn of the British press easily, they could wear it like a *crown*, but when the kids themselves seemed to pick up the attitude of the press and turn their scorn on the Beasties, once that started that wasn't fun, that wasn't something that they loved, it got dangerous. That Liverpool thing was a very dangerous thing. I do not think that Adrock loved being arrested. I don't think that it was traumatic for him, but it was kinda crazy."

Once out of the UK, events calmed down. "When I toured with them in Europe, they was cool guys, I had fun with them," remembers Run. "Runnin' around, doin' shows, just enjoyin' the success. None o' that [the tabloid bad boy image] was true. They was calm, normal guys. I don't think they cared about none o' that stupid stuff. I don't think they worried about what the press was sayin'. They knew who they were and whatever the press thought was what the press thought."

"They got through it, they came back to America, and the record continued to blow up for another year," Adler explains. "That had virtually no impact on their career – it was just a bad week in England."

A bad week, nevertheless, that marked the end of the band's first fifteen minutes of fame, and was enough to put them off visiting the UK for some five years. As the infinitely more tragic stories of murdered rappers Tupac Shakur and Notorious B.I.G. would later prove, there's a price to be paid for allowing a cultivated public image to obscure reality. The Beastie Boys would never make the same mistake again.

Lemon on a Jet Plane

Andrew Mueller

Around the world with U2 April 1997 – February 1998.

"The highest art will be that which in its conscious content
presents the thousandfold problems of the day, the art which
has been visibly shattered by the explosions of last week,
which is forever trying to collect its limbs after yesterday's
crash. The best and most extraordinary artists will be those
who every hour snatch the tatters of their bodies out of the
frenzied cataract of life, who, with bleeding hands and hearts,
hold fast to the intelligence of their time."

Dadaist manifesto, Berlin, 1918

"What's Boner's problem?"

– Beavis & Butthead, USA, 1994

Two hundred miles from here, about a decade ago, four young
Irishmen stood amid the cacti of the Arizona desert and gazed
grimly towards the dusty horizons while Anton Corijn took their
pictures for the cover of *The Joshua Tree*, an album that remains a
benchmark for ascetic introspection. Tonight, the same four
Irishmen will perform songs from an album called *Pop* on a
stage decorated with a fifty-foot-high lemon-shaped mirror ball,
an enormous glowing olive atop a towering swizzle stick, and a
giant golden arch obviously intended to signal associations with
populism and disposability. U2's reinvention, first flagged with
1991's *Achtung Baby* album and subsequent *Zoo TV* tour, has
been an act of total auto-iconoclasm. It's been like watching a
Pope touring the world's cathedrals with a tin of kerosene and a
lighter and has, as such, been well rock'n'roll.

However, there's self-destruction and there's self-destruction, and when U2 open their *PopMart* world tour tonight in Las Vegas's 37,000-seater Sam Boyd Stadium, they deliver an ex-cruciating example of the wrong kind. Beset by technical hitches, grappling with material that seems even less familiar to them than it does to the audience, U2 play a shocker. That they make little attempt to disguise their own disappointment is some mitigation, but not much – it's difficult to extend much sympathy for first-night nerves when tickets are $54.50 a shot. It's perhaps only this consideration that compels the band to grit their teeth and go the distance. If this had been a fight, it would have been stopped.

Las Vegas, we press junketeers have been told, is a logistical rather than a conceptual choice for opening night. If this is true, it's the happiest of coincidences. Las Vegas – Blackpool on steroids – is the city in which the characteristic American refusal to acknowledge that such a thing as vulgarity exists has reached a triumphantly crass apotheosis. In the arcade leading into Caesar's Palace, I stop, entranced, in a foyer where a faux-marble Aph-rodite stands among the ten-cent slot machines. "Wow," says a camcorder-encumbered American next to me. "Isn't it beauti-ful?"

Vegas's casinos are fleetingly amusing but eventually terribly depressing places. At the endless rows of slot machines, people lose and win thousands with a total lack of emotion. I wonder how many of these dead-eyed people feeding in money, pulling a lever, feeding in money, pulling a lever, feeding in money, pulling a lever, are on holiday from repetitive, menial factory jobs. As I sit around the roulette tables, every so often someone will swagger along, throw a ludicrous amount – five hundred, a thousand dollars – on one number and then, when they lose it, shrug and walk away, bearing that no-really-it-didn't-hurt-at-all expression usually seen on batsmen who've just been whacked in the ribs by Allan Donald. It seems bizarre to spend so much money to impress total strangers; there again, I've come to Vegas to watch U2 do exactly that.

If U2 have decided to see what happens when you submit to,

even revel in, the junk, kitsch and flash of popular culture, they've come to ground zero. The only problem is that bringing a fifty-foot lemon-shaped mirror ball to Las Vegas, of all places, and expecting anyone to be impressed, is a bit like trying to attract attention in London by driving around in a red double-decker bus. In a short walk along the Las Vegas Strip from my hotel, I see a pirate ship, King Kong, a blue glass pyramid, the New York City skyline, a volcano that erupts every 15 minutes, and marble dolphins frozen in mid-leap above the fountains next to an automatic walkway. To create a stir here on a purely visual level, U2 would have needed to invest in an entire fifty-foot mirror-ball fruit salad.

Of course, for all the gaudy window-dressing of *PopMart*, it's the music that's supposed to carry it. Tonight, it mostly doesn't, though things start well. In fact, only rarely since the ancients of Babylon finished work on the Ishtar Gate have people made entrances this spectacular.

To a remixed fanfare of M's lone hit "Pop Muzik", U2 enter the arena from under one of the stands along the side. A spotlight tracks their progress through the crows. Bono, his hair cropped and dyed blond, is wearing a boxer's robe and sparring furiously. Edge is clad in a very Las Vegas rhinestone cowboy outfit and looks like an escapee from The Village People. Adam Clayton has drawn the short straw in the outfit department for roughly the thousandth time in U2's history – he wears an orange boiler suit and a face mask and looks like one of those poor Chernobyl technicians who were given a shovel and ten minutes to shift as much glowing rubble as they could off the roof of the reactor before they started growing extra heads. Larry Mullen Jr, consistent throughout U2's image rethinks, has come dressed as Larry Mullen Jr (I've always imagined that, stuffed in some Dublin filing cabinet, there must be the dozens of extravagant costume ideas that the band have presented to Mullen over the years, only to be rebuffed every time with "Well, I thought I'd wear the leather trousers and a T-shirt, again").

At the back of the stage, on the largest LED television screen ever built, the word "Pop" appears in red letters taller than your

house, or taller than your house if you're not a member of U2.
They start with "Mofo", the most explicitly dance-oriented track
from the new album. Immense images of the band fill the screen.
It looks fantastic, and sounds twice as good.

The wires start coming loose almost immediately. Having
established a giddy forward momentum, U2 stick a pole in the
spokes by exhuming their 1980 rabble-rouser "I Will Follow"
and follow that with two relatively undemanding newer songs,
"Even Better Than The Real Thing" and "Do You Feel Loved".
When they go from those into "Pride" and "I Still Haven't
Found What I'm Looking For" there's an almost audible grinding of gears. These two songs were among the most exciting parts
of *Zoo TV* – the former was graced with a spectacular guest
appearance by its subject, Martin Luther King Jr, testifying from
the ether on video, and the latter sounded like a raging defiance of
the temptation to rest on lucrative laurels. Tonight, they just
sound tired, the evening is turning into a bewilderingly timid
exercise in nostalgia, and I'm thinking of that episode of *Yes,
Prime Minister* in which Sir Humphrey is advising Hacker about
his address to the nation, counselling that if he's got nothing new
to say, he should wear a bold modern suit and fill his office with
abstract art.

It gets worse still when U2, hamstrung by sound which is
killing the bottom end and making everything sound like it's
being played down the phone, move down a catwalk to a smaller
stage in the middle of the arena. "If God Will Send His Angels"
is lovely, but "Staring At The Sun" is a disaster, lurching to an
abrupt halt in the middle of the first chorus. "Talk amongst
yourselves," says Bono. "We're just having a family row." They
get all the way through at the second attempt. Edge leads the
crowd in a karaoke singalong of "Daydream Believer".

Some hope that *PopMart* is going to be something more than
watered-down Warholia is provided by "Miami" and "Bullet
The Blue Sky". Both are played with an intensity that verges on
the deranged, and the latter is illustrated with a dazzling animation of Roy Lichtenstein fighter planes, chasing each other across
the immense screen while, around the stadium, perpendicular

lasers point towards the summit of an immense pyramid of light. It's an unabashed steal from Albert Speer's Nuremberg illuminations: that the only lasting cultural legacy of Nazism is stadium rock is an irony U2 underscored during the *Zoo TV* shows by getting the crowds to clap along with a Hitler Youth drummer boy excerpted from Leni Riefenstahl's *Triumph of the Will*. Bono has at last found his voice, along with a bowler hat and a stars'n' stripes umbrella, and is goosestepping along the catwalk in the style of Chaplin's "Great Dictator". This is more like it: if *Zoo TV* marked the first time a band of U2's stature had acknowledged their own absurdity, this may be the first time such a band has asked its audience to do the same.

The rest of the set is an inevitable comedown, and the encores are flat enough to putt on. The giant disco lemon putters slowly down the catwalk in a tornado of dry ice fog, and U2 emerge from inside it. On a better night, this might look like endearing self-mockery, but given what has preceded it, it's a little too close to the pods scene from *This Is Spinal Tap* for comfort. U2 proceed to make rather a madwoman's custard of "Discotheque", follow that with an inconsequential "If You Wear That Velvet Dress" and then engage in an ungainly race with each other to the end of "With Or Without You". They come back on once more, do a shambolic "Hold Me, Thrill Me, Kiss Me, Kill Me" and a desultory "Mysterious Ways" before locating some form to close with a beautifully turned-out "One", illustrated with a touching Keith Haring sequence.

U2 are about the only famous people on earth who don't make an appearance at the after-show party at the venue, or the after-after-show party in Vegas's Hard Rock Café. At both of these gatherings, there is much excitement about the presence of R.E.M., Dennis Hopper, Bruce Willis, Kylie Minogue, Helena Christensen, Winona Ryder, etc., etc., but I'm more interested in the large inflatable *PopMart*-logo-branded lemons suspended from the Hard Rock's ceiling. The more daiquiris I drink, the more convinced I become that one of them would look great on top of my fridge. With the help of some passers-by, a table and two chairs, I get up high enough to get a grip on one and, despite the warnings of a bouncer shouting at me from the ground, remove it from its moorings and climb down.

"Sir, I must ask you . . ."

I was leaving anyway.

My hard-won souvenir nearly goes missing on the way back to the hotel, when I am diverted towards a roulette table somewhere en route. Using an infallible new system based on my birthday, Gianfranco Zola's squad number and covering bets on reds and evens, I do OK, turning 10 dollars into 500. Continuing with the same infallible system, I lose nearly all of it. I totter off to collect what remains of my winnings.

"Sir!" the croupier bellows across the casino floor. "Sir! You forgot your lemon!"

There is one building in Sarajevo that would fit in nicely along the Las Vegas strip. The Holiday Inn, a distended cube of lurid purples, yellows and oranges, can only have been the work of an architect who was totally insensitive to the city's architectural heritage, or a chronic glue-sniffer, or both. The first time I came to Sarajevo, in March 1996, this absurd building, stranded in the open boulevard known as Sniper Alley, was a wreck, shot to pieces. It sat incongruously amid the ruins of the city's other, relatively demure, buildings looking like some bumbling space-craft that had been brought down by crossfire.

The Holiday Inn has been repaired since Sarajevo's war ended in late 1995, though some twisted fragments of stubborn shrapnel still pock the walls. On a grey autumn morning, in a room decorated entirely in brown, a singer, who looks in need of some restoration work himself, is trying to explain what he's doing here.

"There is a history," croaks Bono, "of artists having a response – and they ought to have a response – to situations like this. Dada and surrealism were responses to fascism."

Last night, U2 brought *PopMart* to Sarajevo's Kosevo sta-dium, making good on a five-year-old promise to play in the Bosnian capital. Bono's voice didn't quite make the journey with him.

"They call it Las Vegas throat, did you know that?" says Bono, tentatively rubbing his neck. "It's the desert air. When seasoned old crooners hear of a new boy coming to Las Vegas they all giggle, because they know what's going to happen. We even rang Sinatra's people about this thing, and they just went naaaah, just keep drinking and smoking, it'll sort itself out."

When I first heard that U2 were definitely coming to Sarajevo, I assumed they'd be playing a scratch show with the bare minimum of equipment. When I heard that they were bringing the entire *PopMart* circus – 500 tons of equipment carried by 75 trucks, operated by 250 personnel on sixteen buses and one Boeing 727, with a total daily operating cost of £160,000 – I assumed they'd been out in the sun without hats on. It was less than a year since I'd come to Sarajevo with China Drum, all of whom fitted into one truck, and that had degenerated into the most ludicrous expedition undertaken by man or beast since Scott's to the Antarctic.

"The idea," explains Bono, "was that we'd flash bastard it into town – you know, the big private plane with the lemon on the side, the police escort from the airport, the lot, you saw it, you were there – and play a rock 'n' roll show like rock 'n' roll bands do. Don't patronise these people, just do it. That was the plan. I was gonna give 'em the full whack, you know. I just wasn't able to, because my voice kind of . . . went. But, you know, what happened last night . . . it dwarfed *Pop Mart*. That's what I though was interesting. Arches, lemons, fucking drive-in movie screens, all kind of disappeared, because . . . something else went on, something that I, as an outsider in this city, probably can't fully understand. I just have to say that those were the cards we were dealt, and the crowd made it very special."

I'd been in Sarajevo a month previously, doing a story for the *Sunday Times* about the birth of the city's tourist industry. Just about everything that wasn't moving was upholstered with U2 posters. The concert was all anyone was talking about. Even the staff of Sarajevo's newly reopened tourist office, whose average age was around 70, said they were going. The excitement was about more than a big rock group coming to town: Sarajevo was going to be on CNN because something good was happening in it.

"Well', shrugs Bono, "I don't, as a general rule, suffer from any Catholic guilt, even though I'm half Catholic, but I think for any person who finds success, the instinctive reaction is to try and level the pitch a bit, with your friends, and your family, and I guess in the wider world, which is when you became a real pain in the hole. Or I guess the other extreme is to just put it all up your nose, and I thought I had a great nose, so I wasn't interested in that."

U2 had played a smart game: tickets for the show were sold in Croatia, Slovenia and Yugoslavia, but there was no concert scheduled in Zagreb, Llubljana or Belgrade. Anyone between Austria and Greece who wanted to see U2 was going to have to come to Sarajevo, and they did, in their thousands. On the day of the show, trains had run into Sarajevo for the first time in four years. The city's roads were full of cars bearing Croatian and Yugoslav licence plates. The bars were crowded with people with subtly different accents. There was no trouble – although, earlier this morning, I did see a local market trader knock on the window of a Belgrade-registed car, say something to the clearly affronted driver and walk off looking terribly pleased with themselves; a friend translated the pedestrian's remarks as "I've just fucked your Hungarian mother with her dead horse's dick."

"So no, last night wasn't really what I'd planned," continues Bono, in what sounds a painful rasp. "I'd planned to be in fine voice. I have been in fine voice, of late, and I'd probably have been a terrible pain in the arse if I had pulled that off. It was very hunbling, actually. But maybe that allowed room for Sarajevo to kind of take the gig away from us, which is what they did. They could see that things could go very horribly wrong, but they'd come here, and they'd gone to a lot of trouble, and they were going to make it happen. And they just kind of carried me along. And the band also played with some real spunk, I thought. When I lost it on 'Pride', and Edge started singing it, I thought, fucking hell, now see what it feels like, you bastard, but he did it, you know, he got us there".

The first act on last night had been a local choir. They were followed by Protest, one of the better acts to have emerged from Sarajevo's wartime rock scene. Sikter followed them, starting their set by tearing up the Bosnian national anthem in the style of Hendrix's 'Star Spangled Banner', and playing a blinder after that. When U2 made their entrance, and the *PopMart* stage lit up on cue, the roars had been as much of relief as excitement. In a city which has come to view delivery on promises as very much the exception to the rule, there had been a general view that something would go wrong at the last minute.

In the event, the only thing that went wrong was Bono's voice. On any other night, this might have been catastrophic, but as Bono says, last night it really didn't matter. By the time the giant disco lemon rolled out for the encores, it felt less like another stadium concert, and more like a very, very large party with a band playing in one corner of it. Standing in the middle of it on the mixing desk was an overwhelming experience, if one leavened with a guilt at the privilege of being there without having suffered the same suspension of everyday life that everyone else was celebrating the end of it. "Concerts are one of those things that happen in normal cities," Sikter's drummer Faris had said backstage before the show, twitching with nerves. "Tonight is one of the most important things that's ever happened here – way bigger than the Olympics." Faris is not, in my experience, prone to overstatement. "My father made me some new shoes especially," he laughed.

Two parts of *PopMart* had been tailored to the location. The Karaoke singalong was replaced by Edge delivering a lovely, mournful solo reading of 'Sunday Bloody Sunday', and the encores included the first ever live performance of 'Miss Sarajevo' – the gorgeous song inspired by Bill Carter's film about a wartime beauty pageant, and recorded by U2, Brian Eno and Luciano Pavarotti under the name Passengers. Last night, Eno joined U2 onstage in person, Pavarotti on tape. It had been a tentative performance. "Well, we wrote that song for you,'" Bono said, as it stumbled to a close, "and we can't fucking play it."

When the lights came up at the end of the show, and the crowd started filing out, something strange and wonderful happened. The stand along the left of the stadium, which was filled with ranks of uniformed soldiers serving with the multinational NATO-led Stabilisation Force (SFOR), stood, as one, and applauded the crowd, the people of Sarajevo. The punters leaving the ground stopped, turned around, and clapped back. A self-conscious, embarrassed silence followed, eventually broken by the Spanish SFOR contingent, many wearing their national flag as bandannas, leading an impromptu massed military choir in 'Y Viva Espana' and, then, an altogether surreal line dance to 'The Macerena.'

With me on the mixing desk was the only other British journalist who'd flown out for the show, Mat Smith of the *NME*.

"It's amazing," he said."Every time some idiot musician starts with that hippy-dippy music-bringing-people-together-as-one stuff, we just laugh at them. But look at this . . . they've actually done it. What the hell are we going to write?"

At the Holiday Inn the next morning, Bono tries to give me a hand with that one.

"In the mid-eighties," he says, "we were involved in America, and the concept of the two Americas, and that brought us on the one hand to Central America, Nicaragua and 'Bullet The Blue Sky' and on the other hand to Sun Studios. But it was all part of the same . . . it's sometimes helpful to make a parallel between bands and film-makers.You go for whatever you're doing and just focus on it. And that's one of the reasons our records have real . . . they're caught in their time.When people look at the eighties, they will pick out one of our records, and they'll say that if you want to know what was going on in music, and you want to know what was going on . . . you know, America was what was going on, and this was a response to it. 'Achtung Baby' and 'Zooropa', again, that paints a picture of what was going on. I guess we should start just writing tunes, and just shut the fuck up, but if you're curious, and that's certainly my strongest suit, the tunes get set into a context of some kind . . . and here we are."

Someone comes to tell Bono to get a move on, as U2's plane has to leave.

"I've had, I guess, a few holidays in hell, but I hate that – and you should be careful with that yourself – but the way it works with me, they way it works with the group, is whatever you're doing, you look under every stone of it. So *ZooTV* bought us into that world of television, news, cartoons, Dada, and you end up following that through, and if you do that you end up in Sarajevo one minute and hanging out with some of the most beautiful women in the world the next, and you just get fully into it."

Two months later, by the pool in the exquisite garden behind the impeccably renovated and uproariously expensive Delano Hotel in Miami's South Beach, we are hanging out with some of the most beautiful women in the world, getting fully into it. Photographer Rankin introduces me to Helena Christensen, and one of my chats with Bono is interrupted when he is distracted by Veronica Webb wandering over to say hello. I am inclined to forgive Bono for this, as Veronica Webb wandering over to say hello would be enough to distract a man performing an emergency tracheotomy on his brother.

U2 have pitched camp in the Delano for a couple of weeks while *PopMart* tours the south of the United States. The band's families are here as well – there are seven U2 children – and U2 are flying back to Miami every night after shows in other cities in the lemon-spangled 727. Various friends have flown in for the Miami show, Elvis Costello among them. George Clooney is also staying here ("Hey", says Bono, as we leave the hotel to find a bar showing the Ireland vs Belgium World Cup playoff, "there's Batman playing basketball. Cool") and though he hasn't come as a friend of the band, he seems to leave as one.

Rock tours are not usually such relaxed things to visit, especially not after they've been six months on the road. Most seethe with tensions and paranoias comparable with the last weeks of the Nixon administration, and most regard an itinerant journalist as little more than a handy outlet for those pressures. U2's organisation has the feel of a large and almost suspiciously happy family. It may help that many of their closest staff have associations with the band going back most of the twenty-odd years of

U2's existence. It may also help that many of those closest staff, whether by accident or design, are women.

The four members of U2 are themselves unfailingly courteous and pleasant, certainly more so than men regularly credited with a combined wealth of £300 million really have to be.

Edge, the permanently behatted guitarist, first sees me at some distance past my best when, not long off the flight from London, I descend on his table on the Delano's back porch, jetlagged and margarita-sodden, and interrupt someone else's praise of The Spice Girls with a lengthy rant outlining their defects. Edge cheerfully puts up a case for the defence while I mutter things like "cynical", "vapid", "worse than the plague" and "the Nolan Sisters", and drink someone else's drink, becoming dimly aware that I am talking no sense at all, know nobody here and that everyone has gone very quiet. A hope of salvation arrives in the shape of Elvis Costello; while I don't expect him to remember the nervous nineteen-year-old who interviewed him in Sydney nine years ago, I do expect that the curmudgeonly elder rock'n'roll statesman will take my side. "I'm in the Spice movie," he grins. "I play a barman." I decide that discretion is the better part of valour, and go up to bed, my attempt at a dignified exit hampered by the way the garden furniture keeps jumping in front of me.

Larry Mullen Jr, the strangely ageless drummer whose high-school noticeboard advertisement bought U2 together, introduces himself after a few days and apologises for not wanting to speak on the record on the grounds that "I only feel comfortable sitting at my kit hitting stuff", and besides which, his young son, Elvis, has pulled a table over on himself and hurt his foot. Adam Clayton, the bass player who comes nearest of any of them to mustering the traditional hauteur of the rock'n' roll aristocrat, seems generally thoughtful and oddly shy.

Bono flits between tables in the Delano's garden, dressed all in black with silver sunglasses and the leopard-print loafers Gucci made him to go with the interior of his Mercedes, chatting to those he knows, signing things for those he doesn't. He's a prolific and entertaining talker – I can imagine he gave the Blarney Stone the one kiss it still talks about. Unusually, for

someone as famous as he is, little of what he says is about himself
– he talks seven beats to the bar about things he's read, people
he's met, places he's been. In two espressos flat, he can do
Picasso, the Reverend Cecil William's Glide church in San
Francisco, Daniel Ortega and liberation theology and whether
or not Ireland really stand much of a chance against the Belgians.
Even more unusually, for someone as famous as he, he's also a
generous and genuinely inquisitive listener.

"I like that generosity in Americans," he says later. "We
haven't got the cultural baggage that other bands in the UK
would have, because we're Irish. We don't see America as the
devil like the English do, so we came here early on and we spent a
lot of time here. Being on the road feels like an American idea –
you grow up on Kerouac, and the poetry of the place names, and
what it was like being nineteen or twenty and looking out the
window of a tour bus and thinking it was more like the movies,
not less."

U2's love affair with America has been one of two boundlessly
ambitious entities falling hopelessly for the endless possibilities
of each other. Of the 77 million albums U2 have sold, 30 million
have been bought in America.

In Miani, U2 are playing at the ProPlayer Stadium, home of the
Florida Marlins baseball team. *PopMart* has come a long way, in
every respect, since its inauspicious beginnings in Las Vegas. A
workable tension has been located between the gleeful satire of
consumer culture that flickers on the giant screen, and the songs
from *Pop* which are, beneath the beats and effects, some of the
most intimate and troubled U2 have recorded. During the Miami
show, just before U2 play 'I Still Haven't Found What I'm
Looking For', Bono makes a short speech thanking the crowd for
their patience with his band's unpredictability. "If we keep it
interesting for us," he says, "hopefully it won't be bullshit for
you."

After a triumphant show, in a suite somewhere in the warren of
dressing rooms inside ProPlayer Stadium, Edge can just about
laugh at the memory of Las Vegas; the encore, when he was

forced to his knees to fossick hopelessly for his dropped plectrum in the dry ice while the other three started 'Discotheque' without him and his signature riff was, he says now, "about as Tap as it's ever got". Edge is genial and amusing company, and only makes about a dozen slighting references to my inebriated performance at the Delano the previous evening, which is sweet of him.

U2 have kept Edge's solo 'Sunday Bloody Sunday' in the set since Sarajevo. He's kind enough to let it go when I explain that I'd never liked the song much in its original, martial-drumming, foot-stomping, flag-waving incarnation, that it had seemed to sum up everything that I used to think U2 were: pompous, earnest, and a whole bunch of no fun at all. Stripped down and delivered in a bare whisper, it had worked in Sarajevo, and even removed from that emotive context, it had worked in Miami.

"I thought the song would have a different resonance in Sarajevo," he says, "but not as a band version. I thought if I showcased the lyric and the melody, it might fly. What I discovered was that the song had a completely other side. That's what I find with a lot of our songs, that you can fiddle about with them, but you can't change the essence of them, and it was nice to find a song that we thought we might never play again could still do that. We dropped it on the Unforgettable Fire tour, so it's been nearly ten years."

This must be the weirdest part of the musician's job. Most of us cringe at the memory of things we thought, said or bought when we were younger. But a successful musician never escapes it. Everything ridiculous you did or wore as a youth is a matter of record, part of the fabric of other people's lives.

"Yeah . . . playing the old songs is a bit like what I imagine travelling back in time and meeting yourself would be like. We're quite lucky in that when it comes to the early embarrassing moments, we have so many that it's actually just pointless even trying to defend ourselves. There's so much there that we just have to laugh at, and be thankful that we're still growing, still getting better at what we do. The first few weeks of *PopMart* were . . . well, we'd jumped in at the deep end and hadn't prepared as much as we should have. But not . . . on previous tours, I remember Bono being under such a cloud for hours after coming on stage, but on this tour we're just laughing so much. It's the most fun we've ever had on the road."

Adam Clayton, when he's wheeled before the tape recorder after Edge, offers a similarly sanguine view. As the only member of U2 to have racked up the traditional rock'n'roll accoutrements of court appearances, tabloid scandals, supermodel girlfriends and excess-induced absenteeism (at the end of *Zoo TV* tour in Sydney in 1993, U2 had to play one show with Clayton's guitar tech on bass), Clayton has perhaps had a better view of the bottom of the abyss than the others, but he doesn't have any complaints this evening.

"You can have bad days," he allows, "and every day is a challenge, because the preconceived ideas you had, as a sixteen-year-old joining a pop group, as a twenty-year-old releasing your first album, as a twenty-seven-year-old releasing *The Joshua Tree*, you have to battle against those, you have to get to the essence of what being a musician is, and you have to remember that, well, tonight I could have been playing in the Holiday Inn. By the time showtime comes around, you've got yourself centred. There is a discipline involved, and – I mean, this sounds very Californian – you have to reduce the number of stimuli in your day in order to become a sort of hollow vessel, so by the time you go on stage, you've actually got some energy to run off."

Clayton has a strange accent that isn't quite English and isn't quite Irish.

"What's fun about this now," he continues, "is that an awful lot of the uncertainties have been removed by the fact that we have a history, by now, that indicates that this is probably what we're going to be doing for the rest of our lives. We have a history that says we've done something very hard and very unnatural, for four men to grow together and live with each other for twenty years. I think everyone's a lot more rounded and settled, and realising that this is the most interesting musical engagement we could be involved in."

That's the thing about great bands, though: they're always

more than the sum of their parts. Lennon and McCartney's post-Beatles efforts ran the gamut from the adequate to the excruciating. The Smiths splintered into an occasionally inspired session guitarist and a risible self-parody. Even the ones where you'd think it wouldn't matter go this way, like The Pixies – Black Francis wrote all those fantastic Pixies songs, but listening to his solo album was like wading through knee-deep mud in loose wellies.

"That chemistry," nods Clayton, "is gold dust. If we went off and tried to make solo records, I'm sure they'd be as crap as everyone else's solo records. For some reason, each of us works best in this situation. And that's a nice thing to have figured out. We still all live within twenty minutes of each other. We spend a lot of time with each other, so we can chew a lot of ideas over. Other bands, when they get to our age, there's a couple of divorces, there's a couple of jealousies between members, there are management problems, and it's very hard. We've been lucky, or wise, and we can devote most of our energy to being in U2. We keep a full-time staff on, which a lot of people don't. We're in a unique position, and we do take those risks, and we look like fools sometimes, but other times people say "Yes!", and that's the kind of band I always wanted to be in."

Bono is a restless interviewee, physically and mentally, sitting up and lying down as ideas occur to him. It's the afternoon of the day after the Miami show, and we're sitting in the sunshine in the Delano's garden, roughly equidistant from the swimming pool, the cocktail bar and the giant-sized lawn chess set. Things could probably be worse.

"Are you enjoying Miami? It's a very interesting city. It's a kind of the crossroads between North America and South America . . ."

In Bosnia, Bono had said something about his attraction to the idea of Sarajevo as a cultural crossing place, through in Sarajevo's case it had been between East and West . . . trying not to sound too much like a hijack in search of an underlying theme, I wonder if he sees similarities.

"Exactly. Well, here you have the Catholicism of South America, which is the sexy end of the religion, you know, carnivals . . ."

I'm starting to get used to Bono's associative monologues.

". . . which is something I'm becoming more and more interested in, the carnival, the celebration of the flesh – you know, *carne* meaning meat – before the denial, which is Lent, going into Easter, that kind of thing . . ."

Keeping him to one theme is like trying to cage water – like many people whose understanding of the world has come largely from going places and finding out for themselves, the connections he draws tend to be as individual and eccentric as his experiences, and as he's one of the most famous people on earth, it's safe to assume that his experiences are more individual and eccentric than most. When transcribed into cold hard print, Bono can occasionally read like a stereotypical cosmic rock'n'roll mooncalf, but in person, his intellectual promiscuity just feels like the vigour of a compulsive conversationalist. It's also something I've noticed in a lot of Irish and Scottish friends – a fondness for constructing elaborate, even absurd, theories out of bugger all just for the fun of seeing where the pieces land when the edifice topples over.

". . . and you just get this sense that South America is coming through, you can see it in the writers and film-makers, and this is its interface. You know, South Beach looks like lots of blocks of ice cream, Neapolitan, or . . ."

I'd been thinking that earlier. The violently clashing pastel paint on the beachfront apartment buildings looks ghastly and ridiculous all day, until sunset, when the sky behind them becomes daubed in the exact same colours. Then it looks like heaven, or at least like Ernest Hemingway's idea of it. Except I'd been thinking that the ice cream was more like tutti-frutti. U2 recorded some of *Pop* in Miami.

"Tutti-frutti, OK. Well, we came here to see if there was something here for us, but in the end our record wasn't going to be about any one location. Because sometimes there's almost a physical sense of location, Berlin for *Achtung Baby*, the US for *The Joshua Tree*."

While we talk, passers-by stop to ask Bono for an autograph, or mumble terrified hellos. Bono's lack of annoyance or condescension is startling (I mean, it's annoying me, and I've only been putting up with it for an hour). U2 started young – it feels like they've been there forever, but Bono is only 37 – they've been U2 all their adult lives. It may be that because of this they really don't know any better, but they seem remarkably free of cynicism. They still get excited – they would scarcely have sunk a tidy fortune in taking *PopMart* to Sarajevo otherwise.

"Well," muses Bono, "when you get what you want, what do you do? But we haven't got cynical, you're right. We're still trying to make that record that we hear in our heads, and can't quite play. I guess when we were twenty-three or twenty-four we went through that phase where groups move out of their flats, and into houses, and start wanting to put paintings up on the walls, and they don't want to look like rednecks, so they start reading up on what sort of paintings they should have in their houses, and what Chinese rugs . . . I guess we must have gone through Chinese rug phases, but we were over it coming out of our twenties. The weird thing is that you're left, in a way, with only the right motives. If the reason you joined a band was to get laid, get famous, get rich, well, they all went by the way fairly quickly, so all we're left with is . . . make that record."

U2 in general, and Bono in particular, have often been scoffed at – indeed, back in the dusty-leather-and-white-flags pre-*Achtung Baby* era, I had, occasionally, been party to that scoffing. Scorn is not unusual for a successful rock group. What is unusual is the equanimity with which U2 shrug it off – many are the millionaires who will, given half the chance, bitterly recite every bad review they've ever had. I once spent an afternoon in New York listening to Gavin Rossdale of Bush relate chapter and verse of the critical batterings his band had received, mostly in publications that sold a hundredth of what his records do. I suggested that *a*) next time, he send the journalist a statement of his net worth and a photo of his big house in the country, or vintage car collection, or whatever, and *b*) perhaps he could lighten up. "You don't understand," he replied, and rarely has a truer word been spoken.

"Oh," says Bono, with a dismissive wave of his cigarette, "bands at our level deserve to be humbled. But it was the very gauche nature of where we were at that allowed us entry into a world where much more careful and cooler acts couldn't allow themselves, or depending on your point of view, were too smart to want to visit."

The trouble is that most artists – most people, come to that – condemn themselves to mediocrity because their fear of looking like a fool outweighs their potential for greatness. Hoping that Bono will forgive the impudence, I think it'd be fair to say that this has never looked like a problem for him.

"That's right," he says. "Obviously, it's better to do it in private, but when you're growing up in public, that's hard. People who . . . people who jump off, like . . . like Jimi Hendrix trying to put Vietnam through his amplifier, or like the way Lester Bangs wrote about rock'n'roll, that takes a certain courage. I think one of the things I found difficult in the eighties was this din of voices telling me "But you can't fly, you arsehole". But that's the kind of thing that results in restrained, reasonable music – or, for that matter, restrained, reasonable writing. You must not find yourself tiptoeing."

Pop contains at least two songs, "Staring At The Sun" and "Please", that appear to address the Northern Irish peace process, and concluded with an open letter to Jesus, titled "Wake Up Dead Man".

"Well . . . look. As far as what I actually believe myself goes, I'm not up for discussing it in any detail, because some subjects are too precious for interviews. I let them come out in songs. Also, I haven't got it all figured out, so I don't want to make an arse of myself. But yes, I do feel that there is love and logic behind the universe, and that in recent years that instinct that we all have has been written off, we're reduced to being two-dimensional. There's a heartache that goes with that, or if not a heartache, then certainly a soul-ache, that music . . . I mean, I have great admiration and respect for atheists, though. I feel God would have a lot more time for them than for most people who are part of religion, who seem so odd, to me, or doped, or just believe because they were told to. I think atheists have a certain rigour. In the absence of God, people have promoted a lot of lesser types to the same position, which is quite confusing. Film stars, pop stars, royalty . . . are not actually heroes. Nurses are. Mothers are. Firemen are. Some things are arse about tit."

It must also be difficult trying to maintain a conventional view of religion when you've spent so long being worshipped yourself.

"That's . . . good," he laughs. "I'll have to have a little lie down after that one. Wow, that's great. I'll get out of bed for that. No, basically, but most musicians I know say that the great stuff they kind of stumble on, and the average stuff is what they can claim authorship over. I do still feel that U2 write songs by accident, and maybe that's why we keep shifting ground, to stay out of our depth."

The hapless metaphor is left trying to untangle itself. Bono's away again.

"It all started with the Psalms of David," he continues, with a smile that indicates that he knows he's being preposterous, but is determined to see where this goes. "They were the first blues. There you had man shouting at God: 'Why have you left me? Where have you gone? Who do you think you are anyway?' That's basically what music had been doing since. I'm still a student, so I'm still knocking on Bob Dylan's door . . ."

Ouch.

". . . no pun intended, and I'm still going to turn up to Al Green's church, I'm still going to invite Bob Marley's mother to our gigs, talk to Frank Sinatra, talk to Quincy Jones, just trying to figure it out."

It could be argued that this reverence for their forebears was what got U2 into trouble on *Rattle & Hum,* when they recorded with Dylan and BB King, effectively sneaking into the rock'n'roll hall of fame and hanging their own portraits on the walls. *Rattle & Hum* was derided, and not without reason, as work of epic humourlessness and egomania. Though it did, buried somewhere beneath the homage and piety, contain the line "I don't believe in riches but you should see where I live", which might have been the beginning of U2's rebirth, an acknowledgement that they badly needed to resolve a few contradictions.

"I think you're trying a bit hard, there, but . . . for us, revenge is getting better. I don't think John Lennon ever got over the fact that he was in a pop group, that The Beatles were the girls' group and The Rolling Stones were the boys' one. And that was the greatest gift, in a way, because he was constantly trying to recover from that. So I think that maybe when we were younger we didn't have the brains to say fuck off, what we're doing is more interesting than what you are. Today, to some degree, I can back that up. Back then, we just wondered did people hate our haircuts this much? The answer was yes, of course – and the haircuts were terrible, awful – but it was that very lack of style in this group that led us to soul."

Bono borrows another cigarette from another autograph-hunter. The sun is beginning to set now, and South Beach is enjoying its daily hour of visual harmony between ground and sky. Rankin is making wind-up gestures in the distance, worried that the light will vanish before he gets his photo session, so I ask Bono if he can imagine a life beyond being the singer in U2, the only job he's ever had.

"Yeah . . . I'd like to be alive. I'd like to chase little children across the street with a big stick. I am curious about . . . I love people like Willie Nelson, and Johnny Cash, there's something about their voices as they get older. Boy Dylan's voice on his new album is just . . . I love to write, and I think that's what I'd do if I couldn't sing, or perform. The deadlines that you have to deal with as a journalist are something I'd obviously have a problem with, but I like people who write. Where I'd be writing from, or where I'd be living I don't know, but it's something I'm getting more interested in, and you don't get to do much of it when you're in a band, because the lyrics are your attempt to put the feeling of the music into words."

As we wander down the beach to do the photos, I comment that it can hardly have escaped his notice that, back home in Ireland, there might be more exciting career opportunities awaiting someone with his credentials. After all, if Dana can give the Presidency a shake on the strength of one long-past Eurovision appearance . . .

"Naw," Bono says, and rubs one eye under his silver shades. "I wouldn't move to a smaller house."

Four months or so later, after another *PopMart* show, I'm in a big room full of free drink and freeloading people somewhere underneath Waverley Park, an Australian Rules Football stadium in an inconvenient suburb of Melbourne. I'm in Australia on holiday, reminding my parents what I look like. I'm about to get a fine demonstration of the famous law devised by another great Irish thinker, Murphy. By which I mean that if I ever take someone to a U2 concert whom I'm actually trying to impress, I just know I'll be lucky to sneak into the one-beer-and-a-hundred-straws C-list wing-ding for local radio drones, record company deadwood and spotty competition winners. But the night I take my mother . . .

"Andrew? Bono wants to say hello. Follow me."

Mum, fair play to her, is very cool about the whole thing. She bows her head just slightly when Bono swoops low and kisses her hand, and when he asks her whether she liked the show, she just says she thought it was amazing how much of a racket four young men could make. Someone else I know waves at me, so I go and say hello to them, leaving Mum and Bono to it.

I've seen some weird stuff. But when I look over from the other side of the room at the pair of them still yammering away to each other, I wonder if it gets stranger than this.

On the Road with Gong

Keith Bailey

*When the drumming stops
something terrible happens . . .*

But that's another story – only too well known by any musician who's been on the road for more than five minutes.

Better introduce myself – my name is Keith (well, everyone's gotta be called *something*, right?), better known as Keith the Missile – the (in)famous bass player with Here & Now, and Gong – two obscure, but to my mind beautiful, psychedelic bands, loosely based in the UK, playing convoluted and looping – not to say horribly complicated – music, with pedigrees so long it's better not to even mention them – suffice to say there's quite a few albums from these two outfits knocking around the planet.

I played with Gong for several years – the first time being way back in 1977, and then again from '89 to '94, at which time I left to make way for an even more – ahem – *senior* Gong bassist, Mike Howlett who had decided that he wanted to try *his* hand all over again.

I also run a small booking agency, having built up a list of contacts all over Europe as a player over a twenty year period, and so when I left Gong it wasn't too long before they asked me to return to the fold to work with them as booker/tour manager for Europe.

Things went wonderfully for a good few years – well – *fairly* wonderfully – there were the inevitable personnel changes from time to time – with all the attendant political shenanigans one associates with such upheavals, one of the more significant of which was the reinstatement of one of the original drummers – a guy called Pierre Moerlen – which meant waving goodbye to one of my favourite madcap drummers in the world – Pip Pyle – also a veteran Gongster, albeit during the slightly less successful years.

Plus, of course, there were the occasional spectacular – well . . . *errors* – unwittingly engineered by yours truly . . . Like having an entire Italian tour cancel on you three days before the start of it . . . But hey – we all make mistakes . . . On the whole, though, things were going pretty smoothly right through to May '99 when this story unfolded . . .

Unfolded? More like slowly and inevitably corkscrewed right off the beam and fell apart into Bizarresville Arizona . . . and that's putting it mildly . . .

I guess those of you reading this who're musicians themselves will be only too familiar with the sort of nightmares that sometimes haunt us – most players I've asked own up to having them. Mine usually involve missing the tour bus, and having to get to a major show via incredibly complicated train stations with no signs up to tell you which train is going where – I usually end up staggering across dozens of railway lines, clutching what seems to be a very *heavy* bass, with trains zipping about all over the place, before getting on to what I *hope* is the right one. Then the scene dissolves into a labyrinthian concrete maze of tunnels somewhere below the stage I'm supposed to be playing on. I can hear that the band have started without me, but they sound really thin without a bass-player (or so I tell myself . . .) but try as I might I simply *cannot find my way to the stage* . . . I *never* get to play in these dreams.

Of course, I usually wake up sweating profusely, heart pounding after about ten years of this torment . . .

Only those of you familiar with the agonies of touring/arriving late at shows will understand the intense nervousness, not to mention paranoia, that such a dream can generate.

I digress – but please, bear with me dear reader – it all makes some sort of hideous sense in the end . . .

So anyway, I'd set up a Gong tour for May '99, taking in Belgium, Germany, Austria, Italy and France, ok? Quite a nice little tour, really, even if the money was a *bit* thin on the ground –

the percentages on offer ought to have made up the difference between poverty and a decent wage for the musos concerned. Pierre Moerlen – a real "name" in his own right as a drummer throughout Europe – was still in the driving seat, Mike Howlett was still on bass, the two frontline stars (DAEVID ALLEN and GILLI SMYTHE) were still in place, and there were two new faces in the line-up – MARK HEWINS on guitar and THEO TRAVIS on saxes and flute – the former having already decided that I was the original satanic rip-off artist getting fat (I wish!) on the back of their sweaty endeavours . . . Things were a little fraught, atmosphere wise, between he and I, but I kept my distance, hoping that he would come round if left to work it out for himself . . .

So anyway, there we were, back in the hotel in Hamburg, having played the night before in Belgium, and that same night in the aforementioned Hamburg. They had both been pretty good shows, and we were all feeling nicely relaxed as we sat in the hotel bar, sipping whatever until we felt able to actually sleep . . .

I remember the conversation getting round to something about this being Hamburg, where you could get anything you wanted, literally *anything*, and seeing Pierre, that drummer looking very – well, "uncomfortable" would come somewhere close to the way he looked – and I remembered that he *had* had a serious drug problem at some time in his murky past . . . We've *all* had our little problems at some time or another – drink or drugs – and I just think it's one of those things you have to learn to deal with as a touring musician – learn to deal with it, or get shipped home in a straightjacket. Or a box . . .

So anyway, talk drifted into vacant silences, and after a while we made our separate ways up to the rooms.

The next day was a bit of an early start as the show was in Berlin – about a six-hour drive from Hamburg, so I made sure that everyone was up in plenty of time. Pierre was driving separately from the rest of the band, in his own car, and so I got him a copy of the Berlin town map made, with the venue clearly marked. I really didn't like the idea of him driving separately very much – I saw it as just another opportunity for a cock-up, but he'd insisted right from the start that that was how it had to be. Apparently he'd been involved in a nasty pile-up while travelling in a tour bus once, and said it just made him too nervous to travel that way again. I'd acquiesced, knowing that nothing I could say would change his mind anyway.

So it was no surprise when he asked me for some money that morning – his tour wages to date, plus a sub of about 250 marks, and some petrol money . . . I remember thinking it a bit excessive, but I know how it is with musicians and money sometimes – after all, I've been there myself often enough, right? I paid up, and made sure he knew the get-in time, soundcheck time, onstage time, and all that palaver, and thought no more of it as the tour bus rolled off from the hotel front, Pierre waving from the door. Quite apart from all that, I was well preoccupied with keeping the guitarist sweet enough to last the tour without worrying about mad drummers . . . (Yes, I too believe they are all *completely* crazy . . . As Pip Pyle the archetypal madcap drummer himself once said – "never trust a man who hits things for a living!")

German autobahns ain't what they used to be these days – you're lucky to do 100 km with two lanes, never mind the luxury of three – and so we didn't arrive at the venue in Berlin until about 4.30 p.m. – well after the scheduled time of 3 p.m., to be greeted by a pale and definitely *strained* looking promoter, who rushed us in, talking nineteen to the dozen in heavily accented English, between shouting in – shall we say *Wagnepian* tones at the sound and stage crew, who all looked utterly pissed off with him . . . They'd obviously had to put up with him all day – I already felt sorry for them . . .

I waited until he'd had time to establish what he obviously hoped was his command of the situation before gently informing him that the drummer was making his own way there, and if he hadn't arrived yet, not to worry, he was often a bit late . . .

Our merry promoter's face grew a little paler, but he tried – God bless 'im – to keep his cool – after all, *I* was the tour manager, and I didn't seem too worried.

He began to look paler still when all the backline was set up, the rest of the band had all soundchecked, and there was *still* no sign of yer man. But I got behind the kit – I can play rudimentary sort of drums – most bass players can, y'know – we *do* understand some things, despite all the "what d' you call a guy who hangs around with musicians?" type jokes – and did the necessary, playing a quick number along with the band for the soundman.

Soundcheck over, the band retires to the dressing room to twiddle their thumbs and the promoter collars me. "Zer doors are offnung at exactly acht of zer clock, ja?"

"Ja"

"Ja – ist now sieben of zer clock, ja?"

"Ja"

"Und please, *vere ist zer trummer?*"

"I imagine he's probably stuck in zer traffic jam, ja?" Goddamit, the guy's *getting* to me . . .

"Und ven he get here?"

I suppress the urge to grab his collar and yell, "How the fuck should *I* know?" into his face, contenting myself with an ever so slightly sarcastic: "Just about when he arrives, I should imagine . . . Now if you'll excuse me? I have one or two things to sort out . . . "

I beat a hasty retreat to the dressing room, leaving him wittering on about how he's sold 500 tickets in advance and what if he has to cancel etc.

The dressing room falls silent when I enter – always a bad sign . . .

Gilli looks worried. "Keith, what're we going to do if he doesn't get here?"

"Well, it's only seven – it's still two hours before we go on, let's let it ride for a bit, eh?" That's about the best I can manage. After all, I'm feeling a bit nervous, too.

All eyes are on me; their combined weight is approximately 32 tons . . . why oh why did I give him all that money? Somewhere at the back of my head a malicious little voice cackles, *"He's not coming . . . tee hee hee."*

Fortunately Gilli breaks the tense silence: "Well, *I* think we should start phoning around – I mean Hospitals, Police stations, that sort of thing – I mean it's terrible, anything could have happened . . . He could have had a crash, or got arrested or anything . . ." Her voice trails off as she contemplates the awful possibilities.

There is a definite feeling that most of the boys in the band are trying to keep a positive outlook – you can tell just how hard this is by the sheen of sweat on their brows . . .

The seconds crawl past like men dying in the desert tick . . . tick . . . tick . . . the silence is deafening.

Daevid looks grim, as if he's about to go into one of his famous wizardly rages – I usually manage to disappear when I see one coming, so I get up to go out, saying "I'll just have a look outside – see if he's about . . ."

The promoter is hovering in the corridor outside the dressing room – hurrah!

"You have nothing heard, I think?"

"Spot on, Watson"

Of course, this obscure reference is completely wasted on him, and I make to go past him, but he whips into my path: "Und venn he doesn't come, vat ve do, uh? Zere is zer queue round zer building!"

"Why don't you wind up the pressure a bit more?" I think to myself, saying: "Well, we'll have to cross that bridge when we come to it, mate!"

I can feel the razor edges of incipient paranoia scraping at my already raw nerve endings: "Tell you what though – we haven't missed a show in all the time I've been with this band – which is at least 10 years." I try to sound upbeat, succeding probably, as I see his furrowed brow lighten a little.

"Ja, vell, ve'll be seeing, nicht wahr?"

"Think I'll get some air," I mutter, making for the front of house.

En route I'm waylaid by the soundman: "Hi! What's 'appenin' man?" At least he looks cheerful.

"Absolutely sweet F*** all darlin'!" I drawl casually.

"I reckon he's blown it, myself," he helpfully offers.

I heave a sigh: "Yeah well, I guess you're probably right – what's the time now, anyway?"

"Quarter to."

Jeeze! It really *does* look like we've blown it. I do some rapid calculations – looks like we're going to lose at least £1,500 if we don't do the show – never mind the damage to what we laughingly call our "reputation".

I find myself by the entrance to the venue and, looking out, all I can see is smiling faces. Hundreds and hundreds of 'em . . . My spirits find yet another notch to slide down to . . . What is it about the karma of this band – why do we always seem to blow the best situation?

Suddenly I find my desire for fresh air has evaporated, the thought of having to talk to all those innocent, happy, expectant faces is appalling – what I need now is a stiff drink . . .

I make my way backstage, meeting guess who on the way: "Zo! Vass ist going to happen now?"

"We'll think of something!" I manage – though for the life of me I can't imagine what . . . "Anyway, it's still early days – doors aren't open for – what – ten minutes?"

He looks at his watch: "In exactly acht minuten, I sink!"

"Yeah well, whatever – we're not due on 'til nine though, eh?"

I open the dressing room door to another obviously sudden silence. Everyone looks hopefully up at me; the combined weight of this is definitely somewhere over three hundred tons . . . "Nah, nothin'." I answer the unspoken question.

Daevid takes the lead: "Well, I think we're going to have a start looking at ways to do it without a drummer then."

"Damn – wish I'd brought my beat-box!" Mike Howlett chips in.

"Yeah – at least you only have to punch in the instructions once . . ." An old bass-players' joke. It goes down like a brick in a swimming pool . . .

I realise that there is a distinctly *odd* atmosphere in the room – beyond the obvious worry. I catch the occasional look that I can only describe as *speculative* . . . Something is cooking . . .

The clock ticks on . . .

At acht of zer clock precisely, the promoter finally summons the nerve to enter the dressing room.

"I sink ve open zer doors now, ja?"

Nobody answers so I silently nod my head.

He comes over to me, hovering heavily, if that's possible.

"Und zer trummer?"

Gilli chips in: "He hasn't arrived yet, and we're dreadfully worried – I wonder, would it be possible for you to phone around the local police stations and hospitals? Only if anything *has* happened, we need to know as soon as possible. Would you mind?"

The promoter grows several shades paler and I wonder at Gilli's wisdom . . . Still, I think at least it'll give him something to do. I take his arm and steer him out of the dressing room towards the production office.

My heart sinks further still as we enter the office, for there, smiling somewhat frostily, is my main German contact; an agent I've only spoken to on the 'phone with up 'til now, but I just *know* it's him – he's said he'd see us in Berlin . . . And there was me thinking how impressed he'd be with our professionalism . . .

Introductions are made, and the promoter explains the situation before getting on the phone. The agent looks me over, and smiles again – this time rather like a cat smiling at a mouse . . .

"What're you gonna do if he doesn't show up?" he asks helpfully, his accent is perfect American.

"To be perfectly honest, there's not a lot I *can* do really, is there?" I figure the honest approach is the best thing to follow at this moment. "The band has said they're willing to go on without him; it won't be the same, I know, but it's about all I can offer at the moment – I mean, for all we know, he could be in a ditch somewhere, or in one of your nice clean holding cells – it's just a very unfortunate situation . . ."

"Ja." He agrees, glumly.

The promoter has called about fourteen police stations now, with no success whatsoever, and he's looking increasingly desperate.

I'm feeling completely horrible now myself – Three days into the tour and we've lost the drummer already . . . My confidence is at an all-time low.

It's now 8.30, and I decide there's nothing to be gained by

hanging around the production office, so take the agent along with me to meet the band.

You could cut the atmosphere in the dressing room with a knife now, and the introductions made, a hollow silence descends, only to be broken by our friendly agent: "There were 800 people in last thing I heard, and they're still coming in – it seems a pity we have to disappoint them, doesn't it?"

Our agent mentions this, just as the promoter walks in – "Good timing, mate!" I think to myself . . .

The promoter picks up the thread: "Ja ist ein tausend volk aus there – vat you going to do, huh?" he snarls, through clenched teeth. "I cannot cancel now, verstehe?"

Some people really know how to make you feel good, don't they?

I notice Daevid giving me that *speculative* look again . . . For some reason a distinct feeling of dread washes over me. I struggle with it, trying to let it wash over and through me, hopefully to leave me with a clear mind to deal with whatever happens next. When he sees I'm more or less on top of things again, he approaches, smiling oddly.

"Well Keithy, what'd you think, mate?"

I search my brain for some sort of positive spin to put on the situation . . . nope, nothing in here boys!

"Well," I manage: "there's really not a lot we *can* do, is there? I mean, I don't know about you, but I don't know any drummers in Berlin, let alone anyone capable of learning *your* set . . ."

I believe I mentioned before just how complicated the music of Gong is?

He nods, smiling horribly gently.

"Hey listen, Keithy," he says in dulcet tones. My heart sinks – without knowing why – still deeper . . . "We've been talking about it, and well, you sounded pretty good on the kit in the soundcheck – so what d' you think? Reckon you could handle it? I mean, you've played the set often enough as a bassist, so . . ."

He watches in some amusement as my face reflects the struggle I'm having to take this one on board – he wants *me* to play the drums? I mean, I mentioned my recurring muso's nightmare

earlier on, but even in my worst moments, such an awful prospect
has never occurred to me . . . I mean I can keep time ok – I can
even manage the odd roll from time to time, but that is *no way* the
same as playing a very complicated set to about a thousand
connoisseurs of Gong's highly original sound . . . "NO
WAY!!!" I shout to myself as I look for some way to put this
as gently as possible to the assembled crew, every one of whom's
eyes are now locked on mine – with a combined weight of at least
three thousand tons . . . *Now* I understand what all those speculative looks were about! As I search for the most tactful way to
bow out of this option, I listen with horror as my voice says – with
absolutely *no* volition on my part: "Well . . . I guess you know it's
going to be pretty – well . . . *simplistic?* But yeah, if you can live
with that, I'm willing to give it a go . . ."

My brain goes into a hyper spatial snarl-up as it tries to work
out just why the hell *I said* that, then gives up and goes whimper-
ing into a corner.

"*Good* on yer, Keithy! You'll be ok, mate, just keep it
simple . . ." Daevid is grinning happily as he goes to finish
dressing.

I'm more or less numb internally – save for what's left of my
brain screaming : "WHAT THE FUCK DID YOU SAY *THAT* FOR, BIRD-
BRAIN???!!!" But I still have enough awareness left to notice the
atmosphere in the dressing room is now wildly, manically hy-
percharged, as Mike Howlett (the bass-player) comes over to
discuss strategy with me. Strategy? That's a joke, isn't it? Jeeze,
all I can do is keep time . . . and even that's going to be damn near
impossible, given the sort of time signatures we're talking about
here.

I look up at the clock. It says 8:55 p.m. Oh my *Lord!* We're on
in five minutes – what the hell am I doing? I watch myself
opening my suitcase and rummaging through for a T-shirt to
wear – I know how hot drummers get . . . "Not that *you're* a
drummer, by any stretch of the imagination . . ." my brain
gleefully points out . . . I feel slightly sick . . .

One by one the band come over to clap me on the shoulder.
"Nice one, man . . . Cool! Hey, you're gonna be ok!" etc. etc.

They all try to reassure me, but my mouth is now like nothing so much as a dried up gorilla's armpit . . . Thank God there's no time to think . . . "The bastards knew that," I think to myself – "that's why they left it so long before they asked. . ." Daevid and Mike are hurriedly reshaping the set list.

"Can you handle 'Oily Way?' " They ask me. My mind skitters rapidly through the tune: "God no!" I answer; sounding ridiculously positive – at least *part* of my brain is now reconnected to my vocal chords . . .

The set list completed, everyone looks at me.

"Feeling ok, mate?" Daevid asks.

I draw a deep breath: "Yup! Let's go murder 'em!" I smile at the expectant faces: "Yeah! And quickly! Before they murder *you*!" my mind cackles gleefully . . .

I really don't know *what* I played, or how – that set remains a complete blur to me – but somehow we get through it without a single cat-call *or* a sniper's bullet . . . They even – miracles never cease! – demand an encore!

Then it's all over – or so I think . . .

We get off stage and the band is ecstatic, congratulations are showered over me as the drinks are passed around . . . Even Mark, the new guitarist who thinks I'm the devil incarnate gives me an enthusiastic hug. Blimey!

Daevid strolls over and claps a hand on my shoulder: "Thanks mate!" he says, then pauses before saying: "Y'know, you're the only person on the planet who could've possibly done that – I really appreciate it mate – good on ya!" And he gives my shoulder an affectionate squeeze before going to change out of his stage clothes.

I sit down and reflect on events – "Wow!" "Hey!" And "Wow" again – I can't believe I've actually *done* that!

As I bask in the warm glow of self-satisfaction, the agent comes in.

"Congratulations, my friend!" There is respect in his eyes. "I really thought that was going to be horrible – but you pulled it off, I think – one or two mistakes, but yeah, pretty good! It was well done!"

"Ja auch!" says our promoter: "Zanks a million – you saved our lives I sink!"

I'm beginning to *enjoy* this!

"Ja it was well done!" the agent repeats himself: "but please; I have to ask this one question." He pauses.

I'm still feeling supercharged, and prompt him happily:

"Yeah, go ahead; ask away, mate!"

"What are you going to do tomorrow? You are in Wuppertal, yes? That's very close to Strasbourg, where Pierre Moerlen – your *proper* drummer – lives. He's got quite a fan club there and something tells me they're not going to settle for what *you* can do quite so easily, yes?"

There's an almost audible "pop" as my warm self-congratulatory bubble bursts . . .

"We'll just have to think of something . . ." I hear myself say . . . "Anyway, he may yet turn up . . ."

Just then, our sound engineer comes in, walks over to me, and gives me a hug. "Well *done* mate!" he grins: "I never knew you had it in you! A few mistakes, but otherwise pretty damn good! I only got one complaint all night!"

"Yeah? What was that then?" My *joie de vivre* has totally evaporated now.

"Well, half way through the set this geezer comes up to me an' says "Ziss drummer is scheiss, ja?' He looks at me and grins: "But at least nobody walked out . . ."

I guess that's the best I could've hoped for.

Blurred Vision

Garry Mulholland

Time Out, 18 August 1999.

As the band crash into another selection from their latest album, and the entire Dublin Point begins to pogo wildly, you can't help but grin at the irony. Because, while the English media have decided Blur have betrayed us by turning their backs on fizzy pop and getting all arty on our arses, this huge arena is packed, frantically enthusiastic and – most pertinently – bloody young. So young that I can't spot any over-18s around me on the balcony. Which either means Dublin's teens are easily pleased, or, more likely, that one man's experimental retreat is another boy's great POP! night out. The kids, as always, know best.

And the band? As they hit punky peak after punky peak, you struggle to remember that they've been together ten years, and that they're all in their thirties. That they've survived the nightmares and flops and controversies and terrifying drinking bouts to get here. That they've made enough music to fill a forthcoming 22-CD singles and B-sides box set, and have enough history for an official biography, the savvy and entertaining *3862 Days* by Stuart Maconie. *And* that guitarist Graham Coxon has upcoming exhibitions of his art, and a solo album, and a record label; that bassist Alex James is in a band called Fat Les with a bunch of famous reprobates; that Dave Rowntree dabbles with computer animation; or that Alex and Dave are both pilots, and are helping to raise money to send a spaceship to Mars.

And then there's the singer. Him with the poster-boy grin and the confident swagger. Him that inspired the most vicious inter-band squabble British pop has ever seen. Him that lots of people admire – for his talent and good looks and charisma – but can't

quite bring themselves to like. The band leader, the head boy, the
writer of soundtracks with Michael Nyman *(Ravenous* out soon
on EMI), the father-to-be with artist girlfriend Suzie Winstan-
ley. Where's Damon Albarn's head these days, as he contemplates the latest album, *13* and its detailed descriptions of his
break-up with Elastica's Justine Frischmann? In short – who *are*
Blur, exactly?

Alex

I get to interview bassist Alex James in his beautiful flat in
Covent Garden. At first, it looks as if Mr James is going to live
up to his stereotype beautifully. He welcomes me in as if we've
known each other for years. He's just been prancing round the
front room to Boney M's *Greatest Hits.* He is expressing un-
qualified pleasure at having all his fags bought for him by Camel.
And he is offering me a glass of champagne in the middle of the
afternoon. Except that, once I've accepted, he strolls off and
makes a cup of tea for himself: 'I'm dry at the moment. I was
getting fed up with *this*' (he grips his now-largely-evaporated
beer-belly).

**3862 Days is pretty warts 'n' all for an official
biography . . .**
In some ways it's *too* fuckin' grey! I mean, we have had some fun
as well. Mind you, the photos are a laugh. Fuck me, Damon was
an ugly teenager, wasn't he? Ha! Dave and me have to put up with
that the whole time, Damon and Graham having been at school
together, going on about, 'Whatever happened to old Oofie
Prosser?' or some such.
**You come over as the one who doesn't care what anyone
says about you . . .**
Like anything, that has a lot to do with confidence. For example,
I was riding around on a girl's bike in Bournemouth last weekend. And people were going, 'Look! He's riding a girl's bike!' But
because I know I've got a plane – ha! – it washes off. If I was 15 in
Bournemouth and riding around on a girl's bike, I'd be weeping

myself to sleep at night. And for people who think: He's a cunt with a plane – it's the best way for me to get to work, you cunts! **Blur hold a relatively unique position in British rock at present. You've gradually become more successful, rather than exploded and then sunk. You've been together for ten years, without splitting, or losing members . . .**

. . . Or any deaths. Yeah. When you look at it, the Charlatans and the Manics are probably the only other two bands to have survived. Fuck, it's this business. No wonder the insurance on the car's so expensive.

Damon talks a little in the book about having breakdowns and depressions during the heights of Blurmania.

Aahhh!! They were just fuckin' hangovers, like we all got.

So you become the laddish for who hangs around Soho and gets pissed with famous people.

Yeah, and that's kind of what I wanted. Later, I turned 30 and realised there's something more to life. It's been nice sobering up and having some joy in the mornings. It becomes inelegant, coughing your guts up and feeling shit and talking crap for most of the day. Alcoholism is not a very attractive trait, is it? We definitely are a booze band. There's certainly never been much smack.

Would you accept the irony that, after all that moaning at American rock, your most successful record, 'Song 2', sounds suspiciously like Nirvana?

It's basically Muppet grunge, isn't it? It's also pretty funny that it was banged out in 20 minutes while we waiting for some piece of equipment to turn up. We did an interview with BBC Radio Bristol a couple of years ago, and the DJ gets out this tape and says, 'You're not gonna believe this!' It was an interview with Kurt Cobain, where he asks him what English bands he likes at the moment, and Kurt starts singing 'There's No Other Way'! And we were like, 'Christ! What a nice bloke.' 'Song 2' sounds more like the fucking Offspring than Nirvana – that's the worrying thing.

What are your feelings now about 'the Britpop years'?

I remember going round to everyone and saying. 'This is my

heyday.' Ha! You can't beat that first flush of real success. You walk on water. As far as Britpop was concerned, it was just a reaction to the ruthless, soulless American marketing machine. It was humiliating. In Britain, the music business revolves around being rude to people, swearing a lot, taking drugs and getting drunk and being a genius. In America, it's not enough just to be good. Being a donkey is what sells you a million records. You get the fuckin' art kicked out of you. There, the video is more important than the bassline, which is a sobering thought for bass-players everywhere. I didn't join a band to make videos. Actually, I probably *did* join a band because of 'Rio' by Duran Duran, which is the greatest video moment ever. You can't get on a boat without going down the front and singing that, even if it's a dinghy.

Do you think Damon will make a good dad?
Well, he's been a bit thrown by it, but, yeah. I mean, he's been my dad for the last ten years.

You say in the book that Fat Les's fanbase is made up of 'kids and cunts'.
Some of my best mates are cunts. Keith [Allen] sees the whole thing as a vehicle for his self-glorification, sadly. Even though 'Naughty Christmas' sold 100,000 copies, we lost all our money on it. You don't wanna buy 150,000 copies, do you?

What about the space programme you and Dave have become involved in?
We were sitting in LA one night, wondering why there isn't a British space programme and if we could fund one. A couple of meetings later, we're sitting with a man who plans to send a spacecraft to Mars. I guess it's a vanity thing, really. But it's 1999 and I think we should be making spaceships.

Graham

It's Graham Coxon – the man many of us reckon to be the best guitarist around at present – up next. We meet at Food record label HQ in Camden, where he asks one of the staff if they have beer, but then doesn't take one. He is also off the booze. A professional teenager in his metal-band T-shirt and skatepunk combat pants, he seems wary and hesitant at first, but goes on to enjoy himself immensely. In attitude, mannerism and speaking voice, it's hard to imagine another thirty something who could be more unashamedly childlike.

You still live in Camden. Didn't Britpop mania make you want to go somewhere less hyped?
I like familiarity. When I go to other parts of London I get quite frightened. There's some pretty grim characters in Camden, but I feel safe here. Posh areas are too lofty.
But the book presents you as the member of Blur least comfortable with fame. If that's true, aren't you just too easy to find in Camden?
Sometimes. And that's why I go on the wagon a lot. The first verse of 'Coffee And TV' is about being in The Good Mixer pub and just wondering what on earth I'm doing here, but not feeling inclined to go anywhere else. Because, if I go drinking, it's the only place where I feel I can get a little out of control. There are a lot of boys in there that I've known for a long time who, if things go funny, will make me feel safe. To the locals it's just, 'Oh, him again.' I do get followed home by tourists sometimes. One night it was a whole gaggle of Italian girls. Now, I know a lot of boys are thinking: Phwoar, that's great! But it isn't.
Is Damon more designed for that sort of attention?
Not really. He gets the more aggressive version. He's had burning paper put through his letter box, people having a go at him for being middle-class.
Is it true that you were the least comfortable with the whole 'Parklife' period, and the whole New Lad, Groucho Club thing that Alex and Damon seemed to embody?
I wasn't very happy. Damon would say things and we'd all be tarred with the same brush. I'm still constantly accused of being a Chelsea supporter, When, if I supported any team, it would be Derby where I come from. And I love Alex, but he's very good at winding people up. At that time, the groups I liked were groups I didn't wanna be bigger than. I wanted to be like Dinosaur Jr or

My Bloody Valentine or The Pastels and be on Creation. I remember being on a tube train with Damon when he first said he wanted put brass and different instruments on our records. And I was like, 'What?!' It took me a lot of time to get used to the fact that we were this big pop band.

For a lot of bands, that's the ultimate dream.

Yeah. But you're 24 and these kids are like. . . ten. You don't know why they're there. We were a pop group, but there was always a bit of weirdness and perversity involved. It was more like XTC. In the end, 'Blur' is where we escaped from the jail called pop. The pop car drew ahead, and the weird car, which, because it *is* a weird car, doesn't run as well, broke down, and we mended the wheels. That's why I'm listening to a lot of metal recently, like Motorhead. I like extremes in sound.

You solo album, *The Sky's Too High*, wasn't particularly thrashy. . .

No. Well, it came out of a quiet period. My highlight of the week was going to a place with a lot of other drunks talking about their drunkenness at Camden A.A. which was an extraordinary experience. I'm not sure how public I'm supposed to be about that, but anyway, I don't think I was as bad as I thought. I just needed a kick up the arse.

Any thoughts about Britpop now?

It was horrible, wasn't it? I hate the word 'Brit' and I hate the word 'pop', so Britpop has to be my most hated word. It just meant a mediocre bunch of groups who played in Camden pubs, and people going down the Blow-Up club wearing a Fred Perry with a tie and flares. All the ingredients but all mixed wrong. They reminded me of what Alex says about remixes: it's like giving someone your Labrador to walk and it coming back a poodle.

What's the closest you've been to splitting up?

After touring *The Great Escape*. Damon thought I wasn't interested, and I thought he was insane and had turned into Tommy Steele. In fact, we were just exhausted and had stopped communicating. That's why *The Great Escape* is such a depressing album.

Dave

Drummer Dave Rowntree and I talk the next day in the gardens of
Dublin's Merrion Hotel. He is exactly as the book portrays:
straightforward, friendly, and possessed of a dry wit. A perfect
grounding influence for the three eccentrics in front of him on stage.
He knows that he's the anonymous one, and finds it amusing.

Are you really the most stoical and down-to-earth member of Blur?
People do say that, so I suppose there must be an element of truth
to it – though it doesn't feel like it from this side of my face. It's
not particularly rock 'n' roll, is it? 'Cor, that Ozzy Osbourne!
Isn't he down-to-earth?' Hurhurhur!

As someone from a musical family, did you see yourself becoming a pop star?
My parents were both ex-musicians who'd been badly bitten by
the music business, so they were saying, 'Don't do it for a living.
Do it as a hobby.' To be honest, I'm still not terribly ambitious.
If the band carries on at this level. . . I'm not thinking, 'South
America! We still haven't broken South America!'

When did you make the decision to give up drinking?
Just around the time of *Girls and Boys*. It wasn't a large step to take.
Making the decision is the hardest part. And I've never touched a
drop since. Chemical addiction is a pretty crap thing, it's pretty
weak. It's the psychological addiction that's the hard thing. I gave
up smoking just like that too, after reading this book about it.
There's so much crap talked about addiction. Believe me.

What do you think you would have done if Blur had never happened?
I probably would have emigrated to France, or somewhere.
Actually, I'm probably gonna do that anyway. Before Blur, I
nearly jacked everything in, bought a bus, and drove off with the
hippy convoys. I don't think there's much scope to do your own
thing in England any more. Being in a band is the closest anyone
gets. I would have been an outsider in some way.

What do you think Blur's best idea has been?
Putting out that single on the same day as Oasis. It was an inspired bit of marketing. We should have won an award. Mind you. I managed to keep my head down while it all went off. Ha! There weren't too many people going, 'That fuckin' Dave out of Blur – what a down-to-earth bastard!!!'

Damon

Damon Albarn plays last man. We are still in the ornate Merrion gardens. He describes himself as 'cynical – and older' than when I first interviewed him just before the release of *Parklife* and then scrounges a fag. He's naturally matey, but looks tired, and there are a lot of weary sighs.

Is this a good time to be in Blur?
Well, I've been so busy doing this Kevin Spacey film set in Dublin called *Ordinary Decent People*. I haven't had a day off in six weeks. So I used to find it stressful going on the road, and now it's almost like a day off. I think it's a bit of preparation for fatherhood – being very busy and knackered.
So you're willing to talk about your impending parenthood now?
Yeah. At the beginning, I was just . . . My girl friend's just not interested in having that association. She's an artist in her own right. But there's no point in denying it now.
Do you think that being a father is going to dwarf the whole thing of being a pop star?
Well, *everything*'s been one big event this year. I was recording the soundtrack with Michael Nyman in the mornings and afternoons, the *13* album in the evenings. Then we said we weren't gonna tour, and they made us tour TV stations. Ha! I'm not complaining. But I'm a glutton for punishment. I'm working 18 hours a day. Mind you, I just saw this programme about a Japanese taxi driver working 18-hours days, seven days a week. So I'm not complaining.

Are you a workaholic?

[Sighs] Yes, I am. It's a bit frustrating at times. It's an addiction. It can be very productive, unlike the more conventional addictions. But it's emotionally quite . . . I suppose I'm a fervent devotee of my art.

Dave just told me that there's no such thing as addiction.

I disagree. I've seen a lot of it over the years.

The book portrays you as the driving force in the band, as well as the frontman. The person who wanted it more than anyone else.

Ooh, I dunno. What does that mean? Everyone put in the hours.

But there's more to success than just work. There's drive, focus, ambition . . .

Yes. But, looking at it that way, I become guilty of all our mistakes and our successes, don't I?

Are you?

Well, it depends. We all do our bit. The only thing I regret is that I made *The Great Escape* into a record when I should have made it into a musical. The larger-than-life characters would've worked on stage. Then we could've made *Blur* after *Parklife* and it would've been seamless. I might still do that and add some things – if I could ever go back to writing those sort of songs. If I got really chipper all of a sudden. Haha!

You all seem pretty pissed off with the press at the moment. Why is it . . .

. . . that everyone hates us? Heheheh!!! I know, that's not true. But it seems that way sometimes. 'They're good, *but* . . .' There's always a but.

Do you think that you wind people up?

[Sighs] Well, everyone seems to think so. It's not a deliberate thing. I just think the English lack of sincerity, the ability to be so two-faced, pisses me off sometimes. I don't think I fit in. In that sense, I'm not very English. Or maybe I'm quintessentially English, I don't know. I'm pretty tribalist, I mean, I lived in the East End for ten years, but I'm not allowed to be one of those. Which I'm not, but I *was* born there. And I certainly didn't feel part of anything in Colchester. But I'm associated with the middle class, and you're not allowed to be a creative force if you're middle-class and don't come from anywhere. You're illegitimate. I don't think this sort of thing matters anywhere else but England.

Graham said that fame got really nasty for you at one point, to the degree that you were getting burning things shoved through your letterbox. Is that true?

Yes. But that was an isolated incident. I did hear more Oasis than was good for any individual, though. Out of windows, in shops, in pubs. If someone was sitting next to me, they'd turn up their Walkman so I could hear the Oasis song. I dunno. I went through a period when I thought I was a bit of a star. But I don't think anyone would not have got a bit caught up in it all. I don't think we come across as a band who want to perpetuate our star status. I just realised that living on this planet is a co-operative effort, and that no one is any more special than anyone else. Once you've worked that one out, you're no longer a star.

There's a rumour that has circled the London music biz for years: namely, that the reason the second Elastica album has taken so long is because you wrote the first one. Would you care to comment?

Well . . . [laughs in a slightly stunned manner] There were loads of rumours like that when I was at school. I dunno. Ask Courtney Love. You know. Ask *her* if I wrote Elastica's album.

Sorry, you've bewildered me, so perhaps we'd better move on.

Yeah, we should.

What's this I hear about you training to climb Mount Kilimanjaro?

Erm. I didn't know I was gonna have a baby then. [Long pause] I don't know what to say after that previous question, really.

Sorry if I disturbed you. But everyone gossips about it so I thought I'd ask you face-to-face.

No, no, no. It's just that everyone says that Kurt Cobain wrote Hole's first record.

Yeah. But I can't ask Kurt Cobain about Hole.

Hurhurhur. No, you can't.

And I *can* ask you about Elastica.
Well, you *can*. But I think . . . I've just got a copy of Elastica's new album and I don't know what it is going to sound like at all. And I'm really really interested and I'm sure it's going to be, y'know, better than the first record. It seems pointless to have gone through all that agony and to have not come up with something that will heal all that. It's all about music and if the music's good, does it really matter, y'know, about anything else?

Do you regret admitting that much of the *13* album was about your relationship with Justine Frischmann? Wouldn't it have been better if people had made their own minds up?
Well, I didn't say it. It was an assumption. I didn't deny it, but I didn't issue a press release saying. 'Due to my traumatic break-up, I have been compelled to write these songs.' Hur! They're just about being emotionally very damaged. It doesn't matter who they are about, does it? I do feel like I've come out the other end, and a lot of that is down to the fact that I've just worked solidly. And then I met a wonderful person who had no interest, who'd actually been out of the country when all of the key points of my fame were happening. It's fantastic, really, to get another chance because if you're famous it's difficult.

Do you think the band are more comfortable with you writing from a personal perspective, rather than the 'character comedies' of *Parklife* and *The Great Escape*?
Yeah, definitely, You've got to remember I was brought up in a theatre background, which is a really uncool thing say if you're a rock musician. But I've matured. And I've learnt how to get what I want out of music in a more satisfying way. I'm almost content. Really, being in such a public relationship made it difficult to be direct in the music. I used to get a real ear-bashing if I did anything like that. All I've ever really wanted is a quiet life.

Albarn stays for a while and chats easily, happily. But after the thank yous and goodbyes, as he strides off to the next appointment, he can't resist a parting shot over his shoulder. 'You had a bloody cheek, asking that question about Elastica,' he shouts, still seemingly unwilling to say the words, 'No, I didn't write the first Elastica album.' So I'm surprised when, after the gig, he greets me warmly and invites me to the aftershow party in a bar in town. and even more surprised when, after copious beers, he starts to tell me very personal stuff most of us would be unlikely to tell any stranger, never mind a journalist. At one point, I ask him if he's daring me to write this. At which he simply grins, and insists that it's "down to your own conscience". Complete bullshit, of course, because he knows that no lawyer in their right mind would let us print a word of it. He seems unable to resist stirring the shit, despite his claims to the contrary. One minute generous and affectionate, the next brusque and aggressive, you see how he can inspire love and loyalty yet completely infuriate, all at the same time. But one thing's for sure: if he really wants a quiet life, maybe Damon Albarn should learn how to lie.

Pulp Affliction

Ross Fortune

Time Out, 8 September 1999

The pretty lakeside town of Ithaca is a brutal five-hour drive north-west out of New York City. Hardly a trip into the heart of America's darklands. Yet at journey's end awaits Johnny Dowd – 51 years old, chiselled face, scarred jaw, steel-grey hair and slate-blue eyes. Possessed of a cracker drawl, Dowd is a tough and mysterious figure. Blessed with a gritty, desolate vision, he is responsible for a series of haunting and disturbed songs which infuse the savage art of '50s pulp fiction with the spooked blues devilry of Robert Johnson and lonesome tortured soul of Hank Williams. His music, meanwhile, is something else altogether: a rough-sculpted, hacked and hewn squall of distorted guitars, pounding, clanking rhythms and edgy keyboard sounds that hover and moan, pump and whirl. It is dark and twisted, dirty and sublime stuff.

Dowd released his first album two years ago, aged 49. His second followed earlier this year. Both have garnered deserved acclaim, but so far insufficient success to enable him to give up his day job – running a removals company in Ithaca. 'I'm actually losing money at a pretty scary clip,' he admits, seated in the corner of Zolar Moving Co's long, one-room office which also doubles as his recording studio. 'The better my career has gone, the more money I've lost.' Shifting in his chair – a heftily padded vinyl and chrome affair straight out of a Raymond Chandler movie – he grunts, and stretches out his legs to rest a foot on the sill of the open window. 'But, still, I've gotten damn lucky. I've got a shot at a whole new life, and maybe making a living at it.'

Johnny Dowd was born on Easter Sunday 1948 in Fort Worth,

Texas. He had a Presbyterian upbringing in Pauls Valley, Oklahoma, before moving to Memphis when his parents divorced. In
1969 he was drafted, and spent two years in Berlin. After that, with
an army buddy by the name of Dave Hinkle, he travelled around –
Oklahoma, Georgia, West Virginia, Southern California. Finally,
in a battered and rusty '49 Ford pick-up, Hinkle and Dowd arrived
in Ithaca, New York. 'We had no money at all,' says Dowd.
"That's how we got into the truckin' thing. We put flyers up to
move stuff. To start out, we were mostly just hauling trash in the
pick-up, and then we graduated from trash.' He chuckles, drily.'-
Graduated or de-grad-u-ated. I like the trash-hauling better than
the furniture-moving. actually, But there's more money in furniture. Anyway, we ended up buying a three-quarter ton truck, then
borrowed money to get an ever bigger truck, and one thing led to
another, and 25 years later we're still here.'

During this time Dow played regularly in bands, but ultimately, ended up discouraged. 'I got sick of it,' he says. 'Sick of
the feeling that either I got nothing worth saying or nobody wants
to hear it, or both.' So he quit the band – Neon Baptist – recorded
what became his first album, *Wrong Side Of Memphis*.

'It was real lo-fi, just something I did over a winter after work.
I'd just come up here and experiment. That's why I think that
album has such a claustrophobic feel. It's like somebody was
locked up in a cupboard for six months. All those voices. A
person just talking to themself. Which is basically what it was.'
There is a long pause. 'I think that first album was a little too
much Johnny for a lot of people,' he drawls, with a sparkle in his
eye, chewing on the words.' 'It is for me when I listen to it.'

Dowd's style is distinctive. Songs about the ordinariness of
violence and murder are vividly articulated, and musically too,
powerfully rendered and wrought. Lyrically, it is reminiscent of
the work of cult author Jim Thompson – who has been referred to
as the 'dime-store Dostoevsky' and the 'Camus of crime.' Dowd
readily acknowledges the influence. 'Yeah, he's a great writer. I
read a lot of that shit, before it was hip, you know, I read it when
it came out and it would always have a cover of some chick half-
dressed. That was the closest you could get to pornography when

I grew up, so I'd be stealing those books looking for the dirty parts. I always liked that kind of gangstery stuff, and those kind of films. I sort of think in black and white. I think: lyrically and morally.'

A particularly notable aspect of Dowd's songs is the way they are written in the first person – a device commonplace in fiction and films, but unusual in music (Randy Newman is another rare master of the form). With Dowd assuming the role of the murderer or the deadbeat or loser, the impact is then further heightened by his fearsomely laconic, cornball delivery. Amusingly, celebrated US critic Robert Christgau missed the point entirely, calling Dowd a fake. 'I can tell people are sometimes disappointed that I'm not more obnoxious or more violent,' he shrugs, 'or that I wasn't on death row. Though, for one thing, if I had been on death row, I wouldn't fuckin' be here now, I'd be fuckin dead, y'know. I mean that song, "First There Was A Funeral" is written from the perspective of a dead person!' (A device, incidentally, also employed by Jim Thompson in his book *The Killer Inside Me.*)

'The truth,' growls Dowd, 'is I've been in jail three times. The first time for being drunk and disorderly at a church revival meeting, the second for window peeking and the third for using obscene language in front of a woman. Which is all true, but they aren't exactly the kind of crimes that would make for, like, Jesse James or something.'

Nevertheless, just as Thompson worked out some of his own psychological problems through his writing, Dowd too admits a sense of kinship or culpability with his characters. 'A few years ago, I'd have said I'm just making all this shit up, completely, but as I look back on it I kind of realise, Jesus, that weird shit, that's how you think, you know, that's not this character, that was *your* thoughts, you do feel that way and have felt that way. I guess there's a lot of stuff that went down when I was young, a lot of things that I did. . .' He trails off into silence, staring intently at the floor.

'I've got this new song,' he announces, finally, which starts with the lines, "I was a surfer when I was young/Waves crashing around my head/I hear waves crashing still/As I'm lying here on my bed." Well, if I said, "*He* was a surfer when *he* was young. . ." you can know more about the character, because you're like God, y'know, but then you also got to get into the whole freakin' understanding of the character which to me is really more the province of a good novelist – Flaubert could get into that. But, y'know, I got three minutes and a really loud band. Most of my characters don't know *why* the fuck they're doing what they're doing. They haven't gone to a therapist or nothing.'

'Where I grew up,' he continues, slowly and deliberately, 'the way I was raised, there was right and there was wrong, there was good and there was bad. It wasn't so much about understanding, you were judged by what you did. If you did a bad thing you were a bad person. It wasn't like he did a bad thing 'cos he came from a bad family or something. You were judged on your actions. I mean, I'm a more understanding person now, and I believe you do need to look at that – in real life – but this is rock 'n' roll. This is not real life. Rock 'n' roll is about right and wrong, it is about good and evil. It is about kick out the jams. That's the essence of it.'

In London, at a show at the Water Rats earlier this year, while the band effected a savagely beautiful carnival freakshow of mutant melody and feedback frenzy all around him, Dowd performed the entire gig sitting on a chair – save for one incident. During the song 'No Woman's Flesh' (a dark little number sung by a guy whose drunk-driving has left his wife in a coma) somebody in the audience laughed. Dowd's response was to lurch up yelling in anger, leaning out over the heads of the tightly packed crowd, simultaneously launching wildly into a vicious and violent guitar solo. It was a devastating moment

'Yeah, I remember that,' he recalls, with a trace of a smirk. 'I kind of regret it, 'cos someone might have just told the guy a joke or something, but at the time. . . it's a thing where you just lose it. When I was younger I tended to fly off the handle. I was the kind of person. . . I always thought people were insulting me. I don't feel that way any more. I mean, I do feel that people are insulting me a lot, but I don't react to it. Now I'm kind of thinking: Well, maybe they're right, y'know! But I just kind of lost my temper. I think I probably had one drink past what I should have had. . . two, probably.' He laughs.

In truth, there is a very grim, bleak humour in Dowd's work. It's not something he denies. 'The greatest stuff, a poem or a movie or whatever, it's got to be clicking on all cylinders. It's not a comedy, it's not a tragedy. It's all of that comin' at you at once. That's what's so fuckin' confusing about it. That song "Lonnie" on this album. I mean, it's funny ("He shot himself in the trailer park/A couple of hours before it got dark/Did not die, is paralysed/Can't even wipe the tears from his eyes.") I mean, you think everything is the worst it could be, so you're gonna kill y'self, but you don't kill yourself, and then you find out things weren't as bad as they could be, because now things are really bad and you can't do anything about it. Well, I mean, that's funny, but it's also fuckin' tragic, y'know. It's like someone falling on a banana peel. You could say that's just funny, and some people could say, "Well, no, it's more towards the tragic, the guy's paralysed. . .' There is another long silence. 'I guess if I had a worldview, that would kind of be it.'

Johnny Dowd is a rare talent, a prolific writer, and a legend waiting to happen. He portrays a world out of kilter, a world that is profoundly unsettling – a world that is very real. Significantly, as evidenced on his most recent album, *Pictures From Life's Other Side*, he also has a band who perfectly complement his cracked and guttural voice and vision. In particular, the vocals of Kim Sherwood-Caso possess a stone-cold beauty that punctuate and harmonise, lending a ghostly chill.

And there's more. 'There's stuff from ten or 12 years ago that's probably as good as what we're doing now,' mutters Dowd, matter-of-factly. 'We recorded almost everything – Dave's got a wall of cassettes. I'm probably one of the most recorded people in the freakin' world. If I died now – ching, man! – you could just run with it. Either that or I could just kill somebody and go to jail. Those are my two options for selling a lot of records.'

The Brothers Grim: Oasis

Chris Salmon

Time Out, 19 July 2000.

What with Noel walking off their tour, Liam's marriage crumbling and the new album underperforming, things haven't been going so well for Oasis recently. In these exclusive excoriating interviews, the Gallagher brothers talk more frankly than ever before, and admit that if they're not able to sort out their current batch of problems, the end may well be nigh . . .

LIAM

June 29 Liam Gallagher (27) has been a very busy Manc lately. First, his brother walked out on Oasis's current world tour, after another Bust Up™. Then it became clear that Liam's Stormy Marriage™ to Patsy "who's next?" Kensit was reaching its sad but inevitable end. To make matters worse, Liam was followed to this afternoon's north London photo shoot by paparazzi, and he's got hay fever. Unsurprisingly, although likeable, he's tired, serious and a little stressed. After Liam has posed for photos (his Elvis 'Taking Care Of Business' patch prominent), we sit for a chat.

How's the tour going?
Going good, y'know. Considering Noel's not there.
Does it feel different?
Totally. It's just more punky. Not as professional. Just up and running, banging it out, instead of being a bit . . . dunno. I think we got a bit too slick.
Would you mind Noel not being there if you were a fan?
[Witheringly] Yeah. He writes the songs, you wanna see him

there, don't you? We've just gotta sort it out. He's gotta realise that . . . we've argued before, and we'll argue again. I just wanna be in a band. I don't wanna hear anything about solo albums.

You were getting on pretty well, weren't you?

Yeah, we had been. It's just solo stuff keeps popping up, and I don't like it. It's no good for the band and it's no good for me.

Have you been in touch?

I rang him and he told me to fuck off, so I left it at that. I'll meet him in Dublin the day before the gig and we'll have to have it out there. But we're not splitting up. Even though everyone's saying we should. This is what we do. We've got loads of new songs. There's a new album ready to go.

Do you understand why Noel left?

Yeah, 'cause we were arguing, Y'know, he said things to me, I said things to him. Like you do. And that was it. I just said, "I don't wanna hear about solo albums, you're not putting me on a fucking shelf for a year."

Why do you think he wants to do solo stuff?

I haven't got a clue. People are saying it's 'cause he's got these songs that aren't Oasis. But you make them Oasis, don't ya?

Do you feel there are more eyes on you on stage now?

Nah, 'cause it's a band. Obviously people are into the two brothers thing, but it's not Noel's band, it's not my band. It'd be good if we all worked together instead of Noel just writing things. I think it's time for *us* now, if we're gonna fuckin', y'know, survive.

It must be hard for him, though, having never written with any of you before. Maybe he's threatened by the idea.

I'm sure he is, but there shouldn't be no threat, it's only for the good of the band. He carries the weight of Oasis on his fuckin' shoulders too much. And you can tell he does, in his writing and in everything. It's like "share it out". I'm willing to fuckin' take a chance.

So it's not gonna be a problem getting back with him now?

[Derisively] Nah. We've had arguments before. We're all big boys, we know what we've gotta do. And we were never fucking that close anyway.

How was it through Japan and America?
Japan and America was great. It was just, we were in Barcelona
and Alan had pulled a gig 'cause of his hand and we were sat
about in the dressing room drinking. It was just a pissed-up
fucking argument. And then we had a fight. And he won, I'll give
him that. And he got off and I stayed the night in Barcelona and
he went to Paris and I met him again. I was still pissed up – in the
hotel in Paris and we had another little ding-dong and that's it.
Do you think . . .
[Interrupts] But I'm sure he thought we'd come home after him.
But I thought: Well, fuck that, there's no point. I'm not gonna be
able to get in my house with the press. And once I'm in, I'm not
gonna be able to get out. And I'm not living like that any more.
Fuck it. So I thought: We'll have a crack. It was the first time
we'd ever worked together as a fuckin' band. And it felt nice. And
it's a shame he wasn't here.
Who should be apologising?
Well, I've apologised. I'm man enough to apologise and I'm man
enough to say I was wrong.
So you were out of order?
[Passionately] I was out of order and he was out of order. We
were both totally out of order. We've just gotta fuckin' . . .
[Quietly] I dunno. Y'know, we're always gonna argue.
Are you enjoying life?
[Hesitates] Yeah, it's good, I can't complain. No one's dead, are
they? I've got a beautiful baby and I'm buzzing off him. Shit's
not right at home with me missus, but that'll get sorted. Y'know,
there's no point dwelling on it.
How's London life?
I'm moving, man. Gonna go to the country for a bit.
You're selling the house, aren't you?
Yeah. D'ya wanna buy it?
I wish I could afford it. £1.5 million . . .
More than that, mate. Two point fucking eight. [It's later
reported that the house has been sold for £2.5m.]
What about the whole drink and drugs thing?
No drugs, man, I've had enough. For the time being I've not

given up, but [yawns] I just can't be bothered. Got too much shit going on in my life to be snorting gear. I've got a kid to look after, I've gotta be strong. But I like a pint.

What do you drink?

Anything.

You're not giving that up then?

You can't give up fuckin' booze, man. A couple of pints is okay. And I have a lot of pints. I can drink for England, but you can only drink so much before you're asleep.

You don't think you've ever had a problem with drinking?

I don't think so. No I just like to drink. I could give it up like that, but who am I giving it up for. For some other cunt? If you don't wanna drink then don't drink. If you wanna do summat, do it.

Yeah, but if you're getting rellant . . .

No. I drink 'cause I want to. Not because I need to. It's like, if some shit goes on I don't go 'Oh fuck, I need a drink.' There's no booze in my house. If I was a big heavy fucking drinker, which all these idiots think I am, there'd be beer in my house. It's full of water, my house and the only time I have a drink is when I go to the pub.

Are people saying you shouldn't?

I dunno. Our kid reckons I shouldn't drink. Y'know, I reckon . . . There's a lot of things he shouldn't do.

Isn't he looking out for you? I mean, do you love each other?

I adore him. And if any one bad-mouthed him I'd rip their fuckin' head off. And he'd do the same for me. It's a love-hate relationship. I wanna be him. He wants to be me. Y'know, he wants to be a singer and I want to be a songwriter.

What about your kid? How's he?

He's rocking. He's starting to crawl. He growls. He just goes "grrrr". He don't "go ga ga goo goo".

You like the current album?

I think it's great.

And it's still sold 500,000 copies here.

That's a lot of records. But I don't give a fuck. You can't go

"Right. we're gonna write a record and it's gonna sell *that* amount." It goes where it goes.

The first Stone Roses album sold less than 500,000.

And that's great.

Yeah, and Johnny Hates Jazz sold more. And who remembers Johnny Hates Jazz?

You. You've just mentioned them. You had them on before you came out! And tell you fuckin' what, fair play to him 'cause I hate jazz an' all.

July 12 Oasis pull a show at Roskilde Festival in Denmark, hours after nine fans are killed. Oasis's manager, Marcus Russell meets police who reveal that they don't yet know why people died and haven't made any subsequent security changes. The organisers claim Oasis and Pet Shop Boys (who also cancel) are disrespecting the dead. "Basically, they were asking for the band to go onstage and have Oasis fans dancing on people's graves," Noel tells me later.

July 2 *The Irish Sunday Mirror* carries a story quoting Noel saying of Cork band The Frank And Walters, "Without them I'd be on a building site in Manchester today." Two days on Noel shakes his head. "I couldn't name a song by them," he says.

July 4 Noel Gallagher (33) has been a very lazy Manc lately. After walking out in May, he holidayed at his Ibiza getaway before returning to his Buckinghamshire pad to watch, and enjoy, Euro 2000. We meet in his farmhouse recording studio, surrounded by 37 guitars. Noel is relaxed, bright, friendly, slightly shy, and is pleased to learn from our photographer that Marilyn Manson likes *"Be Here Now"*. Then, for over an hour, he sits and chats about football, Inspiral Carpets and, of course, Liam.

NOEL

Have you spoken to the band?

[Brightly] I haven't, no. I spoke to Marcus [Oasis's manager]. Everybody's on good form, apparently.

Have you read the gig reviews?

[Laughs] I have, yeah. It's ironic. We never got a good review for the first six months of the tour, and as soon as I leave it's like the greatest rock 'n' roll band ever!

Why do you reckon that is?

I have to assume people just don't like me! I mean, the five guys in the group are all brilliant musicians and they're playing brilliant songs, so why wouldn't it be good?

When I was reviewing the new album I did feel the easiest way to write it would be to slag it off . . .

[Nods] Mmm.

These days if you say it's actually quite good, you're laying yourself open. But I reckon "Gas Panic" is one of the best songs you've written.

Well, yeah. I think people expect a bit much. I don't think people think it's a bad album, it's just not this earth-shattering experience. But is any band that important after five albums? What I find . . . not upsetting, but annoying is, like, we've got a single out yesterday. Now, on Monday morning people'll start writing about how it failed to get to Number One, or the top five. But nobody writes how Travis have failed to get to Number One. ["Sunday Morning Call" enters the charts at number four.]

I suppose people expect Oasis to be a bigselling band.

I know, but there has to be a dramatic fucking "Bumph! It's gonna change now!" There can't be just a gradual change over six months. Someone's gotta stand up and say "Fuck. I'm not doin' it any more."

But when Blur came out with the *Blur* album after *The Great Escape*, there was a bit of "Ooh, it's not doing well". Then everyone was like "Who cares?"

I fuckin' envy them in a way because we couldn't go off and make a lo-fi, indie-jungle record. Blur can do that. And Primal Scream can constantly reinvent themselves and The Beta Band can, because they're not considered seminal fuckin' artists. Y'know, we've gotta be constantly in the top five and records have gotta sell millions and tours have gotta be bigger than the last . . . And I don't wanna make fuckin' avantgarde records. I like playing the guitar. I like being in a rock 'n' roll band. But people accuse you of not progressing. Then if you did change they'd say "What are you doing making Krautrock records?"

Does it freak you out reading these good gig reviews?
[Genuinely] No, fuck, no.

How are you in your head?
[Hesitant] I'm really . . . I'm never happy touring at the best of times. Y'know, with me being the spokesman, I get up at ten and before the soundcheck at 5pm I'll have done seven interviews, generally with an interpreter, answering the same questions. The hour and a half on stage is brilliant, but it's just all the bullshit that surrounds it.

Can't you tour on your own terms?
Yeah, but you've gotta have the other five people in the band on the same wavelength. I can't be bothered with the fuckin' rock 'n' rollness of it all. That's not me any more. Whereas everyone else is having the time of their lives.

Liam thinks you expected them to follow you home.
[Surprised] No, not at all. Did I fuck.

Because it was all right in Japan and America . . .
It was brilliant, but y'know, he's made a big deal about this hypothetical fucking' solo career that I'm supposed to be starting. Which is all bollocks. [I only meant] one album of maybe like acousticy, folky stuff in between Oasis records, as a side-project. Now I'm not even sure I can be arsed. It's like if it's gonna cause that much fuckin' trouble, then I can't be bothered.

If you were a punter, how would you feel seeing Oasis without you?
Well in my defence, if anybody wanted their money back they could've seen the promoter. As far as I'm aware everybody turned up. I mean, Oasis was always about Liam Gallagher singing my songs. I think everybody else is totally interchangeable, but out of respect for the British fans I've decided I'm gonna do these gigs and then I'm gonna have a very, very long holiday. And then I'm gonna decide what I wanna do.

Have you had it up to here with Liam?
Oh. I've been up to there with Liam since . . .

I met him for the first time last week. He was pretty much what I expected. Intense, well-meaning, but . . .

[Vehemently] The bottom line is, if Liam's fuckin' sober he's great. But once he's pissed he likes nothing better than to sit in a room and argue. Y'know; "I can drink more than you can drink; My Dad's bigger than your Dad." I mean there's something about me that makes him unhappy, and if I make him that unhappy then I'll, y'know . . .

But he looks up to you, he adores you.

[Passionate] yeah, I adore him as well. But not to the point where I'll sit and be insulted all night, in front of a load of people. I'm not having that off anyone.

Leaving him to it could be the best thing for Oasis. Problem is, he needs to understand your reasons.

Well, I'm quite proud of the fact he's carried on. Y'see, Liam desperately wants to be in charge, and as far as I'm concerned now he is in charge. He needs to prove summat to himself, that he can be the man. But I'm sick of being the endless guest on "The Jerry Springer Show", y'know. "And our next two guests are two brothers from Manchester . . ." It's like, "Aww fuck off, man, I can't be arsed." But you know, Liam's still in his twenties and he's still living the life of a rock star.

But you've got five years on him.

Yeah. But I still don't understand him or the reasons why he's always going off at me. Two or three years ago I'd sit down and try and get inside his head. Now I can't be fuckin' bothered. Until I can see a change in him, what's the fuckin point? Because ultimately the music suffers. You wanna try being in a recording studio with him . . .

He doesn't really understand where you're coming from. He said he tried to apologise.

Yeah, but he's been apologising for six years. And it's not just things about me, he's said some things that are out of order. Things that you shouldn't even think let alone say in front of people who are basically total strangers. It's easy to say you're sorry and it's a different thing meaning it. So he's apologised, big fuckin' deal. Until the next time. But this time there isn't gonna

be a next time, because I've just about had enough of him. And
y'know you're in a hotel room in Paris and you think: Well, I've
got six weeks left in Europe with this twat, or I've got a house in
Ibiza with its own beach. Hmm. This is not a difficult decision to
make.

Is there a chance there might not be a next album?
Well. I've written two songs – that doesn't even constitute a
single. And they were songs I'd written maybe 18 months ago. So
I've gone 18 months without writing anything. And every time I
pick up me guitar or try and write some words, it's just not doing
it for me. As I get older I feel like I need a lot more time. Now you
try and speak to Liam, It's always, "Right, when are we going in
the studio?" And I'm like, "Well, I haven't written any songs."
"Well, when are you gonna write some songs? I'm not fuckin'
having another year off." And I'm like, "You can't force these
things. If it takes me five years to write an album, then you're
gonna have to sit on your arse for five years. Unless *you* go and
write a bunch of fuckin' songs."

I reckon he feels awkward around you.
Yeah, well, we'd be sat on a tour bus and we'd put on a tape and
summat'll come on and he'll go "Who's this?" and you go "Oh,
it's Superstar". And he'll go [aggressively] "Fuck, it's shit".
[Calmly] "Fair enough." [Aggressively] "Who the fuck are they?
So you're into these are ya?" It's like "Well, hang on a minute,
it's only a fuckin' song. I *like* the song. Leave it, man." Before you
know it there's a full-scale argument . . .

But he values your opinion.
Yeah, but why does he have to do that? I don't know. [Sighs] I
was speaking to me mam about it . . . It's like he can't accept the
fact that maybe the band is not the most important thing in my
life any more. When I had two years off, I came back and it was
like, "I'm married, I've got a kid now." And watching my little
girl grow up and go to school is more important than watching the
band develop. He's gotta get his head round that before we can go
any further.

Plus it sounds like he's got shit going on with Patsy.
Well that again, y'know. Everybody in the band has personal

problems, but you should never bring them into the studio or on tour.

C'mon, though: if your marriage was breaking up, it'd be hard for it not to affect you.

I'm sure. [Pauses] I'm sure. But it's nobody else's fault. I mean, I haven't got the answers to his problems. Not at all. But Liam seems to think that because we're not as big as we were five or six years ago, somebody has to have the answers. Y'know: "What are the reasons we don't sell ten million albums any more?" I really don't know. If I knew I'd put it right.

Liam thinks you carry the burden of the band and he's saying he could take more off you.

[Deep breath] Er, it's not that it's a burden, it's just that it's always been like this for me. Liam started doing 50 per cent more interviews on this tour, but it still hasn't taken any workload off me. When we started this tour it was like, we haven't put a record out or played for three years, half the band had gone, there was new members, we were fuckin' on the way to Japan and someone's decided C4 are gonna do an on-the-road documentary, we've got all the journalists in the same hotel. And this is the first *day*. You couldn't go to the bar without [mimes putting dictaphone out] "Can I have a word about this?" And then of course bright spark has to go and say he's gonna break Robbie Williams's nose before we even get on the plane.

That Robbie-Liam thing was a bit silly.

It was just pathetic. I was sat watching CNN in a hotel room in Japan and they had a report from the BRITS and none of it was about who'd won. And then you see fucking Robbie Williams challenging Liam to a fight. And I'm sat there eating my breakfast going "This is not real, this is not happening". But then you pass Liam in the foyer and he's going "Yeah, I'm gonna break his fuckin' legs when I see him". It's like "Will you shut the fuck up, man?"

Beckham and Posh have kind of taken over from you and Liam as the tabloids' most wanted. Do you have any sympathy for them?

Er, I've got sympathy for him 'cause he just seems to be going along with it. I mean, if she wasn't married to him, who's she? Just one of the Spice Girls who can't sing. Whereas he's the best fucking footballer we've got in the country. I mean, you know that documentary they did and she was interviewing him? How can you interview your husband on TV? It's sick. I feel sorry for him, but . . . [laughs] Fuck him, he's a dirty red any way!

How do you think things will be with Liam in Dublin?
The manager phoned me last week and said him and Alan [White, drummer] was saying "Look, we want a meeting before you do these gigs" and I was going "Well fine, all right". And of course, who didn't turn up? So that shows how much it means to him. They think it's gonna be weird, but it's not gonna be weird for me. I don't hate anyone, I haven't fallen out with anyone. It's just I didn't wanna be on the fucking road with him.

Why don't you just play big gigs in capitals where you don't necessarily have to stay in the same hotel, don't have to do any press . . .? It's almost like you take on too much.
Well, that's what I'm saying. We have to sit down at the end of this tour and I've gotta have a big fuckin' think about where we're going and how we're gonna get there. I couldn't just sit down now and go "If we do this, if we do that". But I know what I'm not gonna do is just fuckin' give up making music, just fuckin' sit at home and become a dad. I want my kids to grow up and see me in action, not watch me on some archive footage from fuckin' Knebworth.

Do you think there's a possibility that you're just not gonna bother with Oasis?
Oh course, yeah. But we'll see what happens.

You're more pissed off with it than I thought.
I'm not thinking too much about anything at the moment, just about getting these gigs done and hopefully them being received really well. Then after that . . . See, I've always felt your management or your label never give you enough time. When I was younger I could sit in a room and knock off three songs a day, like "Some Might Say" and "Whatever" and a bunch of B-sides. But y'know, I'm not 26 any more. People think: Aw, give him two weeks and he'll write another album. It's not like that.

Is it pressure?

No, it's just that when I was 26 the most important thing in my entire life was the group and writing songs. But now it's not. I've devoted enough of my time to Oasis. I've given enough, so now I wanna take a bit back. But I never said I was gonna do a solo album and leave the fuckin' band. I just wanna do little things that make it interesting for me. But I've no intention of leaving the band.

Is Liam's drinking the big . . .

[Quickly] For me it is, yeah.

He said: "I just drink till I fall asleep."

Well that's fine, but it's the bit before he falls asleep which is a fuckin' . . . Everybody else finds it really funny, but when you're sat on the end of it. He gets *that far away* from your face, y'know, just going like [incoherently] "Well fuckin', where the fuckin' cunt this." It makes me tired. It gets me down. But he knows that, and the more it gets me down, the more he does it.

It'd be good if you two could sort it out.

Listen. Everytime we fall out it's always this big fuckin' dramatic thing. To me it's just another argument man. It'll sort itself out. It's not as if we're never gonna see each other again. Let's put it this way if I wasn't related to him. I'd have sacked him fuckin' four years ago. But it's not . . . [Quietly] It's deeper than all that.

Perhaps Wembley will be the turning point. That little bit of friction could be the thing that makes it . . .

Y'know, the last gig I did with the band was in Madrid and it was one of the best gigs I've done for years. What I'm really looking forward to is getting onstage at Reading. Because we've gotta follow Primal Scream. And if you can't summon up enough enthusiasm to say, "Right, well, we've gotta be better than them." Y'know, I'm looking forward to going on after them. Then we'll see how good we are."

July 5 Despite Noel's revelation otherwise, *NME* claim they've heard three new tracks.

July 6 Liam insists a new Oasis album is written to be released in January.

July 7 With Liam in Dublin, Patsy Kensit leaves her and Liam's Primrose Hill house. In broad day light. In front of reporters. Wearing a lovely dress. "I'm actually quite relieved," she tells "London Tonight".

July 8 "Patsy Legsit" screams the *Daily Star*, with the *Mirror*'s cover carrying news of Patsy's new fella. Meanwhile, I'm off to Dublin to see Noel and Liam's reunion gig. The route to the 40,000 sell-out Lansdowne Road show is littered with leery, beery men singing and pissing. Naturally, when Liam, the Patron Saint of Laddism, skulks onstage, the crowd go barmy. And although, annoyingly, most of the sound blows into the gusty Dublin night, it's clear Oasis still rock – even if the old stuff does rock most. Liam's voice is as snarlingly majestic as ever, his swagger as cocky. And Noel seems genuinely touched by the spine-tingling crowd reaction to "Don't Look Back In Anger". "We ain't splitting up," growls Liam before the brotherly "Aquiesce", with its chorus of "Because we need each other", after which the brothers shake hands. Later, as they say goodnight to the Dublin masses. Noel tells them, "We'll see you next time." A truce, it seems, has been called.

July 9 The *Irish Sunday People's* front page reveals "Liam's Dublin boozebinge". Apparently, he knocked back 15 pints of Guinness in his hotel. Meanwhile, Noel, we're told, arrived on a different flight and stayed in a different hotel. A truce, then, but not a full-on peace accord.

July 10 "Rock chick to wreck chick" says the *Sun*, splashing pictures of Patsy and her new man over two pages. Thankfully, Liam is keeping "a dignified silence".

And there you have it. Twelve days in the weird, wonderful, ever-changing, tabloid-scrutinised lives of Noel and Liam Gallagher. If Liam can keep his gob shut, they're well poised to reclaim some of their former glories. And if he doesn't, Noel seems likely to walk away. But whatever happens you can be sure the world will be watching. No wonder they called their label Big Brother.

"Can't Help Falling in Love"

Doomed Rock 'n' Roll Marriages

Ike and Tina Turner (1960)

The possible inventor of rock 'n' roll met Annie Mae Bullock in an East St Louis nightclub in 1957. She sang with the band, Ike divorced his wife, and by 1962 he'd married Annie Mae and transformed her into horny little Tina Turner. Within two more years the show had become the Ike and Tina Turner Revue, sporting Ikettes that variously included PP Arnold, Merry Clayton and Bonnie Bramlett. Between then and their final split a year after her appearance as the Acid Queen in the Who's *Tommy* musical in 1975, the two of them had notched up a raft of hit singers and albums. Divorce, superstardom for the former Mrs Turner, end of story.

Well, it might have been if Tina hadn't written her book, *I Tina,* which was made into the film, *What's Love Got To Do With It?* , telling the world in graphic detail that old Ike was a womaniser, a drug-abuser and a dirty, no good, wife-beater. After Tina left him, Ike went through bad times. He was arrested several times for drug violations, income tax evasion and fidding his telephone bill. He served time and signed away his right to sue Disney over the movie *What's Love Got To Do With It?* in return for $45,000. Despite all that, Ike Turner is still one hell of a great rock 'n' roller.

David and Angela Bowie (1970)

When it comes to "open" relationships, the marriage of Mary Angela Barnett to David Robert Jones [Bowie] takes some beating. She was born in Cyprus of American parents; he in Brixton, south London of blue collar London stock. Both of them professed to be bisexual: Angie was expelled from college in Connecticut for having a lesbian affair with another student, and when she and Bowie met, it worked because, "we were laying the same bloke." It is also claimed that the night before their wedding was spent in a threesome with another [female] wedding guest.

His proposal of marriage began: "If you can handle the fact that I'm not in love with you. . ." and it was always planned that part of Angie's role would be as advisor, helping him become what he desired most: a rock star. Rock star he became, and despite having a son together – Duncan Zowie Heywood Bowie – they divorced in 1980. The split was hardly harmonious. In court Bowie claimed that his wife had been a heavy drug user and produced pornographic pictures showing her and other men and women. Bowie won custody of the boy and Angie had to settle for a reported $1000,000 and a gagging order, banning her from revealing details of their marriage together until Zowie reached twenty-one years of age.

Once her "gag" had been removed, Angie revealed much, if not all, in two volumes of autobiography as well as on the Joan Rivers talk show on American TV. Here she revealed that she came home one day and found Bowie in bed with Mick Jagger. Her reaction? She made the two Englishmen a cup of tea. Zowie Bowie revealed how much more sensible he was than his parents when he legally changed his name to Joe.

You can check out what Angie's up to now on her website: http://www. bettyjack.com/angie/index.html. Don't miss the article 'Cyprus – Lands of Passion,' it's a scorcher.

Bill Wyman and Mandy Smith (1989)

What do you call a 48-year old man who courts a thirteen-year old girl? Why, Bill Wyman, of course. Old Bill met "wild child" Mandy at the Brits [British Rock Awards] and kept up a pretence of dating women only half his age whilst he was seeing her "on the quiet". It was lucky for of them that Mandy's mother raised no major objections to the pair seeing each other. When Mandy was sixteen, she broke it off (the relationship), only to fall back into Bill's aged arms for a brief marriage a couple of years later. A year after Bill and Mandy's divorce, the British tabloid press revealed that Bill's son Steven was engaged to Mandy's mum. It must be something in the water.

Michael Jackson and Lisa Marie Presley (1994)

In 1994, just when everyone had given up speculating on Michael Jackson's sexuality, it was announced that he had in fact married Lisa Marie Presley, only daughter of late rock 'n' roll superstar and burger-fancier, Elvis. The wedding took place in the Dominican Republic in May 1994, and not surprisingly, for two months the couple denied that it had even taken place. It was second time around for Presley, whose first marriage to Scientologist and musician Danny Keough, ended in divorce after six years and two children.

Her marriage to Jackson came barely a year after a thirteen-year-old boy accused the former Jackson Five lead vocalist of sexual abuse, while many were concerned for the welfare of "Bubbles", Jackson's pet chimpanzee. Cynics suggested that this could possibly provide a reason for the unexpected troth. For her part, wags put forward the theory that Lisa Marie, who had failed in her bid to launch a singing career, had motives of her own in marrying the "King of Pop". Money almost certainly wasn't a factor. On her twenty-fifth birthday, Presley had inherited the Gracelands fortune of $100 million, whilst her gloved one's assets were estimated to be at least double that.

"Just think," Michael is supposed to have told his new bride a couple of months after the wedding, "nobody thought this would last." And it didn't. Barely twenty months after they'd tied the knot, Lisa told Jackson to "Beat It". In January 1996, Lisa Marie Presley-Jackson filed for divorce, citing irreconcilable differences. In a television interview given six months earlier, Presley was asked if she and Jackson had sex. "Yes! Yes! Yes!" they yelped in unison.

In February 2000, Presley announced that she was to marry

year-old singer-songwriter John Oszajca, whose first album was due for release just a few months later. In August of the same year, Jackson's second wife, Debbie Rowe Jackson, gave birth to a healthy baby boy at the Los Angeles Cedars-Sinai Medical Center. A brother for Bubbles.

Dead End Street

Forget mountain-rescue, parachuting and bodyguarding, the world's most hazardous job is rock musician. If you survive electrocution, drug addiction and over-fondness for the booze, avoid crashing your plane, car or helicopter, and steer clear of suicide, chances are your best friend, wife or record company boss will shoot you in the head. As Patti Smith once remarked: "Not even boot camp is as tough as being in rock 'n' roll." And she should know.

1. "Scary Monsters (And Super Creeps)"
SUDDEN DEATH

Johnny Ace

Christmas night, 1954. An enthusiastic crowd of 3,500 music lovers was enjoying a show at the Civic Auditorium in downtown Houston. Topping the bill were Willie Mae "Big Mama" Thornton, original singer of "Hound Dog", and rising young R&B balladeer, John Alexander Jr, better known as Johnny Ace. Despite having achieved a number one single and half a dozen other hits in the previous two years, Ace was a troubled man who looked older than his twenty-five years. According to one musician on the bill, he "always seemed as if he was just about to hit someone." A rigorous touring schedule coupled with bad eating habits and a love for the bottle had given Ace an extra 40 pounds to carry, and the boyish heart-throb of the pin-ups was starting to look porky and pasty.

While on tour in Florida, Ace had purchased a Harrington & Richardson double-action revolver, which he carried around in an inside jacket pocket, treating it more as a toy than a deadly weapon. He would point it at friends and sometimes he'd even pull the trigger, the hammer clicking on to an empty chamber. Or he'd draw back at the last minute if the gun was loaded. His newest idea of fun was to drive his Oldsmobile at 90 miles an hour and shoot out the zeros in the roadside speed-limit signs.

During the intermission at the Civic Auditorium show, Ace turned up at Mama Thornton's dressing room, accompanied by his girlfriend, Olivia Gibbs, and two of her friends. He had a bottle of vodka in one hand, his pistol in the other, and was waving both of them around. Not one to stand for any such nonsense, the big blues singer prised the weapon away from Ace and saw that there was only one slug in the chamber. Ace demanded the gun back. She reluctantly handed it over, but told him in no uncertain terms not to point it at anyone.

Rising to the perceived challenge, Ace aimed the gun at Olivia Gibbs' friend, Mary Carter, and pulled the trigger. The hammer clicked on to an empty chamber. He then put the pistol to his girlfriend's temple and tried again.

Click. Another empty chamber.

Laughing, Ace pressed the barrel to his own head, saying, "I'll show you it won't shoot," and squeezed the trigger.

Bang! One dead R&B singer.

When Ace's body returned to his hometown of Memphis, an estimated 5,000 people crammed into the 2,000 seater Clayborn Temple Church for the funeral service. Among the mourners were Junior Parker, bandleader Roscoe Gordon, and BB King. As King said later: "Don't ever dare Johnny to do something dangerous' cause the boy would up and do it. Finally that did him in."

It sure did.

Carlton Barrett

Innovative reggae drummer, Carlton Lloyd Barrett, affectionately known as "Carly", was born in Kingston, Jamaica, in

1951. He started playing in the late 1960s, teaming up with his bass-playing brother Aston as the Soul Mates and Rhythm Force. Together they backed Max Romeo and Leroy Brown as the Hippy Boys, were the backbone of the Upsetters, of "Clint Eastwood" and "Cold Sweat" fame, before joining Bob Marley, Peter Tosh and Bunny Wailer as the "Wailing Wailers". Carlton's highly original drumming style – with its distinctive cracking rimshots and dancing cymbals sound – helped make Marley and the Wailers reggae's first truly international successes.

On the evening of 17 April 1987 – Good Friday – Carlton Barrett drove home from the studio and noticed that another car was following. As he walked across the front yard of his Kingston home, a gunman stepped out of the shadows and shot him twice in the head. Carly Barrett was pronounced dead on arrival at hospital. After a brief investigation, the police arrested Carlton's wife, Albertine, her taxi-driving lover, Glenroy Carter, and his friend, Junior Neil. Neil was found guilty of murder, and although Albertine and Carter were sentenced to seven years each for conspiracy, they were released after only a few months on a legal technicality.

Sam Cooke

Soul singer Sam Cook (the "e" came later) was born in Mississippi in 1931, and raised in the "windy city" of Chicago. His father was a Baptist Minister and young Sam sang in church choirs and in gospel groups from the age of nine. Before he'd even left his teens, he'd become lead singer in one of America's hottest gospel outfits, The Soul Stirrers. A huge draw on the gospel circuit, they recorded a string of hits for Specialty Records, including the timeless "Touch The Hem Of His Garment". But Sam had R&B and pop aspirations and, initially under the pseudonym of "Dale Cook", he recorded some non-gospel tracks for Specialty. Despite having Little Richard on the label, owner Art Rupe was afraid of upsetting his fickle gospel customers, and he desperately wanted Cook to carry on with The Soul Stirrers. When Cook insisted on going solo and secular, Rupe sacked him, together with his arranger, Bumps Blackwell.

Although released on the tiny Keen label, their first song together outside Specialty, the self-penned "You Send Me", reached number one in both the pop and R&B charts. Over the next six years, Sam Cooke wrote and recorded some of the finest soul and blues music ever to be slapped on to vinyl. At his best, Sam Cooke had the power to move and groove, and tracks like "Twisting The Night Away", "Shake", "Another Saturday Night" and "Bring It On Home To Me" will be played so long as human beings admit to having souls. Cooke was a committed opponent of racial segregation, both on the road and on record, and after appearing at the prestigious Copacabana nightclub in 1964 in a top hat and carrying a cane, he vowed only to play black clubs from then on. One of his final recordings, the anti-racist anthem, "A Change Is Gonna Come" was released posthumously.

The death of Sam Cooke was sad, unnecessary, and surrounded in mystery and deceit. The facts are that on 11 December 1964, he was shot and then clubbed to death by Mrs Bertha Lee Franklin, manager of the Hacienda Motel in Los Angeles. Although the facts are hazy, the train of events that led to his death were set off earlier the same evening when Sam met a pretty 22-year-old Eurasian woman called Linda Boyer in a Hollywood restaurant called Martoni's. Although married, Cooke had become a heavy drinker after one of his three children had drowned in his swimming pool a year earlier, and he was living away from his wife. Boyer willingly went with him on on a tour of local nightspots, and together they drove to the motel, where they registered as "Mr and Mrs Sam Cooke".

Once in the room, Cooke undressed and – according to Boyer's testimony – forced her to do the same. Whilst he was in the bathroom, she took the opportunity to "escape", grabbing her clothes and his. "I thought he was going to rape me," she told detectives later. When he came out of the bathroom, Cooke was incensed to find not only his prospective bed companion missing, but also his clothes, his wallet containing several thousand dollars, and wedding ring. Raging drunk and dressed only in an overcoat and shoes, Cooke ran to the reception desk where he

demanded to know from Mrs Franklin where Boyer was hiding.
According to the motel-keeper, Cooke was violent and struck her
across the face. "To defend herself," she grabbed a pistol from
underneath the desk and fired three shots, one of which hit Cooke
in the chest. Then she picked up a baseball bat and beat him to
the floor. "I thought he was going to rob me," she later explained. Boyer was picked up half a block away from the motel,
crouched on the floor of a phone booth. At the inquest, Sam
Cooke's death was ruled "justifiable homicide".

Sam Cooke's wallet and wedding ring were never recovered. A
month after the killing, Boyer was convicted of prostitution, and
in 1979, she was sentenced to life imprisonment for murdering
her boyfriend.

King Curtis

On 13 August 1971, ace rock 'n' roll saxophonist Curtis Ousley,
better known as "King Curtis", was stabbed to death during a
fight outside his home in New York City. He was 37-years-old.
Curtis began playing tenor saxophone with Lionel Hampton in
the late 1940s, before turning in sessions for Nat "King" Cole,
Joe Turner, Buddy Holly, Brook Benton, The Drifters and –
most famously – The Coasters. His snappy solos, as typified on
"Yakety Yak", went a long way towards setting the mood of an
era and defining the band's trademark sound. In 1962 he began
cutting records under the name King Curtis and between then
and his death, achieved fifteen *Billboard* chart hits. Curtis also
found time to record and tour with the likes of The Beatles, Sam
Cooke, Aretha Franklin, John Lennon and Wilson Pickett.

At the height of a heatwave in August 1971, Curtis returned
home, carrying an air-conditioner he intended installing in his
apartment at 50 West 86th Street, New York. His way was
blocked by two junkies shooting up on his steps. He asked them
to move, a fight started and one of the men, later identified as
Juan Montanez, stabbed Curtis in the heart with a stiletto. He
was rushed to hospital, but was declared dead on arrival. At the
King's funeral service four days later, his band played a special

hour-long arrangement of "Soul Serenade" as the mourners shuffled in. Jesse Jackson preached the service and Aretha Franklin sang the closing spiritual, "Never Grow Old".

Mal Evans

Former roadie for The Beatles, assistant general manager of their Apple Corps and the man who introduced Badfinger to the Fab Four, mild-mannered Mal had moved to Los Angeles after Apple's collapse. Absorbing the LA vibes maybe a little too well, he developed a fondness for replica guns, including a very realistic Winchester rifle he took pride showing off to friends and neighbours. On 4 January 1976, Evans' girlfriend returned from a shopping expedition to the apartment they shared, and discovered the former "Sixth Beatle" (the band always said that Brian Epstein was the fifth) suicidal and crying, cradling his gun in his lap. Worried that he might be about to do "something stupid" – financial problems had been mooted – she rang friends for help. They (well, what are friends for) called the police. When officers came to arrest him, they found him heavily under the influence of Valium, and mistaking his attempts at humour for gun-play, shot him four times. Mal Evans was dead.

Bobby Fuller

An inventive singer-songwriter, Bobby Fuller formed the Bobby Fuller Four with his brother Randy in 1961, and had their biggest hit with a sparky recording of the Crickets' "I Fought The Law" in 1966. But the Cadillac of success can be a fickle ride and in Bobby's case it came to a lurching stop on 18 July of the same year when his badly beaten body was found in a vehicle in Los Angeles. An autopsy determined that death was due to asphyxia, occasioned through the forced inhalation of gasoline. Police found out that at the time of his death Fuller was seeing a woman called "Melody". Melody was said to have an ex-boyfriend who was a jealous club owner, reputedly with links to organised crime, but before police could interview her, Melody disappeared and the case ran cold. A private investigator hired by Fuller's parents was shot at and quit the case after a few days. Guitarist Jim Reese left California in a hurry less than a week after the funeral, claiming that three sinister men had been to his apartment looking for him; and around the same time, brother Randy Fuller and a roadie were almost run off the road by a car that had been following them.

Marvin Gaye

Marvin Pentz Gay Jr was born on 2 April 1939 in a deprived area of Washington DC, where his father, Marvin Pentz Gay Sr, was a lay minister in the zealous Seventh Day Adventist House of God church. Little Marvin was given a strict upbringing, singing in the choir from the age of three, and there was absolutely no room in his life for TV, movies or dancing. His father was a strict disciplinarian who beat his sons at the slightest sign of disobedience. He preferred not to work – Marvin's mother was sent out of the house at 5 a.m. every morning to clean houses – and his idea of real good fun was to wear his wife's clothing, especially her frilly underwear.

Marvin left school and quit the family home as soon as he was legally able. After joining the Air Force and getting himself discharged in double-quick time for "craziness", in 1957 he started a doowop group called The Marquees, supposedly named after the Marquis de Sade. This brought him to the attention of producer Harvey Fuqua, who took Gay to Berry Gordy and his Tamal and Motown labels. After working as a session drummer and backing singer, at the age of twenty-one, Gay added an "e" to his name, married the boss's 39-year-old sister Anna, and became one of Tamla-Motown's most successful singers. Alternating between his own singles and duets with the likes of Mary Wells, Kim Weston and Tammi Terrell, Marvin Gaye notched up over sixty American pop hits between 1962 and 1969, the most notable being the solo "I Heard It Through The Grapevine" in 1967.

But all was not well. Marvin and Anna fought like cat and dog, with both of them enjoying numerous affairs throughout their stormy marriage, which was somehow destined to last until 1977. In the mid-60s, Gaye discovered stage fright and as this progressively worsened, concerts and singing engagements were often cancelled, sometimes at a moment's notice. Largely because his father was an alcoholic, Gaye managed to stay away from the demon drink, but his cocaine and marijuana intake was astonishing. In 1967 his singing partner and lover Tammi Terrell collapsed into his arms at a concert in Virginia. During the next three years she had six operations on her brain and Gaye's world began to collapse. He spent days by her hospital bedside and when she finally died of a brain tumour in March 1970, aged twenty-four, he all but gave up his career and his life. At her funeral he was visibly disoriented, talking aloud to her and sobbing uncontrollably. Although his religious upbringing led him to believe that suicide was a mortal sin, Gaye publicly threatened to kill himself for the first of several occasions on the day after Tammi's funeral.

Despite his success, Marvin was determined to prove himself outside the music industry. In 1969 he attempted to become a professional footballer, cutting down on his drug and cigarette intake and training rigorously with a couple of friends from the Lions football team. As with other occasions when Gaye attempted to break free, the Motown machine managed to smother this ambition and led him to describe himself as their "slave". He had problems with the tax authorities and partly because of the US Government's involvement in Vietnam, he declared it his civic duty not to let Uncle Sam spend any of *his* money on guns and bombs. Partly inspired by the terrible Vietnam War experiences of his brother, Frankie, the *What's Going On* album of 1971 was self-produced, and declared a masterpiece. But it almost never saw the light of day. Motown considered it too long and "boring", and it was only when Gaye threatened never to record again, did Gordy relent and release it.

Seeing that label mate Diana Ross was getting acting roles, and following brother-in-law Berry Gordy out to Los Angeles, he registered with the William Morris Agency with the intention of getting movie parts. But these were limited to a few minor roles in small blaxploitation films and he soon grew tired of endless auditions. Recording his next album, *Let's Get It On*, the 33-year-old Gaye fell in love with sixteen-year-old Janis Jan Hunter. Within four years she'd had two babies by him and Gaye was turning her on to cocaine and insisting that she take lovers. As his own drug-taking increased, so his life became more bizarre. In October 1977 he and Jan married, but even before his divorce from Anna was fully settled, his new wife was filing for *her* divorce. A year later he signed a new seven-year deal with Motown and a month later filed for bankruptcy, declaring debts of over $6 million. And things got worse.

In an effort to bolster a sagging career and boost his even saggier finances, Gaye went on tour, but audiences were sparse, and he collapsed on-stage in Tennessee due to "physical exhaustion". Compelled by a judge to give Anna the royalties on his next album, he recorded what she took as a personal attack on her, the double album, *Here, My Dear*. It was panned by the critics and sold badly. His recording studio was closed down, his home repossessed and Gaye was arrested and badly beaten by the police when he refused to leave his new mother-in-law's house in LA. Then Jan left him for Teddy Prendergast.

Gaye wrestled his four-year-old son, Frankie, away from Jan and the two of them lived for a time in a bread van in Hawaii. Gaye was taking drugs heavily – when he could afford them – but the rest of the time he was destitute. His mother even pawned the diamonds he had bought her to give to him. The American taxman was demanding he come up with $2 million in back taxes, so Gaye did the only thing he could: he upped and moved to Europe. Ostend businessman Freddy Cousaert, a long-time, fan, took Gaye under his wing and invited him to live with his family in Belgium.

In the meantime Motown had decided to "finish" Gaye's unfinished *In Our Lifetime* album for him and they released it. Gaye was appalled at what they'd done and vowed never to record for Motown again. At Cousaert's urging, CBS bought Gaye's contract from Motown for $1.5 million and in February 1982, he began recording a new album, *Midnight Love*, in Brussels. The first single from the album, "Sexual Healing" was released in the USA in October 1982, and declared the fastest-selling soul single in five years. It stuck to the number one spot like superglue for four months. Never one to accurately read the signs, Gaye decided that it was time to return to LA.

The taxman was still after his $2 million, so in between pursuing Jan and keeping Anna sweet, Gaye embarked on a massive national tour. To keep both sides of his split personality in check, Gaye's personal entourage included his drug-dealer and a preacher, and it soon became obvious that vast amounts of drugs were being consumed and that Marvin Gaye wasn't up to touring. On the first night of a sold-out eight night run at New York's Radio City Music Hall, he turned up nearly two hours late, shouting about how he hated going on stage. According to Pamela Des Barres in her book, *Rock Bottom*, not only was Gaye snorting coke, he was eating it as well. He missed several shows, stripped down to his underwear on stage on three occasions, and found himself back in hospital. His paranoia became intense. Convinced that Jan had hired an assassin, he took to wearing a bullet-proof vest and went about accompanied by roadies armed with sub-machine guns.

Marvin Gaye returned to LA, somehow managed to overcome his hatred of his father and moved back in with his parents. He rarely strayed out of bed, insisting that his mother sleep by his side every night. He rarely ate because he was convinced he was about to be poisoned, and ordered mysterious supplies of drugs and guns to be brought to the house after dark. He snorted coke, watched pornography and attacked the women who were summoned to his bedside.

On the eve of his 45th birthday, 1 April 1984, Marvin Gaye's father was looking for an insurance policy. He called upstairs to his wife, asking he if she knew where it was. His son informed Gaye that if he wanted to speak to his mother, he'd better come upstairs and do it in person. Father stormed up the stairs and began to tell his wife that in future, when he called, "she'd better get off her fat ass and come downstairs". Her son sprang to her defence, attacking his father and sending him sprawling out into

the hallway. In a rage, Gaye ran downstairs. A few moments later
he returned, carrying a .38 revolver. He aimed at his son and
squeezed the trigger.

The force of the bullet threw Marvin Gaye back against the
wall. His father stepped nearer and pumped another slug into his
twitching body.

"On God!" screamed Alberta, Marvin's mother, before sinking to her knees and begging for mercy. But she was safe. Her
husband wasn't abut to shoot her.

Marvin Gaye Sr claimed later that he didn't know that the gun
was loaded with "real bullets". He also said he wasn't aware that
his son was dead until the detectives told him. "I thought he was
kidding me," he told the *Los Angeles Herald*. "I said, 'Oh God of
mercy, oh, oh, oh!, It shocked me. I went to pieces."

In September 1984, Marvin Pentz Gay was found guilty of
voluntary manslaughter and was sentenced to five years proba-
tion. His wife filed for divorce the same year.

Robert Johnson

The life and death of seminal bluesman Robert Johnson has
become the stuff of legend. Says Giles Oakley in his book, *The
Devil's Music*: "There are many conflicting views of the kind of
person he was – drunk, sober, moody, considerate, a womaniser or
a lover – but whatever impression his brief life left on those who
knew him, his music remained to inspire others." Johnson lived
for 27 years and recorded just thirty-odd songs, but even so, today
he is recognised as one of the greatest bluesmen who ever lived.

The bastard son of Julie Ann Majors and farm worker Noah
Johnson, Robert Johnson was probably born on 8 May 1911, in
Hazlehurst, Mississippi. By the age of sixteen, he was working
in cotton fields, but hankered after the life of a travelling
musician. He played under several aliases, including Robert
Sax and Robert Spenser, and was said to have a habit of leaving
places suddenly, occasionally during the break in sets in a club.
He also frequently altered his appearance, telling other musicians it was because he was afraid of the police framing him for

a "murder or something". But the rumour was that he was hiding from someone.

Johnson is thought to have had two wives, his first dying during childbirth in 1930. His first instrument was the harmonica, but he was persuaded to turn to guitar. The persistent rumour is that Robert Johnson waited for the devil at the crossroads, armed with a black cat bone, and sold his soul, in return for the ability to play well. Son House agrees that Johnson was not a particularly good guitar player in his youth, but that he went away and came back much improved. Julio Finn, one-time harmonica-player with Muddy Waters, firmly believes that Johnson made a pact with Satan. He points to Johnson's songs such as "Hellhound of my Trail" and "Me and the Devil Blues", as evidence, and adds that the African religions were still potent forces in Southern Black communities of the 1930s and 1940s. The truth is more mundane. The name of Johnson's probable tutor was Ike Zinnerman, a sinister lone bluesman who claimed that he learned to play the guitar in old country churchyards at night. Guitarists jealous of his talents called Zinnerman the devil, and Johnson's habit of playing with his back to the audience fuelled the rumours. The fact that Johnson developed a cataract on his eye (the "evil" eye) was probably the clincher.

No one knew Johnson was dead until weeks or months after it happened. Blues recordist John Hammond was looking for him for three months before he eventually found out. The date agreed on for Robert Johnson's death is 16 August 1938; the place was Greenwood, Mississippi. Fellow bluesman Son House heard three versions of Johnson's death: that he'd been stabbed by a jealous husband, stabbed by a woman, and poisoned. Johnny Shines, aka "Little Wolf" was told it was something to do with the black arts, and that he fell to his knees and howled like a dog, taking three days to die in agony.

John Lennon

John Lennon, most highly regarded of The Beatles, was shot to death by obsessed stalker, John Chapman on 8 December 1980.

After the release of the *Shaved Fish* compilation album in 1975, he dropped out of the music scene to enjoy life with his wife, Yoko Ono, and their newly-born son, Sean. In 1979 Lennon took out a newspaper advertisement to explain why he'd turned his back on the music business, but barely a year later he and Yoko had signed a new deal with Geffen Records and released an album, *Double Fantasy*. It shot straight to number one of both sides of the Atlantic. The album was an alternating outpouring of love for each other and for their son from the husband and wife team.

At 5.12 on 8 December 1980, Lennon and Ono left their apartment at the Dakota building on Central Park West in New York City, to go to the recording studio to oversee the mastering of possible new singles from the *Double Fantasy* album. A crowd of well-wishers stopped them outside the building and asked for autographs. One of them was Mark Chapman, who wanted Lennon to autograph his copy of *Double Fantasy*.

At approximately 10.50 p.m., John and Yoko arrived back at their apartment, asking the limousine driver to drop them off on the corner of 72nd street. As they walked by the archway leading to the courtyard of the Dakota, a voice shouted, "Mr Lennon!". John turned and recoginsed Mark Chapman, who instantly dropped into a "combat crouch" and fired four shots at the former Beatle. Two shots hit Lennon in his left shoulder and two in the left-hand side of his back. All caused massive internal damage and bleeding.

Mortally wounded, Lennon staggered up the six steps to the concierge's room by the entrance, groaned, "I'm shot", and collapsed on to the floor. Moments later the first police arrived on the scene to find Chapman calmly standing in the same spot from which he'd fired the shots. He'd dropped the pistol after firing it and was waiting to be arrested. The second police unit to arrive took Lennon to Roosevelt Hospital, stretched across the back seat of their patrol car. Officer Moran said that on the way there Lennon was "moaning and groaning" and he asked him, "Are you John Lennon," to which the mortally-injured singer replied, "Yeah". Dr Stephen Lyman of Roosevelt Hospital said that Lennon was dead on arrival. Life was officially pronounced extinct at 11.15 p.m. At the inquest, the Chief Medical Examiner, Dr Gross, said that Lennon died of shock and from loss of blood. "No one could have lived more than a few minutes with such injuries", he added.

Conspiracy theorists have suggested that Mark Chapman had been brainwashed by the CIA to kill Lennon, as Laurence Harvey was in the film of *The Manchurian Candidate*, because he was a threat to incoming president Ronald Reagan. John's son, Sean, has suggested that "it was in the best interests of the United States to have my dad killed." A van driver in California even decorated his vehicle in posters and copies of newspaper articles, suggesting that "Stephen King shot John Lennon." If Mr King or his lawyers are reading this, we would like to point out that we in no way endorse this opinion.

Whoever it was killed John Lennon, whether it was a lone schizophrenic acting under a delusion, or a carefully organised plot orchestrated from the highest levels in government, they extinguished one of the brightest talents the world has ever seen.

The Notorious BIG

Twenty-four-year-old New York rapper, Christopher Wallace, aka "Biggy Smalls", aka "The Notorious BIG, was 75 inches tall, weighed 27 stone, and was as hard as they come. The "Biggy Smalls" name came from a character in the 1975 Bill Cosby film, *Let's Do It Again*, directed by Sydney Poitier. The second Biggy first came to prominence for his work on Mary J. Blige's *What's the 411* album. In 1994 he released a highly successful debut album of his own, the prophetically-titled, *Ready to Die*, and a year later the single "One More Chance" debuted in the *Billboard* pop chart at number five, sharing with Michael Jackson the distinction of the highest debuting single of all time. The Notorious BIG soon became the biggest name in East Coast hip-hop and a target in the vehement feud between East Coast and West Coast rappers. Wallace had already been in trouble with the authorities over alleged gun and drugs violations, but somehow he'd managed to stay "clean". When Tupac Shakur was shot, he was a prime suspect, partly because Tupac had been mouthing off about sleeping with BIG's wife, Faith Evans, and no matter how hard he and Bad Boy label boss Sean "Puffy" Combs protested his innocence, there were those in Los Angeles who'd already made their minds up.

Two days short of the six month anniversary of Tupac Shakur's shooting, BIG found himself in LA for a *Soul Train* Awards event. Early in the morning of 9 March 1997, he was returning to his hotel when a dark-coloured Chevrolet Impala drew up alongside his motorcade. BIG was felled by a hail of bullets in a typical LA-style drive-by shooting. BIG's second album, *Life After Death*, was released three weeks later, and hit the charts at number one. The best of the tracks on the double album was called "You're Nobody ('Til Somebody Kills You)".

Felix Pappalardi

Felix Pappalardi graduated from Michigan Conservatory of Music and began his musical career by playing bass for Greenwich Village folkie Tim Hardin, before making his name as a producer, session-player and arranger. He produced the Youngbloods debut album, as well as *Disraeli Gears*, *Wheels of Fire* and *Goodbye* for Cream. Pappalardi and his wife, Gail Collins, co-wrote "Strange Brew" with Eric Clapton. In 1969 he and guitarist Leslie West formed incredibly loud power-rockers, Mountain, who stunned the audience at Woodstock with their power, clever licks and sheer volume.

After the demise of Mountain, Pappalardi returned to production. Despite impaired hearing (thank you, Mountain) he went to Japan in 1976 and recorded with Japanese band, Creation, before throwing himself wholeheartedly into the New Wave and producing the likes of Cleveland's Dead Boys. On 17 April 1983 he got into an argument with his wife, Gail, who shot him dead. Felix Pappalardi was 43 years old.

Prince Far I

Prince Far I, the Voice of Thunder, was one of Jamaica's most distinctive and endearing musicians. Real name Michael Williams, the Prince was born in 1945 in Spanish Town, Jamaica, and raised in the Waterhouse area of Kingston. After a stint as bouncer at Studio One, he became lead DJ with the Sir Mike the Musical Dragon Sound System, adopting the name King Cry Cry because of his idiosyncrasy of bursting into tears whenever he was *really* angry. Cry Cry recorded with various producers, including Coxsone Dodd, Enos McLeod and Bunny Lee, working out a unique style that earned him the "Voice of Thunder" nickname. Although Far I is invariably described as burly and "a gentle giant", the evidence is that he was only five feet nine inches tall and slight of build. On 15 September 1983, the Prince and his wife were at home in St Catherine, relaxing in front of the television, when attackers smashed their way in through a french window and opened fire on the couple. Far I was killed instantly, his wife was shot twice but pulled through. Her first words on being told of the death of her husband were: "So they finally got him."

Tupac Shakur

Depending on which conspiracy theory you favour, twenty-five-year-old Lesane Crooks (better known as "Tupac Shakur" and "2Pac") was the victim of a feud between LA gangs, faked his own death, or else was killed because he slept with a rival rapper's wife. Born in New York to Black Panther parents, he somehow managed to throw off his East Coast origin and become the figurehead of the West Coast rap scene, signing to Suge Knight's Death Row Records after being bailed out of jail by the label boss after being charged with sexual assault.

Having watched Tyson KO Seldon from a ringside seat at the MGM Grand Hotel in Las Vegas, on 7 September 1996, the multi-million-selling rapper sidled up to an Afro-American fight fan called Orlando Anderson and posed the question, "You from

the South?" Roughly translated, this means: "Are you a meme-
ber of the South Side Crips gang? If so, I'm going to kick your
ass." Getting the wrong answer or maybe no answer at all,
Shakur threw a punch at Anderson's head, knocking him to
the ground, before kicking at his head like a football, with Knight
and the rest of their sizable entourage joining in. It was later
claimed that Shakur had been tipped off by a Death Row records
employee who was with them that Anderson was one of a group of
men who had confronted him and some friends in a sports shop in
Los Angeles a few weeks earlier. In the incident a Death Row
medallion had been snatched as a "trophy". Just the sort of thing
that gets gang-bangers *real* mad.

An hour-and-a-half later, Shakur and Knight were riding
along "the strip", with their bodyguard and friends cruising
behind, when a large white Cadillac pulled up alongside. The
passenger in the Caddy leaned through the window and opened
fire with a Glock .40 calibre handgun. Shakur was shot five time
and Knight, who was driving, suffered a superficial wound to the
head. The record company boss saw how badly injured Tupac
was and shouted, "Don't worry man, we'll get you to hospital!"
The rapper looked at him and said, "I need a hospital? You're the
one shot in the head." He then slipped into a coma from which he
never recovered. Tupac Shakur died in the University of Nevada
Medical Centre six days later. An unofficial version of the story
has Shakur joking with nurses and paramedics on his arrival at
the hospital. Because witnesses to the incident and those involved
with the Death Row posse refused to cooperate with the authorities or speak to the media, facts are hazy.

The conspiracy theories began to surface almost immediately
the first shot was fired. The generally accepted view – said to be
unofficially supported by most police and law enforcement
agencies – is that Orlando Anderson, the victim of the MGM
Grand Hotel beating, was the shooter. His family and friends
deny this, saying that the twenty-three-year-old had not been
involved in any gang activity since a couple of minor incidents in
his teens. Anderson was a high achiever and one of the few kids
from his neighbourhood to graduate high school. And no one

could satisfactorily explain how an unemployed father of four would have access to a large luxury white limousine. Having gained the reputation, probably unwittingly, as Tupac Shakur's assassin, Anderson died eighteen months later, one of three victims of a shoot-out at an LA carwash.

Then there are those who claim that Tupac Shakur faked his own death in order to escape the gang violence. It's a generally accepted truth in certain parts of LA that he now lives in Cuba under an assumed name. In interviews given immediately before the shooting, Tupac seems to indicate a desire to leave the hassle of fame and gang violence behind. Further "evidence" includes the story that Tupac's funeral was suddenly and mysteriously cancelled and the body cremated the day after his "death". Most compelling of all is that Shakur always wore a bulletproof vest, so why wasn't he wearing one to a public event like the Tyson fight? It has been suggested that Suge Knight persuaded Shakur to take off his protective vest, saying it was "too damn hot for that shit." To add further fuel to the fire, Frank Alexander, a Death Row bodyguard was interviewed on Fox 11 News in LA and told how Knight sent twenty bodyguards to their Club 662 destination several hours before they were needed. He also claimed that Knight told the few bodyguards that remained with the party not to pack guns.

Another theory points the finger at New York rapper, the Notorious BIG (real name Christopher Wallace, aka "Biggy Smalls" – *see above*), whose motive was that Tupac was very vocal about sleeping with "BIG's" wife, Faith Evans.

Whoever did away with 2pac – if anyone did – it saw the end of a lifetime sodden with macho violence and pointless feuding. Other highlights of Tupac's criminal career include the accidental shooting of a six-year-old in 1992; an arrest in March '93 for carrying a concealed weapon, and another for shooting two off-duty cops in October of the same year. Shakur was shot four times resisting a mugging in New York, and in November 1994 he was again ambushed outside a studio, this time emerging unscathed. A lucky break, say supporters; a put-up job, say his enemies. Either way, Tupac Shakur's luck finally ran out in September 1996. Probably.

Nancy Spungen

Sid Vicious' fellow Sex Pistol Johnny Rotten described Nancy Spungen as "like the Titanic looking for an iceberg". Although barely twenty, the peroxided groupie had certainly led an eventful life before ending up murdered at New York's Chelsea Hotel on 12 October 1978. She grew up in suburban Philadelphia, and after dropping out of the University of Colorado, moved to New York where she combined the roles of go-go dancer and groupie. Those who are reputed to have "had the pleasure" include Keith Richards, Henry Winkler, Richard Hell and Jerry Nolan of the New York Dolls, who is said to have introduced young Nancy to heroin.

We shall probably never know the exact truth of Nancy Spungen's death, but as he lay dying, Sid Vicious is reputed to have told his "minder", Joe Stevens, his version of events. Both Sid and Nancy were heroin addicts and they'd tried to score some "horse", but their dealer could only give them tranquillisers. They took the downers anyway, but they only served to aggravate Vicious's debilitating "cold turkey" and he set off to randomly bang on doors at the hotel until he got some "proper drugs". A concierge was called and told Sid to stop disturbing the other residents. A fight started and the man broke Sid's nose with a single punch. Back in the room the two "lovers" got into an argument and Nancy slapped Sid's already sore nose. He stabbed her in the side with a hunting knife she'd bought for him in Times Square the previous day. Thinking it wasn't serious, they'd kissed and made up and Sid had gone off to score some methadone from the clinic.

When he returned a few hours' later, Sid couldn't see Nancy in the room and, thinking she'd gone out, he stretched out on the bed and went to sleep. When he woke up he was desperate for a piss, and when he'd staggered into the bathroom, he found her dead body, dressed in black lacy underwear, lying beside the washbasin. Not being an experienced killer, he called the police and confessed to her murder. "I did it because I'm a dog, a dirty dog," said Vicious, as the police led him away.

Peter Tosh

On the afternoon of Saturday 12 September 1987, original Wailer Winston Hubert McIntosh – better known as Peter Tosh – and his wife were entertaining friends at their Kingston home, when three men arrived at their gate, demanding admission. The three were notorious former cocaine dealers who had moved into extortion. Their favoured method was to arrive unannounced at the homes of prominent musicians and other Jamaican celebrities and demand money at gun-point. They'd sold Tosh cocaine in the past and when they'd first arrived at his house the previous day, he thought he'd managed to convince them that he didn't have any spare cash.

Thinking he could reason with them over a spliff and a drink, Tosh invited the men in. Within a few minutes an argument developed and both sides appeared very agitated. Eventually Tosh asked the men to leave. They refused: they weren't about to leave empty-handed twice in two days. By this time all four men were on their feet and Tosh, a martial arts expert, is then thought to have aimed a kung fu kick at the man nearest to him. Tosh was killed instantly by a shotgun fired at pointblank range.

Tosh's 42-year life had been plagued with difficulty and conflict. Although he, together with Bob Marley and Neville O'Riley Livingstone (better known as "Bunny Wailer"), had formed the Wailing Wailers in 1963, eleven years later Island record label boss Chris Blackwell had declared his intention of making Bob Marley the lead singer. Bunny and Tosh both stormed out of separate meetings with Blackwell, but not before Tosh had chased the millionaire around the room with a machete. Peter Tosh never blamed Marley for the split, but he wasn't best pleased when Marley refused to lend him $1,000 to finish his solo *Legalise It* album a couple of years later.

Verbal attacks on the Jamaican government and their political cronies constantly landed Tosh in trouble, and between the late 70s and early 80s he was repeatedly arrested on minor driving and drug charges and subjected to savage beatings. These variously led to a broken arm, stitches to a wound in the fact, a fractured skull and severe concussion.

After his death, one man was arrested and charged with Peter Tosh's murder. After a brief trial he was found guilty and sentenced to be hanged. Tosh left a minimum of ten children, and no will.

King Tubby

Osbourne Ruddock, the distinctly non-tubby "King Tubby", was born in Jamaica 1941. By 1968 he was running his own sound system, the Home Town Hi-Fi, and by means of Tubby's inventiveness and persistence it became famous all over Jamaica. Tubby always mixed live and he concocted many of his effects units himself, included an echo delay unit constructed from a loop tape wound over the heads of an old two-track tape machine. A much imitated King Tubby trademark was to incorporate live sound effect like sirens and gunshots into his mixes. Determined to become a producer in the tradition of Coxsone Dodd and Lee "Scratch" Perry, he spent the early 80s building his own studio in the Waterhouse district of Jamaica. Its first hit, "Temper" by Anthony Red Rose, came soon after it opened in 1985. But fame as a renowned record producer was not on the cards for King Tubby. Early in the morning of 6 February 1989, he'd been in the studio and was returning to his home at 85 Sherlock Crescent, when Tubby was approached by a lone gunman. Seconds later, he lay dead in a pool of his own blood. No motive for his killing was ever discovered and no one has ever been charged with Osbourne Ruddock's death.

Sonny Boy Williamson

Born in Jackson, Tennessee, in 1914, the great harmonica-playing bluesman learned his craft in the company of Sleepy John Estes. John Lee Williamson was known as "Sonny Boy Williamson I" to differentiate him from the younger "Rice" Miller, who was known by the name "Sonny Boy Williamson II" John Lee was a major force in Chicago blues who would certainly have contributed more had not his life been cut tragically short by a

mugger. Williamson was attacked and beaten leaving the Planta-
tion Club in Chicago after a gig. He died of a fractured skull and
other injuries in 1 June 1948.

2. 'Don't Leave Me This Way'
DEATH BY THEIR OWN HAND

Kurt Cobain

One of the finest songwriters of his generation, Cobain was also one
of the most fucked-up junkies ever to die by his own hand. As ever,
the facts are hazy and mostly disputed. On 7 April 1994, the twenty-
seven-year-old Nirvana singer and guitarist was found dead in the
conservatory above the garage of his Seattle home. The accepted
version of events is that he'd shot up some heroin, then opened his
driving license to show his picture as ID, penned a quick suicide
note and blasted a single barrel of the shotgun he'd recently bought
in Stan Baker's Gun Shop into his left temple. It took two days to
discover the body, which was so badly disfigured, it had to be
identified by fingerprints. That's the most widely touted version of
events. Most of these "facts" have since been disputed, in particular
the one about Cobain's head being "blown off". Recently, a police
witness revealed off the record that the shotgun blast damaged his
mouth and brain, but left the face "largely intact". At the same time,
an official police record talks about "substantial damage to the face
and head". Mmmm, confusing.

Not surprisingly, the conspiracy theorists are out in force.
There are those who believe Cobain faked his own death, either as
a way of getting away from the woman he'd married – Hole
singer, Courtney Love – or else, with her knowledge, he'd rigged
it so he could escape his hellish music biz life of drugs and
debauchery for a simple existence in the woods of his childhood.
A large proportion of the Cobain conspiracy clan appear to be
young women with a down on Courtney Love, for whatever
reason. The Internet is littered with sites declaring their hatred
for the poor widow and sites putting forward a host of various
suspects, from the CIA and FBI, to record company executives

and members of Cobain's own family. It's got to be said that the "evidence" put forward by the murder theorists is pretty circumstantial, and revolves around the many inconsistencies in the evidence. A potential "hit-man" had been dredged up who claimed to have been turned down the "job", despite being offered thousands of dollars by "certain parties" to do away with her husband.

Mmmm. And just what was Junior Soprano doing on 5 April 1994?

Ian Curtis

Twenty-three years old Ian Curtis, former lead singer of the inaptly-named Joy Division, hanged himself on 18 May 1989 in the kitchen of his home in Macclesfield, near Manchester, England. An epileptic who had frequently had fits on stage, he was prone to bouts of depression and he'd attempted suicide before. Curtis finally managed to hang himself during a lull between European and American tours. Beside a note that included the words: "At this very moment, I wish I were dead. I just can't cope anymore" was a sleeve of Iggy Pop's *The Idiot*. As fellow bandmember Peter Hook pointed out. "The great tragedy of Ian's death was that all he really wanted to be was successful; and he missed it, by a week". Joy Division's classic 'Love Will Tear Us Apart' single became a massive UK and European hit five days after his death. The band regrouped as New Order.

Tom Evans & Peter Ham (Badfinger)

Although plagued by rumours that they were in fact The Beatles under an assumed name, Badfinger were just about the only continuously successful act on the Fab Four's Apple record label. Badfinger were originally known as The Iveys, an artistically brilliant South Wales foursome, and changed their name in 1969 because it sounded "too Merseybeat". Managed by Bill Collins, the sixty year-old father of actor Lewis (of *The Professionals* fame), a man who would suddenly launch himself into spontaneous push-ups and run up eight flights of stairs to show he wasn't "past it", two of the three main components in Badfinger were guitarist Peter Ham and guitarist-turned-bass-player Tom Evans. After becoming the darlings of Paul McCartney and George Harrison, and despite (some may say because of) Collins' influence, the band found themselves entangled with a shady American manager with alleged Mafia connections. Stan Polley set about tying up their money so tight, even they couldn't get at it.

Unable to pay his mortgage, married and with another child on the way, Ham hanged himself in his garage-cum-studio in Weybridge on 23 April 1975. A note found in a music book he'd been working on contained the PS: "Stan Polley is a soulless [sic] bastard. I will take him with me."

For Tom Evans, the next eight years revolved around a series of disastrous reunion tours where no one got paid, bound up in threats, court cases and legal wrangling. Finally, on 18 November 1983, Tom Evans hanged himself from a tree in his garden. He left no note, but regulars at his local pub planted a tree in his memory. Sick bastards.

Donny Hathaway

Originally a gospel singer, then producer with Curtis Mayfield's Curtom label, performer and writer Hathaway's first hit was a duet with June Conquest, "I Thank You Baby". His greatest hits came in the same vein 1972 and in 1978 with "Where Is The Love?" and "The Closer I Get To You", both top five hits, duetting with Roberta Flack. No one knows why, but on 13 January 1979, Hathaway took the lift to the 15th floor of the Essex House Hotel in New York and flung himself to the ground. He was thirty-two-years-old.

Frankie Lymon

In 1955 Frankie Lymon and the Teenagers had a hit with "Why Do Fools Fall In Love?" Featuring thirteen-year-old New York soprano Frankie, it was to be the first of a half dozen hit singles recorded before Lymon was persuaded in 1959 to seek his fortune as a solo heart throb. The solo career was not a success. Lymon had a drug problem, and his voice had deepened so much it was becoming impossible for him to successfully sing any of his old hits. After a "cure" at Manhattan General Hospital, and a brief stint in the Army that led to a dishonourable discharge, Lymon was arrested for theft and possession of heroin. On 28 February 1968, his dead body was discovered on the floor of his grandmother's bathroom in Harlem. It was a heroin overdose, with the suspicion of suicide. After three wives had disputed the 26-year-old's estate, royalties from the lucrative "Why Do Fools Fall In Love?" were eventually granted to two of the surviving Teenagers, Herman Santiago and Jimmy Merchant.

Phil Ochs

Born in El Paso, Texas in 1940, Phil Ochs was one of the best and most original singer-songwriters of the 1960s. After attending a military academy, he studied journalism at Ohio State University, before moving to New York City in 1961. He became – together with Joan Baez and Bob Dylan – a leading light of the "protest-folk" movement, but whereas the young Zimmerman discovered electricity and a drum kit early on, Ochs stuck close to his roots. "I want to be the first leftwing star", he said at one point, and although highly regarded by those in the know, he remained little more than a cult figure during his life. Ochs' ironic sense of humour is demonstrated by the title of his 1970 *Greatest Hits* ("fifty Phil Ochs fans can't be wrong") album, not a greatest hits collection at all, but a set of new songs and featuring side-players of the calibre of Ry Cooder, members of the Byrds, and James Burton.

In 1971 Ochs exiled himself from the USA and travelled around Europe and Africa. He spent time in London and worked for a while at *Time Out* magazine, before being mysteriously set upon in Africa. This attack left him badly scarred, with irreparably damaged vocal chords. A harsh self-critic before the incident, he became doubly so afterwards. Homesick for a country he disliked, Ochs returned to the USA, where he found the political situation intolerable. He appeared with Dylan at the 1974 benefit concert, 'An Evening With Salvador Allende', and released the scathing single 'Here's To The State Of Richard Nixon'. But Ochs was beginning to look for solutions in the bottom of a glass, and eventually drifted into schizophrenia. He refused to answer to his own name and rechristened himself "John Butler Train". On 9 April 1976, Ochs/Train's dead body was discovered, hanging at his siter's apartment at Far Rockaway, New York.

Del Shannon

At the age of fifty-five, Charles Westover (aka "Del Shannon") decided on 8 February 1990, that a life of rock 'n' roll revival tours was not for him. A member of Alcoholics Anonymous for over a decade and heavily dependent on anti-depressant drugs, the composer and singer of 'Runaway' and 'Hats Off To Larry' pointed a .22 rifle to his head, and pulled the trigger. His wife later sued the drug manufacturers for compensation and settled out of court for an undisclosed sum. Shannon had just completed a new album with Jeff Lynne and wasn't to know that he was about to be asked to become Roy Orbison's replacement in the Travelling Wilburys.

Screamin' Lord Sutch

After his policeman father was killed in the Blitz, David Edward Sutch was raised by his mother in Kilburn, a working class area of war-torn west London. "Lord" was a self-adopted title that was later legitimised by deed-poll. Charged by a desire to perform, Sutch formed his first band – the Raving Savages – in 1959, after passing an audition at Soho's influential Two-I's coffee bar, the launching pad for the likes of Cliff Richard, Tommy Steele, Adam Faith and Paul Raven, aka "Paul Gadd", aka "Gary Glitter". Despite being unable to sing in tune or play any instrument, he became one of Britain's best-loved rock 'n' roll characters, thanks largely to a "Jack The Ripper"-inspired rocky horror stage show that remained virtually unchanged to his death, and a brilliant sense of the absurd.

The Raving Savages played with The Beatles at the Star Club in Hamburg and Mick Jagger and Brian Jones were such fans that they poached band members Carlo Little, Nicky Hopkins and Rick Brown for the first Rolling Stones line-up. Sutch once said: 'When Carlo decided he'd had enough of Jagger, he leant over and handed him a fag packet on which was written the name "Charlie Watts" and a phone number. The rest is history." The Who's drummer Keith Moon often stood in at early Savages gigs and other illustrious past members include Ritchie Blackmore, who left to join Deep Purple, Noel Redding who played bass with Jimi Hendrix and Matthew Fisher, keyboards wizard with Procol Harum. Paul Nicholas, who was to go on to become a musical comedy star, heart-throb, and comedy actor, was another Savages pianist.

Sutch's Atlantic album, *Lord Sutch And Heavy Friends* launched him in America and included contributions from the likes of Jeff Beck and Jimmy Page. The ill-fated Radio Sutch was among the leading British pop radio pirates of the 1960s, and his "political" Monster Raving Loony Party made Sutch a household name in Britain. It all began when Sutch stood for the National Teenager Party in John Profumo's old seat, following the Christine Keeler and Stephen Ward scandal. His policies included votes for eighteen-year-olds, knighthoods for pop stars and a network of commercial radio stations. Law in 2001, but wild stuff in 1963. Later the policies got wilder: campaigning under the slogan "Vote for Insanity, you know it makes sense", he advocated a Jersey branch line to the Channel Tunnel, so that everybody could take advantage of the off-shore tax haven, skiing trips to the EC butter mountain, and the breeding of fish in the European wine lake, so they'd come out pickled. For almost thirty years he stood at every British general election and practically every by-election, entering the *Guinness Book of Records* as the "longest serving political leader."

Sutch's personal life was beset by problems. Barclays Bank threatened to bankrupt him over a £200,000 debt, and only relented when he agreed to sign over ownership of two houses. And the death of his 80-year-old mother on the eve of the 1997 General Election was a severe blow from which he never fully recovered. The raising of the deposit for election candidates from £500 to £5,000 was possibly the last straw, and Screamin' Lord David Sutch put an end to the screamin' when he hanged himself in the hall of his late mother's house in Harrow, west London, on 16 June 1999.

Ross Williams

The ex-lead singer with Christian Death hanged himself in his West Hollywood apartment on 1 April 1998. Bruce Duff of Triple X Records said that Williams' solo career was going well. "I saw him a week ago, I was hanging out with him in a club and he was partying and everything was fine. Most people I know were taken off guard. He didn't leave a note. I don't think there was any real warning. You have to speculate as to why he did it."

Wendy O Williams

The former Plasmatics singer and sex show star, best known for her tight PVC skirts and taped nipples, found it difficult to relate to the relatively quiet life she was living after the rock 'n' roll spotlight moved on. On 2 April 1998, she strolled into the woods near her home in Connecticut and emptied both barrels of a shotgun into her head. Her suicide note included the phrase: "For me, much of the world makes no sense, but my feelings about what I am doing ring loud and clear to an inner ear and a place where there is no self, only calm." A previous attempt as suicide involved trying to knock a knife deep into her chest with a hammer. Unfortunately the blade got stuck in her sternum and she had to go to hospital to have it removed.

3. "Zoom"
PLANES, TRAINS and AUTOMOBILES

Duane Allman

Just twenty-four years of age, Duane Allman of the Allman Brothers Band, was killed on 29 October 1971 in a motorcycle accident near Macon, Georgia. He was hit by a truck travelling in the opposite direction, and, still attached to his bike, he was dragged along for twenty metres. Duane died on the operating table after three hours of surgery. Fifty weeks later, Allman Brothers bass-player Berry Oakley died in an almost identical accident at almost the same location.

Jesse Belvin

Jesse Lorenzo Belvin, writer of the classic 'Earth Angel', was brought up in south Los Angeles and got his first break as vocalist in 1949 with Big Jay McNeely's Three Dots And A Dash. Covers of Sam Cooke songs led some to label him a Cooke copyist, but his singing on such soul and R&B classics as 'Goodnight My Love' (used to close *American Bandstand* for many years) and 'Just To Say Hello', plus his gentle emulation of Elvis Presley, Nat King Cole and Little Richard, point to a versatile performer with a voice that's been compared both to silk and to old granite. In a supreme example of unintentional irony, RCA promoted him as "the black Elvis".

A passionate proponent of racial integration, on 6 February 1960, Belvin played the first concert in Little Rock, Arkansas where the audience wasn't segregated by race. The gig didn't pass without incident. White supremists managed to stop the show twice, urging the white teenagers in the audience to leave, and shouting racist comments at the performers. Belvin had received a number of death threats and after the show he was said to be relieved to be leaving Arkansas. Just outside Fair-hope, Arkansas, driver Charles Shackleford lost control of Belvin's black Cadillac, and it ploughed into a car travelling in the opposite direction. Belvin and Shackleford were killed instantly, Belvin's wife Jo-Ann lingered for two days before she too passed away.

Immediately, rumours circulated that the crash was no accident. The first state trooper on the scene said that the two back types had obviously been tampered with, although this avenue seems not to have been investigated and nothing was ever proved.

The official version, that Shackleford fell asleep at the wheel, has become the accepted truth.

Marc Bolan

The most popular British teen idol in the early 70s, Marc Bolan was the adopted name of London lorry driver's son, Mark Feld. After a brief modelling career and singing in a couple of cult outfits, he formed Tyrannosaurus Rex, originally a "progressive-mystical" duo with Steve Peregrine Took, in 1968. Under the diminutive Bolan's leadership, bongo-player Took left and Tyrannosaurus Rex became electric pop group T.Rex. From 1970's 'Ride A White Swan' to 'I Love To Boogie' in 1976, the hits came thick and fast.

"T.Rextasy" was the biggest thing in Britain since Beatlemania and Bolan began to believe his own hype. He and his wife, June, took over the business dealings and things started to fall apart. Following a tried and tested route, he began to take plenty of cocaine with his brandy and champagne. Bolan's youthful, sleek appearance gradually began to give way to bloated chubbiness, not helped by regular tequila breakfasts. While on a tour of America, he took up with backing singer Gloria Jones and his five-and-a-half year marriage collapsed.

By 1977, Marc Bolan's records were selling in smaller and smaller numbers, but he was given his own series on British children's TV. Although his own performances are near-parodies of what he was capable of in his hey-day, the show did offer an early showcase for punk and New Wave bands like The Damned, Eddie and the Hot Rods and The Jam. The last programme he recorded featured a hastily-rehearsed duet with David Bowie after which Bolan is seen to trip over a microphone cable.

One the evening of 16 September 1977, Marc and Gloria spent a drunken evening at the Speakeasy Club in London's West End, followed by more drinks at Morton's. At around 4 a.m. they headed for home, with Gloria at the wheel of her purple Mini 1275 GT. Between Putney Common and Barnes Common, on a road called Queen's Ride, the car left the tarmac and smashed into a roadside tree. Bolan was killed instantly.

Graham Bond

The common belief is that addled by drink and/or drugs, Graham Bond fell (or jumped) in front of a London Underground train at Finsbury Park Station, on 8 May 1974. Those close to him insist that he was pushed, because of a weird feud with a secretive black magic organisation. But even when pressed, no names are forthcoming. It's true that Bond was seriously obsessed by the "black arts"; two of his later outfits were called Initiation and Holy Magick. But the man who had been so influential in the careers of John McLaughlin, Jack Bruce and Ginger Baker, probably took his secret – if there *was* a secret to take – with him to the grave. Either way, when Graham Bond died, British rock and R&B lost one of its greatest and most innovative talents.

Patsy Cline

Virginia-born country-pop singer Patsy Cline, best known for the haunting ballad 'Crazy', was killed in a plane crash on 5 March 1963, that also claimed the lives of fellow performers Cowboy Copas, Hawkshaw Hawkins and Randy Hughes. She'd already survived a terrible car crash in 1961, after which she'd said: "I think someone's trying to tell me something." A pity she never listened.

Eddie Cochran

Twenty-one-year-old Oklahoma-born rock 'n' roller Eddie Cochran died at St Martin's Hospital in Bristol on Easter Sunday, 1960, after being thrown through the windscreen of a taxi on the way to Heathrow Airport. After completing a very successful British tour at Bristol Hippodrome, he and co-star Gene Vincent were looking forward to returning to USA the following morning. Speeding up the A4 near Bath, the driver suddenly lost

control of the car and the Ford Consul left the road and crashed
into a lamppost. Vincent, who was to suffer leg and back injuries
that plagued him for the rest of his life, survived; and Eddie's
girlfriend, Sharon Sheeley, had her back broken in three places,
her neck in three, and suffered a gash running the length of her
head.

Buddy Holly, The Big Bopper, Ritchie Valens

It was dubbed 'The Day The Music Died' and 3 February 1959,
was certainly a black day for rock 'n' roll. The Winter Dance
Party Tour was an exhausting schlep around North America for
its all-star line-up of Buddy Holly and the Crickets – guitarist
Tommy Allsup, soon-to-be-famous bass-player, Waylon Jen-
nings – The Big Bopper (J.P. Richardson), and seventeen-
year-old Ritchie Valens. Fed up with travelling endlessly on a
cold tour bus with a regularly-malfunctioning heater, Holly hired
a four-seater Beechcraft Bonanza plane from Dwyer Flying
Services to transport The Crickets and himself to their next
venue. The Bopper was down with a bad cold and just before the
plane took off, he and Ritchie Valens managed to swap places
with the Crickets.

The weather was bad that night, with storms in the mountains,
and the pilot was tired and hadn't wanted to fly. What was not
revealed at the time was that he had failed his "instruments only"
flying test and so wasn't really qualified to take off into "nil-
visibility" conditions. The plane came down in a cornfield in
Iowa. No one survived.

Lynyrd Skynyrd

On the last flight before it was due to be traded in, the private
plane belonging to the band Lynyrd Skynyrd crashed into Mississippi swampland on 20 October 1977. The pilot, co-pilot, a
roadie, manager Dean Kilpatrick, and band members Ronnie
Van Zant, Steve Gaines and his sister, Cassie Gaines, were all
killed. Their last album, ironically entitled *Street Survivors* was

recalled by the record company to be given a hasty new cover, removing the picture of the band consumed by flames, that had originally been chosen.

Rick Nelson

On New Year's Eve, 1985, teenage pop singer turned country-rocker, Rick Nelson and his band died when their DC-3 plane crashed on its way to a gig in Dallas. The aircraft had previously been owned by Jerry Lee Lewis, who had got rid of it after a premonition of death.

Otis Redding

The sweet soul singer's triumphant reception at the Monterey Pop Festival in 1967 opened up doors that would have led to mainstream pop stardom – if only Otis Redding had lived. He had been backed by Booker T and the MGs, with guitarist Steve Cropper and the Memphis Horns, and together they'd practically torn the place apart. "If this is what soul music is," wrote one San Francisco hack, "give me more, more, more." As a thank you to the Monterey bookers and audience, he and Cropper wrote the beautiful "(Sittin' On The) Dock Of the Bay" and recorded it three days before he died. On 10 December 1967, Otis's plane crashed into the icy waters of Wisconsin's Lake Monona on the way to a gig. Otis Redding perished, together with four members of his backing group, The Bar-Kays. He was just twenty-six-years old. "(Sittin' On The) Dock of The Bay" reached number one in both the pop and R&B charts four weeks later.

4. "(You're The) Devil In Disguise"
DEATH BY DRINK AND DRUGS

GG Allin

Ask GG Allin what type of music he played and the outrageous East Coaster was liable to tell you: "Mud, rot, cunt-suckin' sleaze trash." Christened Jesus Christ Allin at his religious-nut father's insistence, but later changed by mom to plain Kevin Michael, he started out by playing in local punk bands around New Hampshire. One night someone spiked his drink with LSD in Dunkin' Donuts and Kevin became GG, and GG was wild. *Very* wild; and not a little mad. Staying at a woman's house after a gig in Ann Arbour, he waited for her to wake up and then tortured her by cutting her breasts, stomach and face, dripping hot wax into her wounds, stubbing out cigarettes on her skin and choking her for three days. Allin claimed that the woman was "into it", that she knew it was a form of art. Even so, he pleaded no contest to felonious assault charges and spent eighteen months in prison.

After his release in 1991, GG formed the Murder Junkies with his equally mad brother, Merle. "Prison was the best thing that happened to GG," claims Merle. "It made him more angry, stronger, and it made him realise that he wanted to go out and fuck other people up." Part of GG's act involved pissing and shitting on stage, then he'd slash at his body with knives, before sucking up the mess and eating it. As a result, he was regularly ill with blood poisoning and often arrested. Between 1990 and his death in 1993, GG Allin was arrested fifty-six times. He kept his belongings in a brown paper sack, smashed his teeth out with a microphone and refused to pay taxes. GG's ultimate aim was to kill himself on stage, and he wanted to take as many members of the audience with him as possible. One possible plan involved sticking dynamite up his ass, another centred around a machine-gun. In the end he died of a drug over-dose, weakened by another bout of blood-poisoning. Ironically, it was his audience that did for him at his last ever gig, feeding him pills as he writhed around on the floor, already high on heroin and drunk from a jug of Jim Beam.

John Bonham

The Led Zeppelin drummer (nickname, "Bonzo") was a prank-ster whose hell-raising life on the road masked a pretty staid family life at home – at least to start with. That his childhood idol was Keith Moon, says a lot about what drove Bonzo, both in work and at play. Led Zeppelin's bad boy antics, led from the front by Bonham and road manager Richard Cole, were often pretty unimaginative, restricted to smashing up hotel rooms, food fights and excursions with groupies. Most events took place in America where the tours are longer and people wilder. Fondly-remembered incidents include a young groupie performing a sex exhibition with her Great Dane dog, the famous episode with the "mudshark" at Seattle's Edgewater Inn (Cole insists he was the ringleader and that it was a red snapper), and the time Bonzo filled a bath with fruit, vegetables and groupies and let loose four octopus.

Bonham was a drunk who drank too much, took too many drugs and had a propensity to turn nasty. One night while having sex with six strippers, he led as the band downed sixty screwdriver cocktails between the four of them; on another occasion 280 drinks were consumed by the band, Cole, and manager Peter Grant in a single evening in Frankfurt. During a rock festival in New York, Bonham pulled Jeff Beck's drummer off his stool and did a strip, later repeating the act with Chuck Berry. People had a habit of getting hurt around Led Zeppelin, and if he was in the wrong mood, Bonham was liable to punch a perfect stranger, and forget all about it the next morning. Bonham once attacked and attempted to rape a stewardess on the band's private plane, Starship. Grant and Cole bullied the assorted journalists who were present into silence and the story only came out years later.

By the time Zeppelin recorded their seventh album, *Presence*, Jimmy Page and Bonzo were heavily into heroin and their life resembled a round-the-clock rampage. It wasn't fun any more: it was the beginning of the end. Back in England after a period of tax exile, he crashed his car on the way back from the pub and broke two ribs. On their next European tour, Bonzo fell off his stool after the third song and it was diagnosed as "exhaustion". In September, 1980, Bonham and the band moved into Jimmy Page's new house at Windsor in order to rehearse for another American tour. On the 24th, Bonham popped out to the local pub and drank four quadruple vodkas, before returning to the house, where he drank some more, and passed out on the sofa. He was dragged to a bedroom to sleep it off. By the next morning Bonzo was dead. He'd choked on his own vomit after what was later diagnosed as a drink and heroin overdose. Led Zeppelin disbanded soon afterwards.

Tim Hardin

Most of singer-songwriter Hardin's fame came from other artists recording his songs. And what songs they were: 'If I Were A Carpenter', 'Reason To Believe', and 'Bird On A Wire', to name but three. Towards the end of his life, Hardin's equilibrium was destroyed by heroin. He spent a period in Britain, playing wine bars and folk clubs before returning to the States, lured by talk of a new record deal with Polygram. But it was not to be. On 29 December 1980, just six days after his birthday, Tim Hardin died in Los Angeles of a heroin/morphine overdose.

Jimi Hendrix

Hendrix passed away at the basement flat he and Monika Danneman rented at 22 Lansdowne Terrace, Notting Hill Gate, west London on the morning of 18 September 1970. He had taken nine sleeping pills on top of a pile of booze he'd consumed at Who manager Kit Lambert's party.

Brian Jones

Nineteen-sixty-nine was not a good year for Lewis Brian Hopkin-Jones, otherwise known as Brian Jones. The twenty-seven-year-old had previously been arrested twice for possession of drugs, and had only been saved from prison by top lawyers and by the unexpected intervention of *The Times* newspaper, who quoted William Blake's line: "Who Breaks A Butterfly Upon A Wheel?". Jones was drinking heavily, putting on weight, and the acid and dope he was taking was making him paranoid. He was sure the police were going to bust him for a third time and that the members of his band were conspiring against him. There was also trouble at home. He'd recently bought A.A. Milne's "house at Pooh Corner", Crotchford Farm, and had hired builders under the charge of a guy called Frank Thorogood to renovate the fifteenth-century farmhouse. But the builders were doing less work than partying and whenever Jones confronted them about it, they'd bully him and laugh in his face. At the end of June, Jones had a late night visit from Mick Jagger, Keith Richards and Charlie Watts, who told him that his days in the Stones, the band he was instrumental in founding, were over.

A week later, on 2 July Thorogood and his builders were told that they would have to leave the farm the next morning. That evening Brian Jones, described by witnesses as "completely out of it" and "staggering", decided to go for a late night swim. He'd visited Sri Lanka at the end of 1968 and had been told by an astrologer to "be careful swimming". That night Brian Jones died in the water. The official verdict was "death by misadventure", that he'd drowned whilst under the influence of drugs. Pamela Des Barres, in her book *Rock Bottom*, reports the words of Tom Keylock, who went to visit his dying friend, builder Frank Thorogood, in a north London hospital: "We started talking and he told me he wanted to put his house in order." 'There's something I have to tell you. It will probably shock you . . . It was me did Brian,' he said. 'I just finally snapped, it just happened, that's all there is to it.' "

A.E. Hotchner, author of *Blown Away*, talked to another of the builders, who insisted on the pseudonym of "Marty". "Marty" told him: "There was two guys in particular really had it in for Brian. Been on his back for weeks, I mean always making remarks, the rich fag, all that kinda stuff . . . Anyway this night, Brian was swimming a lot . . . and the girls was watching him. These two guys got pissed about that – they was drinking pretty good by then – it was kind of like when it started, kind of teasing. Sort of grabbing Brian by the leg and pulling him down. They seemed to get more steamed about Brian the more they pushed him down, and I could tell it was turning ugly as hell. Finally one lad wanted to let Brian out, but the other wouldn't let him and they was kind of tugging on him. It got real crazy and the next thing I heard somebody say was he's drowned' . . . and someone said, 'Let's get the hell out of here,' and we ran for it."

When the news of Brian's death was broken to members of the Stones, they were in the studio recording a track for the TV programme, *Top Of The Pops*. Although there are reports that Charlie Watts couldn't stop crying, the band went ahead and recorded the show anyway. The only members of the Rolling Stones who attended Brian Jones' funeral were Bill Wyman and Charlie Watts.

Janis Joplin

Gutsy Janis Joplin, the ballsiest female singer ever, was busted in November 1969 for uttering "vulgar and indecent" language during a show in Tampa, Florida. She gave a cop who was trying to calm the crowd, a piece of her mind. "Don't fuck with these people," she screamed. "Did you buy a $5 ticket? "After leaving Big Brother and the Holding Company, Janis formed a new band with the help of Electric Flag members Mike Bloomfield, Harvey Brooks and Nick Gravenites, retaining Big Brother's Sam Andrew on guitar. The Kozmic Blues Band became the Full Tilt Boogie Band and made the classic *Pearl* album, which was issued unfinished on her death. Janis Joplin died in Hollywood of a heroin overdose on 4 October 1970. She was twenty-seven years old.

Keith Moon

The Charismatic drummer of The Who showed signs of living up to his "Loon" nickname at an early age. "Retarded artistically," wrote one teacher on his report card in 1959, "idiotic in other respects." He got the job in The Who – then called The Detours, later the High Numbers – by getting a friend to tell the band that he could play a lot better than the drummer they already had. He was tried out and it was found to be true. Drug abuse began early: to cope with rigorous touring schedules which often meant two sets in one night, sometimes played at different venues, the band took "speed": "purple heart" pills of amphetamine sulphate. While the rest of the band were taking one or two purple hearts at a time, Keith surprised everyone by gulping down twenty or more. So, when Pete Townshend frustratedly smashed his guitar into his amp one night in a bid to stop the "feed-back", Moon enthusiastically joined in and smashed up his drum kit. Their managers, Kit Lambert and Chris Stamp (brother of actor, Terence), insisted it become part of the act. But only at well-paid gigs.

As The Who became more successful, so Moon's behaviour became more and more outrageous. He routinely drank two bottles of best French cognac a day, topped up with liberal doses of champagne and cocaine. And although the drink and the drugs fuelled his mayhem, there was often method in the madness. Hotel rooms were trashed, but often for a reason other than boredom. In America a hotel manager collared Moon, who was walking around with a ghetto-blaster on his shoulder, and told him to "Turn off that noise!" Before he had time to object, the Loon had dragged the hapless man back to his room and he proceeded to trash it in front of the open-mouthed hotel employee. "*That*," he patiently explained to the stunned hotelier, "Was noise." He then turned up the music: "And *that* is The Who." When Keith Moon threw a television set out of a hotel room window into a swimming pool it wasn't for the sake of seeing it destroyed, it was so he could see the picture as it hit the water. Art, see?

Although a working class lad from Wembley, west London, he adopted a new identity for himself as an English "toff", borrowed partly from observing drinking pals Viv Stanshall and "Legs" Larry Smith of the Bonzo Dog Doo-Dah Band, and co-manager, Chris Stamp. Said Pete Townshend: "He gradually went from talking like a normal Londoner to saying things like 'It must be time for drinky-poos.' It was weird."

Sometimes the pranks went wrong, as when Moon put too much explosive in his drum-kit when the band appeared on the *Smothers Brothers' Comedy Hour* American TV show. The ritual explosion at the end of 'My Generation' turned into something of a minor blood bath, with Moon thrown from his raised platform, a chunk of cymbal embedded in his arm, Pete Townshend's hair on fire and hearing permanently damaged, and the show blown momentarily off the air. Off-camera, guest Bette Davis is said to have swooned into fellow guest Mickey Rooney's arms. More seriously, in January 1970, Moon aide, Neil Boland, was accidentally crushed under the wheel of Moon's pink Rolls Royce, after the drummer had lost control of the car. Moon took it badly and never really forgave himself.

By 1975, Moon had moved to America and bought a beachside property at Malibu. Unfortunately for them both, his next-door neighbour was Steve McQueen, a man who liked his privacy and who relished peace and quiet. After the movie star had called the police a few times and built a high wall between the two properties, Moon decided to get his own back. Who aide Bill Curbishly described how Moon "built a ramp and bought a motorcycle, which was going to go over the wall like Steve McQueen in *The Great Escape*. He got dressed up as Hitler and knocked on McQueen's door, and when McQueen opened it, he got down on his hands and knees and bit McQueen's dog."

Three years later he was fed up with California and moved back to London. Keith and his girlfriend were renting the flat in Mayfair owned by Harry Nilsson, where Mama Cass Elliot had choked to death four years before. By this time Moon was in a bad way. He had put on weight, developed a pot belly and his drumming had become so erratic, the band were close to replacing him. At 4.30 a.m. on 6 September 1978, Keith and Annette returned from a party thrown by Paul McCartney. He played a video of the Vincent Price spoof horror classic, *The Abominable Dr Phibes*, took a handful of sleeping pills and some relaxants called Heminevrin (prescribed to combat his alcoholism and mania), and fell asleep in front of the screen. Three hours later he woke up, and prepared himself a meal of steak and champagne. For dessert he gulped down a few more Heminevrin tablets and went back to bed. Keith Moon never woke up again.

Jim Morrison

By 1971, America had lost its appeal for Jim Morrison, and he upped and moved to Paris, France, taking with him his heroin addiction and desperate drink problem. The States were getting too claustrophobic for the outspoken rocker. Four years earlier, at a Doors concert in New Haven, Connecticut, Morrison had been arrested on stage for "indecent and immoral exhibition, breach of the peace and resisting arrest", after telling the audience how he'd been attacked and maced by a cop backstage for fucking a girl in a shower cubicle. In March 1969 he asked an audience in Miami. "Do you want to see my cock?" They did, and he was arrested for "lewd and lascivious behaviour, public drunkenness and profanity". He received a sentence of sixty days in jail plus a $500 fine and was still fighting the case on appeal when he moved to France.

On 3 July 1971 Jim and his girlfriend Pamela Courson had spent the evening at Rock 'n' Roll Circus on rue de la Seine, where he bought some almost pure Chinese heroin. From here on in the truth begins to blur. It is alleged by some that Jim Morrison OD'd and died in the club and that his body was taken back to Pam's apartment at 17 rue Beautrellis. Officially, he died in the bathtub from heart failure. Pamela's version was that she and Morrison returned home at around 1 a.m. from seeing a Robert Mitchum movie, and Jim had wanted a bath. While in the tub he had a heart attack and died. Conspiracy theorists point to evidence that there was no autopsy and that the name of the doctor who signed the death certificate was forgotten by Pamela and subsequently lost. Morrison had boasted in an interview to *Rolling Stone* magazine that he was going to fake his own death and come back under a new identity. When Courson died barely three years later from another heroin overdose, all kinds of rumours began circulating. The probable, if sad, truth is that Jim Morrison's body does rest in the grave in the Pere Lachaise cemetery the authorities have so much trouble keeping free of graffiti. Nearby are the tombs of Oscar Wilde, Balzac and Chopin. He's in good company.

Gram Parsons

Born in Florida, Cecil Ingram Connor, aka "Gram Parsons", had a short, but eventful life. His father, singer-songwriter Coondog Connor shot himself when the boy was just thirteen and he was raised by a wealthy mother and a stepfather called Bob Parsons. Gram first got into drugs from sampling his mother's supply of tranquillisers, and she died of alcohol abuse the day he graduated college. Gram was sent away to Harvard University, to read Divinity. He didn't last long. Following in the footsteps of his daddy, Gram formed the International Submarine Band to play "cosmic American music" and set about inventing "country-rock" music. He was asked to join the Byrds in 1968, and in three short months he helped them become the first "rock" band to play the Grand Ole Opry, recorded the classic *Sweethearts Of The Rodeo* album, before walking out in disgust at their intention to play Apartheid-bound South Africa.

Parsons formed the Flying Burrito Brothers with fellow ex-Byrd Chris Hillman, hung around with The Rolling Stones and provided an influence that helped Jagger and Richards to compose songs like "Wild Horses" and "Sweet Virginia". In her book, *Rock Bottom*, Jagger's "close personal friend" Pamela Des Barres noted that "Gram and Keith Richards were turning into each other." The Burritos played Altamont with the Stones and on the *Burrito Deluxe* tour, Gram's fear of flying led him to take so many "downers" he had to be taken on to planes in a wheelchair. Gram had become an alcoholic: his spectacular Nudie suits no longer fitted him, but he found rare moments of peace hanging out at a motel in the Joshua Tree desert. During a short space of time Gram's wife left him, his house burnt down and his alcoholic stepfather revealed on a family trip that he'd mixed martinis for his mother in hospital, to speed up her death. On 19 September 1973 Gram Parsons died at the Joshua Tree Inn, after suffering his second overdose in two days.

Elvis Presley

Of course, Elvis Aron Presley is not really dead. The supposed heart attack on 16 August 1977 was faked, and last we heard, Elvis was working in a garage just outside Oldham in Lancashire. But, to preserve his anonymity, we'll pretend that the King really did drop dead on his gold-plated lavatory all those years ago, and that his stomach really was stuffed with hamburger, cherry-pop and eleven different narcotics. It's worth a free re-spray, if nothing else.

If you'd written Elvis as a character in a novel, he'd never get past the first draft. Too over the top, the critics would say; but as the old cliché goes (and I tend to avoid clichés like the plague, so this will really hurt), truth *is* stranger than fiction. Elvis was born, not at "the end of Lonely Street", as some would later claim, but as one half of twins in Tupelo, Mississippi. His brother, Jesse Garon Presley, died during birth. Pop, Vernon, had served prison time for forging cheques and deception and his aim in life was to do as little work as possible. After performing poorly in high school, the young Elvis became a truck-driver with musical aspirations. His motives for making that first record were not (as he later claimed) to give his mother, Gladys, a birthday present, but to see if he really did sound like Dean Martin, as people told him. Y'see, Dean Martin was Elvis's idol, and he'd sussed out that ballads were where the *real* money was. Luckily, Sam Phillips kicked some rock 'n' roll into the boy, and the rest, as those cliché hounds have it, is history.

Some Elvis trivia: Elvis bought his first guitar at Tupelo Hardware Company. The hundred-mile road the Presleys took when they moved from Tupelo to Memphis is now called The Elvis Aron Presley Memorial Highway – or US-78 for short. After Elvis fell out with The Beatles over an imagined slight, Elvis visited US President Richard Nixon and tried to get John Lennon deported. The Church of Elvisology exists and has several thousand members. When he locked himself away at Gracelands with his "Memphis Mafia", Elvis used to send out for pretty young girls in white panties. But the sex he enjoyed was rarely the real thing. He never really got over the notion that full penetration outside marriage was sinful, and his regard for sperm was so great that when any was "accidentally spilled" during heavy petting with a member of his teenage harem, he'd get upset and say, "Oh, look at all those babies we killed." Elvis had not touched his wife, Priscilla, since the night their daughter Lisa Marie was born: he regarded motherhood as too sacred to be sullied by sex.

The only book Elvis was seen reading at Gracelands was *The Physicians's Desk Reference*, which describes the chemistry, effects and proper use of every US-manufactured prescription drug there is. Prescription drugs, together with the teenage girls and fatty junk foods, were Elvis's antidote to the boredom that was threatening to smother his life since Colonel Parker had come up with a price for live performance that no one could afford. Most of his dozens of pills came from the Landmark Pharmacy across the street from Gracelands, and bore the names of members of his "Mafia" who'd be sent along with prescriptions supplied by his pet doctor, "Dr Nick". Despite – or possibly helped by his pill habit – Elvis had a hatred of pot-smokers, acid-takers and low-life junkies. To protect himself he kept a few firearms around the house. In 1970 alone, he spent $19,792 on weapons, and when he died, there were over 250 guns in the building.

Despite all the excess of the later years, Elvis remained "The King". And as everyone knows, there are three Elvis Presleys – the youthful Elvis of Sun Records and hip-shakin', lip-curlin', rebel-rousin' intensity, the middle-aged King of Las Vegas, hamburgers and straining girdles, and the man who specialises in all-over, three coat body spray in Oldham.

Johnny Thunders

The former New York Doll was born John Anthony Genzale Jr on 15 July, 1952. By 1975 the Dolls had transformed into little more than singer David Joansen's backing band, and Thunders left to form The Heartbreakers with Richard Hell and Walter

Lure from Television, and former Dolls drummer Jerry Nolan. From the off, Thunders' notorious drug dependency, coupled with a taste for vast quantities of booze, made for shambolic gigs and even more shambolic off-stage dramas. Late in 1976, they arrived at Heathrow Airport without work permits, intending to support the Sex Pistols on their first national UK tour. But by January 1977, all the dates had been cancelled. Even so Thunders and the Heartbreakers stayed in London, playing their own gigs. Nolan turned most of the Pistols on to heroin, and introduced Sid to his groupie girlfriend, Nancy Spungen.Then they were deported.

The Heartbreakers returned to London, recorded the *LAMF* "Like a mutha-fucker" album and broke up. Thunders teamed up with Pistols Steve Jones and Paul Cook for the short-lived Johnny Thunders' Rebels, before reforming a new line-up Heartbreakers and playing with outfits of various types across America and Europe, One brief interlude was with Sid Vicious in the aptly-named Living Dead. There was no doubt that Thunders' drug habit had just about put his career on hold. It reached the stage where audiences didn't expect him to turn up for his own gigs, and when he did, they often wished he hadn't. In 1981, next to a picture of a "works", American magazine *Trouser Press* declared "Johnny Thunders legally dead", though still playing in a band. The terms "wasted" and "human wreck" were becoming common-place to describe Thunders, and rumours of his death were persistent but invariably unfounded.

On 23 April 1991, the rumour became the true. The thirty-eight-year-old was found dead in a seedy hotel room in New Orleans, surrounded by drug debris. Despite his habit, the first autopsy failed to reveal the cause of death, and "heroin overdose" was added later. The press discovered that Willy Deville was living next door to the hotel and hounded him for comments. He is quoted in *Please Kill Me* by Legs McNeil and Gillian McCain as saying: "It was a tragic end, and I mean, he went out in a blaze of glory, ha, ha, so I thought I might as well make it look real good, you know, out of respect, so I just told everybody that when Johnny died he was laying on the floor with his guitar in his hands. I made that up. When he came out of the St. Peter's Guest House, rigor mortis had set in to such an extent that his body was in a u-shape. When you're laying on the floor in a fetal position, doubled over, well, when the body bag came out, it was in a U.It was pretty awful.''

Sid Vicious

There seemed little doubt at the time that former sex pistol, Sid Vicious (real name John Simon Ritchie), had murdered his groupie-girlfriend, Nancy Spungen, at the Chelsea Hotel in New York. He was certainly on record as admitting it, and once Pistols manager, Malcolm McLaren, had raised the $50,000 bail money, Sid was released on bail after a nightmarish few days at Rikers Island. In prison the twenty-one-year-old had been raped and subjected to endless taunts by his fellow inmates, who resented Vicious's "hard-man" celebrity status. On top of that, he was suffering cold turkey from a heroin habit he'd originally picked up from his victim. Then, as on many occasions in the past, Sid Vicious was not the happiest of young men.

After being released too late to attend Nancy's funeral, Sid slashed at every vein in his body with a smashed lightbulb and a rusty razor. He was rushed to Bellevue psychiatric hospital for observation, but they released him a few days later. On his first night on the town, Sid got into a fight at a club when Todd Smith (brother to Patti) objected to him propositioning his girlfriend. Vicious smashed a bottle into Smith's face and ended up in jail again.

Three months later, Vicious finds himself released into the custody of his mother, Anne. To save her son getting into trouble for buying heroin, mum buys it for him. The drug is close to 100 percent pure and Sid goes to town on it, ending up deader than John Wayne's left lung. Was it accidental or was it suicide? We shall probably never know, but let's give Sid the benefit of the doubt. It is said – and it could very well be an urban myth – that when Anne Beverley, mother to Sid Vicious, returned to London, She dropped the urn containing her son's ashes at Heathrow

Airport, scattering the infamous geezer's remains all over the tarmac. It is also said that when a march was called to commemorate the first anniversary of Sid's death, his loving mother was unable to attend, having been rushed to hospital earlier the same day with a drug overdose.

Gene Vincent

The veteran rock 'n' roller of "Be-Bop-A-Lula" fame survived the car crash that killed Eddie Cochran, but died in Los Angeles on 12 October 1971 from burst ulcers, the result of heavy drink and drug abuse.

Hank Williams

Hank Wiliams, the biggest star of country music, died in the back seat of his chauffeured Cadillac, on 1 January 1953. In his twenty-nine years on earth, he wrote roughly 125 songs, including religious "hymns" and monologues he penned under the name of "Luke the Drifter" Alcoholic, addicted to painkillers as a result of an unbearably painful childhood spine defect, Hank was divorced twice, and yet, despite it all, he was a supreme talent who became the inspiration to every country singer who followed.

On New Year's Day, 1952, Williams was due to play a show in Canton, Ohio. He's had to cancel an appearance in Charleston the previous night after bad weather had prevented his hired plane from taking off. It was decided that Williams would be driven from the Andrew Johnson Hotel in Knoxville by seventeen-year-old Charles Carr, the only man available. Hank was loaded into the caddy, together with a pint of vodka, some chloral hydrate tablets and his pistol. Highway patrolman Swann Kitts pulled the car over for speeding near Rutledge, Tennessee, and remarked that the guy in the backseat looked dead. "Nah, he's only sedated," Carr told him. At around 5.30 in the morning, Carr stopped at a gas station in Oak Hill, West Virginia, to ask for directions. When service station attendant Glen Burdette caught sight of Hank, he knew something was wrong and called the police. There was a third man in the car by then, a relief driver by the name of "Donald Surface" who had been picked up at Bluefield, West Virginia, but he vanished at the first mention of calling in the law and was never traced. Patrolman Howard Jamey answered the call and knew immediately he was looking at a corpse. In Hank's right hand was a note that read "We met, we lived and dear we loved, then comes that fatal day, the love that felt so dear fades away. Tonight love hathe one alone and lonesome, all that I could sing, I you you [sic] still and always will, but that's the poison we have to pay."

The autopsy was conducted by a Russian emigre doctor who barely spoke a word of English. He didn't look for drugs and so didn't find any. His conclusion was that Hank had died of heart failure.

5. "Don't Go Near The Water"
DEATH BY DROWNING

Jeff Buckley

Son of cult singer-songwriter Tim, thirty-year-old Jeff Buckley's star was firmly in the ascent, when he accidentally drowned on 29 May 1997. His debut album *Grace* was greeted as a masterpiece, and executives at Columbia Records were rubbing their hands together in glee at the prospect of a long-term contract with one of the hottest acts of the 1990s. But it was not to be. Buckley and a friend decided to go night swimming in the Mississippi at New Orleans and jumped in fully clothed. A few minutes later Buckley disappeared into the night, and although prompt efforts were made to find him, it was no good. On 4 June his body was finally dicovered, floating near the famous Beale Street.

Randy California

The guitarist and songwriter with Spirit died on 2 January 1997, after a current got the better of him, whilst swimming off the Hawaiian island of Molokai. Before he died, Randy was able to save the life of his twelve-year old son, Quinn.

Dennis Wilson

A drug-and drink-abuser, womaniser and general rock 'n' roll casualty of the Beach Boys' success, by December 1983 the once lithe and muscular blond drummer was bloated and in a pretty bad way. After being beaten up by his estranged wife's boyfriend, Wilson discharged himself from hospital and went to stay on a friend's boat, moored off the Californian coast. On the morning of 28 December, he was up at nine, drinking screwdriver cocktails. After boozing all morning, he toyed with a turkey sandwich and decided he wanted to go swimming in the icy water. Diving the three metres to the sea bottom, he came up with various items of "treasure", the last of which was a photograph in a sterling silver frame. On the next dive, he never resurfaced. As the only surfing Beach Boy, it had been his wish to be buried at sea. A law prohibiting this was overcome by the personal intervention lof President Ronald "Mr Rock 'n' Roll" Reagan, and Dennis Wilson was lowered into the sea from Coast Guard cutter Point Judith at 5.11 p.m. on 4 January 1984.

6. "Jailhouse Rock"
BRUSHES WITH THE LAW
AND ANTISOCIAL BEHAVIOUR

Chuck Berry

When just eighteen years of age, rock 'n' roller Charles Edward Anderson Berry (better known to his "Ding-a-Ling" as "Chuck") was convicted of attempted armed robbery, and served three years in Algoa reformatory School. In 1960 he was sent down for another three year stretch, this time in a Federal prison, for transporting fourteen-year-old prostitute Norine Janice Escalanti, across state lines. He'd picked her up in El Paso, where she was working as a waitress, and she'd joined his tour, travelling through New Mexico, Arizona, Colorado and Missouri. He put her to work as a hat-check girl at his club in St Louis, but fired her soon after – he said it was because he found out she was a prostitute – and sent her home. She filed a complaint. Twenty years later, he spent four months in another Federal penitentiary after underpaying his tax by a cool two hundred grand.

On 27 December, 1989, the *St Louis Post Dispatch* reported that Hosana A. Huck, a former cook at a Berry-owned diner called Southern Air, filed suit for invasion of privacy, alleging that rock 'n' roll's most seminal guitarist had installed video cameras in the women's restrooms. Police confiscated tapes that revealed hundreds of women caught relieving themselves, including shots from an overhead camera revealing the toilet's contents before flushing. Berry later settled out-of-court, according to his lawyer, paying out a total of $1.2 million.

Ian Brown (Stone Roses)

Ian Brown is just the kind of guy you want sitting next to you on a transatlantic flight. In February 1998 he was arrested after harassing a British Airways stewardess on a flight from Paris to Manchester, England. According to press reports, the stewardess was serving duty free goods when she thought she saw the former Stone Roses singer wave her over. Realising that he was just putting something into his pocket, she apologised with another wave. Brown took offence and threatened to cut off her hands for waving at him. She said that he was abusive, pointing his finger at her and speaking in a menacing tone. The captain came out to see what was happening and an argument ensued. After he returned to the cabin to land the plane, Brown spent half a minute pounding on the cockpit door. The pilot radioed ahead and police arrested Brown as he left the plane.

For his part, Brown, aged thirty-five at the time, says that he interpreted the stewardess's wave as "a dismissive gesture". He said that he accepted her apology and was only joking when he threatened to cut her hands off. The pilot, he said, was trying to "wind him up". Ian Brown served his time, but commented later that it was "a lot of fuss over nothing. If I'd been Joe Soap it would never have gone so far." Quite.

James Brown

Feeling good? Sometimes the godfather of Soul was feeling a little *too* good. In 1989, Brown served two years and three months of a six year and three months of a six year sentence after he was chased by police across two states while under the influence of the drug PCP. Earlier the same year, Brown's fourth wife, Adrienne, filed charges alleging that Brown had shot at her as she'd driven away after an argument, and then hit her with a pipe when she'd returned home. He said: "She was just mad because I wouldn't take her on my South American tour." As on three other similar occasions, all charges were later dropped.

A few days later Adrienne was arrested at Augusta airport for possessing PCP, which was found hidden in her bra. Later she claimed that her husband had framed her, but at the time she offered a unique plea, which was not accepted by the court. Adrienne argued that she was entitled to diplomatic immunity because two years earlier Representative D. Douglas Barnard of Georgia had officiated over James Brown Appreciation Day, during which the US congressman proclaimed James Brown to "America's Number-One Ambassador of Soul."In January 1996 Adrienne collapsed and died of heart failure two days after undisclosed cosmetic surgery. She was forty-seven-years old. An autopsy revealed that she had been a heavy drug user for many years and that her stomach contained a cocktail of prescribed and illegal drugs.

In January 1998 the sixty-four-year-old James Brown was admitted to a South Carolina hospital for an addiction to pain-killers. His agent Jeff Allen explained to the *Toronto Star*: "James has had a problem with his back and I don't want to say anything out of place, but he may have gotten addicted to painkillers . . .' He was picked up at his home by sheriff's deputies on a judge's order, after Brown's family had become "concerned about his health". He claimed his daughter hospitalised him against his will after he'd got upset after watching a TV show on poverty-stricken children in South America. Less than a week later he was arrested for possession of marijuana and unlawful use of a firearm. As well as just under an ounce of marijuana, police confiscated a .30 calibre rifle and a .22 calibre semi-automatic handgun. Brown said later: "I need protection. I have guns and I'm going to keep on having guns. Thank God it's a free country." He also claimed he smoked marijuana "because I have bad eyes." The judge ordered James Brown into a ninety-day drug rehab programme.

The Clash

Not surprisingly, The Clash have have lived up to their name when it comes to brushes with the law. In June 1977 Joe Strummer and drummer Topper Headon were arrested for daubing "The Clash" on a wall in london. A few days later, Strummer was fined for stealing pillows from a Holiday Inn. The following March, bassist paul Simonon and Headon were seized after four police cars and a helicopter had been dispatched to Chalk Farm Studios in north London after reports of gunmen on the roof. They'd been shooting at racing pigeons with an air rifle. Strummer and Simonon were then arrested for being drunk and disorderly in Glasgow (more an obligation than a crime, you'd think) and in May 1989 Strummer fell foul of the German authorities when he hit a "fan" over the head with his guitar. After leaving the band and admitting an addiction to heroin, Topper Headon was jailed for fifteen months in 1987 for supplying the drug to a friend who died.

Harry Connick Jr

The smooth band-leader was arrested at JFK airport in New York after being found in possession of a gun. Charges were dropped after Connick agreed to make a commercial warning people against carrying unlicensed firearms.

Spade Cooley

Donnel Clyde Cooley was born in Pack Saddle Creek, Oklahoma, in 1910. The nickname "Spade" came from his almost fanatical devotion to the game of poker. After moving to California in search of work in the early years of the Great Depression, Spade became an occasional movie stand-in for singing cowboy Roy Rogers, and played fiddle at hillbilly dances, before eventually forming his own band. During the Second World War, Spade Cooley and his Orchestra became one of the top Western Swing outfits in the country. Western Swing, a cross between Country dance music and the Big Band Sound typified by Benny Goodman and Glenn Miller, was big, big business on the West Coast back then. Legendary fiddler Bob Wills and his Texas Playboys had moved to Calilfornia in 1943, where audiences as large as 10,000 were boosted by service personnel stationed there during the Second World War.

Spade's biggest hit, "Shame, Shame On You", was recorded in 1945 and led to roles in a shitload of best forgotten films, including *Chatterbox*, *Texas Panhandle* and *The Singing Bandits*, as well as gaining him his own radio and television series. In the late 1940s more than three-quarters of the possible viewing audience tuned in to see "the little man with a big talent in the land of the jigsaw beat" strut his stuff on *The Hoffman Hayride*. Spade developed a taste for outlandish $500 handmade western suits (in the days when $500 could buy you a *very* fine automobile) and his boots were the envy of the upper-crust corral. As a tenderfoot cowboy he made even his friend Roy Rogers look like a rugged son of the desert. After a successful career, Cooley, by now one of California's richest men, gave up the swing in December 1958 and set about building a monumental theme park in the Mojave Desert, to be called Water Wonderland. One of his last recordings was of his own song, the sadly prophetic "You Clobbered me".

A happy retirement was not on the cards for Spade Cooley. In 1945 he had been acquitted on a serious rape charge, and in December of the same year, he'd married his second wife, Ella Mae, a twenty-year-old singer he'd planned to feature in an all-girl hillbilly band he was concocting for TV. "She's the purtiest little filly in the whole of California," he'd tell anyone who'd listen. But all good things must come to an end, and by spring 1961, Spade was hearing rumours that Ella Mae was bragging about sleeping with old pal, Roy Rogers. Spade filed for divorce and won custody of their two daughters, Melody (fourteen) and Donnell (twelve).

In what was described in court as "a wild, drunken attempt to reconcile their wrecked marriage", Spade arrived at Ella Mae's Mojave home on the evening of 3 April, 1961, in a terrible mood. He'd been drinking heavily and chomping pills. The inevitable argument ensued and Cooley started to beat Ella Mae, forcing Melody to watch. He is alleged to have said: "You're going to watch me kill her, Melody. If you don't I'll kill you too. I'll kill us all."

When Melody had been summoned to the ranch, a few minutes earlier, Ella Mae was naked and in the shower, unconscious. Cooley dragged her by her hair to the den and banged her head twice on the floor, calling her a slut. He then screamed, "We'll see if you're dead" and stomped her in the guts before burning her breasts with the cigarette he'd been smoking. Then the phone rang and when Cooley went to answer it, Melody tried unsuccessfully to revive her mother with cold water.

When he came back, he told Melody, "Say nothing to the police or I may have to kill you." Then he stormed out of the room again, and Melody took the opportunity to slip out of the house and run for her life.

Just before midnight the Mojave ambulance service received a call from a man who identified himself as Spade Cooley. He said to send an ambulance quick as his wife had been "bad hurt". The attendants found Ella Mae's body wrapped in a blood-soaked blanket. She was pronounced dead on arrival at Tehachapi Valley Hospital and the sheriff's department was notified. At first Spade told the flatfoots that his wife's injuries had been caused by her falling out of a car. They didn't believe him and faster than you can say "Yee-haw", they charged Donnell Clyde "Spade" Cooley with Murder in the First Degree. Within days, Capitol Records released a song called "Cold, Grey Bars", written by the celebrity convict in his prison cell.

In court Cooley kept Roy Rogers' name out of it. He said that he'd discovered that his wife has been involved in a sex cult that specialised in sodomy. He refused to name names, but is said to have shocked the jury with his lurid accounts of anal penetration and "all manner of other perversions". One juror had to be revived with smelling salts. On 19 August 1961, Cooley was found guilty of Murder One, and following an unsuccessful appeal and some fruitful plea-bargaining, he was sentenced to life imprisonment.

After serving eight years as a model prisoner, it was announced that Cooley was to be released on parole in February 1970. On 23 November 1969 he was granted leave to participate in a benefit concert sponsored by the Alameda County Deputy Sheriffs Association. After a stonkin' performance, including what must have been a somewhat ironic rendition of his hit, 'Shame, Shame on You' ("Runnin' round with other guys, now you think that's mighty wise, dern your heart. Oh, Shame on You!"), he received a standing ovation. Backstage, flushed by his success and already planning for his comeback, fifty-nine year-old Spade Cooley collapsed and died of a heart attack.

Hugh Cornwell

In 1980, the Stranglers guitarist and singer served five weeks of a two month jail sentence for possession of a quantity of drugs. The haul consisted of heroin, cocaine, marijuana and magic mushrooms. To his contemporaries Cornwell was something of an expert on drugs. His drug of choice was speed balls, which he described as "mixing a line of cocaine with a line of heroin. You get the up from the cocaine and then the heroin calms you down, so you don't get paranoid."

Gary Glitter

In November 1999, disgraced 1970s glam-rocker Gary Glitter was sent to prison for four months. The bald, rotund fifty-five-year-old singer pleaded guilty under his own name of Paul Gadd to fifty-four charges of taking and possessing "degrading and hardcore" pornographic pictures of children. Prosecutor John

Royce described the pictures Gadd admitted to taking of children under sixteen years of age, as hardcore paedophile pornography in which "they were forced to engage in a panoply of sexual poses and acts." He'd taken his computer in to a shop in Bristol for repair, and when engineers had discovered just what was on the hard-drive, they immediately called the police. In Hortfield prison, Bristol, Glitter earned £6.10 a week making teddy bears for charity, and was said to have found the life "inside" "hard to bear". Towards the end of his captivity, an anonymous source told the *Sunday Mirror*: "He hasn't showered this week and had to take Valium as he was in such a state."

On his release, after serving a mere two months of the four month sentence, he was driven by an aide to a press conference in Regents' Park, London. There he read a prepared statement. Flanked by four police officers, the millionaire singer looked apprehensive and uneasy as he spoke. "I deeply regret doing what I was sent to prison for. I have served my time. I want to put it all behind me." Glitter then replaced his dark glasses, climbed into his Mercedes and was driven away. After a period spent in hiding in England to fulfil his parole conditions, Glitter intended to go and live in Cuba with a twenty-seven-year-old girlfriend, Yudenia Sosa Martinez. But the Cuban authorities refused him permission to stay. Glitter was last spotted by a British newspaper sailing around Spanish ports in his yacht. It was estimated that at the time of his arrest, Gary Glitter was worth £11 million.

Rick James

Pop-funk singer Rick James, best known for the 'Super Freak' single and for his million-selling debut album, *Come And Get It*, was imprisoned in September 1993, after being tried for the assault and false imprisonment of two women. In July 1991, James and his girlfriend Tania Anne Hijazi was visited at his LA mansion – the same "Xanadu" that once belonged to William Randolph Hearst – by twenty-six-year old masseuse Frances Alley. When she was due to leave, James noticed that his "eight ball" – crack cocaine stash – was missing. "No one fucks with

Rick James in his house," he cried, before forcing her to strip and tying her to a chair. Frances says that James then ordered Tania to heat up a knife over a flame in the kitchen until it was red hot, and then he touched it against the skin around her pubic area. He then pistol-whipped her and poured alcohol on to her knees, before setting it alight with his crack-pipe. She then claimed that he burned her with a lighter, before being untied so that the three of them could go into the bedroom. Besides torturing her, James ordered Alley to perform oral sex on his girlfriend. "Then Tania went down on me," she told the court. 'I was laying on my back, she got on top of me and kind of straddled me and starts peeing on me, my burns and stuff. It hurt real bad." James was charged with assault with a deadly weapon, aggravated mayhem, torture, and "forcible oral copulation".

The second incident took place at the exclusive St James Club and Hotel on Sunset Strip. Here, James and Hijazi beat former Sony Music executive Mary Sauger unconscious and held her against her will for twenty-four-hours in November 1992. The couple were later ordered to pay Ms Sauger $1 million in a civil judgment. All in all, Rick James was sentenced to five years and four months in prison. Hijazi received slightly less time and they married on his release in 1997.

Cured of his crack-cocaine habit, James immediately set about staging a musical comeback. It hit a slight set-back when he was rushed to hospital in November 1998, after suffering a stroke following popping a blood vessel at a concert in Denver. A spokesman for Cedars-Sinai Medical Centre said: "While his recognition and comprehension are fine, he is unable to walk and is in the intensive care unit."

Jerry Lee Lewis

Louisiana-born Lewis has always exhibited an unhealthy fondness for firearms. He gained his nickname, "the Killer", at Bible school, from where he was expelled at the age of fifteen. Jailed at eighteen for stealing a gun, he served his time, took up music, was discovered by Sam Phillips, and went on to become one of rock 'n' roll's greatest innovators, adopting a wild, manic style that many feel is reflective of his own character. He famously married his thirteen- or fourteen-year old cousin, Myra, (her age depends on who you believe), and had to cancel a British tour in 1958, when tabloid newspapers leaked the news. Lewis's background is fundamentalist Christian, with anti-rock preacher Jimmy Swaggart a cousin, so it wasn't surprising when "The Killer" gave up rock 'n' roll altogether in favour of country music in the late 1960s, because rock 'n' roll is "lewd and sinful in the eyes of God". As he said at the time: "I just can't picture Jesus doing a whole lotta shakin'."

By 1974 he was back rockin' and a-rollin', and shooting up his office in Memphis. The businessman next door complained after discovering twenty-five bullet holes in the wall that divided them. In 1976, a pistol-packing Lewis attempted to drive his Caddy through the closed gates at Elvis's Gracelands mansion, and was charged with unlawful weapon possession and intoxication. Later the same year he shot at his bass-player, Norman "Butch" Owens with a .357 Magnum, shattering a glass Coca-Cola bottle and puncturing the bassist's chest. He then castigated him for bleeding on to the Killer's white carpet. The resulting law suit severely dented Lewis's personal fortune and sparked off trouble with the authorities over unpaid taxes.

Lewis's private life has been edged with tragedy. His two sons died in separate accidents, and although his marriage to Myra lasted thirteen years, two of his five ex-wives are now dead. The fourth drowned in a swimming pool in 1982, the fifth a year later from a drugs overdose. The IRS sued Lewis for back taxes and managed to take over his every possession. Eventually the lawyers did a deal and he was allowed to return home to his ranch, which is now one of Mississippi's top tourist attractions.

George Michael

That George Michael had kept his gayness to himself was surprising enough, that it should all come out after a "cottaging" incident in Beverly Hills' Will Rogers Memorial Park (with its sign of Rogers' famous quotation: "I never met a man I didn't like"), kept the tabloids busy for weeks. Born Yorgos Kyriatou Panayiotou, George Michael (well, Yorgos Kyriatou Panayiotou *is* a bit of a mouthful for non-Greeks) was charged with "lewd conduct" after propositioning an undercover cop. "He was quite tasty," said Michael later. "They don't send Karl Malden in there. We're not talking Columbo with his dick out." He pleaded no contest and was sentenced to eighty hours' community service.

Marilyn Manson

In 1999, Craig Marks, editor of *Spin* magazine took Marilyn Manson to court in a $24 million suit, after he claimed the singer and his entourage yelled threats at him after it was discovered that Marilyn Manson wasn't going to be chosen to grace the magazine's next cover. Some of the offending words shouted included: "I can kill you! I can kill your family! I can kill everyone you know!" Manson subsequently filed a counter-suit and the case drags on. Young Brian Warner (as he was in childhood) was reared in Canton, Ohio; when he was eighteen, he and his parents moved to Fort Lauderdale. It has been said that Brian would never have become Marilyn if he'd not been sent to a private Christian school in 1974. "That's where I learned how to deceive and manipulate the system." Another key psychological factor occurred when a stranger broke into the family home and tried to smother the eight-year-old with a pillow. (Suggestions that this may have been a music-loving time traveller have been dismissed as fantasy). A few years later, young Brian found a coffee can in the street. When he opened it up, he was shocked to discover that it contained a human fetus.

Marilyn Manson's act is a freaky, glitzy, occult-inspired show that's the stuff of dreams as well as the stuff of nightmares. It is, he says "designed to speak to the people who understand it and scare the people who don't." In the best rock 'n' roll tradition, he and his band – Twiggy Ramirez, Ginger Fish, Madonna Wayne Gracy and Zim Zum – take the show on the road and continue to live it in their everyday lives. They annoy people in public places, have food fights, smash up motel rooms, set off fire alarms and have even shat in Evan Dando's bathtub. Naughty, naughty. Inevitably their concerts are picketed by Christian protesters. After a show in Syracuse, New York, Manson told a small group of protesters: "You say Jesus loves me. How many of you want to love me? Tonight, how many of you want to come with me and get fucked?" No takers. Somewhat surprisingly, all this goes down well with Dad Warner, who is one of Manson's biggest fans, and, although a greying furniture salesman, travels to as many of his son's shows as he can. "Sometimes," said Manson in an interview in *Rolling Stone*, "I wonder if I'm a character being written, or if I'm writing myself. It's confusing."

Oasis

It's been suggested that the latest bad boys of rock didn't just take musical inspiration from the 1960s bands they so clearly venerate, they also adopted their outrageous lifestyles. The Oasis party kicked off in 1993 and from the off, songwriter Noel Gallagher and his younger, rougher brother, Liam, made no bones about their working class roots. They talked about growing up in a rough part of Manchester, in a world where shop-lifting and joy-riding were as everyday as chips and cheeseburgers. "I've sniffed cans of gas at the age of twelve," said Noel. "Took mushrooms at the age of twelve – proper mushrooms. Not twenty, more like 150. I've done all that." With the success came the money and with the money came excess. Taking drugs "is like having a cup of tea", Noel once remarked. At the 1996 British Pop Awards (the Brits) the brothers managed to insult co-presenters Chris Evans and Michael Hutchence and, refusing to leave the stage, challenged anyone who was "hard enough" to come and remove them. No one bothered. As one Fleet Street hack wrote, somewhat pre-dictably, in 1995: "You can take the Gallaghers out of Man-chester, but you can't take the Manchester out of the Gallaghers." It was like they'd been given the keys to the sweetshop, except it wasn't chocolate bars and sherbet dabs

Liam and Noel liked best, it was cocaine and lager, with Jack Daniels and champagne for chasers.

Back then Oasis were enjoying themselves, and provided you were young enough to appreciate it, it was fun. They brought colour into the greyness of the Major years, and when Tony Blair's New Labour was elected, spin doctors cleverly hinted at how different things were going to be after Noel and Creation record label boss, Alan McGee, were invited to Downing Street for tea and cakes. At first Noel and Liam were equally wild, but never seriously over the top. Said Noel: "Being famous is a good laugh when you're on drugs. You meet people and go 'Naw, nah, fucking nah' and everyone goes, 'Wow, hasn't he got a lot of charisma.' And really you're just hammered." He said that after a while, the house he and wife Meg Matthews shared in Belsize Park had turned into a nightclub: "The bar would always be open and people would just turn up." Then he started having panic attacks. One morning he looked at himself in the mirror and saw yellow skin and bug eyes, and decided that things had to change. He and Meg sold up, bought a house in Buckinghamshire and eased up on the drugs and the drink.

Not so Liam. In 1997 the world was shocked by pictures of him setting upon a fan in Australia and breaking his nose. He's been arrested the previous November in Oxford Street, London; "out of his face" and with a small stash of cocaine in his pocket. It was all beginning to make sense. Liam being cautioned for grabbing a cyclist out of the window of his Mercedes car suddenly seemed like a let-off. Being thrown off a Cathay Pacific flight from Hong Kong to Australia, for lighting up and threatening to stab a crew member. "One panhead told me to shut up," explained Liam. "Some panhead who needs stabbing through the head with a fucking pickax." The on-off-off relationship with professional rock wife, Patsy Kensit, a woman old enough to know better, made the front pages of the tabloids, as did his disappearance in November 1999. It came to a point when Liam quitting Oasis just wasn't news any more. The band survived the departure of original drummer Tony McCarroll, and then guitarist Paul "Bonehead" Arthur and bassist Paul "Guigs" McGuigan in

August 1999, but can it survive the loss of a Gallagher? We'll have to see.

Ozzy Osbourne

"I am something of a madman. I can do nothing in moderation. If it's booze, I drink the place dry. If it's drugs, I take everything and then scrape the carpet for little crumbs. I took LSD every day for five years. I was spending about $1,000 a week on drugs . . . I OD'd about a dozen times."

Ozzy Osbourne.

The former Black Sabbath lead singer is possibly the greatest exponent of the wild rock 'n' roll lifestyle who's not pushing up daisies. Born in Birmingham in 1948, when asked what he wanted to be after he left school, the young John Osbourne said, "a plumber". After stints as plumber's mate, slaughterer, mortuary attendant and car horn-tuner, he turned to burglary and spent three months in Birmingham's Winson Green Prison. While there he tattooed O-Z-Z-Y on his left knuckle and happy faces on both knees, using a sewing needle and a graphite slab. Shortly after his release he was thrown through a plate glass window during a fight with three men.

At the age of eighteen, young John saw that the only sensible way out of his life of crime was to become a rock star, and so with that goal in mind, he renamed himself Zig and put a card in a local music shop window that read: "Ozzy Zig requires gig." Surprisingly it worked and after a series of false starts, a band called Earth was formed. Earth became Black Sabbath and the rest, as they say, is rock 'n' roll history. Although Sabbath were really a blues band to start with, and the only dark thing about them at the time was their name, they fell out with Christian groups early on. In 1971 a track on the *Masters of Reality* album called 'After Forever', which was intended to affirm a belief in God, the church deemed blasphemous. In Memphis their dressing room was mysteriously found to have crosses painted in blood on the walls, and during their set a Satanist leapt on to stage with a

sacrificial knife. After the show, the local witches coven surrounded their hotel and drummer Bill Ward had to scare them
away with a fake hex.

By the mid-1970s, all four members of the band were heavily
into drink and drugs. Especially Ozzy, who was fired from the
band after the *Never Say Die* tour in 1978. For three months after
his dismissal, Oz stayed in his hotel room, ordering pizza, booze
and cocaine to be delivered. Then his wife-to-be Sharon Arden
(daughter of rock manager Don "Machine-gun" Arden) suggested he form his own band. And that's when Ozzy Osbourne
got *really* wild.

Osbourne's first solo tour of America was the *Diary of a
Madman* tour. The crew nicknamed it "Night of the Living
Dead", because so many things went wrong. A crane fell and
crushed $8,000 of synthesisers, the props truck broke down and
the entire band were expelled from their hotel in San Diego after
the management realised just who "John Osbourne" was. It was
part of the contract that twenty-five pounds of raw offal, including calf livers and pig intestines, be provided by the promoter for
Ozzy to throw at the audience. As the tour progressed, the
audience caught on and began bringing their own "raw meat",
which included dead frogs, cats and snakes. Once Ozzy freaked
out totally because when someone threw a toy doll on the stage,
he thought it was a dead baby.

In Des Moines, Iowa, some idiot threw a live bat on stage.
Because of the heat from the lights the bat lay still and, thinking it
was a rubber toy, Ozzy picked it up and bit off its head. He froze
as he realised what he'd done and had to be rushed to hospital to
start a week long course of very painful rabies shots. "It was one
of the biggest mistakes of my life," said Ozzy later, with feeling.
"If you think that rabies shots are funny you should fucking try
them. It's like having a golf ball injected into your arse." After
this, animal rights and welfare groups kept a close eye on Ozzy
Osbourne.

In February 1982, while visiting San Antonio, Texas, Ozzy
was so drunk, Sharon decided to lock up his clothes so that he
couldn't go out and cause any mayhem. But Ozzy wasn't to be

out-done and two hours later he was arrested for urinating on the site of the Alamo, a national shrine. Legend has it that he was wearing one of Sharon's dresses when pulled in, but one of the arresting officers insists he was wearing "athletic shoes with no socks, a T-shirt and a pair of sweatshirts with no underwear." Five months later Ozzy and Sharon were married in Honolulu.

Bizarre Ozzy Facts:

- Ozzy has around eighteen tattoos on his body – and rising. They include a blue dragon with red flames on his right chest and the word "Thanks" on his right palm.
- A superstitious man, Ozzy will not wear anything green.
- His grandfather had a tattoo of a snake which curled round his body from his head down to his toes.
- When Ozzy lived with his wife, Thelma, they took turns feeding the chickens they kept. One day it was Ozzy's turn, but he was too busy drinking. Thelma kept on at him and finally he went outside with a shotgun and blasted them all to hell. On another occasion, he dispatched their seventeen cats in similar fashion.
- To impress executives at Epic records, Sharon arranged for Ozzy to symbolically release two doves from under his cloak as he was introduced. A little (??) drunk and more than a little pissed off by their blase attitude, he bit the head off one of the doves and spat it at them. They were not amused and Sharon had to telephone later and apologise. There is no word on how the dove took it.
- Ozzy is officially banned for life from Salt Lake City, by the Mormon-run council.
- After a heavy drink and drugs binge, he attempted to strangle Sharon, after telling her, "We've decided you've got to die." The police were called and Ozzy ended up in jail. A puzzled Ozzy woke up in his cell and said: "But I was in a Chinese restaurant five minutes ago."
- Without realising it, Ozzy once urinated out of a window on to his loyal audience. There were no complaints.

Axl Rose (Guns N' Roses)

Until Guns N' Roses arrived in Kansas City in July 1991, no one realised just how against home taping singer Axl Rose was. He spotted someone video-taking the band's performance and stage-dived into the audience to grab him. A riot ensued and a quarter of a million dollars' worth of damage was wreaked on the concert hall. A warrant was issued for Rose's arrest and although he dodged process-servers for a year, the unpredictable singer was eventually arrested for assault and property damage the following July at JFK airport, New York. After a nifty piece of pleabargaining, the case against Rose was eventually dropped.

Trouble is no stranger to Axl Rose. He once beat up a man in a bar for suggesting that the tattooed one looked like Jon Bon Jovi, and at the 1992 MTV Awards he told Kurt Cobain (referring to Hole star Courtney Love): "You'd better shut your bitch up or I'm taking you down to the pavement." Charming.

PERMISSIONS

Other titles available from Robinson Publishing

The Mammoth Book of Jokes   Ed. Geoff Tibballs   £6.99 [   ]
Over 6,000 shaggy-dog stories, limericks, puns and put-downs for all occasions.
Quite simply, the ultimate and most accessible compendium of humour ever
written, and fully indexed.

The Mammoth Book of Best   Ed. Gardner Dozois   £9.99 [   ]
New Science Fiction 13
Now in its 13th edition, this enormous anthology offers amazing value for money.

The Mammoth Book of Best   Ed. Stephen Jones   £6.99 [   ]
New Horror 2000
The multiple-award-winning series is now firmly established as the premier annual
showcasing excellence in contemporary dark fantasy and the macabre.

The Mammoth Book of Locked-Room   Ed. Mike Ashley   £6.99 [   ]
Mysteries and Impossible Crimes
The biggest collection of stories with the intention to completely baffle and
confound you. Over 30 stories which will stretch your powers of deduction to the
limits.

Robinson books are available from all good bookshops or direct from the
publishers. Just tick the titles you want and fill in the form below.

TBS Direct
Colchester Road, Frating Green, Colchester, Essex CO7 7DW
Tel: +44 (0) 1206 255777
Fax: +44 (0) 1206 255914
Email: sales@tbs-ltd.co.uk

UK/BFPO customers please allow £1.00 for p&p for the first book, plus 50p for the
second, plus 30p for each additional book up to a maximum charge of £3.00

Overseas customers (inc. Ireland), please allow £2.00 for the first book, plus £1.00
for the second, plus 50p for each additional book.

Please send me the titles ticked above.

NAME (Block letters) . . . .

ADDRESS . . . .

. . . .

POSTCODE . . . .

I enclose a cheque/PO (payable to TBS Direct) for . . . .

I wish to pay by Switch/Credit card

Number . . . .

Card Expiry Date . . . .

Switch Issue Number . . . .